Democracy

Theory and Practice

814

Democracy

Theory and Practice

Edited by

John Arthur

State University of New York
at Binghamton

Wadsworth Publishing Company

Belmont, California
A Division of Wadsworth, Inc.

Philosophy Editor: Kenneth King
Editorial Assistant: Cynthia Campbell
Production Editor: Sara Hunsaker/*Ex Libris*
Design: Vargas/Williams/Design
Print Buyer: Martha Branch
Copy Editor: Sara Hunsaker
Compositor: Kachina Typesetting
Printer: Fairfield Graphics
Cover Painting: *Stump Speaking, or the County Canvass*
by George Caleb Bingham. From the art collection of
Boatmen's National Bank of St. Louis.
Cover Design: Paula Goldstein

This book is printed on acid-free paper that meets
Environmental Protection Agency standards
for recycled paper.

1 2 3 4 5 6 7 8 9 10—96 95 94 93 92

Library of Congress Cataloging-in-Publication Data

Democracy: theory and practice / edited by John Arthur.
p.   cm.
Includes bibliographical references.
ISBN 0-534-17148-6
1. Democracy.   I. Arthur, John.–

JC423.D4414   1991
321.8—dc20   91-25794
                                                        CIP

For Amy, in memory of Andy

Preface

Even the most casual observer of the world scene must be struck by political events in the recent past. From "people power" in the Philippines to the student movement in Tianamen Square to *glasnost* and the failed coup in the Soviet Union, people are demanding the right to elect their leaders. Democracy is also an issue, though in a very different way, in the United States as we debate the role of the Supreme Court in exercising judicial review. Yet, despite the evident importance of the topic, courses on social and political philosophy typically ignore democratic theory. Questions about the political and moral foundation of democratic rule usually give way to discussions of justice, rights, equality, and freedom.

This book is meant to fill that void. It provides a diverse collection of essays on the justifications and limitations of democratic government as well as more practical applications of democratic theory to the workplace, judicial review, legal obligation, voter representation, and campaign reform. Selections are both his-torical and contemporary. They were written by philosophers as well as political scientists and include a few carefully edited legal cases exploring the practical and constitutional implications of the theoretical essays. I hope teachers will find it useful in a variety of courses including political philosophy, philosophy of law, and American government.

Among those who provided helpful comments on the manuscript were several reviewers selected by the publisher, including Michael Margolis, University of Cincinnati; Ronald J. Terchek, University of Maryland; Richard P. Hiskes, University of Connecticut; Kevin J. Cassidy, Fairfield University; Donald Herzog, University of Michigan; Ronald E. Pynn, University of North Dakota; and Charles Drekmeier, Stanford University.

I want to thank Ken King of Wadsworth and Sara Hunsaker for their valuable help in preparing the manuscript.

John Arthur

Contents

Introduction

When we speak of "democratic" government, what exactly does that mean? Does it require nothing more than free and open elections in which representatives are chosen to make laws? Or does it also suggest an active citizenry directly involved in the affairs of government? Put another way, is the democratic ideal the ballot box or the town meeting? Other times, the concept can refer to the ideal that government not only provides for popular participation but also respects individual rights and correctly distributes opportunities and wealth. However defined, these ideas about "democracy" raise philosophical questions, including ones about the justification of democratic procedures.

Though we often assume democratic government is justified, there is wide disagreement about why that might be. Is it because democratic forms express the will of the people, assuring that their desires are satisfied? Or is it because democratic governments are more likely to be just, in the sense that they protect individual rights and provide fair distribution of wealth? Others have claimed that democratic government's strength lies in the effects it has on citizens who participate in the processes of self-government, or that democratic procedures are fair in the sense that they express an underlying commitment to treat all citizens as political equals.

Depending on how we understand the justification of democracy, we may be confronted with other questions about the role of women in democratic government, the lack of democratic control in the workplace, and the possible conflicts between democratic government and capitalist economic systems. Other important problems arise in the context of law in a democracy. Consider, for instance, the role of an unelected Supreme Court in a democratic system when exercising its power of judicial review of legislation. When is it acceptable, or even required, that the desires of the majority be overridden? And why should nine un-

elected judges be allowed, in the name of vague concepts like "freedom of speech," to declare laws enacted by the people's representatives unconstitutional? Other questions involve the obligation of citizens to obey the law. Is there a special obligation to obey simply because the government is democratic? Under what circumstances is civil disobedience justified in a constitutional democracy? These problems, and more, are the focus of this collection.

Essays are divided into two parts: Democratic Theory and Democratic Practice. The four chapters comprising Part One concern the nature and justification of democratic government. Essays in Part Two, Democratic Practice, discuss democracy in the context of the workplace, judicial review, voting procedures, capitalism, and feminism.

The first chapter, **Classical Perspectives,** includes a wide range of essays and provides the groundwork for later discussions. Though many classical thinkers are important in the development of democratic theory, Rousseau and Mill stand out as among the most influential. For students of the United States system, the works of Madison, Hamilton, and Jefferson are a must.

Each of the next three chapters is an elaboration of a different theory of democratic government. Such theories of democracy may be thought of as falling into two broad categories: instrumental and internal. *Instrumental theories* see democratic government as justified because of its good effects, though there is disagreement, of course, on what those consequences might be. Some people view democracy as a means to give expression to the collective will of the people; other people see democracy as a way to encourage, through participation, certain forms of life that are thought valuable. Still others—James Madison, for example—defended the U.S. Constitution on the ground it would protect individual rights and secure justice. Each of these alternatives is explored in the first section.

The second chapter, **The Popular Will Theory,** has roots in the work of James Mill, the father of John Stuart Mill. Here the claim is that democratic procedures are justified because where decisions are made by the majority, the results will reflect the preferences of the majority; democracy reflects, in short, the will of the people. But why, then, should we care about a procedure that gives expression to the people's will? And what, exactly, does that mean? James Mill offers one answer to those questions. Democratic governments allow the will of the majority to override the will of a minority, thereby increasing the total good in society. Instead of serving only a few, government serves the collective interest. But what happens if there is a conflict between the *will* of the people and their *interests*? J. Roland Pennock considers that question, arguing that by understanding clearly the concept of representation we can move toward resolving these familiar issues. Brian Barry's article returns to basics, asking under what circumstances we should be persuaded by the principle that decisions should be decided by majority vote. Although appropriate in some cases, he argues, relying on voting is no guarantee that there will be a determinate outcome expressive of the "will of the people," nor do we normally have grounds for accepting the outcome of a majority vote based simply on the fact a vote was taken. Keith Graham directs his attention to the argument offered by James Mill, questioning whether the outcomes of democratic procedures really do reflect people's interests and whether satisfying interests would justify democracy even if it were possible. In the final selection, William Mitchell argues that those who share the belief that government should efficiently allocate resources among the people based on their preferences should sharply limit political activities undertaken by "representatives" and rely instead on markets.

Chapter 3, **The Best Outcome Theory,** includes a variety of essays that assess democracy and democratic theory from the perspective of its results. Best outcome theories maintain that the case for democracy rests not on its capacity to express the "will of the people" but rather on the effects it has on the citizens who live under it and the type of laws that can be expected to result from democratic processes. The chapter begins with an essay by one of the century's most influential theorists, Joseph Schumpeter. What Schumpeter terms the "modern" theory of democracy describes a movement that began in large part as a reaction to what he saw as the excesses and naiveté of the "classical" model of democracy. Rejecting as outmoded any notion that democratic governments express the will of the people, and skeptical of the capacities of an electorate to govern themselves effectively, Schumpeter and other theorists stress the importance of competition among the elite leaders for votes in an open election. The essay by Friedrich A. Hayek can be seen as an extension of Schumpeter's analysis. Although there is a place for majority voting, he contends, that role is severely limited. Government should seek justice and respect rights, and democratic forms can be of limited use in that enterprise. In the next selection Carole Pateman returns to the classical theories of Rousseau and Mill (along with G. D. H. Cole) in an effort to enrich the concept of democratic government beyond the one offered by Schumpeter and Hayek. Only through active political participation, she reasons, can we hope to become worthy citizens—self-governing and actively democratic. Jane Mansbridge contends it is unclear just how active citizen participation can work in a modern state even if it were a sound objective. Robert Dahl argues, however, that the modern small city is the ideal context in which to realize the ideals of participatory democracy. (Discussions of "workplace democracy" in Chapter 5 extend this discussion.) Jon Elster describes problems with understanding politics in terms of either competitive markets (as defenders of the popular will theory often advocate) or in terms of rational deliberation (as others have suggested). Elster concludes that the truth lies with neither of these two extremes. In the next essay William Nelson offers both a critique of citizen participation, particularly Pateman's, and a defense of democracy based on its tendency to produce the best outcome, which he sees having roots in the thought of James Madison. For Nelson, democratic forms cannot be assessed without a broad understanding of justice and of the likelihood that democratic forms will produce just laws. In the final essay Joseph Raz extends that argument, claiming that democratic government is part of liberalism's larger commitment to the value of autonomy as a way of life.

Each of the theories described so far—popular will and various forms of the best outcome theory—share the assumption that democratic processes are justified *instrumentally*, because of their effects. Disagreements focus on the objectives to be pursued along with the possibility of achieving them. Some theorists see democracy as a means to aggregate preferences, or to serve the interests of the people, others as a way to create good citizens or help assure that policies are just. But some other theorists of democracy offer what might be called an *internal* justification, arguing that the case for democratic government rests on the nature of the democratic process itself rather than on its consequences. Chapter 4, **The Procedural Theory,** looks at this internal justification, focusing in particular on the claim that democratic procedures are inherently fair and express the ideal of equal citizenship. Both Peter Singer and Carl Cohen defend democratic procedures in these terms, contending that only democratic processes allowing each person a vote are compatible with these underlying ideals. Peter Jones pursues these issues further, focusing on the claim that the majority principle expresses the underlying ideal of equality. Behind this claim, he suggests, is the idea that every citizen's interests should be given equal consideration. (In that way, his view is reminiscent of James Mill.) Jones then discusses the related problem of persistent minorities. Charles Beitz first criticizes Singer and others who argue that each citizen is entitled to have an equal opportunity to influence the political process. He goes on, however, to defend his own version of "complex proceduralism" that incorporates elements of proceduralism and best outcome theories.

The remaining three chapters move down somewhat from these lofty heights to consider a range of more practical issues. Chapter 5, **Workplace Democracy,** develops some of the arguments made in previous discussions on political participation. Michael Walzer argues that principles underlying democratic government make it difficult to resist the conclusion that workers should also have control over decisions in the workplace. Robert Dahl's selection then considers the practicability of applying democratic principles to the workplace.

Democracy and the Law, Chapter 6, includes essays on various topics appearing in the intersection of law and democratic theory. Some legal scholars have argued that there is an important but limited role for judicial review in a constitutional democracy—to assure that the political process is fair and genuinely democratic. When judges go beyond their responsibility to police the democratic process, however, they act irresponsibly. That position is outlined and evaluated by Bruce Ackerman. Ronald Dworkin defends a much more activistic role of the Supreme Court, one which, he argues, is entirely compatible with the ideals of democratic government. Cass Sunstein next considers why, in a constitutional democracy, the government might override citizen's private preferences and concludes with a discussion of when such preferences *should* be overridden and of some recent legal issues that revolve around these problems. In the final essay of the chapter, John Rawls considers the nature of the obligation to obey the law and the justification of civil disobedience. On what grounds, he asks, might a citizen reasonably argue that civil disobedience is justified in a constitutional democracy? The chapter concludes with five major Supreme Court opinions in cases involving the democratic process: reapportionment, voting power, voting qualifications, and campaign financing. Carefully edited in order to assure they are accessible to nonlawyers, these four opinions illustrate the practical importance of debates about democratic theory.

The final chapter, **Critical Perspectives,** includes essays critical of democratic government as practiced in western, capitalist societies. Joshua Cohen and Joel Rogers focus on the ways capitalism undermines democratic ideals. Carole Pateman offers a feminist critique of traditional democratic theory (including a critique of her own work reprinted in Chapter 3.)

1
Classical Perspectives

The General Will

Jean-Jacques Rousseau

Jean-Jacques Rousseau was born in 1712 in Geneva, Switzerland. His mother died in childbirth. For ten years Rousseau was raised by his father, who then left the young boy with relatives. After running away at 16, he wandered throughout Europe while he educated himself. Rousseau was a complex and unhappy person. He achieved fame when he won a prize for his essay A Discourse on the Arts and Sciences, *which argued that civilization had an evil influence on people's natural morality. In the years that followed he wrote two novels and numerous political essays.* The Social Contract, *from which the following selection was taken, is his classic work. His books were burned in Paris and Geneva, and Rousseau was forced to flee in order to avoid arrest. He died in poverty in 1788.*

Rousseau's work was extremely influential; indeed he is credited with transforming the public fear of democracy as immoral and unstable into the conviction that it is the only morally acceptable form of government. In the selections reprinted below, Rousseau begins with an account of the origins of the state in the social contract. This leads to discussions of the relationship between the individual and the sovereign, the general will as an expression of the individual in a single body, and, finally, of the role of voting and the will of the majority.

Book I

Chapter V—That It Is Always Necessary to Go Back to a First Convention

. . . There will always be a great difference between subduing a multitude and ruling a society. When isolated men, however numerous they may be, are subjected one after another to a single person, this seems to me only a case of master and slaves, not of a nation and its chief; they form, if you will, an aggregation, but not an association, for they have neither public property nor a body politic. Such a man, had he enslaved half the world, is never anything but an individual; his interest, separated from that of the rest, is never anything but a private interest. If he dies, his empire after him is left disconnected and disunited, as

From Jean-Jacques Rousseau, *The Social Contract* (New York: Charles Scribner's Sons, 1895).

an oak dissolves and becomes a heap of ashes after the fire has consumed it. . . .

Chapter VI—The Social Compact

I assume that men have reached a point at which the obstacles that endanger their preservation in the state of nature overcome by their resistance the forces which each individual can exert with a view to maintaining himself in that state. Then this primitive condition can no longer subsist, and the human race would perish unless it changed its mode of existence.

Now, as men cannot create any new forces, but only combine and direct those that exist, they have no other means of self-preservation than to form by aggregation a sum of forces which may overcome the resistance, to put them in action by a single motive power, and to make them work in concert.

This sum of forces can be produced only by the combination of many; but the strength and freedom of each man being the chief instruments of his preservation, how can he pledge them without injuring himself, and without neglecting the cares which he owes to himself? This difficulty, applied to my subject, may be expressed in these terms:

"To find a form of association which may defend and protect with the whole force of the community the person and property of every associate, and by means of which each, coalescing with all, may nevertheless obey only himself, and remain as free as before." Such is the fundamental problem of which the social contract furnishes the solution.

The clauses of this contract are so determined by the nature of the act that the slightest modification would render them vain and ineffectual; so that, although they have never perhaps been formally enunciated, they are everywhere the same, everywhere tacitly admitted and recognized, until, the social pact being violated, each man regains his original rights and recovers his natural liberty, while losing the conventional liberty for which he renounced it.

These clauses, rightly understood, are reducible to one only, viz., the total alienation to the whole community of each associate with all his rights; for, in the first place, since each gives himself up entirely, the conditions are equal for all; and, the conditions being equal for all, no one has any interest in making them burdensome to others.

Further, the alienation being made without reserve, the union is as perfect as it can be, and an individual associate can no longer claim anything; for, if any rights were left to individuals, since there would be no common superior who could judge between them and the public, each, being on some point his own judge, would soon claim to be so on all; the state of nature would still subsist, and the association would necessarily become tyrannical or useless.

In short, each giving himself to all, gives himself to nobody; and as there is not one associate over whom we do not acquire the same rights which we concede to him over ourselves, we gain the equivalent of all that we lose, and more power to preserve what we have.

If, then, we set aside what is not of the essence of the social contract, we shall find that it is reducible to the following terms: "Each of us puts in common his person and his whole power under the supreme direction of the general will; and in return we receive every member as an indivisible part of the whole."

Forthwith, instead of the individual personalities of all the contracting parties, this act of association produces a moral and collective body, which is composed of as many members as the assembly has voices, and which receives from this same act its unity, its common self (moi), its life, and its will. This public person, which is thus formed by the union of all the individual members, formerly took the name of city, and now takes that of republic or body politic, which is called by its members State when it is passive, sovereign when it is active, power when it is compared to similar bodies. With regard to the associates, they take collectively the name of people, and are called individually citizens, as participating in the sovereign power, and subjects, as subjected to the laws of the State. But these terms are often confused and are mistaken one for another; it is sufficient to know how to distinguish them when they are used with complete precision.

Chapter VII—The Sovereign

We see from this formula that the act of association contains a reciprocal engagement between the public and individuals, and that every individual, contracting so to speak with himself, is engaged in a double relation, viz., as a member of the sovereign towards individuals, and as a member of the State towards the sovereign. But we cannot apply here the maxim of civil law that no one is bound by engagements made with himself; for there is a great difference between being bound to oneself and to a whole of which one forms a part.

We must further observe that the public resolution which can bind all subjects to the sovereign in consequence of the two different relations under which each of them is regarded cannot, for a contrary reason, bind the sovereign to itself; and that accordingly it is contrary to the nature of the body politic for the sovereign to impose on itself a law which it cannot transgress. As it can only be considered under one and the same relation, it is in the position of an individual contracting with himself; whence we see that there is not, nor can be, any kind of fundamental law binding upon the body of the people, not even the social contract. This does not imply that such a body cannot perfectly well enter into engagements with others in what does not derogate from this contract; for, with regard to foreigners, it becomes a simple being, an individual.

But the body politic or sovereign, deriving its existence only from the sanctity of the contract, can never bind itself, even to others, in anything that derogates from the original act, such as alienation of some portion of itself, or submission to another sovereign. To violate the act by which it exists would be to annihilate itself; and what is nothing produces nothing.

So soon as the multitude is thus united in one body, it is impossible to injure one of the members without attacking the body, still less to injure the body without the members feeling the effects. Thus duty and interest alike oblige the two contracting parties to give mutual assistance; and the men themselves should seek to combine in this twofold relationship all the advantages which are attendant on it.

Now, the sovereign, being formed only of the individuals that compose it, neither has nor can have any interest contrary to theirs; consequently the sovereign power needs no guarantee towards its subjects, because it is impossible that the body should wish to injure all its members; and we shall see hereafter that it can injure no one as an individual. The sovereign, for the simple reason that it is so, is always everything that it ought to be.

But this is not the case as regards the relation of subjects to the sovereign, which, notwithstanding the common interest, would have no security for the performance of their engagements, unless it found means to ensure their fidelity.

Indeed, every individual may, as a man, have a particular will contrary to, or divergent from, the general will which he has as a citizen; his private interest may prompt him quite differently from the common interest; his absolute and naturally independent existence may make him regard what he owes to the common cause as a gratuitous contribution, the loss of which will be less harmful to others than the payment of it will be burdensome to him; and,

regarding the moral person that constitutes the State as an imaginary being because it is not a man, he would be willing to enjoy the rights of a citizen without being willing to fulfil the duties of a subject. The progress of such injustice would bring about the ruin of the body politic.

In order, then, that the social pact may not be a vain formulary, it tacitly includes this engagement, which can alone give force to the others—that whoever refuses to obey the general will shall be constrained to do so by the whole body; which means nothing else than that he shall be forced to be free; for such is the condition which, uniting every citizen to his native land, guarantees him from all personal dependence, a condition that ensures the control and working of the political machine, and alone renders legitimate civil engagements, which, without it, would be absurd and tyrannical, and subject to the most enormous abuses.

Chapter VIII—The Civil State

The passage from the state of nature to the civil state produces in man a very remarkable change, by substituting in his conduct justice for instinct, and by giving his actions the moral quality that they previously lacked. It is only when the voice of duty succeeds physical impulse, and law succeeds appetite, that man, who till then had regarded only himself, sees that he is obliged to act on other principles, and to consult his reason before listening to his inclinations. Although, in this state, he is deprived of many advantages that he derives from nature, he acquires equally great ones in return; his faculties are exercised and developed; his ideas are expanded; his feelings are ennobled; his whole soul is exalted to such a degree that, if the abuses of this new condition did not often degrade him below that from which he has emerged, he ought to bless without ceasing the happy moment that released him from it for ever, and transformed him from a stupid and ignorant animal into an intelligent being and a man.

Let us reduce this whole balance to terms easy to compare. What man loses by the social contract is his natural liberty and an unlimited right to anything which tempts him and which he is able to attain; what he gains is civil liberty and property in all that he possesses. In order that we may not be mistaken about these compensations, we must clearly distinguish natural liberty, which is limited only by the powers of the individual, from civil liberty, which is limited by the general will; and possession, which is nothing but the result of force or the right of first occupancy, from property, which can be based only on a positive title.

Besides the preceding, we might add to the acquisitions of the civil state moral freedom, which alone renders man truly master of himself; for the impulse of mere appetite is slavery, while obedience to a self-prescribed law is liberty. But I have already said too much on this head, and the philosophical meaning of the term *liberty* does not belong to my present subject. . . .

Book II

Chapter I—That Sovereignty Is Inalienable

The first and most important consequence of the principles above established is that the general will alone can direct the forces of the State according to the object of its institution, which is the common good; for if the opposition of private interests has rendered necessary the establishment of societies, the agreement of these same interests has rendered it possible. That which is common to these different interests forms the social bond; and unless there were some point in which all interests agree, no society could exist. Now, it is solely with regard to this common interest that the society should be governed.

I say, then, that sovereignty, being nothing but the exercise of the general will, can never be alienated, and that the sovereign power, which is only a collective being, can be represented by itself alone; power indeed can be transmitted, but not will.

In fact, if it is not impossible that a particular will should agree on some point with the general will, it is at least impossible that this agreement should be lasting and constant; for the particular will naturally tends to prefer-

ences, and the general will to equality. It is still more impossible to have a security for this agreement; even though it should always exist, it would not be a result of art, but of chance. The sovereign may indeed say: "I will now what a certain man wills, or at least what he says that he wills;" but he cannot say: "What that man wills tomorrow, I shall also will," since it is absurd that the will should bind itself as regards the future, and since it is not incumbent on any will to consent to anything contrary to the welfare of the being that wills. If, then, the nation simply promises to obey, it dissolves itself by that act and loses its character as a people; the moment there is a master, there is no longer a sovereign, and forthwith the body politic is destroyed.

This does not imply that the orders of the chiefs cannot pass for decisions of the general will, so long as the sovereign, free to oppose them, refrains from doing so. In such a case the consent of the people should be inferred from the universal silence. . . .

Chapter II—That Sovereignty Is Indivisible

For the same reason that sovereignty is inalienable it is indivisible; for the will is either general, or it is not; it is either that of the body of the people, or that of only a portion. In the first case, this declared will is an act of sovereignty and constitutes law; in the second case, it is only a particular will, or an act of magistracy—it is at most a decree.

Chapter III—Whether the General Will Can Err

It follows from what precedes that the general will is always right and always tends to the public advantage; but it does not follow that the resolutions of the people have always the same rectitude. Men always desire their own good, but do not always discern it; the people are never corrupted, though often deceived, and it is only then that they seem to will what is evil.

There is often a great deal of difference between the will of all and the general will; the latter regards only the common interest, while the former has regard to private interests, and is merely a sum of particular wills; but take away from these same wills the pluses and minuses which cancel one another, and the general will remains as the sum of the differences.

If the people came to a resolution when adequately informed and without any communication among the citizens, the general will would always result from the great number of slight differences, and the resolution would always be good. But when factions, partial associations, are formed to the detriment of the whole society, the will of each of these associations becomes general with reference to its members, and particular with reference to the State; it may then be said that there are no longer as many voters as there are men, but only as many voters as there are associations. The differences become less numerous and yield a less general result. Lastly, when one of these associations becomes so great that it predominates over all the rest, you no longer have as the result a sum of small differences, but a single difference; there is then no longer a general will, and the opinion which prevails is only a particular opinion.

It is important, then, in order to have a clear declaration of the general will, that there should be no partial association in the State, and that every citizen should express only his own opinions. Such was the unique and sublime institution of the great Lycurgus. But if there are partial associations, it is necessary to multiply their number and prevent inequality, as Solon, Numa, and Servius did. These are the only proper precautions for ensuring that the general will may always be enlightened, and that the people may not be deceived.

Chapter IV—The Limits of the Sovereign Power

If the State or city is nothing but a moral person, the life of which consists in the union of its members, and if the most important of its cares is that of self-preservation, it needs a universal and compulsive force to move and dispose every part in the manner most expedient for the whole. As nature gives every man an absolute power over all his limbs, and the social pact gives the body politic an absolute power over all its members; and it is this

same power which, when directed by the general will, bears, as I said, the name of sovereignty.

But besides the public person, we have to consider the private persons who compose it, and whose life and liberty are naturally independent of it. The question, then, is to distinguish clearly between the respective rights of the citizens and of the sovereign, as well as between the duties which the former have to fulfill in their capacity as subjects and the natural rights which they ought to enjoy in their character as men.

It is admitted that whatever part of his power, property, and liberty each one alienates by social compact is only that part of the whole of which the use is important to the community; but we must also admit that the sovereign alone is judge of what is important.

All the services that a citizen can render to the State he owes to it as soon as the sovereign demands them; but the sovereign, on its part, cannot impose on its subjects any burden which is useless to the community; it cannot even wish to do so, for, by the law of reason, just as by the law of nature, nothing is done without a cause.

The engagements which bind us to the social body are obligatory only because they are mutual; and their nature is such that in fulfilling them we cannot work for others without also working for ourselves. Why is the general will always right, and why do all invariably desire the prosperity of each, unless it is because there is no one but appropriates to himself this word *each* and thinks of himself in voting on behalf of all? This proves that equality of rights and the notion of justice that it produces are derived from the preference which each gives to himself, and consequently from man's nature; that the general will, to be truly such, should be so in its object as well as in its essence; that it ought to proceed from all in order to be applicable to all; and that it loses its natural rectitude when it tends to some individual and determinate object, because in that case, judging of what is unknown to us, we have no true principle of equity to guide us.

Indeed, so soon as a particular fact or right is in question with regard to a point which has not been regulated by an anterior general convention, the matter becomes contentious; it is a process in which the private persons interested are one of the parties and the public the other, but in which I perceive neither the law which must be followed, nor judge who should decide. It would be ridiculous in such a case to wish to refer the matter for an express decision of the general will, which can be nothing but the decision of one of the parties, and which, consequently, is for the other party only a will that is foreign, partial, and inclined on such an occasion to injustice as well as liable to error. Therefore, just as a particular will cannot represent the general will, the general will in turn changes its nature when it has a particular end, and cannot, as general, decide about either a person or a fact. When the people of Athens, for instance, elected or deposed their chiefs, decreed honors to one, imposed penalties on another, and by multitudes of particular decrees exercised indiscriminately all the functions of government, the people no longer had any general will properly so called; they no longer acted as a sovereign power, but as magistrates. This will appear contrary to common ideas, but I must be allowed time to expound my own.

From this we must understand that what generalizes the will is not so much the number of voices as the common interest which unites them; for, under this system, each necessarily submits to the conditions which he imposes on others—an admirable union of interest and justice, which gives to the deliberations of the community a spirit of equity that seems to disappear in the discussion of any private affair, for want of a common interest to unite and identify the ruling principle of the judge with that of the party.

By whatever path we return to our principle we always arrive at the same conclusion, viz., that the social compact establishes among the citizens such an equality that they all pledge themselves under the same conditions and ought all to enjoy the same rights. Thus, by the nature of the compact, every act of sovereignty, that is, every authentic act of the general will, binds or favors equally all the citizens; so that the sovereign knows only the body of the nation, and distinguishes none of those that compose it.

What, then, is an act of sovereignty properly so called? It is not an agreement between a superior and an inferior, but an agreement of the body with each of its members; a lawful agreement, because it has the social contract as its foundation; equitable, because it is common to all; useful, because it can have no other object than the general welfare; and stable, because it has the public force and the supreme power as a guarantee. So long as the subjects submit only to such conventions, they obey no one, but simply their own will; and to ask how far the respective rights of the sovereign and citizens extend is to ask up to what point the latter can make engagements among themselves, each with all and all with each.

Thus we see that the sovereign power, wholly absolute, wholly sacred, and wholly inviolable as it is, does not, and cannot, pass the limits of general conventions, and that every man can fully dispose of what is left to him of his property and liberty by these conventions; so that the sovereign never has the right to burden one subject more than another, because then the matter becomes particular and his power is no longer competent.

These distinctions once admitted, so untrue is it that in the social contract there is on the part of individuals any real renunciation, that their situation, as a result of this contract, is in reality preferable to what it was before, and that, instead of an alienation, they have only made an advantageous exchange of an uncertain and precarious mode of existence for a better and more assured one, of natural independence for liberty, of the power to injure others for their own safety, and of their strength, which others might overcome, for a right which the social union renders inviolable. Their lives, also, which they have devoted to the State, are continually protected by it; and in exposing their lives for its defense, what do they do but restore what they have received from it? What do they do but what they would do more frequently and with more risk in the state of nature, when, engaging in inevitable struggles, they would defend at the peril of their lives their means of preservation? All have to fight for their country in case of need, it is true; but then no one ever has to fight for himself. Do we not gain, moreover, by incurring, for what insures our safety, a part of the risks that we should have to incur for ourselves individually, as soon as we were deprived of it?

Chapter VI—The Law

By the social compact we have given existence and life to the body politic; the question now is to endow it with movement and will by legislation. For the original act by which this body is formed and consolidated determines nothing in addition as to what it must do for its own preservation.

What is right and conformable to order is such by the nature of things, and independently of human conventions. All justice comes from God, He alone is the source of it; but could we receive it direct from so lofty a source, we should need neither government nor laws. Without doubt there is a universal justice emanating from reason alone; but this justice, in order to be admitted among us, should be reciprocal. Regarding things from a human standpoint, the laws of justice are inoperative among men for want of a natural sanction; they only bring good to the wicked and evil to the just when the latter observe them with every one, and no one observes them in return. Conventions and laws, then, are necessary to couple rights with duties and apply justice to its object. In the state of nature, where everything is in common, I owe nothing to those to whom I have promised nothing; I recognize as belonging to others only what is useless to me. This is not the case in the civil state, in which all rights are determined by law.

But then, finally, what is a law? So long as men are content to attach to this word only metaphysical ideas, they will continue to argue without being understood; and when they have stated what a law of nature is, they will know no better what a law of the State is.

I have already said that there is no general will with reference to a particular object. In fact, this particular object is either in the State or outside of it. If it is outside the State, a will which is foreign to it is not general in relation to it; and if it is within the State, it forms part of it; then there is formed between the whole and its part a relation which makes of it two separate beings, of which the part is one, and

the whole, less this same part, is the other. But the whole less one part is not the whole, and so long as the relation subsists, there is no longer any whole, but two unequal parts; whence it follows that the will of the one is no longer general in relation to the other.

But when the whole people decree concerning the whole people, they consider themselves alone; and if a relation is then constituted, it is between the whole object under one point of view, without any division at all. Then the matter respecting which they decree is general like the will that decreees. It is this act that I call a law.

When I say that the object of the laws is always general, I mean that the law considers subjects collectively, and actions as abstract, never a man as an individual nor a particular action. Thus the law may indeed decree that there shall be privileges, but cannot confer them on any person by name; the law can create several classes of citizens, and even assign the qualifications which shall entitle them to rank in these classes, but it cannot nominate such and such persons to be admitted to them; it can establish a royal government and a hereditary succession, but cannot elect a king or appoint a royal family; in a word, no function which has reference to an individual object appertains to the legislative power.

From this standpoint we see immediately that it is no longer necessary to ask whose office it is to make laws, since they are acts of the general will; nor whether the prince is above the laws, since he is a member of the State; nor whether the law can be unjust, since no one is unjust to himself; nor how we are free and yet subject to the laws, since the laws are only registers of our wills.

We see, further, that since the law combines the universality of the will with the universality of the object, whatever any man prescribes on his own authority is not a law; and whatever the sovereign itself prescribes respecting a particular object is not a law, but a decree, not an act of sovereignty, but of magistracy.

I therefore call any State a republic which is governed by laws, under whatever form of administration it may be; for then only does the public interest predominate and the commonwealth count for something. Every legitimate government is republican; I will explain hereafter what government is.

Laws are properly only the conditions of civil association. The people, being subjected to the laws, should be the authors of them; it concerns only the associates to determine the conditions of association. But how will they be determined? Will it be by a common agreement, by a sudden inspiration? Has the body politic an organ for expressing its will? Who will give it the foresight necessary to frame its acts and publish them at the outset? Or how shall it declare them in the hour of need? How would a blind multitude, which often knows not what it wishes because it rarely knows what is good for it, execute of itself an enterprise so great, so difficult, as a system of legislation? Of themselves, the people always desire what is good, but do not always discern it. The general will is always right, but the judgment which guides it is not always enlightened. It must be made to see objects as they are, sometimes as they ought to appear; it must be shown the good path that it is seeking, and guarded from the seduction of private interests; it must be made to observe closely times and places, and to balance the attraction of immediate and palpable advantages against the danger of remote and concealed evils. Individuals see the good which they reject; the public desire the good which they do not see. All alike have need of guides. The former must be compelled to conform their wills to their reason; the people must be taught to know what they require. Then from the public enlightenment results the union of the understanding and the will in the social body; and from that the close cooperation of the parts, and, lastly, the maximum power of the whole. Hence arises the need of a legislator. . . .

Book IV

Chapter I—That the General Will Is Indestructible

So long as a number of men in combination are considered as a single body, they have but one will, which relates to the common preservation and to the general well-being. In such a case all the forces of the State are vigorous and simple, and its principles are clear and luminous; it has no confused and conflicting interests; the common good is everywhere plainly manifest and only good sense is required to perceive it. Peace, union, and equality are foes to political subtleties. Upright and simpleminded men are hard to deceive because of their simplicity; allurements and refined pretexts do not impose upon them; they are not even cunning enough to be dupes. When, in the happiest nation in the world, we see troops of peasants regulating the affairs of the State under an oak and always acting wisely, can we refrain from despising the refinements of other nations, who make themselves illustrious and wretched with so much art and mystery?

A State thus governed needs very few laws; and in so far as it becomes necessary to promulgate new ones, this necessity is universally recognized. The first man to propose them only gives expression to what all have previously felt, and neither factions nor eloquence will be needed to pass into law what every one has already resolved to do, so soon as he is sure that the rest will act as he does.

What deceives reasoners is that, seeing only States that are ill-constituted from the beginning, they are impressed with the impossibility of maintaining such a policy in those States; they laugh to think of all the follies to which a cunning knave, an insinuating speaker, can persuade the people of Paris or London. They know not that Cromwell would have been put in irons by the people of Berne, and the Duke of Beaufort imprisoned by the Genevese.

But when the social bond begins to be relaxed and the State weakened, when private interests begin to make themselves felt and small associations to exercise influence on the State, the common interest is injuriously affected and finds adversaries; unanimity no longer reigns in the voting; the general will is no longer the will of all; opposition and disputes arise, and the best counsel does not pass uncontested.

Lastly, when the State, on the verge of ruin, no longer subsists except in a vain and illusory form, when the social bond is broken in all hearts, when the basest interest shelters itself impudently under the sacred name of the public welfare, the general will becomes dumb; all, under the guidance of secret motives, no more express their opinions as citizens than if the State had never existed; and, under the name of laws, they deceitfully pass unjust decrees which have only private interest as their end.

Does it follow from this that the general will is destroyed or corrupted? No; it is always constant, unalterable, and pure; but it is subordinated to others which get the better of it. Each, detaching his own interest from the common interest, sees clearly that he cannot completely separate it; but his share in the injury done to the State appears to him as nothing in comparison with the exclusive advantage which he aims at appropriating to himself. This particular advantage being excepted, he desires the general welfare for his own interests quite as strongly as any other. Even in selling his vote for money, he does not extinguish in himself the general will, but eludes it. The fault that he commits is to change the state of the question, and to answer something different from what he was asked; so that, instead of saying by a vote: "It is beneficial to the State," he says: "It is beneficial to a certain man or a certain party that such or such a motion should pass." Thus the law of public order in assemblies is not so much to maintain in them the general will as to ensure that it shall always be consulted and always respond. . . .

Chapter II—Voting

We see from the previous chapter that the manner in which public affairs are managed may give a sufficiently trustworthy indication of the character and health of the body politic. The more that harmony reigns in the assemblies, that is, the more the voting approaches unanimity, the more also is the general will predominant; but long discussions, dissensions, and uproar proclaim the ascendancy of private interests and the decline of the State. . . .

There is but one law which by its nature requires unanimous consent, that is, the social compact, for civil association is the most voluntary act in the world: every man being born free and master of himself, no one can, under any pretext whatever, enslave him without his assent. To decide that the son of a slave is born a slave is to decide that he is not born a man.

If, then, at the time of the social compact, there are opponents of it, their opposition does not invalidate the contract, but only prevents them from being included in it; they are foreigners among citizens. When the State is established, consent lies in residence; to dwell in the territory is to submit to the sovereignty.

Excepting this original contract, the vote of the majority always binds all the rest, this being a result of the contract itself. But it will be asked how a man can be free and yet forced to conform to wills which are not his own. How are opponents free and yet subject to laws they have not consented to?

I reply that the question is wrongly put. The citizen consents to all the laws, even to those which are passed in spite of him, and even to those which punish him when he dares to violate any of them. The unvarying will of all the members of the State is the general will; it is through that that they are citizens and free. When a law is proposed in the assembly of the people, what is asked of them is not exactly whether they approve the proposition or reject it, but whether it is comformable or not to the general will, which is their own; each one in giving his vote expresses his opinion thereupon; and from the counting of the votes is obtained the declaration of the general will. When, therefore, the opinion opposed to my own prevails, that simply shows that I was mistaken, and that what I considered to be the general will was not so. Had my private opinion prevailed, I should have done something other than I wished; and in that case I should not have been free.

This supposes, it is true, that all the marks of the general will are still in the majority; when they cease to be so, whatever side we take, there is no longer any liberty.

In showing before how particular wills were substituted for general wills in public resolutions, I have sufficiently indicated the means practicable for preventing this abuse; I will speak of it again hereafter. With regard to the proportional number of votes for declaring this will, I have also laid down the principles according to which it may be determined. The difference of a single vote destroys unanimity; but between unanimity and equality there are many unequal divisions, at each of which this number can be fixed according to the condition and requirements of the body politic.

Two general principles may serve to regulate these proportions: the one, that the more important and weighty the resolutions, the nearer should the opinion which prevails approach unanimity; the other, that the greater the dispatch requisite in the matter under discussion, the more should we restrict the prescribed difference in the division of opinions; in resolutions which must be come to immediately, the majority of a single vote should suffice. The first of these principles appears more suitable to laws, the second to affairs. Be that as it may, it is by their combination that are established the best proportions which can be assigned for the decision of a majority.

Constitutional Democracy

James Madison, Alexander Hamilton, and Thomas Jefferson

Like many of their contemporaries, the framers of the United States Constitution did not seek to establish a democratic government but instead a "Republican" one. Though committed to avoiding monarchy, they were also keenly aware of the dangers inherent in electoral processes. Recent experiences under the Articles of Confederation had convinced them of the dangers of majority rule. So while the government they created did not ignore the will of the people, neither did it place the reins of power squarely in their hands. Madison and the others used two strategies to ensure that the new government would not be led astray: separation of powers and indirect representation. Rather than a single, elected assembly the new government proposed a bicameral assembly, a president chosen independently from the Congress, and a judiciary comprised of judges appointed for life. Each branch was to have limited powers specified in advance. In addition to those checks, the individual states were to retain a substantial amount of power. Indirect representation was the rule rather than the exception: only the lower branch of the Congress, the House, was directly elected. Senators were originally chosen by state legislators (which were themselves mostly bicameral); the President was chosen by an Electoral College, whose members were themselves originally chosen by state legislators; and the judiciary was to be appointed by the President (not popularly elected) with the "advise and consent" of the Senate (not proportionately representative and indirectly elected). Judges were then given lifetime tenure, removable only for "treason or other high crimes and misdemeanors."

James Madison was the prime architect of the new Constitution, and the selections which follow include the most important statements of his philosophical position. Both Madison and Alexander Hamilton played a key role in the protracted struggle for ratification in the months following the convention. This material begins with selections from The Federalist Papers, *a series of essays written by Madison, Hamilton, and John Jay for New York newspapers in which they advocated adoption of the new Constitution. The final two selections are letters written by Jefferson to Madison along with Madison's response to Jefferson.*

From *The Federalist Papers*, Clinton Rossiter, ed. (New York: New American Library, 1961); and *The Papers of Thomas Jefferson, 1789–1790*, Julien P. Boyd, ed. (Princeton, NJ: Princeton University Press, 1961).

Federalist—Number 10

James Madison

Among the numerous advantages promised by a well constructed Union, none deserves to be more accurately developed than its tendency to break and control the violence of faction. The friend of popular governments, never finds himself so much alarmed for their character and fate, as when he contemplates their propensity to this dangerous vice. . . .

By a faction I understand a number of citizens, whether amounting to a majority or minority of the whole, who are united and actuated by some common impulse of passion, or of interest, adverse to the rights of other citizens, or to the permanent and aggregate interests of the community.

There are two methods of curing the mischiefs of faction: the one, by removing its causes; the other, by controlling its effects.

There are again two methods of removing the causes of faction: the one by destroying the liberty which is essential to its existence; the other, by giving to every citizen the same opinions, the same passions, and the same interests.

It could never be more truly said than of the first remedy, that it is worse than the disease. Liberty is to faction, what air is to fire, an aliment without which it instantly expires. But it could not be a less folly to abolish liberty, which is essential to political life, because it nourishes faction, than it would be to wish the annihilation of air, which is essential to animal life, because it imparts to fire its destructive agency.

The second expedient is as impracticable, as the first would be unwise. As long as the reason of man continues fallible, and he is at liberty to exercise it, different opinions will be formed. As long as the connection subsists between his reason and his self-love, his opinions and his passions will have a reciprocal influence on each other; and the former will be objects to which the latter will attach themselves. The diversity in the faculties of men from which the rights of property originate, is not less an insuperable obstacle to the uniformity of interests. The protection of these faculties is the first object of Government. From the protection of different and unequal faculties of acquiring property, the possession of different degrees and kinds of property immediately results: and from the influence of these on the sentiments and views of the respective proprietors, ensues a division of the society into different interests and parties.

The latent causes of faction are thus sown in the nature of man; and we see them everywhere brought into different degrees of activity, according to the different circumstances of civil society. A zeal for different opinions concerning religion, concerning Government and many other points, as well of speculation as of practice; an attachment to different leaders ambitiously contending for pre-eminence and power; or to persons of other descriptions whose fortunes have been interesting to the human passions, have in turn divided mankind into parties, inflamed them with mutual animosity, and rendered them much more disposed to vex and oppress each other, than to co-operate for their common good. So strong is this propensity of mankind to fall into mutual animosities, that where no substantial occasion presents itself, the most frivolous and fanciful distinctions have been sufficient to kindle their unfriendly passions, and excite their most violent conflicts. But the most common and durable source of factions, has been the various and unequal distribution of property. Those who hold, and those who are without property, have ever formed distinct interests in society. Those who are creditors, and those who are debtors, fall under a like discrimination. A landed interest, a manufacturing interest, a mercantile interest, a monied interest, with many lesser interests, grow up of necessity in civilized nations, and divide them into different classes, actuated by different sentiments and views. The regulation of these various and interfering interests forms the principal task of modern Legislation, and involves the spirit of party and faction in the necessary and ordinary operations of Government.

No man is allowed to be a judge of his own cause; because his interest would certainly bias his judgment, and, not improbably, corrupt his integrity. With equal, nay with greater reason, a body of men, are unfit to be both judges and parties, at the same time; yet, what are many of the most important acts of legislation, but so many judicial determinations, not indeed concerning the rights of single persons, but concerning the rights of large bodies of citizens; and what are the different classes of legislators, but advocates and parties to the causes which they determine? Is a law proposed concerning private debts? It is a question to which the creditors are parties on one side, and the debtors on the other. Justice ought to hold the balance between them. Yet the parties are and must be themselves the judges; and the most numerous party, or, in other words, the most powerful faction must be expected to prevail. Shall domestic manufactures be encouraged, and in what degree, by restrictions on foreign manufactures? are questions which would be differently decided by the landed and the manufacturing classes; and probably by neither, with a sole regard to justice and the public good. The apportionment of taxes on the various descriptions of property, is an act which seems to require the most exact impartiality; yet, there is perhaps no legislative act in which greater opportunity and temptation are given to a predominant party, to trample on the rules of justice. Every shilling with which they over-burden the inferior number, is a shilling saved to their own pockets.

It is in vain to say, that enlightened statesmen will be able to adjust these clashing interests, and render them all subservient to the public good. Enlightened statesmen will not always be at the helm: Nor in many cases, can such an adjustment be made at all, without taking into view indirect and remote considerations, which will rarely prevail over the immediate interest which one party may find in disregarding the rights of another, or the good of the whole.

The inference to which we are brought, is, that the *causes* of faction cannot be removed; and that relief is only to be sought in the means of controlling its *effects*.

If a faction consists of less than a majority, relief is supplied by the republican principle, which enables the majority to defeat its sinister views by regular vote: It may clog the administration, it may convulse the society; but it will

be unable to execute and mask its violence under the forms of the Constitution. When a majority is included in a faction, the form of popular government on the other hand enables it to sacrifice to its ruling passion or interest, both the public good and the rights of other citizens. To secure the public good, and private rights, against the danger of such a faction, and at the same time to preserve the spirit and the form of popular government, is then the great object to which our enquiries are directed: Let me add that it is the great desideratum, by which alone this form of government can be rescued from the opprobrium under which it has so long labored, and be recommended to the esteem and adoption of mankind.

By what means is this object attainable? Evidently by one of two only. Either the existence of the same passion or interest in a majority at the same time, must be prevented; or the majority, having such co-existent passion or interest, must be rendered, by their number and local situation, unable to concert and carry into effect schemes of oppression. If the impulse and the opportunity be suffered to coincide, we well know that neither moral nor religious motives can be relied on as an adequate control. They are not found to be such on the injustice and violence of individuals, and lose their efficacy in proportion to the number combined together; that is, in proportion as their efficacy becomes needful.

From this view of the subject, it may be concluded, that a pure Democracy, by which I mean, a Society, consisting of a small number of citizens, who assemble and administer the Government in person, can admit of no cure for the mischiefs of faction. A common passion or interest will, in almost every case, be felt by a majority of the whole; a communication and concert results from the form of Government itself; and there is nothing to check the inducements to sacrifice the weaker party, or an obnoxious individual. Hence it is, that such Democracies have ever been spectacles of turbulence and contention; have ever been found incompatible with personal security, or the rights of property; and have in general been as short in their lives, as they have been violent in their deaths. Theoretic politicians, who have patronized this species of Government, have erroneously supposed, that by reducing mankind to a perfect equality in their political rights, they would, at the same time, be perfectly equalized and assimilated in their possessions, their opinions, and their passions.

A Republic, by which I mean a Government in which the scheme of representation takes place, opens a different prospect, and promises the cure for which we are seeking. Let us examine the points in which it varies from pure Democracy, and we shall comprehend both the nature of the cure, and the efficacy which it must derive from the Union.

The two great points of difference between a Democracy and a Republic are, first, the delegation of the Government, in the latter, to a small number of citizens elected by the rest: secondly, the greater number of citizens, and greater sphere of country, over which the latter may be extended.

The effect of the first difference is, on the one hand to refine and enlarge the public views, by passing them through the medium of a chosen body of citizens, whose wisdom may best discern the true interest of their country, and whose patriotism and love of justice, will be least likely to sacrifice it to temporary or partial considerations. Under such a regulation, it may well happen that the public voice pronounced by the representatives of the people, will be more consonant to the public good, than if pronounced by the people themselves convened for the purpose. On the other hand, the effect may be inverted. Men of factious tempers, of local prejudices, or of sinister designs, may by intrigue, by corruption or by other means, first obtain the suffrages, and then betray the interests of the people. The question resulting is, whether small or extensive Republics are most favorable to the election of proper guardians of the public weal: and it is clearly decided in favor of the latter by two obvious considerations.

In the first place it is to be remarked that however small the Republic may be, the Representatives must be raised to a certain number, in order to guard against the cabals of a few; and that however large it may be, they must be limited to a certain number, in order to guard against the confusion of a multitude. Hence the number of Representatives in the

two cases, not being in proportion to that of the Constituents, and being proportionally greatest in the small Republic, it follows, that if the proportion of fit characters, be not less, in the large than in the small Republic, the former will present a greater option, and consequently a greater probability of a fit choice.

In the next place, as each Representative will be chosen by a greater number of citizens in the large than in the small Republic, it will be more difficult for unworthy candidates to practise with success the vicious arts, by which elections are too often carried; and the suffrages of the people being more free, will be more likely to centre on men who possess the most attractive merit, and the most diffusive and established characters.

It must be confessed, that in this, as in most other cases, there is a mean, on both sides of which inconveniences will be found to lie. By enlarging too much the number of electors, you render the representative too little acquainted with all their local circumstances and lesser interests; as by reducing it too much, you render him unduly attached to these, and too little fit to comprehend and pursue great and national objects. The Federal Constitution forms a happy combination in this respect; the great and aggregate interests being referred to the national, the local and particular, to the state legislatures.

The other point of difference is, the greater number of citizens and extent of territory which may be brought within the compass of Republican, than of Democratic Government; and it is this circumstance principally which renders factious combinations less to be dreaded in the former, than in the latter. The smaller the society, the fewer probably will be the distinct parties and interests composing it; the fewer the distinct parties and interests, the more frequently will a majority be found of the same party; and the smaller the number of individuals composing a majority, and the smaller the compass within which they are placed, the more easily will they concert and execute their plans of oppression. Extend the sphere, and you take in a greater variety of parties and interests; you make it less probable that a majority of the whole will have a common motive to invade the rights of other citizens; or if such a common motive exists, it will be more difficult for all who feel it to discover their own strength, and to act in unison with each other. Besides other impediments, it may be remarked, that where there is a consciousness of unjust or dishonorable purposes, communication is always checked by distrust, in proportion to the number whose concurrence is necessary.

Hence it clearly appears, that the same advantage, which a Republic has over a Democracy, in controlling the effects of a faction, is enjoyed by a large over a small Republic—is enjoyed by the Union over the States composing it. Does this advantage consist in the substitution of Representatives, whose enlightened views and virtuous sentiments render them superior to local prejudices, and to schemes of injustice? It will not be denied, that the Representation of the Union will be most likely to possess these requisite endowments. Does it consist in the greater security afforded by a greater variety of parties, against the event of any one party being able to outnumber and oppress the rest? In an equal degree does the increased variety of parties, comprised within the Union, increase this security. Does it, in fine, consist in the greater obstacles opposed to the concert and accomplishment of the secret wishes of an unjust and interested majority? Here, again, the extent of the Union gives it the most palpable advantage.

The influence of factious leaders may kindle a flame within their particular States, but will be unable to spread a general conflagration through the other States: a religious sect, may degenerate into a political faction in a part of the Confederacy; but the variety of sects dispersed over the entire face of it, must secure the national Councils against any danger from that source: a rage for paper money, for an abolition of debts, for an equal division of property, or for any other improper or wicked project, will be less apt to pervade the whole body of the Union, than a particular member of it; in the same proportion as such a malady is more likely to taint a particular county or district, than an entire State.

In the extent and proper structure of the Union, therefore, we behold a Republican remedy for the diseases most incident to Republican Government. And according to the degree of pleasure and pride, we feel in being

Republicans, ought to be our zeal in cherishing the spirit, and supporting the character of Federalists.

Federalist—Number 51

James Madison

To what expedient then shall we finally resort for maintaining in practice the necessary partition of power among the several departments, as laid down in the Constitution? The only answer that can be given is, that as all these exterior provisions are found to be inadequate, the defect must be supplied, by so contriving the interior structure of the government, as that its several constituent parts may, by their mutual relations, be the means of keeping each other in their proper places. Without presuming to undertake a full development of this important idea, I will hazard a few general observations, which may perhaps place it in a clearer light, and enable us to form a more correct judgment of the principles and structure of the government planned by the convention.

In order to lay a due foundation for that separate and distinct exercise of the different powers of government, which to a certain extent, is admitted on all hands to be essential to the preservation of liberty, it is evident that each department should have a will of its own; and consequently should be so constituted, that the members of each should have as little agency as possible in the appointment of the members of the others. . . .

But the great security against a gradual concentration of the several powers in the same department, consists in giving to those who administer each department, the necessary constitutional means, and personal motives, to resist encroachments of the others. The provision for defence must in this, as in all other cases, be made commensurate to the danger of attack. Ambition must be made to counteract ambition. The interest of the man must be connected with the constitutional rights of the place. It may be a reflection on human nature, that such devices should be necessary to control the abuses of government. But what is government itself but the greatest of all reflections on human nature? If men were angels, no government would be necessary. If angels were to govern men, neither external nor internal controls on government would be necessary. In framing a government which is to be administered by men over men, the great difficulty lies in this: You must first enable the government to control the governed; and in the next place, oblige it to control itself. A dependence on the people is no doubt the primary control on the government; but experience has taught mankind the necessity of auxiliary precautions.

This policy of supplying by opposite and rival interests, the defect of better motives, might be traced through the whole system of human affairs, private as well as public. We see it particularly displayed in all the subordinate distributions of power; where the constant aim is to divide and arrange the several offices in such a manner as that each may be a check on the other; that the private interest of every individual, may be a sentinel over the public rights. These inventions of prudence cannot be less requisite in the distribution of the supreme powers of the state.

But it is not possible to give to each department an equal power of self defence. In republican government the legislative authority, necessarily, predominates. The remedy for this inconveniency is, to divide the legislature into different branches; and to render them by different modes of election, and different principles of action, as little connected with each other, as the nature of their common functions, and their common dependence on the society, will admit. . . .

There are moreover two considerations particularly applicable to the federal system of America, which place that system in a very interesting point of view.

First. In a single republic, all the power surrendered by the people, is submitted to the administration of a single government; and usurpations are guarded against by a division of the government into distinct and separate departments. In the compound republic of America, the power surrendered by the people, is first divided between two distinct governments, and then the portion allotted to each, subdivided among distinct and separate departments. Hence a double security arises to the rights of the people. The different governments will control each other; at the same time that each will be controlled by itself.

Second. It is of great importance in a republic, not only to guard the society against the oppression of its rulers; but to guard one part of the society against the injustice of the other part. Different interests necessarily exist in different classes of citizens. If a majority be united by a common interest, the rights of the minority will be insecure. There are but two methods of providing against this evil: The one by creating a will in the community independent of the majority, that is, of the society itself; the other by comprehending in the society so many separate descriptions of citizens, as will render an unjust combination of a majority of the whole, very improbable, if not impracticable. The first method prevails in all governments possessing an hereditary or self appointed authority. This at best is but a precarious security; because a power independent of the society may as well espouse the unjust views of the major, as the rightful interests, of the minor party, and may possibly be turned against both parties. The second method will be exemplified in the federal republic of the United States. Whilst all authority in it will be derived from and dependent on the society, the society itself will be broken into so many parts, interests and classes of citizens, that the rights of individuals or of the minority, will be in little danger from interested combinations of the majority. In a free government, the security for civil rights must be the same as for religious rights. It consists in the one case in the multiplicity of interests, and in the other, in the multiplicity of sects. The degree of security in both cases will depend on the number of interests and sects; and this may be presumed to depend on the extent of country and number of people comprehended under the same government. This view of the subject must particularly recommend a proper federal system to all the sincere and considerate friends of republican government: Since it shews that in exact proportion as the territory of the union may be formed into more circumscribed confederacies or states, oppressive combinations of a majority will be facilitated, the best security under the republican form, for the rights of every class of citizens, will be diminished; and consequently, the stability and independence of some member of the government, the only other security, must be proportionally increased. Justice is the end of government. It is the end of civil society. It ever has been, and ever will be pursued, until it be obtained, or until liberty be lost in the pursuit. In a society under the forms of which the stronger faction can readily unite and oppress the weaker, anarchy may as truly be said to reign, as in a state of nature where the weaker individual is not secured against the violence of the stronger: And as in the latter state even the stronger individuals are prompted by the uncertainty of their condition, to submit to a government which may protect the weak as well as themselves: So in the former state, will the more powerful factions or parties be gradually induced by a like motive, to wish for a government which will protect all parties, the weaker as well as the more powerful. It can be little doubted, that if the state of Rhode Island was separated from the confederacy, and left to itself, the insecurity of rights under the popular form of government within such narrow limits, would be displayed by such reiterated oppressions of factious majorities, that some power altogether independent of the people would soon be called for by the voice of the very factions whose misrule had proved the necessity of it. In the extended republic of the United States, and among the great variety of interests, parties and sects which it embraces, a coalition of a majority of the whole society could seldom take place on any other principles than those of justice and the general good; and there being thus less danger to a minor from the will of the major party, there must be less pretext also, to provide for the security of the former, by introducing into the government a will not dependent on the latter; or in other words, a will independent of the society itself. It is no less certain than it is important, notwithstanding the contrary opinions which have been entertained, that the larger the society, provided it lie within a practicable sphere, the more duly capable it will be of self government. And happily for the *republican cause*, the practicable sphere may be carried to a very great extent,

by a judicious modification and mixture of the *federal principle*.

Federalist—Number 63

James Madison

Among the criticisms leveled against the proposed U.S. Constitution was the undemocratic nature of the U.S. Senate. Senators were to serve for six years, they were to be chosen by state legislatures rather than elected, and each state, however large or small, was to have the same number of Senators. Madison answered each of these in The Federalist Papers. *Here he argues, apparently paradoxically, that the Senate is responsible to the people in a way the House of Representatives is not, despite the fact that House members stand for election every two years.*
—EDITOR

I add, as a *sixth* defect, [of a republic lacking a Senate] the want, in some important cases, of a due responsibility in the government to the people, arising from that frequency of elections which in other cases produces this responsibility. This remark will, perhaps, appear not only new, but paradoxical. It must nevertheless be acknowledged, when explained, to be as undeniable as it is important.

Responsibility, in order to be reasonable, must be limited to objects within the power of the responsible party, and in order to be effectual, must relate to operations of that power, of which a ready and proper judgment can be formed by the constituents. The objects of government may be divided into two general classes: the one depending on measures which have singly an immediate and sensible operation; the other depending on a succession of well-chosen and well-connected measures, which have a gradual and perhaps unobserved operation. The importance of the latter description to the collective and permanent welfare of every country needs no explanation. And yet it is evident that an assembly elected for so short a term as to be unable to provide more than one or two links in a chain of measures, on which the general welfare may essentially depend, ought not to be answerable for the final result any more than a steward or tenant, engaged for one year, could be justly made to answer for places or improvements which could not be accomplished in less than half a dozen years. Nor is it possible for the people to estimate the *share* of influence which their annual assemblies may respectively have on events resulting from the mixed transactions of several years. It is sufficiently difficult, at any rate, to preserve a personal responsibility in the members of a *numerous* body, for such acts of the body as have an immediate, detached, and palpable operation on its constituents.

The proper remedy for this defect must be an additional body in the legislative department, which, having sufficient permanency to provide for such objects as require a continued attention, and a train of measures, may be justly and effectually answerable for the attainment of those objects.

Thus far I have considered the circumstances which point out the necessity of a well-constructed Senate only as they relate to the representatives of the people. To a people as little blinded by prejudice or corrupted by flattery as those whom I address, I shall not scruple to add that such an institution may be sometimes necessary as a defence to the people against their own temporary errors and delusions. As the cool and deliberate sense of the community ought, in all governments, and actually will, in all free governments, ultimately prevail over the views of its rulers; so there are particular moments in public affairs when the people, stimulated by some irregular passion, or some illicit advantage, or misled by the artful misrepresentations of interested men, may call for measures which they themselves will afterwards be the most ready to lament and condemn. In these critical moments, how salutary will be the interference of some temperate and respectable body of citizens, in order to check the misguided career and to suspend the blow mediated by the people against themselves, until reason, justice, and truth can regain their authority over the public mind? What bitter anguish would not the people of Athens have often escaped if their government had contained so provident a safeguard against the tyranny of their own passions? Popular liberty might then have escaped the indelible reproach of decree-

ing to the same citizens the hemlock on one day and statues on the next.

It may be suggested that a people spread over an extensive region cannot, like the crowded inhabitants of a small district, be subject to the infection of violent passions or to the danger of combining in pursuit of unjust measures. I am far from denying that this is a distinction of peculiar importance. I have, on the contrary, endeavored in a former paper to show that it is one of the principal recommendations of a confederated republic. At the same time, this advantage ought not to be considered as superseding the use of auxiliary precautions. It may even be remarked that the same extended situation which will exempt the people of America from some of the dangers incident to lesser republics will expose them to the inconveniency of remaining for a longer time under the influence of those misrepresentations which the combined industry of interested men may succeed in distributing among them.

It adds no small weight to all these considerations to recollect that history informs us of no long-lived republic which had not a senate. Sparta, Rome, and Carthage are, in fact, the only states to whom that character can be applied. In each of the two first there was a senate for life. The constitution of the senate in the last is less known. Circumstantial evidence makes it probable that it was not different in this particular from the two others. It is at least certain that it had some quality or other which rendered it an anchor against popular fluctuations; and that a smaller council, drawn out of the senate, was appointed not only for life, but filled up vacancies itself. These examples, though as unfit for the imitation as they are repugnant to the genius of America, are, notwithstanding, when compared with the fugitive and turbulent existence of other ancient republics, very instructive proofs of the necessity of some institution that will blend stability with liberty. I am not unaware of the circumstances which distinguish the American from other popular governments, as well ancient as modern; and which render extreme circumspection necessary, in reasoning from one case to the other. But after allowing due weight to this consideration it may still be maintained that there are many points of similitude which render these examples not unworthy of our attention. Many of the defects, as we have seen, which can only be supplied by a senatorial institution, are common to a numerous assembly frequently elected by the people, and to the people themselves. There are others peculiar to the former which require the control of such an institution. The people can never wilfully betray their own interests; but they may possibly be betrayed by the representatives of the people; and the danger will be evidently greater where the whole legislative trust is lodged in the hands of one body of men than where the concurrence of separate and dissimilar bodies is required in every public act.

The difference most relied on between the American and other republics consists in the principle of representation, which is the pivot on which the former move, and which is supposed to have been unknown to the latter, or at least to the ancient part of them. The use which has been made of this difference, in reasonings contained in former papers, will have shown that I am disposed neither to deny its existence nor to undervalue its importance. I feel the less restraint, therefore, in observing that the position concerning the ignorance of the ancient governments on the subject of representation is by no means precisely true in the latitude commonly given to it. Without entering into a disquisition which here would be misplaced, I will refer to a few known facts in support of what I advance.

In the most pure democracies of Greece, many of the executive functions were performed, not by the people themselves, but by officers elected by the people, and *representing* the people in their *executive* capacity.

Prior to the reform of Solon, Athens was governed by nine Archons, annually *elected by the people at large.* The degree of power delegated to them seems to be left in great obscurity. Subsequent to that period we find an assembly, first of four, and afterwards of six hundred members, annually *elected by the people;* and *partially* representing them in their *legislative* capacity, since they were not only associated with the people in the function of making laws, but had the exclusive right of originating legislative propositions to the people. The senate of Carthage, also, whatever might be its power or the duration of its

appointment, appears to have been elective by the suffrages of the people. Similar instances might be traced in most, if not all, the popular governments of antiquity.

Lastly, in Sparta we meet with the Ephori, and in Rome with the Tribunes; two bodies, small indeed in number, but annually *elected by the whole body of the people,* and considered as the *representatives* of the people, almost in their *plenipotentiary* capacity. The Cosmi of Crete were also annually *elected by the people,* and have been considered by some authors as an institution analogous to those of Sparta and Rome, with this difference only, that in the election of that representative body the right of suffrage was communicated to a part only of the people.

From these facts, to which many others might be added, it is clear that the principle of representation was neither unknown to the ancients nor wholly overlooked in their political constitutions. The true distinction between these and the American governments lies *in the total exclusion of the people in their collective capacity,* from any share in the *latter,* and not in the *total exclusion of the representatives of the people* from the administration of the *former.* The distinction, however, thus qualified, must be admitted to leave a most advantageous superiority in favor of the United States. But to insure to this advantage its full effect, we must be careful not to separate it from the other advantage, of an extensive territory. For it cannot be believed that any form of representative government could have succeeded within the narrow limits occupied by the democracies of Greece. . . .

Federalist—Number 78

Alexander Hamilton

. . . Whoever attentively considers the different departments of power must perceive that, in a government in which they are separated from each other, the judiciary, from the nature of its functions, will always be the least dangerous to the political rights of the Constitution; because it will be least in capacity to annoy or injure them. The Executive not only dispenses honors, but holds the sword of the community. The legislature not only commands the purse, but prescribes the rules by which the duties and rights of every citizen are to be regulated. The judiciary, on the contrary, has no influence over either the sword or the purse; no direction either of the strength or of the wealth of the society; and can take no active resolution whatever. It may truly be said to have neither FORCE nor WILL, but merely judgment; and must ultimately depend upon the aid of the executive arm even for the efficacy of its judgment. . . .

Some perplexity respecting the rights of the courts to pronounce legislative acts void, because contrary to the Constitution, has arisen from an imagination that the doctrine would imply a superiority of the judiciary to the legislative power. . . . It is far more rational to suppose, that the courts were designed to be an intermediate body between the people and the legislature, in order, among other things, to keep the latter within the limits assigned to their authority. The interpretation of the laws is the proper and peculiar province of the courts. A constitution is, in fact, and must be regarded by the judges, as a fundamental law. It therefore belongs to them to ascertain its meaning, as well as the meaning of any particular act proceeding from the legislative body. If there should happen to be an irreconcilable variance between the two, that which has the superior obligation and validity ought, of course, to be preferred; or, in other words, the Constitution ought to be preferred to the statute, the intention of the people to the intention of their agents.

Nor does this conclusion by any means suppose a superiority of the judicial to the legislative power. It only supposes that the power of the people is superior to both; and that where the will of the legislature, declared in its statutes, stands in opposition to that of the people, declared in the Constitution, the judges ought to be governed by the latter rather than the former. They ought to regulate their decisions by the fundamental laws, rather than by those which are not fundamental. . . .

It can be of no weight to say that the courts, on the pretence of a repugnancy, may substitute their own pleasure to the constitutional intentions of the legislature. This might as well happen in the case of two contradictory statutes; or it might as well happen in every

adjudication upon any single statute. The courts must declare the sense of the law; and if they should be disposed to exercise WILL instead of JUDGMENT, the consequence would equally be the substitution of their pleasure to that of the legislative body. The observation, if it prove any thing, would prove that there ought to be no judges distinct from that body.

If, then, the courts of justice are to be considered as the bulwarks of a limited constitution against legislative encroachments, this consideration will afford a strong argument for the permanent tenure of judicial offices, since nothing will contribute so much as this to that independent spirit in the judges which must be essential to the faithful performance of so arduous a duty.

This independence of the judges is equally requisite to guard the Constitution and the rights of individuals from the effects of those ill humors, which the arts of designing men, or the influence of particular conjunctures, sometimes disseminate among the people themselves, and which, though they speedily give place to better information, and more deliberate reflection, have a tendency, in the meantime, to occasion dangerous innovations in the government, and serious oppressions of the minor party in the community. . . . Until the people have, by some solemn and authoritative act, annulled or changed the established form, it is binding upon themselves collectively, as well as individually; and no presumption, or even knowledge, of their sentiments, can warrant their representatives in a departure from it, prior to such an act. But it is easy to see, that it would require an uncommon portion of fortitude in the judges to do their duty as faithful guardians of the Constitution, where legislative invasions of it had been instigated by the major voice of the community. . . .

Letter from Thomas Jefferson to James Madison

Paris, September 6, 1789.

Dear Sir, — I sit down to write to you without knowing by what occasion I shall send my letter. I do it because a subject comes into my head which I would wish to develope a little more than is practicable in the hurry of the moment of making up general despatches.

The question, Whether one generation of men has a right to bind another, seems never to have been started either on this or our side of the water. Yet it is a question of such consequences as not only to merit decision, but place also, among the fundamental principles of every government. The course of reflection in which we are immersed here on the elementary principles of society has presented this question to my mind; and that no such obligation can be transmitted I think very capable of proof. I set out on this ground which I suppose to be self evident, "*that the earth belongs in usufruct to the living;*" that the dead have neither powers nor rights over it. The portion occupied by any individual ceases to be his when himself ceases to be, and reverts to the society. If the society has formed no rules for the appropriation of its lands in severalty, it will be taken by the first occupants. These will generally be the wife and children of the decedent. If they have formed rules of appropriation, those rules may give it to the wife and children, or to some one of them, or to the legatee of the deceased. So they may give it to his creditor. But the child, the legatee or creditor takes it, not by any natural right, but by a law of the society of which they are members, and to which they are subject. Then no man can by *natural right* oblige the lands he occupied, or the persons who succeed him in that occupation, to the paiment of debts contracted by him. For if he could, he might during his own life, eat up the usufruct of the lands for several generations to come, and then the lands would belong to the dead, and not to the living, which would be reverse in our principle. What is true of every member of the society individually, is true of them all collectively, since the rights of the whole can be no more than the sum of the rights of individuals. . . .

What is true of a generation all arriving to self-government on the same day, and dying all on the same day, is true of those on a constant course of decay and renewal, with this only difference. A generation coming in and going out entire, as in the first case, would have a right in the 1st year of their self dominion to contract a debt for 33. years, in the 10th.

for 24. in the 20th. for 14. in the 30th. for 4. whereas generations changing daily, by daily deaths and births, have one constant term beginning at the date of their contract, and ending when a majority of those of full age at that date shall be dead. The length of that term may be estimated from the tables of mortality, corrected by the circumstances of climate, occupation &c. peculiar to the country of the contractors. . . .

I suppose that the received opinion, that the public debts of one generation devolve on the next, has been suggested by our seeing habitually in private life that he who succeeds to lands is required to pay the debts of his ancestor or testator, without considering that this requisition is municipal only, not moral, flowing from the will of the society which has found it convenient to appropriate the lands become vacant by the death of their occupant on the condition of a paiment of his debts; but that between society and society, or generation and generation there is no municipal obligation, no umpire but the law of nature. We seem not to have perceived that, by the law of nature, one generation is to another as one independent nation to another. . . .

On similar ground it may be proved that no society can make a perpetual constitution, or even a perpetual law. The earth belongs always to the living generation. They may manage it then, and what proceeds from it, as they please, during their usufruct. They are masters too of their own persons, and consequently may govern them as they please. But persons and property make the sum of the objects of government. The constitution and the laws of their predecessors extinguish them, in their natural course, with those whose will gave them being. This could preserve that being till it ceased to be itself, and no longer. Every constitution, then, and every law, naturally expires at the end of 19. years. [*Jefferson has argued that half of the voters will be dead in 19 years.*—ED.] If it be enforced longer, it is an act of force and not of right.

It may be said that the succeeding generation exercising in fact the power of repeal, this leaves them as free as if the constitution or law had been expressly limited to 19. years only. In the first place, this objection admits the right, in proposing an equivalent. But the power of repeal is not an equivalent. It might be indeed if every form of government were so perfectly contrived that the will of the majority could always be obtained fairly and without impediment. But this is true of no form. The people cannot assemble themselves; their representation is unequal and vicious. Various checks are opposed to every legislative proposition. Factions get possession of the public councils. Bribery corrupts them. Personal interests lead them astray from the general interests of their constituents; and other impediments arise so as to prove to every practical man that a law of limited duration is much more manageable than one which needs a repeal. . . .

Turn this subject in your mind, my Dear Sir, and particularly as to the power of contracting debts, and develope it with that perspicuity and cogent logic which is so peculiarly yours. Your station in the councils of our country gives you an opportunity of producing it to public consideration, of forcing it into discussion. At first blush it may be rallied as a theoretical speculation; but examination will prove it to be solid and salutary. It would furnish matter for a fine preamble to our first law for appropriating the public revenue; and it will exclude, at the threshold of our new government the contagious and ruinous errors of this quarter of the globe, which have armed despots with means not sanctioned by nature for binding in chains their fellow-men. . . .

Letter from James Madison to Thomas Jefferson

NEW YORK, February 4, 1790.

DEAR SIR, — Your favor of January 9, inclosing one of September last, did not get to hand till a few days ago. The idea which the latter evolves is a great one, and suggests many interesting reflections to Legislators, particularly when contracting and providing for public debts. Whether it can be received in the extent to which your reasonings carry it is a question which I ought to turn more in my thoughts than I have yet been able to do before I should be justified in making up a full

opinion on it. My first thoughts lead me to view the doctrine as not *in all respects* compatible with the course of human affairs. I will endeavour to sketch the grounds of my skepticism. "As the Earth belongs to the living, not to the dead, a living generation can bind itself only; in every Society, the will of the majority binds the whole; according to the laws of mortality, a majority of those ripe for the exercise of their will do not live beyond the term of 19 years; to this term, then, is limited the validity of every act of the society, nor can any act be continued beyond this term, without an *express* declaration of the public will." This I understand to be the outline of the argument.

The acts of a political society may be divided into three classes:

1. The fundamental constitution of the Government.
2. Laws involving some stipulation which renders them irrevocable at the will of the Legislature.
3. Laws involving no such irrevocable quality.

1. However applicable in theory the doctrine may be to a Constitution, it seems liable in practice to some weighty objections.

Would not a Government, ceasing of necessity at the end of a given term, unless prolonged by some Constitutional Act previous to its expiration, be too subject to the causality and consequences of an interregnum?

Would not a Government so often revised become too mutable and novel to retain that share of prejudice in its favor which is a salutary aid to the most rational Government?

Would not such a periodical revision engender pernicious factions that might not otherwise come into existence, and agitate the public mind more frequently and more violently than might be expedient?

2. In the second class, of acts involving stipulations, must not exceptions, at least to the doctrine, be admitted?

If the earth be the gift of *nature* to the living, their title can extend to the earth in its *natural* state only. The *improvements* made by the dead form a debt against the living, who take the benefit of them. This debt cannot be otherwise discharged than by a proportionate obedience to the will of the Authors of the improvements.

But a case less liable to be controverted may, perhaps, be stated. Debts may be incurred with a direct view to the interests of the unborn, as well as of the living. Such are debts for repelling a Conquest, the evils of which descend through many generations. Debts may even be incurred principally for the benefit of posterity. Such, perhaps, is the debt incurred by the United States. In these instances the debts might not be dischargeable within the term of 19 years.

There seems, then, to be some foundation in the nature of things, in the relation which one generation bears to another, for the *descent* of obligations from one to another. Equity may require it. Mutual good may be promoted by it. And all that seems indispensable in stating the account between the dead and the living is, to see that the debts against the latter do not exceed the advances made by the former. Few of the incumbrances entailed on nations by their predecessors would bear a liquidation even on this principle.

3. Objections to the doctrine, as applied to the third class of acts, must be merely practical. But in that view alone they appear to be material.

Unless such temporary laws should be kept in force by acts regularly anticipating their expiration, all the rights depending on positive laws, that is, most of the rights of property, would become absolutely defunct, and the most violent struggles ensue between the parties interested in reviving, and those interested in reforming the antecedent state of property. Nor does it seem improbable that such an event might be suffered to take place. The checks and difficulties opposed to the passage of laws, which render the power of repeal inferior to an opportunity to reject, as a security against oppression, would here render the latter an insecure provision against anarchy. Add to this that the very possibility of an event so hazardous to the rights of property could not but depreciate its value; that the approach of the crisis would increase the effect; that the frequent return of periods superseding all the obligations dependent on antecedent laws and usages must, by weakening the sense of them, co-operate with motives to licenciousness already too powerful; and

that the general uncertainty and vicissitudes of such a state of things would, on one side, discourage every useful effort of steady industry pursued under the sanction of existing laws, and, on the other, give an immediate advantage to the more sagacious over the less sagacious part of the Society.

I can find no relief from such embarrassments but in the received doctrine that a *tacit* assent may be given to established Governments and laws, and that this assent is to be inferred from the omission of an express revocation. It seems more practicable to remedy by well-constituted Governments the pestilent operation of this doctrine in the unlimited sense in which it is at present received, than it is to find a remedy for the evils necessarily springing from an unlimited admission of the contrary doctrine.

Is it not doubtful whether it be possible to exclude wholly the idea of an implied or tacit assent, without subverting the very foundation of Civil Society?

On what principle is it that the voice of the majority binds the minority? It does not result, I conceive, from a law of nature, but from compact founded on utility. A greater proportion might be required by the fundamental Constitution of Society, if under any particular circumstances it were judged eligible. Prior, therefore, to the establishment of this principle, *unanimity* was necessary; and rigid Theory accordingly presupposes the assent of every individual to rule which subjects the minority to the will of the majority. If this assent cannot be given tacitly, or be not implied where no positive evidence forbids, no person born in Society could, on attaining ripe age, be bound by any acts of the majority, and either a unanimous renewal of every law would be necessary as often as a new member should be added to the Society, or the express consent of every new member be obtained to the rule by which the majority decides for the whole.

If these observations be not misapplied, it follows that a limitation of the validity of all Acts to the computed life of the generation establishing them is in some cases not required by theory, and in others not consistent with practice. They are not meant, however, to impeach either the utility of the principle as applied to the cases you have particularly in view, or the general importance of it in the eye of the Philosophical Legislator. On the contrary, it would give me singular pleasure to see it first announced to the world in a law of the United States, and always kept in view as a salutary restraint on living generations from *unjust and unnecessary* burdens on their successors. This is a pleasure, however, which I have no hope of enjoying. The spirit of Philosophical legislation has not prevailed at all in some parts of America and is by no means the fashion of this part, or of the present Representative Body. The evils suffered or feared from weakness in Government and licencious-

ness in the people have turned the attention more towards the means of strengthening the powers of the former, than of narrowing their extent in the minds of the latter. Besides this it is so much easier to descry the little difficulties immediately incident to every great plan than to comprehend its general and remote benefits, that further light must be added to the Councils of our Country before many truths which are seen through the medium of Philosophy become visible to the naked eye of the ordinary politician.

Considerations on Representative Government

John Stuart Mill

John Stuart Mill's life was extraordinary, by almost any account. Mill was born in 1806 and died in 1873. His father, James Mill, along with economist David Ricardo and legal philosopher John Austin, was among the most devoted followers of Jeremy Bentham. James Mill authored numerous books, including a history of British India, but his most important works were defenses of utilitarianism and democratic government (selections from his "Essay on Government" are reprinted in Section 2). Like Bentham, the senior Mill held that human behavior is best understood in terms of self-interest and that government serves the common good by promoting the happiness of its citizens. Happiness, in turn, was assumed to refer to pleasure and the absence of pain.

James resolved to raise his son, John Stuart, according to sound utilitarian principles. With Bentham's help he developed a plan that included keeping the boy away from other children and a rigorous tutoring program. By the age of three John Stuart had learned Greek; next he pursued mathematics, Latin, and history and by twelve he was studying logic and political economy. At fourteen he went to France to live with Bentham's brother, and a year later he studied law with John Austin, then professor at University College, London. At twenty he entered a depression that lasted five years, during which he rejected Bentham's narrow hedonism in favor of a more complex conception of human well-being. At twenty-four he began a relationship with Harriet Taylor. She was married, but, despite that, the relationship lasted two decades until her husband John Taylor died. After John Stuart Mill and Harriet Taylor were married they withdrew from "insipid society" and the gossip they had endured for many years. The two lived happily together for seven years until her death. Mill served briefly as a member of Parliament, and died in France after being defeated for re-election. Mill's works include the On Liberty *(1859),* Utilitarianism *(1863), and* On the Subjection of Woman *(1869).*

Mill contends that democracy's strength lies in its effects on the character of those who live under it, by encouraging citizens to develop their intellectual and moral capacities. Mill then discusses the concept of representation and the legitimate role of elected officials, together with the difficult problem of assuring that minorities are given adequate say in the decision-making process. The selection concludes with a defense of plural voting.

From John Stuart Mill, *Considerations On Representative Government* (1861).

That the Ideally Best Form of Government Is Representative Government

It has long (perhaps throughout the entire duration of British freedom) been a common saying, that if a good despot could be ensured, despotic monarchy would be the best form of government. I look upon this as a radical and most pernicious misconception of what good government is; which, until it can be got rid of, will fatally vitiate all our speculations on government.

The supposition is, that absolute power, in the hands of an eminent individual, would ensure a virtuous and intelligent performance of all the duties of government. Good laws would be established and enforced, bad laws would be reformed; the best men would be placed in all situations of trust; justice would be as well administered, the public burthens would be as light and as judiciously imposed, every branch of administration would be as purely and as intelligently conducted, as the circumstances of the country and its degree of intellectual and moral cultivation would admit. I am willing, for the sake of the argument, to concede all this; but I must point out how great the concession is; how much more is needed to produce even an approximation to these results than is conveyed in the simple expression, a good despot. Their realisation would in fact imply, not merely a good monarch, but an all-seeing one. He must be at all times informed correctly, in considerable detail, of the conduct and working of every branch of administration in every district of the country, and must be able, in the twenty-four hours per day which are all that is granted to a king as to the humblest labourer, to give an effective share of attention and superintendence to all parts of this vast field; or he must at least be capable of discerning and choosing out, from among the mass of his subjects, not only a large abundance of honest and able men, fit to conduct every branch of public administration under supervision and control, but also the small number of men of eminent virtues and talents who can be trusted not only to do without that supervision, but to exercise it themselves over others. So extraordinary are the faculties and energies required for performing this task in any supportable manner, that the good despot whom we are supposing can hardly be imagined as consenting to undertake it, unless as a refuge from intolerable evils, and a transitional preparation for something beyond. But the argument can do without even this immense item in the account. Suppose the difficulty vanquished. What should we then have? One man of superhuman mental activity managing the entire affairs of a mentally passive people. Their passivity is implied in the very idea of absolute power. The nation as a whole and every individual composing it, are without any potential voice in their own destiny. They exercise no will in respect to their collective interests. All is decided for them by a will not their own, which it is legally a crime for them to disobey. What sort of human beings can be formed under such a regimen? What development can wither their thinking or their active faculties attain under it? On matters of pure theory they might perhaps be allowed to speculate, so long as their speculations either did not approach politics, or had not the remotest connection with its practice. On practical affairs they could at most be only suffered to suggest; and even under the most moderate of despots, none but persons of already admitted or reputed superiority could hope that their suggestions would be known to, much less regarded by, those who had the management of affairs. A person must have a very unusual taste for intellectual exercise in and for itself, who will put himself to the trouble of thought when it is to have no outward effect, or qualify himself for functions which he has no chance of being allowed to exercise. The only sufficient incitement to mental exertion, in any but a few minds in a generation, is the prospect of some practical use to be made of its results. It does not follow that the nation will be wholly destitute of intellectual power. The common business of life, which must necessarily be performed by each individual or family for themselves, will call forth some amount of intelligence and practical ability, within a certain narrow range of ideas. There may be a select class of *savants,* who cultivate science with a view to its physical uses, or for the pleasure of the pursuit. There will be a bureaucracy, and persons in training for the bureaucracy, who will be taught at least some empirical maxims of government and public administration. There may be, and often has been, a systematic organisation of the best mental power in the country in some special direction (commonly military) to promote the grandeur of the despot. But the public at large remains without information and without interest on all the greater matters of practice; or, if they have any knowledge of them, it is but a *dilettante* knowledge, like that which people have of the mechanical arts who have never handled a tool. Nor is it only in their intelligence that they suffer. Their moral capacities are equally stunted. Wherever the sphere of action of human beings is artificially circumscribed, their sentiments are narrowed and dwarfed in the same proportion. The food of feeling is action: even domestic affection lives upon volunary good offices. Let a person have nothing to do for his country, and he will not care for it. It has been said of old, that in a despotism there is at most but one patriot, the despot himself; and the saying rests on a just appreciation of the effects of absolute subjection, even to a good and wise master. . . . Leaving things to the Government, like leaving them to Providence, is synonymous with caring nothing about them, and accepting their results, when disagreeable, as visitations of Nature. With the exception, therefore, of a few studious men who take an intellectual interest in speculation for its own sake, the intelligence and sentiments of the whole people are given up to the material interests, and, when these are provided for, to the amusement and ornamentation, of private life. But to say this is to say, if the whole testimony of history is worth anything, that the era of national decline has arrived: that is, if the nation had ever attained anything to decline from. If it has never risen above the condition of an Oriental people, in that condition it continues to stagnate. But if, like Greece or Rome, it had realised anything higher, through the energy, patriotism, and enlargement of mind, which as national qualities are the fruits solely of freedom, it relapses in a few generations into the Oriental state. And that state does not mean stupid tranquillity, with security against change for the worse; it often means being overrun, conquered, and reduced to domestic slavery, either by a stronger despot, or by the nearest barbarous people who retain along with their savage rudeness the energies of freedom.

Such are not merely the natural tendencies, but the inherent necessities of despotic government; from which there is no outlet, unless in so far as the despotism consents not to be despotism; . . .

There is no difficulty in showing that the ideally best form of government is that in which the sovereignty, or supreme controlling power in the last resort, is vested in the entire aggregate of the community; every citizen not only having a voice in the exercise of that ultimate sovereignty, but being, at least occasionally, called on to take an actual part in the government, by the personal discharge of some public function, local or general.

To test this proposition, it has to be examined in reference to the two branches into which, as pointed out in the last chapter, the inquiry into the goodness of a government conveniently divides itself, namely, how far it promotes the good management of the affairs of society by means of the existing faculties, moral, intellectual, and active, of its various members, and what is its effect in improving or deteriorating those faculties.

The ideally best form of government, it is scarcely necessary to say, does not mean one which is practicable or eligible in all states of civilisation, but the one which, in the circumstances in which it is practicable and eligible, is attended with the greatest amount of beneficial consequences, immediate and prospective. A completely popular government is the only polity which can make out any claim to this character. It is pre-eminent in both the departments between which the excellence of a political constitution is divided. It is both more favourable to present good government, and promotes a better and higher form of national character, than any other polity whatsoever.

Its superiority in reference to present well-being rests upon two principles, of as universal truth and applicability as any general propositions which can be laid down respecting human affairs. The first is, that the rights and interests of every or any person are only secure from being disregarded when the person interested is himself able, and habitually disposed, to stand up for them. The second is, that the general prosperity attains a greater height, and is more widely diffused, in proportion to the amount and variety of the personal energies enlisted in promoting it.

Putting these two propositions into a shape more special to their present application; human beings are only secure from evil at the hands of others in proportion as they have the power of being, and are, self-*protecting;* and they only achieve a high degree of success in their struggle with Nature in proportion as they are self-*dependent,* relying on what they themselves can do, either separately or in concert, rather than on what others do for them.

The former proposition—that each is the only safe guardian of his own rights and interests—is one of those elementary maxims of prudence, which every person, capable of conducting his own affairs, implicitly acts upon, wherever he himself is interested. . . .

It is an adherent condition of human affairs that no intention, however sincere, of protecting the interests of others can make it safe or salutary to tie up their own hands. Still more obviously true is it, that by their own hands only can any positive and durable improvement of their circumstances in life be worked out. Through the joint influence of these two principles, all free communities have both been more exempt from social injustice and crime, and have attained more brilliant prosperity, than any others, or than they themselves after they lost their freedom. Contrast the free states of the world, while their freedom lasted, with the contemporary subjects of monarchical or oligarchical despotism. . . . Their superior prosperity was too obvious ever to have been gainsaid: while their superiority in good government and social relations is proved by the prosperity, and is manifest besides in every page of history. . . .

Thus stands the case as regards present well-being; the good management of the affairs of the existing generation. If we now pass to the influence of the form of government upon character, we shall find the superiority of popular government over every

other to be, if possible, still more decided and indisputable.

This question really depends upon a still more fundamental one, viz., which of two common types of character, for the general good of humanity, it is most desirable should predominate—the active, or the passive type; that which struggles against evils, or that which endures them; that which bends to circumstances, or that which endeavours to make circumstances bend to itself.

The commonplaces of moralists, and the general sympathies of mankind, are in favour of the passive type. Energetic characters may be admired, but the acquiescent and submissive are those which most men personally prefer. The passiveness of our neighbours increases our sense of security, and plays into the hands of our wilfulness. Passive characters, if we do not happen to need their activity, seem an obstruction the less in our own path. A contented character is not a dangerous rival. Yet nothing is more certain than that improvement in human affairs is wholly the work of the uncontented characters; and, moreover, that it is much easier for an active mind to acquire the virtues of patience than for a passive one to assume those of energy.

Of the three varieties of mental excellence, intellectual, practical, and moral, there never could be any doubt in regard to the first two which side had the advantage. All intellectual superiority is the fruit of active effort. Enterprise, the desire to keep moving, to be trying and accomplishing new things for our own benefit or that of others, is the parent even of speculative, and much more of practical, talent. The intellectual culture compatible with the other type is of that feeble and vague description which belongs to a mind that stops at amusement, or at simple contemplation. The test of real and vigorous thinking, the thinking which ascertains truths instead of dreaming dreams, is successful application to practice. . . . With respect to practical improvement, the case is still more evident. The character which improves human life is that which struggles with natural powers and tendencies not that which gives way to them. The self-benefiting qualities are all on the side of the active and energetic character: and the habits and conduct which promote the advantage of each individual member of the community must be at least a part of those which conduce most in the end to the advancement of the community as a whole.

But on the point of moral preferability, there seems at first sign to be room for doubt. I am not referring to the religious feeling which has so generally existed in favour of the inactive character, as being more in harmony with the submission due to the divine will. Christianity as well as other religions has fostered this sentiment; but it is the prerogative of Christianity, as regards this and many other perversions, that it is able to throw them off. Abstractedly from religious considerations, a passive character, which yields to obstacles instead of striving to overcome them, may not indeed be very useful to others, no more than to itself, but it might be expected to be at least inoffensive. Contentment is always counted among the moral virtues. But it is a complete error to suppose that contentment is necessarily or naturally attendant on passivity of character; and useless it is, the moral consequences are mischievous. Where there exists a desire for advantages not possessed, the mind which does not potentially possess them by means of its own energies is apt to look with hatred and malice on those who do. The person bestirring himself with hopeful prospects to improve his circumstances is the one who feels good-will towards others engaged in, or who have succeeded in, the same pursuit. And where the majority are so engaged, those who do not attain the object have had the tone given to their feelings by the general habit of the country, and ascribe their failure to want of effort or opportunity, or to their personal ill luck. But those who, while desiring what others possess, put no energy into striving for it, are either incessantly grumbling that fortune does not do for them what they do not attempt to do for themselves, or overflowing with envy and ill-will towards those who possess what they would like to have.

There are, no doubt, in all countries, really contented characters, who not merely do not seek, but do not desire, what they do not already possess, and these naturally bear no ill-will towards such as have apparently a more favoured lot. But the great mass of seeming contentment is real discontent, combined with indolence or self-indulgence, which, while taking no legitimate means of raising itself, delights in bringing others down to its own level. And if we look narrowing even at the cases of innocent contentment, we perceive that they only win our admiration when the indifference is solely to improvement in outward circumstances, and there is a striving for perpetual advancement in spiritual worth, or at least a disinterested zeal to benefit others. The contented man, or the contented family, who have no ambition to make any one else happier, to promote the good of their country or their neighbourhood, or to improve themselves in moral excellence, excite in us neither admiration nor approval. We rightly ascribe this sort of contentment to mere unmanliness and want of spirit. The content which we approve is an ability to do cheerfully without what cannot be had, a just appreciation of the comparative value of different objects of desire, and a willing renunciation of the less when incompatible with the greater. These, however, are excellences more natural to the character, in proportion as it is actively engaged in the attempt to improve its own or some other lot. He who is continually measuring his energy against difficulties learns what are the difficulties insuperable to him, and what are those which, though he might overcome, the success is not worth the cost. He whose thoughts and activities are all needed for, and habitually employed in, practicable and useful enterprises, is the person of all others least likely to let his mind dwell with brooding discontent upon things either not worth attaining, or which are not so to him. Thus the active, self-helping character is not only intrinsically the best, but is the likeliest to acquire all that is really excellent or desirable in the opposite type.

The striving, go-ahead character of England and the United States is only a fit subject of disapproving criticism on account of the very secondary objects on which it commonly expends its strength. In itself it is the foundation of the best hopes for the general improvement of mankind. . . .

Now there can be no kind of doubt that the passive type of character is favoured by the government of one or a few, and the active self-helping type by that of the Many.

Irresponsible rulers need the quiescence of the ruled more than they need any activity but that which they can compel. Submissiveness to the prescriptions of men as necessities of nature is the lesson inculcated by all governments upon those who are wholly without participation in them. The will of superiors, and the law as the will of superiors, must be passively yielded to. But no men are mere instruments or materials in the hands of their rulers who have will or spirit or a spring of internal activity in the rest of their proceedings: and any manifestation of these qualities, instead of receiving encouragement from despots, has to get itself forgiven by them.

Very different is the state of the human faculties where a human being feels himself under no other external restraint than the necessities of nature, or mandates of society which he has his share in imposing, and which it is open to him, if he thinks them wrong, publicly to dissent from, and exert himself actively to get altered. No doubt, under a government partially popular, this freedom may be exercised even by those who are not partakers in the full privileges of citizenship. But it is a great additional stimulus to any one's self-help and self-reliance when he starts from even ground, and has not to feel that his success depends on the impression he can make upon sentiments and dispositions of a body of whom he is not one. It is a great discouragement to an individual, and a still greater one to a class, to be left out of the constitution; to be reduced to plead from outside the door to the arbiters of their destiny, not taken into consultation within. The maximum of the invigorating effect of freedom upon the character is only obtained when the person acted on either is, or is looking forward to becoming, a citizen as fully privileged as any other. What is still more important than even this matter of feeling is the practical discipline which the character obtains from the occasional demand made upon the citizens to exercise, for a time and in their turn, some social function. It is not sufficiently considered how little there is in most men's ordinary life to give any largeness either to their conceptions or to their sentiments. Their work is a routine; not a labour of love, but of self-interest in the most elementary form, the satisfaction of daily

wants; neither the thing done, nor the process of doing it, introduces the mind to thoughts or feelings extending beyond individuals; if instructive books are within their reach, there is no stimulus to read them; and in most cases the individual has no access to any person of cultivation much superior to his own. Giving him something to do for the public, supplies, in a measure, all these deficiencies. If circumstances allow the amount of public duty assigned him to be considerable, it makes him an educated man. Notwithstanding the defects of the social system and moral ideas of antiquity, the practice of the dicastery and the ecclesia raised the intellectual standard of an average Athenian citizen far beyond anything of which there is yet an example in any other mass of men, ancient or modern. The proofs of this are apparent in every page of our great historian of Greece; but we need scarcely look further than to the high quality of the addresses which their great orators deemed best calculated to act with effect on their understanding and will. A benefit of the same kind, though far less in degree, is produced on Englishmen of the lower middle class by their liability to be placed on juries and to serve parish offices; which, though it does not occur to so many, nor is so continuous, nor introduces them to so great a variety of elevated considerations, as to admit of comparison with the public education which every citizen of Athens obtained from her democratic institutions, must make them nevertheless very different beings, in range of ideas and development of faculties, from those who have done nothing in their lives but drive a quill, or sell goods over a counter. Still more salutary is the moral part of the instruction afforded by the participation of the private citizen, if even rarely, in public functions. He is called upon, while so engaged, to weigh interests not his own; to be guided, in case of conflicting claims, by another rule than his private partialities; to apply, at every turn, principles and maxims which have for their reason of existence the common good; and he usually finds associated with him in the same work minds more familiarised than his own with these ideas and operations, whose study it will be to supply reasons to his understanding, and stimulation to his feeling for the general interest. He is made to feel himself one of the public, and whatever is for their benefit to be for his benefit. Where this school of public spirit does not exist, scarcely any sense is entertained that private persons, in no eminent social situation, owe any duties to society, except to obey the laws and submit to the government. There is no unselfish sentiment of identification with the public. Every thought or feeling, either of interest or of duty, is absorbed in the individual and in the family. The man never thinks of any collective interest, of any objects to be pursued jointly with others, but only in competition with them, and in some measure at their expense. A neighbour, not being an ally or an associate, since he is never engaged in any common undertaking for joint benefit, is therefore only a rival. Thus even private morality suffers, while public is actually extinct. Were this the universal and only possible state of things, the utmost aspirations of the lawgiver or the moralist could only stretch to make the bulk of the community a flock of sheep innocently nibbling the grass side by side.

From these accumulated considerations it is evident that the only government which can fully satisfy all the exigencies of the social state is one in which the whole people participate; that any participation, even in the smallest public function, is useful; that the participation should everywhere be as great as the general degree of improvement of the community will allow; and that nothing less can be ultimately desirable than the admission of all to a share in the sovereign power of the state. But since all cannot, in a community exceeding a single small town, participate personally in any but some very minor portions of the public business, it follows that the ideal type of a perfect government must be representative.

Of the Proper Functions of Representative Bodies

In treating of representative government, it is above all necessary to keep in view the distinction between its idea or essence, and the particular forms in which the idea has been clothed by accidental historical developments, or by the notions current at some particular period.

The meaning of representative government is, that the whole people, or some numerous portion of them, exercise through deputies periodically elected by themselves the ultimate controlling power, which, in every constitution, must reside somewhere. This ultimate power they must possess in all its completeness. They must be masters, whenever they please, of all the operations of government. There is no need that the constitutional law should itself give them this mastery. It does not in the British Constitution. But what it does give practically amounts to this. . . .

But while it is essential to representative government that the practical supremacy in the state should reside in the representatives of the people, it is an open question what actual functions, what precise part in the machinery of government, shall be directly and personally discharged by the representative body. Great varieties in this respect are compatible with the essence of representative government, provided the functions are such as secure to the representative body the control of everything in the last resort.

There is a radical distinction between controlling the business of government and actually doing it. The same person or body may be able to control everything, but cannot possibly do everything; and in many cases its control over everything will be more perfect the less it personally attempts to do. The commander of an army could not direct its movements effectually if he himself fought in the ranks, or led an assault. It is the same with bodies of men. Some things cannot be done except by bodies; other things cannot be well done by them. It is one question, therefore, what a popular assembly should control, another what it should itself do. . . . In the first place, it is admitted in all countries in which the representative system is practically understood, that numerous representative bodies ought not to administer. The maxim is grounded not only on the most essential principles of good government, but on those of the successful conduct of business of any description. No body of men, unless organised and under command, is fit for action, in the proper sense. Even a select board, composed of few members, and these specially conversant with the business to be done, is always an inferior instrument to some one individual who could be found among them, and would be improved in character if that one person were made the chief, and all the others reduced to subordinates. What can be done better by a body than by any individual is deliberation. When it is necessary or important to secure hearing and consideration to many conflicting opinions, a deliberative body is indispensable. . . .

Instead of the function of governing, for which it is radically unfit, the proper office of a representative assembly is to watch and control the government: to throw the light of publicity on its acts: to compel a full exposition and justification of all of them which any one considers questionable; to censure them if found condemnable, and, if the men who compose the government abuse their trust, or fulfil it in a manner which conflicts with the deliberate sense of the nation, to expel them from office, and either expressly or virtually appoint their successors. This is surely ample power, and security enough for the liberty of the nation. In addition to this, the Parliament has an office, not inferior even to this in importance; to be at once the nation's Committee of Grievances, and its Congress of Opinions; an arena in which not only the general opinion of the nation, but that of every section of it, and as far as possible of every eminent individual whom it contains, can produce itself in full light and challenge discussion; where every person in the country may count upon finding somebody who speaks his mind, as well or better than he could speak it himself—not to friends and partisans exclusively, but in the face of opponents, to be tested by adverse controversy; where those whose opinion is overruled, feel satisfied that it is heard, and set aside not by a mere act of will, but for what are thought superior reasons, and commend themselves as such to the representatives of the majority of the nation; where every party or opinion in the country can muster its strength, and be cured of any illusion concerning the number or power of its adherents; where the opinion which prevails in the nation makes itself manifest as prevailing, and mar-

shals its hosts in the presence of the government, which is thus enabled and compelled to give way to it on the mere manifestation, without the actual employment, of its strength; where statesmen can assure themselves, far more certainly than by any other signs, what elements of opinion and power are growing, and what declining, and are enabled to shape their measures with some regard not solely to present exigencies, but to tendencies in progress. Representative assemblies are often taunted by their enemies with being places of mere talk and *bavardage*. There has seldom been more misplaced derision. I know not how a representative assembly can more usefully employ itself than in talk, when the subject of talk is the great public interests of the country, and every sentence of it represents the opinion either of some important body of persons in the nation, or of an individual in whom some such body have reposed their confidence. A place where every interest and shade of opinion in the country can have its cause even passionately pleaded, in the face of the government and of all other interests and opinions, can compel them to listen, and either comply, or state clearly why they do not, is in itself, if it answered no other purpose, one of the most important political institutions that can exist anywhere, and one of the foremost benefits of free government. Such "talking" would never be looked upon with disparagement if it were not allowed to stop "doing;" which it never would, if assemblies knew and acknowledged that talking and discussion are their proper business, while *doing*, as the result of discussion, is the task not of a miscellaneous body, but of individuals specially trained to it; that the fit office of an assembly is to see that those individuals are honestly and intelligently chosen, and to interfere no further with them, except by unlimited latitude of suggestion and criticism, and by applying or withholding the final seal of national assent. . . . But the very fact which most unfits such bodies for a Council of Legislation qualifies them the more for their other office—namely, that they are not a selection of the greatest political minds in the country, from whose opinions little could with certainty by inferred concerning those of the nation, but are, when properly constituted, a fair sample of every grade of intellect among the people which is at all entitled to a voice in public affairs. Their part is to indicate wants, to be an organ for popular demands, and a place of adverse discussion for all opinions relating to public matters, both great and small; and, along with this, to check by criticism, and eventually by withdrawing their support, those high public officers who really conduct the public business, or who appoint those by whom it is conducted. Nothing but the restriction of the function of representative bodies within these rational limits will enable the benefits of popular control to be enjoyed in conjunction with the no less important requisites (growing ever more important as human affairs increase in scale and in complexity) of skilled legislation and administration. . . .

Of True and False Democracy, Representation of All, and Representation of the Majority Only

It has been seen that the dangers incident to a representative democracy are of two kinds: danger of a low grade of intelligence in the representative body, and in the popular opinion which controls it; and danger of class legislation on the part of the numerical majority, these being all composed of the same class. We have next to consider how far it is possible so to organise the democracy as, without interfering materially with the characteristic benefits of democratic government, to do away with these two great evils, or at least to abate them, in the utmost degree attainable by human contrivance.

The common mode of attempting this is by limiting the democratic character of the representation, through a more or less restricted suffrage. But there is a previous consideration which, duly kept in view, considerably modifies the circumstances which are supposed to render such a restriction necessary. A completely equal democracy, in a nation in which a single class composes the numerical majority, cannot be divested of certain evils; but those evils are greatly aggravated by the fact that the democracies which at present exist are not equal, but systematically unequal in favour of the predominant class. Two very different ideas are usually confounded under the name democracy. The pure idea of democracy, according to its definition, is the government of the whole people by the whole people, equally represented. Democracy as commonly conceived and hitherto practised is the government of the whole people by a mere majority of the people, exclusively represented. . . . The former is synonymous with the equality of all citizens; the latter, strangely confounded with it, is a government of privilege, in favour of the numerical majority, who alone possess practically any voice in the State. This is the inevitable consequence of the manner in which the votes are now taken, to the complete disfranchisement of minorities. . . . That the minority must yield to the majority, the smaller number to the greater, is a familiar idea; and accordingly men think there is no necessity for using their minds any further, and it does not occur to them that there is any medium between allowing the smaller number to be equally powerful with the greater, and blotting out the smaller number altogether. In a representative body actually deliberating, the minority must of course be overruled; and in any equal democracy (since the opinions of the constituents, when they insist on them, determine those of the representative body) the majority of the people, through their representatives, will outvote and prevail over the minority and their representatives. But does it follow that the minority should have no representatives at all? Because the majority ought to prevail over the minority, must the majority have all the votes, the minority none? Is it necessary that the minority should not even be heard? Nothing but habit and old association can reconcile any reasonable being to the needless injustice. In a really equal democracy, every or any section would be represented, not disproportionately, but proportionately. A majority of the electors would always have a majority of the representatives; but a minority of the electors would always have a minority of the representatives. Man for man they would be as fully represented as the majority. Unless they are, there is not equal government, but a government of inequality and privilege: one part of the people rule over the rest: there is a part whose fair and equal share of influence in the representation is withheld from them; contrary to all just government, but, above all, contrary to the principle of democracy, which professes equality as its very root and foundation.

The injustice and violation of principle are not less flagrant because those who suffer by them are a minority; for there is not equal suffrage where every single individual does not count for as much as any other single individual in the community. But it is not only a minority who suffer. Democracy, thus constituted, does not even attain its ostensible object, that of giving the powers of government in all cases to the numerical majority. It does something very different: it gives them to a majority of the majority; who may be, and often are, but a minority of the whole. All principles are most effectually tested by extreme cases. Suppose then, that, in a country governed by equal and universal suffrage, there is a contested election in every constituency, and every election is carried by a small majority. The Parliament thus brought together represents little more than a bare majority of the people. This Parliament proceeds to legislate, and adopts important measures by a bare majority of itself. What guarantee is there that these measures accord with the wishes of a majority of the people? Nearly half the electors, having been outvoted at the hustings, have had no influence at all in the decision; and the whole of these may be, a majority of them probably are, hostile to the measures, having voted against those by whom they have been carried. Of the remaining electors, nearly half have chosen representatives who, by supposition, have voted against the measures. It is possible, therefore, and not at all improbable, that the opinion which has prevailed was agreeable only to a minority of the nation, though a majority of that portion of it whom the institutions of the country have erected into a ruling class. If democracy means the certain ascendancy of the majority, there are no means of insuring that but by allowing every individual figure to tell equally in the summing up. Any minority left out, either purposely or by the play of the machinery,

gives the power not to the majority, but to a minority in some other part of the scale.

The only answer which can possibly be made to this reasoning is, that as different opinions predominate in different localities, the opinion which is in a minority in some places has a majority in others, and on the whole every opinion which exists in the constituencies obtains its fair share of voices in the representation. . . . This is strikingly exemplified in the United States; where, at the election of President, the strongest party never dares put forward any of its strongest men, because every one of these, from the mere fact that he has been long in the public eye, has made himself objectionable to some portion or other of the party, and is therefore not so sure a card for rallying all their votes as a person who has never been heard of by the public at all until he is produced as the candidate. Thus, the man who is chosen, even by the strongest party, represents perhaps the real wishes only of the narrow margin by which that party outnumbers the other. Any section whose support is necessary to success possesses a veto on the candidate. Any section which holds out more obstinately than the rest can compel all the others to adopt its nominee; and this superior pertinacity is unhappily more likely to be found among those who are holding out for their own interest than for that of the public. The choice of the majority is therefore very likely to be determined by that portion of the body who are the most timid, the most narrow-minded and prejudiced, or who cling most tenaciously to the exclusive class-interest; in which case the electoral rights of the minority, while useless for the purposes for which votes are given, serve only for compelling the majority to accept the candidate of the weakest or worst portion of themselves. . . . But real equality of representation is not obtained unless any set of electors amounting to the average number of a constituency, wherever in the country they happen to reside, have the power of combining with one another to return a representative. This degree of perfection in representation appeared impracticable until a man of great capacity, fitted alike for large general views and for the contrivance of practical details—Mr. Thomas Hare—had proved its possibility by drawing up a scheme for its accomplishment, embodied in a Draft of an Act of Parliament: a scheme which has the almost unparalleled merit of carrying out a great principle of government in a manner approaching to ideal perfection as regards the special object in view, while it attains incidentally several other ends of scarcely inferior importance.

According to this plan, the unit of representation, the quota of electors who would be entitled to have a member to themselves, would be ascertained by the ordinary process of taking averages, the number of voters being divided by the number of seats in the House: and every candidate who obtained that quota would be returned, from however great a number of local constituencies it might be gathered. The votes would, as at present, be given locally; but any elector would be at liberty to vote for any candidate in whatever part of the country he might offer himself. Those electors, therefore, who did not wish to be represented by any of the local candidates, might aid by their vote in the return of the person they liked best among all those throughout the country who had expressed a willingness to be chosen. This would, so far, give reality to the electoral rights of the otherwise virtually disfranchised minority. But it is important that not those alone who refuse to vote for any of the local candidates, but those also who vote for one of them and are defeated, should be enabled to find elsewhere the representation which they have not succeeded in obtaining in their own district. It is therefore provided that an elector may deliver a voting paper, containing other names in addition to the one which stands foremost in his preference. His vote would only be counted for one candidate; but if the object of his first choice failed to be returned, from not having obtained the quota, his second perhaps might be more fortunate. He may extend his list to a greater number, in the order of his preference, so that if the names which stand near the top of the list either cannot make up the quota, or are able to make it up without his vote, the vote may still be used for some one whom it may assist in returning. To obtain the full number of members required to complete

the House, as well as to prevent very popular candidates from engrossing nearly all the suffrages, it is necessary, however many votes a candidate may obtain, that no more of them than the quota should be counted for his return: the remainder of those who voted for him would have their votes counted for the next person on their respective lists who needed them, and could by their aid complete the quota. To determine which of a candidate's votes should be used for his return, and which set free for others, several methods are proposed, into which we shall not here enter. He would of course retain the votes of all those who would not otherwise be represented; and for the remainder, drawing lots, in default of better, would be an unobjectionable expedient. The voting papers would be conveyed to a central office, where the votes would be counted, the number of first, second, third, and other votes given for each candidate ascertained, and the quota would be allotted to every one who could make it up, until the number of the House was complete: first votes being preferred to second, second to third, and so forth. . . .

In the first place, it secures a representation, in proportion to numbers, of every division of the electoral body: not two great parties alone, with perhaps a few large sectional minorities in particular places, but every minority in the whole nation, consisting of a sufficiently large number to be, on principles of equal justice, entitled to a representative. Secondly, no elector would, as at present, be nominally represented by some one whom he had not chosen. Every member of the House would be the representative of a unanimous constituency. He would represent a thousand electors, or two thousand, or five thousand, or ten thousand, as the quota might be, every one of whom would have not only voted for him, but selected him from the whole country; not merely from the assortment of two or three perhaps rotten oranges, which may be the only choice offered to him in his local market. Under this relation the tie between the elector and the representative would be of a strength, and a value, of which at present we have no experience. Every one of the electors would be personally identified with his representative, and the representative with his constituents. Every elector who voted for him would have done so either because, among all the candidates for Parliament who are favourably known to a certain number of electors, he is the one who best expresses the voter's own opinions, or because he is one of those whose abilities and character the voter most respects, and whom he most willingly trusts to think for him. The member would represent persons, not the mere bricks and mortar of the town— the voters themselves, not a few vestrymen or parish notabilities merely. All, however, that is worth preserving in the representation of places would be preserved. Though the Parliament of the nation ought to have as little as possible to do with purely local affairs, yet, while it has to do with them, there ought to be members specially commissioned to look after the interests of every important locality: and these there would still be. In every locality which could make up the quota within itself, the majority would generally prefer to be represented by one of themselves; by a person of local knowledge, and residing in the locality, if there is any such person to be found among the candidates, who is otherwise well qualified to be their representative. It would be the minorities chiefly, who being unable to return the local member, would look out elsewhere for a candidate likely to obtain other votes in addition to their own.

Of all modes in which a national representation can possibly be constituted, this one affords the best security for the intellectual qualifications desirable in the representatives. At present, by universal admission, it is becoming more and more difficult for any one who has only talents and character to gain admission into the House of Commons. The only persons who can get elected are those who possess local influence, or make their way by lavish expenditure, or who, on the invitation of three or four tradesmen or attorneys, are sent down by one of the two great parties from their London clubs, as men whose votes the party can depend on under all circumstances. On Mr. Hare's system, those who did not like the local candidates, or who could not succeed in carrying the local candidate they preferred, would have the power to fill up their voting papers by a selection from all the persons of national reputation, on the list of candidates, with whose general political principles they were in sympathy. Almost every person, therefore, who had made himself in any way honourably distinguished, though devoid of local influence, and having sworn allegiance to no political party, would have a fair chance of making up the quota; and with this encouragement such persons might be expected to offer themselves, in numbers hitherto undreamt of. Hundreds of able men of independent thought, who would have no chance whatever of being chosen by the majority of any existing constituency, have by their writings, or their exertions in some field of public usefulness, made themselves known and approved by a few persons in almost every district of the kingdom; and if every vote that would be given for them in every place could be counted for their election, they might be able to complete the number of the quota. In no other way which it seems possible to suggest would Parliament be so certain of containing the very élite of the country.

Of the Extension of the Suffrage

Whoever, in an otherwise popular government, has no vote, and no prospect of obtaining it, will either be a permanent malcontent, or will feel as one whom the general affairs of society do not concern; for whom they are to be managed by others; who 'has no business with the laws except to obey them,' nor with public interests and concerns except as a looker-on. What he will know or care about them from this position, may partly be measured by what an average woman of the middle class knows and cares about politics, compared with her husband or brothers.

Independently of all these considerations, it is a personal injustice to withhold from any one, unless for the prevention of greater evils, the ordinary privilege of having his voice reckoned in the disposal of affairs in which he has the same interest as other people. If he is compelled to pay, if he may be compelled to fight, if he is required implicitly to obey, he should be legally entitled to be told what for; to have his consent asked, and his opinion counted at its worth, though not at more than its worth. There ought to be no pariahs in a full-grown and civilized nation; no persons disqualified, except through their own default. Every one is degraded, whether aware of it or not, when other people, without consulting him, take upon themselves unlimited power to regulate his destiny. And even in a much more improved state than the human mind has ever yet reached, it is not in nature that they who are thus disposed of should meet with as fair play as those who have a voice. Rulers and ruling classes are under a necessity of considering the interests and wishes of those who have the suffrage; but of those who are excluded, it is in their option whether they will do so or not and however honestly disposed, they are in general too fully occupied with things which they *must* attend to, to have much room in their thoughts for anything which they can with impunity disregard. No arrangement of the suffrage, therefore, can be permanently satisfactory, in which any person or class is peremptorily excluded; in which the electoral privilege is not open to all persons of full age who desire to obtain it.

There are, however, certain exclusions, required by positive reasons, which do not conflict with this principle, and which, though an evil in themselves, are only to be got rid of by the cessation of the state of things which requires them. I regard it as wholly inadmissible that any person should participate in the suffrage, without being able to read, write, and, I will add, perform the common operations of arithmetic. Justice demands, even when the suffrage does not depend on it, that the means of attaining these elementary acquirements should be within the reach of every person, either gratuitously, or at an expense not exceeding what the poorest, who earn their own living, can afford. If this were really the case, people would no more think of giving the suffrage to a man who could not read, than of giving it to a child who could not speak; and it would not be society that would exclude him, but his own laziness. When society has not performed its duty, by rendering this amount of instruction accessible to all, there is some hardship in the case, but it is a hardship that

ought to be borne. If society has neglected to discharge two solemn obligations, the more important and more fundamental of the two must be fulfilled first: universal teaching must precede universal enfranchisement. . . .

It is also important, that the assembly which votes the taxes, either general or local, should be elected exclusively by those who pay something towards the taxes imposed. Those who pay no taxes, disposing by their votes of other people's money, have every motive to be lavish, and none to economize. As far as money matters are concerned, any power of voting possessed by them is a violation of the fundamental principle of free government; a severance of the power of control, from the interest in its beneficial exercise. It amounts to allowing them to put their hands into other people's pockets, for any purpose which they think fit to call a public one; which in some of the great towns of the United States is known to have produced a scale of local taxation onerous beyond example, and wholly borne by the wealthier classes. . . .

However this may be, I regard it as required by first principles, that the receipt of parish relief should be a peremptory disqualification for the franchise. He who cannot by his labour suffice for his own support, has no claim to the privilege of helping himself to the money of others. By becoming dependent on the remaining members of the community for actual subsistence, he abdicates his claim to equal rights with them in other respects. Those to whom he is indebted for the continuance of his very existence, may justly claim the exclusive management of those common concerns, to which he now brings nothing, or less than he takes away. As a condition of the franchise, a term should be fixed, say five years previous to the registry, during which the applicant's name has not been on the parish books as a recipient of relief. . . . Nonpayment of taxes, when so long persisted in that it cannot have arisen from inadvertence, should disqualify while it lasts. These exclusions are not in their nature permanent. They exact such conditions only as all are able, or ought to be able, to fulfil if they choose. They leave the suffrage accessible to all who are in the normal condition of a human being: and if any one has to forego it, he either does not care sufficiently for it, to do for its sake what he is already bound to do, or he is in a general condition of depression and degradation in which this slight addition, necessary for the security of others, would be unfelt, and on emerging from which, this mark of inferiority would disappear with the rest.

In the long run, therefore (supposing no restrictions to exist but those of which we have now treated), we might expect that all, except that (it is to be hoped) progressively diminishing class, the recipients of parish relief, would be in possession of votes, so that the suffrage would be, with that slight abatement, universal. That it should be thus widely expanded, is, as we have seen, absolutely necessary to an enlarged and elevated conception of good government. Yet in this state of things, the great majority of voters, in most countries, and emphatically in this, would be manual labourers; and the twofold danger, that of too low a standard of political intelligence, and that of class legislation, would still exist, in a very perilous degree. It remains to be seen whether any means exist by which these evils can be obviated.

They are capable of being obviated, if men sincerely wish it; not by any artificial contrivance, but by carrying out the natural order of human life, which recommends itself to every one in things in which he has no interest or traditional opinion running counter to it. In all human affairs, every person directly interested, and not under positive tutelage, has an admitted claim to a voice, and when his exercise of it is not inconsistent with the safety of the whole, cannot justly be excluded from it. But though every one ought to have a voice—that every one should have an equal voice is a totally different proposition. When two persons who have a joint interest in any business, differ in opinion, does justice require that both opinions should be held of exactly equal value? If with equal virtue, one is superior to the other in knowledge and intelligence—or if with equal intelligence, one excels the other in virtue—the opinion, the judgment, of the higher moral or intellectual being, is worth more than that of the inferior: and if the institutions of the country virtually assert that they are of the same value, they assert a thing which is not. . . .

Every one has a right to feel insulted by being made a nobody, and stamped as of no account at all. No one but a fool, and only a fool of a peculiar description, feels offended by the acknowledgment that there are others whose opinion, and even whose wish, is entitled to a greater amount of consideration than his. To have no voice in what are partly his own concerns, is a thing which nobody willingly submits to; but when what is partly his concern is also partly another's, and he feels the other to understand the subject better than himself, that the other's opinion should be counted for more than his own, accords with his expectations, and with the course of things which in all other affairs of life he is accustomed to acquiesce in. It is only necessary that this superior influence should be assigned on grounds which he can comprehend, and of which he is able to perceive the justice. . . .

If there existed such a thing as a really national education, or a trustworthy system of general examination, education might be tested directly. In the absence of these, the nature of a person's occupation is some test. An employer of labour is on the average more intelligent than a labourer; for he must labour with his head, and not solely with his hands. A foreman is generally more intelligent than an ordinary labourer, and a labourer in the skilled trades than in the unskilled. A banker, merchant, or manufacturer, is likely to be more intelligent than a tradesman, because he has larger and more complicated interests to manage. In all these cases it is not the having merely undertaken the superior function, but the successful performance of it, that tests the qualifications; for which reason, as well as to prevent persons from engaging nominally in an occupation for the sake of the vote, it would be proper to require that the occupation should have been persevered in for some length of time (say three years). Subject to some such condition, two or more votes might be allowed to every person who exercises any of these superior functions. The liberal professions, when really and not nominally practised, imply, of course, a still higher degree of instruction; and wherever a sufficient examination, or any serious conditions of education, are required before entering on a profession, its members could be admitted at once to a plurality of votes. The same rule might be applied to graduates of universities; and even to those who bring satsifactory certificates of having passed through the course of study required by any school at which the higher branches of knowledge are taught, under proper securities that the teaching is real, and not a mere pretence. . . .

Let me add, that I consider it an absolutely necessary part of the plurality scheme, that it be open to the poorest individual in the community to claim its privileges, if he can prove that, in spite of all difficulties and obstacles, he is, in point of intelligence, entitled to them. There ought to be voluntary examinations at which any person whatever might present himself, might prove that he came up to the standard of knowledge and ability laid down as sufficient, and be admitted, in consequence, to the plurality of votes. A privilege which is not refused to any one who can show that he has realized the conditions on which in theory and principle it is dependent, would not necessarily be repugnant to any one's sentiment of justice: but it would certainly be so, if, while conferred on general presumptions not always infallible, it were denied to direct proof.

2

The Popular Will Theory

Essay on Government

James Mill

James Mill was born in Scotland in 1773, the son of a shoemaker. He married Harriet Burrow in 1806, and they had nine children, of whom John Stuart was the oldest. Among his earlier works is a highly regarded three volume work The History of India, *which won him a position at the East India Trading Company. A disciple of Jeremy Bentham, Mill joined the "Philosophical Radicals" and worked to further the utilitarian ideals through legal reform. His writing included work in history, psychology, economics, and politics. He also wrote a series of articles for the* Encyclopedia Britannica, *which were published between 1816 and 1823. In these articles he attempted to apply utilitarian principles to various topics. His most important article was his "Essay on Government."*

Mill begins with the assumption that human behavior can be explained by individual self-interest, and that the common good is the sum of each individual's own good. The key question for politics is how to assure that the desires of individuals to exercise their will over others can be properly channeled. Politics is essentially a contest of will, and rulers tend to use power to conform the will of the community to their own will rather than expressing the will of the people as a whole. Government can place power in the hands of the many (democracy), the few (aristocracy), or the one (monarchy.) None of these is satisfactory, however, which leads Mill to representative government. Here, he argues, is the best hope of finding a system that expresses the will of the people and thereby serves the larger interest rather than the narrow goals of the few. But, says Mill, the arrangement of a representative system requires delicate consideration of such matters as duration of office and the qualifications of office holders.

I. *The End of Government; viz. the Good or Benefit for the Sake of which it exists.* The question with respect to Government is a question about the adaptation of means to an end. Notwithstanding the portion of discourse which has been bestowed upon this subject, it is surprising to find, on a close inspection, how few of its principles are settled. The reason is, that the ends and means have not been analyzed; and it is only a general and undistinguishing conception of them, which is found in the minds of the greatest number of men. Things, in this situation, give rise to interminable disputes; more especially when the deliberation is subject, as here, to the strongest action of personal interest. . . .

The end of Government has been described in a great variety of expressions. By Locke it was said to be 'the public good;' by others it has been described as being 'the greatest happiness of the greatest number.' These, and equivalent expressions, are just; but they are defective, inasmuch as the particular ideas which they embrace are indistinctly announced; and different conceptions are by means of them raised in different minds, and even in the same mind on different occasions. . . .

We may allow, for example, in general terms, that the lot of every human being is determined by his pains and pleasures; and that his happiness corresponds with the degree in which his pleasures are great, and his pains are small.

Human pains and pleasures are derived from two sources: — They are produced, either by our fellow-men, or by causes independent of other men.

From James Mill, "Essay on Government" (1820).

We may assume it as another principle, that the concern of Government is with the former of these two sources; that its business is to increase to the utmost the pleasures, and diminish to the utmost the pains, which men derive from one another. . . .

II. *The Means of attaining the End of Government; viz. Power, and Securities against the Abuse of that Power.* Two things are here to be considered; the power with which the small number are entrusted; and the use which they are to make of it.

With respect to the first, there is no difficulty. The elements, out of which the power of coercing others is fabricated, are obvious to all. Of these we shall, therefore, not lengthen this article by any explanation.

All the difficult questions of Government relate to the means of restraining those, in whose hands are lodged the powers necessary for the protection of all, from making bad use of it.

Whatever would be the temptations under which individuals would lie, if there was no Government, to take the objects of desire from others weaker than themselves, under the same temptations the members of Government lie, to take the objects of desire from the members of the community, if they are not prevented from doing so. Whatever, then, are the reasons for establishing Government, the very same exactly are the reasons for establishing securities, that those entrusted with the powers necessary for protecting others make use of them for that purpose solely, and not for the purpose of taking from the members of the community the objects of desire.

III. *That the requisite Securities against the Abuse of Power, are not found in any of the simple Forms of Government.* There are three modes in which it may be supposed that the powers for the protection of the community are capable of being exercised. The community may undertake the protection of itself, and of its members. The powers of protection may be placed in the hands of a few. And, lastly, they may be placed in the hands of an individual. The Many, The Few, The One; These varieties appear to exhaust the subject. It is not possible to conceive any hands, or

combination of hands, in which the powers of protection can be lodged, which will not fall under one or other of those descriptions. And these varieties correspond to the three forms of Government, the Democratical, the Aristocratical, and the Monarchical.

It will be necessary to look somewhat closely at each of these forms in their order.

1. *The Democratical.* — It is obviously impossible that the community in a body can be present to afford protection to each of its members. It must employ individuals for that purpose. Employing individuals, it must choose them; it must lay down the rules under which they are to act; and it must punish them, if they act in disconformity to those rules. In these functions are included the three great operations of Government — Administration, Legislation, and Judicature. The community, to perform any of these operations, must be assembled. This circumstance alone seems to form a conclusive objection against the democratical form. To assemble the whole of a community as often as the business of Government requires performance would almost preclude the existence of labour; hence that of property; and hence the existence of the community itself.

There is another objection, not less conclusive. A whole community would form a numerous assembly. But all numerous assemblies are essentially incapable of business. It is unnecessary to be tedious in the proof of this proposition. In an assembly, everything must be done by speaking and assenting. But where the assembly is numerous, so many persons desire to speak, and feelings, by mutual inflammation, become so violent, that calm and effectual deliberation is impossible.

It may be taken, therefore, as a position, from which there will be no dissent, that a community in mass is ill adapted for the business of Government. There is no principle more in conformity with the sentiments and the practice of the people than this. The management of the joint affairs of any considerable body of the people they never undertake for themselves. What they uniformly do is, to choose a certain number of themselves to be the actors in their stead. Even in the case of a common Benefit Club, the members choose a

Committee of Management and content themselves with a general control.

2. *The Aristocratical.* — This term applies to all those cases, in which the powers of Government are held by any number of persons intermediate between a single person and the majority.

The source of evil is radically different, in the case of Aristocracy, from what it is in that of Democracy.

The Community cannot have an interest opposite to its interest. To affirm this would be a contradiction in terms. The Community within itself, and with respect to itself, can have no sinister interest. One Community may intend the evil of another; never its own. This is an indubitable proposition, and one of great importance. The Community may act wrong from mistake. To suppose that it could from design, would be to suppose that human beings can wish their own misery. . . .

We have already observed, that the reason for which Government exists is, that one man, if stronger than another, will take from him whatever that other possesses and he desires. But if one man will do this, so will several. And if powers are put into the hands of a comparatively small number, called an Aristocracy, powers which make them stronger than the rest of the community, they will take from the rest of the community as much as they please of the objects of desire. They will, thus, defeat the very end for which Government was instituted. The unfitness, therefore, of an Aristocracy to be entrusted with the powers of Government, rests on demonstration.

3. *The Monarchical.* — It will be seen, and therefore words to make it manifest are unnecessary, that, in most respects, the Monarchical form of Government agrees with the Aristocratical, and is liable to the same objections.

If Government is founded upon this, as a law of human nature, that a man, if able, will take from others anything which they have and he desires, it is sufficiently evident that when a man is called a King, it does not change his nature; so that when he has got power to enable him to take from every man what he pleases, he will take whatever he pleases. To suppose that he will not, is to affirm that Government is unnecessary; and that human be-

ings will abstain from injuring one another of their own accord. . . .

That one human being will desire to render the person and property of another subservient to his pleasures, notwithstanding the pain or loss of pleasure which it may occasion to that other individual, is the foundation of Government. The desire of the object implies the desire of the power necessary to accomplish the object. The desire, therefore, of that power which is necessary to render the persons and properties of human beings subservient to our pleasures, is a grand governing law of human nature.

What is implied in that desire of power; and what is the extent to which it carries the actions of men; are the questions which it is necessary to resolve, in order to discover the limit which nature has set to the desire, on the part of a King, or an Aristocracy, to inflict evil upon the community for their own advantage.

Power is a means to an end. The end is, every thing, without exception, which the human being calls pleasure, and the removal of pain. The grand instrument for attaining what a man likes is the actions of other men. Power, in its most appropriate signification, therefore, means, security for the conformity between the will of one man and the acts of other men. This, we presume, is not a proposition which will be disputed. The master has power over his servant, because when he wills him to do so and so, — in other words, expresses a desire that he would do so and so, he possesses a kind of security that the actions of the man will correspond to his desire. The general commands his soldiers to perform certain operations, the King commands his subjects to act in a certain manner, and their power is complete or not complete, in proportion as the conformity is complete or not complete between the actions willed and the actions performed. The actions of other men, considered as means for the attainment of the objects of our desire, are perfect or imperfect, in proportion as they are or are not certainly and invariably correspondent to our will. There is no limit, therefore, to the demand of security for the perfection of that correspondence. . . . With respect to the rulers of a community, this at least is certain, that they have a desire for the conformity between their will and the actions of every man in the community. And for our present purpose, this is as wide a field as we need to embrace. . . . As it has been demonstrated that there is no limit to the number of men whose actions we desire to have conformable to our will, it follows, with equal evidence, that there is no limit to the command which we desire to possess over the objects which ensure this result.

It is, therefore, not true, that there is, in the mind of a King, or in the minds of an Aristocracy, any point of saturation with the objects of desire. The opinion, in examination of which we have gone through the preceding analysis, that a King or an Aristocracy may be satiated with the objects of desire, and, after being satiated, leave to the members of the community the greater part of what belongs to them, is an opinion founded upon a partial and incomplete view of the laws of human nature. . . .

The chain of inference, in this case, is close and strong, to a most unusual degree. A man desires that the actions of other men shall be instantly and accurately correspondent to his will. He desires that the actions of the greatest possible number shall be so. Terror is the grand instrument. Terror can work only through assurance that evil will follow any want of conformity between the will and the actions willed. Every failure must, therefore, be punished. As there are no bounds to the mind's desire of its pleasure, there are of course no bounds to its desire of perfection in the instruments of that pleasure. There are, therefore, no bounds to its desire of exactness in the conformity between its will and the actions willed; and, by consequence, to the strength of that terror which is its procuring cause. Every, the most minute, failure must be visited with the heaviest infliction: and, as failure in extreme exactness must frequently happen, the occasions of cruelty must be incessant.

We have thus arrived at several conclusions of the highest possible importance. We have seen, that the very principle of human nature upon which the necessity of Government is founded, the propensity of one man to possess himself of the objects of desire at the cost of another, leads on, by infallible sequence, where power over a community is attained, and nothing checks, not only to that degree of plunder which leaves the members (excepting always the recipients and instruments of the plunder) the bare means of subsistence, but to that degree of cruelty which is necessary to keep in existence the most intense terror.

The world affords some decisive experiments upon human nature, in exact conformity with these conclusions. . . .

VI. *In the Representative System alone the Securities for good Government are to be found.* What then is to be done? For, according to this reasoning, we may be told that good Government appears to be impossible. The people, as a body, cannot perform the business of Government for themselves. If the powers of Government are entrusted to one man, or a few men, and a Monarchy, or governing Aristocracy, is formed, the results are fatal: And it appears that a combination of the simple forms is impossible.

Notwithstanding the truth of these propositions, it is not yet proved that good Government is unattainable. For though the people, who cannot exercise the powers of Government themselves, must entrust them to some one individual or set of individuals, and such individuals will infallibly have the strongest motives to make a bad use of them, it is possible that checks may be found sufficient to prevent them. The next subject or inquiry, then, is the doctrine of checks. . . .

There can be no doubt, that, if power is granted to a body of men, called Representatives, they, like any other men, will use their power, not for the advantage of the community, but for their own advantage, if they can. The only question is, therefore, how they can be prevented? In other words, how are the interests of the Representatives to be identified with those of the community?

Each Representative may be considered in two capacities; in his capacity of Representative, in which he has the exercise of power over others, and in his capacity of Member of the Community, in which others have the exercise of power over him.

If things were so arranged, that, in his capacity of Representative, it would be impossible for him to do himself so much good by mis-government, as he would do himself harm in his capacity of member of the community, the object would be accomplished. . . . [T]he amount of power assigned to the checking body cannot be diminished beyond a certain amount. It must be sufficient to overcome all resistance on the part of all those in whose hands the powers of Government are lodged. But if the power assigned to the Representative cannot be diminished in amount, there is only one other way in which it can be diminished, and that is, in duration.

This, then, is the instrument; lessening duration is the instrument, by which, if by any thing, the object is to be attained. The smaller the period of time during which any man retains his capacity of Representative, as compared with the time in which he is simply a member of the community, the more difficult it will be to compensate the sacrifice of the interests of the longer period, by the profits of mis-government during the shorter.

This is an old and approved method of identifying, as nearly as possible, the interests of those who rule, with the interests of those who are ruled. It is in pursuance of this advantage, that the Members of the British House of Commons have always been chosen for a limited period. If the Members were hereditary, or even if they were chosen for life, every inquirer would immediately pronounce that they would employ, for their own advantage, the powers entrusted to them; and that they would go just as far in abusing the persons and properties of the people, as their estimate of the powers and spirit of the people to resist them would allow them to contemplate as safe. . . .

In the principle of limiting the duration of the power delegated to the Representatives of the people, is not included the idea of changing them. The same individual may be chosen any number of times. The check of the short period, for which he is chosen, and during which he can promote his sinister interest, is the same upon the man who has been chosen and rechosen twenty times, as upon the man who has been chosen for the first time. And there is good reason for always re-electing the man who has done his duty, because the longer he serves, the better acquainted he becomes with the business of the service. . . .

The general conclusion, therefore, which is evidently established is this; that the benefits of the Representative system are lost, in all cases in which the interests of the choosing body are not the same with those of the community.

It is very evident, that if the community itself were the choosing body, the interest of the community and that of the choosing body would be the same. The question is, whether that of any portion of the community, if erected into the choosing body, would remain the same?

One thing is pretty clear, that all those individuals whose interests are indisputably included in those of other individuals, may be struck off without inconvenience. In this light may be viewed all children, up to a certain age, whose interests are involved in those of their parents. In this light, also, women may be regarded, the interest of almost all of whom is involved either in that of their fathers or in that of their husbands.

Having ascertained that an interest, identical with that of the whole community, is to be found in the aggregate males, of an age to be regarded as *sui juris,* who may be regarded as the natural Representatives of the whole population, we have to go on, and inquire, whether this requisite quality may not be found in some less number, some aliquot part of that body.

As degrees of mental qualities are not easily ascertained, outward and visible signs must be taken to distinguish, for this purpose, one part of these males from another. Applicable signs of this description appear to be three; Years, Property, Profession or Mode of Life. . . .

With respect to the first principle of selection, that of age, it would appear that a considerable latitude may be taken without inconvenience. Suppose the age of forty were prescribed, as that at which the right of Suffrage should commence; scarcely any laws could be made for the benefit of all the men of forty which would not be laws for the benefit of all the rest of the community. . . .

We come next to the inquiry, whether the interest of a body of electors, constituted by the possession of a certain amount of property or income, would be the same with the interest of the community?

It will not be disputed, that, if the qualification were raised so high that only a few hundreds possessed it, the case would be exactly the same with that of the consignment of the Electoral Suffrage to an Aristocracy. . . .

It is not easy to find any satisfactory principle to guide us in our researches, and to tell us where we should fix. The qualification must either be such as to embrace the majority of the population, or some thing less than the majority. Suppose, in the first place, that it embraces the majority, the question is, whether the majority would have an interest in oppressing those who, upon this supposition, would be deprived of political power? If we reduce the calculation to its elements, we shall see that the interest which they would have, of this deplorable kind, though it would be something, would not be very great. Each man of the majority, if the majority were constituted the governing body, would have something less than the benefit of oppressing a single man. If the majority were twice as great as the minority, each man of the majority would only have one-half the benefit of oppressing a single man. In that case, the benefits of good Government, accruing to all, might be expected to overbalance to the several members of such an elective body the benefits of misrule peculiar to themselves. Good Government, would, therefore, have a tolerable security. Suppose, in the second place, that the qualification did not admit a body of electors so large as the majority, in that case, taking again the calculation in its elements, we shall see that each man would have a benefit equal to that derived from the oppression of more than one man; and that, in proportion as the elective body constituted a smaller and smaller minority, the benefit of misrule to the elective body would be increased, and bad Government would be insured.

It seems hardly necessary to carry the analysis of the pecuniary qualification, as the principle for choosing an elective body, any farther.

We have only remaining the third plan for constituting an elective body. According to the scheme in question, the best elective body is that which consists of certain classes, professions, or fraternities. The notion is, that when these fraternities or bodies are represented, the community itself is represented. The way in which, according to the patrons of this theory, the effect is brought about, is this.

Though it is perfectly true, that each of these fraternities would profit by misrule, and have the strongest interest in promoting it; yet, if three of four such fraternities are appointed to act in conjunction, they will not profit by misrule, and will have an interest in nothing but good Government.

According to the ideas of Lord Liverpool, the landholders ought to be represented; the merchants and manufacturers ought to be represented; the officers of the army and navy ought to be represented; and the practitioners of the law ought to be represented. Other patrons of the scheme have added, that literary men ought to be represented. And these, we believe, are almost all the fraternities, which have been named for this purpose, by any of the advocates of representation by clubs. To insure the choice of Representatives of the landholders, landholders must be the choosers; to insure the choice of Representatives of the merchants and manufacturers, merchants and manufacturers must be the choosers; and so with respect to the other fraternities, whether few or many. Thus it must be at least in *substance;* whatever the form, under which the visible acts may be performed. According to the scheme in question, these several fraternities are represented *directly,* the rest of the community is *not* represented directly; but it will be said by the patrons of the scheme, that it is *represented virtually,* which, in this case, answers the same purpose. . . . Unless the patrons of this theory can prove to us, contrary to all experience, that a common interest cannot create an *esprit de corps* in men in combinations, as well as in men individually, we are under the necessity of believing, that an *esprit de corps* would be formed in the classes separated from the rest of the community for the purposes of Representation; that they would pursue their common interest; and inflict all the evils upon the rest of the community to which the pursuit of that interest would lead.

It is not included in the idea of this union for the pursuit of a common interest, that the clubs or sets of persons appropriated to the business of Representation should totally harmonize. There would, no doubt, be a great mixture of agreement and disagreement among them. But there would, if experience is any guide, or if the general laws of human nature have any power, be sufficient agreement to prevent their losing sight of the common interest; in other words, for insuring all that abuse of power which is useful to the parties by whom it is exercised.

The real effect of this motley Representation, therefore, would only be to create a motley Aristocracy; and, of course, to insure that kind of misgovernment which it is the nature of Aristocracy to produce, and to produce equally, whether it is a uniform, or a variegated Aristocracy; whether an Aristocracy all of landowners; or an Aristocracy in part landowners, in part merchants and manufacturers, in part officers of the army and navy, and in part lawyers. . . .

We have seen, that, unless the Representative Body are chosen by a portion of the community the interest of which cannot be made to differ from that of the community, the interest of the community will infallibly be sacrificed to the interest of the rulers. . . .

Political Representation: An Overview

J. Roland Pennock

Representatives sometimes find themselves forced to choose between policies that express the will of the people or ones expressing the people's genuine interests. In this essay, J. Roland Pennock addresses this and other problems associated with political representation. Beginning with an analysis of the concept, asking what it means to "prepresent" others, he then develops a theoretical account of what responsible officials should do when undertaking to represent others. It is first of all a mistake, argues Pennock, to suppose only those elected to office can or should act as representatives. Pennock uses various examples to explore different theories of representation, claiming that the dichotomy between a trustee charged with acting in the people's interest and a delegate who should act in accord with their desires is most fundamental to any theory of representation. Whether a representative should serve the interests or express the will of the people is an issue that can best be approached by paying close attention to the particular context in which the issues have arisen, he argues. Pennock concludes with a brief discussion of another conflict representatives sometimes face, between their duties to represent their district and their nation as a whole.

"Our common conceptions of representation are obsolete."[1] So declared Heinz Eulau at a recent meeting of the American Political Science Association. . . .

A few years ago, H. B. Mayo reached a similar conclusion. "Democratic theory," he wrote, "has little to gain from talking the language of representation, since everything necessary to the theory may be put in terms of (a) legislators (or decision-makers) who are (b) legitimated or authorized to enact public policies, and who are (c) subject or responsible to public control at free elections. The difficulties of policy-makers are practical," he continued, "and there is no need to confuse democratic politics by a theory that makes the difficulties

From J. Roland Pennock, "Political Representation: An Overview," *Nomos X: Representation,* J. Roland Pennock and John W. Chapman, eds. (New York: Atherton, 1968), pp. 3–24. Some footnotes omitted.

appear to be metaphysical or logical within the concept of representation."[2]

Statements like these, coming from both empirical and theoretical directions, might well give pause to anyone who would give further serious consideration to the subject. . . .

My argument will proceed along two lines. The first will point out that parts of the government other than elected representatives (members of the legislature) serve representative functions and that the concept of representation then links or relates to each other these various carriers of representative roles. The second point will be that even the personnel more specifically thought of as "representatives," i.e., members of an elective legislature, have various roles from which frequently emerge conflicting directives that can be reconciled only by reference to some superior set of norms. It is suggested here that, in some measure, the concept of representation, *considered in the specific contexts in which it is applied,* provides this superior set of norms. Much that would be hopelessly vague considered in the abstract becomes more precise in actual application. In making this second point I shall give some indication of the relation between the theory of representation and certain analyses and empirical studies of legislative roles.[3]

To guard against misconceptions, certain explanatory notes are in order here. In the first place, I assume that the word "representation" may not always have had the same meaning and that it may not always mean the same thing today in different countries. Where the context does not indicate otherwise, I am speaking of Anglo-American usage in the twentieth century.

Second, while I shall deal mainly with the "concept" of representation, I shall refer also to various "theories" of representation. The two may be kept mutually distinct, but they tend to merge; and just where the line is to be drawn between them is in a measure arbitrary. For instance, if the word meant—as it does not—that a "representative" was a person who should do what and only what his constituents demanded of him, one would not need a "theory" about his proper role. The substance of such a theory would have been incorporated into the definition. If, on the other

hand, the word meant that a representative was a person empowered to do whatever he chose on behalf of those whom he represented, and this was all it meant, then only a theory about how representatives should behave could supply such a normative element. In other words, in default of general agreement upon a single theory, no theory would become part of the definition, but the latter would tend to be supplemented by two or more alternative theories. Incidentally, this explains why I said above that representation "may" not always have had the same meaning. Whether the meaning of the term itself varied depends upon how much of the attendant theory one tries to pack into the definition.

Finally, as has been already implied, it will not be argued that all elements of vagueness can be eliminated from the term. Nor is vagueness always a vice; indeed, in moderation, it may be a virtue! Ponder that popular (and useful) term in modern political science, "consensus"; or consider "power," "liberty," "cleavage," or "the public interest." Imprecise terms, in this case terms that lay down a standard (as contrasted with a rule) of conduct, often have the virtue of holding together, before the mind's eye, related though distinct ideas. They show linkages and continuities that might otherwise be overlooked. Synthesis as well as analysis has its uses in contributing to the understanding of systems of all kinds, including political systems. As the use of the word "standards" may suggest, terms with some element of vagueness are especially likely to be required where norms are involved, but the examples of "power," "consensus," and "cleavage" show that not only normative terms are difficult to render precise.

Political Representation Not Confined to the Democratic State

In considering political representation in its broadest sense, we should remember that the idea of political representation is by no means modern or confined to the democratic state. In a proper use of the word, all legitimate governments are "representative." Thus medieval kings were thought to be made legitimate not only by hereditary right and divine ordination but also by the acclaim of the nobles. They owed their authority also, at least in some dim past, to the people more generally, or so it was widely held. It was part of their office as well to see that justice was done, "to protect the poor as well as the rich in the enjoyment of their rights."[4] Even that great apostle of Divine Right, James I, considered himself trustee for the realm, though accountable to no one but God for the execution of that trust.

Thomas Hobbes, absolutist of a different sort, insisted that his sovereign was representative of the polity, having been authorized to rule by the unanimous voices of the citizenry. While, as Hanna Pitkin says, this was "formal" rather than "substantive" representation,[5] and is an example of the opposite of the delegate theory of representation, yet Hobbes' sovereign, like James I, had a duty to maintain justice and serve the interest of the people, it being understood (as far as Hobbes is concerned) that their primary interest was security. Finally, it will do no harm to remind ourselves that even the modern totalitarian dictator, even Hitler, sought legitimacy by claiming to represent the people. Ultimate power and final responsibility were his, said the Führer, because through him the true spirit of the German people found expression. He also sought to authenticate his legitimacy by claiming the constitutional legality of his regime and by subsequent reliance upon plebiscites. And of course he was recognized by the governments of other states as the authorized spokesman, the representative, of the German people.

It will be noted that the two main claims of monarchs and dictators from which their legitimacy appears to have derived were (1) the contention that they stood for, gave expression to, and supported the interests (and, we should add, ideals and aspirations) of their people; and (2) the argument that they were in some fashion authorized to act (generally within variously stated or implied limits) in their behalf. All this is not of mere historical interest, nor applicable only to nondemocratic states. *All* regimes obtain legitimacy by being in some degree representative or at least convincing their subjects that they are. One of the

traditional arguments for absolute monarchy has been that the monarch could have no interest that conflicted with that of the welfare of the realm, since his greatness varied directly with its greatness.

As certain elements of the realm became dissatisfied with the operation of this theory, they demanded a more responsive form of representation, one over which they had control. Thus today the man in the street tends to think of elected officers and especially of the elected legislature as *the* representative body and of its members as *the* representatives. Elections are thought of as providing the great sanction for assuring representative behavior. Above all else, they supply the element of authorization, keeping it current. It is reasonable to believe that they tend to secure governmental action in the interest of those whom they are supposed to represent, both by enforcing accountability and by giving some indication of what the people consider their interests to be.[6]

The Bureaucracy and Representation

Yet it would be a great mistake to assume that elections are the only means by which persons in positions of authority are encouraged to act representatively, even today, or that elected officers are the only ones whose behavior is in a measure representative. Members of the bureaucracy, even though they may be practically immune from even indirect elective pressure, are expected to exercise their discretionary authority subject at least to some guidance by the norms of representation.[7] . . . However, in one of its meanings, the concept of representation is normative in the ethical sense; and like all such norms, it has a certain force of its own, without reliance upon externally imposed sanctions. This, of course, is not to deny that the discretionary powers delegated to administrative officials may not in some cases be so great that internalized norms (either of a representational or of a professional variety) are an inadequate assurance of representative behavior . . .

In arguing that administrators, especially

those having broad discretionary powers or exercising great influence on the making of policy, are acting in a representative role, I do not mean that this is the only role they play or even that the role in this context calls for the same behavior as it would in a legislative context. The circumstances associated with the establishment of the authority in question, especially the terms of the basic legislation, may indicate that the wishes of a particular segment of the polity, perhaps a particular industry, are to be given exceptional weight in the exercise of this authority. Or they may suggest that representation in this case should veer sharply away from the responsiveness-to-desire pole toward that of estimation of public interest. Naturally, the first type of situation might be expected to prevail where the powers to be exercised have their major impact on the section of the public in question and where the issues are such that this public would normally have the most relevant information or expertise. The powers of the United States Department of Agriculture over acreage allotments, under the Agricultural Adjustment Act, would be a good example.

A rather different situation, which also frequently leads to the demand for a more "representative" bureaucracy, is found where a new policy has been established, let us say for the benefit of some group deemed to be especially in need of governmental assistance. This demand may result in the creation of a new agency, independent of other departments and staffed as far as possible by personnel who are highly sympathetic with the new policy. They may therefore be expected to be especially concerned to find out the desires and interests (particularly the "needs") of the group in question. The "poverty program" and its Office of Economic Opportunity provide an obvious example. . . .

Elected Representatives: General Theory

Let us turn to my second theme, elected representatives, which has already been briefly introduced. First, in speaking of "elected rep-

resentatives" I am referring to members of a legislature with power, collectively, to make laws and determine national policy. In principle, elected representatives need have no such power. They might be simply advisory or expressive. Thus a modern elective legislator—at least in the Anglo-American tradition—is not simply a representative. He has powers that do not necessarily adhere to representing. But whatever else he may be, whatever roles he may play, he is a representative and therefore should act representatively, subject to the norms of representation, whatever they may be. In the United States, the same is true of the President: he performs his functions as President in a representative capacity, subject therefore to the norms attached to this concept as they apply in the context of his office.

Whether leadership is to be considered as an aspect of representing, as entailed by it, or as a necessary means to performing the representative function, is of no real importance; but a discussion of representation without reference to leadership would lack an important element. Those who seek to represent large numbers of people are bound to find that consensus, even majority opinion, is often lacking. Likewise they may be convinced that what their constituents seem to desire and what is in their real interest or in the national interest, as the case may be, are far apart. In either case, the optimal performance of their function calls for leadership, for forming or re-forming public opinion, and for building consensus, thus easing the task of representation by lessening the tension between its frequently conflicting norms of reflecting constituency desires and pursuing constituency and national interest. That is to say, the very fact that representatives are severally related to distinct localities strongly implies that they have a special obligation to look after the desires and interests of the people in those localities (or the national interest as seen by the voters in those localities). Clearly, at least in the United States, this is the accepted theory. The difference between the United States and Great Britain will be discussed later on.

When we were talking about a monarch or dictator professing to represent a realm, with no authorized intermediary spokesmen, the question of whose view of the national interest should be considered did not arise. But now that attention has shifted to a group of elected intermediaries, close enough to their constituents that it is possible for them to know the views of the majority on a few issues, that question does arise. We now have the outlines of four distinct theories about the duty of a representative. These theories may be stated in the following propositions:

1. The representative should act in support of what he believes an effective majority of his constituency desires.
2. The representative should act in support of what he believes is in the constituency's interest.
3. The representative should act in support of what he believes the nation (or an effective majority of it) desires.
4. The representative should act in support of what he believes is in the nation's interest. . . .

It will be observed that these theories rely heavily upon the distinction between "interest" and "desire." Because the first of these terms, in particular, is notoriously ambiguous or vague, I must digress to discuss the meaning intended here. I believe that for present purposes the world's ambiguities can be confined within reasonable limits. When I speak of the "interest" of a person, or a constituency, or a nation, I mean "advantage." An action, policy, law, or institution is in the interest of a person if it increases his opportunity to get what he desires, including the realization of his aspirations and ideals. To spell this out a little further, the distinction I am intending to make between "desire" and "interest" is the distinction between what is immediately demanded and what in the long run, with the benefit of hindsight, would have been preferred or would have contributed to the development of the individual into a person capable of making responsible decisions.

If, after the representative has done his best to form an enlightened opinion, he believes that a given measure would in fact improve, for example, the economic or educational level of his constituency, other things being equal he would be entitled to conclude that it is in their interest. Of course, most of the time he will be making the kind of judgments that involve weighing an advantage against a disadvantage (both being incurred by the same course of action), just as an individual tries to decide whether something is in his interest. All that can be demanded is that the representative make this kind of judgment as wisely and impartially as he can. In most cases the standard will not be more vague than the one we all must use for our private choices. The same will be true when a decision must be made between what is judged to be a great advantage for a sizable minority and a lesser advantage for a bare majority. All this must be within the framework of what the society in question has established (whether or not in the form of a written constitution) as proper for the state to do — i.e., it must respect recognized rights.

To return now from definitional digression to our discussion of theories of representation, it is well known that American legislators do not all adopt the same theory. At least, when they are asked about how they view their roles, some stress the delegate concept, while others say they consider themselves trustees. . . . The thesis that will be advanced here, however, is that, regardless of what they may say, legislators in fact do not have this wide a choice. It will be argued further that the common understanding of representation itself, shaped partly by the circumstances, provides guidance, even though the area of "common understanding" is not complete.

Delegate Versus Trustee

Among these theories, it is probably safe to say that the dichotomy between acting as a delegate and acting as a trustee is most fundamental. It also seems clear that neither pole of this dichotomy is adequate to explain democratic representation in the modern Anglo-American tradition. For a representative to act purely and simply as a delegate would be to make him functionless most, if not all, of the time, for it is seldom clear precisely what a constituency, or even its majority, wishes. Most of the individuals who compose it either do not know enough or do not care enough (or both) about the issues on which their representatives must vote to have clear opinions of their own; and even when opinions are formed, a majority is likely to be lacking. Representing a constituency is not like representing a client, whose wishes, on a single issue at least, are presumably unitary. A constituency, on the contrary, is rarely unified, even on a single question. Of course, in some cases a clear majority has a definite view on an issue. It might be argued that in such cases the representative should act as a delegate, supporting the majority's desires even though he believes these desires are contrary to their own interests. Thinking for himself and deliberating on the basis of discussion with others, in other words, should be reserved for cases where no clear majority opinion unopposed by an intense minority exists. This is, to be sure, a logically possible position. My own view is that it would not be held by many thoughtful people who consider the implication of the legislative situation, with its opportunities for discussion, deliberation, and obtaining information. In any case, the burden of proof under these circumstances would certainly be on the legislator to justify voting contrary to the majority will.

Similarly, in other ways, what "representation" entails is affected by the context of the office of elected legislator. For instance, if the general attitude of the people in a given constituency were, let us say, anti-French, one would properly say that a person who held that attitude was, other things being equal, "representative" of the constituency. It would not follow, however, that a representative elected by this constituency should vote for anti-French policies, regardless of other considerations. Interests would also need to be taken into account.

But the interest pole of the desire-interest axis is also untenable. . . . In fact, it appears to be generally agreed that representation in a democratic context makes the satisfaction of popular desire itself a legitimate interest, thus blunting the sharpness of the contrast between representation of desires and representation of interests. It seems clear, then, that the proper role of a political representative today is generally believed to fall somewhere between these poles, as several contributors to

this volume maintain. Thus, it is argued here, the prevailing concept of political representation itself gives some guidance for the reconciliation of these conflicts.

Let us consider the delegate-trustee issue in the light of a series of examples illustrating various combinations of strong or weak (and positive or negative) majority desires, strong or weak (and positive or negative) minority desires, and strong or weak (and positive or negative) convictions on the part of the representative as to the constituency's real interest. Suppose it is a question of whether funds should be spent on a fish hatchery and a research institute to study certain diseases that have been limiting the local fish supply, or whether they should be spent on improving the roads. Assuming that motorists outnumber anglers by a staggering ratio, it is not unlikely that a majority, while not feeling very strongly about the matter, might oppose the hatchery, whereas only the minority would have very strong feelings about it and support it. Suppose also that the legislator's own study convinced him that the hatchery and research institute were, on balance, more in the public interest than the additional funds for roads (perhaps partly because of a putative lift to the tourist industry and, through it, to the economy as a whole). Under these circumstances a vote for the fishermen would seem to be in order. If, however, his informed judgment was clearly in the contrary direction, he should vote for the roads. But what if it seemed to him a toss-up? Should he follow the rather passive majority or the relatively small but demanding minority? To this question no pat answer is available. If electoral considerations point in one direction or the other, that fact in itself would be significant and it would be right to allow them to govern.

Now take a proposal to fluoridate the water supply. Polls reveal that 45 per cent of the electorate are mildly in favor of the plan, 40 per cent are indifferent, and 15 per cent are violently opposed and strongly organized. (The medical association, comprising about 0.5 per cent of the population, is on record as strongly favoring the proposal.) The representative in question, having read the literature submitted to him by the medical association and by the antifluoridation society, as well as that supplied by the public health authorities, is firmly convinced that the fears expressed by the "antis" are groundless and that in the long run fluoridation would be a great advantage to all members of the society. Here again the duty of the representative seems clear enough: to vote for fluoridation. Suppose, however, that the campaign of the "antis" has been highly successful. Opinion polls show the following distribution:

Strongly pro	10%
Weakly pro	20%
Indifferent	10%
Weakly anti	30%
Strongly anti	30%

How should the legislator "represent" his constituents in this situation, still assuming that he is convinced that no harm to health or the security of the country, and a great deal of good, will come of the move? It would appear that we are now in a gray zone where the norms of representation are at best ambiguous. A strong majority will oppose a strong general interest. He might argue (to himself) that, while the satisfaction of desire is always a good in itself and exerts a claim upon the representative, the claim is weakened when the desire is clearly based upon a misconception of the facts. Such a weakened claim might be overridden by the strong claim based upon the enlightened view of interest. This would be my conclusion on the facts as stated.

As another example, let us consider proposed anti-closed-shop ("right-to-work") legislation. We shall assume a widespread popular prejudice against the closed shop, while the pressure groups of business and organized labor (the latter being considerably the larger but a minority of the electorate) line up, respectively, pro and con. This case is in some ways similar to the preceding one; but the question of "interest" here is much less susceptible to objective determination, and opinion among the experts is more sharply divided. Assuming that the vote must be "yes" or "no," the presumption would appear to be for following the legislator's own instructed judgment of what was in the constituency's interest.

But now suppose that a substantial segment of business sided with labor on the issue (find-

ing that the closed shop made for greater stability of labor relations). In this situation, even though the two made up only a sizable minority of the electorate, there would be a strong argument that representation of the people (a weighted amalgam of their desires and their interests) called for siding with the minority, unless the legislator's own instructed judgment of constituency interest pointed strongly in the opposite direction.

The very way in which these hypothetical cases have been discussed indicates that the concept of representation, while giving a fairly clear answer to some of the dilemmas created by the multiple roles that a democratic legislator must play, is bound to leave large gray areas. Two devices for narrowing these areas are open to him. First, he may (and should) exert leadership in his constituency to narrow the gap between effective desire and constituency interest as he perceives it. The second means, likely to be effective in more cases than the first, is to find some accommodation between the opposing groups, some modification of the original proposal that, at best, might accomplish what each was really after and, at the least, might minimize the frustration of one side without seriously alienating the other. In the case of the anti-closed-shop proposal, a law that permitted the union shop might fill this requirement.

We need not cite further examples, although other combinations of weak and strong, and minority and majority desires and interests are possible and undoubtedly are found in practice. . . . Members of a legislative body must cooperate with each other in a multitude of ways, of which accepting the leadership of recognized party leaders in the legislative chamber is one, but not the only one. This role may call for behavior in certain cases that is not apparently compatible with what the representative norms would seem to demand. Yet even the requirements imposed by the existence of a group of friends in the legislature who frequently support each other's interests in very informal return for like conduct on the part of other members of the group may be indirectly in the interests of the constituents of each of these members. Thus, whether or not the "consensual role" is thought of as distinct from "representation," it in fact may, and, I would argue, should, serve the same ends and be subject ultimately to the same tests of correctness. It is useful to point it out as a separate item; but it would be a mistake not to recognize it as a part of a larger whole whose norms help to define its legitimate claims.

Now a word about electoral considerations, a factor that was deliberately put aside in the preceding discussion. Suppose that our model representative, having made the kind of analysis we have been discussing, decides that he ought to vote for X. At this point he considers the probable effect of this course of action on his chances for re-election and decides that they will be decidedly diminished. What effect, if any, should this have on his decision, if he is to stick to the norms of "representing"? In the first place, it might properly serve as a warning to recheck his previous calculations and judgments. Perhaps he had misjudged the intensity of certain desires. Assuming, however, that he found no reason to alter his appraisal, he might have decided to support what he felt to be the true interest of his constituency against its own misguided judgment (for example, in the fluoridation case). Now if indeed he were convinced, after careful study, that this would cost him his seat, should that fact, within the norms of representation, affect his decision? (We must assume that his vote in the legislative body might determine the outcome.) It would appear that the only rational way for him to go about answering this question would be to estimate the alternative to his occupying the seat and the balance of representativeness for the constituency, on all issues, if his opponent held it. By this judgment, barring party and national interest considerations, to be discussed below, he must be bound. In considering the practical operation of this formula, it must be borne in mind that if, for example, voting for fluoridation would cost him his seat, it is highly probable that his opponent would also vote for fluoridation.[8]

But one must consider the question of whether in certain instances a representative may have a higher duty than to represent his constituency (still putting aside considerations of party and national interest). The clearest, if not the only, case would be that of a matter of conscience, a case where justice or moral right might be thought to conflict with constituency desire and possibly even with constituency interest. The case of segregation naturally comes to mind. Of course, if a segregationist constituency has elected an integrationist, knowing him to be such and in the absence of any pledge on his part to support the constituency views in this matter, no problem arises. They have waived any right to object; they have made the judgment that, all things considered, he will represent them better than any alternative that is open to them.[9] But suppose he has kept silent (or equivocated) on the subject and that he is certain that if he cast an integrationist vote it would cost him his seat at the next election. If he acts as a representative, he must go contrary to his conscience (i.e., to another ethical norm).[10] He faces a dilemma in which he must choose between ethical norms, a not unusual circumstance in life, and he must work out his solution by calculating and weighing consequences or by whatever other means his ethical principles may demand.

What about the relation of a representative to the minority in his constituency? Do people who did not vote for him and do not expect to vote for him have any claim upon him? Should he take their desires or their interests into account? If we speak now of their desires insofar as they are opposed to those of the majority (and no more intense) and of their interests insofar as they are in irreconcilable conflict with those of the majority—and this is a substantial narrowing of the issue, justified by what has already been taken into account by the preceding analysis—the answer would seem to be that the minority is entitled to consideration within the bounds set by the underlying consensus in the society in question. In addition to recognized rights, this consensus would normally include commonly accepted notions of justice.

Thus a geographically isolated minority would have a claim on all representatives to supply them with police protection—or bomb shelters—in the same proportion to need as in other parts of the country. At least as far as desire rather than interest is taken into account, this may seldom be a real issue, for one would not normally expect to find situations in which common notions of justice were accepted and yet the majority desired to neglect a minority in this way. Still, consideration of the treatment of Negroes in many places suggests that a wide gap between the implications of generally accepted standards and expressed desires is quite possible.

District Versus Nation

The second big problem for representational theory, after that of desire versus interest, is that of part versus whole, constituency versus nation. The tension appears only as one moves toward the interest pole of the representational standard; for no one would think that a representative should be influenced, per se, by the demands (as distinct from the interests) of any constituents but his own, even though they included every citizen of the country save his own constituents. But let us suppose it is a question of a direct conflict between what he is convinced is the national interest on the one hand, and, on the other hand, what both he and his constituents are convinced is their interest. What then?

The situation posed is not likely to occur very often. On most questions the constituency will not be looking. That is to say, very few of its members will have any opinion; nor would an impartial observer believe that the public policy issue involved raised any question of conflict between the constituency and the nation. So we are dealing with the exceptional situation. We are not here considering the question of whether the representative should act solely as a delegate. As at least a partial "trustee," he must inform himself so that he can determine the constituency interest. As a member of a deliberative assembly he should also discuss the matter with his colleagues in further search of sound judgment. But beyond all this, does his membership in an assembly with responsibility for national policy imply pursuit of what Burke called the "general reason of the whole"? Perhaps it would be better to ask, as we did when discussing obligations toward the minority: What is the underlying consensus on the subject in this society? Some obligation on the part of all to support the welfare of the whole is implied by citizenship in any body politic. Without it a body politic would not exist. Surely, then, per-sons who are selected to represent others in the government of that body politic must, inter alia, be expected to represent their interest in and obligation to the whole (even when the constituents themselves might be inclined to overlook it).

This much would appear to be clear. The strength of the obligation of a representative to support the national as opposed to the local interest, where the two clearly conflict, is a function of several factors. First of all, it must be judged in terms of some inevitably crude estimate of the strength in the particular case of each of the interests involved, local and national. Second, the system of government itself is relevant. In Britain, Parliament (including its "Government") is the only vehicle for representation in the legislative process. In the United States, on the other hand, the division of labor and responsibility among President, Senate, and House of Representatives somewhat alters the situation, the implication being that the representatives of lesser areas than the whole have some special obligation to espouse local interests. Finally, it is partly a matter of the strength of the particular national consensus. It would appear at least a priori probable that the national consensus in Great Britain is stronger than it is in the United States. (To get a clearer picture of the extent to which this is true would be an interesting aim for an empirical study.) Conceivably, the generally accepted theory in a given country might be that the general interest would be best secured by each locality (through its elected representatives) pursuing its own particular interest exclusively. I personally doubt whether many people in the United States, barring a few sophisticated political scientists, accept this view.[11]

Furthermore, it is perhaps fair to say that where a strong and highly visible local interest seems to be opposed to the national interest, the representative may have to face the possibility of defeat at the next election and thus be forced to make the kind of calculation of alternative that has been described here. Frequently, too, it may be fruitless or detrimental for the representative to vote for the national interest against that of his constituency. Take the case of pork barrel legislation. It may be assumed that the net effect of the legislation will be detrimental to the national welfare but beneficial to the constituency of the representative in question. It is likely that if, during the bill's formulation, he refused to commit himself to support it, he would lose his district's "pork" while not defeating the bill. Under such circumstances, the only effective line for the representative to take is to try to combine with other representatives to create institutionalized procedures to inhibit this sort of legislation. It is a measure of the "national" consensus in Britain that, in the form of the procedure for private bill legislation, just such action has been taken. . . .

In conclusion, it will be recalled that this essay began by considering the way in which a regime as a whole is representative. It now appears that the representativeness of a modern democratic government is not achieved through any single channel. In the United States, three sets of constituencies elect representatives at the federal level alone. Moreover, the bureaucracy, and an informal but effective additional form of representation, that of organized groups, provide other avenues of representation.[12] There is good reason for this variety. For a person to be represented with respect to all of his interests with which government concerns itself is immensely difficult and inevitably partial and inaccurate, as Rousseau recognized with typical hyperbole. Accountability enforced by elections is one device, a crude one, for making government representative. It has been suggested here that an idea of what representation means, a set of ethical norms, also plays a role. The existence of numerous and varied avenues of representation, each by virtue of its own peculiar nature, seeing, reflecting, attempting to effectuate a slightly different facet of that great conglomerate of desires and interests that make up the electorate, probably produces a more tolerable result than could be accomplished by any one of them alone.

Notes

1. "Legislators and Magistrates," mimeographed; paper delivered at the meetings of the American Political Science Association, September 1966.

2. H. B. Mayo, *An Introduction to Democratic Theory* (New York: Oxford University Press, 1960), p. 103.

3. In this connection I have in mind especially the extensive and valuable study of *The Legislative System* by John C. Wahlke, Heinz Eulau, William Buchanan, and LeRoy C. Ferguson (New York: Wiley, 1962).

4. R. W. and A. J. Carlyle, *Medieval Political Theory* (Edinburgh & London: William Blackwood & Sons, 1915), III, 33.

5. Hanna Pitkin, *The Concept of Representation* (Berkeley: University of California Press, 1967).

6. Hard data on such questions of causation are difficult to secure. It was V. O. Key's cautious conclusion, after surveying the data, that constituency opinion is one of the factors influencing the votes of legislators. He also concluded that legislators frequently have considerable freedom of choice (freedom from constituency pressure) and that they tend to exercise this choice in a way that suggests a relation between the votes they cast and the characteristics of the constituency (as revealed by demographic data). V. O. Key, Jr., *Public Opinion and American Democracy* (New York: Knopf, 1961), pp. 486–87.

7. It is at least an arguable position to contend that, as the policy role of bureaucracies in both England and the United States has increased, and as this role has become more widely recognized, the ideal of administrative "neutrality" has weakened and the demand to strengthen popular control over those administrators who in fact make policy in important matters has grown. One thinks, for example, of Britain's recently created specialized select committees for the supervision of administration. . . .

8. It is because electoral considerations do play this role, which it is argued here they should, that the matter of apportionment . . . is important. It must be recognized, however, that evidence may be found in support of the proposition that well-apportioned and malapportioned legislatures arrive at very similar policy results. Thomas R. Dye, "Malapportionment and Public Policy in the United States," *Journal of Politics*, 27 (1965), 586–601. Insofar as this finding is generally true, it is at least consistent with the proposition that ethical norms of representation are not without effect.

9. This reasoning makes the not improbable

assumption that on such a salient issue as one involving a sharp conflict between the conscience of the representative and the majority will of the constituency an alternative would have been presented (through the primary election or otherwise) had the majority not been prepared to make the judgment imputed to them in the text.

10. For the sake of sharpening the issue, it is assumed that constituency desire, and possibly even constituency interest, might reasonably be judged so strong in this case as to override any consideration of an opposing national interest. In fact, it will be only in the rarest of cases that the issue between the dictates of conscience and those of representational norms will be in such direct conflict.

11. One of the writer's experiences during a British by-election is illustrative of the national differences in question. The constituency was heavily agricultural and highly marginal. On being asked about the attitude of the (traditionally Conservative) farmers toward the election, a Conservative party official showed great moral indignation over the fact that some farmers were actually considering voting for the Labor candidate just because of certain promised agricultural benefits—and contrary, it was implied, to what they must know was the national interest! It seems unlikely that any American politician could make such an argument with a straight face.

12. To have considered the judiciary, especially in the United States, as itself being, in a measure, a representative organ would not have been inaccurate but would have extended the essay beyond reasonable limits. It should at least be noted, however, that in the very decisions considered in this volume—those dealing with the apportionment of legislative representatives—the court was acting in a way it considered representative of the democratic ideals. It attributed these ideals to the Constitution, but perhaps one may be forgiven for suspecting that it found them in the evolving Constitutional morality of the nation rather than in the words of the document or the intention of the framers.

Is Democracy Special?

Brian Barry

One reason democratic procedures are sometimes thought attractive is that it seems only reasonable when opinion is divided on an issue to adopt the policy preferred by the majority (what Barry terms the "majority principle"). Beginning with a brief discussion of the nature of democratic procedures, Barry goes on to assess that claim. Using an example of a vote taken among five people about whether to allow smoking in their railroad car, he describes the four assumptions on which the majority principle rests. Without those four, he argues, the majority principle is neither determinate of a particular result nor would it be acceptable. That indeterminacy, however, raises problems for any defense of democracy that rests on the claim it is possible to express the collective will by somehow aggregating the majority's preferences. Barry concludes with a discussion of the extent to which these four assumptions hold in the actual world of politics.

From Brian Barry, "Is Democracy Special?" in Peter Laslett and James Fishkin, eds. *Philosophy, Politics and Society*, 5th series (New Haven: Yale University Press, 1979), pp. 156–164, 166–171. Reprinted by permission. Some footnotes omitted.

. . . By a democratic procedure I mean a method of determining the content of laws (and other legally binding decisions) such that the preferences of the citizens have some formal connection with the outcome in which each counts equally. Let me make four comments on this definition.

First, I follow here those who insist that 'democracy' is to be understood in procedural terms. That is to say, I reject the notion that one should build into 'democracy' any constraints on the content of the outcomes produced, such as substantive equality, respect for human rights, concern for the general welfare, personal liberty or the rule of law. The only exceptions (and these are significant) are those required by democracy itself as a procedure. Thus, some degree of freedom of communication and organization is a necessary condition of the formation, expression and aggregation of political preferences. And in a state (as against a small commune, say) the only preferences people can have are preferences for general lines of policy. There are not going to be widely-held preferences about whether or not Mr Jones should be fined £10 for speeding or Mrs Smith should get supplementary benefit payments of £3.65 per week. At most there can be preferences for a speeding tariff or for general rules about eligibility for supplementary benefit. If magistrates or civil servants are arbitrary or capricious, therefore, they make democracy impossible.

Second, I require that there should be a formal connection between the preferences of the citizens and the outcomes produced. My intention in specifying a formal connection is to rule out cases where the decision-making process is *de facto* affected by the preferences of the citizens but not in virtue of any constitutional rule. Thus, eighteenth century England has been described as 'oligarchy tempered by riot'.[1] But however efficacious the rioters might be I would not say that their ability to coerce the government constituted a democratic procedure. In the concluding words of the judge appointed to enquire into riots in West Pakistan in 1953: 'But if democracy means the subordination of law and order to political ends—then Allah knoweth best and we end the report.'[2]

Third, by 'some formal connection' I intend

deliberately to leave open a variety of possible ways in which democratic procedures might be implemented. In particular, I wish to include both voting on laws by the citizens at large and voting for representatives who exercise the law-making function. I shall take either of these to constitute 'some formal connection with the outcome' in the sense required by the definition: in the first case the citizens choose the laws and in the second they choose the law-makers (in both cases, of course, within the limits of the choice presented to them).

Finally, the phrase 'each counts equally' has to be read in conjunction with the preceding phrase 'some formal connection with the outcome'. That is to say, nothing is suggested by the definition of democratic procedure about equality of actual influence on outcomes. The equality is in the formal aspect: each adult citizen is to have a vote (only minor exceptions covering a tiny proportion of those otherwise eligible being allowed) and there are to be no 'fancy franchises' giving extra votes to some.

What about the notion that each vote should have an 'equal value'? This is valid if we construe it as a formal requirement. If there are two constituencies each of which returns one representative, the value of a vote is obviously unequal if one constituency contains more voters than another.[3] To talk about 'equal value' except in this *a priori* sense is, in my view, sheer muddle. In recent years, for example, supporters of systems of proportional representation in Britain have succeeded in scoring something of a propaganda victory by pressing the idea that the vote for a candidate who comes third (or lower) in a plurality system is 'wasted' and the people who vote for the candidate are 'effectively disfranchised'. But then why stop there? The only way of making sense of this argument is by postulating that anyone who voted for a candidate other than the actual winner—even the runner-up—was 'effectively disfranchised'; and it was not long before some academics stumbled on this amazing theoretical breakthrough.[4] I do not think that anyone of ordinary intelligence would be found saying of an election for, say, the post of president of a club: 'I didn't vote for the winning candidate. In other words my vote didn't help elect anybody. And that means I was effectively disfranchised'. It is a little alarming that such palpably fallacious reasoning should have the power to impose on people when the context is a parliamentary election.

There is one simple, and, on the face of it, attractive, reason for giving special weight to laws arrived at by democratic procedures, namely that, on any given question about which opinion is divided, the decision must, as a matter of logic, accord with either the preferences of the majority or the preferences of the minority. And, by something akin to the rule of insufficient reason, it seems difficult to say why the decision should go in the way wanted by the minority rather than in the way wanted by the majority.

Obviously, even if the majority principle were accepted, there would still be a gap between the majority principle and democratic procedures as I have defined them. The implication of the majority principle is, fairly clearly, that the best form of democratic procedure is that which permits a vote on issues by referendum. There is no guarantee that elected representatives will on every issue vote in such a way that the outcome preferred by a majority of citizens will be the one chosen. However much we cry up the effects of electoral competition in keeping representatives in line, there is no theoretical reason for expecting that a party or coalition of parties with a majority will always do what a majority of voters want. (Persistent non-voters will in any case have their preferences disregarded by competitive parties—though it may be noted that this is equally so in a referendum.) Even a purely opportunistic party would not necessarily be well-advised to back the side on every issue that the majority supports, as Anthony Downs pointed out.[5] And in practice no party is purely opportunistic—indeed a purely opportunistic party would in most circumstances be an electoral failure because it would be too unpredictable. The party or parties with a legislative majority are therefore always liable to have a package of policies approved of by a majority and policies opposed by a majority. (On many other issues, there may be no single policy with majority support, but that is a complication in the specification of the majority principle that I shall discuss below.)

All this, however, is not as damaging for democratic procedures as might be supposed. For it may surely be said that no method for selecting law-makers and governments that was *not* democratic (in the sense defined) could provide a better long-run prospect of producing outcomes in accord with the majority principle. However disappointed an adherent of the majority principle might be in the actual working of democratic procedures, it is hard to see what he or she would stand to gain by helping to secure their overthrow. . . .

I have suggested, then, that the majority principle provides fairly strong backing for democratic procedures. What now has to be asked, of course, is whether there is any reason for accepting the majority principle. The view that there is something natural and inevitable about it was expressed forcefully by John Locke in paragraphs 95–9 of the *Second Treatise*. The argument is tied up with Locke's consent theory of political authority but can, I think, be detached from it. The nub is that if there is going to be a body capable of making binding decisions then it 'must move one way' and 'it is necessary the Body should move that way whither the greater force carries it, which is the *consent of the majority*'. Locke adds that 'therefore we see that in Assemblies impowered to act by positive Laws where no number is set by that positive Law which impowers them, the *act of the Majority* passes for the act of the whole, and of course determines, as having by the Law of Nature and Reason, the power of the whole'.[6]

In my first book, *Political Argument*, I put forward the example of 'five people in a railway compartment which the railway operator has omitted to label either "smoking" or "nosmoking"' each of whom 'either wants to smoke or objects to others smoking in the vicinity'.[7] (I should have added that the carriage should be understood as one of the sort that does not have a corridor, so the option of changing compartments is not open.) I still think that the example was a good one. Unless all five can reach agreement on some general substantive principle—that in the absence of positive regulation there is a 'natural right' to smoke or a 'natural right' for any one person to veto smoking—it is difficult to see any plausible alternative to saying that the outcome should correspond to majority preference.

The position of someone who is outvoted but refuses to accept the decision is difficult to maintain. As I have suggested, quite persuasive arguments can be made for saying that the decision should not simply reflect the number of people who want to smoke as against the number who dislike being in the presence of smokers. But, since opposing principles can be advanced, the existence of relevant principles does not seem to offer a sound basis for resistance to a majority decision. Or suppose that one of the travellers happens to be the Archbishop of Canterbury. He might claim the right to decide the smoking question on the basis either of his social position or on the basis of his presumptive expertise in casuistry. If his claim is accepted by all the other passengers, no decision-making problem arises because there is agreement. If not all the fellow-passengers accept his claim, however, it again seems difficult to see how the question can be settled except by a vote. And if he finds himself in the minority it must be because he has failed to convince the others (or more than one of them) of his claim to authority. He may continue to maintain that it should have been accepted, just as a believer in the natural right to smoke may continue to maintain that the others should have accepted that principle. But in the face of actual non-acceptance, the case for bowing to the majority decision looks strong.

On further analysis, however, we have to recognize that the 'naturalness' of the majority principle as a way of settling the dispute rests on several features of the particular example which are not commonly found together. I am therefore now inclined to say that it was a good example in the sense that it illustrated well the case for the majority principle but that it was in another sense a bad example because of its special features. I shall single out four, the first three of which make the majority principle determinate while the fourth makes it acceptable. First, we implicitly assume that the people in the compartment have to make only this one decision. Second, only two alternatives are envisaged: smoking or non-smoking. Third, the decision-making constituency is not open to doubt. And fourth, nothing has been said to suggest that the outcome on the issue is

of vital importance for the long-term well-being of any of those involved.

To begin with, then, let us retain the feature from the original case that the decisions to be made are dichotomous (that is to say, there are only two alternatives to choose between) but now say that several different decisions have to be taken. In addition to the question whether to permit smoking the passengers also have to decide whether to allow the playing of transistor radios. Suppose that a vote is taken on each question and there is a majority against each. It may be that a majority of the passengers would nevertheless prefer permitting both to prohibiting both, if they were given a choice in those terms.

Let us assign the following symbols: W is no smoking, X is smoking allowed; Y is no playing of radios, Z is playing allowed. The preferences of the five passengers (A, B, C, D and E) are in descending order as in Table 8.1.[8]

Rank order	A	B	C	D	E
1	WZ	WZ	XY	WY	WY
2	XZ	XZ	XZ	WZ	XY
3	WY	WY	WY	XY	WZ
4	XY	XY	WZ	XZ	XZ

Table 1

In a straight vote A, B, D and E all prefer W to X, and C, D and E prefer Y to Z, so the outcome would be W and Y. But the pair WY is less well liked than the opposite pair XZ by A, B and C.

We now ask: what does the majority principle prescribe in a situation like this? Are we committed to the view that neither smoking nor playing radios should be allowed, because there is a majority against each? Or can we take account of the fact that there is a majority in favour of overturning the result of the two separate votes and substituting their opposites?

The case just presented is consistent with each person's preferences on smoking being independent of what is decided about radio playing, and vice versa. But, in most political matters, this assumption of 'separability' does not hold. What we favour on one issue depends on how other issues are settled. Some things are complementary: we don't want to vote for buying the land unless there is going to be a majority for spending money on the building that is proposed to go on the land. Others are competitive: if expensive project X is going to be funded, we don't want to vote for expensive project Y as well, but if project X is going to be defeated, we would favour project Y. In such a case, the whole concept of a majority on a single issue becomes indeterminate, because each person's preference depends on his or her expectations about the way the other relevant issues are going to be decided. And the outcome if issues are packaged together depends on the way the packaging is done.

A further difficulty is that as soon as we aggregate two or more dichotomous decisions we get a choice between more than two outcomes, and there is then the possibility that no one is capable of getting a majority over each of the others in a pair-wise vote. (In the jargon of collective choice theory, there is no Condorcet winner among the alternatives.) Thus, in the example I set out, I pointed out that A, B and C prefer XZ to WY. But I could have gone on to say that C, D and E prefer XY to XZ, that A, B and D prefer WZ to XY, and that C, D and E prefer WY to WZ. Since, as we already know, A, B and C prefer XZ to WY, it is clear that we have here a cycle including all four possible combinations. No outcome is capable of getting a majority over each of the others and so the majority principle offers no guidance.

The simplest way of generating a situation in which there are cyclical majorities is to have a choice between three possible outcomes. Suppose that our passengers consider three candidates for a binding rule about smoking: X (no smoking), Y (smoking but only of cigarettes) and Z (smoking of pipes and cigars as well as cigarettes). There may, of course, be an outright majority for one outcome. . . .

The trouble is that there may not be any outcome that is capable of getting majority support against any other (or, in the case of even numbers, two that are equally good . . .). Thus, suppose now that D and E do not like to smoke cigarettes and, if they cannot smoke their pipes, would prefer a smoke-free environment to one contaminated by C's cigarette smoke. Then the preference matrix

becomes as in Table 8.3. We now pit each possible outcome against each other in a series of three pairwise comparisons and get the result that X beats Y (A, B, D and E prefer it), Z beats X (C, D and E prefer it) and Y beats Z (A, B and C prefer it). Thus, a quite plausible distribution of preferences generates a 'paradox of voting' in which the majorities arising from pairwise comparisons form a cycle.

Rank order	A and B	C	D and E
1	X	Y	Z
2	Y	Z	X
3	Z	X	Y

Table 3

The two sources of indeterminacy in the majority principle that I have so far been pointing out may be considered rather dull and technical, incapable of arousing political passions. This is by no means true. Consider, for example, the importance that both sympathizers of President Allende and apologists for the coup that overthrew him and the regime have attached in their polemics to the question whether or not he had majority support for his policies. Given a political set-up with three blocs, Allende was able to come into power as President on a bare plurality; and the Popular Unity Coalition that supported him never achieved a majority of votes cast. It was on the basis of these facts that the junta claimed legitimacy in terms of the majority principle for overthrowing the constitutional government. On the other side, however, it may be argued that 'one cannot infer that those who opposed Allende necessarily supported a military coup, especially the bloody one that ensued following his overthrow. Thus there is little evidence that a majority of Chileans wanted Allende overthrown by the military.'[9]

It is not my intention to join in this debate, merely to point out that, where the majority principle is indeterminate, generals find it worth appealing to it and scholars find it worth rebutting that appeal. However, if we measure the importance of a question by the blood spilt over it (and I find it hard to think of a better criterion) the importance of the third reason for the indeterminacy of the majority principle can hardly be denied. The question is the deceptively innocent one: majority of *what?*

In the railway carriage example this is not a problem. If the decision about permitting or prohibiting smoking is to be made according to majority preference there can be no doubt that the people whose preferences should be taken into account are the five people in the railway carriage who will be affected by the decision. But when the question is the boundaries of political entities—empires, supranational organizations, federations, nation states, provinces or other sub-divisions—and their respective decision-making powers, the question 'who is included?' is an explosive one.

There is no need to labour the point. The briefest survey is enough. In Western Europe, after centuries of wars between states, civil wars, and heavy-handed centralizing government, Northern Ireland is paralyzed by conflict, Scottish nationalism is a powerful force, the centralized Belgian state has been virtually partitioned, unfinished business from the nineteenth century still hangs over the Swiss Jura and the Alto Adige, while in Spain Basque and Catalan separatism are stirring again after the long freeze. In Eastern Europe almost every state has claims on the territory of at least one other. Order, of a kind, is maintained by the Soviet Union, which is itself a patchwork of nationalities held together by coercion. And nobody is taking bets on the existence of Yugoslavia in ten years time. In North America, Quebec has a separatist government, and the unity of the country is in question. In the Middle East three wars have been fought over the boundaries of Israel and no end is in sight. In Africa, the boundaries bequeathed by the colonial powers, after a period of surprising stability (interrupted only by the Biafran and Katagan secessions) are coming under pressure in the Horn of Africa, and the trouble looks as if it may well spread further in coming years. The Indian subcontinent has seen first the convulsion of the creation of Pakistan and then the almost equally bloody process of its splitting into two; while in India the states have had to be reconstituted, amid a good deal of disorder, in an attempt to satisfy the aspirations of linguistic groups. There are few parts of the world where boundaries are not a potential source of serious conflict, and where we do not hear that there are (e.g. China) this is as likely to reflect our ignorance as the absence of potential conflict.

The only thing that has to be established, beyond the existence of conflicts over boundaries, is that the majority principle has no way of solving them, either in practice or in theory. In practice, the majority principle, so far from alleviating conflicts over boundaries, greatly exacerbates them. It may be tolerable to be ruled over by a cosmopolitan autocracy, like the Austrian empire, or a more or less even-handed colonial power like the British in India. But to be subject to a majority of different language, religion or national identity is far more threatening. In an area where nationalities are intermingled, like the Balkans, every move to satisfy majority aspirations leaves the remaining minorities even more vulnerable.

On a theoretical level, any use of the majority principle in order to establish boundaries must involve begging the question. Locke, to do him credit, saw that the majority principle could come into play only after the constituency has been identified, but he finessed the problem by resorting to the fiction that those who are to form 'one body' all individually agree to do so. This approach obviously fails to provide any guidance in any situation where it is actually needed, that is to say where people are disagreeing about the 'body' they want to be members of. . . .

Meanwhile, it should be noted that the upshot of the discussion is that any attempt to justify boundaries by appealing to the majority principle must be void. You can have as many referenda as you like, and show every time that over half of the people within the existing boundaries approve of them, but you cannot use that to prove to a minority that wants to secede that they ought to acquiesce in the *status quo*. If their loyalty is to be awakened, other and better arguments—backed by deeds rather than votes—are needed.

Suppose, however, that the composition of the group that is to be subject to a common policy is not at issue, and that the two more technical sources of indeterminacy are absent, does that make the majority principle unassailable? Of course not. The fourth and last of the special features of the railway carriage case that I singled out was that, as the story had been told, we had no reason to suppose that the question of smoking or not smoking was of vital importance to any of the people involved. (It might be said that smoking is inherently a vital interest in that being smoked at lowers one's expectation of life; but, if we put it as a question of interests, is a few minutes more life a greater interest than the freedom of the addict from withdrawal symptoms?) Suppose, however, that one of the passengers suffers from severe asthma or emphysema, and that being subjected to tobacco smoke is liable to precipitate a dangerous attack. No doubt one would hope that this fact, when explained, would lead the others to agree not to smoke, however many of them would like to. But say that it does not. It seems clear to me that the person at risk would be behaving with an almost insane disregard for his or her interests in accepting a majority decision to allow smoking. The obvious recourse would be, I presume, to pull the communication cord and bring the train to a grinding halt.

It might be argued that nothing said here shows that the majority principle lacks universality: it still applies but in some cases the reason it provides for obedience is overridden by a more pressing consideration, such as self-protection against a risk of substantial harm. However, it does not seem to me that this is a correct representation of the position. Where the decision is sufficiently threatening to the vital interests of (some of) those affected by it, its pedigree is neither here nor there.

Take for example a group of youths like those in *The Clockwork Orange* who beat up strangers for fun. Would we be inclined to say 'Well, at least there's one redeeming feature: they choose their victims by majority vote'? I think not. This example of course raises the question of constituency, since the victim is outside the decision-making group. But if we modify it so that the members of a group decide by majority vote to beat up one of their own number I still do not think that the chosen victim has less reason to resist or escape

than he would if the decision were taken by a strong-arm leader. I do not see any significant respect in which my modified example of the railway passengers differs from that. I suppose that someone might adduce the difference between deliberately causing harm and doing something whose known but unintended consequences are harmful, but that is not in my view a morally relevant distinction.

The political parallels hardly need to be filled in. No minority can be, or should be, expected to acquiesce in the majority's trampling on its vital interests. Unfortunately the parallel to pulling the communication cord—bringing the state, or that part of its policy that is objectionable, to a grinding halt—is a much more messy business and carries the risk of incurring costs much higher than a £25 fine. But the principle is clear enough. Nobody but a moral imbecile would really be prepared to deliver himself over body and soul to the majority principle. . . .

Notes

1. W. J. M. Mackenzie, *Power, Violence, Decision* (Harmondsworth: Penguin, 1975), p. 151.

2. Quoted in Hugh Tinker, *Ballot Box and Bayonet: People and Government in Emergent Asian Countries* (Chatham House Essays, 5; London: Oxford University Press, 1964), p. 83.

3. This is, it may be noted, the line taken by the U.S. Supreme Court in its decision requiring redistricting to secure approximately equal constituencies. (The leading case is Reynolds *v.* Sims, 377 U.S. 533 (1964).)

4. An analysis with whose general line I concur is Paul E. Meehl, 'The Selfish Voter Paradox and the Thrown-Away Vote Argument', *The American Political Science Review* LXXI (1977): pp. 11–30.

5. A. Downs, *An Economic Theory of Democracy* (New York: Harper and Brothers, 1957), pp. 55–60.

6. John Locke, *Two Treatises of Government*, ed. Peter Laslett (New York: The New American Library, Mentor Book, 1965), pp. 375–6.

7. B. M. Barry, *Political Argument* (London: Routledge and Kegan Paul, 1965), p. 312.

8. Adapted from Appendix, Example I (p. 69) of Nicholas R. Miller, 'Logrolling, Vote Trading, and the Paradox of Voting: A Game-Theoretical Overview', *Public Choice* 30 (1977): pp. 49–75.

9. James Petras and Morris Morley, 'Chilean Destabilisation and Its Aftermath', *Politics* XI (1976): pp. 140–8 at p. 145.

Democracy and Interests

Keith Graham

In this chapter from his recent book, Keith Graham weighs carefully the assumptions behind James Mill's claim that representative democracy is justified because it can best achieve the underlying purpose of government: satisfaction of interests. Graham rejects this argument, questioning whether government is best understood as an attempt to satisfy interests as well as whether democratic government could achieve that even if it were the objective. It is far from clear, he thinks, that people's interests can be identified with their expressed preferences, or that a genuinely democratic system can successfully compute and aggregate them.

The Interests Argument

A defence of democracy is likely to connect in some way with the thought, familiar since the Renaissance, that individual human beings as such are important. If we then try to explain what it is which gives them this importance, one form our answer may take is that each individual human being has interests which they can express and which they have a right to pursue. The virtue which may then be claimed for democratic arrangements is that they ensure that this will be done. Here we have an argument in terms of interests, popularly known as the 'shoe-pinching argument': only the individual can know where the shoe pinches. If we begin, therefore, from the assumption that any individual's interests constitute a legitimate demand, then the claimed

From Keith Graham, *The Battle of Democracy* (Totowa, NJ: Barnes and Noble, 1986), pp. 21–30. Reprinted by permission.

merit of a system of rule by the people is that it extends a proper influence to the shoe-wearer. It enables individuals to express their preferences, and since this is what determines subsequent policy it maximises the satisfaction of those preferences. The alternative to this would be to exclude the interests of some individuals from having an influence on the outcome, or else to suppose that for such influence to operate it is unnecessary to consult those whose interests are in question. And neither of these, it may be felt, is supportable since they involve either not caring that some people's shoes pinch or else supposing, implausibly, that someone *other* than the wearer knows best where they do pinch.

How strong is this interests argument? Notice that it explicitly identifies what is in people's interests with the preferences they themselves express. There is a powerful tradition which gives privileged status, in this way, to people's own perceptions of where their interests lie. But that tradition is open to challenge. Formally, the idea that someone's interests can simply be 'read off' from their own expressed views is refuted by the fact that people change their minds. If I hold conflicting views at different times about where my interests lie, then at least sometimes I must be wrong. Informally, the infallibility of such judgments is refuted whenever we, as observers, see that someone will make a mess of their life, say in a choice of career or partner, in following what they judge is in their interest.

In a more theoretical vein, the identification of people's interests with their expressed preferences may be challenged in a number of ways. Most abstractly, there are grounds for claiming in a fashion reminiscent of Kant that preferences or desires are themselves a species of judgment, that they are therefore amenable to criticism in the light of what is reasonable, and that in consequence it is perfectly possible for someone to make *mistakes* in their preferences. Again, it is a commonplace that desires and preferences do not arise from pure reflexion on the part of the individual; rather, they are subject to considerable social influence. This brings with it the possibility that a social system may itself work against an individual's interests and at the same time be productive of desires and references which are similarly inimical to that individual's interests. The mere fact that this is a possibility suggests that a conceptual distance must be maintained between interests and desires. This leaves the difficult question how interests *are* to be identified. We might then identify them not with the desires an agent happens to have but those the agent *would* have *if* he or she were forming those desires rationally and/or autonomously. Alternatively, we might identify interests in an 'objective' way, by reference to what would make an individual flourish, regardless of what their own actual or hypothetical desires were.

Regardless of whether these ways of identifying interests will fare any better than the original way, a proponent of the interests argument might object that the difficulties raised in the last two paragraphs are directed against a stronger version of it than anyone actually needs to hold. It could be maintained that individuals have, not infallible knowledge of their interests, but probably a better knowledge than some unknown and remote person in a position of great power over them. In any

case, it might reasonably be felt that only they themselves can safely be relied upon to *pursue* their interests. If that is so, then a better result might still follow, in terms of the satisfaction of interests, from democratic decision-making rather than some imposed form of decision. Alternatively, it might be held that there is merely a presumption in favour of individuals being the best judges of their interests, but one which can be defeated only by compelling evidence to the contrary.

At this stage the issue is indeterminate. But this may in fact work against grounding acceptance of democracy in the interests argument. For suppose that compelling evidence of a particular kind were available: suppose that some undemocratic regime were able to make the trains run on time and were highly successful at providing facilities which were in an obvious way good for human beings. Should we not then have to say that this regime was in fact ministering to individuals' interests?

Now a proponent of the interests argument might refuse to allow that this *is* a possibility, and give as the reason that it could not be in anyone's interests to be treated as one is in an undemocratic regime. This response is to the point, but it fundamentally alters the nature of the grounding for democracy, and brings the present argument much closer to alternatives still to be considered. For it would no longer be a case of tracing a contingent connexion between democracy and individuals' interests described independently of commitment to particular political forms; rather, those interests are now themsleves beginning to be specified in a way which favours the treatment accorded in a democratic as opposed to an undemocratic regime. We should then have to consider (as we shall) what it is about people which might give them such an interest.

If we confine our attention to interests which can be specified independently of political form, however, it is clear that our hypothetical question is a source of embarrassment for the interests argument. Democracy as rule by the people is interpreted and justified in that argument as a system in which people's interests are maximised because decisions are determined by their own preferences. In the conceivable circumstance that some *other* type of system in fact maximises interests, then we no longer have any reason for supporting democracy.

At this point we have a choice. Anyone placing a very high premium on the satisfaction of individuals' interests will not shrink from accepting this consequence, and will argue that democracy is not necessarily the preferable form of decision-making in all circumstances. Others will feel that the rejection of democracy is too high a price to pay, that there is something deeply repugnant in subjecting people to undemocratic forms of decision-making which cannot be offset by gains elsewhere. For them the interests argument will carry a commitment (albeit a hypothetical one) which they are not prepared to accept. In that case an alternative grounding will need to be given to justify subscription to democracy, and it will be natural to concentrate attention on what it is about human beings which explains this repugnance and makes democracy an appropriate arrangement for them. . . .

Interests and the Form of Democracy

If we leave aside these difficulties in the interests argument, the question still remains what form of democracy it would license. In terms of the original analogy we might ask what degree of control the shoe-wearer is supposed to have over the shoe-maker, and indeed whether these should be distinct roles at all.

The natural home, as it were, of the interests argument is utilitarianism—a version of it is put forward for instance by James Mill in his *Essay on Government*. There the argument is that rule of the few will produce a government in the interests of the few, a result which will be avoided if power is in the hands of the whole community, as in a democracy. If the point is that there is something disproportionate in the interests of the few prevailing, this has an egalitarian ring to it, which might be thought to be reinforced by the general egalitarian thrust present in Bentham's version of utilitarianism, according to

which each is to count for one and none for more than one. Does this perhaps suggest a form of democracy in which power is diffused in a more radically egalitarian way than we are accustomed to meet with, one in which individuals exert more direct control on a more equal basis over decisions which affect their lives? James Mill does not himself draw that inference but comes down in favour of a representative system where power is distributed very unequally among citizens; but we may not be convinced by this, particularly when we recall that strand of the original argument which suggests that individuals will at least have a better idea of their own interests than some remote person in power over them. That can easily be construed as a criticism of existing representative systems, where a small number of elected politicians determine the conditions of life of large numbers of people, as well as of undemocratic systems.

However, we must remember that it would be self-defeating for the interests argument to accord any independent weight to considerations of equality. If an equal distribution of political power did in fact maximise satisfaction of individual interests that would be a reason, from the perspective of this argument, for insisting upon that distribution. But it might not. Even if each individual's interest is to be equally considered, it might be that interest-satisfaction would be maximised by some individuals' handing over political power to representatives appointed to act upon their behalf. Much will turn on such issues as how far individuals *can* be expected to have an accurate and reliable view about their own interests and their satisfaction. If we hold strong enough views on their unreliability then we can embrace representative systems involving relatively little prior responsiveness to individuals' opinions. We can say with Edmund Burke that it is the duty of a representative to follow what his own conscience tells him is the interest of his electors, rather than sacrificing this to the electors' own opinions.

Indeed, there is a long intellectual pedigree, going back at least to Adam Smith's 'invisible hand' theory, to theories which suggest that a given result is likely to be obtained precisely by people's acting in some *other* way than with the conscious intention to realise it. In a context closely related to the present one, David Miller has recently argued that there is no *a priori* reason why legislation should not be produced which accords with electors' preferences, even though they have no direct control over it and it is the prerogative of elected leaders who merely respond to the electorate's preferences by anticipation. In the same way, he suggests, there is no *a priori* reason why a market economy in which producers act so as to maximise profits should not in fact work so as to satisfy consumers' desires.[1] Whilst this is true in both cases, we should recognise that some considerable *a posteriori* argument will be required in order to establish that such a happy coincidence of outcome is achievable in this roundabout way. So too for our own case, which concerns interests rather than (necessarily) preferences and desires. That was the point of my earlier criticism: we simply do not know, in advance of a complicated weighing of evidence, whether a system in which elected leaders initiate policies with only indirect influence from the populace at large will serve the interests of the populace, just as we cannot say, without pronouncing on some complicated theories, whether people can be systematically mistaken about their true interests. But if these issues remain unsettled whilst our commitment to a particular form of decision-making is not in doubt, then we must look elsewhere for a complete account of the grounds for that commitment.

As soon as we introduce other considerations besides interests into those grounds, a further qualification must be placed on Miller's argument. Pursuing the analogy between market society and the struggle for power in parliamentary democracy, he suggests that if 'a model shows how the pursuit of private ends may lead under the appropriate conditions to social goals being achieved, then anyone who shares those goals must endorse the model—at least pending an alternative theory which shows how the goals in question may be achieved more effectively'. That fits the interests argument very well and demonstrates how it can end up supporting an interpretation of 'rule by the people' which exactly matches existing political institutions (always assuming that it can deliver the required *a posteriori* argument). But for anyone who departs from the pure version of the interests argument, the principle enunciated by Miller will not necessarily hold. We might, for example, wish to see the satisfaction of interests maximised but still believe that there are important constraints on how this is achieved, that there are some things you just cannot do to people for the sake of that goal. It is a common characteristic of our thinking to be concerned not just with objectives but with observing various constraints in achieving them. That explains, for example, why we face a dilemma when confronted with cases of paternalism, if this is defined as intervening in someone's life against their will but for their benefit. The benefit considered in itself is something we welcome, but the manner of its achievement causes us to hesitate over whether it is legitimately secured or not.

Conflict of Interests

For the interests argument, the ideal situation would be one where all participants to a decision had a clear and correct conception of where their interests lay and acted in concert to realise them. That would furnish a perfectly straightforward interpretation of 'rule by the whole people'. But apart from the other difficulties we have noticed, there is a further problem about coincidence and divergence of interests.

We have so far spoken as if the computation and joint realisation of people's interests would be unproblematic, but this is not so. For example, even if two people agree that it is in their respective interests that a given state of affairs should obtain, they may differ over what route furnishes the best way of achieving that state of affairs. That is the simplest case. Where there is disagreement over *which* state of affairs should obtain, there are more difficulties. If there are any cases where people do not just happen to have differing interests but *necessarily* come into conflict, because of the relations they stand in to each other, matters are more serious still.

What are we to do in such cases? At a minimum we can review the situation, reconsider and see if resolution of the conflict is possible. We can search for unnoticed interests which individuals hold in common. We can perhaps 'trade' in such a way that I relinquish my preference for one outcome or state of affairs in exchange for your support on some other issue. Or we can make the move from thinking purely in terms of individual interests to group, and perhaps a general, interest. Each of these strategies will be attended by problems of its own; but in any case, unless they result in one hundred per cent success, a residual problem will remain. Provided the sum total of individual interests has all the figures on one side, so to speak, we can say that the people are ruling because their interest is being realised. But if some individuals' interests are being met while others are not, then the people as a whole are not ruling, because the people do not, in the sense required by this argument, constitute a whole.

At this point the natural move is to settle for majority voting. This, after all, fits in very well with the aspirations of the interests argument in so far as we have described it as being concerned to *maximise* interests. If we make certain simplifying assumptions (such as, once again, ignoring intensities of preference if interests are identified with preferences) and ignore the fact that interests can be served to a greater or lesser degree, then to meet the interests of most people is necessarily to maximise interests. So why not ensure that the people rule by having an arrangement which allows them to express views about their interests, count the results and act accordingly?

The first problem is this. Either such a summing process allows us to arrive at something which can reasonably be called the people's interest or it does not. If it does not, then we have not yet found any basis for adopting a majoritarian procedure as an expression of rule by the people. But even it if does, the relation between individual and general interest remains problematic. Where my interest and the general interest diverge or conflict—an inherent possibility in a majoritarian system—it still has to be shown why the results thrown up by such a procedure should have any impact on my convictions or my actions. . . .

We might try to remedy this by adverting to the mathematics of the argument. The reason for an individual's accepting a *system* of majority decision-making, it might be said, is that on each occasion when a decision is made the interests of more individuals will be met than not (at worst, 51 per cent as against 49 per cent). Therefore, this is a system in which an individual has a better than 50/50 chance of having his or her interests met. Contrast this with the only alternative (leaving aside complete consensus)—some form of non-majority or minority rule—in which no such guarantee can be given.

One crucial unstated assumption underlies this argument: that the majority is a shifting entity, not constantly composed of the same group of individuals. For an individual who is in a permanent minority, and indeed for one who is in a minority more than on average, the mathematics of majority rule has negative appeal. In this connexion two actual cases often cited are those of blacks in the United States and Catholics in Northern Ireland, who, it is said, constitute permanent minorities with shared interests and are in just that position. If democracy itself, therefore, is not to suffer from negative appeal in these circumstances then it will have to be dissociated from majority rule.

Moreover, even leaving aside these difficulties, it is plain that this argument will at most help with only one half of the motivational problem. . . . It may display the appeal of a system which most of the time serves an individual's interests; but it does nothing to explain why such an individual should accept the decision of that system on a particular occasion when to do so will run counter to his or her interests. On the contrary, for as long as we continue to think solely in terms of the individual's interests, it displays the appeal of going along with the system when its deliverances, in the form of majority verdicts, coincide with one's own wishes, but of abandoning it when this ceases to be so.

Now of course we can reply that to do this is unfairly to make exceptions in one's own favour or to treat others unequally, and it may be important to say this. But to make these points is to swing the argument into a new orbit and to forsake the attempt to ground democracy only in interests. . . .

Often the interests argument has been pursued with a background assumption about human motivation, namely that individuals always do act egoistically so as to further their own individual interests, or that it is rational for them to do so. On that assumption the very idea of participation in a political process at all becomes problematic, since the 'cost' of doing so will frequently outweigh the increased likelihood of any 'benefits' so obtained. (From a purely self-interested point of veiw, why should I bother to vote, or take part in political activity, if the outcome is likely to remain the same whether I do so or not?) No doubt for the purpose of a particular kind of axiomatic theorising assumptions of this kind are fruitful, but as straightforward theses about human nature they look more questionable. The conception of rationality which stigmatises altruism as irrational can be challenged and the allegedly universal self-interestedness of human behaviour is breached at the very least by actions whose aim is to benefit one's immediate family circle rather than oneself—a more significant breach of the egoistic assumption than might at first appear.

However, although bringing group as well as individual interests into the reckoning will help with the general problem of conflict between individual and collective, it will not of itself deal with the motivational problem. For unless the group is extended to embrace the entire population, exactly similar difficulties to those already encountered will crop up again. It will be a tautology that it is in any group's interests to accept decisions which serve its interests, but not to accept decisions which go against its interests and therefore not to accept democratic decisions as such.

Note

1. David Miller, "The Competitive Model of Democracy" in *Democratic Theory and Practice*, G. Duncan, (ed.) (Cambridge: Cambridge U. Press, 1983), pp. 133–155.

Efficiency, Responsibility, and Democratic Politics

William C. Mitchell

In this essay William Mitchell discusses the political and economic implications of what he terms the "collectivization" of government. Beginning with the assumption that individuals seek to maximize their own utility, he argues that while such behavior serves well in the context of a market, it leads to bad policies and irresponsible conduct by politicians. This is because monopolistic power and coercion are the hallmarks of the political system, while in a market the decision to pursue self-interest benefits others as well as the individual making the decision. As voters demand that they receive something for nothing, politicians are encouraged to make decisions which benefit sub-groups at the expense of the general good. Time and resources are wasted seeking redistribution rather than in production. Though individually rational, political participation is collectively irrational.

From William C. Mitchell, "Efficiency, Responsibility, and Democratic Politics." Reprinted by permission of New York University Press from *Liberal Democracy*, NOMOS XXV, edited by J. Roland Pennock and John W. Chapman. Copyright © 1983 by New York University, pp. 343–373.

In politics, more than anywhere else, we have no possibility of distinguishing between being and appearance.

—Hannah Arendt, *On Revolution*

Today, nearly all social phenomena have become politicized, and almost all social difficulties are assumed to have only political solutions. The politicizing of life can be seen in every basic relation: between parents and children, between husband and wife, employers and unions, businessmen and consumers, professors and students, between races, between men and women. All this stands in sharp contrast to an earlier period when individuals perceived their difficulties as essentially private and to be dealt with privately through private institutions of family, church, and the market. Today, the initiative is collective and the solution bureaucratic.

Collectivizing society inevitably leads to aggrandizement of the state and enshrinement of power. Politicians and bureaucrats become more significant in our lives than businessmen, and public institutions supplant the private. Coercion and compulsory philanthropy replace voluntary agreements and persuasion. Individuals increasingly must seek permission to "do their own thing." As a result, the individual has become more dependent on the state, a dependence that leads necessarily to personal frustration, impotence, anger, and irresponsibility. The discrepancy between reality and millennium promised by the intellectual "left" only makes these realities more difficult to explain and accept. Conflict, passion, hatred, revolution are now made respectable by social theorists while the ideals of eighteenth- and nineteenth-century liberalism are derided as an amusing ideology of the not-so-wonderful past when men were enslaved by the industrial revolution.

My theme is this: As society becomes more collectivized, responsible individual participation and governmental rationality are seriously weakened. A diminished sense of responsibility leads, in turn, to greater conflict and injustice in the distribution of wealth and income than might otherwise be obtained through market and other private choices. More generally, public policy is characterized by extraordinary perversities from which

come hopelessness and anger. Since one is not in command of one's fate in a collectivized society, blind adjustment, i.e., irrational conduct, is not only permitted but exalted. I cannot believe that much good will result from these developments.

Responsible Participation in Markets and Politics

The many and varied roles we play in a modern democracy help to shape our perceptions, beliefs, and values. Because the activities of a modern market economy and democracy are decentralized, specialized, and intricate, we cannot expect that all social effects or consequences of actions taken by individuals will be considered. Both ignorance and disincentives combine to produce ill-considered or "irresponsible" choices and policies. We must assume, too, that people find it difficult to assign "responsibility" correctly. We do not know to whom credit is due for our good fortune nor whom to blame when things go wrong.

My argument is simple: Utility-maximizing individuals find fewer incentives for responsible behavior in the polity than in the market. Indeed, collective choice, whether direct or representative, is unusually productive of both irresponsible conduct and irrational policies. Collective choice generates frustration, alienation, and impotence in individuals and extraordinary collective inefficiencies and inequities. To politicize life is to invite individuals to ignore the consequences of their choices. Since voting is acting for others one might assume that each would consider social consequences, or so romantic democrats would have us believe. I maintain that we act most responsibly when we act on our own behalf within well-defined property rights and liability rules. That leads me to a definition of "responsibility."

Responsibility is defined in a slightly unfamiliar way as rational choice. Rational choice, in turn, is defined as decisions that take full accounting of relevant consequences, i.e., the costs and benefits of alternatives. An efficient or responsible choice is, therefore, one in which all possible gains are exhausted; it is no longer possible to make anyone better-off without someone else being less well-off. Few individuals and no great societies attain perfect efficiency in the employment of resources. Rather, efficiency is concerned with moves in the right direction, i.e., putting resources into more highly valued uses. When resources are misallocated less-valued uses dominate choices. Foregone productive contributions are greater than the value of the existing or actual contribution of resources. The source of misallocation may be attributed chiefly to ignorance—to the allocation of resources at prices that do not reflect true costs and future preferences, income and prices. Accordingly, opportunities are presented to the better-informed or lucky to profit by these misallocations. An individual who discovers these unexploited opportunities redirects the flow of resources and thereby makes himself and others better-off. This is responsible market behavior.

Unfortunately, the responsible entrepreneur may earn greater profits by not considering all costs. These unaccounted costs are known variously as externalities, spillover or neighborhood effects, and social costs. In many activities social costs considerably exceed private costs, as in air and water pollution, congestion, deforestation and employment damaging to the health or development of the employee. Too many of these unintended bads will be produced by private markets. Hence, resources are misallocated. Although people act rationally in ignoring these costs, they are real and will be paid by someone.

Moralizing about these matters is not likely to solve anything as long as each continues to see a huge gap between the high cost to him of "responsible" behavior and the low cost of "irresponsible" behavior—especially when he thinks that his own sacrifice will make no noticeable difference to the community, and will not induce others to follow his lead. Every private act has social consequences; the more completely these consequences are taken into account, the more satisfactory will be the resulting allocation of resources. Since the spillovers of private choices become larger in advanced society, we should attend to more

effective ways of assigning responsibility to people for their actions.

So-called irresponsible action resulting in externalities is actually not an imperfection or failure of the market so much as it is a political failure. More efficient allocations of resources can be achieved by assigning responsibility through voluntary exchange on the basis of property rights that are more fully specified. What is needed is not more restriction on property rights but rather their extension into those areas that are presently treated as communal property. Nothing invites irresponsible conduct so much as resources "owned" by everyone. We should devise institutions that internalize relevant costs and benefits. Internalization forces people to consider consequences because they are brought home to them. Accordingly, individuals become more responsible.

The market system obviously fails to internalize all externalities. Still, it does manage to handle an extraordinary number of externalities. In particular, the market induces people to do good by enabling them to capture a share of the benefits for themselves. Surely most writers believe in copyrights! Every new or improved commodity is made because people expect to exchange their own work for something they want. While the market does internalize many costs and benefits it may fail to calculate long-term or intergenerational allocations. Whether a political process could do a better job is debatable. Just as future consumers are unable to register their demands so, too, the unborn voter has no voice.

Whereas the market encourages production of the right goods it may not always call forth the right amounts. Political activity (or politics), however, may do neither; worse, it stimulates unproductive transfer activity. Rational thought in politics is devoted not to the discovery of new ideas, new products, new resources, new and more efficient means of production but to new means of exploitation. One cannot readily redistribute wealth and income in the economy without doing good for others; since making oneself better-off through political means ordinarily requires less than unanimous consent, doing good at the expense of others is facilitated. Such behavior is irresponsible.

Political Settings

The unique and rather disturbing aspects of politics gain significance when contrasted with the economics of a market economy. The economy generates resource allocation through a host of individual transactions. These transactions take place on the basis of private property and freedom of contract. There are rules for deciding who owns each piece of property. Each person has substantial control over the use of his property. Property can change hands only by free exchange or by free gift. A person's wealth increases rapidly if he gets large gifts, if he produces, if others are willing to offer high prices for what he owns, and if he saves wisely. Because of free contract, no one is forced to accept a position that he thinks inferior to that his original property secures. If anyone can produce something that is more valuable than the resources used up, then he can gain from its production. If he can find other people who trade things that he regards as more valuable than what he gives up, then he can gain from exchange. Under certain well-known conditions, freedom of exchange leads to an optimal allocation of resources. The role of prices in this entire process is of extraordinary importance, for prices constitute the essential information sellers and buyers need in making their respective decisions.

Collective choice, on the other hand, is based on some specified, minimal agreement, and choices are binding on all. Coercion is, therefore, a hallmark of the political system. In the market men generally act directly for themselves, but most public decisions are made by representatives or fiduciaries rather than by individual voters. Still, every representative and voter is a potential dictator in that each attempts to choose for all others as well as for oneself. Benevolent would-be dictators though we may be, we attempt to impose our values, views, policies and preferences on all others if only because laws must be of general application. A market choice, on the other hand, is not an attempt to persuade or impose that choice on other consumers.

In addition to being coercive, polities can exist only if their governments possess monopoly powers. Governments do not tolerate competitors. Accordingly, citizens cannot switch to competing bureaucracies whenever they become dissatisfied with a service. "Voting with one's feet" has, therefore, distinct and readily apparent limitations as an effective control over politicians and bureaucrats, whereas in the market it (or "exit") is common practice.

Although governments are monopolies, they engage in peculiar economic decision-making. They are not permitted to seek profits. Instead, the government normally finances its activities by payments from taxpayers unrelated to specific goods or services. When government distributes services and goods, it does so at zero prices or less-than-cost prices. The beneficiaries pay unequal "prices" for the same services. Markets, on the other hand, charge a uniform price to all regardless of personal and economic characteristics. The very existence of prices enables not only precise but systematic comparison of values and costs. In the world of politics most services go unpriced.

That governments engage in these odd forms of fiscal behavior has enormous consequences not only for the overall allocation of resources, distribution of welfare and burdens, but also for the daily life of citizens, politicians, and bureaucrats. Economists and public choice theorists are exploring choices in terms of their efficiency and equity. Political scientists have examined some of this behavior but have, for the most part, chosen to emphasize non-monetary interrelations of personality and politics. While many of these investigations are valuable, most appear to have been conducted without knowledge of the political setting. Without an understanding of the distinctive properties of the political process and government one lacks at least part of the explanation of irresponsible conduct.

In order to analyze the actual processes by which irresponsibility is generated in politics and minimized in markets we must examine on the one hand the immediate situations and incentives of politicians, voters, bureaucrats and buyers and sellers, on the other.

My analysis assumes that all behavior is self-interested. Insofar as this assumption is valid it follows that abolishing self-interest is fruitless; it also follows that abolition of private property in the instruments of production, for example, brings no fundamental change in human nature. Any set of political and economic institutions, including socialism, creates characteristic patterns of incentives and costs. The abolition of property or the administering of public property does not remove private control over and private use of resources. Someone, somehow, administers the resources, determining the opportunities for their employment and thus tempts public decision makers to make use of public resources at the expense of the general public.

Voters and Voting: Ignorance, Illusion and Confusion

While voting rights or "assets" are typically distributed to adults universally, equally, and free of charge, they cannot be used without incurring some cost. The costs may have an enormous range, but they are rarely in accord with the benefits that might be sought by voting. Just as the vote is given all, regardless of knowlege, effort and achievement, so that same vote cannot be bought and sold. I point to these fundamental properties of the vote because none of them is conducive to responsible choice. Because voting rights are free and universal, there is little incentive to develop expertise, to specialize, and to economize in their exercise. Voters can rationally remain ignorant. In a market equivalent ignorance would impose severe penalties.

Normally, prospective voters face a highly biased and discouraging situation. They not only confront powerful constraints but have only the slightest influence over outcomes. They have influence without having real choices. More exactly, their choices can be exercised only at prearranged times. These opportunities would be analogous to a market in which consumers were asked to supply themselves with goods for a four-year stretch without rights to return. And, unlike the con-

sumer faced with a plethora of marginal choices, the voter faces binary, i.e., either/or, and future-oriented or uncertain options. One cannot have a little more or a little less of a candidate nor even a little more or less public expenditures and revenues. In two-party systems the choice generally presented is one involving homogeneous promises, or between "Tweedledee" and "Tweedledum." Were genuine choices offered no expression of intensity would be permitted and while tie-in purchases are rare in the market, they are characteristic of politics. Furthermore, the voter is confined to a single constituency; he is unable to vote for favorite politicians in districts other than his own.

The voter is free of a "reality test" in the sense that (a) he has little incentive to be informed, and (b) he need not consider the fiscal consistency of his choices. Voters rarely face price tags and explicit contracts on policies. If they did, they could not enforce compliance from politicians; no court will uphold campaign promises. Voters can only choose "process" characteristics and hope for the best.[1] Typically, consumers buy "results" rather than promises and leave the process to those who specialize in producing the goods and services. While any purchase is made under some uncertainty, the uncertainty confronting the voter is far greater.

A reduced sense of reality and disconnection of benefits and costs accounts not only for irresponsibility but also for apathy. The paradox of participation, i.e., the lessened value of one's vote as the electorate grows, is felt by the lowliest of voters. No such paradox exists in the market. In any event, the ordinary citizen is likely to view himself in an uncontrollable system. So he expends less effort on political issues than he spends on almost any economic choice. As usual, Schumpeter was right when he wrote:

> It will help to clarify the point if we ask ourselves why so much more intelligence and clearheadedness show up at a bridge table than in, say, political discussion among non-politicians. At the bridge table, we have a definite task; we have rules that discipline us; success and failure are clearly defined; and we are prevented from behaving irresponsibly because every mistake we make will not only im-

mediately tell us but also be immediately allocated to us. These conditions, by their failure to be fulfilled for political behavior of the ordinary citizen, show why it is that in politics he lacks the alertness and judgment he may display in his profession.[2]

Consider now the citizen-voter as citizen-consumer in a "government store." The store is, of course, operated by politicians and bureaucrats, all of whom are expected to serve in "the public interest." The government store is, then, a sort of cooperative. But it is a peculiar one in that it is destined to frustrate its members. Most of our public goods and an increasing volume of private goods are being offered in these "stores." These goods have no price tags but differential prices (taxes) are imposed, having little to do with the evaluations of the citizen-consumer. Not only are prices absent but consumers are required to finance unwanted goods or goods in unwanted quantities. Unlike the market, consumption is not subject to consumer discretion.

Consumer advocates have found private markets wanting in protections for the consumer; so they support government regulation. Suppose now that we ask for consumer protection in the political market. Surely protection is needed when government administers more than a third of the GNP. Unlike government, and unless they have monopoly power, private firms can neither require consumers to purchase goods nor charge differential prices. Furthermore, firms operate under laws of contract and tort, whereas the public producers can be sued only with their own consent. Many public services are of such a nature that consumer appraisal of them is all but impossible. Many political decisions are confounded by the presence of goods that have not been bought and sold and are therefore unpriced. People cannot decide whether these goods are worth having in what amounts by comparing price to cost. Nor can they choose among goods on the basis of comparative prices.

In effect, the producer does the judging, as is clearly the case when professors grade their students. Like professors, governments decide what to produce, in what quantities, and to whom it will go. Neither faces an independently generated demand curve. In fact,

the demand for many public services is decided by the politicians and bureaucrats rather than by the ultimate consumers. . . . While private advertisers must appeal to a vast number of individuals to change demand, governmental agencies need appeal only to small numbers of congressmen, suppliers of resources, and beneficiaries of specific services. Of course, the money for advertising comes not from sales but from unknown taxpayers who know not the uses being made of their untagged dollars.

William Buckley, in an obvious play on a famous passage from Galbraith's *The Affluent Society*, suggests that our "social imbalance" has a political explanation:

A modern Justine could in New York City, wake up in the morning in a room she shares with her unemployed husband and two children, crowd into a subway in which she is hardly able to breathe, disembark at Grand Central and take a crosstown bus which takes twenty minutes to go the ten blocks to her textile loft, work a full day and receive her paycheck from which a sizeable deduction is withdrawn in taxes and union fees, return via the same ordeal, prepare supper for her family and tune up the radio to full blast to shield the children from the gamey denunciations her next-door neighbor is hurling at her husband, walk a few blocks past hideous buildings to the neighborhood park to breathe a little fresh air, and fall into a coughing fit as the sulphur dioxide excites her latent asthma, go home, and on the way lose her handbag to a purse-snatcher, sit down to oversee her son's homework only to trip over the fact that he doesn't really know the alphabet even though he had his fourteenth birthday yesterday, which he spent in company of a well-known pusher. She hauls off and smacks him, but he dodges and she bangs her head against the table. The ambulance is slow in coming and at the hospital there is no doctor in attendance. An intern finally materializes and sticks her with a shot of morphine, and she dozes off to sleep. And dreams of John Lindsay.[3]

That politics might have something to do with unemployment, union monopoly, education, transit, and medical services seems reasonable.

While citizens may be victimized by governments, they are continuously encouraged to get something for nothing. While the same motive prevails in the economy, price tags veto the wish. Not so in the polity; one can get something for nothing because government, with its coercive powers, can award benefits to some while it charges others. As the LSE [London School of Economics] joke about the democratic process goes: "Give me your vote, and I'll give you somebody else's money!" So universally accepted is this practice that redistribution is now widely viewed as a major function of government. So powerful is the conviction that eminent economists—Lester Thurow,[4] Harold M. Hochman[5] and James D. Rodgers[6]—treat redistribution as a pure public good. That suggests a close look at those who spend some people's money on others.

Politicians: Vote Gathering and Irresponsibility

We can understand the politician's contribution to irresponsibility once we appreciate his incentives, disincentives, and resources. My analysis proceeds in much the same manner as the analysis of voters and voting. The results are similar in that behavior is peculiar but hardly irrational given the rules of the game.

Those who occupy decision-making posts gain them by a competitive struggle for votes from utility-maximizing but mostly uninformed, part-time voters. The quest for votes encourages the politician to take short-run perspectives and buy support. He opts for programs that will be highly visible to specific groups, each of whom he expects or hopes will contribute to his coalition of minorities at election time. He rewards those whose support is most contingent rather than those of whom he is sure: money must be spent in the "right" places at the "right times." And, it must be spent in the "right" ways! For example, politicians prefer programs that confer benefits through regulation or tax reductions rather than outright transfers. Accordingly, the politician is able to advance the welfare of some without arousing and annoying others. Legislative review is also avoided. Welfare payments "in-kind" are preferred to income grants, but this practice may reflect taxpayer

rather than beneficiary interests. In any event, he can spend money in ways denied the private businessman and the consumer. They must decide within a known budget constraint; they confront opportunity costs in a most direct manner. This is not so for most politicians, who decide both spending and tax policies without the constraint of a fixed fund. Log-rolling is a typical consequence; if one interest group is gaining an "unfair" advantage, the response of legislators is not to end the "injustice," but to seek similar advantages for their own constituents. While log-rolling makes compelling political sense it has slight economic justification. Still, it is a basic political process.

Spending programs must ultimately be financed by someone, some way, for as the cliché now has it, "there ain't no such thing as a free lunch." Unless constrained by Constitutional rule or an alert and informed electorate, politicians may ignore the Friedman dictum. But even these "controls" offer no guarantee of responsible action, because the redistributive preferences of voters outweigh their concern for collective efficiencies. Voters and politicians alike can simultaneously advocate massive spending, lower taxes, and balanced budgets without going broke.

Tax policies are the obverse of spending decisions, i.e., the politician attempts to diffuse taxes over as many people as possible. Taxes may be made less visible and onerous by shifting them to non-voters, making payment less noticeable, and changes in bases and rates as gradual as possible. As in spending politicians are concerned with the impact of taxing on marginal voters and votes, not with the efficiency of markets. Most legislators are uninterested in the economist's criterion of fiscal neutrality; if market intervention or inefficient regulation will garner more votes they will be done in spite of known inefficiencies.

Regardless of ideology, politicians encourage citizens to use the political system. Once the polity has significant control over the economy citizens must resort to political activity if they are to protect or advance personal welfare. Their activity necessarily creates work, status, and power for the politicians. So they will select policies that make voters still more dependent on the state: a politician will, for example, advise people to seek state aid rather than take an independent private course of action. In the aftermath of the Mount St. Helens eruption, Northwest politicians, regardless of party, attempted to outdo one another in well-publicized efforts to obtain federal disaster monies, rather than advising local residents to leave the area. Politicians are most reluctant to tell obsolescent industries and occupations to heed the market signals. Instead, they protect the dying with tariffs, import quotas, subsidies, favorable tax legislation—all those schemes known as the "new protectionism." State support for local interests demonstrates care, a compassion that cannot be demonstrated with efficient policies. The latter will always appear as cold and impersonal long-run solutions. Again, we conclude that the politician is simply uninterested in efficiency; his attitude is dictated . . . by the truly important political consideration of *whose* gains and *whose* losses. The ever-present prospect of receiving great benefits at little or no extra personal cost brings forth a persistent demand for redistribution.

The invisible hand of self-interest has produced remarkable results in the marketplace, but the same practice applied to political intervention in the economy may work in reverse. The universal pursuit of protection and redistribution—import quotas, fuel allocations, legalized monopolies, tax privileges, etc.—may so encumber the system as to generate a gigantic prisoners' dilemma in which everyone ends up worse-off. This may be one of the great tragedies of modern democracies: The better a political system performs in representing the narrow interests of its citizens, the worse it may be at managing its economy. If each citizen's collective interests are overwhelmed by the promise and necessity of seeking more immediate gains from redistribution, then all will share a smaller GNP. The fundamental problem for the politician stems from his having to satisfy ever-increasing demands for larger shares from a possibly less productive economy and more reluctant taxpayers. His dilemma is eased somewhat by the ignorance of consequences that is so characteristic of politics: The people who are helped by any particular policy

are often those who have not struggled for it, while those who are injured include many who know not the source of their difficulties.

Aside from a necessary and important interest in the fiscal behavior of elective officials, we must take note of certain other facts and incentives. Politicians have become full-time professionals, earning considerable salaries, commanding many valuable perquisites of office, but having little influence on bureaucrats and the programs they administer. In the political division of labor, politicians must pay for most of the decision costs of policy-making and governing. They do not take on the external costs of their policies. Hence they want to reduce decision costs but show little desire to reduce externalities levied at the rest of us. That the politician treats the federal budget as a "common pool resource" should occasion no surprise.[7] When private and public costs diverge, as they do in politics, one may expect fiscal irresponsibility.

Those who seek elective office are seldom those who would find an entrepreneurial career attractive. Once one grasps the differences between government and business, the reasons are apparent. Political life is much more exciting, ego-rewarding, and visible than private business. If few can name very many public officials, fewer still can name any of the top 500 businessmen.

In business appearance and reality cannot long be separated; in the crudest sense, this means there is a "bottom line" to discipline executives. Profits, or the lack thereof, can be disguised only in the very short run. In government there is no stock market, and that is why a politician or an entire administration can play at image-making. The very criteria of political success are controversial. Having returned to private life after a stint in government, many businessmen have noted that appearance is much more important than reality, a distinction that would not even occur in the business world. In politics power depends on what others think you have in the way of influence. Frequently people appear to have influence when they have none or little; occasionally, politicians seem not to have influence when in fact they are quite powerful. Would-be politicians soon learn that diligent cultivation of appearances is of the utmost importance.

Aspiring politicians also learn that while the appearance of consistency may or may not be the hobgoblin of small minds, it is important for a political career. Businessmen are expected and entitled to change their minds about future action as conditions change. Responsible decision-making demands adaptability. In politics those who vacillate are accused of inconsistency by other politicians, the Russians, and the press, as was Jimmy Carter. In consequence, much political language is double-talk. Politicians go to great lengths to avoid appearing to have changed their principles, priorities, and assessments. The media exploit these linguistic gymnastics, because mistakes and inconsistencies are newsworthy. Businessmen are not subjected to this kind of scrutiny; money does the talking.

Politicians interested in imagery learn, too, the importance of posing as the person who not only devised a policy but convinced others to go along. Who gets to announce policies and when are matters of the highest strategic import. Inclusion in decision-making is of primary significance to politicians; to be excluded is costly not only to his constituents but for his reputation. That is why congressmen insist on having pictures taken with the President and, more importantly, of having the President appear to be listening or congratulating.

If appearances and reality are so inconsistent and power so critical, we should expect that those who go into politics either are or soon become vain, shallow, and unprincipled. All too often, politics seems tantamount to expedience. Everyone is obliged to say what we cannot possibly believe, promise the impossible, force practitioners to reckon with fools, flatter people who repel us, deprecate those we esteem, and all this for the sake of power whose possession will prove disappointing. Milton Friedman, in a recent *Newsweek* column, observed that

> Most members of Congress are honest, decent people whom you and I would be proud to have as personal friends and whom we would trust implicitly to tell us the truth and to honor their obligations. Yet, as "public servants," they consistently behave very differently, making assertions that they know to be untrue,

making promises that they know will not be kept. Voting for legislation that they know to be undesirable.[8]

Politicians speak often but say as little of consequences as possible. Historians inform us that Lincoln was a partial exception for he did not make a single campaign speech in 1860 and refused to answer any questions about his intentions. He said he would stand on his "record." Ironically, politicians must dress up their virtue of compromising in the language of "principle," the greatest of political vices. In the phrase, "Words that Succeed and Policies that Fail," Murray Edelman conveys much of what I have attempted to characterize as compassion without responsibility.[9]

Aside from the fact that politicians are forced to conceal, shift positions, smooth feelings, evade, and the like, their task is extraordinarily difficult. They are expected to rush in where the market fears to tread, providing services such as defense and clean air that the market ignores. But the dictates of economic efficiency are of little appeal and guidance in the public sector. The criterion of efficiency simply dictates that the best policy is that which yields the largest net benefits; questions of who is to get how much of the benefits and who is to pay how much of the costs are not addressed. Economists may know how to choose between two housing projects but not know how to advise a politician on which one to support, because they cannot advise on who should have better housing. The politician has no such out from choice. When equity is not relevant, as in the provision of public goods, the politician faces an equally difficult task—deciding how much or the optimal supplies of both public goods and bads. Public choice theory is fairly certain that no institutional arrangements can provide a definitive answer to this question. Some citizens will always prefer more than is offered; others with differing tastes will always prefer less, whatever the amount supplied. But once the decision is made to supply a particular quantity of a public good, the same amount is available to all. As a result, and unlike the market, individuals cannot adjust their consumption. If all individuals must "consume" the same amount, many are going to be frustrated. Politicians must live with this fact.

Bureaucratic Appearances and Reality

We continue our inquiry into the divergence of appearance and reality by examining bureaucracy and its incumbents the bureaucrats. Again, we discover a gulf leading to irresponsible conduct as well as a number of other well-known bureaucratic maladies, including even severe personality disorders. Once more the analysis is not meant to condemn intelligent, well-educated, hard-working servants of the public; in fact, most bureaucrats display all of these virtues. Ironically, dedicated and efficient effort may violate the norm of [efficiency] and, of course, infringe upon individual freedom. In the words of Stephan Michelson, we are dealing with the "working bureaucrat and the nonworking bureaucracy."[10]

Bureaucrats work within the powerful constraints of a formal, hierarchical organization whose mission is defined by legislative fiat and whose task is to supply the public with not-for-profit services. The bureau finances its activities not by the sale of services but from a periodic budgetary commitment provided by the legislative branch. These funds are based on the government's right to print money, collect taxes, issue tax-free bonds, and even conscript and expropriate. Needless to say, private firms are denied these unique financial instruments. Public organizations so financed are not likely to go out of business, since they can shape the demand for their own services by collusion with private suppliers, beneficiaries, and, of course, interested politicians. Once an agency is in the budget, it is borne along year after year without close legislative oversight and certainly without the daily scrutiny of a marketplace.

These external differences tend to be more significant than the internal differences between a private firm and a public agency. However, one important internal difference pertains to the working conditions of employees; private competitive firms place much greater reliance on financial rewards and employment sanctions. Higher-level employees may obtain a substantial proportion of their income in the form of contingent claims, i.e., bonuses and stock options, and their employment is far less secure. In addition, government agencies account for their finances in a radically different way from that of profit-making firms. Accounts in private enterprises include both a balance sheet and an accrual-based income statement. Hardly any government agency prepares a balance sheet, and no decisions are made on "bottom-line" considerations, i.e., on the basis of net worth. Cash flow statements are used by agencies because capital expenditures are budgeted at time of purchase and never again. Private firms are quite flexible in their capital decisions since they shift capital expenditures on the basis of expected returns. Public agencies, on the other hand, are relatively inflexible since sales are not important. Instead, entrenched beneficiaries are able to maintain services even when public demand has shifted to other services. One might, therefore, claim that new agencies tend to be capital-deficient, while established agencies are capital-rich.

These curious economics of bureaucracies are not in the least peculiar to politics, a point made with considerable imagination by Gordon Tullock[11] and Anthony Downs[12] and with rigor by William A. Niskanen, Jr.[13] Public bureaucracies, operated by some 14 million employees, many strongly unionized, and several million more part-time employees, are now an electoral group that cannot be ignored.[14] Of greater significance, however, is the role played by bureaucrats in managing the economy, in supplying public goods, and redistributing income. Bureaucracies can and typically do ignore the marginal cost/benefit nexus in deciding their levels of operation; in short, they expand their services as far beyond that point as the size of the consumer surplus will permit. Excessive production then constitutes exploitation of those who finance the excess capacities and levels of operation. We should be careful to note that this form of exploitation is frequently done in the guise of "doing good," and meeting "social" or "merit" needs. Bureaucracies provide services and goods but not always in accord with citizen preferences; some people get more than they want and obviously are willing to finance. Even if production is excessive, the intended beneficiaries may complain because of insufficient personal allocations, excessive red tape, inopportune investigations, impersonality, and arbitrary decisions.

Bureaucracies and the political processes that decide their financing are notoriously inadequate in accurately and speedily reflecting societal preferences. A bureaucracy is, nevertheless, able to reflect its own preferences for larger budgets and have those preferences enacted. The important point here is that bureaucrats will want higher levels of public output, not because their preferences are necessarily different but because they face a different constraint; in this case, the relative prices of public and private goods confronting bureaucrats are different from those confronting the citizenry. For the same level of utility, bureaucrats will prefer a mix that contains more public goods and fewer private goods. As producer roles are more significant for the average citizen-voter, so too is the producer role more important to a government worker than is his other role as a citizen-voter. The stakes are larger and the chances greater that one can affect one's fate as a producer than as a consumer and citizen.

While private producers are constrained by the market to keep costs down, such incentives are largely nonexistent or weak in the public sector. In fact, the dominant incentives work in exactly the opposite direction. A bureaucrat gains status, income, and power by supervising more subordinates and not by what he produces in the way of valuable services to the public. It is in the interest of higher-level bureaucrats to overstaff their agencies and to increase the flow of paper or even the complexity of the organization. Making work for the agency has a payoff for every member, at the expense of citizens. The drive is to use as much as possible to achieve any given output. Legislators need to know that these costs are highly visible so that the agency has a persuasive rationale for a still larger budget. As was noted above, a bureaucracy can shift its demand curve in order to justify greater appropriations, but the same result can also be attained by increasing the alleged costs or by charging below-cost prices. When prices are reduced and/or below-cost prices adopted, demand for the service will increase.

Bureaucracies are meddlesome, inefficient, and therefore irresponsible. The extent of their costly behavior varies from one agency to another, from one time to another, from one nation to another, but it is always limited somewhat by prevailing institutions and the contrary interests of citizens. Unfortunately, the costs of organizing these opposing interests are far higher than might ideally be the case and certainly higher than the costs of efficient rent-seeking by the bureaucracies themselves.

Negative-Sum Games, Harm and Failure

One acts positively to further one's welfare. That social costs or externalities [*i.e., effects of bargains on third parties*—ED.] may follow is incidental—a consequence that is unintentional and often unknown at the moment of decision. If the externalities are negative, complaints are certain and political action demanded; if operations are beneficial, few speak out. While one acts politically to advance personal welfare, this is mostly achieved not by seeking mutually desired exchanges but through negative and even destructive actions taken with the express purpose of harming others. Voters, bureaucrats, and politicians act against other members of the polity. Policies are deliberately enacted that restrict the alternatives available to others. Indeed the state is the enemy of Paretian choice. And, worse, Fromm's "escape from freedom" has become a fear of freedom for other people. As M. Bruce Johnson aptly observes:

> More and more products and activities that were voluntarily chosen by private decision are becoming involuntarily imposed, restricted, or eliminated by state mandate. Yet, it does not follow that because we are all one people, we all want the same diets, automobiles, medical

services, pension benefits, and environmental amenities—or that we all are willing to bear the same costs to obtain a given benefit.[15]

George Stigler is unfortunately correct in asserting that Uncle Sam is really "Uncle Same" in his bureaucratic treatment of citizens, except, of course, at tax and subsidy times.[16]

Because the imposition of harm is so characteristic of political action, we should expect that as society is politicized, zero-sum and, increasingly, negative-sum games will replace the positive-sum games of the market. Potential benefactors turn to the state as the lowest-cost way of protecting themselves and intentionally or not imposing their own values on others. Evidently, politicians and bureaucrats are willing to supply the demand for security; evidently, many intellectuals and others are willing to justify their claims.

Since imposition of harm is so characteristic of political action, we should probably expect that politics will attract those who wish to see others controlled or harmed. In the worst circumstances sadists will go into politics, and in less horrendous situations well-meaning ideologists wanting to save mankind will crusade for ill-conceived reforms.

Those concerned about the failures of markets and market economies have a legitimate concern. We should worry also about the modern democratic polity and its impact on individualism and responsible conduct. Since the polity is treated by many as a substitute rather than a complement to the market, analysis of political, as opposed to economic, failure becomes imperative.

Failure is indigenous to politics. The polity, unlike the economy, is characterized by costly and infrequent trading, expensive information, high organizational and entry costs, many externalities. The consequences of any decision are therefore less fully thrust upon the political than the market participant. To offset this tendency of reduced cost-bearing, special constraints are imposed on officials and public employees. But such contraints, adopted in the interest of responsibility, are a poor substitute for the internalization of consequences. They contribute mightily to inflexibility. More importantly, the failure or inability of politics to internalize costs and bene-

fits induces the kind of irresponsible behavior described as inefficient by public choice theorists and irrational by some political psychologists. As society becomes increasingly politicized, we may expect more of both public inefficiency and private irresponsibility.

Individuals are rarely ennobled by political action; instead, they are enticed to become less informed, less fair-minded, and less responsible. The waste of scarce resources is a tragic yet inevitable consequence of political choice.

Political Dynamics and Political Participation

Readers may find my analysis and its implications disturbing if not downright perverse, outlandish, or even churlish. Nowhere might these reactions be more quick and strong than on the important issue of political participation in a democracy. For the obvious conclusion is that "participatory" democracy is bound further to weaken our sense of responsibility, already woefully weak.

Nevertheless, given the assumption of utility maximization and the unique properties of public choice, participation is eminently rational. To be sure, the motivation assumed here may not possess the ethical qualities many political philosophers seem to prefer and, indeed, may even believe prevail. Still, my analysis should be understood as favoring individual and organizational political effort. We are in the grip of a new political dynamic.

Regardless of the reasons for the growth of the "State," the facts are that taxation consumes a major portion of current income; that government is the single largest purchaser of goods and services; that regulation of individuals, businesses, etc., is pervasive and costly (an estimated $2 billion in administrative costs and $100 billion per year in compliance costs);[17] that changing rules, expenditures, taxes and regulations alter property rights which, in turn, affect the income and wealth of every single citizen; and finally, that federal transfer payments totalled more than $300 billion in 1980.[18] *In a world like ours "participation" in politics and administration be-*

comes mandatory. We are driven to it. A mundane happening illustrates our predicament. After the Carter Administration forced recreational boat owners to purchase and install expensive anti-pollution devices and then proposed that weekend boating during energy shortages be banned, the membership of the Boat Owners Association soon increased from 50,000 to its current level of more than 80,000.[19] Democratic politics becomes both more aggressive and more defensive. The advocates of participatory democracy will get their way for reasons they will not like and try to ignore.

There is more to the dynamic of our situation than these facts suggest. In attempting to improve their lot, people do not merely adjust to economic contingency. They alter the rules and policies to their own advantage. The effort they will expend to alter rules and policies depends on the relationship between costs and expected gains. This is the rational principle that explains the political dynamic of collectivistic liberalism.

What appears to have happened over the past century is nothing less than a dramatic shift in the cost-benefit schedules of political action. While the state has always provided basic services and redistributed income and wealth, we observe rapid intensification during the twentieth century. As this has occurred, the returns from using the political process have increased at a far greater rate than the also mounting costs. Almost any economic decision can now be challenged in the political arena and with a reasonable expectation of success. To be sure, as more citizens have entered politics and as their pressure has become more continuous and professionalized, the costs have increased. But the ratio has widened, and that is the crucial calculation. The question is no longer one of participation, if it ever was, but of the shape of effective action. . . .

The conclusion is that the liberal democratic welfare state has generated a distinctive form of politics. People try to obtain income and wealth at the expense of others and attempt to protect themselves against government. Economic man has put on political clothes. While a definitive estimate of outcomes is probably impossible, there does seem to be considerable agreement among analysts of redistributive politics and economics that (1) income and wealth are redistributed both vertically and horizontally; (2) that almost every citizen is both beneficiary and donor; (3) that significant transfers take place among members of the same income bracket; (4) that lower-income groups have made significant gains during the past forty years; (5) that total transfers have not altered the basic market distribution by very much; and finally, (6) that inequality prevails.[20]

All this is very costly, i.e., the opportunity costs are enormous since the energy expended is not productive. The person busy in the halls of government advancing his own prosperity is obviously not working for others. These opportunity costs are probably unmeasurable. Anyway, the overall distribution remains unequal and, as noted throughout this essay, many programs are perverse. Contrary to liberal intention and expectation, many of the rich become richer and some of the poor, poorer. After all the frenetic action and transfers, most people still occupy the same relative positions. Rational individual and group action will increase transaction costs, produce a smaller social product, and in the end leave most worse off. This is the disastrous dynamic of our democracy. But not to seek subsidies when others may be expected to, and not to demand tax privileges when others do, makes no sense. Everyone is caught up in a tragedy of the budgetary "commons." These "games" are neither ennobling nor socially optimal.

In the words of Robert A. Dahl, ". . . the making of governmental decisions is not a majestic march of great majorities united upon certain matters of policy. It is the steady appeasement of relatively small groups."[21] We face the dilemma of individual and collective rationality, that general ruin can be the outcome of rational action.[22]

Political "participation" is self-interested and rational, yet in the long term highly irrational. This finding goes against conventional radical wisdom. Political participation is usually held to be an intrinsic good and productive of good consequences. A healthy democracy is one in which citizens participate in public-spirited ways, more or less continuously, enjoy the comradeship of cooperative action and, of course, resolve social problems. The polity is really a commune writ large. Others consider democracy an arena for class conflicts, yet one in which fighting stops short of violence. Both views make political participation the most significant and noble of human actions. Our present politics is not what Hannah Arendt had in mind.

Curiously, economic behavior is generally considered mundane, selfish, uninteresting and even "unproductive." Neither saints nor heroes appear in the marketplace! This being the case, no one worries about economic life except that it is seen as demeaning, inhuman, and a realm of domination. Markets are zero-sum games. They exhibit fraud, coercion, monopoly, and capitalistic pathologies. Political action is treated as selfless, communal, exhilarating, and productive. If so, some thinkers have some difficulty in explaining why so rewarding an activity is so unattractive to so many Americans. The answer is found, not in the opportunity costs of politics, but in the institutional and policy constraints imposed by "establishments," "power elites" and "corporate pluralism."

But surely this attitude is mistaken. Political "participation" is far more intense than our pollsters and radicals think. Indeed, one cannot be apolitical; even the simple act of "not voting" or declaring that one "doesn't know" are political acts because they have consequences for the resolution of political and economic issues. Likewise, to obey or disobey a law, to pay or cheat on one's taxes, to receive or not receive a subsidy, to sing or not sing the national anthem, to watch a TV newscast, to love or hate one's country are political statements. Americans are a highly politicized people and becoming more so, as are the British. Given the importance of government they have no choice.

"Participatory" politics is not well informed. Why does a highly politicized people remain ignorant of political strategy and public policies? Again, the competitive dynamic provides the answer. We have marketized, not humanized, politics.

Politics is highly uncertain. Reduction of uncertainty is costly and not often worth anyone's while. In these discouraging conditions few are apt to become expert in political matters. Instead, the individual will become an ideologue or depend upon hired experts to represent him. In consequence, the distribution of political information is highly skewed.

Throughout this essay I have maintained that the polity remains an inferior mechanism to the market when it comes to the allocation of scarce resources between myriad and conflicting individual preferences. All markets, of course, work imperfectly compared to the ideals of the textbooks. Still, the realities of imperfect markets—externalities, consumer ignorance, advertising, monopoly, oligopoly, non-optimal provisions of public goods—are overwhelmed by the universality and magnitude of public failure. While this failure is intractable democracy remains superior to other forms of politics because individual liberty and preferences are honored as ideals, and institutions of collective choice at least make some effort to discern and act upon them. Finally, I, for one, have not despaired of the possibilities of institutional reform. Certain recently proposed constitutional amendments pertaining to the fiscal and monetary powers of government provide more suitable settings for enacting efficient policies. Moreover, recent imaginative work on "demand revelation" reveals means of coping with the free-rider problem, as well as offering further testimony to the inventiveness of the human mind.[23] While collective choice stands in the sharpest contrast to the market, marginal improvements are possible. But of all improvements the most effective is a steady diminution of the scope of government.

Notes

1. Thomas Sowell, *Knowledge and Decisions* (New York: Basic Books, 1980), pp. 140–141.

2. Joseph A. Schumpeter, *Capitalism, Socialism and Democracy, third edition* (New York: Harper and Row, 1975), p. 261.

3. William F. Buckley, Jr., *The Unmasking of a Mayor* (New York: Viking Press, 1966), pp. 30–31, as quoted in Richard E. Wagner, "Advertising and the Public Economy: Some Preliminary Ruminations," in David G. Tuerch (ed.), *The Po-*

litical Economy of Advertising (Washington, D.C.: American Enterprise Institute, 1978), p. 98.

4. Lester C. Thurow, "The Income Distribution as a Pure Public Good," *Quarterly Journal of Economics*, 85 (May 1971), pp. 327–336.

5. Harold M. Hochman, "Individual Preferences and Distributional Adjustment," *American Economic Review*, LXII (May 1972), pp. 353–360.

6. Harold M. Hochman and James D. Rodgers, "Pareto Optimal Redistribution," *American Economic Review*, LIX (September 1969), pp. 542–557.

7. John Baden and Rodney D. Fort, "Natural Resources and Bureaucratic Predators," *Policy Review* (Winter 1980), pp. 69–81.

8. Milton Friedman, "Balanced on Paper," *Newsweek* (June 23, 1980), p. 68.

9. Murray Edelman, *Political Language: Words that Succeed and Policies that Fail* (New York: Academic Press, 1977).

10. Stephan Michelson, "The Working Bureaucrat and the Non-Working Bureaucracy," in Carol H. Weiss and Allen H. Barton (eds.), *Making Bureaucracies Work* (Los Angeles: Sage Publications, 1980), pp. 175–200.

11. Gordon Tullock, *The Politics of Bureaucracy* (Washington, D.C.: Public Affairs Press, 1965).

12. Anthony Downs, *Inside Bureaucracy* (Boston: Little, Brown & Co., 1967).

13. William A. Niskanen, Jr., *Bureaucracy and Representative Government* (Chicago: Aldine-Atherton, 1971), p. 137.

14. Winston C. Bush and Arthur T. Denzau, "The Voting Behavior of Bureaucrats and Public Sector Growth," in Thomas E. Borcherding (ed.), *Budgets and Bureaucrats* (Durham, N.C.: Duke University Press, 1977).

15. M. Bruce Johnson, "The Economics and America's Third Century," in Robert I. Rooney and M. Bruce Johnson, *The Economics of America's*

Third Century: A Discussion (Los Angeles: The International Institute for Economic Research, 1978), p. 23.

16. George J. Stigler, "The Government of the Economy," *A Dialogue on the Proper Economic Role of the State* (Selected Papers No. 7, Graduate School of Business, University of Chicago, 1963).

17. Roy Ash, *The Political World, Government Regulation, and Spending* (Los Angeles: International Institute for Economic Research, 1979), p. 5.

18. Edgar K. Browning and Jacqueline M. Browning, *Public Finance and the Price System* (New York: Macmillan Publishing Co., 1980), p. 194.

19. Brooks Jackson, "Reagan Plan to Tax Yachts and Boats Has Owners Angry," *Wall Street Journal* (May 8, 1981), p. 29.

20. See, for example, Edgar K. Browning, *Redistribution and the Welfare System* (Washington, D.C.: American Enterprise Institute, 1975); James N. Morgan *et al.*, *Income and Welfare in the United States* (New York: McGraw-Hill Book Company, 1972); and especially, Morton Paglin, "The Measurement and Trend of Inequality: A Basic Revision," *The American Economic Review*, 65 (September 1975), pp. 598–609.

21. Robert A. Dahl, *A Preface to Democratic Theory* (Chicago: University of Chicago Press, 1956), p. 146.

22. The relationship between rational individual choice and collective irrationality is imaginatively explored in Jon Elster, *Ulysses and the Sirens* (Cambridge: Cambridge University Press, 1979); J. Roland Pennock, *Democratic Political Theory* (Princeton: Princeton University Press, 1979); and E. L. Jones, *The European Miracle* (Cambridge: Cambridge University Press, 1981).

23. Edward Clarke, *Demand Revelation and the Provision of Public Goods* (Cambridge: Ballinger Publishing Co., 1980).

3

The Best
Outcome
Theory

Classical and Modern Theories of Democracy

Joseph Schumpeter

The "classical" theory of democracy came in for a good deal of criticism around the time of the second world war. Among the most influential of these critics was Joseph Schumpeter. Schumpeter served as Minister of Finance in the Austrian government, but when Nazism began to emerge he gave up his professorship in Berlin and moved to the United States. His most famous work, from which the following selections are taken, was Capitalism, Socialism and Democracy. *It was first published in 1942.*

In it, Schumpeter undertakes to show why the classical theories of democracy are inadequate both as descriptions of the way democratic governments actually function and as justifications for democratic institutions and practices. In its place he proposes a more "realistic" theory, one which better describes reality and which does not imagine government to be capable of the impossible—expressing the "will of the people." His "realistic" theory, far more minimalist, emphasizes competition among potential leaders to win office and the limited role in government of the average citizen.

I. The Classical Doctrine of Democracy

The Common Good and the Will of the People

The eighteenth-century philosophy of democracy may be couched in the following definition: the democratic method is that institutional arrangement for arriving at political decisions which realizes the common good by making the people itself decide issues through the election of individuals who are to assemble in order to carry out its will. Let us develop the implications of this.

It is held, then, that there exists a Common Good, the obvious beacon light of policy, which is always simple to define and which every normal person can be made to see by means of rational argument. There is hence

From Joseph Schumpeter, *Capitalism, Socialism and Democracy*, 3rd ed. (New York: Harper and Row, 1950). Copyright © 1942 by Joseph Schumpeter. Reprinted by permission of HarperCollins Publishers.

no excuse for not seeing it and in fact no explanation for the presence of people who do not see it except ignorance—which can be removed—stupidity and anti-social interest. Moreover, this common good implies definite answers to all questions so that every social fact and every measure taken or to be taken can unequivocally be classed as "good" or "bad." All people having therefore to agree, in principle at least, there is also a Common Will of the people (= will of all reasonable individuals) that is exactly coterminous with the common good or interest or welfare or happiness. The only thing, barring stupidity and sinister interests, that can possibly bring in disagreement and account for the presence of an opposition is a difference of opinion as to the speed with which the goal, itself common to nearly all, is to be approached. Thus every member of the community, conscious of that goal, knowing his or her mind, discerning what is good and what is bad, takes part, actively and responsibly, in furthering the former and fighting the latter and all the members taken together control their public affairs. . . .

As soon as we accept all the assumptions that are being made by this theory of the polity—or implied by it—democracy indeed acquires a perfectly unambiguous meaning and there is no problem in connection with it except how to bring it about. Moreover we need only forget a few logical qualms in order to be able to add that in this case the democratic arrangement would not only be the best of all conceivable ones, but that few people would care to consider any other. It is no less obvious however that these assumptions are so many statements of fact every one of which would have to be proved if we are to arrive at that conclusion. And it is much easier to disprove them.

There is, first, no such thing as a uniquely determined common good that all people could agree on or be made to agree on by the force of rational argument. This is due not primarily to the fact that some people may want things other than the common good but to the much more fundamental fact that to different individuals and groups the common good is bound to mean different things. . . . If we are to argue that the will of the citizens *per se* is a political factor entitled to respect, it must first exist. That is to say, it must be something more than an indeterminate bundle of vague impulses loosely playing about given slogans and mistaken impressions. Everyone would have to know definitely what he wants to stand for. This definite will would have to be implemented by the ability to observe and interpret correctly the facts that are directly accessible to everyone and to sift critically the information about the facts that are not. Finally, from that definite will and from these ascertained facts a clear *and prompt* conclusion as to particular issues would have to be derived according to the rules of logical inference—with so high a degree of general efficiency moreover that one man's opinion could be held, without glaring absurdity, to be roughly as good as every other man's. And all this the modal citizen would have to perform for himself and independently of pressure groups and propaganda, for volitions and inferences that are imposed upon the electorate obviously do not qualify for ultimate data of the democratic process. The question whether these conditions are fulfilled to the extent required in order to make democracy work should not be answered by reckless assertion or equally reckless denial. It can be answered only by a laborious appraisal of a maze of conflicting evidence. . . .

This instance of course is not an isolated one. If results that prove in the long run satisfactory to the people at large are made the test of government *for* the people, then government *by* the people, as conceived by the classical doctrine of democracy, would often fail to meet it.

Human Nature in Politics

It remains to answer our question about the definiteness and independence of the voter's will, his powers of observation and interpretation of facts, and his ability to draw, clearly and promptly, rational inferences from both. . . .

During the second half of the last century, the idea of the human personality that is a homogeneous unit and the idea of a definite will that is the prime mover of action have been steadily fading—even before the times of Théodule Ribot and of Sigmund Freud. In particular, these ideas have been increasingly discounted in the field of social sciences where the importance of the extra-rational and irrational element in our behavior has been receiving more and more attention. Of the many sources of the evidence that accumulated against the hypothesis of rationality, I shall mention only two.

The one—in spite of much more careful later work—may still be associated with the name of Gustave Le Bon, the founder or, at any rate, the first effective exponent of the psychology of crowds *(psychologie des foules)*. By showing up, though overstressing, the realities of human behavior when under the influence of agglomeration—in particular the sudden disappearance, in a state of excitement, of moral restraints and civilized modes of thinking and feeling, the sudden eruption of primitive impulses, infantilisms and criminal propensities—he made us face gruesome facts that everybody knew but nobody wished to see and he thereby dealt a serious blow to the picture of man's nature which underlies the classical doctrine of democracy and democratic folklore about revolutions. No doubt there is much to be said about the narrowness of the factual basis of Le Bon's inferences which, for instance, do not fit at all well the normal behavior of an English or Anglo-American crowd. Critics, especially those to whom the implications of this branch of social psychology were uncongenial, did not fail to make the most of its vulnerable points. But on the other hand it must not be forgotten that the phenomena of crowd psychology are by no means confined to mobs rioting in the narrow streets of a Latin town. Every parliament, every committee, every council of war composed of a dozen generals in their sixties, displays, in however mild a form, some of those features that stand out so glaringly in the case of the rabble, in particular a reduced sense of responsibility, a lower level of energy of thought and greater sensitiveness to nonlogical influences. Moreover, those phenomena are not confined to a crowd in the sense of a physical agglomeration of many people. Newspaper readers, radio audiences, members of a party even if not physically gathered together are terribly easy to work up into a psychological crowd and into a state of frenzy in which attempt at rational argument only spurs the animal spirits.

The other source of disillusioning evidence that I am going to mention is a much humbler one—no blood flows from it, only nonsense. Economists, learning to observe their facts more closely, have begun to discover that, even in the most ordinary currents of daily life, their consumers do not quite live up to the idea that the economic textbook used to convey. On the one hand their wants are nothing like as definite and their actions upon those wants nothing like as rational and prompt. On the other hand, they are so amenable to the influence of advertising and other methods of persuasion that producers often seem to dictate to them instead of being directed by them. The technique of successful advertising is particularly instructive. There is indeed nearly always some appeal to reason. But mere assertion, often repeated, counts more than rational argument and so does the direct attack upon the subconscious which takes the form of attempts to evoke and crystallize pleasant associations of an entirely extra-rational, very frequently of a sexual, nature.

The conclusion, while obvious, must be drawn with care. In the ordinary run of often repeated decisions the individual is subject to the salutary and rationalizing influence of favorable and unfavorable experience. He is also under the influence of relatively simple and unproblematical motives and interests which are but occasionally interfered with by excitement. Historically, the consumers' desire for shoes may, at least in part, have been shaped by the action of producers offering attractive footgear and campaigning for it; yet at any given time it is a genuine want, the definiteness of which extends beyond "shoes in general" and which prolonged experimenting clears of much of the irrationalities that may originally have surrounded it. Moreover, under the stimulus of those simple motives consumers learn to act upon unbiased expert advice about some things (houses, motorcars) and themselves become experts in others. It is simply not true that housewives are easily fooled in the matter of foods, *familiar* household articles, wearing apparel. And, as every salesman knows to his cost, most of them have a way of insisting on the exact article they want.

This of course holds true still more obviously on the producers' side of the picture. No doubt, a manufacturer may be indolent, a bad judge of opportunities or otherwise incompetent; but there is an effective mechanism that will reform or eliminate him. Again Taylorism rests on the fact that man may perform simple handicraft operations for thousands of years and yet perform them inefficiently. But neither the intention to act as rationally as possible nor a steady pressure toward rationality can seriously be called into question at whatever level of industrial or commercial activity we choose to look.

And so it is with most of the decisions of daily life that lie within the little field which the individual citizen's mind encompasses with a full sense of its reality. Roughly, it consists of the things that directly concern himself, his family, his business dealings, his hobbies, his friends and enemies, his township or ward, his class, church, trade union or any other social group of which he is an active member—the things under his personal observation, the things which are familiar to him independently of what his newspaper tells him, which he can directly influence or manage and for which he develops the kind of responsibility that is induced by a direct relation to the favorable or unfavorable effects of a course of action.

Once more: definiteness and rationality in thought and action* are not guaranteed by this familiarity with men and things or by that sense of reality or responsibility. Quite a few other conditions which often fail to be fulfilled would be necessary for that. For instance, generation after generation may suffer from irrational behavior in matters of hygiene and yet fail to link their sufferings with their noxious habits. As long as this is not done, objective consequences, however regular, of course do not produce subjective experience. Thus it proved unbelievably hard for humanity to realize the relation between infection and epidemics: the facts pointed to it with what to us seems unmistakable clearness; yet to the end of the eighteenth century doctors did next to nothing to keep people afflicted with infectious disease, such as measles or smallpox, from mixing with other people. And things must be expected to be still worse whenever there is not only inability but reluctance to recognize causal relations or when some interest fights against recognizing them.

Nevertheless and in spite of all the qualifications that impose themselves, there is for everyone, within a much wider horizon, a narrower field—widely differing in extent as between different groups and individuals and bounded by a broad zone rather than a sharp line—which is distinguished by a sense of reality or familiarity or responsibility. And this field harbors relatively definite individual volitions. These may often strike us as un-

*Rationality of thought and rationality of action are two different things. Rationality of thought does not always guarantee rationality of action. And the latter may be present without any conscious deliberation and irrespective of any ability to formulate the rationale of one's action correctly. The observer, particularly the observer who uses interview and questionnaire methods, often overlooks this and hence acquires an exaggerated idea of the importance of irrationality in behavior. This is another source of those overstatements which we meet so often.

intelligent, narrow, egotistical; and it may not be obvious to everyone why, when it comes to political decisions, we should worship at their shrine, still less why we should feel bound to count each of them for one and none of them for more than one. If, however, we do choose to worship we shall at least not find the shrine empty.

Now this comparative definiteness of volition and rationality of behavior does not suddenly vanish as we move away from those concerns of daily life in the home and in business which educate and discipline us. In the realm of public affairs there are sectors that are more within the reach of the citizen's mind than others. This is true, first, of local affairs. Even there we find a reduced power of discerning facts, a reduced preparedness to act upon them, a reduced sense of responsibility. We all know the man—and a very good specimen he frequently is—who says that the local administration is not his business and callously shrugs his shoulders at practices which he would rather die than suffer in his own office. High-minded citizens in a hortatory mood who preach the responsibility of the individual voter or taxpayer invariably discover the fact that this voter does not feel responsible for what the local politicians do. Still, especially in communities not too big for personal contacts, local patriotism may be a very important factor in "making democracy work." Also, the problems of a town are in many respects akin to the problems of a manufacturing concern. The man who understands the latter also understands, to some extent, the former. The manufacturer, grocer or workman need not step out of his world to have a rationally defensible view (that may of course be right or wrong) on street cleaning or town halls.

Second, there are many national issues that concern individuals and groups so directly and unmistakably as to evoke volitions that are genuine and definite enough. The most important instance is afforded by issues involving immediate and personal pecuniary profit to individual voters and groups of voters, such as direct payments, protective duties, silver policies and so on. Experience that goes back to antiquity shows that by and large voters react promptly and rationally to any such chance. But the classical doctrine of democracy evidently stands to gain little from displays of rationality of this kind. Voters thereby prove themselves bad and indeed corrupt judges of such issues, and often they even prove themselves bad judges of their own long-run interests, for it is only the short-run promise that tells politically and only short-run rationality that asserts itself effectively.

However, when we move still farther away from the private concerns of the family and the business office into those regions of national and international affairs that lack a direct and unmistakable link with those private concerns, individual volition, command of facts and method of inference soon cease to fulfill the requirements of the classical doctrine. What strikes me most of all and seems to me to be the core of the trouble is the fact that the sense of reality is so completely lost. Normally, the great political questions take their place in the psychic economy of the typical citizen with those leisure-hour interests that have not attained the rank of hobbies, and with the subjects of irresponsible conversation. These things seem so far off; they are not at all like a business proposition; dangers may not materialize at all and if they should they may not prove so very serious; one feels oneself to be moving in a fictitious world.

This reduced sense of reality accounts not only for a reduced sense of responsibility but also for the absence of effective volition. One has one's phrases, of course, and one's wishes and daydreams and grumbles; especially, one has one's likes and dislikes. But ordinarily they do not amount to what we call a will—the psychic counterpart of purposeful responsible action. In fact, for the private citizen musing over national affairs there is no scope for such a will and no task at which it could develop. He is a member of an unworkable committee, the committee of the whole nation, and this is why he expends less disciplined effort on mastering a political problem than he expends on a game of bridge.*

*It will help to clarify the point if we ask ourselves why so much more intelligence and clear-headedness show up at a bridge table than in, say, political discussion among non-polititians. At the bridge table we have a definite task; we have rules that discipline us; success and failure are clearly defined; and we are prevented from behaving irresponsibly because every mistake we

The reduced sense of responsibility and the absence of effective volition in turn explain the ordinary citizen's ignorance and lack of judgment in matters of domestic and foreign policy which are if anything more shocking in the case of educated people and of people who are successfully active in non-political walks of life than it is with uneducated people in humble stations. Information is plentiful and readily available. But this does not seem to make any difference. Nor should we wonder at it. We need only compare a lawyer's attitude to his brief and the same lawyer's attitude to the statements of political fact presented in his newspaper in order to see what is the matter. In the one case the lawyer has qualified for appreciating the relevance of his facts by years of purposeful labor done under the definite stimulus of interest in his professional competence; and under a stimulus that is no less powerful he then bends his acquirements, his intellect, his will to the contents of the brief. In the other case, he has not taken the trouble to qualify; he does not care to absorb the information or to apply to it the canons of criticism he knows so well how to handle; and he is impatient of long or complicated argument. All of this goes to show that without the initiative that comes from immediate responsibility, ignorance will persist in the face of masses of information however complete and correct. It persists even in the face of the meritorious efforts that are being made to go beyond presenting information and to teach the use of it by means of lectures, classes, discussion groups. Results are not zero. But they are small. People cannot be carried up the ladder.

Thus the typical citizen drops down to a lower level of mental performance as soon as he enters the political field. He argues and analyzes in a way which he would readily recognize as infantile within the sphere of his real interests. He becomes a primitive again. His thinking becomes associative and affective. And this entails two further consquences of ominous significance.

make will not only immediately tell us but also be immediately allocated to us. These conditions, by their failure to be fulfilled for the political behavior of the ordinary citizen, show why it is that in politics he lacks all the alertness and the judgment he may display in his profession.

First, even if there were no political groups
trying to influence him, the typical citizen
would in political matters tend to yield to extra-rational or irrational prejudice and impulse. The weakness of the rational processes
he applies to politics and the absence of effective logical control over the results he arrives
at would in themselves suffice to account for
that. Moreover, simply because he is not "all
there," he will relax his usual moral standards
as well and occasionally give in to dark urges
which the conditions of private life help him to
repress. But as to the wisdom or rationality of
his inferences and conclusions, it may be just
as bad if he gives in to a burst of generous
indignation. This will make it still more difficult for him to see things in their correct proportions or even to see more than one aspect
of one thing at a time. Hence, if for once he
does emerge from his usual vagueness and
does display the definite will postulated by the
classical doctrine of democracy, he is as likely
as not to become still more unintelligent and
irresponsible than he usually is. At certain
junctures, this may prove fatal to his nation.

Second, however, the weaker the logical
element in the processes of the public mind
and the more complete the absence of rational
criticism and of the rationalizing influence of
personal experience and responsibility, the
greater are the opportunities for groups with
an ax to grind. These groups may consist of
professional politicans or of exponents of an
economic interest or of idealists of one kind or
another or of people simply interested in stag-
ing and managing political shows. The sociology of such groups is immaterial to the argument at hand. The only point that matters
here is that, Human Nature in Politics being
what it is, they are able to fashion and, within
very wide limits, even to create the will of the
people. What we are confronted with in the
analysis of political processes is largely not a
genuine but a manufactured will. And often
this artefact is all that in reality corresponds to
the *volonté générale* of the classical doctrine. So
far as this is so, the will of the people is the
product and not the motive power of the political process.

The ways in which issues and the popular
will on any issue are being manufactured is
exactly analogous to the ways of commercial
advertising. We find the same attempts to contact the subconscious. We find the same technique of creating favorable and unfavorable
associations which are the more effective the
less rational they are. We find the same eva-
sions and reticences and the same trick of producing opinion by reiterated assertion that is
successful precisely to the extent to which it
avoids rational argument and the danger of
awakening the critical faculties of the people.
And so on. Only, all these arts have infinitely
more scope in the sphere of public affairs than
they have in the sphere of private and professional life. The picture of the prettiest girl
that ever lived will in the long run prove
powerless to maintain the sales of a bad cigarette. There is no equally effective safeguard
in the case of political decisions. Many decisions of fateful importance are of a nature
that makes it impossible for the public to experiment with them at its leisure and at moderate cost. Even if that is possible, however,
judgment is as a rule not so easy to arrive at as
it is in the case of the cigarette, because effects
are less easy to interpret.

But such arts also vitiate, to an extent quite
unknown in the field of commercial advertising, those forms of political advertising that
profess to address themselves to reason. To
the observer, the anti-rational or, at all events,
the extra-rational appeal and the defenseless-
ness of the victim stand out more and not less
clearly when cloaked in facts and arguments.
We have seen above why it is so difficult to
impart to the public unbiased information
about political problems and logically correct
inferences from it and why it is that information and arguments in political matters will
"register" only if they link up with the citizen's
preconceived ideas. As a rule, however, these
ideas are not definite enough to determine
particular conclusions. Since they can themselves be manufactured, effective political
argument almost inevitably implies the attempt to twist existing volitional premises into
a particular shape and not merely the attempt
to implement them or to help the citizen to
make up his mind.

Thus information and arguments that are
really driven home are likely to be the servants
of political intent. Since the first thing man will
do for his ideal or interest is to lie, we shall
expect, and as a matter of fact we find, that
effective information is almost always adulter-

ated or selective and that effective reasoning in politics consists mainly in trying to exalt certain propositions into axioms and to put others out of court; it thus reduces to the psycho-technics mentioned before. The reader who thinks me unduly pessimistic need only aks himself whether he has never heard—or said himself—that this or that awkward fact must not be told publicly, or that a certain line of reasoning, though valid, is undesirable. If men who according to any current standard are perfectly honorable or even high-minded reconcile themselves to the implications of this, do they not thereby show what they think about the merits or even the existence of the will of the people?

There are of course limits to all this. And there is truth in Jefferson's dictum that in the end the people are wiser than any single individual can be, or in Lincoln's about the impossibility of "fooling all the people all the time." But both dicta stress the long-run aspect in a highly significant way. It is no doubt possible to argue that given time the collective psyche will evolve opinions that not infrequently strike us as highly reasonable and even shrewd. History however consists of a succession of short-run situations that may alter the course of events for good. If all the people can in the short run be "fooled" step by step into something they do not really want, and if this is not an exceptional case which we could afford to neglect, then no amount of retrospect common sense will alter the fact that in reality they neither raise nor decide issues but that the issues that shape their fate are normally raised and decided for them. More than anyone else the lover of democracy has every reason to accept this fact and to clear his creed from the aspersion that it rests upon make-believe.

II. Another Theory of Democracy

Competition for Political Leadership

I think that most students of politics have by now come to accept the criticisms leveled at the classical doctrine of democracy in the preceding chapter. I also think that most of them agree, or will agree before long, in accepting another theory which is much truer to life and at the same time salvages much of what sponsors of the democratic method really mean by this term. Like the classical theory, it may be put into the nutshell of a definition.

It will be remembered that our chief troubles about the classical theory centered in the proposition that "the people" hold a definite and rational opinion about every individual question and that they give effect to this opinion—in a democracy—by choosing "representatives" who will see to it that that opinion is carried out. Thus the selection of the representatives is made secondary to the primary purpose of the democratic arrangement which is to vest the power of deciding political issues in the electorate. Suppose we reverse the roles of these two elements and make the deciding of issues by the electorate secondary to the election of the men who are to do the deciding. To put it differently, we now take the view that the role of the people is to produce a government, or else an intermediate body which in turn will produce a national executive or government. And we define: the democratic method is that institutional arrangement for arriving at political decisions in which individuals acquire the power to decide by means of a competitive struggle for the people's vote.

Defense and explanation of this idea will speedily show that, as to both plausibility of assumptions and tenability of propositions, it greatly improves the theory of the democratic process.

First of all, we are provided with a reasonably efficient criterion by which to distinguish democratic governments from others. We have seen that the classical theory meets with difficulties on that score because both the will and the good of the people may be, and in many historical instances have been, served just as well or better by governments that cannot be described as democratic according to any accepted usage of the term. Now we are in a somewhat better position partly because we are resolved to stress a *modus procedendi* the presence or absence of which it is in most cases easy to verify.

For instance, a parliamentary monarchy like the English one fulfills the requirements of the democratic method because the monarch is practically constrained to appoint to cabinet office the same people as parliament would elect. A "constitutional" monarchy does not qualify to be called democratic because electorates and parliaments, while having all the other rights that electorates and parliaments have in parliamentary monarchies, lack the power to impose their choice as to the governing committee: the cabinet ministers are in this case servants of the monarch, in substance as well as in name, and can in principle be dismissed as well as appointed by him. Such an arrangement may satisfy the people. The electorate may reaffirm this fact by voting against any proposal for change. The monarch may be so popular as to be able to defeat any competition for the supreme office. But since no machinery is provided for making this competition effective the case does not come within our definition.

Second, the theory embodied in this definition leaves all the room we may wish to have for a proper recognition of the vital fact of leadership. The classical theory did not do this but, as we have seen, attributed to the electorate an altogether unrealistic degree of initiative which practically amounted to ignoring leadership. But collectives act almost exclusively by accepting leadership—this is the dominant mechanism of practically any collective action which is more than a reflex. Propositions about the working and the results of the democratic method that take account of this are bound to be infinitely more realistic than propositions which do not. They will not stop at the execution of a *volonté générale* but will go some way toward showing how it emerges or how it is substituted or faked. What we have termed Manufactured Will is no longer outside the theory, an aberration for the absence of which we piously pray; it enters on the ground floor as it should.

Third, however, so far as there are genuine group-wise volitions at all—for instance the will of the unemployed to receive unemployment benefit or the will of other groups to help—our theory does not neglect them. On the contrary we are now able to insert them in exactly the role they actually play. Such volitions do not as a rule assert themselves directly. Even if strong and definite they remain latent, often for decades, until they are called to life by some political leader who turns them into political factors. This he does, or else his agents do it for him, by organizing these volitions, by working them up and by including eventually appropriate items in his competitive offering. The interaction between sectional interests and public opinion and the way in which they produce the pattern we call the political situation appear from this angle in a new and much clearer light.

Fourth, our theory is of course no more definite than is the concept of competition for leadership. This concept presents similar difficulties as the concept of competition in the economic sphere, with which it may be usefully compared. In economic life competition is never completely lacking, but hardly ever is it perfect. Similarly, in political life there is always some competition, though perhaps only a potential one, for the allegiance of the people. To simplify matters we have restricted the kind of competition for the leadership which is to define democracy, to free competition for a free vote. The justification for this is that democracy seems to imply a recognized method by which to conduct the competitive struggle, and that the electoral method is practically the only one available for communities of any size. But though his excludes many ways of securing leadership which should be excluded, such as competition by military insurrection, it does not exclude the cases that are strikingly analogous to the economic phenomena we label "unfair" or "fraudulent" competition or restraint of competition. And we cannot exclude them because if we did we should be left with a completely unrealistic ideal. Between this ideal case which does not exist and the cases in which all competition with the established leader is prevented by force, there is a continuous range of variation within which the democratic method of government shades off into the autocratic one by imperceptible steps. But if we wish to understand and not to philosophize, this is as it should be. The value of our criterion is not seriously impaired thereby.

Fifth, our theory seems to clarify the relation that subsists between democracy and individual freedom. If by the latter we mean the existence of a sphere of individual self-government the boundaries of which are historically variable—*no* society tolerates absolute freedom even of conscience and of speech, *no* society reduces that sphere to zero—the question clearly becomes a matter of degree. We have seen that the democratic method does not necessarily guarantee a greater amount of individual freedom than another political method would permit in similar circumstances. It may well be the other way round. But there is still a relation between the two. If, on principle at least, everyone is free to compete for political leadership by presenting himself to the electorate, this will in most cases though not in all mean a considerable amount of freedom of discussion *for all*. In particular it will normally mean a considerable amount of freedom of the press. This relation between democracy and freedom is not absolutely stringent and can be tampered with. But, from the standpoint of the intellectual, it is nevertheless very important. At the same time, it is all there is to that relation.

Sixth, it should be observed that in making it the primary function of the electorate to produce a government (directly or through an intermediate body) I intended to include in this phrase also the function of evicting it. The one means simply the acceptance of a leader or a group of leaders, the other means simply the withdrawal of this acceptance. This takes care of an element the reader may have missed. He may have thought that the electorate controls as well as installs. But since electorates normally do not control their political leaders in any way except by refusing to reelect them or the parliamentary majorities that support them, it seems well to reduce our ideas about this control in the way indicated by our definition. Occasionally, spontaneous revulsions occur which upset a government or an individual minister directly or else enforce a certain course of action. But they are not only exceptional, they are, as we shall see, contrary to the spirit of the democratic method.

Seventh, our theory sheds much-needed light on an old controversy. Whoever accepts the classical doctrine of democracy and in consequence believes that the democratic method is to guarantee that issues be decided and policies framed according to the will of the people must be struck by the fact that, even if that will were undeniably real and definite, decision by simple majorities would in many cases distort it rather than give effect to it. Evidently the will of the majority is the will of the majority and not the will of "the people." The latter is a mosaic that the former completely fails to "represent." To equate both by definition is not to solve the problem. Attempts at real solutions have however been made by the authors of the various plans for Proportional Representation.

These plans have met with adverse criticism on practical grounds. It is in fact obvious not only that proportional representation will offer opportunities for all sorts of idiosyncrasies to assert themselves but also that it may prevent democracy from producing efficient governments and thus prove a danger in times of stress. But before concluding that democracy becomes unworkable if its principle is carried out consistently, it is just as well to ask ourselves whether this principle really implies proportional representation. As a matter of fact it does not. If acceptance of leadership is the true function of the electorate's vote, the case for proportional representation collapses because its premises are no longer binding. The principle of democracy then merely means that the reins of government should be handed to those who command more support than do any of the competing individuals or teams. And this in turn seems to assure the standing of the majority system within the logic of the democratic method, although we might still condemn it on grounds that lie outside of that logic.

Majority Rule

Friedrich A. Hayek

Like Schumpeter, Friedrich Hayek sees a limited but important role for democratic processes. Hayek begins by distinguishing democracy from liberalism, arguing that liberalism offers the sounder theory of government. Majority rule should be understood as a means to an end, not as the end itself; by understanding it that way, he claims, we can see clearly democracy's real advantages as well as the limitations that should be placed on democratic processes. Although democratic procedures are justified as a method of settling disputes, they do not guarantee the correct decision. For that task, he argues, society must rely on political philosophers for guidance.

Though men be much governed by interest, yet even interest itself, and all human affairs, are entirely governed by opinion.
—David Hume

1. Equality before the law leads to the demand that all men should also have the same share in making the law. This is the point where traditional liberalism and the democratic movement meet. Their main concerns are nevertheless different. Liberalism (in the European nineteenth-century meaning of the word, to which we shall adhere throughout this chapter) is concerned mainly with limiting the coercive powers of all government, whether democratic or not, whereas the dogmatic democrat knows only one limit to government—current majority opinion. The difference between the two ideals stands out most clearly if we name their opposites: for democracy it is authoritarian government; for liberalism it is totalitarianism. Neither of the two systems necessarily excludes the opposite of the other: a democracy may well wield totalitarian powers, and it is conceivable that an authoritarian government may act on liberal principles.

Like most terms in our field, the word "democracy" is also used in a wider and vaguer sense. But if it is used strictly to describe a

From Friedrich A. Hayek, *The Constitution of Liberty* (Chicago: University of Chicago Press, 1960), pp. 103–117. Reprinted by permission.

method of government—namely, majority rule—it clearly refers to a problem different from that of liberalism. Liberalism is a doctrine about what the law ought to be, democracy a doctrine about the manner of determining what will be the law. Liberalism regards it as desirable that only what the majority accepts should in fact be law, but it does not believe that this is therefore necessarily good law. Its aim, indeed, is to persuade the majority to observe certain principles. It accepts majority rule as a method of deciding, but not as an authority for what the decision ought to be. To the doctrinaire democrat the fact that the majority wants something is sufficient ground for regarding it as good; for him the will of the majority determines not only what is law but what is good law.

About this difference between the liberal and the democratic ideal there exists widespread agreement. There are, however, those who use the word "liberty" in the sense of political liberty and are led by this to identify liberalism with democracy. For them the ideal of liberty can say nothing about what the aim of democratic action ought to be: every condition that democracy creates is, by definition, a condition of liberty. This seems, to say the least, a very confusing use of words.

While liberalism is one of those doctrines concerning the scope and purpose of government from which democracy has to choose, the latter, being a method, indicates nothing about the aims of government. Though "democratic" is often used today to describe particular aims of policy that happen to be popular, especially certain egalitarian ones, there is no necessary connection between democracy and any one view about how the powers of the majority ought to be used. In order to know what it is that we want others to accept, we need other criteria than the current opinion of the majority, which is an irrelevant factor in the process by which opinion is formed. It certainly provides no answer to the question of how a man ought to vote or of what is desirable—unless we assume, as many of the dogmatic democrats seem to assume, that a person's class position invariably teaches him to recognize his true interests and that therefore the vote of the majority always expresses the best interests of the majority.

2. The current undiscriminating use of the word "democratic" as a general term of praise is not without danger. It suggests that, because democracy is a good thing, it is always a gain for mankind if it is extended. This may sound self-evident, but it is nothing of the kind.

There are at least two respects in which it is almost always possible to extend democracy: the range of persons entitled to vote and the range of issues that are decided by democratic procedure. In neither respect can it be seriously contended that every possible extension is a gain or that the principle of democracy demands that it be indefinitely extended. Yet in the discussion of almost any particular issue the case for democracy is commonly presented as if the desirability of extending it as far as possible were indisputable.

That this is not so is implicitly admitted by practically everybody so far as the right to vote is concerned. It would be difficult on any democratic theory to regard every possible extension of the franchise as an improvement. We speak of universal adult suffrage, but the limits of suffrage are in fact largely determined by considerations of expediency. The usual age limit of twenty-one and the exclusion of criminals, resident foreigners, non-resident citizens, and the inhabitants of special regions or territories are generally accepted as reasonable. It is also by no means obvious that proportional representation is better because it seems more democratic. It

can scarcely be said that equality before the law necessarily requires that all adults should have the vote; the principle would operate if the same impersonal rule applied to all. If only persons over forty, or only income-earners, or only heads of households, or only literate persons were given the vote, this would scarcely be more of an infringement of the principle than the restrictions which are generally accepted. It is also possible for reasonable people to argue that the ideals of democracy would be better served if, say, all the servants of government or all recipients of public charity were excluded from the vote. If in the Western world universal adult suffrage seems the best arrangement, this does not prove that it is required by some basic principle.

We should also remember that the right of the majority is usually recognized only within a given country and that what happens to be one country is not always a natural or obvious unit. We certainly do not regard it as right that the citizens of a large country should dominate those of a small adjoining country merely because they are more numerous. There is as little reason why the majority of the people who have joined for some purposes, be it as a nation or some supernational organization, should be regarded as entitled to extend the scope of their power as far as they please. The current theory of democracy suffers from the fact that it is usually developed with some ideal homogeneous community in view and then applied to the very imperfect and often arbitrary units which the existing states constitute.

These remarks are meant only to show that even the most dogmatic democrat can hardly claim that every extension of democracy is a good thing. However strong the general case for democracy, it is not an ultimate or absolute value and must be judged by what it will achieve. It is probably the best method of achieving certain ends, but not an end in itself. Though there is a strong presumption in favor of the democratic method of deciding where it is obvious that some collective action is required, the problem of whether or not it is desirable to extend collective control must be decided on other grounds than the principle of democracy as such.

3. The democratic and the liberal traditions thus agree that whenever state action is re-

quired, and particularly whenever coercive rules have to be laid down, the decision ought to be made by the majority. They differ, however, on the scope of the state action that is to be guided by democratic decision. While the dogmatic democrat regards it as desirable that as many issues as possible be decided by majority vote, the liberal believes that there are definite limits to the range of questions which should be thus decided. The dogmatic democrat feels, in particular, that any current majority ought to have the right to decide what powers it has and how to exercise them, while the liberal regards it as important that the powers of any temporary majority be limited by long-term principles. To him it is not from a mere act of will of the momentary majority but from a wider agreement on common principles that a majority decision derives its authority.

The crucial conception of the doctrinaire democrat is that of popular sovereignty. This means to him that majority rule is unlimited and unlimitable. The ideal of democracy, originally intended to prevent all arbitrary power, thus becomes the justification for a new arbitrary power. Yet the authority of democratic decision rests on its being made by the majority of a community which is held together by certain beliefs common to most members; and it is necessary that the majority submit to these common principles even when it may be in its immediate interest to violate them. It is irrelevant that this view used to be expressed in terms of the "law of nature" or the "social contract," conceptions which have lost their appeal. The essential point remains: it is the acceptance of such common principles that makes a collection of people a community. And this common acceptance is the indispensable condition for a free society. A group of men normally become a society not by giving themselves laws but by obeying the same rules of conduct. This means that the power of the majority is limited by those commonly held principles and that there is no legitimate power beyond them. Clearly, it is necessary for people to come to an agreement as to how necessary tasks are to be performed, and it is reasonable that this should be decided by the majority; but it is not obvious that this same majority must also be entitled to determine

what it is competent to do. There is no reason why there should not be things which nobody has power to do. Lack of sufficient agreement on the need of certain uses of coercive power should mean that nobody can legitimately exercise it. If we recognize rights of minorities, this implies that the power of the majority ultimately derives from, and is limited by, the principles which the minorities also accept.

The principle that whatever government does should be agreed to by the majority does not therefore necessarily require that the majority be morally entitled to do what it likes. There can clearly be no moral justification for any majority granting its members privileges by laying down rules which discriminate in their favor. Democracy is not necessarily unlimited government. Nor is a democratic government any less in need of built-in safeguards of individual liberty than any other. It was, indeed, at a comparatively late stage in the history of modern democracy that great demagogues began to argue that since the power was now in the hands of the people, there was no longer any need for limiting that power. It is when it is contended that "in a democracy right is what the majority makes it to be" that democracy degenerates into demogoguery.

4. If democracy is a means rather than an end, its limits must be determined in the light of the purpose we want it to serve. There are three chief arguments by which democracy can be justified, each of which may be regarded as conclusive. The first is that, whenever it is necessary that one of several conflicting opinions should prevail and when one would have to be made to prevail by force if need be, it is less wasteful to determine which has the stronger support by counting numbers than by fighting. Democracy is the only method of peaceful change that man has yet discovered.

The second argument, which historically has been the most important and which is still very important, though we can no longer be sure that it is always valid, is that democracy is an important safeguard of indiviual liberty. It was once said by a seventeenth-century writer that "the good of democracy is liberty, and the courage and industry which liberty begets."[1] This view recognizes, of course, that democracy is not yet liberty; it contends only that it is more likely than other forms of government to

produce liberty. This view may be well founded so far as the prevention of coercion of individuals by other individuals is concerned: it
can scarcely be to the advantage of a majority
that some individuals should have the power
arbitrarily to coerce others. But the protection
of the individual against the collective action
of the majority itself is another matter. Even
here it can be argued that, since coercive power must in fact always be exercised by a few, it
is less likely to be abused if the power entrusted to the few can always be revoked by
those who have to submit to it. But if the
prospects of individual liberty are better in a
democracy than under other forms of government, this does not mean that they are certain.
The prospects of liberty depend on whether
or not the majority makes it its deliberate object. It would have little chance of surviving if
we relied on the mere existence of democracy
to preserve it.

The third argument rests on the effect
which the existence of democratic institutions
will have on the general level of understanding of public affairs. This seems to me the
most powerful. It may well be true, as has been
often maintained, that, in any given state of
affairs, government by some educated elite
would be a more efficient and perhaps even a
more just government than one chosen by
majority vote. The crucial point, however, is
that, in comparing the democratic form of
government with others, we cannot take the
understanding of the issues by the people at
any time as a datum. It is the burden of the
argument of Tocqueville's great work, *Democracy in America,* that democracy is the only
effective method of educating the majority.
This is as true today as it was in his time.
Democracy is, above all, a process of forming
opinion. Its chief advantage lies not in its
method of selecting those who govern but in
the fact that, because a great part of the population takes an active part in the formation of
opinion, a correspondingly wide range of persons is available from which to select. We may
admit that democracy does not put power in
the hands of the wisest and best informed and
that at any given moment the decision of a
government by an elite might be more beneficial to the whole; but this need not prevent us
from still giving democracy the preference. It

is in this dynamic, rather than in its static,
aspects that the value of democracy proves
itself. As is true of liberty, the benefits of
democracy will show themselves only in the
long run, while its more immediate achievements may well be inferior to those of other
forms of government.

5. The conception that government should
be guided by majority opinion makes sense
only if that opinion is independent of government. The ideal of democracy rests on the
belief that the view which will direct government emerges from an independent and
spontaneous process. It requires, therefore,
the existence of a large sphere independent of
majority control in which the opinions of the
individuals are formed. There is widespread
consensus that for this reason the case for
democracy and the case for freedom of speech
and discussion are inseparable.

The view, however, that democracy provides not merely a method of settling differences of opinion on the course of action to be
adopted but also a standard for what opinion
ought to be has already had far-reaching
effects. It has, in particular, seriously confused
the question of what is actually valid law and
what ought to be the law. If democracy is to
function, it is as important that the former can
always be ascertained as that the latter can
always be questioned. Majority decisions tell us
what people want at the moment, but not what
it would be in their interest to want if they
were better informed; and, unless they could
be changed by persuasion, they would be of no
value. The argument for democracy presupposes that any minority opinion may become a majority one.

It would not be necessary to stress this if it
were not for the fact that it is sometimes represented as the duty of the democrat, and particularly of the democratic intellectual, to accept
the views and values of the majority. True,
there is the convention that the view of the
majority should prevail so far as collective action is concerned, but this does not in the least
mean that one should not make every effort to
alter it. One may have profound respect for
that convention and yet very little for the wisdom of the majority. It is only because the
majority opinion will always be opposed by
some that our knowledge and understanding

progress. In the process by which opinion is formed, it is very probable that, by the time any view becomes a majority view, it is no longer the best view: somebody will already have advanced beyond the point which the majority have reached. It is because we do not yet know which of the many competing new opinions will prove itself the best that we wait until it has gained sufficient support.

The conception that the efforts of all should be directed by the opinion of the majority or that a society is better according as it conforms more to the standards of the majority is in fact a reversal of the principle by which civilization has grown. Its general adoption would probably mean the stagnation, if not the decay, of civilization. Advance consists in the few convincing the many. New views must appear somewhere before they can become majority views. There is no experience of society which is not first the experience of a few individuals. Nor is the process of forming majority opinion entirely, or even chiefly, a matter of discussion, as the overintellectualized conception would have it. There is some truth in the view that democracy is government by discussion, but this refers only to the last stage of the process by which the merits of alternative views and desires are tested. Though discussion is essential, it is not the main process by which people learn. Their views and desires are formed by individuals acting according to their own designs; and they profit from what others have learned in their individual experience. Unless some people know more than the rest and are in a better position to convince the rest, there would be little progress in opinion. It is because we normally do not know who knows best that we leave the decision to a process which we do not control. But it is always from a minority acting in ways different from what the majority would describe that the majority in the end learns to do better.

6. We have no ground for crediting majority decisions with that higher, superindividual wisdom which, in a certain sense, the products of spontaneous social growth may possess. The resolutions of a majority are not the place to look for such superior wisdom. They are bound, if anything, to be inferior to the decisions that the most intelligent members of the group will make after listening to all opinions: they will be the result of less careful thought and will generally represent a compromise that will not fully satisfy anybody. This will be even more true of the cumulative result emanating from the successive decisions of shifting majorities variously composed: the result will be the expression not of a coherent conception but of different and often conflicting motives and aims.

Such a process should not be confused with those spontaneous processes which free communities have learned to regard as the source of much that is better than individual wisdom can contrive. If by "social process" we mean the gradual evolution which produces better solutions than deliberate design, the imposition of the will of the majority can hardly be regarded as such. The latter differs radically from that free growth from which custom and institutions emerge, because its coercive, monopolistic, and exclusive character destroys the self-correcting forces which bring it about in a free society that mistaken efforts will be abandoned and the successful ones prevail. It also differs basically from the cumulative process by which law is formed by precedent, unless it is, as is true of judicial decisions, fused into a coherent whole by the fact that principles followed on earlier occasions are deliberately adhered to.

Moreover, majority decisions are peculiarly liable, if not guided by accepted common principles, to produce over-all results that nobody wanted. It often happens that a majority is forced by its own decisions to further actions that were neither contemplated nor desired. The belief that collective action can dispense with principles is largely an illusion, and the usual effect of its renouncing principles is that it is driven into a course by the unexpected implications of former decisions. The individual decision may have been intended only to deal with a particular situation. But it creates the expectation that wherever similar circumstances occur the government will take similar action. Thus principles which had never been intended to apply generally, which may be undesirable or nonsensical when applied generally, bring about future action that few would have desired in the first instance. A government that claims to be committed to no principles and to judge every problem on its merits usually finds itself having to observe principles not of its own choosing and being led into action that it had never contemplated. A phenomenon which is now familiar to us is that of governments which start out with the proud claim that they will deliberately control all affairs and soon find themselves beset at each step by the necessities created by their former actions. It is since governments have come to regard themselves as omnipotent that we now hear so much about the necessity or inevitability of their doing this or that which they know to be unwise.

7. If the politician or statesman has no choice but to adopt a certain course of action (or if his action is regarded as inevitable by the historian), this is because his or other people's opinion, not objective facts, allow him no alternative. It is only to people who are influenced by certain beliefs that anyone's response to given events may appear to be uniquely determined by circumstances. For the practical politician concerned with particular issues, these beliefs are indeed unalterable facts to all intents and purposes. It is almost necessary that he be unoriginal, that he fashion his program from opinions held by large numbers of people. The successful politician owes his power to the fact that he moves within the accepted framework of thought, that he thinks and talks conventionally. It would be almost a contradiction in terms for a politician to be a leader in the field of ideas. His task in a democracy is to find out what the opinions held by the largest number are, not to give currency to new opinions which may become the majority view in some distant future.

The state of opinion which governs a decision on political issues is always the result of a slow evolution, extending over long periods and proceeding at many different levels. New ideas start among a few and gradually spread until they become the possession of a majority who know little of their origin. In modern society this process involves a division of functions between those who are concerned mainly with the particular issues and those who are occupied with general ideas, with elaborating and reconciling the various principles of action which past experience has suggested. Our views both about what the consequences of our actions will be and about what we ought to aim at are mainly precepts that we have acquired as part of the inheritance of our society. These political and moral views, no less than our scientific beliefs, come to us from those who professionally handle abstract ideas. It is from them that both the ordinary man and the political leader obtain the fundamental conceptions that constitute the framework of their thought and guide them in their action.

The belief that in the long run it is ideas and therefore the men who give currency to new ideas that govern evolution, and the belief that the individual steps in that process should be governed by a set of coherent conceptions, have long formed a fundamental part of the liberal creed. It is impossible to study history without becoming aware of "the lesson given to mankind by every age, and always disregarded—that speculative philosophy, which to the superficial appears a thing so remote from the business of life and the outward interest of men, is in reality the thing on earth which most influences them, and in the long run overbears any influences save those it must itself obey."[2] Though this fact is perhaps even less understood today than it was when John Stuart Mill wrote, there can be little doubt that it is true at all times, whether men recognize it or not. It is so little understood because the influence of the abstract thinker on the masses operates only indirectly. People rarely know or care whether the commonplace ideas of their day have come to them from Aristotle or Locke, Rousseau or Marx, or from some professor whose views were fashionable among the intellectuals twenty years ago. Most of them have never read the works or even heard the names of the authors whose conceptions and ideals have become part of their thinking.

So far as direct influence on current affairs is concerned, the influence of the political philosopher may be negligible. But when his ideas have become common property, through the work of historians and publicists, teachers and writers, and intellectuals generally, they effectively guide developments. This means not only that new ideas commonly begin to exercise their influence on political action only a generation or more after they have first been stated but that, before the contributions of the speculative thinker can exercise such influence, they have to pass through a long process of selection and modification.

Changes in political and social beliefs necessarily proceed at any one time at many different levels. We must conceive of the process not as expanding over one plane but as filtering slowly downward from the top of a pyramid, where the higher levels represent greater generality and abstraction and not necessarily greater wisdom. As ideas spread downward, they also change their character. Those which are at any time still on a high level of generality will compete only with others of similar character, and only for the support of people interested in general conceptions. To the great majority these general conceptions will become known only in their application to concrete and particular issues. Which of these ideas will reach them and gain their support will be determined not by some single mind but by discussion proceeding on another level, among people who are concerned more with general ideas than with particular problems and who, in consequence, see the latter mainly in the light of general principles.

Except on rare occasions, such as constitutional conventions, the democratic process of discussion and majority decision is necessarily confined to part of the whole system of law and government. The piecemeal change which this involves will produce desirable and workable results only if it is guided by some general conception of the social order desired, some coherent image of the kind of world in which the people want to live. To achieve such an image is not a simple task, and even the specialist student can do no more than endeavor to see a little more clearly than his predecessors. The practical man concerned with the immediate problems of the day has neither the interest nor the time to examine the interrelations of the different parts of the complex order of society. He merely chooses from among the possible orders that are offered him and finally accepts a political doctrine or set of principles elaborated and presented by others.

If people were not at most times led by some system of common ideas, neither a coherent policy nor even real discussion about particular issues would be possible. It is doubtful whether democracy can work in the long run if the great majority do not have in common at least a general conception of the type of society desired. But even if such a conception exists, it will not necessarily show itself in every majority decision. Groups do not always act in accordance with their best knowledge or obey moral rules that they recognize in the abstract any more than individuals do. It is only by appealing to such common principles, however, that we can hope to reach agreement by discussion, to settle conflict of interests by reasoning and argument rather than by brute force.

8. If opinion is to advance, the theorist who offers guidance must not regard himself as bound by majority opinion. The task of the political philosopher is different from that of the expert servant who carries out the will of the majority. Though he must not arrogate to himself the position of a "leader" who determines what people ought to think, it is his duty to show possibilities and consequences of common action, to offer comprehensive aims of policy as a whole which the majority have not yet thought of. It is only after such a comprehensive picture of the possible results of different policies has been presented that democracy can decide what it wants. If politics is the art of the possible, political philosophy is the art of making politically possible the seemingly impossible.

The political philosopher cannot discharge his task if he confines himself to questions of fact and is afraid of deciding between conflicting values. He cannot allow himself to be limited by the positivism of the scientist, which confines his functions to showing what is the case and forbids any discussion of what ought to be. If he does so, he will have to stop long before he has performed his most important function. In his effort to form a coherent picture he will often find that there are values which conflict with one another—a fact which most people are not aware of—and that he must choose which he should accept and which reject. Unless the political philosopher is prepared to defend values which seem right to him, he will never achieve that comprehensive outline which must then be judged as a whole.

In this task he will often serve democracy

best by opposing the will of the majority. Only a complete misapprehension of the process by which opinion progresses would lead one to argue that in the sphere of opinion he ought to submit to majority views. To treat existing majority opinion as the standard for what majority opinion ought to be would make the whole process circular and stationary. There is, in fact, never so much reason for the political philosopher to suspect himself of failing in his task as when he finds that his opinions are very popular. It is by insisting on considerations which the majority do not wish to take into account, by holding up principles which they regard as inconvenient and irksome, that he has to prove his worth. For intellectuals to bow to a belief merely because it is held by the majority is a betrayal not only to their peculiar mission but of the values of democracy itself.

The principles that plead for the self-limitation of the power of the majority are not proved wrong if democracy disregards them, nor is democracy proved undesirable if it often makes what the liberal must regard as the wrong decision. He simply believes that he has an argument which, when properly understood, will induce the majority to limit the exercise of its own powers and which he hopes it can be persuaded to accept as a guide when deciding on particular issues.

9. It is not the least part of this liberal argument that to disregard those limits will, in the long run, destroy not only prosperity and peace but democracy itself. The liberal believes that the limits which he wants democracy to impose upon itself are also the limits within which it can work effectively and within which the majority can truly direct and control the actions of government. So long as democracy constrains the individual only by general rules of its own making, it controls the power of coercion. If it attempts to direct them more specifically, it will soon find itself merely indicating the ends to be achieved while leaving to its expert servants the decision as to the manner in which they are to be achieved. And once it is generally accepted that majority decisions can merely indicate ends and that the pursuit of them is to be left to the discretion of the administrators, it will soon be believed also

that almost any means to achieve those ends are legitimate.

The individual has little reason to fear any general laws which the majority may pass, but he has much reason to fear the rulers it may put over him to implement its directions. It is not the powers which democratic assemblies can effectively wield but the powers which they hand over to the administrators charged with the achievement of particular goals that constitute the danger to individual freedom today. Having agreed that the majority should prescribe rules which we will obey in pursuit of our individual aims, we find ourselves more and more subjected to the orders and the arbitrary will of its agents. Significantly enough, we find not only that most of the supporters of unlimited democracy soon become defenders of arbitrariness and of the view that we should trust experts to decide what is good for the community, but that the most enthusiastic supporters of such unlimited powers of the majority are often those very administrators who know best that, once such powers are assumed, it will be they and not the majority who will in fact exercise them. If anything has been demonstrated by modern experience in these matters, it is that, once wide coercive powers are given to governmental agencies for particular purposes, such powers cannot be effectively controlled by democratic assemblies. If the latter do not themselves determine the means to be employed, the decisions of their agents will be more or less arbitrary.

General considerations and recent experience both show that democracy will remain effective only so long as government in its coercive action confines itself to tasks that can be carried out democratically. If democracy is a means of preserving liberty, then individual liberty is no less an essential condition for the working of democracy. Though democracy is probably the best form of limited government, it becomes an absurdity if it turns into unlimited government. Those who profess that democracy is all-competent and support all that the majority wants at any given moment are working for its fall. The old liberal is in fact a much better friend of democracy than the dogmatic democrat, for he is concerned with preserving the conditions that make democracy workable. It is not "antidemocratic" to try to persuade the majority that there are limits beyond which its action ceases to be beneficial and that it should observe principles which are not of its own deliberate making. If it is to survive, democracy must recognize that it is not the fountainhead of justice and that it needs to acknowledge a conception of justice which does not necessarily manifest itself in the popular view on every particular issue. The danger is that we mistake a means of securing justice for justice itself. Those who endeavor to persuade majorities to recognize proper limits to their just power are therefore as necessary to the democratic process as those who constantly point to new goals for democratic action.

Notes

1. Sir John Culpepper, *An Exact Collection of All the Remonstrances* (London, 1643), p. 266.
2. J. S. Mill, "Bentham" (London and Westminster Review, 1838), reprinted in *Dissertations and Discussions*, 3d Ed. (London, 1875), p. 330.

A Participatory Theory of Democracy

Carole Pateman

In this essay, taken from her book Participation and Democratic Theory, *Carole Pateman explains and defends a participatory theory of democracy based on three thinkers: J. J. Rousseau, J. S. Mill, and G. D. H. Cole. According to contemporary critics of the classical view, such as Schumpeter, the classical theory is both unrealistic in its assessment of voters and blind to the importance of leadership. According to those critics, voters are a relatively unimportant part of the political process, and although popular education is important for stability, too much political participation is dangerous. Pateman is concerned to meet the criticisms. The ideal, for the classical theorists, was of "rational and active democratic man"—an ideal they believed could only be realized through education and industrial organization. In the context of their argument, she claims, that ideal is both attractive and workable.*

Rousseau might be called the theorist *par excellence* of participation, and an understanding of the nature of the political system that he describes in *The Social Contract* is vital for the theory of participatory democracy. Rousseau's entire political theory hinges on the individual participation of each citizen in political decision making and in his theory participation is very much more than a protective adjunct to a set of institutional arrangements; it also has a psychological effect on the participants, ensur-

From Carole Pateman, *Participation and Democratic Theory* (Cambridge: Cambridge University Press, 1970), pp. 22–44. Reprinted by permission. Some footnotes omitted.

ing that there is a continuing interrelationship between the working of institutions and the psychological qualities and attitudes of individuals interacting within them. It is their stress on this aspect of particpation and its place at the centre of their theories that marks the distinctive contribution of the theorists of participatory democracy to democratic theory as a whole. Although Rousseau was writing before the modern institutions of democracy were developed, and his ideal society is a non-industrial city-state, it is in his theory that the basic hypotheses about the function of participation in a democratic polity can be found.[1]

In order to understand the role of participation in Rousseau's political theory it is essential to be clear about the nature of his ideal participatory political system, as this has been subject to widely differing interpretations. Firstly, Rousseau argued that certain economic conditions were necessary for a participatory system. As is well known Rousseau advocated a society made up of small, peasant proprietors, i.e. he advocated a society of economic equality and economic independence. His theory does not require absolute equality as is often implied, but rather that the differences that do exist should not lead to political inequality. Ideally, there should be a situation where no 'citizen shall be rich enough to buy another and none so poor as to be forced to sell himself' and the vital requirement is for each man to own some property— the most sacred of the citizen's rights—because the security and independence that this gives to the individual is the necessary basis on which rest his political equality and political independence.[2]

If these conditions are established the citizens can assemble as equal and independent individuals, yet Rousseau also wanted them to be interdependent, the latter being necessary if the independence and equality are to be preserved. This is not so paradoxical as it sounds because the participatory situation is such that each citizen would be powerless to do anything without the co-operation of all the others, or of the majority. Each citizen would be, as he puts it, 'excessively dependent on the republic' (1968, p. 99, bk. II, ch. 12), i.e. there would be an equal dependence of each individual on all the others viewed collectively as sovereign, and independent participation is the mechanism whereby this interdependence is enforced. The way in which it works is both simple and subtle. It is possible to read the *Social Contract* as an elaboration of the idea that laws, not men, should rule, but an even better formulation of the role of participation is that men are to be ruled by the logic of the operation of the political situation that they had themselves created and that this situation was such that the possibility of the rule of individual men was 'automatically' precluded. It is because the citizens are independent equals, not dependent on anyone else for their vote or opinion, that in the political assembly no one need vote for any policy that is not as much to his advantage as to the advantage of any other. Individual X will be unable to persuade others to vote for his proposal that gives X alone some advantage. In a crucial passage in the *Social Contract* Rousseau asks 'how should it be that the general will is always rightful and that all men constantly wish the happiness of each but for the fact that there is no one who does not take that word "each" to pertain to himself and in voting for all think of himself?'[3] In other words, the only policy that will be acceptable to all is the one where any benefits and burdens are equally shared; the participatory process ensures that political equality is made effective in the decision-making assembly. The substantive policy result is that the general will is, tautologically, always just (i.e affects all equally) so that at the same time individual rights and interests are protected and the public interest furthered. The law has 'emerged' from the participatory process and it is the law, not men, that governs individual actions.[4]

Rousseau thought that the ideal situation for decision making was one where no organised groups were present, just individuals, because the former might be able to make their 'particular wills' prevail. Rousseau's remarks about groups follow directly from what he says about the operation of the participatory process. He recognised that there would inevitably be 'tacit associations', i.e. unorganised individuals who were united by some common interest, but it would be very difficult for such a tacit association to obtain support for a policy to its special advantage because of the conditions under which participation takes place. If it was impossible to avoid organised associations within the community then, Rousseau argues, these should be as numerous and as equal in political power as possible. That is, the participatory situation of individuals would be repeated so far as the groups were concerned, and none could gain at the expense of the rest. Rousseau says nothing, not surprisingly, about the internal authority structure of such groups but his basic analysis of the participatory process can be applied to any group or association.[5]

This analysis of the operation of Rousseau's particpatory system makes two points clear; first, that 'participation' for Rousseau is participation in the making of decisions and second, that it is, as in theories of representative government, a way of protecting private interests and ensuring good government. But participation is also considerably more than this in Rousseau's theory. Plamenatz (1963) has said of Rousseau that 'he turns our minds . . . to considering how the social order affects the structure of human personality' (vol. I, p. 440), and it is the psychological impact of social and political institutions that is Rousseau's main concern; which aspect of men's characters do particular institutions develop? The crucial variable here is whether or not the institution is a participatory one and the central function of participation in Rousseau's theory is an educative one, using the term 'education' in the widest sense. Rousseau's ideal system is designed to develop responsible, individual social and political action through the effect of the participatory process. During this process the individual learns that the word 'each' must be applied to himself; that is to say, he finds that he has to take into account wider matters than his own immediate private interests if he is to gain co-operation from others, and he learns that the public and private interest are linked. The logic of the operation of the participatory system is such that he is 'forced' to deliberate according to his sense of justice, according to what Rousseau calls his 'constant will' because fellow citizens can always resist the implementation of inequitable demands. As a result of participating in decision making the individual is educated to distinguish between his own impulses and desires, he learns to be a public as well as a private citizen. Rousseau also believes that through this educative process the individual will eventually come to feel little or no conflict between the demands of the public and private spheres. Once the participatory system is established, and this is a point of major importance, it becomes self-sustaining because the very qualities that are required of individual citizens if the system is to work successfully are those that the process of participation itself develops and fosters; the more the individual citizen participates the better able he is to do so. The human results

that accrue through the participatory process provide an important justification for a participatory system.

Another aspect of the role of participation in Rousseau's theory is the close connection between participation and control and this is bound up with his notion of freedom. A full discussion of Rousseau's use of this latter concept is not necessary here, but it is inextricably bound up with the process of participation. Perhaps the most famous, or notorious, words that Rousseau ever wrote were that a man might be 'forced to be free' and he also defined freedom as 'obedience to a law one prescribes to oneself'.[6] Some of the more fanciful and sinister interpretations that have been placed on the first words would not have been possible if Rousseau's concept of freedom had been placed firmly in the context of participation, for the way in which an individual can be 'forced' to be free is part and parcel of the same process by which he is 'forcibly' educated through participating in decision making. Rousseau argues that unless each individual is 'forced' through the participatory process into socially responsible action then there can be no law which ensures everyone's freedom, i.e. there can be no general will or the kind of just law that the individual can prescribe to himself. While the subjective element in Rousseau's concept of freedom—that under such a law the individual will feel unconstrained, will *feel* free—has often been commented upon, it is usually overlooked that there is an objective element involved as well. (Though this is not to say that one accepts Rousseau's definition of freedom as consisting in obedience.) The individual's actual, as well as his sense of, freedom is increased through participation in decision making because it gives him a very real degree of *control* over the course of his life and the structure of his environment. Rousseau also argues that freedom requires that he should exercise a fair measure of control over those that execute the laws and over representatives if an indirect system is necessary.[7] In the introduction to his recent translation of the *Social Contract* Cranston criticises Rousseau for never, in that work, seeing institutions as a threat to freedom (Rousseau, 1968, p. 41). This criticism precisely misses the point. The participatory institutions of the *Social Contract* cannot be a threat to freedom just because of the logic of their operation, because of the interrelationship between the authority structure of institutions and the psychological orientations of individuals. It is the whole point of Rousseau's argument that the (existing) non-participatory institutions do pose such a threat, indeed, they make freedom impossible—men are everywhere 'in chains'. The ideal institutions described in the *Social Contract* are ideal because Rousseau regards their operation as guaranteeing freedom.

Rousseau also sees participation as increasing the value of his freedom to the individual by enabling him to be (and remain) his own master. Like the rest of Rousseau's theory the notion of 'being one's own master' has come in for a good deal of criticism, although Cranston strikes a new note when he refers to it as the ideal of a footman and so, presumably, not worth serious consideration—but that is too easy a dismissal of the idea.[8] In the eighth *Letter from the Mountain* Rousseau says that freedom consists 'moins à faire sa volonté qu'a n'être pas soumis à celle d'autrui; elle consiste encore à ne pas soumetre la volonté d'autrui à la nôtre. Quiconque est maître ne peut être libre.' (1965, vol II, p. 234). That is, one must not be master of another; when one is master of oneself and one's life, however, then freedom is enhanced through the control over that life that is required before it is possible to describe the individual as his 'own master'. Secondly, the participatory process ensures that although no man, or group, is master of another, all are equally dependent on each other and equally subject to the law. The (impersonal) rule of law that is made possible through participation and its connection with 'being one's own master' gives us further insight into the reason why Rousseau thinks that individuals will conscientiously accept a law arrived at through a participatory decision-making process. More generally, it is now possible to see that a second function of participation in Rousseau's theory is that it enables collective decisions to be more easily accepted by the individual.

Rousseau also suggests that participation has a third, integrative function; that it increases the feeling among individual citizens that they 'belong' in their community. In a sense integration derives from all the factors mentioned already. For example, the basic economic equality means that there is no disruptive division between rich and poor, there are no men like the one Rousseau disapprovingly mentions in *Émile* who, when asked which was his country, replied 'I am one of the rich' (1911, p. 313). More important is the experience of participation in decision making itself, and the complex totality of results to which it is seen to lead, both for the individual and for the whole political system; this experience attaches the individual to his society and is instrumental in developing it into a true community.

This examination of Rousseau's political theory has provided us with the argument that there is an interrelationship between the authority structures of institutions and the psychological qualities and attitudes of individuals, and with the related argument that the major function of participation is an educative one. These arguments form the basis of the theory of participatory democracy as will become clear from the discussion of the theories of J. S. Mill and Cole. The theories of these two writers reinforce Rousseau's arguments about participation but more interestingly in these theories the theory of participatory democracy is lifted out of the context of a city-state of peasant proprietors into that of a modern political system.

John Stuart Mill, in his social and political theory, as in other matters, started out as a devoted adherent of the doctrines of his father and of Bentham, which he later severely criticised, so that he provides an excellent example of the differences between the theories of representative government and participatory democracy. However, Mill never completely rejected these early teachings and by the end of his life his political theory was composed of a mixture of all the diverse influences that had affected him. He never managed satisfactorily to synthesise these—the task is probably an impossible one—and this means that there is a profound ambiguity between the participatory foundations of his theory and some of his more practical proposals for the establishment of his 'ideally best polity'.

Echoes of the utilitarian view of the purely protective function of participation can be found in Mill's mature politcal theory. For example, he says in *Representative Government*—which expressed the principles 'to which I have been working up during the greater part of my life'—that one of the greatest dangers of democracy lies in 'the sinister interest of the holders of power: it is the danger of class legislation . . . And one of the most important questions demanding consideration . . . is how to provide efficacious securities against this evil'.[9] For Mill, however, Bentham's notion of 'good government' only dealt with part of the problem. Mill distinguished two aspects of good government. First, 'how far it promotes the good management of the affairs of society by means of the existing faculties, moral, intellectual, and active, of its various members' and this criterion of good government relates to government seen as 'a set of organised arrangements for public business' (1910, pp. 208 and 195). Mill criticised Bentham for building his political theory on the assumption that this aspect was the whole. He wrote in the essay on *Bentham* that all that the latter could do

> is but to indicate means by which in any given state of the national mind, the material interests of society can be protected; . . . (his theory) can teach the means of organising and regulating the merely *business* part of the social arrangements . . . He committed the mistake of supposing that the *business* part of human affairs was the whole of them (Mill's emphasis) (1963, p. 102).

In J. S. Mill's estimation the merely business aspect of government is the least important; fundamental is government in its second aspect, that of 'a great influence acting on the human mind', and the criterion to be used to judge political institutions in this light is 'the degree in which they promote the general mental advancement of the community, including under that phrase advancement in intellect, in virtue, and in practical activity and efficiency' (1910, p. 195). In this respect Bentham's theory has nothing to say. Mill sees government and political institutions first and foremost as educative in the broadest sense of that word. For him the two aspects of government are interrelated in that a necessary condition of good government in the first, busi-

ness, sense is the promotion of the right kind of individual character and for this the right kind of institutions are necessary (1963, p. 102). It is primarily for this reason, not because such a form of government will be in the universal interest, that Mill regards popular, democratic government as the 'ideally best polity'. Thus, he is against a benevolent despotism, which a he points out, could, if it were all-seeing, ensure that the 'business' side of government were properly carried out, because, as he asks, 'what sort of human beings can be formed under such a regimen? What development can either their thinking or their active faculties attain under it? . . . Their moral capacities are equally stunted. Wherever the sphere of action of human beings is artificially circumscribed, their sentiments are narrowed and dwarfed . . .' (1910, pp. 203–4).

It is only within a context of popular, participatory institutions that Mill sees an 'active', public-spirited type of character being fostered. Here, again, we find the basic assertion of the theorists of participatory democracy of the interrelationship and connection between individuals, their qualities and psychological characteristics, and types of institutions; the assertion that responsible social and political action depends largely on the sort of institutions within which the individual has, politically, to act. Like Rousseau, Mill sees these qualities being as much developed by participation as existing beforehand and thus the political system has a self-sustaining character. Nor does Mill regard it as necessary that citizens should perform the sort of logical and rational calculations that Schumpeter asserted were necessary. He remarks in *Representative Government* that it would not be a rational form of government that required 'exalted' principles of conduct to motivate men, though he assumes that there is a certain level of political sophistication and public-spiritedness in the 'advanced' countries to whom this theory is addressed (1910, p. 253). Mill sees the educative function of participation in much the same terms as Rousseau. He argues that where the individual is concerned solely with his own private affairs and does not participate in public affairs then the 'self-regarding' virtues suffer, as well as the capacities for responsible public action remaining undeveloped. 'The man never thinks of any collective interest, of any object to be pursued jointly with others, but only in competition with them, and in some measure at their expense' (1910, p. 217). The 'private money-getting occupation' of most individuals uses few of their faculties and tends to 'fasten his attention and interest exclusively upon himself, and upon his family as an appendage of himself;—making him indifferent to the public . . . and in his inordinate regard for his personal comforts, selfish and cowardly' (1963, p. 230). The whole situation is changed, however, when the individual can participate in public affairs; Mill, like Rousseau, saw the individual in this case being 'forced' to widen his horizons and to take the public interest into account. That is, the individual has to 'weigh interests not his own; to be guided, in the case of conflicting claims, by another rule than his private partialities; to apply, at every turn, principles and maxims which have for their reason of existence the common good' (1910, p. 217).

So far, Mill's theory has been shown to reinforce rather than add to Rousseau's hypothesis about the educative function of participation but there is another facet of Mill's theory which does add a further dimension to that hypothesis, a necessary dimension if the theory is to be applied to a large-scale society. I have already quoted from one of Mill's reviews of de Tocqueville's *Democracy in America*. This work was a decisive influence on Mill's political theory, in particular with the part which deals with local political institutions. Mill was very impressed with de Tocqueville's discussion of centralisation and the dangers inherent in the development of a mass society (dangers made familiar now by modern sociologists also impressed by that analysis). In the *Political Economy* Mill declares that 'a democratic constitution not supported by democratic institutions in detail, but confined to the central government, not only is not political freedom, but often creates a spirit precisely the reverse'.[10] In his review of Volume II of de Tocqueville's book Mill argues that it is no use having universal suffrage and participation in national government if the individual has not been prepared for this participation at local level; it is at this level that he learns how to govern himself. 'A political act, to be done only once in a few

years, and for which nothing in the daily habits of the citizen has prepared him, leaves his intellect and his moral dispositions very much as it found them' (1963, p. 229). In other words, if individuals in a large state are to be able to participate effectively in the government of the 'great society' then the necessary qualities underlying this participation have to be fostered and developed at the local level. Thus, for Mill, it is at local level where the real educative effect of participation occurs, where not only do the issues dealt with directly affect the individual, and his everyday life but where he also stands a good chance of, himself, being elected to serve on a local body (1910, p. 347–8). It is by participating at the local level that the individual 'learns democracy'. 'We do not learn to read or write, to ride or swim, by being merely told how to do it, but by doing it, so it is only by practising popular government on a limited scale, that the people will ever learn how to exercise it on a larger' (1963, p. 186).

In a large-scale society representative government will be necessary and it is here that a difficulty arises; are Mill's practical proposals about representation compatible with the fundamental role he assigns to the educative function of participation in his theory? In his practical proposals Mill does not take his own arguments about participation seriously enough and this is largely because of ideas about the 'natural' state of society which are mixed in with the rest of his social and political theory.

Bentham and James Mill had thought that education, in the narrow, 'academic' sense of that term, was the major way of ensuring responsible political participation on the part of the 'numerous classes', and John Stuart Mill never really rejected this view. One of Mill's main concerns was how a political system could be achieved where the power was in the hands of an élite—the educated élite (in the narrow sense). A well cultivated intellect, he thought, was usually accompanied by 'prudence, temperance, and justice, and generally by all the virtues which are important in our intercourse with others'.[11] It was persons already well educated (the 'instructed') that Mill regarded as the 'wisest and best' men and whom he thought should be elected to office at all political levels. He considered that democracy was inevitable in the modern world, the problem was to so organise things that democratic political institutions would be compatible with the 'natural' state of society, a state where 'worldly power and moral influence are habitually exercised by the fittest persons whom the existing state of society affords' and where the 'multitude' have faith in this 'instructed' minority who will rule.[12] Mill, it should be noted, did not want a situation where the multitude was deferential in the unthinking, habitual sense of that word. Indeed, he thought that the time was past when such a thing was possible; 'the poor have to come out of their leading strings . . . whatever advice, exhortation, or guidance is held out to the labouring classes, must henceforth be tendered to them as equals and accepted by them with their eyes open'.[13] The élite had to be accountable to the many and it was the reconciliation of élite rule with accountability that Mill saw as the 'grand difficulty' in politics. His answer to this problem gives rise to the ambiguity in his theory of participation.

From Mill's theory about the educative function of participation one would expect his answer to this problem would be that the maximum amount of opportunity should be given to the labouring classes to participate at local level so they would develop the necessary qualities and skills to enable them to assess the activities of representatives and hold them accountable. But Mill says nothing of the sort. His practical proposals for achieving a 'natural' but ideal political system are quite different. Mill distinguished between 'true democracy', which gives representation to minorities (and to this end Mill enthusiastically espoused Hare's proportional representation scheme), and the ideal system. The former did not solve the problem of ensuring that his educated élite had a preponderant influence; that ideal system could only come about under a system of plural voting based on educational attainment, 'though everyone ought to have a voice—that everyone should have an equal voice is a totally different proposition.'[14] Thus, Mill rejects Rousseau's argument that for effective participation political equality is necessary. Mill also implicitly uses a different definition of 'participation' from Rousseau, for he did not think that even the elected representatives

should legislate but only accept or reject legislation prepared by a special commission appointed by the Crown; the proper job of representatives is discussion (1910, p. 235 ff.).

A further illustration of this point is Mill's comment on the form that the ideal suffrage should take. He says that it is 'by political discussion that the manual labourer, whose employment is a routine, and whose way of life brings him in contact with no variety of impressions, circumstances, or ideas, is taught that remote causes, and events which take place far off, have a most sensible effect even on his personal interests' (1910, p. 278).

One might raise the question, with Mill's practical proposals for the achievement of the ideally best polity and his implicit definition of participation, of whether participation would have the educative effect he postulated. The important point about Rousseau's paradigm of direct participation is that the participatory process was organised in such a way that individuals were, so to speak, psychologically 'open' to its effects. But none of this obtains in Mill. The majority are branded by the suffrage system as political inferiors and cannot resist the implementation of disadvantageous policies; if a predetermined élite are to gain political power why should the majority even be interested in discussion? Mill seems unaware of any inconsistency in the various elements of his theory but it is difficult to see how his kind of participation is to fulfil its allotted role. Even with universal suffrage and decision making by representatives there would not be such a 'strongly' educative environment as that provided by Rousseau's direct participatory system and the problem of how far Rousseau's model can be replicated in modern conditions will be taken up later. Here it should be noted that Mill's educationally crucial local political level might give scope for direct participation in decision making.

The stress on local political institutions is not the only extension that Mill makes to the hypothesis about the educative effect of participation, but before discussing this other aspect it is useful to note that Mill agrees with Rousseau about the other two functions of participation. The whole argument about the 'critical deference' of the multitude rests partly on the suggestion that participation aids the acceptance of decisions and Mill specifically points to the integrative function of participation. He says that through political discussion the individual 'becomes consciously a member of a great community' (1910, p. 279) and that whenever he has something to do for the public he is made to feel 'that not only the common weal is his weal, but that it partly depends on his exertions' (1963, p. 230).

Perhaps the most interesting aspect of Mill's theory is an expansion of the hypothesis about the educative effect of participation to cover a whole new area of social life—industry. In his later work, Mill came to see industry as another area where the individual could gain experience in the management of collective affairs, just as he could in local government. Mill saw the real value of the various theories of socialism and co-operation that were being advocated, and sometimes tried out, in his day as lying in their potential as means of education. As might be expected he was suspicious of those schemes that were centralist in character; as Robson points out, Mill in the *Chapters on Socialism* gives his approval to 'such socialist schemes as depend on voluntary organisation in small communities and which look to a national application of their principles only through the self-multiplication of the units' (1968, p. 245). In such a form of organisation widespread participation could be accommodated. Mill saw co-operative forms of industrial organisation leading to a 'moral transformation' of those that took part in them (he also thought they would be more productive, but that was partly a result of the 'transformation'). A co-operative organisation would lead, he said, to 'friendly rivalry in the pursuit of a good common to all; the elevation of the dignity of labour; a new sense of security and independence in the labouring class; and the conversion of each human being's daily occupation into a school of the social sympathies and the practical intelligence'.[15] Just as participation in the government of the collective interest in local politics educates the individual in social responsibility so participation in the management of the collective interest of an industrial organisation fosters and develops the qualities in the individual that he needs for public activities. 'No soil,' says Mill, could be more conducive to the training of the individual to feel 'the public interest his own' than a 'communist association'.[16] Just as Mill regarded democracy as inevitable in the modern world so he saw some form of co-operation as inevitable in industry; now that the labouring classes had come out of their 'leading strings' the employer/employee relationship would not be maintainable in the long run, some form of co-operation must take its place. In the *Political Economy* Mill discusses what form this might take and he comes to the conclusion that if 'mankind is to continue to improve' then in the end one form of association will predominate, 'not that which can exist between a capitalist as chief, and workpeople without a voice in the management, but the association of the labourers themselves on terms of equality, collectively owning the capital with which they carry on their operations, and working under managers elected and removable by themselves.'[17]

In the same way that participation in local government is a necessary condition for participation at the national level because of its educative or 'improving' effect, so Mill is suggesting that participation in the 'government' of the workplace could have the same impact. These wider implications of Mill's arguments about the importance of education are usually overlooked, yet they are of great significance for democratic theory. If such participation in the workplace is to be possible then the authority relationship in industry would have to be transformed from the usual one of superiority-subordination (managers and men) to one of co-operation or equality with the managers (government) being elected by the whole body of employees just as representatives at the local level are elected. That is to say, the political relations in industry, using the word 'political' in a wide sense, would have to be democratised. Moreover it is possible to go further; Mill's argument about the educative effect of participation in local government and in the workplace could be generalised to cover the effect of participation in all 'lower level' authority structures, or political systems. It is because this general hypothesis can be derived from their theories that I have referred to these writers as theorists of the participatory society. Society can be seen as being composed of various political systems, the structure of authority of which has an important effect on the psychological qualities and attitudes of the individuals who interact within them; thus, for the operation of a democratic polity at national level, the necessary qualities in individuals can only be developed through the democratisation of authority structures in all political systems.

We might also note at this point that there is another dimension to this theory of participation. Apart from its importance as an educative device, participation in the workplace—a political system—can be regarded as political participation in its own right. Thus industry and other spheres provide alternative areas where the individual can participate in decision making in matters of which he has first hand, everyday experience, so that when we refer to 'participatory democracy' we are indicating something very much wider than a set of 'institutional arrangements' at national level. This wider view of democracy can be found in the political theory of G. D. H. Cole, to which we now turn.

A discussion of Cole's theory—and here we shall be dealing solely with his early writings—is of particular interest because his theory is not only set in the context of a modern, industrialized society but it is very much a theory *of* such a society. The remarks which Mill made about participation in industry, though illuminating for our purposes, were peripheral to his main body of social and political theory, but for Cole it is industry that holds the key that will unlock the door to a truly democratic polity. In his theory of Guild Socialism Cole worked out a detailed scheme of how a participatory society might be organised and brought into being which is of considerable intrinsic interest, although we shall be concerned with the principles that underlay this scheme rather than the blueprint itself. Another significant aspect of Cole's work of this period was the very great influence of Rousseau. There were other influences also, William Morris and Marx, for instance, but Cole frequently quotes Rousseau; the spirit of the latter pervades his work and many of Cole's basic concepts are derived from Rousseau. This is an additional reason for examining Cole's work. Discussions of Rousseau's political theory usually reach the conclusion

that it is of little relevance today (and it is sometimes suggested that the influence that it has had has been positively pernicious). I have already argued that Rousseau's theory provides the starting point and the basic material for any discussion of the participatory theory of democracy and Cole's theory provides one attempt to translate the insights of Rousseau's theory into a modern setting.

Cole's social and political theory is built on Rousseau's argument that will, not force, is the basis of social and political organisation. Men must co-operate in associations to satisfy their needs and Cole begins by looking at 'the motives that hold men together in association' and the 'way in which men act through association in supplement and complement to their actions as isolated or private individuals' (1920, pp. 6 and 11). To translate their will into action in a way that does not infringe upon their individual freedom, Cole argues that men must participate in the organisation and regulation of their associations. The idea of participation is central to his theory. 'I assume', he says, echoing Mill's criticism of Bentham's political theory, 'that the object of social organisation is not merely material efficiency, but also essentially the fullest self-expression of all the members.' Self-expression 'involves self-government' and this means that we must 'call forth the people's full participation in the common direction in the affairs of the community' (1920, p. 208). This, in turn, involves the fullest freedom of all members for 'freedom is to find perfect expression' (1918, p. 196). Cole also says, again following Rousseau, that the individual is 'most free where he cooperates with his equals in the making of laws'.[18]

Cole's theory is a theory of associations. Society as he defined it is a complex of associations held together by the wills of their members'.[19] If the individual is to be self-governing then he not only has to be able to participate in decision making in all the associations of which he is a member but the associations themselves have to be free to control their own affairs (Cole regarded the interference of the state as the main danger here), and if they were to be self-governing in this sense then they have to be roughly equal in political power. In *The World of Labour* Cole argues that the suppression of groups in the French Revolution was an historical accident because of the privileges they then happened to possess, and he adds that 'in recognizing that where there must be particular associations, they should be evenly matched, Rousseau admits the group principle to be inevitable in the great state. We may then regard the new philosophy of groups as carrying on the true egalitarian principles of the French Revolution' (1913, p. 23).

This theory of associations is linked to his theory of democracy through the principle of function, 'the underlying principle of social organisation' (1920, p. 48). Cole thought that 'democracy is only real when it is conceived in terms of function and purpose' and the function of an association is based on the purpose for which it was formed (1920a, p. 31). Every association that 'sets before itself any object that is of more than the most rudimentary simplicity finds itself compelled to assign tasks and duties, and with these powers and a share of authority, to some of its members in order that the general object may be effectively pursued' (1920, p. 104). That is, representative government (in the wide sense of that latter term) is necessary in most associations. In Cole's view existing forms of representation are *mis*representation for two reasons. First, because the principle of function has been overlooked, the mistake has been made of assuming that it is possible for an individual to be represented as a whole and for all purposes instead of his being represented in relation to some well-defined function. Second, under the existing parliamentary institutions the elector has no real choice of, or control over, his representative, and the system actually denies the right of the individual to participate because 'having chosen his representative, the ordinary man has, according to that theory, nothing left to do except to let other people govern him'. A system of functional representation, on the other hand, implies 'the constant participation of the ordinary man in the conduct of those parts of the structure of Society with which he is directly concerned, and which he has therefore the best chance of understanding'.[20]

Thus in Cole's theory there is a distinction between the existence of representative 'institutional arrangements' at national level and democracy. For the latter the individual must be able to participate in all the associations with which he is concerned; that is to say, a participatory society is necessary. The democratic principle, Cole says, must be applied 'not only or mainly to some special sphere of social action known as "politics", but to any and every form of social action, and, in especial, to industrial and economic fully as much as to political affairs' (1920a, p. 12). This notion is in fact implicit in Cole's 'new philosophy of groups' that he built on the foundation laid by Rousseau, for it is to apply Rousseau's insights about the functions of participation to the internal organisation of all associations and organisations. For Cole, therefore, like Mill, the educational function of participation is crucial, and he also emphasises that individuals and their institutions cannot be considered in isolation from each other. He remarks in *Guild Socialist Restated* that if Guild Socialist theory was largely a theory of institutions this was not because

> it believes that the life of men is comprehended in their social machinery, but because social machinery, as it is good or bad, harmonious or discordant with human desires and instincts, is the means either of furthering, or of thwarting, the expression of human personality. If environment does not, as Robert Owen thought, make character in an absolute sense, it does direct and divert character into divergent forms of expression (1920a, p. 25).

Like Mill, Cole argued that it was only by participation at the local level and in local associations that the individual could 'learn democracy'. 'Over the vast mechanism of modern politics the individual has no control, not because the state is too big, but because he is given no chance of learning the rudiments of self-government within a smaller unit' (1919, p. 157). Actually, Cole has rather disregarded the implications of his own arguments here; the fact that the modern state *is* so big is one important reason for enabling the individual to participate in the 'alternative' political areas of society, a fact that Cole's writings show him to be well aware of.

The important point, however, is that in Cole's view industry provided the all-important arena for the educative effect of participation to take place; for it is in industry that, outside Government, the individual is involved to the greatest extent in relationships of superiority and subordination and the ordinary man spends a great deal of his life at work. It was for this reason that Cole exclaimed that the answer that most people would give to the question 'what is the fundamental evil in our modern society?' would be the wrong one: 'they would answer POVERTY, when they ought to answer SLAVERY' (1919, p. 34). The millions who had been given the franchise, who had formally been given the means to self-government had in fact been 'trained to subservience' and this training had largely taken place during the course of their daily occupation. Cole argued that 'the industrial system . . . is in great measure the key to the paradox of political democracy. Why are the many nominally supreme but actually powerless? Largely because the circumstances of their lives do not accustom or fit them for power or responsibility. A servile system in industry inevitably reflects itself in political servility' (1918, p. 35). Only if the individual could become self-governing in the workplace, only if industry was organised on a participatory basis, could this training for servility be turned into training for democracy and the individual gain the familiarity with democratic procedures, and develop the necessary 'democratic character' for an effective system of large-scale democracy.[21]

For Cole, like Rousseau, there could be no equality of political power without a substantive measure of economic equality and his theory provides us with some interesting indications of how the economic equality in Rousseau's ideal society of peasant proprietors might be achieved in a modern economy. In Cole's view 'the abstract democracy of the ballot box' did not involve real political equality; the equality of citizenship implied by universal suffrage was only formal and it obscured the fact that political power was shared very unequally. 'Theoretical democrats', he said, ignored 'the fact that vast inequalities of wealth and status, resulting in vast inequalities of education, power and control of environment, are necessarily fatal to any real democracy, whether in politics or any other sphere.'[22]

One of Cole's major objections to the capitalist organisation of industry was that under it labour was just another commodity and so the 'humanity' of labour was denied. Under the Guild Socialist system this humanity would be fully recognised, which would mean 'above all else, the recognition of the right . . . to equality of opportunity and status' (1918, p. 24). It is the latter that is really important; only with the equalisation of status could there be the equality of independence that, as we have seen from the discussion of Rousseau's theory, is crucial for the process of participation. Cole thought that there would be a move toward the equalisation of incomes, final equality arising through the 'destruction of the whole idea of remuneration for work done' (1920a, pp. 72–3), but the abolition of status distinctions plays a larger role in his theory. Partly this would come about through the socialisation of the means of production under a Guild Socialist system because classes would then be abolished (by definition—Cole used the term in a Marxian sense), but of more (practical) importance were two other factors. Under a participatory system there would no longer be one group of 'managers' and one group of 'men', the latter having no control over the affairs of the enterprise, but one group of equal decision makers. Secondly, Cole saw a participatory organisation of industry leading to the abolition of the fear of unemployment for the ordinary man, and so to the abolition of the other great status distinction, inequality in security of tenure of employment.

However, although Cole's democratic theory hinges on the establishment of this equality of status in industry, he was (despite Schumpeter's strictures on this point) very conscious of the problem of the preservation of leadership under such a democratic system, and he thought that the principle of function provided an answer. If representation (leadership) was organised on a functional basis then it was possible to have 'representatives' rather than 'delegates'. The latter seemed necessary because it appeared to be the only way that control could be exercised by the electorate given that 'as soon as the voters have exercised their votes their existence as a group lapses until the time when a new election is required'. Functional associations, by contrast, can have a continuous existence, so can continually advise, criticise and, if necessary, recall the representative. They also have an additional merit in that 'not only will the representative be chosen to do a job about which he knows something, but he will be chosen by persons who know something of it too'.[23]

Although Cole regarded 'material efficiency' as only one object of social and political organisation, he thought that a participatory society would be superior in this respect also. Under conditions of economic security and equality the profit motive—the motive of 'greed and fear'—would be replaced by the motive of free service and workers would see that their efforts were for the benefit of the whole community. He thought that there existed large untapped reserves of energy and initiative in the ordinary man that a participatory system would call forth; it was self-government that was the key to efficiency. The workers would never be persuaded to give of their best 'under a system which from any moral standpoint is utterly indefensible'.[24]

The main interest for our purpose in Cole's specific plan for self-government in the workshop and other spheres, Guild Socialism, is that it provides us with one man's notion, in great detail, of what a participatory society might look like. Cole put forward several versions, but the most theoretically pluralist is to be found in *Guild Socialism Restated* on which this, very brief, account is based.[25] The Guild Socialist structure was organised, vertically and horizontally, from the grass roots upward and was participatory at all levels and in all its aspects. The vertical structure was to be economic in nature—for on good functionalist principles the political and economic functions in society were to be separated. On the economic side production and consumption were also differentiated. What are usually thought of as 'guilds' were actually to be the unit of organisation on the production side. In the economic sphere Cole also proposed the setting up of consumer co-operatives, utility councils (for provision of gas, etc.), civic guilds to take care of health, education, etc., and

cultural councils to 'express the civic point of view'—and any other *ad hoc* bodies that might prove necessary in a particular area. The workshop was to be the basic 'building block' of the guild and, similarly, the grass root unit of each council, etc., was to be small enough to allow the maximum participation by everyone. Each guild would elect representatives to the higher stages of the vertical structure, to local and regional guilds and councils, and at the highest level, to the Industrial Guilds Congress (or its equivalent).

The purpose of the horizontal (political) structure was to give expression to 'the communal spirit of the whole society'. Each town or country area would have its own commune where the basic unit would be the ward, again to allow maximum individual participation, and representatives would be elected from the guilds, etc., and any other local bodies to the commune on a ward basis. The next horizontal layer was to be composed of regional communes, bringing together both town and country and the regional guilds, and at the apex would be found the National Commune which would, Cole thought, be a purely co-ordinating body neither functionally, historically nor structurally continuous with the existing state.

The precise merits or demerits of this particular blueprint do not concern us here; as Cole himself said, 'the principles behind guild socialism are far more important than the actual forms of organisation which guild socialists have thought out' (1920c, p. 7), and it is with these principles, the principles underlying the theory of participatory democracy, and the question of their empirical relevance at the present time, that we are concerned.

The very great difference between the theories of democracy discussed in this chapter and the theories of those writers whom we have called the theorists of representative government makes it difficult to understand how the myth of one 'classical' theory of democracy has survived so long and is so vigorously propagated. The theories of participatory democracy examined here were not just essays in prescription as is often claimed, rather they offer just those 'plans of action and specific prescriptions' for movement towards a (truly) democratic polity that it has been suggested are lacking. But perhaps the strangest criticism is that these earlier theorists were not, as Berelson puts it, concerned with the 'general features necessary if the (political) institutions are to work as required', and that they ignored the political system as a whole in their work. It is quite clear that this is precisely what they were concerned with. Although the variable identified as crucial in those theories for the successful establishment and maintenance of a democratic political system, the authority structures of non-Governmental spheres of society, is exactly the same one that Eckstein indicates in his theory of stable democracy, the conclusions drawn from this by the earlier and later theorists of democracy are entirely different. In order that an evaluation of these two theories of democracy can be undertaken I shall now briefly set out (in a similar fashion to the contemporary theory of democracy above), a participatory theory of democracy drawn from the three theories just discussed.

The theory of participatory democracy is built round the central assertion that individuals and their institutions cannot be considered in isolation from one another. The existence of representative institutions at national level is not sufficient for democracy; for maximum participation by all the people at that level socialisation, or 'social training', for democracy must take place in other spheres in order that the necessary individual attitudes and psychological qualities can be developed. This development takes place through the process of participation itself. The major function of participation in the theory of participatory democracy is therefore an educative one, educative in the very widest sense, including both the psychological aspect and the gaining of practice in democratic skills and procedures. Thus there is no special problem about the stability of a participatory system; it is self-sustaining through the educative impact of the participatory process. Participation develops and fosters the very qualities necessary for it; the more individuals participate the better able they become to do so. Subsidiary hypotheses about participation are that it has an integrative effect and that it aids the acceptance of collective decisions.

Therefore, for a democratic polity to exist it is necessary for a participatory society to exist, i.e. a society where all political systems have been democratised and socialisation through participation can take place in all areas. The most important area is industry; most individuals spend a great deal of their lifetime at work and the business of the workplace provides an education in the management of collective affairs that it is difficult to parallel elsewhere. The second aspect of the theory of participatory democracy is that spheres such as industry should be seen as political systems in their own right, offering areas of participation additional to the national level. If individuals are to exercise the maximum amount of control over their own lives and environment then authority structures in these areas must be so organised that they can participate in decision making. A further reason for the central place of industry in the theory relates to the substantive measure of economic equality required to give the individual the independence and security necessary for (equal) participation; the democratising of industrial authority structures, abolishing the permanent distinction between 'managers' and 'men' would mean a large step toward meeting this condition.

The contemporary and participatory theories of democracy can be contrasted on every point of substance, including the characterisation of 'democracy' itself and the definition of 'political', which in the participatory theory is not confined to the usual national or local government sphere. Again, in the participatory theory 'participation' refers to (equal) participation in the making of decisions, and 'political equality' refers to equality of power in determining the outcome of decisions, a very different definition from that in the contemporary theory. Finally, the justification for a democratic system in the participatory theory of democracy rests primarily on the human results that accrue from the participatory process. One might characterise the participatory model as one where maximum input (participation) is required and where output includes not just policies (decisions) but also the development of the social and political capacities of each individual, so that there is 'feedback' from output to input.

Many of the criticisms of the so-called 'classical' theory of democracy imply that the latter theory has only to be stated for it to become obvious that it is unrealistic and outmoded. With the participatory theory of democracy this is far from the case; indeed, it has many features that reflect some of the major themes and orientations in recent political theory and political sociology. For example, the fact that it is a model of a self-sustaining system might make it attractive to the many writers on politics who, explicitly or implicitly, make use of such models. Again, similarities between the participatory theory of democracy and recent theories of social pluralism are obvious enough, although these usually argue only that 'secondary' associations should exist to mediate between the individual and the national polity and say nothing about the authority structures of those associations'. The wide definition of the 'political' in the participatory theory is also in keeping with the practice in modern political theory and political science. One of the advocates of the contemporary theory of democracy, Dahl (1963, p. 6), has defined a political system as 'any persistent pattern of human relationships that involves to a significant extent power, rule or authority'. All this makes it very odd that no recent writer on democratic theory appears to have reread the earlier theorists with these concerns in mind. Any explanation of this would, no doubt, include a mention of the widely held belief that (although these earlier theories are often said to be descriptive) 'traditional' political theorists, especially theorists of democracy, were engaged in a largely prescriptive and 'value-laden' enterprise and their work is thus held to have little direct interest for the modern, scientific, political theorist. . . .

Bibliography

Cole, G. D. H. (1913) *The World of Labour*, G. Bell and Sons, London.

—— (1915), "Conflicting Social Obligations", *Proceedings of the Aristotelian Society, vol. xv*, pp. 140–59.

—— (1918), *Labour in the Commonwealth*, Headley Bros., London.

—— (1919), *Self-government in Industry*, G. Bell and Sons, London.

—— (1920), *Social Theory*, Metheun, London.

—— (1920a), *Guild Socialism Restated*, Leonard Parsons, London.

—— (1920b), *Chaos and Order in Industry*, Metheun, London.

Dahl, R. A. (1963) *Modern Political Analysis*, Prentice-Hall, New Jersey.

Mill, J. S. (1910) *Representative Government*, Everyman ed.

—— (1924), *Autobiography*, World's Classics, ed.

—— (1963), *Essays on Politics and Culture*, Himmelfarb, G., ed., New York.

—— (1965), *Collected Works*, Robson, J. M., ed., University of Toronto Press.

Plamenatz, J. (1963), *Man and Society*, Longmans, London.

Rousseau, J. J. (1911) *Emile*, Everyman, ed.

—— (1965), *The Political Writings*, Vaughan, C. E., ed., Blackwell, Oxford.

—— (1968), *The Social Contract*, Cranston, M., trans., Penguin Books.

Notes

1. The political system described in *The Social Contract* was not a democracy according to Rousseau's usage of the term. For him, a 'democracy' was a system where the citizens executed as well as made the laws and for that reason it was fit only for gods (bk. III, ch. 4). It might be noted here that as Rousseau's is a direct, not representative system, it does *not* conform to Schumpeter's definition of 'classical' democratic theory.

2. Rousseau (1968), bk. II, ch. II, p. 96, and (1913), p. 254.

3. Rousseau (1968), bk. II, ch. 4, p. 75. See also p. 76, 'the general will is an institution in which each necessarily submits himself to the same conditions which he imposes on others.'

4. Apropos of Schumpeter's 'classical' definition it is something of a misnomer to say that Rousseau's citizens decide 'issues'. What they do by participating is to come up with the right answer to a problem (i.e. the general will). There will not necessarily be a right answer in the case of an

'issue' as we understand the term in the political conditions of today. Nor is an ability to make 'logical inferences' required. Quite the contrary, the whole point of the participatory situation is that each independent but interdependent individual is 'forced' to appreciate that there is only one right answer, to apply the word 'each' to himself.

5. Rousseau (1968), bk. II, ch. 3, p. 73.

6. Rousseau (1968), bk. I, ch. 7, p. 64, and bk. I, ch. 8, p. 65.

7. See Rousseau (1968, bk. III, ch. 18, p. 148) and (1953, pp. 192 ff.).

8. Rousseau (1968, p. 42).

9. Mill (1910), Preface and p. 254.

10. Mill (1965), bk. V, ch. XI, §6, p. 944.

11. Quoted in Robson (1967, p. 210).

12. Mill (1963, p. 17). Mill contrasts this state to the present one, a state of 'transition' where old institutions and doctrines have been 'outgrown' and the multitude have lost their faith in the instructed and are 'without a guide' (p. 3).

13. Mill (1965), bk. IV, ch. VII, §2, p. 763.

14. Mill (1910, p. 283). In his *Autobiography* Mill admitted that the proposal for plural voting found favour with nobody (1924, p. 218).

15. Mill (1965), bk. IV, ch. VII, §6, p. 792.

16. Mill (1965), bk. II, ch. I, §3, p. 205. Mill uses the word 'communist' more loosely than we do today.

17. Mill (1965), bk. IV, ch. VII, §6, p. 775. See also §§ 2, 3, 4.

18. Cole (1919, p. 182). But Cole did not accept that freedom consisted in obedience to these laws; he regarded laws as 'the scaffolding of hu-man freedom; but they are not part of the building' (1918, p. 197).

19. Cole (1920a, p. 12). It should, perhaps, be noted that Cole did not see the whole life of the individual encompassed in these groups. Much of his life, and some of its most valuable aspects, found expression outside association; the individual is 'the pivot on which the whole system of institutions turns. For he alone has in him the various purposes of the various institutions bound together in a single personality' (1918, p. 191).

20. Cole (1920, p. 114); see also pp. 104–6.

21. Implicit in all Cole's writings on the necessity of a participatory society is the hypothesis that participation will have an integrative effect. This underlies his many references to 'community' and the importance he attaches to local participatory institutions where men can learn the 'social spirit'. In the industrial sphere it is the basis of the assumption that the new form of organisation would lead to co-operation and fellowship in a community of workers instead of the usual industrial conflict. See Cole (1920, p. 169) and (1920a, p. 45).

22. Cole (1920a, p. 14); see also (1913, p. 421).

23. Cole (1920, pp. 110–13). Such a system would go part of the way to meeting objections often raised about the amount of 'rationality' that a democratic system requires of the voter. Cole like the other theorists of the participatory society took the view that 'rationality' was, at least in part, acquired through the process of participation.

24. Cole (1919, p. 181) and (1920b, p. 12).

25. Cole (1920a).

The Limits of Friendship

Jane J. Mansbridge

In this essay, Jane J. Mansbridge raises a variety of objections against participatory democracy. She begins by describing the ideals underlying participation: equality, unanimity and direct democracy. But, she argues, as small groups of friends become large associations of strangers these ideals are transformed. Though sometimes workable among small groups, the ideals cannot be fully realized in a larger political association comprised of people with widely different viewpoints. Indeed, smallness often brings coercion rather than equality. The solution, she suggests, may lie in some combination of representative democracy and smaller participatory groups. But the answer does not lie in mass assemblies that try to achieve the ideals of participation.

In the last ten years, many small organizations staffed by middle-class young people of the New Left have operated as "participatory democracies." Every major city and every rural area to which young people have migrated has had its free schools, food coops, law communes, women's centers, hot lines, and health clinics organized along "participatory" lines.

The term "participatory democracy," apparently coined by Arnold Kaufman in 1960, came into widespread use after 1962, when the Students for a Democratic Society (SDS) gave it a central place in their founding Port Huron Statement. What the term meant then was unclear, and has become less clear since, as it has been applied to virtually any form of organization that brings more people than usual into the decision-making process.

In many radical organizations, however, "participatory democracy" has been more than a slogan. It has implied specific mechanisms for making decisions (1) in such a way that each member sees him- or herself as equal to others in the organization; (2) by unanimity and not by majority rule; (3) by direct democ-

From Jane J. Mansbridge, "The Limits of Friendship," in *Nomos XVI: Participation in Politics*, J. Roland Pennock and John W. Chapman, eds. (New York: New York University Press, 1977), pp. 246–266. Some footnotes omitted.

racy and not through representatives; (4) in face-to-face assembly, not by referenda.

These principles began as the principles of friendship. As Aristotle suggests, friendship is an equal relation, it does not grow or maintain itself well at a distance, and its expression is in unanimity. The participatory vision seeks to extend the mode of friendship to larger groups, and beyond voluntary associations to decision making on the job and in the neighborhood. It attempts to derive the formal, public procedures of government from the informal arrangements of friendship.

Yet the participatory democracy of the New Left is more than a return to familistic, "ancient" or primitive social organization. It embodies ideals—like those of political equality and individual rights—that are the result of several centuries of rational-bureaucratic thought. Participatory democrats demand that actions be taken and decisions be made according to the universalistic criteria to which they are accustomed in a public polity. In constant tension between the informal intimacy of a friendship and the formal, public nature of a government, these small democracies must also face the related tension between their members' conflicting desires for a life in common and for individual autonomy. They handle these tensions by making the same formulae—political equality, unanimity, direct democracy—carry two contradictory burdens. Each formula must, in one or another of its incarnations, both create a community in which an individual is one with others and protect the same individual against the others in that community.

As participatory democracies grow from small groups of close acquaintances to larger associations of strangers, each formula changes its function. The ideal of equality, which a small group of friends experiences as mutual respect, becomes, as the group grows larger, an insistence on exact equality of power. The ideal of unanimity, which among friends reflects similarity in goals, becomes with growth an individual's veto against actions of the majority. Face-to-face contact, which friends value for the pleasure of coming together, becomes in a larger group the insurance that no decision escapes each individual's scrutiny. Distrust replaces trust, and the natural equality, unanimity, and directness of friendship are transformed into rules whose major purpose is the protection of the individual.

Aristotle wrote that "friendship appears to hold city-states together."[1] Friendship also appears to hold participatory democracies together until they evolve into polities that only aggregate and protect individual interests. This essay examines the changes in the functions of political equality, unanimity, and direct democracy that accompany such an evolution. It concludes that, in order to achieve the goals they originally set for themselves, participatory democracies must stay small, stable, and voluntary enough to remain real groups of friends. Building participatory organizations therefore requires a federation of small friendship groups and an ideology that accepts the limitations of participation in larger polities.

Political Equality

Members of a group can become interested in the equal division of power for at least three reasons. They may want to shore up the group's commitment to the equal worth of each member, insuring equality of respect. They may want each member to develop responsibility, feelings of control, and political skill. And they may want to protect members equally against the impositions of others. The first goal, equal worth and equal respect, is the most closely linked to the conditions of friendship. This is usually the initial reason that a small organization self-consciously pursues social, functional, and political equality.

Equal Worth

Almost every small organization of the New Left has gone through the experience of trying to eliminate inequalities of status, interest, functional importance, and power among the jobs in the organization. In Vietnam Summer, a radical political group active in 1967, the political staff itself helped organize a "revolt of the secretaries," because "some of the members of the political staff seemed embarrassed that, often for the first time in their Movement experience, they had others to do their 'shit work' for them.[2] As a result of this upheaval, the secretaries began to advise local organizing projects while the political staff did its own typing.

Why? In the first place, as the Greeks said quite simply, "friendship is equality."[3] Children, who idolize their elders and enjoy dominating younger siblings, like best to play with others their own age. They want to be met and understood, challenged but not overwhelmed. Among adults, friendships form among those who feel in some way on a par, and any situation which puts people in clearly unequal roles is a threat to the friendship between them. Participatory democrats want the exhilaration, mutual trust, and reciprocity of working with equals. They want colleagues, not secretaries.

Second, their empathy prevents these young people from settling for an organization divided into a corps of equals and a maintenance crew. It makes them uneasy about asking others to play roles that they would not want to play themselves. They would be mistaken if they assumed that everyone else shared their own preferences in task, responsibility, or working conditions. But they are rarely mistaken in assuming that all members of an organization want at least to be regarded as equal to the others in worth, value, and dignity.

Natural friendships are built on equality of respect. In would-be friendships, like Vietnam Summer, members use political equality to strengthen their commitment to each others' equal worth. They never succeed perfectly, for no one can respect all others equally. However, the constant attempt to make power more equal can keep the ideal of equal respect vividly present. Institutions devised to spread power equally guarantee some attention to each member. A goal of equal power encourages those who would otherwise concentrate only on their tasks to recognize the psychological effects of their actions on other members of the organization. Finally, the very fact that an organization cares for its individual members enough to worry about equality of power may also contribute to an individual's self-esteem. For self-respect normally depends upon the respect of others, and the ideal of equal power publicly affirms each member's worth.

By concentrating on this one means of fostering equal respect, participatory democracies sometimes neglect other means. One can encourage situations in which people see each other as competent in roles they all consider important. Equal respect can also arise from moments of emotional identification. In the first flush of discovering their common history, women in the radical women's movement felt a tremendous sense of "sisterhood." To feel that all women were your sisters meant that all other differences, or inequalities, faded into insignificance beside the overwhelming understanding that you had, so to speak, grown up together—shared the same fears, troubles, ways of coping, humiliations, and joys. In the era of sisterhood, institutional reminders of the distinctions and inequalities of the larger society became intolerable. We found too much in each woman to respect.

To the extent that we feel we share experience with another, we feel alike, and hence in some sense equal. We think of this underlying experience when we say that although human beings may be unequal in "outward" qualities, they are equal "underneath." Our common experience allows us to view others as somehow independent of their social roles and ti-

tles, which are clearly unequal. Blood brothers and sisters, unequal in skills, often feel these sentiments of identity and equality of respect. Workers, blacks, Jews, women, nationalists—all groups with a common past—can, in stressing that past, evoke feelings of identity and equality. "Fraternity" does not contradict the ideal of equality, . . . but rests on a perception of underlying likeness.

The shared experience that develops a perception of likeness may be deliberately and consciously created. It need not come from a distant past. War, working together under stress, a common "transcendant" experience, or self-revelation in consciousness-raising sessions and encounter groups can quickly create mutual identification, empathy, and respect. In young participatory democracies, a sense of experimentation, of difference from the outside world, and even of struggle against that world, reinforces the members' points of common identity. The small size of the group allows an intense interaction that soon becomes meaningful common history. The experience of identification is a firm basis for equality of respect. When that emotional identification begins to weaken, however, participatory democracies, rather than trying to strengthen it directly, usually turn to a formal commitment to political equality.

In most participatory democracies, the commitment to political equality means a good deal more than the conventional "one person, one vote." In one women's group in New York, each member took twelve disks as a meeting began, having to spend one each time she spoke. Most participatory groups, if they do not ask a different person to chair each meeting, use a "rotating chair," by which each participant after speaking calls on the next, in order to prevent the domination of one chairperson. Large meetings break down into small groups to enable everyone to speak. Keniston reports that in Vietnam Summer,

individuals who were not informed about the issues were sometimes included in policy-making discussions; while the "natural" leaders with the greatest experience, the best ideas, and the surest grasp of the facts sometimes deliberately refrained from voicing their opinions lest they appear to dominate.[4]

Behind such drastic departures from traditional procedures lies the attempt not only to shore up with political institutions a crumbling equality of respect, but also to allow all members to develop their faculties through political participation and to protect their interests equally in the decision-making process.

Self-development

The argument from personal development through political participation appears constantly in the theoretical literature, although it is rarely considered by participatory democrats themselves. Philosophers from Aristotle through Hegel to T. H. Green have suggested that the social and political arrangements of the state should function to help citizens develop their faculties. J. S. Mill added an egalitarian twist by using this general principle as an argument for extending the suffrage. . . . The Port Huron Statement assumed that participatory democracy would "develop man's unfulfilled capacities for reason, freedom and love," and foster his "unrealized potential for self-cultivation, self-direction, self-understanding and creativity."[5]

Yet widespread power, rather than equal power, suffices for this purpose. According to various versions of this argument, members of a polity ought to acquire a sense of responsibility for others in the community. They ought to have the experience of control over some of the larger events that affect their lives. They ought to be able to acquire political skills through the experiences of debating, writing, finding a compromise, standing firm, trying to solve problems, thinking about public issues. None of these different forms of self-development logically requires an equal distribution of power. Individual needs inevitably vary if "need" is defined by psychic or educational benefit. Reducing political inequality helps spread the opportunity for political development. But optimal individual growth depends on flexibility, variety, and the experience of taking as much responsibility as one wants or can stand. It does not depend on an exactly equal division of power.

Equal Protection of Interests

It is when significant conflicts of interest emerge that those affected begin to worry whether the division of power is precisely equal. Liberal tradition sees political equality primarily as a means, in a situation of conflict, to the equal protection of individual interests. Locke argued that each person, giving up in civil society his natural right to defend his interests by force, acquired the right to have those interests protected by the government to the same extent as did other individuals. The right to a "fair and equal Representative" became in Locke's civil society the individual's guarantee of protection.

The extension of a "right" to protect one's interests equally to all sane, mature human beings in a polity has taken generations. The first conceptual step seems to have been extending the ancient idea of equal protection of the law, in which the relevant category entitled by right to equal protection was that of all human beings within a polity, to the right of all sane, mature members of that category to participate in making the law. The second step is from the right to participate to the right to equally weighted participation. The Supreme Court of the United States, without specific mandate in the Constitution and presumably following the logic implicit in the right to vote, itself began this last step when it decided that votes in state and federal elections must be votes of equal weight.

Once competing interests have arisen, the Liberal argument from equal protection of interests leads participatory democrats to seek mechanisms—such as direct democracy, speaking quotas, even the self-censorship of influential members—that give each participant not just an equally weighted vote, but, as far as possible, equal power throughout the decision-making process. A vote of equal weight will not suffice to protect an individual's interests if that individual is deprived of power in spheres other than the ballot box. If the objective is to benefit the poor as much as the rich and the shy as much as the aggressive, provision must be made for the poor or shy to have as much power, electoral and nonelectoral, as the rich and the aggressive.

A major problem with this argument from equal protection of interests is that the standard analogy with voting poses the issue as one of "rights." This suggests an absolute ideal that is neither intuitively appealing nor, in most cases, practical. A democrat might prefer to conclude that if the exercise of power confers benefits, a just society would provide those benefits equally to everyone unless there were compelling reasons to do otherwise. This is not the same as saying that there is an absolute right to equal power, but it does imply that equal power is a goal of importance to be weighed against other competing goals.

Weighing the Costs

Most people assume that the costs of a more equal distribution of power are prohibitively high, whatever the benefits of bolstered equal respect, increased political education, and the equal protection of interests. They fear that more equal participation in decision making will impair the quality of the final product and the efficiency of production.

We do not have a great deal of empirical evidence about how equalizing power within organizations affects their level of efficiency. Warren Bennis and Philip Slater suggest that when creativity, innovation, adaptability, and responsiveness are at a premium, more equal influence in decision making produces a better product. The experiences of Israeli kibbutzim suggest that it is possible to have much more equality in economic and political structures than we now have in the United States without impairing either the quality or the quantity of the goods and services produced. Just as we can probably redistribute income quite a lot without reducing incentives to work, so we may be able to redistribute power far more than we usually imagine without having an adverse effect on the quality or quantity of the product.

Beyond a certain point in any process, attempts to ensure absolutely equal power in every decision will reduce output. The higher the value one puts on the benefits of equal respect, political education and equal protection, the higher the price one will be willing to pay in output. Many participatory democrats are willing to reduce the quantity and perhaps also the quality of production quite dramatically in order to increase equality. Responding to Isaiah Berlin's example of a symphony, some participatory democrats would certainly

argue that if the roles of conductor and players could not be rotated or the prestige of the jobs made more equal, the musicians should consider playing music that does not require a conductor, such as chamber music or some forms of jazz.

Yet even for those participatory democrats who are not especially concerned about output, the pursuit of absolute equality has high costs. By denying the existence of any inequality of power, participatory democrats lose accountability. Minimal inequalities in power do exist in all groups because all groups evolve norms and sanctions. As soon as two human beings come together, they set up rules that allow them to predict and control each others' behavior. In various ways they punish disapproved behavior and reward the approved. Through this process any society or group, no matter how free of formal hierarchy, comes to have its most and least favored members, with corresponding inequalities in the sanctions these individuals can threaten and the rewards they can bestow. One can alter the character and magnitudes of these distinctions, but pretending that none exist only obscures their effects.

Inequalities in energy, in interest, in available time and expertise, or in any other quality valued by a group, always result in de facto inequalities in power. If this inequality is not acknowledged, and a group has grown so large that each member does not have an intimate acquaintance with all its operations, it becomes difficult to know who has had a major impact on a decision, to hold that person to account, and to replace him or her if necessary. Informal social connections and informal sources of information become more important in determining influence than do either the amount of time spent in the organization or the considered opinions of the membership. No one knows where to go for accurate information; those without inside knowledge feel manipulated. Eliminating formal leadership, and therefore accountability, does not eliminate inequality, but drives it underground.

Every society or group also requires a division of labor, no matter how elementary. In a friendship group, in spite of some division of labor, each member is in one sense irreplaceable. The loss of that member makes a great hole in the group, changing its meaning for the others. As the groups grows, different kinds of work usually become differentially important. Some members become less replaceable and therefore more "equal" than others. Participatory democracies consequently try to avoid the division of labor or rotate jobs to make such division temporary. When specialization becomes absolutely necessary, they try to insure that all specialties have equal prestige.

In practice, this often means that participatory groups unconsciously focus on areas in which none of the members has any special expertise. The radical women's movement, for example, has a strong norm of referring whenever possible to personal experience. One function of this norm is to place all members on an equal footing by eliminating the advantage of those who have learned from books or from research. While such an emphasis promotes equal respect, it also makes less likely any enterprise that demands technical expertise and makes large long-term projects almost impossible.

Participatory groups' eagerness to make space for the timid and inexperienced, letting them try their wings without the numbing comparison to others who can do it better, can also make those with skills reluctant to develop them. Members may begin to devalue their skills and therefore themselves. An extremely able and energetic woman in one participatory organization concluded dubiously of herself, "I don't think that I think that I am more competent than people in any sense—well, in some sense I do, in terms of organizing things, I guess, . . ." and later reflected about competence that "It's no longer something that you can go on feeling good about."

Any calculation of the costs and benefits of trying to achieve strict political equality has to take account of a group's real reasons for wanting such equality. If the goal is primarily to promote equal respect among the members, equal political power in every decision will sometimes be less effective than shared experience and the opportunity for members to know each other on more than one functional level. If the goal is to promote the individual political growth of members of the group, a distribution according to need of the opportu-

nity to exercise responsibility and control will almost always be more effective than a quantitatively equal apportionment of power. A plethora of small responsibilities, the rotation of office, specific training, and the general encouragement of competence give the experience of citizenship and control and teach political skills. The precisely equal distribution of power makes most sense as an ideal in a polity where decisions are made and are perceived as being made to the benefit or detriment of sets of individuals, under the assumption that the interests of those individuals ought to be protected equally. This conception of polity is not that of a friendship.

Unanimity

Just as the growth of a group and the divergence of its goals change the meaning of equality from natural mutual respect to a defensive insistence on equal power, so too growth and divergence change the procedure of unanimity or "consensus" from a device for knitting a friendship together into a public weapon against coercion.

The institution of unanimity in decision making was not invented by modern participatory democrats. It is the traditional method for making decisions in communities that conceive of themselves as one body, without faction. Aristotle said of the Greek city-states that "unanimity, which seems akin to friendship, is the principal aim of legislators. They will not tolerate faction at any cost." . . . And an SDS article on draft resistance exhorts:

You are a serious resistance: don't vote on issues, discuss them until you can agree. All the pain of long meetings amounts to a group which knows itself well, [and] holds together with a serious, human spirit. . . .[6]

Rousseau saw majority vote as the hallmark of a polity where "in every heart the social bond is broken:"

As long as several men in assembly regard themselves as a single body, they have only a single will. . . . But when the social bond begins to be relaxed and the State to grow weak, . . . opinion is no longer unanimous. . . .[7]

Those traditional societies that stress group cohesion—the Indian, Japanese, or Javan village councils, for example—make their decisions without a vote. Early New England town meetings rarely tabulated their votes and did not enter the results in the minutes, preferring to maintain the fiction of unanimity. Committees, political caucuses, street gangs, and experimental small groups tend to make their decisions by consensus.

In traditional societies, insistence on consensus often works not so much to resolve conflicts as to prevent them from arising. Maintaining the unity of the group is more important than the benefits of open conflict resolution. Participatory groups value this unity. They assume that the group can be fundamentally of one mind and that differences can be worked out either by rational discussion or by emotional transcendence. One food coop member suggested as an answer to his group's problems, "Just put an ounce of grass in each order," and expected conflicts to be resolved in the emotional unity of the group.

Moments of consensual unity do make a profound impression on the participants. One woman describes a crisis meeting in a radical newspaper as "the first political meeting I ever went to where I really understood consensus."

It was such an exciting meeting—almost everybody talked—there were about thirty women in the room—and it went from about a total split to finally someone saying, "Listen, if we can't do that we don't deserve the paper," and then everybody saying, "Right on!" It was one of the few meetings where it goes around and then people just really come together and say "Far out!" You know it's right. It was such a *high* . . . it was wonderful. It was such a high.

In a small friendship group, unanimity expresses the desire of the group to act as one. As the group extends its boundaries but still remains a small and homogeneous community, it preserves the procedures of unanimous consensus in order to preserve its unity. This is the point at which Mike, of Boston's North End, worried about the effect of a vote. It is the point at which Aristotle's legislators tried to bring about unanimity. It is also, however, the point at which the procedure of unanimity comes to protect the rights of the less aggressive, less verbal, or the minority, by giving

them a potential veto, making it more likely that others will listen to them and try to understand their points of view. One woman argued for consensus rather than majority rule within her organization on the grounds that:

Minority groups get trashed* so easily. . . . One thing about consensus is that in order to reach it, you need to have discussion and really go over things so that people understand them. The trouble with majority rule is that it's so easy just to make the decision, and nobody understands.

Consensus protects the minority from being "trashed" by allowing it to command sufficient attention from the majority to make its position understood. Consensus guarantees respect and listening, by right.

Finally, as the group becomes a public polity and important conflicts of interest develop, the *liberum veto* of consensus turns into a negative weapon, allowing every member of the association to carve out his or her own bill of rights, a minimum area of noninterference. In a debate on consensus as one radical constitution was hammered out, I heard most often as an argument for the procedure of unanimity, "I don't trust anyone except myself!"

This bitter, self-protective refusal to be coerced by a majority has the most force when the potential harm to the minority is most immediately obvious, as it would be if the group were going to take illegal action. But within an organization, a specific subgroup like lesbians, who have had the experience of being in a permanent minority, may also fear the slow, subtle process of having their interests in that organization consistently weakened. They see themselves in the position of the South before 1860, and like Calhoun they want a constitution that gives them a veto. Given their generally left wing politics, most members of a participatory organization have had the experience of being in a permanent minority on national issues, and thus suspicion of majority rule is widespread.

*"Trashing," which originally meant looting and breaking windows in a riot, involves hurting a person in a way that treats him with disrespect. Here it refers to the way a dominant majority within the group might callously ignore the interests and feelings of a minority.

Yet consensus, while encouraging some minorities to talk, subdues others. One meeting that I considered a triumph of consensus broke into small groups for half a day at the beginning to give everyone a chance to speak, took an entire weekend to go over each issue carefully, and eventually brought potentially irreconcilable positions into harmony. The final decisions were made unanimously. Months afterwards, however, one of the participants could say, "I found myself agreeing with things at the first mass meeting that if I'd been voting I certainly wouldn't have agreed to. Consensus is often bullying unless it's a clear consensus."

Voting by secret ballot rather than oral consensus protects the more insecure members of the community. As a participant in a town meeting reported, "If you vote by ballot you haven't got to get up and voice your opinion, you haven't got to,—ah—you can vote yes or no and nobody's going to know the difference." When middle-class students met with working- and lower-class people in assemblies of more than twenty in Chicago's JOIN, "voting was more democratic [than the process of reaching oral unanimity] . . . because the community people, intimidated by the verbalism of the student organizers, felt free to cast ballots as they wished."[8]

When unanimity comes to be used in a public and formal manner to protect the individual rights of those participants who dare to use it as a veto, it also has the contradictory effects of creating deadlock and forcing other participants into positions contrary to their wishes. In this incarnation, it may not be the most effective protection against coercion.

Face-to-Face Direct Democracy

Growth also brings changes in the meaning of direct, face-to-face decision making. A small group gains much of its energy from the pleasure its members take in face-to-face contact. Because face-to-face relations are the cement of friendship, when a group grows or begins to diverge in its goals, its members institute

face-to-face meetings as a way to correct inaccuracies of perception, iron out differences, and create a spirit of community. They oppose referenda, for referenda do not allow the discussion that brings about a real consensus. They oppose representation, for it deprives the membership of the experience of citizenship. Finally, when major conflicts of interest develop, members demand face-to-face meetings as a protection against the potential coercion of an elite. They now perceive referenda as giving them control at only one stage of the process, when a question has been formulated, discussed, worded and placed, perhaps manipulatively, on the ballot. They now perceive representation as allowing a small group to make decisions in its own interest rather than in the interest of the members.

At this last stage, the legacy of Liberal consent theory provides a rationale for the requirements of both direct democracy and unanimity, for in Locke's nature every man is presumptively free and thus bound in civil society only by laws to which he has given his consent. . . .

To young Americans brought up on consent theory, who lived most of their lives with a war to which they in no way consented, such words strike home. The authors of the Port Huron Statement believed that "the felt powerlessness of ordinary people" depended on "the actual structural separation of the people from power." The Statement did not explicitly recommend direct democracy, but members of SDS, following its implicit logic, rejected representation in their internal governmental structure. Wave after wave of leaders in the New Left soon became willing to mix direct democracy with representation. However, the continuation of the Vietnam War and other bitter disappointments in national politics intensified the distrust of representative institutions from below. As one young woman put it, "Everyone just has so much experience with representative democracy not working. The only way to influence anything is to be directly in on it." The traditional Anglo-American fear of power, the suspicion that in elections a voter is only a means to an end he may not suspect, the homely knowledge that people who run for office are not like those they claim to represent, the proud conviction of individual uniqueness—all make representation suspect once the group grows beyond the bounds of mutual trust.

Yet direct democracy is not the perfect instrument either for producing cohesion or for preventing coercion. Unless there is practically no conflict, face-to-face assembles, designed to produce feelings of community, can backfire and intimidate the less self-reliant. Face-to-face communication, despite its many advantages, usually increases the level of emotional tension. Where there are persistent conflicts, open hostility may develop. Because the fear of such hostility and disagreement is, at least in American society, an important cause of nonparticipation in politics, some citizens will forgo their chance to participate in face-to-face politics rather than expose themselves to what they feel is a frightening experience.

Residents of a Vermont town say again and again of the town meeting that "all it is is more or less a fight, a big argument," observe that there are "too damn many arguments," or sum it up by exclaiming, "I just don't like disagreeable situations!" A woman in the radical women's movement reports, "I don't go to meetings anymore. They depress me." The causes are the same. Face-to-face participation in political decisions, rather than creating community, may frighten away the very people it is supposed to bring into more active participation.

When conflicts become extreme, direct democracy is used to guard against the domination of a few. However, replacing representative with direct democracy does not eliminate differences in power. Electing a representative may visibly deprive a voter of day-to-day control, but the unregulated marketplace of time and energy in a direct democracy often creates an even greater distance between the active and the ordinary members.

The Chicago high-school student who wants a direct democracy because "No one can represent me. I'm the only one who knows what I'm thinking and no one else can present my views," fears for his individuality. Representation forces him into anonymity, identified only with an interest or set of interests. But for most people the practical effect of a mass meeting is worse—it results in complete invisibility.

Small groups allow each person to communicate his or her views, either through speaking or through general demeanor. In large assemblies, however, most people express themselves only by voting after the discussion has come to an end. They can contribute to the emotional tone of the discussion by murmuring, cracking jokes with their neighbors, shuffling their feet, or in other ways indicating their approbation or discontent, but as individuals they are not likely to make an impression on the assembled body. They might decide that their views have been expressed adequately by others, thus turning the mass meeting into another form of representative democracy. But because participants have no way of selecting speakers to represent them, their views may not be represented at all.

Coercion and Community

No one of the principles of participatory democracy inevitably requires the others. A polity may have political equality without unanimity, unanimity without equality, and face-to-face direct democracy without either unanimity or equality. Yet in participatory democracies these three principles do serve many of the same ends, depending on where the organization lies on a spectrum from unity to diversity, informality to formality. In the small friendship group, equality, unanimity, and direct contact work to create a feeling of community, a sense of mutual claim. In the larger polity with diverse goals, the same procedures work to protect the individual members of the group against coercion. In most real participatory democracies (no longer friendships but not yet universalistic polities) equality, unanimity, and direct democracy must at the same time knit the group together and protect individuals against the group.

This double function derives from the underlying hope of all participatory organizations, small and large, to create a society which is at once unitary and noncoercive. Like the otherwise dissimilar ideals of suburban "good government" and the "withering away of the state," the participatory ideal implies that some process, whether emotional or rational, can bring about solutions that are best for all and untainted by coercion.

This ideal can never be fully realized. No two people have identical interests. Nor can an individual in contact with others fully escape the coercive effects of their expectations and the sanctions they may impose. Friends are able to compromise their interests and submit to group norms in a way they *feel* is free and spontaneous. They do not perceive costs in the relationship as costs; they do not perceive mutual sanctions held against each other as sanctions.

"When the social bond is broken," however, conflicts sometimes require that one party explicitly win or lose, rather than those conflicts being compromised, transfigured, or their implications ignored in the warmth of friendship. At the same time the "free rider" who takes no responsibility must be subjected to overt rather than covert coercion. As a group grows larger, it becomes necessary either to bear unresolved conflicts and the strain of greatly disparate contributions or to find a substitute for friendship's "spontaneous," "costless" compromise and compliance. The two possible substitutes are intensified social pressure or the institution of rational-legal rules and sanctions. Most participatory groups, still modeling themselves on friendships, choose intensified social pressure. To recognize explicitly that the nature of their group had changed would lead them to consider more formal standards.

Although the unitary polity is seductive to the imagination and at times immensely fulfilling to its members, such a system does not always meet everyone's needs. Small size itself is often more coercive than large, for a small group can exert more intense pressure on its members, and in a large group the dissident can more easily find an ally. The small group is a powerful instrument of behavior change. In a nonparticipatory society, individuals, like those who join encounter or consciousness-raising groups, may use a group's pressure to change themselves in ways they have freely chosen. But if membership is no longer fully voluntary, the small group can become an instrument for inculcating the values of a particular political system, in the manner of Hitler's Jugendbund or of a corporation that employs "participative" techniques. Even in the absence of conscious state or corporate direction, if every member of a society or work-

place were expected to participate politically through such a group, individuals might no longer feel or be free to use participation for their own ends. They might easily be drawn into groups whose ends they did not share and find themselves manipulated in ways they did not intend.

The assumption of one common interest is not, in fact, as appropriate to a neighborhood or workplace group as to a small voluntary association. In the 1970s in the United States most groups that operate on a participatory basis have a membership self-selected from a small group of friends or potential friends, similar in age, life style, and aspiration. They are usually young, unencumbered by children or ties to a given geographical area. They are relatively free to leave the association if it does not fill their needs. Most actual neighborhoods and jobs, however, attract individuals who have no such prior attachment or common goals, who may not want to make the commitment to any group, or to a new group, and who are also, once established, less able to leave. A unitary community may not be what they want or need. At least in the United States labor unions that have preserved a fictional unanimity turn out be be more coercive than those few that have legitimated conflict and faction.

Within a large workplace or neighborhood, small groups may be able to form on the basis of common values, aspirations, and personal liking. But since the small group is such a powerful force, the option of leaving and joining another group must always be open, and any organization composed of small groups will require a mechanism for helping people shift from group to group. For most people, getting together with new people, learning to trust them, committing oneself to them, and then leaving for either work or personal reasons is a traumatic process. A system of small groups, if it is to include mobility, almost demands the self-reliant, autonomous personality it hopes to create.

Decentralization

While members of large participatory democracies use participatory procedures to protect themselves from coercion, their more deeply held goal is a society in which coercion will seem nonexistent—a friendship. They are trying to create in their participatory democracies what Robert Redfield called a "folk society." This is a society with little division of labor, direct and consensual in nature. It is a society so small that everybody knows everybody well, in which "all human beings admitted to the society are treated as persons; one does not deal impersonally ('thing fashion') with any other participant in the little world of that society."[9]

A sound instinct for self-preservation draws people to such associations, where they can find refuge from an intensely competitive society in mutual respect. It is not strange that when their associations grow beyond the bounds of a close-knit friendship group, members should try to retain the equality of respect, the directness and the unanimity that marked their earlier experience.

Yet when a participatory organization expands and its members' goals diverge, mechanisms that at one time served to maintain the sense of community come to be used by individuals against the group. The principles of equality, unanimity and direct, face-to-face democracy, applied in a changed context may not always serve their new purpose of protection well, and may make it difficult for the less aggressive, or those without the right social contacts, to develop and grow within the organization. The principle of equal power can paralyze an organization, hide the real dynamics of decision making, drive competent people out, and promote a sense of lassitude and irresponsibility. The principle of unanimity can intimidate the nonverbal and the insecure, and produce immobility. The principle of direct, face-to-face democracy can work to benefit those with the time for meetings, the social contacts that make those meetings enjoyable, and the self-confidence to speak in them.

If the goal of a more participatory society is to provide its members with a context of equal respect, direct control over events that affect them and the opportunity for self-development, it must be based on groups small enough to work as friendships. The small group, like a true friendship, can come to accept its members as they are and can give them support for growing in ways they choose. It can serve as a buffer against the pressures of a manipulative society, allowing its members to choose their own pace and direction of development.

If, however, the goal of a participatory society is to protect individual interests equally, that society has already grown beyond the point of "selfless" friendship. New institutions are required in keeping with the new purpose. The most common response at this point is to establish a system in which the members periodically elect decision-makers to represent their interests. This may be a good system for ensuring equal protection, but, aside from the obvious difficulties in guaranteeing accountability and equality of representation, it does not provide the psychological or developmental benefits of participatory democracy.

Perhaps what we need are organizations that combine small participatory groups as primary units with a reformed representative democracy for making larger-scale decisions. Such organizations could probably do more than traditional representative ones to ensure that all their members' interests were protected equally, since they would bring more people into watchful, active participation. A mixture of small groups and representative democracy could also do more for individual psychological development, as small participatory groups would give their members opportunities to work with others, take responsibility for others, and gain a prouder sense of themselves. Finally, the small groups in such a "mixed" organization could provide their members with a refuge of equal respect.

The problems of arranging genuinely supportive small groups and designing representative institutions which can tie them together make the enterprise I suggest difficult. The real obstacle, however, is that no one now wants such organizations. Most reformers seek only to expand the right to representation, e.g., by having workers elect their managers or by having neighborhoods elect their school boards. Participatory activists, seduced by the experiences they have tasted on a smaller scale and perhaps by the power that accrues to activists in a large "unitary" group, envision the ideal large organization and even the ideal nation-state as friendships. Yet both solutions remain fatally flawed. Traditional representative structures seldom help people to develop their faculties or to reduce their sense of powerlessness. Participatory systems based on mass assemblies fail when they try to stretch the principles of direct, face-to-face, consensual, egalitarian democracy beyond the bounds of friendship.

Notes

---

1. Aristotle, *Ethics,* trans. John Warrington (New York: Everyman's Library, 1963). p. 167.

2. Kenneth Keniston, *The Young Radicals* (New York: Harcourt, Brace and World, 1968), p. 160.

3. "Philotes isotes legetai," Aristotle, *Ethics,* p. 174.

4. Keniston, *Young Radicals,* p. 166.

5. "The Port Huron Statement," in Paul Jacobs and Saul Landau, eds. *The New Radicals* (New York: Vintage Books, 1966), p. 154.

6. Dee Jacobsen, "We've Got to Reach Our Own People" (1967), quoted in Staughton Lynd, "Prospects for the New Left," *Liberation* 13 (January 1971), 22.

7. Jean-Jacques Rousseau, *The Social Contract,* trans. G. D. H. Cole (New York: Dutton, 1950), p. 102. Rousseau assumed that a city as large as Rome, at 400,000, could act as a single body (pp. 89–90).

8. Lynd, "Prospects," p. 22.

9. Robert Redfield, "The Folk Society," *The American Journal of Sociology,* 52 (1947), 301.

The City in the Future of Democracies

Robert Dahl

Beginning with an imaginary debate at a constitutional convention among people trying to design an ideal democratic system in the year 2000, Robert Dahl explores a question that has been in the background for much of the preceding discussion: What is the ideal size of a democratic government? Different sized political units, he argues, demand different conceptions of democracy. Indeed, he points out, there is nothing wrong with imagining democratic government to be like a set of "Chinese boxes" — each with its own integrity and identity. The task, then, is to locate the ideal size for genuine participatory democracy. The nation, he argues, is too immense to be fully self-governing; nor can the town or workplace fill the bill. The right answer, he contends, is the city. If organized, run correctly, and kept to the right size, the city holds out the best prospect for meaningful self-government.

This is a somewhat modified and condensed version of an address by Robert Dahl, "The City in the Future of Democracies," originally printed in the *American Political Science Review,* 61 (December 1967), pp. 953–970. Some footnotes omitted.

I

I have a fantasy in which a modern Constitutional Convention assembles a group of fifty-five men or thereabouts whose commitment to democracy and whose wisdom are not in doubt. Their task is to design democratic institutions suitable for this small planet in the year 2000. And so they come to the problem of the unit.

Being learned, as well as wise, naturally they recall the city-state. Well, says one, since full civic participation is possible only if the number of citizens is small, let us arrange for a world of small democratic city-states. Let the unit of democracy, then, be the small city.

Ah, says another, you forget that the world of the 21st century is not ancient Greece. You even forget that ancient Greece was the setting for a highly defective international system. The trouble with the small city in the modern world is that there are too many problems it cannot cope with, because they go beyond its boundaries. Think of some of the problems of American cities: revenues, transportation, air and water pollution, racial segregation, inequality, public health . . . I would make the list longer, but it is already long enough to show that the small city is obviously an inappropriate unit and that we have to locate democracy in a larger unit. I urge that we consider the metropolis.

But, says a third, even the boundaries of the metropolis are smaller than the kinds of problems you mention. The legal boundaries of metropolis are an obsolete legacy of the past. What we need is metropolitan governments with legal boundaries extending to the limits of the metropolitan area itself, boundaries set not by obsolete patterns of settlement but by present densities.

Your argument is persuasive, says a fourth, but you do not carry it far enough. Demographers and planners now tell us that in the United States, to take one example, there is an uninterrupted urban area on the East Coast extending from Virginia to Maine. Even your metropolitan governments will be too small there. And in the future much of the world will surely be as densely settled as our Eastern seaboard. Consequently, I believe that we must design regional democracies, controlled by democratic governments responsive to the electorate of a whole region.

Well, says a fifth, I notice you have already bypassed such things as states and provinces, which is all to the good, since they are as anachronistic as the small city. But you will have to agree that even if you carve up the world into regional governments big enough, for instance, to cover the Eastern seaboard, you cannot expect these units to be adequate for very long. With the population of the world reaching six billion, or ten billion, most of the United States will soon be a vast, undifferentiated, urban mass. Other countries are headed in the same direction. There is, then, a good deal to be said for the only traditional unit that enjoys consensus and allegiance on a scale commensurate with the problems. I mean, of course, the nation-state. If we were to think of the United States as one city, as we shall have to do in the future, it is obvious that the proper unit to bound our sovereign electorate cannot be smaller than the United States. With minor changes here and there, the nation-state is probably good for another century or so. So let us proceed to make use of it by eliminating the powers of all the intermediate units, which are, after all, only obstacles that permit local groups to frustrate national majorities.

But, objects a sixth, you are still too much the victim of the past to think clearly about the future. Obviously our very existence depends on our capacity to create a government that will subordinate the nation-state to a larger legal order. Just as your villages, towns, cities, metropolises, and regions are too small to cope singlehandedly with their problems, so too is your nation-state, even one as big as the United States, the USSR, or China. The fatal flaw of the nation-state is its inablity to eliminate interstate violence; and because of our genius for violence we can now destroy the species. Even prosaic problems are now beyond the control of the nation-state: the efficiencies that come from world markets, monetary problems, the balance of trade, the movement of labor and skills, air and water pollution, the regulation of fishing, the dissemination of nuclear weapons. . . . I know it is bold, but we must plan for a world government, and to us that surely means a democratic world government. The appropriate electorate for the 21st century is nothing smaller than the human race. The only legitimate majority is the majority of mankind.

At this point there is a tumult of objections and applause. Finally the first speaker gains the floor. Each speaker, he says, has been more persuasive than the last. But, he adds, I simply cannot understand how my learned friend, the last speaker, proposes to govern the world, if he has in mind, as I thought, a single world-wide electorate, a single parliament, a single executive, all attempting to represent that nonexistent monstrosity, a single world-wide majority. I say that even if it would miraculously hold together, which I doubt, a democracy with six billion citizens is no democracy at all. I, for one, do not wish to be only one six-billionth part of any government. One may as well accept a despot and have done with the Big Lie that what we have is a democracy.

Ah, the advocate of a democratic world government now replies, of course I meant that there would be subordinate governments, which would be democracies.

I thank my learned colleague for this important clarification, says the advocate of the small city-state. I now propose that these subordinate governments consist of units about the size of small cities.

Again there is tumult. The speaker who now gains the floor is the one who had earlier spoken in behalf of the metropolis. Hold on, he objects, if we are to have a subordinate unit, surely it must be one large enough to deal with the problems of an urban society. Obviously this unit should be the metropolis. . . .

Suddenly it becomes as clear to everyone at the Constitutional Convention as it has become to you that the argument over the unit has gone completely around in a circle, that it has now started all over again, that it has no logical terminus, that it could go on forever. Perhaps that is why we still talk about the city-state.

For the logic seems unassailable. Any unit you choose smaller than the globe itself—and that exception may be temporary—can be shown to be smaller than the boundaries of an urgent problem generated by activities of some people who are outside the particular unit and hence beyond its authority. Rational control over such problems dictates ever larger units, and democratic control implies a larger electorate, a larger majority. Yet the larger the unit, the greater the costs of uniform rules, the larger the minorities who cannot prevail, and the more watered down is the control of the individual citizen. Hence the argument for larger units does not destroy the case for small units. What it does is to make a seemingly small but radical shift in the nature of the arguments.

For we drop completely the notion so dear to the Greeks and early Romans that to be legitimate a unit of government must be wholly autonomous. With autonomy we also drop the belief that there is a single sovereign unit for democracy, a unit in which majorities are autonomous with respect to all persons outside the unit and authoritative with respect to all persons inside the unit. Instead we begin to think about appropriate units of democracy as an ascending series, a set of Chinese boxes, each larger and more inclusive than the other, each in some sense democratic, though not always in quite the same sense, and each not inherently less nor inherently more legitimate than the other.

Although this may be a discomforting and alien conception in some democratic countries where political tradition has focused on the overriding legitimacy, autonomy, and sovereignty of the nation-state and of national majorities, even in these countries the evolution of pluralistic institutions has vastly modified the applicability of monistic conceptions of democracy. And of course in democracies with federal systems, like Switzerland, Canada, and the United States, or in nonfederal countries like the Netherlands that inherit a political tradition powerfully shaped by federalism and the legitimacy of pluralist institutions, to see the units of democracy as a set of Chinese boxes is very much easier—though even in these countries it will take some rethinking and a vast amount of institution building before any of us can think easily about the nation-state as a Chinese box nested in yet larger ones of equal legitimacy.

Our imaginary Constitutional Convention, and our Chinese boxes do not, of course, bring us much closer to a solution to our original problem of the appropriate unit for democracy. But they do suggest that there is not necessarily a single kind of unit, whether it be city-state or nation-state, in which majorities have some specially sacred quality not granted to majorities in other units, whether smaller or larger, more or less inclusive.

A Frenchman, perhaps even an Englishman, or any strong believer in majority rule will tell me that surely in one of these boxes there must be a majority that is sovereign, or else conflicts between different majorities, one of which may in a larger perspective be only a minority, can never be resolved. I ask, very well, a majority of what unit? And my critic will say, the majority, naturally, of the nation. To which I reply, *why* is this more sacred than the others? Because it is larger? But I can point to still larger majorities in the making of this world. Will you remain faithful to your answer when your nation is a unit in a world polity? Or will you not, instead, revert to federalist conceptions? Anyway, I might add, in a number of federal countries, including some rather old and respectable representative democracies, citizens have grown moderately accustomed to the idea that national majorities—or rather their spokesmen—are not necessarily more sacred than majorities or minorities in certain kinds of less inclusive units. This is logically untidy, and it requires endless readjustments as perspectives and levels of interdependence change. But it makes for a better fit with the inevitable pluralistic and decentralizing forces of political life in nation-states with representative governments.

The hitherto unreported debate at our imaginary Convention also suggests that in a world of high population densities, ease of communication, and great interdependence, where autonomy is in fact impossible short of the earth itself, we confront a kind of dilemma that the Greeks could hardly have perceived. Let me suggest it by advancing a series of propositions:

The larger and more inclusive the unit, the more its government can regulate aspects of the environment that its citizens want to regulate, from air and water pollution and racial justice to the dissemination of nuclear weapons.

Yet the larger and more inclusive a unit with a representative government, and the more complex its tasks, the more participation must be reduced for most people to the single act of voting in an election.

Conversely, the smaller the unit, the greater the opportunity for citizens to participate in the decisions of their government, yet the less of the environment they can control.

Thus for most citizens, participation in very large units becomes minimal and in very small units it becomes trivial. At the extremes, citizens may participate in a vast range of complex and crucial decisions by the single act of casting a ballot; or else they have almost unlimited opportunities to participate in decisions over matters of no importance. At the one extreme, then, the people vote but they do not rule; at the other, they rule—but they have nothing to rule over.

These are extreme cases, and if they were all there were, it would be a discouraging prospect. But may there not be others in between?

Before we turn to this question, I want you to notice that our hypothetical Constitutional Convention and the Chinese boxes also hint at the possibility that we may need different models of democracy for different kinds of units. I see no reason to think that all kinds of units with democratic institutions and practices do, can, or should behave in the same way—no reason, then, why we should expect democracy in a committee, in a city, and in a nation to be the same either in fact or in ideal. If we expect that representative government in the nation-state is roughly equivalent to democratic participation in a committee then we are bound to be misled in our understanding of political life, in our hopes, and in our strategies for changing the world from what it is to what it ought to be.

II

If the nation-state is too immense, and if interdependence and population densities render the autonomous self-governing city-state too costly, are there units powerful enough, autonomous enough, and small enough to permit, and in the right circumstances to encourage, a body of citizens to participate actively and rationally in shaping and forming vital aspects of their lives in common? Is there, in this sense, an optimal unit?

There are a number of candidates for this position. Occasionally, for example, one still runs across a nostalgia for the village—a nostalgia strongest, I suspect, among people who have never lived in small towns. There are also suggestions going back nearly a century that we shift our search for the democratic unit away from the government of the state to the government of nonstate institutions such as the workplace, business firm, corporation, or industry. And lately there has been a resurgence of interest, especially among young political activists, in the old and recurring idea of reconstructing democracy around small units that would offer unlimited opportunities for participation.

Although I cannot possibly do justice here to these various alternatives, I would like to venture a few comments on each.

The fragmented and even shattered community in which modern man seems condemned to live tempts one to suppose that the appropriate unit for democratic life might be the village or small town. Only there, it might be thought, could one ever hope to find a center of life small enough so that it permits wide participation and small enough besides to foster the sense of unity, wholeness, belonging, of membership in an inclusive and solitary community which we sometimes seem to want with such a desperate yearning. Speaking for myself, I doubt whether man can ever recapture his full sense of tribal solidarity. Like childhood itself, there is no returning to the childhood of man. What is more, the attempt to satisfy this craving, if carried far on a densely packed globe, leads not to community but to those hideously destructive forms of tribalism that this century has already seen too much of.

Anyway, I suspect that the village probably never was all that it is cracked up to be. The village, including the preindustrial village, is less likely to be filled with harmony and solidarity than with the oppressive weight of repressed deviation and dissent which, when they appear, erupt explosively and leave a lasting burden of antagonism and hatred. I have not been able to discover much evidence of the consensual *Gemeinschaft* in descriptions of the small town of Springdale in upstate New York, or St. Denis in Quebec, or Peyrane, the village in the Vaucluse, or the small English town of Glossop near Manchester, or the peasant village of Montegrano in south Italy, or the Tanjore village in south India that André Béteille recently described.

Here, for example, is how Horace Miner saw political life in the French-Canadian parish of St. Denis thirty years ago:

> Politics is a topic of continual interest and one which reaches fever heat during election time . . . The whole parish is always divided between the "blues" or Conservatives, and the "reds." Party affiliations follow family lines and family cliques and antagonisms. The long winter *veillées* are attended almost invariably by family groups of similar political belief. Constituents of each party have a genuine dislike for those of the other . . . Election time is one of great tension, of taunts and shouting as parishioners get their evening mail . . . Insults are common, and many speaking acquaintances are dropped. During the last election the minority candidate had to have one meeting in the parish in secret, another open but under provincial police protection . . . Campaigns reach their climax with the *assemblée contradictoire*, at which both candidates speak. Characteristically at these meetings there are organized strong-arm tactics, drinking, and attempts to make each candidate's speech inaudible . . .
>
> The chicanery of politicians is a byword in the parish. Factional strife threatens the life of every organized association . . . On the whole the associational life of the community is weak. The people are not joiners.[1]

Thus village democracy before the demos was ruined by industrialization and urbanization!

If the democratic village seems hardly worth seeking in this industrial and postindustrial epoch, the prospect is all the more appealing that democracy might be extended to the place where most adult citizens spend most of their time—their place of work. Professional people with a great deal of autonomy, academics who enjoy an extraordinary amount of autonomy and a fair measure of self-government in our universities, executives and adminstrators who see authority relationships from above rather than from below, all are likely to underestimate the consequences for the average citizen in a modern industrial society flowing from the fact that at his place of work he is a rather low-level subordinate in a system of hierarchical relationships. Although the term democracy has been prostituted in the service of employee relationships, the fact is that practically everywhere in the world, the industrial workplace—the factory, industry, or corporation, whether owned privately or publicly—is no democracy in any sense consistent with our usage in the realm of the state. "The idea of a factory, nationalized or privately owned," it has been said, "is the idea of command."[2] The factory, the enterprise, the industry, the corporation is a hierarchy; it may be an aristocracy, an oligarchy, a monarchy, a despotism, but it is not a democracy. This is as true in socialist economies as in capitalist and mixed economies. A century ago Engels asserted that hierarchy would be necessary in the factory even under socialism, that even in a socialist enterprise the worker would lose his autonomy. . . .

Whether the workplace should be democratized, and if so how and how much, are questions that need to be distinguished from the problem of regulating the enterprise, industry, or corporation to ensure that it accomplishes the social and public functions that are the only reason the rest of us are willing to grant its vast legal rights, privileges and immunities, and extraordinary power. If democratic states have become immense, so have corporations. There are privately owned corporations that have gross annual revenues greater than the GNP of most countries of the world, that spend annually sums greater than the entire budgets of the governments of most of the nation-states in the world. To ensure that these immense resources and powers are used for public purposes is a staggering problem. But internal democracy in the factory, firm, industry, or corporation is not necessarily a more effective means of public control than regulating a hierarchically administered firm by competition and the price system, by a

regulatory agency, by government ownership, or by various combinations of these and other possibilities. Indeed, even if the modern corporation were internally democratic, no matter whether it were public or private and no matter whether it were to operate in an economy predominantly privately owned or predominantly publicly owned, I do not think we any more than the Soviets or Yugoslavs would want to dispense entirely with such external controls as competition and the price system. In short, no system of *internal* control negates the need for a system of *external* controls that compel or induce those who exercise authority within the enterprise, whether these managers are chosen by and are accountable to stockholders, workers, or the state, to employ their power and resources for jointly beneficial purposes rather than for exploiting consumers.

But even if we can distinguish the problem of internal democracy from that of external control, the problem does not vanish. It is true that in many developed countries with representative governments, trade-union power has substituted bargaining for undiluted hierarchy in the control of wages and working conditions. But even where they are most powerful, labor unions have by no means created a democratic factory or industry; moreover, as a result more of apathy than of repression, few unions anywhere have developed a really high degree of internal democracy. Aside from a few scattered instances elsewhere, the most massive, ambitious, and far-reaching experiment in democraticizing the workplace has been taking place in Yugoslavia since 1950. Sober studies suggest that while the system of workers' control has problems—some of them, like apathy and Michels' iron law of oligarchy, familiar to every student of democratic organizations—it might well prove to be a viable system of internal control. If it does, it will surely stand as an alternative with a very great appeal—at least in the long run—to workers in other industrial nations. If workers can participate in the government of their factories in Yugoslavia, and if these factories prove to be relatively efficient, surely the whole question of internal democracy will come alive in other countries.

Yet even if it should prove to be possible,

efficient, and desirable, I do not believe that democracy in the workplace is a substitute for democracy in the state. For one thing, I doubt whether democracy in the workplace can be preserved indefinitely unless there is democracy in the state. Moreover, where an opposition party is illegal in the state, opposition in the factory has distinct limits. Finally—and this is the most important point—the workplace is not as important as the state and with increasing leisure it may grow less so. To accept as a focus for self-government a type of unit that is and must be concerned with only a small part of the range of collective concerns would be to trivialize the democratic idea. I find it hard to believe that man's aspiration toward rational control over his environment by joint action with his fellow men will ever be satisfied by democraticizing the production of aspirin, cars, and television sets.

III

Any form of political participation that cannot be performed more or less simultaneously but must be carried on sequentially runs into the implacable barrier of time. Time's relentless arrow flies directly to the Achilles heel of all schemes for participatory democracy on a grand scale. It is easy to show that any unit small enough for all the members to participate fully (where each member has the opportunity to present his views and have them discussed) cannot be larger than a working committee. If you doubt this, I ask you to sit down with pencil and paper and do a few exercises with various assumptions as to the time available for decisions and the time required for each participant to make his point or at least present his point of view. You will quickly see how cruel is time's neutral guillotine. Or let me simply evoke your own experience with committees to remind you how quickly a committee grows too large for every member to participate fully. Or consider the experience of legislative committees, cabinets, regulatory commissions, judicial bodies. Would we not all agree that an effective working committee can have no more than—let us err on the side of

generosity—thirty to forty members? Drawing on their own experience, most readers, I imagine, would cut these figures by a half or two-thirds.

Now if the great advantage of a unit the size of a working committee is that it allows full participation by its members, its great drawback, from a democratic point of view, is that unless it is a representative body or an agent of a representative body it ought not be given much public authority. Either the unit, though small, is granted authority because it represents a much larger number of citizens; or else, not being a representative body, it has little authority other than to recommend and advise; or else, if it has much power and is not a representative body, its power is illegitimate. In an interdependent society, any significant power wielded by a body the size of a working committee is bound to have important effects on citizens not sitting on that committee. Consequently either the committee is representative or its power is illegitimate. We can hardly espouse the small, self-governing, fully participatory unit as a normative goal if it is illegitimate. If it is representative, then it is no longer a body in which all citizens can participate fully. We have run into a cul-de-sac, as you see, and so we must get back to the starting point.

Some of you may regard this as a pessimistic analysis. It is, I admit, a very large fly in the ointment. Like death, it may be a brutal and perhaps even a tragic limit on man's possibilities, but I do not see why this conclusion must lead to pessimism. The idea of democracy would never have gotten off the ground if enthusiastic democrats had not been willing to settle for something a good deal less than complete and equal participation by all citizens in all decisions. It is worth recalling that in Athens, where the opportunities for free male citizens to participate in running the city seem to have been about as great as they have ever been anywhere, citizens were chosen for what was probably the most coveted participation in the life of the polis—a seat on the Council of Five Hundred, the inner council, or the various administrative boards—by lot or, in the case of the Board of Generals, by election, and to that extent these bodies were instances of representative government and not direct democracy. Participation in the Assembly, which met about once a month, was scarcely the fullest flowering of participatory democracy. I have been to enough town meetings myself to know something of their limitations. If you think of a town meeting in which a quorum sometimes required the presence of 6,000 people, where maybe as many as 30–40,000 were eligible to attend, and where perhaps 4–5,000 were frequently present, it is obvious that most Athenian citizens must have lived their lives without once speaking to their fellow citizens in the Assembly. That, one judges from the reports in Thucydides, was a forum that gave preference to orators.

Nonetheless, I doubt—although we shall never know—whether many Athenians felt frustrated because their opportunities to participate were not as unlimited as their skies. Between the working committee and the nation-state there is, I think, a critical threshold of size, below which the opportunities for participation can be so great and so fairly meted out that no one feels left out and everyone feels that his viewpoint has been pretty fairly attended to. Athens was far too large for the democracy of the working committee; de facto it had to employ a certain amount of representation. Yet I suspect that it was below the critical threshold. And even if we now reject as unattainable the ideal of full, equal, and direct participation by all citizens in all collective decisions—the ideal of committee democracy—we can still search for a unit that remains within this critical threshold for widespread participation.

IV

We have travelled a long trail and turned into a number of branching paths in our quest but we have not found a unit that seems optimal for rational self-government. The journey would have been much longer had we taken the time to explore the byways as carefully as they deserve. Yet if we keep going, I think that we shall finally end up about at the place where the Greeks left off: somewhere within view of the democratic city.

Yet what we come to is not the Greek city, nor can it be; not the polis, then, but a democratic city that would be consistent with the presence of the nation-state, the institutions of representative government, a level of technology beyond anything the Greeks dreamed of, and huge populations densely spread over the face of our shrunken earth.

If the ancient Greeks were the first truly modern people, choice shaped by geography and historical accident made them also city people. So, too, choice shaped by demography and technology makes us a city people. But even if the Greeks were a city people and though they were modern in almost every important sense, our cities must differ in fact and in ideal from their actual and ideal cities. For one thing, the proportion of the residents of a modern democratic city eligible to participate in political life will be very much larger— something like half of the population, so that even a city of 100,000 will have around 50,000 adult citizens. Much more quickly than the Greeks, we reach the limits of direct democracy. Moreover, the citizens of a modern city will also be highly mobile. A resident of Athens was a citizen only if his ancestors were Athenians; in any modern city, many citizens are recent arrivals, or are about to move to another city. . . .

As a result of our mobility, socialization into the political life of the modern democratic city is enormously more difficult for us than for the Greeks. Then, too, the Greek city was completely autonomous in ideal and pretty much so in fact. Our cities are not autonomous in fact nor would many of us offer total autonomy as an ideal. Finally, the citizen of a Greek city ordinarily had one inclusive loyalty to the city of his ancestors and to its gods. He invested in his city a kind of engagement in comparison with which patriotism in the nation-state must seem either shallow or strident. But the citizens of our modern cities will have no single loyalty and no single community; they will have multiple loyalties to many associations; and nowhere will they find the all-inclusive community.

If for these reasons a modern city cannot be a polis, we can nonetheless reasonably hope one day to achieve great democratic cities. As the optimum unit for democracy in the 21st century, the city has a greater claim, I think, than any other alternative.

To begin with, from now on into the next century man seems clearly destined to live in cities. If to live in cities is our fate, to live in great cities is our opportunity. Is it not of some significance that of the four great waves of experimentation in the West with popular government, during three of these—the Greek, the Roman, and the medieval communes of north Italy—popular governments managed to construct cities of exceptional and enduring beauty?

Yet during the fourth wave, that of representative democracy in the nation-state, we have so far failed most profoundly in our cities. Is it too much to hope that we might be on the verge of a fifth wave, the age of the democratic city within the democratic nation-state? By we, I mean of course, the whole of the Western democratic world and its offshoots. But most of all, I mean we here in the United States.

City building is one of the most obvious incapacities of Americans. We Americans have become an urban people without having developed an urban civilization. Though we live in cities, we do not know how to build cities. Perhaps because we have emerged so swiftly out of an agrarian society, perhaps because so many of us are only a generation or two removed from farm and field, small town and peasant village, we seem to lack the innate grasp of the essential elements of the good city that was all but instinct among Greeks, Romans, and the Italians of the free communes. Our cities are not merely noncities, they are anticities—mean, ugly, gross, banal, inconvenient, hazardous, formless, incoherent, unfit for human living, deserts from which a family flees to the greener hinterlands as soon as job and income permit, yet deserts growing so rapidly outward that the open green space to which the family escapes soon shrinks to an oasis and then it too turns to a desert.

One advantage of the city as a unit for democratic government is, then, that it confronts us with a task worthy of our best efforts because of its urgency, its importance, its challenge, the extent of our failure up to now, and its promise for the good life lived jointly with fellow citizens.

These considerations point to another asset of the city as a democratic unit. While the city is not and cannot be autonomous, the policies of city hall and the totality of city agencies and activities are so important to our lives that to participate in the decisions of the city means, or anyway can mean, participating in shaping not merely the trivial but some of the most vital aspects of our environment. I say shaping and not totally controlling because the city is only one of our Chinese boxes. But it is in the city and with the powers and resources made available to cities that we shall deal with such crucial problems as the education of our children, our housing, the way we travel to and from our place of work, preventive health measures, crime, public order, the cycle of poverty, racial justice and equality—not to mention all those subtle and little understood elements that contribute so heavily to the satisfaction of our desires for friendship, neighborhood, community, and beauty.

V

Yet if the city and its government are important to us, can the good city today be small enough to remain below that critical threshold for wide participation that I mentioned a moment ago?

The existence of a few giant metropolises here and there may mislead us as to fact and possibility. Only a modest percentage of the world's population lives even today in the giant metropolis. Indeed, in 1960 only one-fifth of the people of the world lived in cities over 100,000. It is true that in the most urbanized region of the world, North America, in 1960 six out of every ten people lived in cities over 100,000. Yet even in the United States, less than one out of every ten lived in cities over a million.

It will take some doing, but we do not have to end up all jammed together in the asphalt desert of the large metropolis—unless that is really what we want. And Americans pretty clearly do not want to live in the large metropolis but rather in cities of modest dimensions. For example, in a survey by Gallup in 1966 nearly half the respondents living in cities of 500,000 and over said they would like to live somewhere else—suburb, small town, farm; by contrast, few of the people living in suburb or town wanted to move to the big cities. About three out of four respondents were distressed by the prospect that their own community will double in population. Census figures for the past several decades tell us that Americans have been acting out these preferences.

What, then, is the optimum size for a city? Although this question, which so far as I know was first asked by political philosophers in Athens over 2,000 years ago, is no longer a subject of discussion among political scientists, scholars in various fields have provided a considerable amount of analysis and evidence to bear on the question. It is only fair to warn you that all answers are still highly controversial; yet a good deal of evidence supports the view that the all-around optimum size for a contemporary American city is almost surely far less than the size of our giant cities, very likely less than 1 million, and probably less than half that. Indeed, the possibility cannot be ruled out that a city under 100,000 could be, and perhaps often is, a more satisfactory place to live in for most people than something bigger.

The matter is, as I said, still highly debatable; yet it is interesting that there is no worthwhile evidence at present demonstrating, for example, that governments of cities over 50,000 manage to achieve any significant economies of scale. The few items on which increasing size does lead to decreasing unit costs, such as water and sewerage, are too small a proportion of total city outlays to lead to significant economies; and even these reductions are probably offset by rising costs for other services, such as police protection.

Per capita city expenditures increase with the size of city, at least in the United States. In 1960 the mean expenditure for U.S. cities over 150,000 was $123 per capita compared with $70 per capita for cities in the 25–50,000 range. Yet there is no evidence that these higher costs per capita provide residents of large cities with a better life, taking it in the round, than the life enjoyed by residents of smaller cities. If it costs more in a city of a million than in a city of 25,000 to build, maintain, and police a park within walking distance of every citizen, then higher per capita expenditures for parks in big cities hardly signify that their residents have better public services than residents of smaller cities. What is more, the outlays in larger cities are actually less for some key functions than in smaller cities. For example, even though larger cities employ more persons per capita in public administration than smaller cities, per capita employment in education is on the average lower in larger cities than in small cities.

Roads and highways nullify the older economic advantage of the metropolis as a market and a source of specialized labor. . . .

The oft-cited cultural advantages of the metropolis are also largely illusory. On the basis of his research on American cities, Duncan estimates that the requisite population base for a library of "desirable minimum professional standards" is 50–75,000, for an art museum, 100,000, "with a somewhat higher figure for science and historical museums." Yet, even though larger cities have larger libraries, the circulation of library books per capita markedly decreases with size of city. There is also a negative correlation between city size and per capita museum attendance. Moreover, just as smaller cities can retain their collective identities and yet form a larger economic unit, thanks to ease of transportation and communication, so we have barely begun to explore the ways in which small cities by federating together for specific purposes might enjoy all of the cultural advantages of the large city and yet retain their individual identities, the pleasures of living in communities of lower densities and more open spaces, and relatively greater opportunities for political participation.

When we think about the size of a city in which a high culture may flourish, it is instructive to recall that during the Renaissance the city that produced Machiavelli and, I think it fair to say, an outpouring of great paintings, sculpture, and architecture beyond anything we Americans have yet created, had a population of around a hundred thousand. This was probably about the population of the city of Venice during the Renaissance. When Michelangelo chiseled out his Moses and painted his frescoes in the Sistine Chapel, Rome may have had as few as 40,000 residents.

Now what is strangely missing from the discussion of the optimum size of cities is the voice of the political scientist. The question is, of course, broader than the problem of what size of city may be optimal for a democratic political life. One might prefer a giant city to a smaller community even if the larger city were not optimal for democracy. But political life is not trivial. Surely political criteria have a place among the criteria for the optimum size of cities; and among these political criteria surely one of the most important is whether a city is beyond the threshold for widespread participation.

It seems obvious that if a city small enough to permit widespread participation were also optimal in other respects, then that unit would have a truly exceptional role to play in a democratic civilization. For no other unit, surely, would at once be so important and so accessible: a unit that could be—indeed must be—clothed with great powers and considerable autonomy if it is to manage its problems, yet a unit small enough so that citizens could participate extensively in determining the ways in which the city's great powers could be used. Unlike almost every other unit of which I can think, the city need not be so huge that, like the nation-state, it reduces the participation of most citizens to voting, nor so small that its activities must be trivial.

The city has at least one more advantage: it has great potentialities as a unit for educating citizens in civic virtue. We are approaching a crisis in the socialization of citizens into the political life of the democratic nation-state, a crisis that the challenges of nation building, democratization, and overcoming the most blatant evils of industrialization have delayed or obscured. There are signs of malaise among young people, among the very citizens who shortly before the dawn of the 21st century will have become—to use the word that has now become a mindless cliché—the establishment. If the malaise were only American, one could put it down to television, overpermissive child rearing, the persistence of an unpopular and ugly war, or other causes more or less specific to the United States; but there are signs of this malaise among youth in almost all the democratic countries.

I am not going to try to explain here a phenomenon too compex for brief analysis. But a part of the phenomenon—I don't know how much it is symptom and how much underlying cause—is a belief that the government of the nation-state is remote, inaccessible, and unresponsive, a government of professionals in which only a few can ever hope to participate actively and a still smaller number can ever gain great influence after years of dedication to political life.

What we need, what they need, and what some of them are trying to create (often with incredible ignorance of elementary political wisdom) is a political unit of more truly human proportions in which a citizen can acquire confidence and mastery of the arts of politics—that is, of the art required for shaping a good life in common with fellow citizens. What Pericles said of Athens, that the city is in general a school of the Grecians, may be said of every city of moderate size: it is a marvelous school. I have no doubt that a modern city even of moderate size is a good deal more complicated than Athens was. It has a much greater need for highly trained professionals, permanent administrative agencies, full-time leaders. Yet in the main, its problems are, I believe, within reach of the average citizen. And I believe it may be easier for citizens to reason about the good life and the ways to reach it by thinking in the more immediate and palpable context of the city than in the context of the nation-state or international politics. Even if solving the problems of the city is not quite enough for the good life, it is a great, indispensable, and comprehensible prerequisite.

VI

What I have presented is not a program but a perspective, not a prophecy but a prospect. It is not a solution to the problems of the city or of democracy, but a viewpoint from which to look at the problems of democracy and the city. If it does not lead directly to the answers, it might nonetheless help one to see the questions.

I have already suggested one implication of this way of looking at things—if popular governments in the modern world are a series of Chinese boxes, then we obviously need different models, theories, and criteria of excellence for each. I may seem to be repeating only what was commonly said nearly two centuries ago as ideas about representative government began to develop, that we cannot judge representative government in the nation-state as if it were or could be democracy in a committee, or, for that matter, a town meeting. Yet it is interesting to me that we have made so little of these palpable and evidently inherent differences in the performance of different kinds of units, all of which we are prone to call democratic.

Yet if the democratic city lies somewhere between democracy in the committee or in the town meeting and representative government in the nation-state, then it would be important to know what the similarities and differences are, and what standards of excellence we can apply to one but not the other. Even the democratic city, I fear, cannot satisfy anyone who has a vision of leaderless and partyless democracy, for at its best the politics of the democratic city will be more like a competitive polyarchy than a committee; organized parties and interest groups are more likely to exist than the free and spontaneous formation and dissolution of groups for every issue; a full-time leader or activist will exert more influence than any of his followers; institutionalized conflict is more likely than uncoerced consensus. Yet these are hunches that do no more than point to new worlds that need exploring.

The perspective I have been describing also bears on the way we think about units of government intermediate between nation-state and city. An American obviously must take the fifty states into account. These are too solidly built to be done away with and I don't propose to break any lances tilting against them. Yet in the perspective I am suggesting the states do not stand out as important institutions of democratic self-government. They are too big to allow for much in the way of civic participation—think of California and New York, each about as large in population as Canada or Yugoslavia and each larger than 80 percent of the countries of the world. Yet an American state is infinitely less important to citizens of that state than any democratic nation-state is to its citizens. Consequently the average Amer-

ican is bound to be much less concerned about the affairs of his state than of his city or country. Too remote to stimulate much participation by their citizens, and too big to make extensive participation possible anyway, these units intermediate between city and nation are probably destined for a kind of limbo of quasi-democracy. They will be pretty much controlled by the full-time professionals, whether elected or appointed. Moreover, many of the problems that states have to deal with will not fit within state boundaries. It cannot even be said that the states, on the whole, can tap any strong sentiments of loyalty or like-mindedness among their citizens. Doubtless we shall continue to use the states as important intermediate instruments of coordination and control—if for no other reason than the fact that they are going institutions. But whenever we are compelled to choose between city and state, we should always keep in mind. I think, that the city, not the state, is the better instrument of popular government.

This argument also applies to megalopolis, to the city that is *not* a city, to the local government that is *not* a local government. The city of New York, for example, has about the same population as Sweden or Chile. It is twice as large as Norway, three times the size of New Zealand. To regard the government of New York as a local government is to make nonsense of the term. If the Swedes were to rule their whole country from Stockholm with no local governments, I am quite sure that we would begin to question whether the people of Sweden could rightly be called self-governing. Where, we might ask the Swedes, are your local governments? But should we not ask the same thing of New Yorkers: Where are *your* local governments? For purely historical and what to me seem rather irrational reasons, we continue to regard the government of the giant metropolis as if it were a local government, when we might more properly consider it as the equivalent of a state or a provincial government—and hence badly in need of being broken up into smaller units for purposes of local government. If it turns out that the government of a metropolis cannot be decentralized to smaller territorial units, then should we not quite openly declare that the metropolis cannot ever be made into a democratic city? This may be an inconvenient truth, but if it is true, it may be—like much truth— liberating in the end.

Yet I must admit that problems like these involving the metropolis demand more than we now know. The metropolis is a world to be explored, so let us explore it, hoping that we may discover how even it might be turned into a democratic city. . . .

Notes

1. Horace Miner, *St. Denis* (Chicago: U. of Chicago Phoenix Books, 1939), pp. 58–61.
2. Graham Wootton, *Workers, Unions and the State* (London: Routledge and Kegan Paul, 1966), p. 36.

The Market and the Forum: Three Varieties of Political Theory

Jon Elster

In this essay, Jon Elster discusses three views of democratic politics. First, according to social choice theory, politics is a matter of individuals who pursue private interests and eventually compromise with each other. There is no clear break between what goes on in the market and the political realm, and the problem for politics is to reach decisions that reflect individual preferences. Elster criticizes this social choice view on two grounds: that expression *of preferences is not a reliable guide to actual preferences and, second, that even* actual *preferences are not a suitable guide to political decisions. The second model is associated with Habermas, and seeks to replace the model of the market with the forum, i.e., with "rational discourse." However, Elster finds numerous problems with this: "discussion" may not be the best response to people who act nonmorally, and such rational discussion has many "vulnerabilities" which he describes. The third model, which he compares to J. S. Mill, sees politics from neither extreme. While rejecting the market view, it also refuses to divorce political activity completely from it. Public life is neither a means to pursue private interests nor an autonomous realm of debate in which the good life is realized. In truth, he argues, politics resembles various other activities like games and science. It can be valuable and satisfying, but only if people assume there is an independent standard of right or justice.*

I want to compare three views of politics generally, and of the democratic system more specifically. I shall first look at social choice theory, as an instance of a wider class of theo-

From Jon Elster, "The Market and the Forum: Three Varieties of Political Theory," in *Foundations in Social Choice Theory,* John Elster and Aanund Hylland, eds. (Cambridge: Cambridge University Press, 1986), pp. 103–128. Reprinted by permission of the author. Some footnotes omitted.

ries with certain common features. In particular, they share the conception that the political process is instrumental rather than an end in itself, and the view that the decisive political act is a private rather than a public action, viz. the individual and secret vote. With these usually goes the idea that the goal of politics is the optimal compromise between given, and irreducibly opposed, private interests. The other two views arise when one denies, first, the private character of political behaviour and then, secondly, goes on also to deny the instrumental nature of politics. According to the theory of Jürgen Habermas, the goal of politics should be rational agreement rather than compromise, and the decisive political act is that of engaging in public debate with a view to the emergence of a consensus. According to the theorists of participatory democracy, from John Stuart Mill to Carole Pateman, the goal of politics is the transformation and education of the participants. Politics, on this view, is an end in itself—indeed many have argued that it represents the good life for man. I shall discuss these views in the order indicated. I shall present them in a somewhat stylized form, but my critical comments will not I hope, be directed to strawmen.

I

Politics, it is usually agreed, is concerned with the common good, and notably with the cases in which it cannot be realized as the aggregate outcome of individuals pursuing their private interests. In particular, uncoordinated private choices may lead to outcomes that are worse for all than some other outcome that could have been attained by coordination. Political institutions are set up to remedy such *market failures,* a phrase that can be taken either in the static sense of an inability to provide public goods or in the more dynamic sense of a breakdown of the self-regulating properties usually ascribed to the market mechanism. In addition there is the redistributive task of politics . . . According to the first view of politics, this task is inherently one of interest struggle and compromise. The obstacle to agreement is not only that most individuals want redistribution to be in their favour, or at least not in their disfavour. More basically consensus is blocked because there is no reason to expect that individuals will converge in their views on what constitutes a just redistribution.

I shall consider social choice theory as representative of the private-instrumental view of politics, because it brings out supremely well the logic as well as the limits of that approach. Other varieties, such as the Schumpeterian or neo-Schumpeterian theories, are

closer to the actual political process, but for that reason also less suited to my purpose. For instance, Schumpeter's insistence that voter preferences are shaped and manipulated by politicians tends to blur the distinction, central to my analysis, between politics as the aggregation of given preferences and politics as the transformation of preferences through rational discussion. And although the neo-Schumpeterians are right in emphasizing the role of the political parties in the preference-aggregation process, I am not here concerned with such mediating mechanisms. In any case, political problems also arise within the political parties, and so my discussion may be taken to apply to such lower-level political processes. In fact, much of what I shall say makes better sense for politics on a rather small scale—within the firm, the organization or the local community—than for nationwide political systems.

In very broad outline, the structure of social choice theory is as follows. (1) We begin with a *given* set of agents, so that the issue of a normative justification of political boundaries does not arise. (2) We assume that the agents confront a *given* set of alternatives, so that for instance the issue of agenda manipulation does not arise. (3) The agents are supposed to be endowed with preferences that are similarly *given* and not subject to change in the course of the political process. They are, moreover, assumed to be causally independent of the set of alternatives. (4) In the standard version, which is so far the only operational version of the theory, preferences are assumed to be purely ordinal, so that it is not possible for an individual to express the intensity of his preferences, nor for an outside observer to compare preference intensities across individuals. (5) The individual preferences are assumed to be defined over all pairs of individuals, i.e. to be complete, and to have the formal property of transitivity, so that preference for A over B and for B over C implies preference for A over C.

Given this setting, the task of social choice theory is to arrive at a social preference ordering of the alternatives. . . . The ordering should satisfy the following criteria. (6) Like the individual preferences, it should be complete and transitive. (7) It should be Pareto-optimal, in the sense of never having one option socially preferred to another which is individually preferred by everybody. (8) The social choice between two given options should depend only on how the individuals rank these two options, and thus not be sensitive to changes in their preferences concerning other options. (9) The social preference ordering should respect and reflect individual preferences, over and above the condition of Pareto-optimality. This idea covers a variety of notions, the most important of which are *anonymity* (all individuals should count equally), *nondictatorship* (a fortiori no single individual should dictate the social choice), *liberalism* (all individuals should have some private domain within which their preferences are decisive), and *strategy-proofness* (it should not pay to express false preferences). . . . I shall discuss two sets of objections, both related to the assumption of given preferences. I shall argue, first, that the preferences people choose to express may not be a good guide to what they really prefer; and secondly that what they really prefer may in any case be a fragile foundation for social choice.

In actual fact, preferences are never 'given', in the sense of being directly observable. If they are to serve as inputs to the social choice process, they must somehow be *expressed* by the individuals. The expression of preferences is an action, which presumably is guided by these very same preferences. It is then far from obvious that the individually rational action is to express these preferences as they are. Some methods for aggregating preferences are such that it may pay the individual to express false preferences, i.e. the outcome may in some cases be better according to his real preferences if he chooses not to express them truthfully. The condition for strategy-proofness for social choice mechanisms was designed expressly to exclude this possibility. It turns out, however, that the systems in which honesty always pays are rather unattractive in other respects. We then have to face the possibility that even if we require that the social preferences be Pareto-optimal with respect to the expressed preferences, they might not be so with respect to the real ones. Strategy-proofness and collective rationality, therefore,

stand and fall together. Since it appears that the first must fall, so must the second. It then becomes very difficult indeed to defend the idea that the outcome of the social choice mechanism represents the common good, since there is a chance that everybody might prefer some other outcome.

Amos Tversky has pointed to another reason why choices—or expressed preferences—cannot be assumed to represent the real preferences in all cases.[1] According to his 'concealed preference hypothesis', choices often conceal rather than reveal underlying preferences. This is especially so in two sorts of cases. First, there are the cases of anticipated regret associated with a risky decision. Consider the following example (from Tversky):

> On her twelfth birthday, Judy was offered a choice between spending the weekend with her aunt in the city (C), or having a party for all her friends. The party could take place either in the garden (GP) or inside the house (HP). A garden party would be much more enjoyable, but there is always the possibility of rain, in which case an inside party would be more sensible. In evaluating the consequences of the three options, Judy notes that the weather condition does not have a significant effect on C. If she chooses the party, however, the situation is different. A garden party will be a lot of fun if the weather is good, but quite disastrous if it rains, in which case an inside party will be acceptable. The trouble is that Judy expects to have a lot of regret if the party is to be held inside and the weather is very nice.
>
> Now, let us suppose that for some reason it is no longer possible to have an outside party. In this situation, there is no longer any regret associated with holding an inside party in good weather because (in this case) Judy has no other place for holding the party. Hence, the elimination of an available course of action (holding the party outside) removes the regret associated with an inside party, and increases its overall utility. It stands to reason, in this case, that if Judy was indifferent between C and HP, in the presence of GP, she will prefer HP to C when GP is eliminated.

What we observe here is the violation of condition (8) above, the so-called 'independence of irrelevant alternatives'. The expressed preferences depend causally on the set of alternatives. We may assume that the real preferences, defined over the set of possible outcomes, remain constant, contrary to the case to be discussed below. Yet the preferences over the *pairs* (choice, outcome) depend on the set of available choices, because the 'costs of responsibility' differentially associated with various such pairs depend on what else one 'could have done'. Although Judy could not have escaped her predicament by deliberately making it physically impossible to have an outside party, she might well have welcomed an event outside her control with the same consequence.

The second class of cases in which Tversky would want to distinguish the expressed preferences from the real preferences concerns decisions that are unpleasant rather than risky. For instance, 'society may prefer to save the life of one person rather than another, and yet be unable to make this choice'. In fact, losing both lives through inaction may be preferred to losing only one life by deliberate action. Such examples are closely related to the problems involved in act utilitarianism versus outcome utilitarianism. One may well judge that it would be a good thing if state *A* came about, and yet not want to be the person by whose agency it comes about. The reasons for not wanting to be that person may be quite respectable, or they may not. The latter would be the case if one were afraid of being blamed by the relatives of the person who was deliberately allowed to die, or if one simply confused the causal and the moral notions of responsibility. In such cases the expressed preferences might lead to a choice that in a clear sense goes against the real preferences of the people concerned.

A second, perhaps more basic, difficulty is that the real preferences themselves might well depend causally on the feasible set. One instance is graphically provided by the fable of the fox and the sour grapes. . . . [T]he cause of his holding them to be sour was his conviction that he would in any case be excluded from consuming them, and then it is difficult to justify the allocation by invoking his preferences. Conversely, the phenomenon of 'counter-adaptive preferences'—the grass is always greener on the other side of the fence, and the forbidden fruit always sweeter—is also baffling for the social choice theorist, since it implies that such preferences, if respected, would not be satisfied—and yet the whole point of respecting them would be to give them a chance of satisfaction.

Adaptive and counter-adaptive preferences are only special cases of a more general class of desires, those which fail to satisfy some substantive criterion for acceptable preferences, as opposed to the purely formal criterion of transitivity. I shall discuss these under two headings: autonomy and morality.

Autonomy characterizes the way in which preferences are shaped rather than their actual content. Unfortunately I find myself unable to give a positive characterization of autonomous preferences, so I shall have to rely on two indirect approaches. First, autonomy is for desires what judgment is for belief. The notion of judgment is also difficult to define formally, but at least we know that there are persons who have this quality to a higher degree than others: people who are able to take account of vast and diffuse evidence that more or less clearly bears on the problem at hand, in such a way that no element is given undue importance. In such people the process of belief formation is not disturbed by defective cognitive processing, nor distorted by wishful thinking and the like. Similarly, autonomous preferences are those that have not been shaped by irrelevant causal processes—a singularly unhelpful explanation. To improve somewhat on it, consider, secondly, a short list of such irrelevant causal processes. They include adaptive and counter-adaptive preferences, conformity and anti-conformity, the obsession with novelty and the equally unreasonable resistance to novelty. In other words, preferences may be shaped by adaptation to what is possible, to what other people do or to what one has been doing in the past—or they may be shaped by the desire to differ as much as possible from these. In all of these cases the source of preference change is not in the person, but outside him—detracting from his autonomy.

Morality, it goes without saying, is if anything even more controversial. (Within the

Kantian tradition it would also be questioned whether it can be distinguished at all from autonomy.) Preferences are moral or immoral by virtue of their content, not by virtue of the way in which they have been shaped. Fairly uncontroversial examples of unethical preferences are spiteful and sadistic desires, and arguably also the desire for positional goods, i.e. goods such that it is logically impossible for more than a few to possess them. The desire for an income twice the average can lead to less welfare for everybody, so that such preferences fail to pass the Kantian generalization test. [*Act only on maxims you can consistently will to become universal law.*—Ed.] Also they are closely linked to spite, since one way of getting more than others is to take care that they get less—indeed this may often be a more efficient method than trying to excel.

To see how the lack of autonomy may be distinguished from the lack of moral worth, let me use *conformity* as a technical term for a desire caused by a drive to be like other people, and *conformism* for a desire to be like other people, with anti-conformity and anti-conformism similarly defined. Conformity implies that other people's desires enter into the causation of my own, conformism that they enter irreducibly into the description of the object of my desires. Conformity may bring about conformism, but it may also lead to anti-conformism, as in Theodore Zeldin's comment that among the French peasantry 'prestige is to a great extent obtained from conformity with traditions (so that the son of a non-conformist might be expected to be one too').[2] Clearly, conformity may bring about desires that are morally laudable, yet lacking in autonomy. Conversely, I do not see how one could rule out on *a priori* grounds the possibility of autonomous spite, although I would welcome a proof that autonomy is incompatible not only with anti-conformity, but also with anti-conformism.

We can now state the objection to the political view underlying social choice theory. It is, basically, that it embodies a confusion between the kind of behaviour that is appropriate in the market place and that which is appropriate in the forum. The notion of consumer sovereignty is acceptable because, and to the extent that, the consumer chooses between

courses of action that differ only in the way they affect him. In political choice situations, however, the citizen is asked to express his preference over states that also differ in the way in which they affect other people. This means that there is no similar justification for the corresponding notion of the citizen's sovereignty, since other people may legitimately object to social choice governed by preferences that are defective in some of the ways I have mentioned. A social choice mechanism is capable of resolving the market failures that would result from unbridled consumer sovereignty, but as a way of redistributing welfare it is hopelessly inadequate. If people affected each other only by tripping over each other's feet, or by dumping their garbage into one another's backyards, a social choice mechanism might cope. But the task of politics is not only to eliminate inefficiency, but also to create justice—a goal to which the aggregation of prepolitical preferences is a quite incongruous means.

This suggests that the principles of the forum must differ from those of the market. A long-standing tradition from the Greek *polis* onwards suggests that politics must be an open and public activity, as distinct from the isolated and private expression of preferences that occurs in buying and selling. In the following sections I look at two different conceptions of public politics, increasingly removed from the market theory of politics. Before I go on to this, however, I should briefly consider an objection that the social choice theorist might well make to what has just been said. He could argue that the only alternative to the aggregation of given preferences is some kind of censorship or paternalism. He might agree that spiteful and adaptive preferences are undesirable, but he would add that any institutional mechanism for eliminating them would be misused and harnessed to the private purposes of power-seeking individuals. Any remedy, in fact, would be worse than the disease. This objection assumes (i) that the only alternative to aggregation of given preferences is censorship, and (ii) that censorship is always objectionable. . . . I shall now discuss a challenge to the first assumption, viz. the idea of a *transformation* of preferences through public and rational discussion.

II

Today this view is especially associated with the writings of Jürgen Habermas on 'the ethics of discourse' and 'the ideal speech situation'. As mentioned above, I shall present a somewhat stylized version of his views, although I hope they bear some resemblance to the original.[3] The core of the theory, then, is that rather than aggregating or filtering preferences, the political system should be set up with a view to changing them by public debate and confrontation. The input to the social choice mechanism would then not be the raw, quite possibly selfish or irrational, preferences that operate in the market, but informed and other-regarding preferences. Or rather, there would not be any need for an aggregating mechanism, since a rational discussion would tend to produce unanimous preferences. When the private and idiosyncratic wants have been shaped and purged in public discussion about the public good, uniquely determined rational desires would emerge. Not optimal compromise, but unanimous agreement is the goal of politics on this view.

There appear to be two main premises underlying this theory. The first is that there are certain arguments that simply cannot be stated publicly. In a political debate it is pragmatically impossible to argue that a given solution should be chosen just because it is good for oneself. By the very act of engaging in a public debate—by arguing rather than bargaining—one has ruled out the possibility of invoking such reasons. To engage in discussion can in fact be seen as one kind of self-censorship, a pre-commitment to the idea of rational decision. Now, it might well be thought that this conclusion is too strong. The first argument only shows that in public debate one has to pay some lip-service to the common good. An additional premise states that over time one will in fact come to be swayed by considerations about the common good. One cannot indefinitely praise the common good 'du bout des lèvres', for—as argued by Pascal in the context of the wager—one will end up having the preferences that initially one was

faking. This is a psychological, not a conceptual premise. To explain why going through the motions of rational discussion should tend to bring about the real thing, one might argue that people tend to bring what they mean into line with what they say in order to reduce dissonance, but this is a dangerous argument to employ in the present context. Dissonance reduction does not tend to generate autonomous preferences. Rather one would have to invoke the power of reason to break down prejudice and selfishness. By speaking with the voice of reason, one is also exposing oneself to reason.

To sum up, the conceptual impossibility of expressing selfish arguments in a debate about the public good, and the psychological difficulty of expressing other-regarding preferences without ultimately coming to acquire them, jointly bring it about that public discussion tends to promote the common good. . . .

I now want to set out a series of objections—seven altogether—to the view stated above. I should explain that the goal of this criticism is not to demolish the theory, but to locate some points that need to be fortified. I am, in fact, largely in sympathy with the fundamental tenets of the view, yet fear that it might be dismissed as Utopian, both in the sense of ignoring the problem of getting from here to there, and in the sense of neglecting some elementary facts of human psychology.

The *first objection* involves a reconsideration of the issues of paternalism. Would it not, in fact, be unwarranted interference to impose on the citizens the obligation to participate in political discussion? One might answer that there is a link between the right to vote and the obligation to participate in discussion, just as rights and duties are correlative in other cases. To acquire the right to vote, one has to perform certain civic duties that go beyond pushing the voting button on the television set. There would appear to be two different ideas underlying this answer. First, only those should have the right to vote who are sufficiently *concerned* about politics to be willing to devote some of their resources—time in particular—to it. Secondly, one should try to favour *informed* preferences as inputs to the voting process. The first argument favours participation and discussion as a sign of interest, but does not give it an instrumental value in itself. It would do just as well, for the purpose of this argument, to demand that people should pay for the right to vote. The second argument favours discussion as a means to improvement—it will not only select the right people, but actually make them more qualified to participate.

These arguments might have some validity in a near-ideal world, in which the concern for politics was evenly distributed across all relevant dimensions, but in the context of contemporary politics they miss the point. The people who survive a high threshold for participation are disproportionately found in a privileged part of the population. At best this could lead to paternalism, at worst the high ideals of rational discussion could create a self-elected elite whose members spend time on politics because they want power, not out of concern for the issues. As in other cases, to be discussed later, the best can be the enemy of the good. I am not saying that it is impossible to modify the ideal in a way that allows both for rational discussion and for low-profile participation, only that any institutional design must respect the trade-off between the two.

My *second objection* is that even assuming unlimited time for discussion, unanimous and rational agreement might not necessarily ensue. Could there not be legitimate and unresolvable differences of opinions over the nature of the common good? Could there not even be a plurality of ultimate values?

I am not going to discuss this objection, since it is in any case preempted by the *third objection*. Since there are in fact always time constraints on discussions—often the stronger the more important the issues—unanimity will rarely emerge. For any constellation of preferences short of unanimity, however, one would need a social choice mechanism to aggregate them. One can discuss only for so long, and then one has to make a decision, even if strong differences of opinion should remain. This objection, then, goes to show that the transformation of preferences can never do more than supplement the aggregation of preferences, never replace it altogether.

This much would no doubt be granted by most proponents of the theory. True, they would say, even if the ideal speech situation

can never be fully realized, it will nevertheless improve the outcome of the political process if one goes some way towards it. The *fourth objection* questions the validity of this reply. In some cases a little discussion can be a dangerous thing, worse in fact than no discussion at all, viz. if it makes some but not all persons align themselves on the common good. The following story provides an illustration:

> Once upon a time two boys found a cake. One of them said, 'Splendid! I will eat the cake.' The other one said, 'No, that is not fair! We found the cake together, and we should share and share alike, half for you and half for me.' The first boy said, 'No I should have the whole cake!' Along came an adult who said, 'Gentlemen, you shouldn't fight about this: you should *compromise*. Give him three quarters of the cake.'[4]

What creates the difficulty here is that the first boy's preferences are allowed to count twice in the social choice mechanism suggested by the adult: once in his expression of them and then again in the other boy's internalized ethic of sharing. And one can argue that the outcome is socially inferior to that which would have emerged had they both stuck to their selfish preferences. . . .

A *fifth objection* is to question the implicit assumption that the body politic as a whole is better or wiser than the sum of its parts. Could it not rather be the case that people are made more, not less, selfish and irrational by interacting politically? The cognitive analogy suggests that the rationality of beliefs may be positively as well as negatively affected by interaction. On the one hand there is . . . 'groupthink', i.e. mutually reinforcing bias. On the other hand there certainly are many ways in which people can, and do, pool their opinions and supplement each other to arrive at a better estimate. Similarly autonomy and morality could be enhanced as well as undermined by interaction. Against the pessimistic view of Reinhold Niebuhr that individuals in a group show more unrestrained egoism than in their personal relationships, we may set Hannah Arendt's optimistic view:

> American faith was not all based on a semireligious faith in human nature, but on the contrary, on the possibility of checking

human nature in its singularity, by virtue of human bonds and mutual promises. The hope for man in his singularity lay in the fact that not man but men inhabit the earth and form a world between them. It is human worldliness that will save men from the pitfalls of human nature.[5]

Niebuhr's argument suggests an aristocratic disdain of the *mass,* which transforms individually decent people—to use a characteristically condescending phrase—into an unthinking horde. While rejecting this as a general view, one should equally avoid the other extreme, suggested by Arendt. Neither the Greek nor the American assemblies were the paradigms of discursive reason that she makes them out to be. The Greeks were well aware that they might be tempted by demagogues, and in fact took extensive precautions against this tendency. The American town surely has not always been the incarnation of collective freedom, since on occasion it could also serve as the springboard for witch hunts. The mere decision to engage in rational discussion does not ensure that the transactions will in fact be conducted rationally, since much depends on the structure and the framework of the proceedings. The random errors of selfish and private preferences may to some extent cancel each other out and thus be less to be feared than the massive and coordinated errors that may arise through group-think. On the other hand, it would be excessively stupid to rely on mutually compensating vices to bring about public benefits as a general rule. I am not arguing against the need for public discussion, only for the need to take the question of institutional and constitutional design very seriously.

A *sixth objection* is that unanimity, were it to be realized, might easily be due to conformity rather than to rational agreement. I would in fact tend to have more confidence in the outcome of a democratic decision if there was a minority that voted against it, than if it was unanimous. I am not here referring to people expressing the majority preferences against their real ones, since I am assuming that something like the secret ballot would prevent this. I have in mind that people may come to change their real preferences, as a result of seeing which way the majority goes. Social psychology has amply shown the strength of this bandwagon effect, which in political theory is also known as the 'chameleon' problem. It will not do to argue that the majority to which the conformist adapts his view is likely to pass the test of rationality even if his adherence to it does not, since the majority could well be made up of conformists each of whom would have broken out had there been a minority he could have espoused.

To bring the point home, consider a parallel case of non-autonomous preference formation. We are tempted to say that a man is free if he can get or do whatever it is that he wants to get or do. But then we are immediately faced with the objection that perhaps he only wants what he can get, as the result of some such mechanism as 'sour grapes'. We may then add that, other things being equal, the person is freer the more things he wants to do which he is not free to do, since these show that his wants are not in general shaped by adaptation to his possibilities. Clearly, there is an air of paradox over the statement that a man's freedom is greater the more of his desires he is not free to realize, but on reflection the paradox embodies a valid argument. Similarly, it is possible to dissolve the air of paradox attached to the view that a collective decision is more trustworthy if it is less than unanimous.

My *seventh objection* amounts to a denial of the view that the need to couch one's argument in terms of the common good will purge the desires of all selfish arguments. There are in general many ways of realizing the common good . . . Each such arrangement will, in addition to promoting the general interest, bring an extra premium to some specific group, which will then have a strong interest in that particular arrangement. The group may then come to prefer the arrangement because of that premium, although it will argue for it in terms of the common good. Typically the arrangement will be justified by a causal theory—an account, say, of how the economy works—that shows it to be not only *a* way, but the only way of promoting the common good. The economic theories underlying the early Reagan administration provide an example. I am not imputing insincerity to the proponents of these views, but there may well be an element of wishful thinking. Since social scientists disagree so strongly among themselves as to how societies work, what could be more human than to pick on a theory that uniquely justifies the arrangement from which one stands to profit? The opposition between general interest and special interests is too simplistic, since the private benefits may causally determine the way in which one conceives of the common good.

These objections have been concerned to bring out two main ideas. First, one cannot assume that one will in fact approach the good society by acting as if one had already arrived there. . . . When others act non-morally, there may be an obligation to deviate not only from what they do, but also from the behaviour that would have been optimal if adopted by everybody. In particular, a little discussion, like a little rationality or a little socialism, may be a dangerous thing. If, as suggested by Habermas, free and rational discussion will only be possible in a society that has abolished political and economic domination, it is by no means obvious that abolition can be brought about by rational argumentation. I do not want to suggest that it could occur by force—since the use of force to end the use of force is open to obvious objections. Yet something like irony, eloquence or propaganda might be needed, involving less respect for the interlocutor than what would prevail in the ideal speech situation.

As will be clear from these remarks, there is a strong tension between two ways of looking at the relation between political ends and means. On the one hand, the means should partake of the nature of the ends, since otherwise the use of unsuitable means might tend to corrupt the end. On the other hand, there are dangers involved in choosing means immediately derived from the goal to be realized, since in a non-ideal situation these might take us away from the end rather than towards it. A delicate balance will have to be struck between these two, opposing considerations. It is in fact an open question whether there exists a ridge along which we can move to the good society, and if so whether it is like a knife-edge or more like a plateau.

The second general idea that emerges from the discussion is that even in the good society, should we hit upon it, the process of rational discussion could be fragile, and vulnerable to adaptive preferences, conformity, wishful thinking and the like. To ensure stability and robustness there is a need for structures—political institutions or constitutions—that could easily reintroduce an element of domination. We would in fact be confronted, at the political level, with a perennial dilemma of individual behaviour. How is it possible to ensure at the same time that one is bound by rules that protect one from irrational or unethical behaviour—and that these rules do not turn into prisons from which it is not possible to break out even when it would be rational to do so?

III

It is clear from Habermas's theory, I believe, that rational political discussion has an *object* in terms of which it makes sense. Politics is concerned with substantive decision-making, and is to that extent instrumental. True, the idea of instrumental politics might also be taken in a more narrow sense, as implying that the political process is one in which individuals pursue their selfish interests, but more broadly understood it implies only that political action is primarily a means to a non-political end, only secondarily, if at all, an end in itself. In this section I shall consider theories that suggest a reversal of this priority, and that find the main point of politics in the educative or otherwise beneficial effects on the participants. And I shall try to show that this view tends to be internally incoherent, or self-defeating. The benefits of participation are by-products of political activity. Moreover, they are *essentially* by-products, in the sense that any attempt to turn them into the main purpose of such activity would make them evaporate. It can indeed be highly satisfactory to engage in political work, but only on the condition that the work is defined by a serious purpose which goes beyond that of achieving this satisfaction. If that condition is not fulfilled, we get a narcissistic view of politics—corresponding to various consciousness-raising activities familiar from the last decade or so.

My concern, however, is with political theory rather than with political activism. I shall argue that certain types of arguments for political institutions and constitutions are self-defeating, since they justify the arrangement in question by effects that are essentially by-products. Here an initial and important distinction must be drawn between the task of justifying a constitution *ex ante* and that of evaluating it *ex post* and at a distance. I argue below that Tocqueville, when assessing the American democracy, praised it for consequences that are indeed by-products. In his case, this made perfectly good sense as an analytical attitude adopted after the fact and at some distance from the system he was examining. The incoherence arises when one invokes the same arguments before the fact, in public discussion. Although the constitution-makers may secretly have such side effects in mind, they cannot coherently invoke them in public.
. . .

Tocqueville, in a seeming paradox, suggested that democracies are less suited than aristocracies to deal with long-term planning, and yet are superior in the long-run to the latter. The paradox dissolves once it is seen that the first statement involves time at the level of the actors, the second at the level of the observer. On the one hand, 'a democracy finds it difficult to coordinate the details of a great undertaking and to fix on some plan and carry it through with determination in spite of obstacles. It has little capacity for combining measures in secret and waiting patiently for the result'.[6] On the other hand, 'in the long run government by democracy should increase the real forces of a society, but it cannot immediately assemble at one point and at a given time, forces as great as those at the disposal of an aristocratic government'.[7] The latter view is further elaborated in a passage from the chapter on 'The Real Advantages Derived by American Society from Democratic Government':

> That constantly renewed agitation introduced by democratic government into political life passes, then, into civil society. Perhaps, taking everything into consideration, that is the greatest advantage of democratic government, and I praise it much more on account of what it causes to be done than for what it does. It is

incontestable that the people often manage public affairs very badly, but their concern therewith is bound to extend their mental horizon and to shake them out of the rut of ordinary routine . . . Democracy does not provide a people with the most skillful of governments, but it does that which the most skillful government often cannot do: it spreads throughout the body social a restless activity, super-abundant force, and energy never found elsewhere, which, however little favoured by circumstances, can do wonders. Those are its true advantages.[8]

The advantages of democracies, in other words, are mainly and essentially by-products. The avowed aim of democracy is to be a good system of government, but Tocqueville argues that it is inferior in this respect to aristocracy, viewed purely as a decision-making apparatus. Yet the very activity of governing democratically has as a by-product a certain energy and restlessness that benefits industry and generates prosperity. Assuming the soundness of this observation, could it ever serve as a public justification for introducing democracy in a nation that had not yet acquired it? The question is somewhat more complex than one might be led to think from what I have said so far, since the quality of the decisions is not the only consideration that is relevant for the choice of a political system. The argument from *justice* could also be decisive. Yet the following conclusion seems inescapable: if the system has no inherent advantage in terms of justice or efficiency, one cannot coherently and publicly advocate its introduction because of the side effects that would follow in its wake. There must be a *point* in democracy as such. If people are motivated by such inherent advantages to throw themselves into the system, other benefits may ensue—but the latter cannot by themselves be the motivating force. It the democratic method is introduced in a society solely because of the side effects on economic prosperity, and no one believes in it on any other ground, it will not produce them.

Tocqueville, however, did not argue that political activity is an end in itself. The justification for democracy is found in its effects, although not in the intended ones, as the strictly instrumental view would have it. More to the point is Tocqueville's argument for the jury system: 'I do not know whether a jury is useful to the litigants, but I am sure that it is very good for those who have to decide the case. I regard it as one of the most effective means of popular education at society's disposal.'[9] This is still an instrumental view, but the gap between the means and the end is smaller. Tocqueville never argued that the effect of democracy was to make politicians prosperous, only that it was conducive to general prosperity. By contrast, the justification of the jury system is found in the effect on the jurors themselves. And, as above, that effect would be spoilt if they belived that the impact on their own civic spirit was the main point of the proceedings.

John Stuart Mill not only applauded but advocated democracy on the ground of such educative effects on the participants. In current discussion he stands out both as an opponent of the purely instrumental view of politics, that of his father James Mill, and as a forerunner of the theory of participatory democracy. In his theory the gap between means and ends in politics is even narrower, since he saw political activity not only as a means to self-improvement, but also as a source of satisfaction and thus a good in itself. . . . Yet this very way of paraphrasing Mill's view also points to a difficulty. Could it really be the case that participation would yield a benefit even when the hoped-for results are nil . . .? Is it not rather true that the effort is itself a function of the hoped-for result, so that in the end the latter is the only independent variable? When Mill refers, critically, to the limitations of Bentham, whose philosophy 'can teach the means of organising and regulating the merely *business* part of the social arrangement', he seems to be putting the cart before the horse. The non-business part of politics may be the more valuable, but the value is contingent on the importance of the business part.

For a fully developed version of the non-instrumental theory of politics, we may go to the work of Hannah Arendt. Writing about the distinction between the private and the public realm in ancient Greece, she argues that:

Without mastering the necessities of life in the household, neither life nor the 'good life' is

possible, but politics is never for the sake of life. As far as the members of the *polis* are concerned, household life exists for the sake of the 'good life' in the *polis*.[10]

The public realm . . . was reserved for individuality; it was the only place where men could show who they really and inexchangeably were. It was for the sake of this chance, and out of love for a body politic that it made it possible to them all, that each was more or less willing to share in the burden of jurisdiction, defence and administration of public affairs.[11]

Against this we may set the view of Greek politics found in the work of M. I. Finley. Asking why the Athenian people claimed the right of every citizen to speak and make proposals in the Assembly, yet left its exercise to a few, he finds that 'one part of the answer is that the *demos* recognised the instrumental role of political rights and were more concerned in the end with the substantive decisions, were content with their power to select, dismiss and punish their political leaders'.[12] Elsewhere he writes, even more explicitly: 'Then, as now, politics was instrumental for most people, not an interest or an end in itself.'[13] Contrary to what Arendt suggests, the possession or the possibility of exercising a political right may be more important than the actual exercise. Moreover, even the exercise derives its value from the decisions to be taken. Writing about the American town assemblies, Arendt argues that the citizens participated 'neither exclusively because of duty nor, and even less, to serve their own interests but most of all because they enjoyed the discussions, the deliberations, and the making of decisions'.[14] This, while not putting the cart before the horse, at least places them alongside each other. Although discussion and deliberation in other contexts may be independent sources of enjoyment, the satisfaction one derives from *political* discussion is parasitic on decision-making. Political debate is about what to *do*— not about what ought to be the case. It is defined by this practical purpose, not by its subject-matter.

Politics in this respect is on a par with other activities such as art, science, athletics or chess. To engage in them may be deeply satisfactory, if you have an independently defined goal such as 'getting it right' or 'beating the opposition'. A chess player who asserted that he played not to win, but for the sheer elegance of the game, would be in narcissistic bad faith—since there is no such thing as an elegant way of losing, only elegant and inelegant ways of winning. When the artist comes to believe that the process and not the end result is his real purpose, and that defects and irregularities are valuable as reminders of the struggle of creation, he similarly forfeits any claim to our interest. The same holds for E. P. Thompson, who, when asked whether he really believed that a certain rally in Trafalgar Square would have any impact at all, answered: 'That's not really the point, is it? The point is, it shows that democracy's alive . . . A rally like that gives us self-respect. Chartism was terribly good for the Chartists, although they never got the Charter.'[15] Surely, the Chartists, if asked whether they thought they would ever get the Charter, would not have answered: 'That's not really the point, is it?' It was because they believed they might get the Charter that they engaged in the struggle for it with the seriousness of purpose that also brought them self-respect as a side effect.

IV

I have been discussing three views concerning the relation between economics and politics, between the market and the forum. One extreme is 'the economic theory of democracy', most outrageously stated by Schumpeter, but in essence also underlying social choice theory. It is a market theory of politics, in the sense that the act of voting is a private act similar to that of buying and selling. I cannot accept, therefore, Alan Ryan's argument that 'On any possible view of the distinction between private and public life, voting is an element in one's public life.' The very distinction between the secret and the open ballot shows that there is room for a private-public distinction within politics. The economic theory of democracy, therefore, rests on the idea that the forum should be like the market, in its purpose as well as in its mode of functioning. The purpose is defined in economic terms, and the mode of functioning is that of aggregating individual decisions.

At the other extreme there is the view that the forum should be completely divorced from the market, in purpose as well as in institutional arrangement. The forum should be more than the distributive totality of individuals queuing up for the election booth. Citizenship is a quality that can only be realized in public, i.e. in a collective joined for a common purpose. This purpose, moreover, is not to facilitate life in the material sense. The political process is an end in itself, a good or even the supreme good for those who participate in it. It may be applauded because of the educative effects on the participants, but the benefits do not cease once the education has been completed. On the contrary, the education of the citizen leads to a preference for public life as an end in itself. Politics on this view is not *about* anything. It is the agonistic display of excellence, or the collective display of solidarity, divorced from decision-making and the exercise of influence on events.

In between these extremes is the view I find most attractive. One can argue that the forum should differ from the market in its mode of functioning, yet be concerned with decisions that ultimately deal with economic matters. Even higher-order political decisions concern lower-level rules that are directly related to economic matters. Hence constitutional arguments about how laws can be made and changed, constantly invoke the impact of legal stability and change on economic affairs. It is the concern with substantive decisions that lends the urgency to political debates. The ever-present constraint of *time* creates a need for focus and concentration that cannot be assimilated to the leisurely style of philosophical argument in which it may be better to travel hopefully than to arrive. Yet within these constraints arguments form the core of the political process. If thus defined as public in nature, and instrumental in purpose, politics assumes what I believe to be its proper place in society.

Notes

1. Tversky, A. (1981) 'Choice, preference and welfare: some psychological observations', paper

presented at a colloquium on 'Foundations of social choice theory', Ustaoset (Norway).

2. Zeldin, T. (1973) *France 1848–1945*, Vol. 1 (Oxford: Oxford University Press), p. 134.

3. I rely on Habermas, J. (1982) Diskursethik—notizen zu einem Begrundingsprogram. Mimeographed.

4. Smullyan, R. (1980) *This Book Needs No Title* (Englewood Cliffs, N.J.: Prentice-Hall), p. 56.

5. Arendt, H. (1973) *On Revolution* (Hammondsworth: Pelican Books), p. 174.

6. Tocqueville, A. de (1969) *Democracy in America* (New York: Anchor Books), p. 229.

7. Ibid., Tocqueville, p. 224.

8. Ibid., Tocqueville, pp. 243–244.

9. Ibid., Tocqueville, p. 275.

10. Ibid., Arendt, p. 37.

11. Ibid., Arendt, p. 41.

12. Finley, M. I. (1976) 'The freedom of the citizen in the Greek world', reprinted as Ch. 5 in M. I. Finley, *Economy and Society in Ancient Greece* (London: Chatto and Windus, 1981), p. 83.

13. Finley, M. I. (1981) 'Politics', in M. I. Finley (ed.), *The Legacy of Greece* (Oxford: Oxford University Press), p. 31.

14. Ibid., Arendt, p. 119.

15. Sunday Times, 2 November 1980.

Open Government and Just Legislation: A Defense of Democracy

William Nelson

William Nelson begins with a critical discussion of Carole Pateman's account of political participation. While rejecting her view, Nelson nevertheless contends that political participation is critical for understanding the justification of democracy. Using James Madison's theory as a backdrop, Nelson defends participation on the basis of its beneficial effects on the citizens and because the laws emerging from democratic political structures tend to be more just than ones emerging from other political forms. Nelson next explores the conditions that a government must satisfy if its laws are to be morally justified. Those conditions, he claims, can be found in John Rawls' concept of a "well ordered society" in which the principles on which government rests represent a possible consensus among free and independent persons. Then in the final section Nelson returns to the writing of John Stuart Mill, offering an interpretation and then a defense of his theory of representative government.

Participation and Virtue

According to Carole Pateman . . . a participatory society is desirable in itself, not for its

From William N. Nelson, *On Justifying Democracy* (Boston: Routledge and Kegan Paul, 1980), pp. 48–51, 96–104, and 106–121. Reprinted by permission. Some footnotes omitted.

legislative consequences. But this can be misleading. While the value of a participatory society is not supposed to lie in its effects on legislation or policy, she does think its value lies in some of its other effects. Like many participation theorists, Pateman follows J. S. Mill when he says that one criterion for good government is 'the virtue and intelligence of the human beings composing the community'.

The most important aim of government should be 'to promote the virtue and intelligence of the people themselves'.[1] The desirability of a participatory society, as she sees it, derives from its positive effects on the character of members of society. Indeed, one of her reasons for advocating the goal of a participatory society—a society in which all associations are run by participation of their members—is her belief that desirable character traits will develop most readily in smaller associations in which people can become more deeply involved. Participation in national politics is less likely to have the same effects.

It seems to me that considerations of this type are at least relevant to the justification of a system of government. It could be argued, I suppose, that the proper function of government is the regulation of interactions among persons but not the alteration of their character. But it could be replied that governmental forms inevitably have some effect on human character; and, at least to the extent that this is true, the nature of these effects is relevant to the evaluation of governmental forms. Moreover, even if we regard regulation of interactions as the primary concern of government, it seems reasonable to suppose that people's characters will tend to affect the quality of their interactions. My quarrel with this form of participation theory, then, does not concern the type of argument offered, but the details of the argument. Consider, for example, the kind of effects on character on which Pateman focuses. These fall into several groups. First, active participation (especially in small associations or in the work-place) is supposed to lead people to develop a 'responsible' character, to enhance group harmony, develop a sense of cooperation and a sense of community, and to lead to willing acceptance of group decisions. Second, it leads people to feel that they are free, that they are their own master, and to increase their sense of political efficacy (and thus their desire to participate more fully), and it teaches them how to participate effectively. Finally, it leads them to develop active, non-servile characters, democratic or nonauthoritarian personality structures, and it leads them to broaden their horizons and to appreciate the viewpoints and perspectives of others.[2]

The foregoing is not an exhaustive list of all the character traits Pateman mentions, but it is a representative collection. The division into groups is not Pateman's. I add it because it seems to me that different complexes of these character traits are relevant to the task of justification in different ways. Basically, I want to argue that most of the character traits Pateman discusses either are not clearly desirable traits, or are desirable only on the assumption that we have already decided to have a participatory society. Partly because of the limited nature of her aims, and partly because of general features of the justification of political institutions which I shall discuss, the apparent circularity here does not entirely vitiate her argument. Nevertheless, it does mean that the considerations she advances in favor of participatory democracy constitute less than a full, independent justification.

Consider some of the traits Pateman discusses. The traits in the first two groups are, in a way, complementary. The traits in the second group—a sense of efficacy, a feeling of freedom and of being one's own master—are traits that lead people to want to participate more extensively in group decisions. The idea seems to be that participation breeds more participation. Thus, *if* we wish a society in which decisions are fully democratic—in which they are made by participation of those affected—we can be reassured that the process of democratization will tend to be self reinforcing. While the traits collected in the second group have to do with the participatory society's tendency to remain democratic, the traits in the first group have to do with its tendency to remain stable. If Pateman is right about the traits in this group, participation will lead people to acquiesce in group decisions, at least so long as these are made by participatory means. Her conclusions, then, are very different from the conclusions of a number of the revisionist writers who think that increased levels of participation may lead to social instability. Pateman's interest in these questions about stability and the level of participation clearly derives from her concern to answer the revisionists' charge that participation may endanger stability as well as their claim that political apathy is simply natural for people. Her general argument, I think, is that increased participation and stable democracy are *both* possible so long as we democratize the *whole* society instead of just national political institutions. Now, I am neither competent to answer the empirical questions here nor particularly interested in them. Even if a stable, participatory society is possible, my question is why we should try to bring it about?

The third group of character traits to which Pateman refers may seem to provide an answer to my questions. Nonauthoritarian personality structures, nonservile characters and the ability to appreciate the viewpoint of others may well seem like intrinsically good traits. This depends, of course, on just how we understand these phrases. For example, if a nonauthoritarian is (in part) someone who tends to acquiesce in majority decisions, no matter how outrageous, it seems to me undesirable. (This problem of interpretation figures in a number of questions here. For example, I took a 'sense of community' to be relevant primarily to a willingness to go along with community decisions, but Pateman may think of it in other ways too.) At the very least, the desirability of many of the traits Pateman mentions seems to depend on the assumption that we have a democratic society. Thus, the ability to appreciate the viewpoints and needs of others will at least be more important in a democratic, participatory society than it will be in other kinds of society. This does not make it irrelevant to the justification of a participatory society, but it does suggest that Pateman is not sufficiently aware of the complexity of the justificatory task she faces.[3] Ultimately, it seems to me, we need a reasonably well articulated moral theory. Given such a theory, it would be interesting to know whether a particular kind of political system would produce intrinsically good character structures, as defined by such a theory. But the relation between character, morality and institutions is likely to be more complex than that. Presumably, a moral theory will both lay down certain standards that laws or policies are supposed to meet and offer an account of human virtue and human good. Now, if the political system were so designed that it would produce the right laws or

policies no matter what people were like, the effects of the institutions on their character would be important only insofar as the morality directly implied specific standards for judging character. It is likely, however, that the effect of institutions on legislation would depend in part on the character of people occupying institutional positions. Hence, in most cases, the evaluation of the institutions would depend in part on the effect of those institutions on people's character. Roughly, we want institutions that will affect people in such a way that such people, operating those institutions, will produce the most nearly ideal laws and policies. John Stuart Mill, I think, sees the relation between institutional choice and individual character in just this way.[4] He does evaluate institutions in part by their effects on character, but a moral theory—utilitarianism—serves as the foundation of the argument. Without such a foundation, the argument would be radically incomplete. It would rest, as does Pateman's argument, on a merely conventional list of vaguely specified 'democratic' character traits. We need to go further than that. . . .

What we need to do, if we are to offer an argument for democracy capable of convincing those who are not already convinced democrats, is to begin with an independent account of what is morally desirable and why it is morally desirable. If we can then argue, in terms of such an account, that democracy is desirable itself, or has desirable consequences, we will have made some progress. This is what I shall attempt to do in this chapter. The task will require an excursion into moral theory, and then a discussion of how a representative democracy might be expected to work so as to produce government acceptable from the perspective of the kind of moral theory I shall sketch. . . .

The theory I shall develop in this chapter will be an instrumental theory. I shall argue that democracy is desirable largely because of its good effects—because it tends to produce good laws and policies, or, at least, to prevent bad ones. But this kind of theory has been subjected to serious criticism, perhaps most notably by Robert Dahl in his widely read *Preface to Democratic Theory*.[5] Since some of Dahl's arguments can be taken to be general arguments against any justification of the type I shall attempt, I must discuss Dahl's critique of Madison before proceeding with the program I have outlined.

Dahl on Madison

The first chapter of *Preface to Democratic Theory* is a critique of what Dahl takes to be the Madisonian theory of democracy. Democracy, on this theory, is American constitutional democracy with its complex system of checks on the power of majorities. Madison's argument for this system, according to Dahl, is that a republican form of government, circumscribed by checks on the power of majorities, is necessary to prevent tyranny. The absence of either popular elections or constitutional checks and balances will lead to tyranny (Dahl, 11).[6] This is a justification of constitutional democracy in terms of its substantive effects, and Dahl argues that it fails. He criticizes it on two grounds. First, assuming that we know what tyranny is, Dahl argues that Madison's justification seems to be based on a false empirical generalization. Second, he argues that we cannot really even test this generalization since we cannot give an adequate account of what tyranny is. True, we could define 'tyranny' in such a way that any nonrepublican government or government without separation of powers, was, by definition, tyrannical. But that kind of definition makes the argument trivial and uninteresting. The argument is interesting only if we begin with an independent definition of 'tyranny', but no such definition is adequate.

The first objection presupposes that the second is mistaken, so it is hard to see just how we are to take it. Still, it seems reasonable to say that, on any initially plausible account of tyranny, there are possible nontyrannical governments that lack the kind of constitutional restraints on the power of majorities that we find in the United States Constitution. Great Britain is a good enough example (Dahl, 13). Moreover, common sense, together with a good deal of social theory, suggests that noninstitutional, psychological restraints can be just

as effective as legal restraints in preventing abuse of power (Dahl, 17–19).[7] So, it seems doubtful that a constitutional democracy of the sort Madison had in mind is necessary to prevent tyranny.

The second objection is the more fundamental one. If it is successful, it will undermine any attempt to justify a system of government by reference to a substantive moral goal like the avoidance of tyranny. How exactly does the objection go? To define 'tyranny' in terms of the deprivation of natural rights is not to define it adequately unless we can "specify a process by which specific natural rights can be defined in the context of some political society" (Dahl, 23). Any attempt to do so in a way consistent with other elements of a theory like Madison's will fail, so, "tyranny seems to have no operational meaning in the context of political decision-making" (Dahl, 24). Now, the general point here presumably is not limited to definitions of 'tyranny' or definitions of 'natural rights'. The point, rather, is that a justification of a form of government based on the claim that that government will produce certain kinds of legislation requires a precise account of the kind of legislation in question. Otherwise, it will be impossible to determine the truth of the key premise in the argument. Dahl thinks he has an argument to rule out any adequate account, but I believe his argument fails.

There are two problems with Dahl's argument. First, he demands more of an adequate definition than he needs to demand, and, second, even given his overly strong requirement, he fails to demonstrate that it cannot be met. The second point is the easier one to make. Dahl argues by elimination. He considers only three possible theories of natural rights: that each person has a right to do whatever he wants; that each has a right to do whatever is not unanimously condemned, and, that each has a right to do whatever is not condemned by a majority. Dahl holds each of these theories to be either impractical or inconsistent with other elements of a theory like Madison's. (The third, for example, seems to rule out the possibility of majority tyranny (Dahl, 23–4).) But these are not all the possible theories of natural rights; so we cannot conclude that there is *no* adequate theory. And what a strange collection of theories Dahl has chosen to discuss! Moral theorists do not generally take seriously accounts of moral rights that make those rights depend on how people happen to vote. (What if they are immoral?) But here Dahl seems to be a victim of his decision to require not just a clear and precise account of the ethical goals to be attained by the political process, but an account that determines, *by some decisive political process,* what those goals involve. This brings us back to the first of the two problems mentioned above: Dahl demands more of an adequate definition than he needs to demand.

At the very least, Dahl requires that a definition of natural rights be operational. There are serious philosophical problems about the requirement of operational definition in any area of inquiry.[8] But, even if we assume that something like the requirement of operational definition is reasonable, I think Dahl requires too much. Everyone would agree, I suppose, that reasonable clarity and precision is desirable. No doubt one idea associated with operational definition is just this idea. The proponents of operational definition want to be able to say what does and does not follow from this or that proposition—what its truth conditions are. But they also want the presence or absence of these truth conditions to be subject to public determination. They want an account of truth conditions such that there will be virtually no room for disagreement about whether or not they are satisfied. Most would agree, however, that verifiability *in principle* is the most we can require. The most we can require is that, for each proposition, if we had the time, resources and so on, we could get near universal agreement on the truth or falsity of the proposition. . . .

If we want a political system that will make laws, if we want these laws to be an effective determinant of conduct, and if we want to penalize those who violate the laws, we need clear criteria, about which there can be little disagreement, by means of which we can determine what the law requires and who has complied with it. It is not enough that this be determinable merely *in principle.* We need procedures that will terminate in a reasonably short period of time. When we attach practical consequences to the truth or falsity of certain

propositions, we need practical, decisive procedures by which to determine their truth or falsity. Dahl, I want to suggest, confuses the requirement of decisive procedures appropriate in political contexts with the weaker requirements of clarity and verifiability in principle which may be appropriate in some theoretical contexts. It is for this reason that Dahl considers only accounts of natural rights stated in terms of procedures like majority rule.

I do not want to deny the importance of decisive, practical procedures in political systems. The question how we should go about justifying our choice of procedures is an important one just because we need some procedures. It is a difficult question just because no procedure can capture the moral criteria by which we evaluate political decisions. But the question whether a given system or procedure is justified is not itself a political question; it is a theoretical question. We do not need a decisive procedure to settle the question of the justifiability of our political decision procedures. Still, if we are to defend democracy, as Madison evidently did, by arguing that it tends to have results of a certain kind, it is incumbent on us to give a reasonably clear account of the kind of result we have in mind. To this extent, I agree with Dahl. But when Dahl objects that there is no way to clarify Madison's goal of nontyranny, he bases his objection on a survey of an absurdly small and irrelevant sample of possible attempts to clarify this goal. Apparently, this is because he requires more than clarity, and more even than what is normally demanded by those who require operational definitions.

Conceivably, Dahl was dimly aware of this kind of problem when he allowed himself to assume, at the beginning of his discussion of Madison, that we do have a clear enough understanding of what constitutes tyranny to evaluate Madison's central empirical claim—the claim that republican government with separation of powers is necessary for nontyrannical government. Dahl thinks it obvious, indeed, that there are governments significantly different from Madison's constitutional democracy that nevertheless manage to be nontyrannical. But now we should look again at this criticism. I do not want to quibble about the interpretation of Madison's writings in *The Federalist;* but, clearly, some theories *like* the theory Dahl attributes to Madison are immune to Dahl's criticisms. Thus, one might argue for some form of constitutional democracy not on the ground that it is *necessary* for decent government, but on the ground that it is more likely than other forms of government to lead to decent government. In sum, then, Dahl's arguments fall far short of ruling out any attempt to justify democracy in terms of the moral quality of its likely substantive results.

Morality and Just Government

The most important question about the system of laws and institutions making up the state is whether they satisfy the conditions morality lays down for such systems. Morality determines the limits of the permissible for systems of laws and institutions as well as for individual conduct. It has been said that 'justice is the first virtue of institutions.'[9] If this is so, it is so because a reasonable moral theory assigns a kind of priority to considerations of justice or because, in such a theory, considerations referred to as considerations of justice are just those relevant to the assessment of institutions. I have no objection to this way of speaking, but it leaves us with the following question: when it is true that legal, political or economic institutions are just, what does this involve? This is a substantive moral question. It can be answered only within a substantive theory. I shall argue for democracy, here, on the ground that it tends to produce specific laws and policies that are just. I am assuming that this kind of argument is sufficient to justify a political system, or at least to create a strong presumption in its favor. Suppose someone says that this kind of argument is irrelevant—that the crucial question concerns not the effects of the system, but its intrinsic features, whether it is fair, for example. I have no *general* argument against this position. I have attempted to reply to specific theories of this type in earlier chapters. I hope to establish, in this chapter, at least the possibility of a coherent, plausible justification in terms

of effects. Skepticism about the possibility of such a theory, as voiced by Dahl for example, may well be one reason for the prevalence of "procedural" theories.

If we are to argue that democracy satisfies principles of justice, and if this requires us to argue that democracy is well designed to produce just laws and policies, we clearly must say something about what justice, and morality in general, require. One way to carry out a defense of democracy along these lines would be this: offer an account of which laws are morally good laws, and then try to show that democracies tend to have good laws and that other governments do not. (Dahl used something analogous to this procedure to discredit Madison's contention that democracy is necessary for good government.) There are other possibilities, however. . . . The mechanics of democracy are such, I shall argue, that, given certain assumptions about human nature, democracy will automatically tend to produce morally acceptable results. Now this kind of argument, like the others I have mentioned, seems to presuppose a clear account of which laws are morally good laws. I shall have something to say along these lines, but most of my argument will proceed at a higher level of abstraction. Instead of offering anything like a complete account of what morality requires, I shall suggest an account of what a (reasonable) morality is. This account will embody conditions which must be satisfied by any acceptable moral principles. I shall then argue that, following the procedures of (a kind of) constitutional democracy, we will tend to come up with laws that are justifiable in terms of principles satisfying the conditions of acceptability for moral principles. The general idea is this: the tests that a law has to pass to be adopted in a constitutional democracy are analogous to the tests that a moral principle must pass in order to be an acceptable moral principle.

What conditions must a principle satisfy in order to be an acceptable moral principle? What conditions must a set of principles satisfy if they are to constitute an adequate morality? What principles are true moral principles? It is natural to think that the answer to these questions depends on an account of the function of morality: true moral principles are principles that perform the function of moral principles.

Looking at the problem in this way generates difficult questions. If two distinct sets of principles would equally well perform the function of morality, for example, is each set a set of true principles? More fundamental, however, is the question whether there is any such thing as *the* function(s) of morality. And how do we know when we have found it (them)? I do not have definitive answers to these questions. Nevertheless, I shall propose an account of morality in terms of its functions. The account I offer is not the only possible account of its kind. Others have been, or might be, offered. But neither is my account idiosyncratic. My suggestions about the function of morality should seem familiar both to theorists (since it is borrowed from other theorists) and to ordinary people. I think they are plausible suggestions. More important, whether or not what I offer here correctly captures the "essence" of morality seems to me *relatively* unimportant. What is more important is that we have reason to be interested in morality as I conceive it. The functions of morality, on my account, are important functions. We have reason to be interested in principles or rules performing these functions, and we have reason to be interested in the truth or falsity of judgments made with respect to these rules. In any case, I believe it is better to leave off these preliminary discussions and turn to the account itself. We will be in a better position to decide what to do with the account when we have it before us.

A Conception of Morality

Minimally, a morality can be described by a system of rules or principles proscribing some kinds of harmful or dangerous conduct and enjoining certain kinds of beneficial conduct. Such rules constitute a system of constraints or boundaries determining the limits of the permissible. To speak of these rules as constraints is to emphasize their overriding character; when moral considerations conflict with other considerations, moral considerations take precedence. Moral rules, as so far described, can be usefully distinguished into two groups. (1)

Some rules proscribe or enjoin actions that are either harmful or useful in themselves, regardless of what other people are doing; (2) Some rules enjoin actions which will either prevent harm or promote benefits just in case they are generally performed.[10] Rules of type (2) may be either direct rules, enjoining specific types of conduct, or indirect rules requiring simply that people adhere to whatever specific rules or conventions are being generally adhered to.[11] When I speak here of rules governing actions, I include actions establishing or altering institutional structures. When I speak of rules requiring that we benefit or refrain from harming people, I do not mean to exclude rules requiring that we benefit some of the expense of others. Thus, moral rules can include rules for settling disputes when one gains only at the expense of another, and they can also include rules governing the distribution or redistribution of goods.

Even if any morality includes rules of the sort described here, it does not follow that such rules exhaust the content of morality, nor, more importantly, does it mean that any such set of rules constitutes an *adequate* morality. What more is necessary? Let me begin by considering John Rawls's notion of a 'well-ordered society'. A society is well-ordered, he says, when it is "effectively regulated by a public conception of justice." More specifically, "(1) everyone accepts and knows that the others accept, the same principles of justice, and (2) the basic social institutions generally satisfy and are generally known to satisfy these principles." In a well-ordered society, "while men may put forth excessive demands on one another, they nevertheless acknowledge a common point of view from which their claims may be adjudicated." The shared, public system of principles constitutes "the fundamental charter of a well-ordered human association."[12]

Pretty clearly, the notion of a well-ordered society admits of degrees. Consensus on principles can be more or less perfect, and institutions can vary in the degree to which they satisfy the conditions laid down in the shared moral principles. In a perfectly well-ordered society, though, there will be complete agreement on principles for evaluating actions and common institutions. Moreover, I take it, there will be agreement that these principles are final (Rawls, 135–6). These principles are the *fundamental charter* of a well-ordered association. When these principles apply to a specific decision, they are taken to override any other considerations that might also apply. Thus, the shared, public system of rules in a well-ordered society plays the same role in the life of the community earlier assigned to moral rules in general. It is regarded as a system of *constraints* determining the limits of the permissible.

When a proposal is agreed to be contrary to the shared system of principles, it will be rejected by all. On the other hand, there may well be disagreement about the acceptability, *all things considered,* of proposals consistent with the shared morality. Nor is this the only source of disagreement and strife. While there is agreement, in a well-ordered society, on fundamental principles, there may not be agreement on the consequences of their application to particular cases. Typically, there will be agreement on what is relevant to a given decision, but there may well be disagreement on the truth or falsity of some statement that all regard as relevant. Nevertheless, the knowledge that there is agreement on ends strengthens "the bonds of civic friendship" (Rawls, 5), and mitigates the otherwise divisive effects of disagreement on specific matters of policy.

I want to suggest that one important function of a morality is to serve as the public system of constraints on action agreed to by citizens in a well-ordered society. A test for an *adequate* morality is that its principles be able to perform this function. The more stable a system of principles—the greater its capacity to continue to perform this function as a society grows and changes—the more adequate it is.

In general, then, those parts of a morality relevant to the assessment of laws and institutions consist of a system of final rules compliance with which tends to prevent harm or produce benefits. An adequate morality is a system of such rules on which there could be an enduring consensus. It is a system of rules that could be accepted by all members of society as principles determining the absolute limits of the permissible. Now, the idea of focusing on what could be agreed to or on

what could constitute a consensus is like the idea that seems to underlie much moral theory in the social contract tradition.[13] There are, of course, differences within that tradition. Some theorists, for example, see moral principles as principles that *would* be agreed to in more or less idealized situations. Others hold that moral principles are principles actually agreed to in actual situations. The position I have sketched here is like those theories emphasizing hypothetical agreement since it asserts that an adequate morality is a system of principles that could be accepted by everyone, even if none is accepted now. On the other hand, it is like theories emphasizing an actual agreement in that it says a morality constitutes a possible consensus among actual people. . . .

One way in which my theory resembles other contract theories is that it seems to be subject to some of the same criticisms. Consider this question: why should we believe that real people ought to comply with the principles that ideal people would agree to in some hypothetical situation? This objection corresponds to the question about my theory, why should we believe that people ought to comply with rules that could, or even do, constitute a consensus on fundamental constraints on conduct? This question could be interpreted in different ways. (1) It might be the question whether we have any reason to be interested in the requirements of such systems of rules. (2) It could be the question whether what people would agree to has anything to do with what *morality* requires of them . . .

I have suggested that we think of a morality as a system of overriding constraints on action compliance with which tends to produce benefits or prevent harm and which could serve as the fundamental charter of a well-ordered society. I have not said that any system of rules with these two properties is an adequate morality. The properties mentioned are necessary conditions. Are there other necessary conditions? The question whether the rules imagined here would be a morality no doubt stems partly from the feeling that the class of acceptable rules needs to be narrowed down further. At the very least, one might say, a set of principles is an adequate morality only when it represents a possible consensus *among free and independent persons.* We could imagine a kind of slave society in which the slaves themselves are so dehumanized that they would accept the slaveholders' rationale for their common institutions. But, given the modification suggested here, that would not show that these institutions were morally acceptable. To show this, we would have to show that principles permitting such institutions *would* be acceptable to all concerned even if they were free from its dehumanizing effects.

The requirement that a set of principles be a potential *stable* consensus—a consensus that would endure over time—will tend to rule out some seemingly unfair sets of principles in some societies. When there is social mobility, so that any person (or any person's child) might occupy most any position in society, people will be reluctant to accept principles giving special, permanent advantages even to their own social class. And, if they do, consensus on those principles will tend to break down as people who have known those advantages come to occupy less advantageous positions. However, in a rigid caste society, we would find neither of these kinds of check on the adoption of principles that look grossly unfair. A caste society with a caste morality may be a stable, well-ordered society. It does make some difference, then, whether we make it a necessary condition for a morality's being adequate that it constitute a possible, stable consensus among free and independent persons. But should we say this?

I shall argue here that people generally have reason to promote and comply with principles satisfying the conditions I have so far laid down; and I shall argue that people generally have a greater interest in such principles when those principles would be acceptable under conditions of freedom and independence. I do not believe this is a *proof* that principles satisfying the conditions in question constitute an adequate morality. If one holds that, by definition, moral principles are principles on which people have a reason to act, then my argument is relevant to such a proof. Be that as it may, the argument does serve as a partial justification of the kind of principles I have in mind, at least to those who share a certain ideal of social cooperation. Moreover, if I am correct, morality as I conceive it can

perform what might be regarded as one of its characteristic functions: people can successfully appeal to its principles in order to criticize the conduct of others or to justify their own.[14]

With or without the added requirement that principles be acceptable to free and independent persons, what reason do we have to take an interest in moral principles as described here? Suppose, to begin with, that we are in a well-ordered society. If so, there will be a set of fundamental principles on which people agree, and it will be agreed that these principles determine the limits of the permissible. They entail a set of constraints on conduct within which, it is agreed, we must confine ourselves. They will require that we refrain from harming one another in various ways, and they will require that we benefit one another in various ways. Also, in a well-ordered society, legal, political and economic institutions will be justifiable from the perspective of these shared principles, and it will be agreed that this is so. Now, on these assumptions, we will want others to comply with our shared principles insofar as we stand to benefit (or to avoid harm) as a result of their compliance. More interesting, it will generally be in the interest of each individual to conform to those shared principles himself and to develop the general disposition to do so. It will also generally be in the interest of each that basic institutions continue to be justifiable in terms of the society's shared principles. The argument for these conclusions is pretty straightforward. Given a general belief in certain fundamental constraints, and given a normal interest in the opinions of others, each will want to *appear* to limit his behavior by those constraints. But the easiest way to appear to conform to principles, usually, is to conform to them! And, if one has an interest in such general conformity, one has an interest in developing the general disposition to conform. Moreover, given an interest in conforming to shared principles, each has an interest in minimizing conflict between the requirements of these principles and the constraints and requirements of institutions. When one benefits from institutional constraints on others, one wants to be able to justify those constraints.

When one is able to make use of institutions to his advantage, one wants to be able to justify one's conduct to others. All this requires, however, that the institutions themselves be justifiable in terms of shared, public principles.

In a well-ordered society, under plausible assumptions about human motives, people generally have a reason to conform to shared principles of morality. Do they have *more* reason to conform to principles acceptable to free and independent persons than to principles that are not? Most people are concerned about the opinions of others, and this concern, at the very least, makes them want to appear to conform to shared principles. The reasons for this will vary from person to person. Some, perhaps, will simply want to avoid criticism. Even then, they will do well to cultivate a general disposition to conform, since actual conformity virtually guarantees the appearance of conformity, and alternative strategies can involve costly calculation and planning. But most of us, to a greater or lesser degree, do not want merely to appear to comply with generally accepted standards. We want, in Philippa Foot's nice phrase, "to live openly and in good faith with [our] neighbors."[15] Not only do we want to avoid the consequences of hypocrisy (always being on guard, trying to keep our lies consistent and so on), but we find lying and deceit intrinsically unpleasant. We do not want to have to conceal; we want our lives to be able to stand inspection. All this, of course, strictly requires only that we comply with whatever restrictions people actually believe in. But if it makes us feel uncomfortable to have to conceal our conduct from others, it will hardly satisfy us to know that we can justify our conduct to others only because they have come to accept certain principles under duress or some psychological constraint. At least the latter attitude seems a natural extension of the former. For many of us, then, some of the same considerations that lead us to take an interest in the requirements of shared principles will lead us also to take a greater interest in requirements that would be acceptable to people choosing freely and independently.

I have argued so far only that people in a well-ordered society have a reason to comply with generally accepted principles. But I have said that a morality consists of a set of principles that *would* perform the function of the public conception of justice in a well-ordered society. Do we have a reason to take an interest in a morality—in principles that would serve this function—when we are not in a well-ordered society? Does this property of a morality give us a reason to take an interest in it when it is not generally accepted? Most of us, I think, do have a reason to want principles to be generally accepted, and to comply with principles that could be generally accepted even when no such principles are now accepted. So long as we wish to be able to justify our conduct to others, we have reason to comply with rules that others *could* be led to accept; we also have reason to try to get those principles accepted. To this point, the argument is like the argument for complying with rules actually accepted in a well-ordered society. But suppose many people accept principles—racist principles might be an example—that are *inconsistent* with principles that could be generally accepted. In this case, conduct that *could* be justified to everyone, in the long run, could not be justified to many people in the short run. In this kind of situation, it is far from clear that individuals have a reason to care about what morality requires. At least, whether a given person has reason to act according to principles that could be generally accepted will depend to a far greater extent on particular motives and features of his situation that are likely to differ from those of others. It will depend on the extent to which he must deal with members of racial minorities, for example; and it will depend on whether his desire to be able to justify his conduct to others is based on a mere desire to avoid ostracism and reprisals, or on a respect for persons as persons.

Aside from the desire to be able to justify our conduct to others, it should be remembered, we have other reasons to want certain kinds of general principles adopted and complied with. According to the theory under consideration, a morality is not just any system of principles that can be generally accepted and publicly avowed. It is a system of principles requiring some beneficial conduct and proscribing some harmful conduct. But then, insofar as we stand to benefit (or avoid harm) from compliance on the part of others, we have reason to want them to comply. Thus, we have an additional, independent reason to push for the acceptance of principles that could gain general acceptance and that people could therefore have a reason to comply with. One reason people have for complying with rules depends on the acceptability of those rules to other people. So, our interest in compliance on the part of others also gives us an interest in the general acceptability of those rules. It leads us to try to find systems of constraints that are, intuitively speaking, fair as well as beneficial.

Let me summarize. An adequate morality, I have suggested, can be described by a set of principles or rules having, at least, the following properties: (1) Compliance with the principles tends to produce benefits or prevent harm; (2) The principles could serve as the shared, public principles constituting a stable, "fundamental charter of a well-ordered human association" as Rawls understands this notion; and (3) The principles could perform this function in a society of free and independent persons. The idea is that it is a necessary condition for a system's being an adequate morality that it satisfy these conditions, but I did not argue for this conclusion directly. What I argued is that we have reason to want *some* such set of principles accepted and generally complied with. If some set is accepted and complied with, we have reason to comply ourselves and to urge continued compliance on the part of others. We have reason to treat them with the seriousness normally accorded a morality.

It should be emphasized that the arguments in this section depend on empirical assumptions, and that the conclusions hold only other things being equal. First, the arguments depend clearly on assumptions about human motives and interests, like the assumption that we are not generally indifferent to the opinions of others; and they depend on assumptions about our circumstances, like the assumption that it is costly and difficult to conceal one's conduct. These assumptions *could* be false, but I think they are not. Second, the

extent to which one has a reason to comply with the directives of morality (as conceived here) will depend on the extent to which others accept and comply with those directives. If no one accepted principles with the properties of an adequate morality, people would have much less reason to try to develop and comply with such principles. Still, it is hard to imagine a complete lack of consensus on principles within subgroups in a society anyhow; and, in the absence of a rigid caste structure, people would tend to comply with principles most widely accepted and therefore most widely acceptable. The long run tendency is toward general compliance with, and general acceptance of, principles that have the properties of an adequate morality. But, even if this is right, it does not follow at all that each person will always have an overriding reason to comply with such principles in particular cases.[16]

At the beginning of the section before this one, I asked what conditions a political system had to satisfy in order to be morally acceptable, and I said that this question is itself a substantive moral question. In this section, I have offered a partial account of the nature of an adequate morality, but I have said virtually nothing about its substantive content. If I am right, of course, the substantive requirements of morality will depend on what kinds of principles people can agree to under certain conditions and for certain purposes. What I shall argue in the next two sections is that familiar institutions of representative democracy tend to foster consensus on adequate principles of morality, and consequently tend to produce law and policy decisions consistent with these principles. The argument will depend in part on the precise nature of representative institutions and it will also presuppose some of the motivational assumptions I have introduced in this section in arguing that people have reason to care about the requirements of an adequate morality. The idea that this argument constitutes a *justification* for democracy depends on an assumption about what the substantive requirements of an adequate morality would be. Specifically, I assume that an adequate morality will include requirements that laws and social policy must satisfy, and I assume that it will not require anything of political decision procedures other than that they tend to produce acceptable laws and policies.

Democracy and Just Government: Mill's Argument

In this section I shall offer an interpretation and defense of the theory of democracy John Stuart Mill presented in *Considerations on Representative Government*.[17] I think Mill's justification of representative government is, in its main lines, reasonable. Other philosophers have suggested similar arguments, and Mill's argument needs to be supplemented at certain points; but I shall begin with Mill here, partly because he has sometimes been misinterpreted, and partly because, properly interpreted, he makes the case about as well as anyone.

According to Mill, the "ideally best form of government," the "form of government most eligible in itself," is representative government (Mill, 35–6). What does Mill mean by "most eligible in itself," and what, in his view, are the criteria for good government in general? Basic to Mill's theory of government is the idea that different systems of government are appropriate in different societies and in different stages in the development of a given society. The form of government ideally best in itself, then, is not the form of government best under all circumstances. Instead, the idea is this: We consider all possible states of society, and we suppose that each is governed by the form of government best for that state of society. Each form of government, then, is operating in its most propitious circumstances, and we say that the society that is best governed has the form of government that is best in itself. In Mill's words, that government is "most eligible in itself . . . which, if the necessary conditions existed for giving effect to its beneficial tendencies, would, more than all others, favor and promote not some one improvement, but all forms and degrees of it" (Mill, 35).

That form of government is best in itself

which, given propitious circumstances, has the best effects. Government, according to Mill, is a *means* to certain ends (Mill, 15). But to what ends? What is the function of government? In Mill's view, there are two *criteria* for a good government. On the one hand, government must "promote the virtue and intelligence of the people" in the community. On the other hand, the "machinery" of government must be "adapted to take advantage of the amount of good qualities which may at any time exist and make them instrumental to the right purposes" (Mill, 25–6). As many commentators have noted, Mill tends to emphasize the first of these criteria. What has not generally been noticed is that possession of these criteria—of these *marks* of good government—is not what *makes* the government good. What *makes* the government good is its having good effects. Virtuous citizens and appropriate governmental "machinery" are marks of good government because they are what makes it possible for government to produce the right effects. This is quite clear from the way in which Mill introduces the idea of concentrating on the personal qualities of the citizenry. He begins by considering the problem of the administration of justice. An effective and fair judicial system requires intelligent, honest and fair-minded citizens: witnesses must be reliable, judges must refrain from taking bribes, jurors must be willing and able to consider the merits of a case dispassionately, and so on (Mill, 24). Mill uses the same example in order to explain the importance of the "machinery" of government.

> The judicial system being given, the goodness of the administration of justice is in the compound ratio of the worth of the men composing the tribunals, and the worth of the public opinion which influences or controls them. But all the difference between a good and a bad system of judicature lies in the contrivances adopted for bringing whatever moral and intellectual worth exists in the community to bear upon the administration of justice and making it duly operative on the result (Mill, 26).

The tendency of a government to promote the virtue of its citizens, together with the quality of its "machinery," are *criteria* of good government because governments that promote virtue and have the right machinery tend to perform the function of governments well. But the *function* of a government is to produce good decisions and good legislation—in general, to promote "the aggregate interests of society" (Mill, 16). An ideal form of government, then, will be a government that is in harmony with itself. It will consist of institutions that affect people's character in such a way that people with that kind of character, operating those institutions, will tend to produce the best laws and decisions. To show that a form of government is desirable, one would need, in principle, to begin with an account of the goals to be achieved—an account of good legislation, for example. One would then have to demonstrate that, given the machinery of government, and given the effects of that form of government on the citizenry, we could expect good laws and policies.

Mill is a utilitarian. He holds, as noted above, that government should be so designed that it promotes "the aggregate interests of society." Why does he think that representative government is the form of government most likely to achieve this goal? In part, of course, the answer is that representative government is not the best form of government under *all* conditions. If, for example, citizens have acquired neither the willingness to acquiesce in *necessary* authority, nor sufficient will to take an active role in government, representative government will fail (Mill, Chapter 3). Nevertheless, Mill holds, once the requisite conditions have been satisfied, representative government is superior to any other form of government, under *any* conditions. Why?

The "ideally best form of government," Mill says,

> is that in which the sovereignty, or supreme controlling power in the last resort, is vested in the entire aggregate of the community, every citizen not only having a voice in the exercise of that ultimate sovereignty, but being, at least occasionally, called on to take an actual part in the government by the personal discharge of some public function, local or general (Mill, 42).

This kind of government, Mill says, will both make good use of people as they are, and will

tend to improve them in such a way that they will govern even better as time passes. People will be secure from bad government because they will be "self-*protecting*" and they will be able to improve their collective lot because they will become "self-*dependent*" (Mill, 43). In a popular form of government, the chance of injustice will be reduced because each person will stand up for his own rights. And no one stands up for a person's rights better than that person himself. Moreover, a system in which people have some control over their political situation breeds an active, vigorous citizenry. According to Mill, not only will active persons do a better job of protecting their rights, but also, active as opposed to passive persons will promote the long term interests of society. Self government protects people against abuses, it breeds the type of citizen who will be vigilant in protecting himself, and it breeds in everyone the attitudes that a society must have in its rulers if it is to advance (Mill, 43–52).

Parts of Mill's position—the idea that democracy protects individuals against injustice by giving them a chance to stand up for their own rights, for example—are familiar to most of us.[18] But the question is whether it is really *true* that individual rights are protected in a democracy. In what kind of a democracy, operating under what kinds of voting rules, do rights get protected? Throughout most of Chapter 3, Mill seems to be thinking of a direct democracy. He concludes the chapter thus:

> it is evident that the only government that can fully satisfy all the exigencies of the social state is one in which the whole people participate; that any participation, even in the smallest public function is useful; that the participation should everywhere be as great as the general degree of improvement of the community will allow; and that nothing less can be ultimately desirable than the admission of all to a share in the sovereign power of the state. But since all cannot, in a community exceeding a single small town, participate personally in any but some very minor portions of the public business, it follows that the ideal type of a perfect government must be representative (Mill, 55).

This is a non sequitur. If direct democracy is ideal, but unfeasible, it does not follow that the feasible alternative most similar, namely representative democracy, is therefore the best of the feasible alternatives. It may be the best, but we need further argument to show this. Specifically, we would need to show that it will perform functions like that of protecting the rights of individuals as well as any alternative. There are clearly difficult questions here. For example, will everyone be represented, or represented equally well, in a representative democracy? And will it make a difference whether Parliament operates on a simple majority rule or on some alternative kind of rule?

Even if we imagine that some kind of direct democracy is possible, and assume that people are vigorous in the protection of what they take to be their own rights and interests, it does not follow that each person's rights *will* be protected in a direct democracy. In Chapter V [*where Nelson discussed economic or popular will theories*—ED.] we looked at some attempts to predict the outcome of democratic decision-making processes under various assumptions about voting rules, and on the assumption that each individual would be vigorous in trying to achieve his own ends. Mill does not offer anything like this kind of analysis of democratic decision-making, but our earlier discussions should remind us that there is no guarantee that everyone will get his way. Quite the contrary. The problem of majority tyranny is still a serious problem.

As it happens, Mill does devote some later chapters (Chapter 7, especially) to the problem of designing a method of representation in which all shades of opinion achieve representation in Parliament. However, everyone's being represented in Parliament does not guarantee that everyone's rights will be respected in parliamentary decisions. After all, even direct democracy does not guarantee protection for everyone, since people may have diametrically opposed opinions as to what their rights are, and there is no reason to believe, a priori, that the person who is correct will prevail.

Mill would reply, I believe, that this objection is based on a misunderstanding of the way in which democracy works to protect people's rights. It is not because everyone has a vote that each person's rights are protected. Having a vote does not guarantee being on the winning side. The important thing about democratic government—whether direct democracy or representative democracy—is that the processes of decision-making and administration are carried out in the *open*. It is not that everyone will always have his or her way, but that whatever is done will be done in *public*. Administrators and legislators will be forced to *defend* their actions in public.

The proper function of a representative parliament, according to Mill, is not to administer, nor even to legislate, if by this we mean to write bills and enact statutes. If only because it is too large and diverse, it is ill suited to these tasks (Mill, 71–7). Its proper function is:

> to watch and control the government: to throw the light of publicity on its acts: [and] to compel a full exposition and justification of all of them which anyone considers questionable; . . . Parliament [is] at once the nation's Committee of Grievances and its Congress of Opinions—an arena in which not only the general opinion of the nation, but that of every section of it, and as far as possible of every eminent individual whom it contains, can produce itself in full light and challenge discussion; where every person in the country may count upon finding somebody who speaks his mind, as well or better than he could speak it himself, not to friends and partisans exclusively, but in the face of opponents, to be tested by adverse controversy; where those whose opinion is overruled feel satisfied that it is heard and set aside not by a mere act of will, but for what are thought superior reasons . . . (Mill, 81–2).

Why think that this kind of open government, open debate of public policy, willingness to consider grievances seriously and respond to them, will lead to good government? Why think, for that matter, that representatives will properly discharge their responsibility to publicize the activities of government, to publicize criticism of the government, and to debate the issues seriously? Won't there be a temptation, for example, simply to ignore demands for justification when they proceed from small minorities? There are two kinds of questions here. On the one hand, there are questions about the likelihood that elected representatives will perform the functions expected of them according to the theory. On the other hand, there is the question whether, even if they do, the result will be morally good government. Mill offers, at best, only partial answers to these questions.

In a way, each of the two questions I have raised here is a question concerning the character of citizens. How will they respond to demands for justification from others? What will they regard as an acceptable justification? When will they be willing to limit their demands on others? To what extent will they feel that they need to justify their conduct to others? The questions I have raised above are also questions about what morality requires. What is the relation between a policy's being acceptable to members of a community—its being justifiable in the sense that it is acceptable—and its being *morally* justifiable?

Now, in Mill's view, a major advantage of democracy is that it improves the character of its citizens. On the one hand, he thinks it will produce active, self assertive persons concerned with improving their environment. Perhaps more important, when citizens are required "to exercise, for a time and in their turn, some social function," this mitigates the fact that there is little "in most men's ordinary life to give any largeness either to their conceptions or to their sentiments". When a person is required to serve on juries, or to serve in local office, "[he] is called upon, while so engaged, to weigh interests not his own; to be guided, in case of conflicting claims, by another rule than his private partialities; to apply, at every turn, principles and maxims which have for their reason of existence the common good" (Mill, 53–4).

As I read Mill, assumptions something like these are crucial to his theory. The open and public character of government in a representative democracy is a *desirable* feature of that kind of government only if we assume that open discussion of governmental policy tends to result in good policy choices, or at least tends to prevent bad choices. The plausibility of this assumption depends, in turn, on assumptions about the kind of policy that citizens will find acceptable. What Mill wants to claim is that the very process of open discussion leads people to adopt reasonable moral

principles. It works both directly and indirectly. To the extent that citizens already have good character, public discussion of governmental policy alternatives results in good policy. To the extent that citizens lack good character, public discussion and debate tends to improve their character by leading them, for example, to appreciate the situation of others.

The question is whether any of this is true. If Mill wishes to claim that participating in government, listening to public debate of political issues, discussing these issues with acquaintances and so forth, will lead people to adopt any specific set of moral principles—utilitarian principles, for example—it is not clear how he could defend his claim. But it may be possible to provide a plausible defense of a less specific claim. Recall Rawls's conception of a 'well-ordered society' discussed in the preceding section: A well-ordered society is a society governed by commonly accepted principles of justice. Now, it does seem plausible that, when matters of public policy are subject to frequent public debate, and when most individuals are called upon, from time to time, "to exercise some public function," that citizens will attempt to formulate principles in terms of which they will be able to defend their positions to others. Similarly, to the extent that political leaders must defend their positions publicly, they will have to formulate principles and conceptions of the common good in terms of which they can justify their positions. At least, given open institutions, and given the kind of motivational assumptions discussed in the preceding section, public functionaries will attempt to formulate coherent justifications for their policies; and these justifications will have to be capable of gaining widespread public acceptance. Such justifications will have to represent a kind of possible consensus— a possible "fundamental charter of a well-ordered society." But principles like this satisfy at least a necessary condition for adequate moral principles. And if we assume a populace sufficiently well educated to understand the consequences of legislative proposals, laws that can pass the test of public justifiability will tend to be morally justifiable laws.

Summary, Objections and Qualifications

Mill's theory of representative government, I have claimed, embodies a justification of the kind appropriate for a system of government. The argument is that representative government tends to produce morally acceptable laws and policies. At least, it tends to produce laws and policies within the bounds of the permissible as determined by reasonable moral principles. The argument needs to be filled out with a general account of moral principles; and I have attempted to provide a partial account which, when conjoined with Mill's argument, makes the argument plausible. The idea is this: Morality is a system of constraints on conduct which people could jointly acknowledge as the constraints determining the form of their association together. Thus, a good system of government is a system that leads people to formulate mutually agreeable conceptions of fundamental constraints, and it is a system that leads them to adopt laws and policies compatible with such constraints.[19] A system of representative government with an educated, responsible citizenry, and with representatives who understand their responsibility to promote serious, open discussion of governmental policy—a *public* government, we might call it—should have these consequences.

Is public government, as conceived here, feasible? This question could have different meanings. Many recent disputes about the feasibility of democratic institutions have focused on the difference between representative systems and direct democracy of one kind or another. Thus, those more or less sympathetic to current institutions have objected to advocates of greater participation—the town meeting model—that it is just impossible to operate a national government that way.[20] But clearly there is no such problem about a system of representative government. We already have one. On the other hand, existing institutions and practices are not above criticism from the perspective of the kind of theory suggested here. If there is a single idea

that is central to Mill's theory, it is the idea of *open* government. In a society of any great size it is clear that the ideal of open government depends for its realization on a variety of institutions. A vigorous free press, free not only from legal limitations, but also from more subtle forms of intimidation, is clearly essential. Open meetings laws—"Sunshine Laws"—are also a natural step toward this ideal, as are proposals to broadcast congressional hearings and even sessions of congress. Such changes, evidently desirable in terms of this theory, are also possible.

The real problems of feasibility are not problems about the possibility of necessary institutions. They have to do with whether people—both citizens and officials of government—will comply with the spirit of open government. There is a nest of problems here. People, I have claimed, naturally want to be able to justify their conduct to others. They want their own actions and their institutions to be acceptable from the perspective of mutually acceptable principles. If Mill is right, the institutions of representative government, especially when they require some citizen participation at least at some level, tend to foster the development of this natural desire. When this desire is prevalent, open government conducted in a spirit of candor and openness tends to be good government. But, the prevalence of this desire does not itself guarantee that government will be so conducted. Quite simply, well-meaning elected officials, wanting to enact justifiable policies, may lack faith in the public, and thus may decide to act undemocratically. In the short run, at least, they will not necessarily be acting wrongly. The argument for democracy, as conceived here, is an argument in terms of its long run tendencies. In the short run, it requires faith. Even in a society of well-meaning persons, democracy is not necessarily stable; it is liable to degenerate into nondemocratic alternatives.

Another kind of instability afflicts democracies. The advantage of democracy is that it *moralizes* the process of government.[21] It encourages both citizens and representatives to think of legislation and policy-making in terms of what can be justified; and it leads them to formulate principles and conceptions of the common good in terms of which they can carry out the process of justification. The result, at best, is a stable, well-ordered society, as Rawls understands this notion, with virtual unanimity on fundamental principles underwriting common laws and institutions. But another possibility is a politics built around entrenched, irreconcilable ideologies: a society divided into warring camps. What *morality* requires in a case like this cannot be specified in the abstract. Perhaps one of the ideologies is actually a reasonable morality. Perhaps neither is. In any case, there is no guarantee that the democratic process will result in reasonable laws and policies under these conditions, and it is possible that democracy itself will not long survive.[22]

A good question for empirical study is the question under what conditions the "moralizing" tendencies of democratic politics will tend to produce desirable results and under what conditions they will not. One might think that a crucial variable would be the method of voting. Specifically, one might think a simple majority rule, either in the election of representatives or in the legislative process itself, would encourage the development of ideologies with less than universal appeal. Something closer to a unanimity rule seems more appropriate, given the emphasis on unanimity in my theory. But, as we have seen in earlier chapters, the unanimity rule is equivalent to the rule of one when that one happens to favor the status quo. Unless we assume that the status quo has some privileged status in morality, the unanimity rule is not clearly preferable to the majority rule. The ideal of democratic politics sketched here is that, whatever policies we adopt, they will have to be *justifiable* in terms of widely acceptable principles. Under majority rule, a decision *not* to change is subject to the same requirement.

Variables other than voting rules may well be even more important. The size of the community and the quality of communications, the character and educational level of citizens, and the presence or absence of castes or patterns of segregation are all likely to influence the quality of political debate and, hence, the quality of legislation. Again, it will take empirical investigation to determine just what variables affect the *moral* quality of legislation as I understand this notion here. It seems to me likely, for example, that the pressures for just legislation will be greater in a society to which people feel committed than in a society from which emigration is easy or attractive. But this conjecture requires verification.[23]

It is worth recalling, briefly, Dahl's criticism of Madison. Madison claimed, according to Dahl, that American constitutional procedures are strictly *necessary* if we are to avoid tyranny, and Dahl ridiculed that idea. I think it is also clear that no system of political institutions, by itself, is *sufficient* to prevent tyranny. I suspect Dahl would agree fully. But if there is reason to believe that democratic institutions are morally preferable to nondemocratic alternatives, they must increase the likelihood that laws and policies will conform to the requirements of an adequate morality. Whether they will do so in a particular case probably depends on factors of the kinds I have mentioned.

Many theorists have argued for democracy on the ground that it tends to protect the rights of individuals, and, in general, to produce just laws and policies. But the arguments tend to be weak. True, people have a chance to exercise their grievances, argue for their rights, and exercise their franchise in defense of their positions. But what we need to know is whether legitimate claims will tend to prevail and illegitimate claims to lose. Why think that? I have offered a way to strengthen the argument by suggesting assumptions about human motivation, about the dynamics of representative government, and about the nature of morality. The argument depends especially on these assumptions about morality. I have assumed that an adequate morality constitutes a kind of possible point of agreement among people concerning the limits of the permissible in their common affairs. At the beginning of this chapter, I suggested that other attempted justifications of democracy tend to assume the value of what they are trying to justify. When they assume a moral theory, for example, the moral theory is just what critics of democracy are likely to regard as in need of justification. Now, I can imagine someone objecting to the conception of morality advanced here in much the same way: The idea that what is morally right has anything to do with what people believe, or are willing to accept, or whatever, might well seem to be presupposed by a belief in democracy; and that presupposition is what bothers critics of democracy. I have some sympathy with this objection. It is probably correct, and worth noting, that unless there is *some* systematic connection between people's needs, preferences, etc., and what morality requires, then it is doubtful that democracy can be morally justified. On the other hand, we need not assume, and I do not assume here, that morality simply requires doing what the majority prefers, or that all preferences and desires need to be given equal weight, or even that they be weighted in proportion to their subjective intensity. It is more complicated than that. Moreover, I have made at least some effort to show that the conception of morality assumed here is reasonable on independent grounds. . . .

Notes

---

1. J. S. Mill, *Considerations on Representative Government* (Indianapolis and New York: Bobbs-Merrill, 1958), 25.

2. Pateman, *op. cit.,* 24–5, 29–31, 45–6, 63–4, 74.

3. Pateman herself, it should be noted, is not so much interested in questions of justification. Her main concern is with questions of feasibility.

4. Mill, *op. cit.,* 5–6, 15, 24–5.

5. Robert Dahl, *Preface to Democratic Theory* (Chicago: University of Chicago Press, 1956). (Subsequent references in the text to "Dahl" are to this volume.)

6. Control of "factions" is also supposed to be necessary, but that is irrelevant to my argument here.

7. We have seen that some of the participation theorists, as well as those with whom they disagree, have been concerned with the psychological prerequisites of stable, decent government. Some of the former, of course, argue that extensive participation contributes to the development of the relevant psychological conditions.

8. See Carl Hempel, "Empiricist Criteria of Cognitive Significance: Problems and Changes" in his *Aspects of Scientific Explanation* (Chicago: Free Press. 1956).

9. John Rawls, *A Theory of Justice* (Cambridge, Mass.: Harvard University Press, 1971), p. 3.

10. Trivial examples include such rules as "everyone stop on red and go on green." Some examples are instances of coordination problems in which everyone gains *if and only if* everyone follows some rule. Other examples are analogous to the prisoners' dilemma in which universal cooperation is sufficient, but not necessary for the production of some shared benefit. The latter cases, of course, present serious problems of instability. For an interesting discussion of coordination problems, see David Lewis, *Convention* (Cambridge, Mass.: Harvard University Press, 1969). For the prisoners' dilemma, see Luce and Raiffa, *Games and Decisions* (New York: Wiley, 1957), chap. 5. On the relation between these problems and the requirements of morality, see David Gauthier, "Morality and Advantage," *Philosophical Review* 76 (October 1967): 460–475.

11. The so-called 'Principle of Fairness' is an example of such a rule. See Rawls, *A Theory of Justice*, sec. 18.

12. Rawls, *A Theory of Justice*, p. 5. (Subsequent references in the text to "Rawls" are to this volume.)

13. Among modern writers, Rawls is the best known proponent of a kind of hypothetical contract theory, though there are others. Gilbert Harman conceives of morality as a kind of actual agreement among actual persons. See "Moral Relativism Defended," *Philosophical Review* 84 (January 1975); *The Nature of Morality* (New York: Oxford University Press, 1977), chaps. 5–8; and "Relativistic Ethics: Morality as Politics," *Midwest Studies in Philosophy,* 3 (University of Minnesota: Morris, 1978), pp. 109–121.

14. For the distinction between *proof* and *justification* I have in mind, see Rawls, *A Theory of Justice*, sec. 87, esp. pp. 580–581.

15. Philippa Foot, "Morality as a System of Hypothetical Imperatives," *Philosophical Review* 81 (July 1972), p. 314. The argument in the text relies heavily on Mrs. Foot's work, especially on the concluding pages of her "Moral Beliefs," *Proceedings of the Aristotelian Society* 58 (1958–9). See also Rawls, *A Theory of Justice*, sec. 86.

16. One person's belief that others comply with the rules does not, in itself, necessarily give that person a reason to comply himself. For some people, at least, complying with the rules, by itself, is not a convention in David Lewis's sense of the term. (See "Languages, Language and Grammar" in *On Noam Chomsky: Critical Essays,* ed. G. Harman (New York: Doubleday 1974), p. 255.) Conformity to some moral rules is unstable, at least among some people: while each benefits if everyone complies, universal conformity is not necessary. But, it may well be true, in most groups, that, if each complies with *and* professes belief in the rules, each thereby has reason to profess belief in *and* comply with the rules. This conjunctive regularity may come to have the status of a convention.

17. [Chapters 3, 5, and 6 reprinted in this volume.] References in the text to Mill are to the Bobbs-Merrill edition (Indianapolis and New York: 1958).

18. See, for example, Benn and Peters, *The Principles of Political Thought* (New York: Free Press, 1965), p. 414ff; and Carl Cohen, *Democracy* (Athens, Ga: University of Georgia Press, 1971), sec. 14.3.

19. Compare Rawls, *A Theory of Justice:* "Justice as fairness begins with the idea that where common principles are necessary and to everyone's advantage, they are to be worked out from the viewpoint of a suitably defined initial situation of equality . . . the constitutional process should preserve the equal representation of the original position to the degree that this is feasible" (pp. 221–222).

20. See Robert Dahl, *After the Revolution* (New Haven and London: Yale University Press, 1970) and "Democracy and the Chinese Boxes" in *Frontiers of Democratic Theory,* ed. H. Kariel (New York: Random House, 1970).

21. Benn and Peters, *The Principles of Political Thought,* p. 416.

22. Some writers, it seems to me, are excessively concerned about this prospect and hold that moralizing or ideological tendencies should be resisted in favor of the politics of compromise among (mere) interest groups. At least, this is the impression I get from S. M. Lipset, "The Paradox of American Politics," *The Public Interest* 41 (Fall 1975).

23. For discussion of this idea, see Albert Hirschman, *Exit, Voice and Loyalty* (Cambridge, Mass.: Harvard University Press, 1970).

Liberalism, Skepticism, and Democracy

Joseph Raz

Raz begins his essay with a discussion of the position that moral disagreement or moral skepticism provides the basis of democratic government and individual liberty. Rejecting such claims, he then considers the argument that democratic procedures rest on the fact that people have expressed a belief or a preference and have nothing to do with the reasons for their vote or the soundness of those reasons. Raz also rejects this approach, arguing that democratic government is justified because democratic governments serve the well-being of people. The legitimacy of democratic governments is based on their ability to give sound decisions. In the final sections Raz discusses "value pluralism" (the view that there are many different valuable ways of life) and autonomy (understood in terms of self-definition among a range of valuable alternatives). Ultimately, he claims, "perfectionist" liberalism's commitment to freedom rests on belief in the value of autonomy. He concludes with a brief discussion of the importance of public culture and the response "perfectionist" liberalism should make to those who advocate or live ignoble lives.

From Joseph Raz, "Liberalism, Skepticism, and Democracy," *Iowa Law Review,* Vol. 74, No. 4 (May, 1989). Reprinted by permission. Some footnotes omitted.

Our culture combines a dedication to individual freedom with bitter disagreements about its limits. In a way the disagreements tell of the strength of the commitment to freedom. They result from controversies concerning the reasons for that commitment, which lead to differences in our understanding of its meaning and limits. The fact that individual freedom is supported by so many currents of thought, by so many religious and philosophical tendencies in our society, is evidence of the strength of our commitment to this ideal and of its centrality to our culture.

Nor should the alternative ways of understanding the value of individual freedom be thought of as necessarily incompatible. There are indeed many powerful arguments in support of this ideal, and they are largely mutually reinforcing, although they differ in detail, and therefore, part company round the edges. All this means is that in some instances the case for freedom is supported by only some of the myriad reasons which bolster it in the majority of cases.

Some of the best arguments for individual freedom are of a practical, or pragmatic, cast. One points to the success, cultural and economic, that the free play of ideas and the spirit of enterprise have brought to the countries which encouraged them. Another argument points to the contribution of respect for individual freedom to social stability, and individual prosperity, in a world riven by fundamental moral and religious disagreements. Respect for individual liberties provides the *modus vivendi* necessary for the stability of pluralistic societies. It also ensures that not only members of ideological groups which are temporarily in the ascendancy, but the bulk of the population, can enjoy relative prosperity. A third argument rests on the principled limitations on the ability of any government or any large bureaucracy to achieve complex moral goals and on the inevitable undesirable by-products of bureaucratic interventions.

I mention these powerful pragmatic arguments only in order to say that the fact that I am not going to consider them does not mean that I underestimate their importance. But my concern in this Article is with some moral arguments for respecting individual freedom. In certain quarters there is in the air an atmosphere of moral privatization, of a tendency to separate morality from the state. According to these trends, morality is a matter of which we know little, something on which objective judgment is impossible, something which should be left to the individual. The state should keep out of morality. At most it should merely hold the ring, providing impartial adjudication among private opinions.

People who hold such views often regard them as supporting individual freedom. By excluding the state from the moral realm, or from all but procedural morality, they seek to leave individuals free to pursue their hearts' content. I think that in the main such views are misguided and dangerous. They are based on confused reasoning, and they give freedom a bad name. They present a morally anemic argument for freedom. The case for individual liberty is alleged to rest on the weakness of morality, or on our inability to understand moral issues. Partly because of this, such arguments tend to encourage toleration bred by indifference to others, toleration which is excessively individualistic in spirit. I begin this Article by criticizing the view that moral skepticism or moral fallibility provides an important moral foundation for respecting individual liberty. . . . I conclude with a brief summary of an alternative view defending individual liberty as a positive value, as an element in the moral ideal of the free person.* It will become clear that this view of freedom is not infected by the individualism of which liberals are often accused.

Skeptical Themes

A. Skeptical Liberality

As a teacher I am constantly surprised at the deep roots of value skepticism among the better educated in our society. Every year, when the new students arrive, I am reminded that while very few people are thorough skeptics, many are half skeptics. That is, while people

---

*It hardly needs saying that there are many other principled, moral arguments in support of individual freedom which I neither examine nor mention here.

do have their views and their principles, they often combine them with general skepticism and agnosticism about values. They hold that there is no way of "objectively" establishing or justifying any value judgments. Every person's view is just his view. Somebody else will have a conflicting view, and there is little more to be said on the matter. As I have said, this attitude is generally part of an outlook which is vaguely supportive of individual freedom. Since no one can really show that his view is better than that of the next person, everyone should tolerate the view of the next person. Sociologically, skepticism tends to be connected with weak respect for freedom. It leads to toleration based not on valuing the freedom of others, but on distance, sometimes on mutual incomprehension. Freedom is protected not because it is valuable, but because there is no moral sanction for anything, not even for the suppression of freedom.

I am not concerned with the familiar and vexing question of the coherence of various forms of skepticism. Rather our interest is confined to the relation between skepticism and toleration. Global value skepticism, *i.e.,* the claim that no knowledge can be gained on any moral issue, and more broadly, on any question involving values, not only cannot serve as a basis for belief in toleration, but is inconsistent with it. It denies that we can have any reason to believe in toleration. It is true that global skepticism also rules out intolerant attitudes and policies which are rooted in principles and in values. This, however, merely leaves people free to pursue actions and policies which do not depend on any belief in the validity of any principles or values. It is doubtful whether people, liberated from the constraining influence of their value beliefs, are more likely to follow tolerant policies rather than intolerant ones or any arbitrary mix of actions.

Such global value skepticism leaves little room for any justification of general policies. It normally is thought that it leaves open the possibility of self-interested justifications, but their relevance, and therefore their availability, are doubtful. On appropriate occasions, self-interest can in some sense justify, or at any rate explain, why certain people support a policy. It is to their advantage, or so they believe. But that does not show that the policy is justified and is normally irrelevant to its justification. Furthermore, theories which aim to show that morality rests on enlightened self-interest, along Hobbesian lines, are not skeptical theories. Hence those who believe that under fairly common conditions tolerant policies are in every person's long-term interests, whatever their plausibility, are not advancing skeptical arguments. When self-interest can justify general policies of toleration, skepticism is at an end. The impossibility of showing that global skepticism paves the road to toleration is conceptual.

Global skepticism is to be distinguished from local skepticism, that is, the view that we cannot obtain knowledge on certain particular issues. For example, some people claim that no one can know the answers to questions such as whether punishment deters, whether fetuses are human beings, or whether solitary confinement is a form of torture. Local skepticism is no more successful in supporting a general policy of tolerance. It all depends on what we are ignorant about. Sometimes ignorance would lead to what may be regarded as a more tolerant attitude. Ignorance about the value of capital punishment may, when combined with other suitable premises, support its abolition. In other cases, however, the rational outcome is likely to be nontolerant. Ignorance about the status of fetuses may well justify criminal prosecution of anyone who is an accomplice to an abortion.

B. Corrigibility and Tolerance

Skepticism, whether local or global, holds little promise for any political theorist. The realization that our beliefs may be mistaken should not, however, be confused with skepticism. Does our fallibility provide an argument for toleration? It is certainly often thought to do so, but is the argument cogent?

The connection is in the common belief that realization of our fallibility justifies reducing our confidence in our own beliefs. If they may be right and I may be wrong, does it not follow that I am not entitled to be confident that I am right, and should not that lead me to adopt a tolerant attitude toward their views? Should realization of my fallibility undermine my confidence in my beliefs? Should I be less than certain that I am sitting in my room writing this simply because it is possible, as it surely is, that in fact I am lying in bed dreaming, or with my brain stimulated to produce delusions and false beliefs? This familiar chain of thought reflects deep confusions about the reasons for certainty or for doubt.

Justified certainty rests not on a belief in infallibility, but on a belief that one is not in fact mistaken, that there is no reason to suspect a mistake, and every reason, based on evidence and on one's situation, to trust one's beliefs. I am absolutely certain tht George Bush is today President of the United States, that Australia is in the Southern Hemisphere, that the British Parliament sits in London, *etc.* Although I may be wrong each time, I am absolutely certain of these beliefs, and rightly so.

The point is that uncertainty is an awareness of a flaw ("the document appears to have been interfered with"), inadequate evidence, or an inferior situation one is in ("I'm too far away to tell," "the light is misleadingly bright"). Mere realization of fallibility is not a discovery of a flaw, but an awareness of the conditions of knowledge. The possession of knowledge depends on the exercise of skills and judgment. They are capabilities which can be used and abused, whose use can be successful or may misfire. Becoming aware of our fallibility can amount to no more than realization of this fact.

The fact that to realize that we may be wrong is merely to realize something about the conditions of knowledge may be obscured by the view that sometimes we have infallible beliefs. Mathematics is often thought to be an example. It is then felt that fallible beliefs are flawed, that they lack whatever it is which gives infallible beliefs that quality. The simple fact is that in general, mathematical beliefs are as fallible as any others, and the many mistakes committed by everyone, from a young pupil to an expert mathematician, demonstrate this. It is true that there are propositions, such as that I have a body, and including some simple mathematical propositions, such as that $2 + 2 = 4$, acceptance of which is not revisable. These are propositions which fix the use of our basic concepts and determine our fun-

damental orientation in the world. Even to doubt them is incoherent. Rejecting them is a sign of conceptual confusion or ignorance. Severe cases mark cognitive collapse, or even insanity. But such beliefs, far from being the standard and norm of all rational beliefs, are exceptional and in many ways unlike normal beliefs. For example, while we can have evidence for these basic beliefs, our confidence in them does not depend on such evidence. These are highly difficult and contentious issues which we cannot explore here. The crucial point is that ordinary knowledge is fallible.

Recognition that fallibility is part of the conditions of ordinary knowledge underpins the attitude of critical rationality. It includes realization of the corrigibility and revisability of all ordinary beliefs, precisely because of our fallibility, and a readiness to re-examine our beliefs as necessary. Critical rationality has political implications. Its desirability argues for political institutions which adopt that attitude, and which allow adequate opportunities for periodic re-evaluation of public policies. What counts as adequate is a difficult question which need not detain us here. Suffice it to say that there is no general answer suitable to all cases. The same is true of ordinary personal beliefs. Some of our beliefs should be reexamined periodically, whereas others, while open to revision if contrary evidence is forthcoming, need not be subject to routine re-evaluation. Sometimes it is appropriate to embrace certain beliefs on fairly slender evidence, while at others an assurance that the matter was thoroughly investigated is a condition of rationality.

The requirements of critical rationality affect the structures of institutions and the processes of decisionmaking more than they affect the substance of policies. Still, these requirements yield a powerful constraint on substantive policies. Other things being equal, policies which are incompatible with the existence and proper functioning of political institutions whose actions and policies are open to re-evaluation and revision should be avoided. Certain ways of running the secret service, *e.g.,* which may have various advantages, should nonetheless be avoided because they presuppose the absence of the kind of accountability that critical rationality requires.

As a consequence, the realization of the possibility of error suggests that, other things being equal, one should prefer policies which provide for reversible measures over those which rely on irreversible ones.* This is one of the traditional arguments against capital punishment. Clearly, liberal thinkers traditionally have paid much attention to the implications of the requirements of critical rationality. Equally clearly, these arguments do not support as great a degree of toleration and pluralism as advocated by traditional liberal theories.

So far we have considered only the principled, global belief in the possibility of error. Error is more likely in some areas than others. Thus, realization that our knowledge of nuclear technology and its implications is very incomplete, and therefore, that our beliefs in issues of nuclear safety are particularly vulnerable to doubt, is a reason against the use of nuclear power. This caution may be reinforced by the fact that the results of accidents or of long-term contamination through the proliferation of radioactive material can be catastrophic, so that even a small risk of error may be sufficient to inhibit action.

The special danger of error in particular areas has, therefore, further political implications which go beyond the general adoption of an attitude of critical rationality and apply even to those who do not wish to adopt it as a matter of general principle. These implications, just like those of local skepticism, bear no special relation to liberal theories and do not in general lend support to tolerant rather than to intolerant policies. I suspect that if a general trend can be discerned in the way in which local doubts operate, it is in favor of a cautious and conservative attitude. In general such doubts tend to affect new, or relatively recent, policies more than long-established ones, as the consequences of the latter are better known. Of new policies, radical departures and far-reaching innovations do more often give rise to doubts than small-scale amendments to existing policies. Cautious conservatism is sometimes perceived as

*But the fact that it is not a strong argument against allowing houses to be demolished by their owners shows that this preference is not in general a very strong one.

supporting toleration. In fact it merely favors the status quo. It supports toleration only if you already practice it.

C. The Vulnerability of Values

It is sometimes thought that we are particularly prone to error on questions of value, or alternatively that bureaucracies are particularly vulnerable to error in such matters. It is of great importance to realize that even if this is so, advocates of toleration can find little comfort in this fact. When debating the use of nuclear energy we have a choice between its use and its rejection. Our ignorance of the hazards of the nuclear industry does not infect our actions if we avoid developing that industry. If you do not use radioactive material you avoid the hazards of radioactivity. Is there anything comparable regarding the hazards of morality and of value? There can be only if some of our actions carry moral significance whereas their omission does not. I suspect that this is not the case. In particular it seems plausible that if any action carries moral significance, so does its omission. The very fact that an action is morally significant confers significance on its omission. If there is a duty to perform an act then it is wrong not to perform it. The same seems to be true in all matters of value.

Whatever the truth of this matter, it is itself a moral issue. If I am wrong, then I made a wrong moral judgment. In other words, the proposition that we can avoid moral mistakes and errors by avoiding actions which are morally significant is a moral proposition which, if all moral propositions are particularly vulnerable to error, is itself particularly vulnerable. It follows that even if morality is particularly vulnerable there is no way to avoid the risk of error. If there is a range of actions whose performance escapes moral significance, then this is itself a matter of moral judgment which is liable to the enhanced risk of error of all moral propositions.

It may be worth adding that despite the popularity of the view that all value judgments are particularly vulnerable to error, this is not a view which can survive even the most cursory examination. Are we really more liable to error when we hold that torturing the innocent is wrong than when we think that the nuclear energy industry is safer than coal mining (as the chairman of the (British) Central Electricity Generating Board assures us)? There are no general theoretical reasons to think so.

One natural line of retreat from the view that all value judgments are suspect is to the contention that whatever the general vulnerability to mistake of value judgments, those made by public authorities are particularly vulnerable. The reasons given above concerning the general argument from vulnerability apply to and defeat this contention as well. A more modest version of it is, however, the most important argument for limited government. It tries to isolate certain ranges of issues regarding which public authorities are particularly prone to error. Various such areas can be identified. To an extent they depend on the structure and constitution of particular authorities. One familiar general observation, however, seems appropriate. In mass, highly mobile societies, public authorities are particularly ill-adapted to judge matters in which having the right moral feelings, the proper moral sensibilities, is of particular importance. They are more suited to dealing with abstract principles, with general rights and duties than with matters of moral character, personal relations, etc. Such matters are better kept, as far as possible, within the private sphere and out of the public domain.*

D. Reasonable Disagreement

Another common theme in this context is that disagreement over value judgments is often reasonable disagreement. Questions of the good, of the meaning of life, and of right action are ones over which reasonable people disagree and which admit of reasonable doubt and reasonable disagreement.

Should the fact that someone reasonably disagrees with me weaken the trust I have in my view? A simple example shows that in

general it should not do so. If I am found guilty of a crime I may agree that the case against me was proved beyond reasonable doubt. I may agree, in other words, that the jury not only reasonably doubted my protestations of innocence, but was rationally compelled by the evidence to convict me, without in the least losing faith in my own innocence.

This case has the following special feature. The jury is likely to believe that I know whether I am guilty or not. When it finds me guilty it also comes to the conclusion that I probably am lying about my innocence. When I find them reasonable, I find reasonable their belief that I am lying. Most cases are not like that. In most cases one party has no reason to think that the other has special access to the truth. On the contrary, the typical case is one in which one person finds another's conflicting belief reasonable, given the evidence available to the other person, his experience in the matters concerned, *etc.*, but believes that his own experience or evidence are superior. That is why his confidence is not shaken by the reasonable disagreement.

If others doubt my true and reasonable belief or disagree with it, their doubt and disagreement are reasonable when, through no fault of their own, they do not have evidence of the same quality that I have, but their evidence is sufficient for them, given their degree of understanding and expertise in the matter, to base a judgment on, or else when the evaluation of the evidence is sufficiently difficult to make error not really surprising, given normal human capacities. Thus T. Nagel points out that even when people share the same evidence they may reasonably disagree due to differences in judgment understood as differences in the assessment of the evidence.

I may think that it would be reasonable for someone else either to believe or not to believe *p* on the evidence available to me . . . yet find that I do believe it. Perhaps in that case I must also judge that it would not be reasonable for *me*, as I am, not to believe it on that evidence. . . .*

*Nagel, *Moral Conflict and Political Legitimacy*, 16 PHIL. & PUB. AFF. 215, 235 (1987).

---

*The difficulties in following this advice are vividly illustrated by the standing of women within the family. On the one hand, one wishes to keep such personal matters out of the political domain. On the other hand, the abuse of women by their husbands in some contemporary cultures makes this unacceptable.

Evidently, such divergence of evidence or its evaluation can easily arise in circumstances which cast no doubt on the solidity of my beliefs. Knowing this, I may be rational to remain unmoved in the face of reasonable disagreement. Naturally, the fact that someone reasonably disagrees with me may, in appropriate circumstances, call into action my attitude of critical rationality. I will want to reassess my belief in order to be satisfied that I am right and the other person is wrong. But I may do so, reinforcing my original conviction, without denying that the other person's disagreement was and remains reasonable.

While not necessarily spreading doubt, the existence of a reasonable disagreement has moral implications. Those who act wrongly because of a reasonable mistake should be excused (though they may still have to make amends). Similarly, the fact that wrongdoing was based on a reasonable mistake affects our judgment of the character and virtue of the offenders. But none of this should induce one to desist from acting on beliefs with which others reasonably disagree. That seems to indicate that reasonable disagreement provides a limited basis for toleration. It may appear to support moderation in penal policies. One should not criminalize actions undertaken because of a reasonable belief that they are right. But this exaggerates the true significance of this consideration. The very fact that an act is prohibited by law may affect the reasonableness of a belief that it is an innocent act.

To take account of this, the degree of toleration based on reasonable disagreement is limited to the following: One should not criminalize actions undertaken because of a reasonable belief that they are right, if that belief will remain reasonable even if they are prohibited by law. Given this qualification, and given that reasonable disagreement bars neither public policies nor legislation based on the beliefs disagreed with, other than direct criminal prohibitions, it is evident that only a very limited measure of toleration can be derived from this consideration.

The emphasis in the previous remarks is on the reasonableness of a person's beliefs. It is interesting that the very fact that someone holds certain beliefs is an argument for tolera-tion, regardless of their reasonableness. Think of a person who has a distorted view of the significance of sex in life. Assume that he neither harms nor affects others in any unfair way. His interest only is at stake. Can we make him better by making him conform to some other sets of beliefs, even though he continues to reject them? In such matters the only way to help him is to bring about a change of belief in him. We must act through his own attitudes and beliefs or not act at all. This is a powerful consideration in favor of toleration on many matters, which does not depend on any belief being reasonable. It supports tolerating the unreasonable as well. But it is an argument of limited scope. It is an argument for tolerating the conduct of those who have certain beliefs. It is no argument for letting them have a free hand in developing, retaining, or propagating any beliefs, however wrong.

E. Semi-Skepticism and Neutrality

Some people have in mind a more radical epistemic attitude when they talk of reasonable disagreement. Consider an example. John believes in a life of change, variety, and free experimentation. Joanna disagrees. She believes that people should be loyal to the traditions, tastes, and practices they were brought up on. But Joanna regards John's view as a reasonable one. To be precise, she thinks that these are matters over which it is impossible to find conclusive arguments either way. John has strong arguments to support his view. Though she disagrees with him, she thinks that he is as likely to be right as she is. She does not think that anything follows from that by itself. But she also believes that all people are entitled to be respected. The combination of people's right to respect with the fact that their views on the meaning of life, even those she believes to be wrong, are equally likely to be right, implies that they should be left to conduct their lives each by his or her own light.

Normally the proper reaction to such a situation is to suspend belief. If two mutually exclusive views are equally likely to be right, then we do not have adequate reason to accept either of them. One may argue, however, that given that one has to carry on with the business of life (we assume that suicide is not an acceptable option), then one is more likely to have a good life if guided by some conception of the good than by none. Since one has no reason to change from the conception one has, it is best to remain faithful to it, even while realizing that it is not more likely to be correct than the next person's.

Is this cognitive attitude logically possible? The difficulty is that having a certain belief commits one to disbelieving its contradictory. Joanna is supposed to believe in a certain conception of the good but also to believe that its contradictory is as likely to be true as it is. To assume that one believes a proposition (*i.e.*, believes it to be true) while one regards it as no more likely to be true than its contradictory is to allow a radical rupture between belief and belief that one's belief is justified. This may be logically impossible. The best way to understand Joanna's attitude is to say that she acts as if a certain conception of the good is correct, but without believing it to be correct.

This is an unstable state of mind, full of internal tensions. It seems an unpromising foundation for any far-reaching political principle. Does it in fact lend support for toleration? We should ask whether Joanna has any reason to believe that others will be better off if they live by their own conceptions of the good rather than by hers? By hypothesis the answer is no. She believes that her conception of the good is as likely to be right as any of its competitors and, therefore, has no reason deriving from considerations of the good of others to think that they are better off living in the ways they believe to be best than if they follow her ideals. It is true that she does not think that they will be better off following her ideals. She cannot endorse a policy favoring her ideals as against theirs for the good it will do them. But she may have plenty of other reasons to wish for such a policy, most notably that it may help her in pursuit of her ideals. If she has any reason to adopt a tolerant policy, this must derive from other considerations. One such consideration, already noted, is the restriction on the imposition of practices not believed in.

The tenuousness of one's beliefs, even if less than in the extreme case of Joanna, may provide an additional reason against interference with others, though it is not one

based on their interests. Joanna may rightly feel reluctant to take the responsibility for other people's affairs, which her interference will bring with it. The chances that she will be doing them harm rather than good are too great. But this is an argument about what is the right action for her, not about what is best for them. If they carry on their lives as they wish, then their success or failure is their responsibility. If Joanna makes them follow her ideals, their fortune is, at least in part, her responsibility. She may find a reason for noninterference in a principle that people should not assume responsibility for others' lives unless they have a clear and substantial reason to do so.

This weak principle of noninterference is both important practically and interesting theoretically. Its theoretical interest is in that it is not a logical principle (as, *e.g.,* "intentional action is justified only if based on a valid reason"), for it imposes a "burden of proof" heavier than is required by logic. On the other hand, as was remarked above, it is not based on simple concern for the well-being of others. It is a principle governing each person's own proper attitude toward others, as an element of an articulation of the doctrine of the good life. It establishes a presumption against interference, a weak "mind your own business" presumption, as governing the proper attitude toward others. It is part of an attempt to strike a balance between concern for the good of all and a more self-directed attitude as the proper attitude for people to adopt. The practical importance of the principle is great, though dispersed. Even though there is no reason to believe that Joanna's attitude is a justified universal one, it is beyond doubt the proper attitude on numerous diverse occasions. On all such occasions the principle "do not interfere except for a clear and substantial reason" comes into its own and forms a powerful force for toleration.

So far we have been examining the implications, if any, of individual disagreement, that is, of the fact that this or that person disagrees with us. Suppose, however, that disagreement is general in our society. Does that make a difference? Some people regard the general controversiality of many value judgments as the foundation of a policy of toleration. This view seems much more plausible. If a view is controverted by many, then it is likely to be controverted by some who have the evidence and the sense to evaluate it. They may be mistaken, but on the other hand, they may be right, and the mistake may be mine. An attitude of critical rationality suggests that error is quite likely in such cases. Though of course reexamining the evidence and finding an explanation suggesting that the others, and not I, are in error will allay these doubts to a considerable extent.

Although these considerations apply to all controversial beliefs, there are special reasons to regard controversy as a mark of error in matters of value. First, there are no moral experts. There is no moral science, no hidden, yet-to-be-discovered bits of moral evidence. There is a sense, though it is not easy to explain, in which morality is entirely on the surface, and the basic moral factors are available for all to see. Controversy, therefore, does acquire special significance. Second, it is arguable that values are, at least partly, constituted by social practices. This would explain the absence of moral experts and the fact that the moral facts necessary to establish moral principles are available for all to see. It also would reinforce the suspicion that moral controversy is a sign that something is wrong. If practices play a constitutive role in establishing values, then controversy may show a defect in the constitution of the relevant value, not merely in its recognition. We shall return briefly to these matters. For present purposes suffice it to note that these last ruminations took us a long way beyond skepticism towards a partially societal-based account of morality. . . .

Democracy and Preference

There can be little doubt that it is wrong to disadvantage one person because another person *believes* that the first has mistaken views or leads a misguided life. That a person has certain beliefs is rarely a reason for treating anyone one way or another. It is important here to emphasize that this is in agreement with the way people perceive their own deliberations. Consider a person, call her Jane, who may be an official or an ordinary citizen about to vote on the allocation of a benefit to or its withdrawal from another, call him James, who applied for it. Imagine that Jane believes that James is cruel to his parents and that in accordance with this belief she intends to vote against him. She would be irrational to think that her belief that he is cruel to his parents is a reason for denying James his request. She believes that James's cruelty to his parents, not her belief that he is cruel, is a valid reason for denying him the benefit. This is seen most clearly if we imagine that the decision is not hers, but that she argues for denying James the benefit before the appointed tribunal. She will rely on James's cruelty. But she will not say, indeed it makes no sense for her to say, "I believe that he is cruel. Therefore, regardless of whether he really is, there is reason to deny him the benefit he has applied for." The same is true in general of all agents. They believe in the existence of facts which they take to be reasons for certain actions. But they do not take the fact that they hold these beliefs, as distinguished from the truth of these beliefs, as such reasons.

It is possible, of course, that while Jane does not and should not regard the fact of her having certain beliefs as a reason, others should so regard it. In particular it is possible that the political system, being a democratic one, regards not the truth of Jane's belief, but the fact that she has it, and that because of it she has formed a certain preference, as the reason for accepting her vote as influencing the outcome of political decisions. This conclusion seems to be forced on us by the very logic of democratic government. It appears to be based on the principle that people should use their votes to express their preferences, and that people's preferences should count as such, just because they are people's preferences, regardless of whether they are good or bad, true (*i.e.*, reflecting true beliefs) or false. The rationale for democratic political decisions, according to this view, disregards the internal aspects of people's votes. It disregards the fact that people view their votes as justified only if they are based on true beliefs. Democratic theory regards the vote itself, the bare expression of a belief, as the justification of political decisions.* . . .

If that is the foundation of democracy then there is a powerful argument for suppressing some of our beliefs when we come to vote. The principle that one should not disadvantage other people because one *believes* them to be wrong, or their preferred style of life to be worthless or demeaning, is, on this view, consistently violated by democratic regimes that give effect to votes which reflect beliefs concerning the morality or value of other people's characters, actions, or styles of life. Hence this understanding of democracy leads once more to the familiar conclusion that one should lead one's own life by one's beliefs, and let others lead their lives by theirs. One should refrain from relying on one's beliefs about the value of different styles of life, *etc.,* when voting or deciding public policies.

Yet there is a puzzle in this view of democracy. According to it the reason a vote counts is different from the reason for which it is cast. My reason for voting to abolish capital punishment is that it is morally wrong. But the "system's" reason for counting my vote is that I cast it. The system is alleged to be indifferent to my reason, indifferent to the true moral merit of capital punishment and concerned only with counting heads. There seems to be both something right and something wrong here. On the one hand, my vote counts even if it is based on a false belief. So it seems that my belief, rather than the fact which is my reason for it, matters. On the other hand, if my subjective belief is all that matters, why should I, in forming it, agonize about the rights and wrongs of the issues concerned? Why shouldn't I just express any belief or preference that comes first to mind? Why should I, as we all believe I should, try to form an in-

formed judgment, *i.e.,* one responsive to the truth?

We begin to see the way through this puzzle when we realize that it is not limited to democracy. It has wider ramifications, for it is tied up with the very structure of authority, democratic or otherwise. Take a typical case. The authority with power to license drugs for public use approves of drugs on the ground that they are safe. It regards the safety of the drugs, and not its own beliefs about their safety, as proper ground for its action. It investigates each case in order to reach a conclusion which conforms to the facts and is willing to change its belief when it turns out to be at odds with the facts. At the same time it is inevitably the case that its decision is binding because it represents its bona fide belief, not because it is a sound decision. Mistaken decisions are equally binding. It would not be an authority if it did not have the power to err.

It is therefore tempting to say that the reason for the authority's action is that it *believes* its action to be justified. That, and not the actual justification of its action, assures it of its binding force. Yet at the same time the reason for this is that acknowledging the validity of an authority's decision whatever its soundness, *i.e.,* without making its soundness a condition of its validity, is deemed to be more likely to lead to action supported by sound reason than any alternative method of deciding what to do. In the terminology of two-level rule-based justifications, the authority's belief in the soundness of the decision brings the decision under a rule which is itself justified because it is likely to lead to action in accord with sound reason, and not because it leads to action conforming to the authority's preferences.

In other words, it is the truth or soundness of the decisions which counts ultimately. Truth and soundness provide the argument for the legitimacy of the authority. Honest belief is merely a necessary means to the goal. An authority is legitimate only if its honest belief is, at least in the long run, a reliable indicator of the correct course of action to take.

One appealing misconception needs to be sorted out. There is a view of democracy which suggests that while the previous remarks are true of authority in general, things

---

*This argument has the consequence that tactical voting, in which a person votes in a way that does not express his preference on the main issue of the vote in order to prevent an outcome he fears, or for any other reason, is condemned as contrary to the democratic principle. To simplify the argument I will not raise this objection to the understanding of democracy discussed in the text. On my own understanding of democracy, tactical voting is often legitimate.

are otherwise with democratic authority. It is best understood as premised on the belief that the good for people is to have their preferences satisfied. Its purpose is simply to assure each person that his preferences will count together with those of all others. This attempt to view utilitarianism as the necessary underpinning of democracy fails like all versions of preference-satisfaction utilitarianism because it misconceives individual well-being. People flourish and their lives are fulfilled and successful to the extent that they successfully engage in worthwhile activities, pursuits, and relationships. Success in the sense of preference satisfaction is only part of this story. To contribute to a person's well-being the success has to be in a worthwhile, valuable activity, pursuit, or relationship. This is attested to by the fact that preferences are reason-based and are held and valued by those who have them because they believe that they are preferences for what is valuable and worthwhile.

We can distinguish various kinds of political issues. Some have to do with deciding between right and wrong. Some concern the setting up of frameworks for individual lives, and for individual choices, to enable people to live in a decent, worthwhile environment and to have valuable choices. In these and many similar decisions, the value or merit of various choices is the primary ground of political action. Reliance on belief in that value is the way one aims at the value within structures of authority. Of course, some decisions are different. Some decisions concern a choice among goods, where there is no reason, independent of the subjective tastes and inclinations of the population, to prefer one to the others. In such cases it is proper to choose in accordance with people's tastes. If everyone prefers baseball to football then all resources should go to baseball. If some prefer the one game and some the other, a just distribution should be achieved, and it may well be sensitive to the numbers who share the different tastes. But even here we do not expect the electorate simply to vote for their own preference, but rather to vote for a package of measures which represent a just distribution of the goods concerned, given their own and other people's preferences.

This brief discussion, which is meant to be

no more than a reply to one important way of justifying democratic institutions, is incomplete in various ways. One is in not discussing the intrinsic desirability of democracy as offering means of participating in the public life of one's community. The argument is not meant to deny or to minimize the importance of that fact. But it is meant to suggest that democracy can be justifiably used to this end only if it meets the instrumentalist condition explained above, *i.e.,* only if it leads, by and large, to good government. The interrelations between the instrumental and the participatory elements of democracy become complicated in two ways. First, because participation is valuable in itself, providing opportunities for it through democratic constitutional arrangements is a value which may justify putting up with some shortfall in other dimensions of performance. This does not compromise the central role of the instrumental aspect of democratic governments, as of any government. It merely allows its partial compromise if necessary to secure the goal of participation. Second, within a certain range, valuable goals are those endorsed by society collectively. In such matters participation, assuming that it is the proper way to determine social goals, is necessary for the system of government to discharge its instrumentalist goal.

Democracy is best understood as a political system allowing individuals opportunities for informed participation in the political process whose purpose is the promotion of sound decisions. Democracy is justified inasmuch as it is necessary to serve the well-being of people. It shares the general structure of authority and relies, for its legitimacy, on its ability to deliver sound decisions.

Liberalism and Autonomy

A. Autonomy and Value Pluralism

If what we have said so far is right, then beliefs about the value of people's lives, while never being themselves the grounds of political decisions, have their role in the process of political deliberation about the true grounds of decisions. These grounds are considerations of what does and what does not contribute to people's well-being, which options and what aspects of the common culture are valuable and to be encouraged and which are ignoble and to be discouraged. No value judgments are discounted. In voting for political measures one gives full weight to all one's beliefs. The idea that I should apply my beliefs about the good life to the conduct of my own life, but not to public policies which affect the fortunes of others, does not find any support in the arguments we have canvassed.

But this is precisely the view that many liberal thinkers have been shrinking from. It entrusts governments with the job of deciding what is good for people. What happens to the cause of freedom now? The fear that all liberals face is twofold. First, there is the fear of a bureaucratic, dogmatic, insensitive, and inefficient big brother trying to lead our lives for us. Second, there is the fear of a government fired by ideals trying to reshape people for their own good and imposing a uniform pattern of life on all. The first fear concerns the competence of governments in pursuing ideals of the good. The second rejects uniformity and insists on individual autonomy.

As I said at the outset, the response to the worry about competence will not concern us today. It is in essence a pragmatic, rather than a principled, response. There is no reason to think that governmental ignorance, incompetence, and insensitivity affect uniformly and overwhelmingly all the issues involved. It is likely to manifest itself more in some areas than in others, and the best response to it seems to vary from country to country and from issue to issue. It is the fear of uniformity and the insistence on the value of autonomy, of self-definition, that is the most immediate source of our moral fears. Can that concern be reconciled with the view that governments are to protect and promote, inasmuch as it is within their competence to do so, the well-being of individuals?

Fear of uniformity and of the denial of individual autonomy has led many liberal writers to insist that the state should have nothing to do with the promotion of ideals of the good life. This in turn has led to the impoverishment of their understanding of human flourishing and of the relations between individual well-being and a common culture. Instead one should denounce the rejection of autonomy and the embracing of uniformity as misguided conceptions of individual well-being. Only through a conception of well-being based on autonomy and value pluralism can we restore the true perspective of the role of morality in politics. Let me explain.

"Pluralism" is often used to indicate a position according to which different ways of life and different conceptions of the good should be tolerated regardless of their moral value. "Value pluralism" as used here marks a different and competing idea. It represents the view that there are many different and incompatible valuable ways of life. Different occupations (e.g., the physician, the politician, the miner, the police officer, the artist, the athlete, the academic) and different styles of life (e.g., that of the single person, of a member of a large family, of the lover of the open country or of metropolitan cities) call forth different qualities, develop different aspects of people's personalities and suppress others. Some people have such distinctive abilities and disabilities that they can find fulfillment in one way only. But most of us have it in us, at least when we are still young, to develop in different directions, to become different persons. The point I am anxious to stress is one which I hope is implicitly generally recognized. It is that many of the routes open to us in our lives are both incompatible and valuable. They are valuable in that each style of life, each pursuit is good and contributes to the well-being of the persons engaged in it. They are incompatible in that no person can combine all of them in one single life as they call on different qualities and require the relative neglect or even suppression of other qualities which are good in themselves. It is this value multiplicity, this incompatibility of much that is valuable that I mean by value pluralism.

Value pluralism is intimately associated with autonomy. The latter has two major aspects. The first is that of self-definition. It is the thought that what we are is, in significant respects, what we become through successive choices during our lives, that our lives are a continuous process of self-creation. This is not the rather repugnant thought of people having and pursuing life plans. It does not pre-suppose, though it is compatible with, a reflective attitude to one's life as a whole, or the setting to oneself of life-long targets, or of considering and evaluating one's course in life in a very reflective, intellectual way. Some people are like that. Most are not. The idea of self-definition is nonetheless crucial in understanding their lives and its meaning. They make themselves into what they finally turn out to be through successive small and medium-size decisions, through drifting as much as through steering a course for themselves. Self-definition tells of a view of individual well-being which emphasizes the importance of activity in judging the success of a life, and rejects a sharp separation of the goodness of a person and the goodness of that person's life. One is what one is making oneself into through the conduct of one's life. Or at least this is so to a significant degree.

The second aspect of the idea of autonomy goes well beyond self-definition. It is that autonomy is valuable only if one steers a course for one's life through significant choices among diverse and valuable options. The underlying idea is that autonomous people had a variety of incompatible opportunities available to them which would have enabled them to develop their lives in different directions. Their lives are what they are because of the choices made in situations where they were free to go various different ways. The emphasis here is on the range of options available to the agent. This points to a connection between autonomy and pluralism. A pluralistic society, we may say, not only recognizes the existence of a multiplicity of values, but also makes their pursuit a real option available to its members. But it is not merely that autonomy and pluralism require the availability of a wide range of options. They are also at one in requiring that those be valuable options.

We value autonomy to the extent that it adds to the well-being of the autonomous person. We regard the fact that a life was autonomous as adding value to it. We think of our own lives and the lives of others as better for having been developed autonomously. But we value autonomous choices only if they are choices of what is valuable and worthy of choice. Those who freely choose the immoral,

ignoble, or worthless we judge more harshly precisely because their choice was free. If a person drifts into a wasteful, self-degrading way of life because he knows no better, because he never had the chance to develop differently, we judge his life for what it is worth, but mitigate our judgment of him because he had no choice. No such mitigation is available to those who freely and deliberately choose the same immoral, ignoble, or worthless life, having had opportunities to choose otherwise. This shows that autonomy does not always lead to the well-being of the autonomous person. It can make his life worse if it leads him to embrace immoral or ignoble pursuits. Autonomy contributes to one's well-being only if it leads one to engage in valuable activities and pursuits.

A conception of individual well-being which combines autonomy and value pluralism meets the liberal question of how a political pursuit of ideals of the good can be combined with an attitude of toleration and respect for individual freedom. Perfectionist liberalism has firm moral foundations. On the one hand, on this conception governments' function is to protect and promote, within the bounds of their competence, the well-being of people. On the other hand, we claimed that people prosper through a life of self-definition consisting of free choices among a plurality of incompatible but valuable activities, pursuits, and relationships, *i.e.*, a plurality of valuable and incompatible styles and forms of life. This value pluralism, and not skepticism, or value neutrality, is the liberal bulwark against uniformity, against a society imposing through its government or otherwise a uniform vision of the ideal form of life on its population. Furthermore, given that the flourishing life is the self-created life, *i.e.*, a life engaged in freely chosen valuable activities and pursuits, it is not a life which governments or anyone else can give to people, let alone impose on them. Autonomy speaks of an active life freely engaged in by the agent. It is incompatible with any vision of morality being thrust down people's throats.

Hence a government dedicated to pluralism and autonomy cannot make people good. To be autonomous they have to choose their own lives for themselves. Governments, and other people generally, can help people flourish, but only by creating the conditions for autonomous life, that is, primarily by guaranteeing that an adequate range of diverse and valuable options shall be available to all. Beyond that they must leave individuals free to make of their lives what they will.

B. The Importance of the Common Good

So far I have tried to draw a picture of perfectionist liberalism which bases the liberal respect for freedom on a political concern for the well-being of individuals. One of the virtues of this form of liberalism is that its doctrine of freedom is moored in a wider conception of the good person and the good society, rather than being cut off from them as is the case with liberal doctrines of moral neutrality and others. This is the clue to the way to rid liberalism of its association with self-centered individualism.

The clue is in the dependence of autonomy on the environment. The life of the autonomous person is distinctive not by what it is, but by how is came to be what it is. It is marked by the fact that it could have been otherwise and became what it is through the choices of that person. It is marked by the fact that the autonomous agent had many options which he rejected. To show that a person had an autonomous life we have to look not only at him but also at his environment. One is autonomous only if one lives in an environment rich with possibilities. Concern with autonomy is concern with the environment.

The environment determines whether one has the conditions of autonomy and it is the conditions of autonomy which are, up to a point, the charge of political institutions. Governments cannot make people have a flourishing autonomous life. That is up to each one to see to himself. But governments can help put people in conditions where they are able to have that kind of life by protecting and promoting the creation of the environment which makes such a life a possibility. Toleration as respect for individual freedom not only is consistent with, it in fact requires concern for and involvement with others.

It is important to see that this is not merely a moral requirement of concern for all. It is also, to a degree, a precondition of having the required environment oneself. The availability of options depends in part on private goods, *e.g.*, money. But options also depend on public goods, which are available to all and which serve all. Public goods lie at the foundations of most options. Options are to a considerable degree socially defined. A British coal miner is someone engaged in extracting coal. But he is also someone whose job involves certain patterns of relations with colleagues and bosses, certain patterns of work routines and leisure times, etc. And beyond all that he is someone whose fortunes are affected by the public images and myths of coal mining, the images of physical hard work, dirt and blackness, courage and danger, camaraderie, and a long tradition of loyalty and struggle, of belonging to the aristocracy of the working class, etc. Those for whom there is a real option of becoming a coal miner or of leaving the mines have a choice whose meaning is partly determined by a public culture which contributes to making mining what it is.

It is much the same not only for all occupations but also for all leisure activities, such as stamp collecting, train spotting, jazz music, and amateur photography, which are all recognized forms of social activity with their attendant rewards, traditions, and public images determining their social status and thus their meaning for individuals who may or may not choose to engage in them: The same is true of personal relations. Marriage, friendships, parenthood, and the others are all molded and patterned by the common culture which determines to a very considerable degree the bounds of possible options available to individuals.

The conditions of autonomy require an environment rich in possibilities. In that they require an appropriate public culture, for it is the public culture which to a considerable degree determines the nature and quality of the opportunities available in a society. But to the extent that the conditions of autonomy require a suitable public culture, they depend on the common good, that is, on a good which if available to one is available to all and whose benefits can be had by all without competition or conflict.

We should not, of course, underestimate the degree to which our society involves competition for resources. Nor should we underestimate the severity of the distributional problems which a morality of personal autonomy gives rise to with its requirement that an adequate range of diverse and valuable options be within the reach of all. It is important, however, to see clearly the crucial role of a suitable common culture sustaining and defining the options available in a society. Recognition of the importance of such a common culture leads to the rejection of moral individualism. It also dispels any impression that an autonomy-based morality encourages self-centered and socially indifferent attitudes, or that it regards social relations as based on negotiated agreements.

An autonomy-sustaining common culture is a presupposition of the freedom of one and all. People concerned with their own autonomy must be concerned with the flourishing of the common culture. They must be concerned with the existence of one major condition for the autonomy of all.

C. Tolerating the Bad

A liberal democracy assigns its political institutions, in addition to the job of providing for basic needs when necessary, the tasks of marking sound boundaries within which individuals may act freely without the consent of all those who are affected by their actions, and of protecting and enhancing the common services and the common culture which will enable those individuals to pursue worthwhile options within the area in which they have the freedom to act.

The idea I am trying to convey is that people's preferences should be freely pursued only within certain bounds. They should be free to engage in valuable activities, pursuits, and relationships within the limits set by consideration for the interests of others. They should be free to do so because such activities, pursuits, and relationships contribute to their well-being. Thus, the function of government, besides the provision of a minimal protective net guaranteeing the satisfaction of basic needs, is to demarcate the boundaries of such freedom of action so as to enhance, inasmuch

as is in its power, the quality of the options it makes available to people.

All this raises one major question. The picture this pluralistic and autonomy-based liberalism suggests is one in which the community and its institutions foster and encourage a wide range of diverse forms of life among which individuals are left freely to choose. But those are all good and valuable types of activity and forms of life. What of those which are immoral and ignoble? I do not mean merely those which are considered to be immoral or ignoble but which are in fact alright. People will be protected against the results of misjudgments by constitutional policies instilling caution and moderation. The question I am raising concerns the fate of those whose activities and preferences are really immoral or ignoble. Is it not the essence of liberalism that they too should be defended? The answer to this is a qualified yes. They should be defended to the extent that this is necessary for the protection of their autonomy.

The threat to their position arises out of the fact that autonomously choosing the immoral detracts from one's well-being. Given that governments' task is the promotion of well-being and that they are required to protect and promote autonomy only to the extent that it contributes to people's well-being, it seems to follow that they need not respect people who pursue immoral or ignoble activities and that such activities may be suppressed by governmental action. Where is liberal toleration now?

This argument is, however, fallacious and its intolerant conclusions exaggerated. It is true that the perfectionist liberal who encourages the community and its political institutions to foster pluralism and autonomy sees no value in the protection of immoral and demeaning options as such. The community and its institutions are fully justified in trying to discourage, inasmuch as they can, the availability of such options. Both in fostering a common culture and in providing access to its opportunities one should act with discrimination to encourage the good and the valuable and to discourage the worthless and the bad.

Discouragement should, however, be sensitive to the fact that the means must be appropriate to the ends and that they must respect the basic principle that people should be allowed to pursue their well-being, *i.e.,* that their autonomy be respected at all times. This principle requires discrimination in the means used by the authorities for discouraging victimless immoralities. Those means should not infringe people's autonomy, which is the foundation of their well-being. This means that governments should not use repressive measures, and in particular that they should neither criminalize nor employ coercion to discourage victimless immoralities. For such measures interfere with people's general standing as autonomous human beings. They do not merely make it more difficult for people to engage in a specific worthless activity. Criminalization and other repressive measures deny people, to a substantial degree, control over the course of their lives. By attaching the stigma of criminal conviction, by disrupting people's lives through the processes of trial and conviction, and often through imprisonment, they affect not merely the ability to engage in one particular activity by the general control one has over the course of one's life. Such an infringement of personal autonomy may be justified by the need to protect the autonomy of others. But when it is not justified by this need, when the matter concerns victimless offenses, then respect for the autonomy of the individual dictates a policy of toleration which goes well beyond the recognition of the plurality of values and extends to tolerating victimless immoralities.

To conclude, the moral roots of our concern for individual freedom lie in an appreciation of the importance of personal autonomy to the prosperity of the individual. This leads both to an active encouragement of the freedom of people to guide their own lives by successive choices from an adequate range of valuable options and to a passive toleration of misguided choices at least to the extent that, subject to the need to protect the interests of others, no measures will be adopted by the state which infringe the autonomy of individuals however misguided their choices may be. For their autonomy is a condition of their prosperity in modern societies.*

Finally, because the value of political freedom lies in providing the conditions for personal autonomy and because personal autonomy can be realized only in a society which maintains an appropriate public culture, the freedom of one individual depends on the freedom of others. Of course, there are many conflicts of interests among individuals and disputes as to whether the freedom of one should be purchased at a cost to others. But beyond this stands vindicated the traditional precept that no person can be free except in a society of free people. Concern for individual freedom leads directly to concern for the condition of society as a whole.

*My argument is confined to modern industrial societies. Moreover, as it stands, it does not apply to enclaves of traditional premodern communities within our societies.

4

The Procedural Theory

Democracy as Fair Compromise

Peter Singer

Peter Singer begins his essay by distinguishing three models illustrating different pro-cedures a group might follow in making a decision whether to subscribe to a controversial newspaper. He goes on to argue that the third, democratic procedure has special legitimacy because it represents a fair compromise — it gives everybody an unequal share of influence in the decision. Singer then turns to the problem of the rights of minorities, arguing that there is a stronger case for disobedience when the right in question is necessary for the maintenance of the democratic procedure itself than when it is not.

The Models

I take as my basic model a common-room association of a university college, similar to those at Oxford. At Oxford colleges, the Junior Common Room is the political body of all the undergraduate students. It functions in a manner similar to student unions at many other universities. Because of its small size, however, and because it is easier for members to meet together in a residential college, it suits my purposes slightly better than a students' union at a large, non-residential university would. The accuracy of my account as an account of how Oxford common-room associations function is, of course, immaterial. I will just stipulate that the following facts hold, and the reader can regard the model as a purely hypothetical construct. The relevant facts, then, are these. Membership of the common-room association is automatic for all members of the college. Subscriptions to the association are taken from college fees, so one can withdraw from the association only by withdrawing from the college altogether. This would be highly inconvenient, and to with-

draw from one college without joining another is, we shall say, out of the question. Any other college to which one went would have a similar common-room association to which one would also have to belong. The common-room association has been in existence for as long as anyone can remember, and if any records of its origin ever existed, they have been lost. So none of the members knows how the association was originally set up, or for what purposes. Every member simply found the association in existence when he joined the college.

This is the basic model. I will now describe three variants of it. Consider first an association in which all the important decisions about what the association shall do, how its money be spent, and so on, are made by one man, known as the Leader. The origin of this particular system is to be found in the immediate past history of the common-room association. Some time ago, the man who is now the Leader claimed that the decision-procedure then operating had led to stupid decisions, not in the real interests of the association. Henceforth, he would make all the decisions himself, guided by the interests of the members. If anyone objected, they were invited to fight it out with the Leader's friends, who were the best fighters in the association. No one objected. Since taking power, the Leader's decisions have accorded reasonably well with his promise to rule in the interests of all.

One of the tasks which the association has carried out for as long as anyone can remember is the selection of a number of newspapers for the common room, to be paid for from general funds, and read by whoever wants to read them. So that all may read these papers, there is a regulation that no one is to remove papers from the common room until they have been there for a week. One day, the Leader decides that the common room should subscribe to a new paper, which I shall call *The News*. A member of the college, who will be called the Dissenter, objects to the newspaper, not for personal or aesthetic reasons, but because the paper carries out a scurrilous campaign against the minority of black people in the country, implying that blacks are always dirty, lazy, and dishonest, and should not be allowed to mix with whites. This campaign, we shall say, manages to keep within the bounds of the law. The Dissenter finds the very presence of the paper in the common-room offensive; he also fears that if other common-room members, less aware than he is of the paper's bias and distortion, read the paper regularly, it will inflame latent prejudices and they will come to discriminate against the two or three black members of the college. (Once again, whether this would really happen is not relevant for our purposes; if the reader finds the example implausible he can substitute one of his own. It would not matter if the Dissenter's objection to *The News* was on the grounds of obscenity, or because it was a propaganda sheet for the armed forces.)

The Dissenter asks the Leader to reconsider his decision, but the Leader is unmoved. The Dissenter then decides to take stronger action. He goes into the common-room every morning, before the other members are about, and removes the paper.

For comparison, consider now two common-room associations similar to the above in every respect, except for the methods of taking decisions. Firstly, consider an association in which decisions are still made by one man, but he did not have to seize power, and he does not have to intimidate opponents with threats of violence. In this association there has been a tradition, for as long as can be remembered, that the person who has been a

member of the college for the longest time— the Senior Member—makes all the decisions (there is a recognized method for determining who of those who entered in the same year is the most senior). The Senior Member is expected to decide in the interests of all, and it is, again, reasonable to claim that he does so.

As in the first association, the decision to subscribe to *The News* is taken, the Dissenter vainly puts his case to the Senior Member, and finally resorts to removing the paper.

In the final association, the custom is and, so far as is known, always has been, for decisions to be taken by a vote of the whole association at a general meeting, the majority view prevailing. The Dissenter attends these meetings, and votes according to his opinions. Sometimes motions which he favours are carried, sometimes they are lost. When a motion is carried, those who voted against it accept it, and do not hinder its being put into effect, although they may try to get the decision changed at subsequent meetings. At the meetings, all members are free to speak, subject only to some necessary procedural restrictions. The meetings are conducted fairly, and the votes tallied accurately. . . .

Fairness and Compromise

[A]lthough the decision-making power in the second model association is unequally distributed, the Senior Member can still contend that it is fairly distributed, because there is adequate reason for him to have complete power. Now in the dispute of *The News*, the Dissenter's action (removing the paper) is an attempt to assume complete power in respect to whether members of the association shall read the paper. Like the Senior Member, the Dissenter can claim that there is good reason for him to exercise more than an equal share of power over this issue—because, say, he is the only member of the association fully aware of the harmful tendencies of the paper. The Dissenter could put forward this justification of his action in all three model associations. In the first two associations, it is a claim against the claims of the Leader and Senior Member. In the third association, where the decision-making power is evenly distributed, the Dissenter's claim is against all the other members. His claim will be challenged by other members who, having voted in favour of subscribing to the paper, will consider him to be mistaken about its harmful tendencies, or perhaps about the importance of these tendencies. The Dissenter, after all, is acting on his own judgement about this. The other members have their own judgements too, which they sincerely believe correct. In claiming that his own judgement entitles him to a greater say in the matter than the others, the Dissenter is making a claim which the others could make, and which, if many of them did make, would be incompatible with the continued existence of a peaceful decision-procedure. . . .

The decision-procedure of the third association, in which all members have equal say in decisions, and then accept the result, is a paradigm of a fair compromise. It is, obviously, a beneficial compromise, since a peaceful settlement of disputes is better than settlement by force. The benefit of peaceful settlement would, however, also be achieved if everyone accepted any other decision-procedure. The distinction between the associations is that it is only in the third association that the nature of the decision-procedure makes it possible for everyone to refrain from acting on his own judgement about particular issues without giving up more than the theoretical minimum which it is essential for everyone to give up in order to achieve the benefits of a peaceful solution to disputes. It is the fairness of the compromise by which force is avoided that gives rise to the stronger reason for accepting the decision-procedure of the third association. This may seem a strange thing to say, since I have previously argued that abstract discussion cannot prove the third system to be fairer than the second. My point depends upon a distinction between 'absolute fairness' and the kind of fairness which is limited by what can be achieved in a given situation—or as I shall call it, perhaps rather loosely, 'fairness as a compromise'.

When we say that an arrangement is fair, we often mean not that it is absolutely fair, but

that it is fair given the conditions under which the arrangement is made. These conditions may include a certain amount of ignorance, or a lack of agreement in a situation in which agreement is essential. For example, if we were called upon to judge between two claimants to a sum of money, and after hearing both sides we were of the opinion that although the claims were incompatible, there was no way of telling which was the better, we might think it fair to divide the money between the two. If the claims were to something which could not be divided, we might toss a coin to decide. Under the circumstances, this would be a fair compromise, although from the point of view of one who had 'absolute' knowledge, and thus knew which of the claimants was entitled to the money, it could be said to be unfair because it gives as much to the party who deserves none as to the party who deserves all.

For a different example, in which a compromise is required not so much because of ignorance as to what is absolutely fair, as because of the need to come to some agreement, we might take a dispute between husband and wife as to who should get up when the baby cries at night. The wife may say that the husband should get up, because she attends to the baby all day, while the husband feels that the wife should get up, since he has worked all day. They both feel, equally strongly, that their own position is correct. Agreement on the merits of the matter cannot be reached, but some agreement is essential, since neither wants the baby to cry unattended. A fair compromise under these circumstances would be for the husband and wife to take it in turns in getting up. This is a compromise because both parties give up some part of what they claim, in order to reach an agreement which is even more important than having their own way on the particular issue. There could, of course, be other compromise solutions. If the husband were, in the last resort, prepared to let the baby cry all night, while the wife were not, she might have to settle for some other arrangement, for instance, that she would get up every week-night, and the husband only at weekends. This would still be a compromise—both parties are still giving up something—but it would no longer be a fair compromise. The unequal arrangement is not based on any recognition that the husband's case is the better one. It is based merely on the greater strength of his position.

I hope that these examples have made the notion of 'fairness as a compromise' reasonably clear. When the merits of incompatible claims cannot be ascertained, or when agreement on the merits of such claims cannot be reached, a procedure like tossing a coin, or dividing what is in dispute equally, is the fairest course that can be taken. It is generally to be preferred to allowing superior force to settle the issue.

It should be obvious from what has been said before that a society which disagrees fundamentally over the kind of decision-procedure it should have is in a state appropriate for fair compromise. The various incompatible claims that are being made cannot be settled by rational argument, nor is it likely that they can be settled by any decision-procedure, since it is precisely the decision-procedure that is in dispute. As the Italian anarchist Errico Malatesta once argued:

> If you choose 100 partisans of dictatorship, you will discover that each of the hundred believes himself capable of being, if not sole dictator, at least of assisting very materially in the dictatorial government. The dictators would be those who, by one means or another, succeeded in imposing themselves on society.
> And, in course of time, all their energy would inevitably be employed in defending themselves against the attacks of their adversaries . . .[1]

Malatesta thought that this was a reason against having any government at all; it seems to me that it counts at least as strongly in favour of the obvious compromise solution of giving everyone an equal voice in decisions, and if we think that, men being what they are, some government is preferable to no government, we will prefer a fair compromise solution to the anarchist solution.

As a further illustration of the need for compromise, consider the fate of the proposal made by John Stuart Mill, which I have already mentioned, that while everyone should have at least one vote, those with superior education and intelligence should have additional votes. As Mill himself said, later in life, this was a proposal which found favour with no one. The reason, I think, is not that it would obviously be unfair to give more votes to better qualified people, but rather that it would be impossible to get everyone to agree on who was to have the extra votes. Mill seems to have believed that the uneducated would accept the claims of the educated, and agree that education was a proper qualification for having a greater voice in decisions. Yet even now, when everyone has one vote, there are frequent complaints about 'pointy-headed intellectuals' who think they know better than ordinary men how the country should be run. Assuming that we did believe Mill's system of voting to be perfectly fair, it would still be a brave, or rather a foolhardy, man who would put it forward as a serious proposal. In view of the row such a proposal would stir up, it would be wise to put aside beliefs about what is perfectly fair, and settle for the sort of compromise represented by 'one man, one vote'.

The decision procedure of the third association, then, is a fair compromise between the competing claims to determine what the association shall do, because it gives no advantage to any of the parties to the dispute. (It would be more accurate to say: it gives no inbuilt advantages. It may give an advantage to a particularly persuasive speaker, but this is an incidental and probably minor factor. If this were felt to prejudice the fairness of the compromise, however, it would be possible to avoid it, at some cost, by allowing chance to determine who shall take decisions, in rotation. The ancient Greeks used this method. Our disinclination to do so is probably based on the feeling that the incidental unfairness involved in a system like that of the third association does not justify the presumably inferior decisions that would be the result of distributing power by lot.) As a fair compromise, it is greatly preferable to a 'fight to the finish' over each controversial issue. Fairness as a compromise is all that can be expected because, as we have seen, it is extraordinarily difficult to decide—let alone to reach agreement on—what is a sufficient reason for an unequal distribution of power.

The point I am making can also be seen as a point about the different implications of a resort to force in different situations. The Dissenter, in removing *The News*, is resorting to force against the decision-procedure of his association, no matter what that decision-procedure is. But the position he takes in respect of the used of force is importantly different in the third model. Disobedience to a system which is a fair compromise implies willingness to impose one's own views on the association. It is an attempt to gain, by force, greater say than others have about what should be done (or, in the case of disobedience intended not to affect a particular issue, but to lead to the overthrow of the decision-procedure in operation and its replacement by some other decision-procedure, an attempt to have greater say about what sort of decision-procedure there is to be). This is not necessarily true of disobedience to a decision in which the Dissenter was denied the participation that he would have had under a fair compromise. In the first and second associations, disobedience is compatible with willingness to accept a fair compromise whereby one's own views have no more influence than those of anyone else. When there is no fair compromise, one can disobey in order to obtain a decision-procedure which does represent a fair compromise. To disobey when there already is a fair compromise in operation is necessarily to deprive others of the say they have under such a compromise. To do so is to leave the others with no remedy but the use of force in their turn.

What all this amounts to is that there are strong reasons for playing one's part in supporting and preserving a decision-procedure which represents a fair compromise. To disobey under these circumstances is to reject the compromise and to attempt to use force to impose one's views on others. . . . I have argued that a system like that of the third model association, in which every member has a vote, is a fair compromise. To this an important objection can be made. It is best put by means of a hypothetical example. Assume that in our third association there is a minority of people who are marked off from the other members in some way—let us say, they are blacks, while the majority are white. Over a period of time, and at various general meetings, decisions are taken which put the black

members at a disadvantage. For example, at one meeting it is proposed that black members should not occupy armchairs when doing so leads to a white member having to sit on one of the less comfortable benches. The blacks vote against this proposal, but it is carried. The same happens with other proposals, and when at subsequent meetings the blacks attempt to get the decisions rescinded, they are consistently outvoted by the solid white majority. Surely all this makes the decision-procedure no more than a travesty of a fair compromise.

The objection must be accepted. In the circumstances described, it is clear that the fact that each member has an equal vote is insufficient to ensure that the system operates as a fair compromise between all parties. . . .

Rights Against the Majority

There is a tradition in democratic thought which links democracy with a theory of rights. Majority rule, according to this tradition, is only a part of democracy, or at least, of 'constitutional democracy', which is the only kind of democracy worth the name. Just as essential to democracy are limits on the scope of majority action, limits which leave to the individual inviolable freedoms, beyond the legitimate reach of the majority. The classic statement of this view is the American Declaration of Independence:

> We hold these truths to be self-evident: that all men are created equal; that they are endowed by their Creator with certain inalienable rights; that among these are life, liberty and the pursuit of happiness; that to secure these rights, governments are instituted among men, deriving their just powers from the consent of the governed; that whenever any form of government becomes destructive of these ends it is the right of the people to alter or to abolish it . . .

It is hardly surprising that the belief that democracy involves respect for rights should be most widely held in the United States, but it can also be found almost everywhere democratic ideas are to be found. A powerful defence of disobedience can be based on it. If men have inviolable rights, that is, rights which ought never to be violated, any decision which denies these rights can have no moral claim to be obeyed. So the reasons for obedience for which I have argued must be treated as having limits which make them inapplicable when the majority decision interferes with rights.

In order to discuss this line of thought, it will be convenient to deal separately with two classes of rights: those that are essential for the preservation of a system of government sufficiently like that of our third model association to give rise to the reasons for obedience for which I have argued, and those which are not essential for this. I will first consider rights in the former group, and to facilitate discussion I will revert to the third model association.

Imagine that in the third association there is a majority of members who strongly dislike certain views held by a few members on how the association should be run. Naturally, the few cannot put their views into effect, since they are a minority, but they hope that they will eventually convert a majority of members to their views. In order to prevent this, the majority pass a motion that no one should be allowed to speak in support of these views. What reaction to this decision would be in accordance with the aspects of the decision-procedure of the third model association which give rise to the special reasons for obeying it? (For convenience, I shall refer to these aspects as 'democratic principles'.)

A selective restriction of the right to free speech is contrary to democratic principles. By a selective restriction, I mean one which picks out certain views, and says that no one may speak or write in favour of these views, although other views are not proscribed; alternatively, a selective restriction might prevent some people from supporting any political views at all, while allowing others to support whatever views they like. In either case, the restriction destroys the fair compromise which is the basis of democratic obligations, since it favours some members of the society over others—some have the means of winning other members over to their views, others do not.

A restriction of the right to free speech which was not selective but total would appear not to favour any particular members of the society over others. It is difficult, however, to imagine such a proposal being made seriously, outside a Trappist monastery. Even the most totalitarian states bombard their citizens with the views of the ruling clique. In a democracy, free speech has obvious advantages in promoting informed decision-making, which is more likely to be right than uninformed decision-making. Nevertheless, the idea of a total ban is of theoretical interest, because it suggests that not every ban on free speech will be undemocratic. If people wished to avoid debating issues almost as much as they wished to avoid fighting over them, they might accept as a fair compromise a system in which issues were decided by a vote, but no one was allowed to speak for or against any proposal. More realistically, a democratic society may adopt procedural rules which limit the amount of debate on any issue, or the amount of canvassing that any candidate for office may do. These rules are all restrictions on free speech, but they are restrictions which apply equally to everyone, no matter who he is and what views he supports. Unlike selective restrictions, they do not violate the principle of fair compromise, and so do not affect this democratic reason for obedience. Selective restrictions do vitiate this reason for obedience. Where there are selective restrictions on free speech, those considering whether to disobey do not have to take into account this specifically democratic reason for obedience.

It is perhaps anomalous that the argument just advanced applies in a more straightforward way to any decisions reached by the association while the decision restricting freedom of speech is operative, than to the original motion itself, since this motion was passed under conditions of free speech, and therefore under a fair decision-procedure. It seems to follow that the fairness of the decision-procedure up to and including this decision is a reason for accepting and participating in it, and that this participation gives rise to a further reason for obedience, in the normal way. It is only to later decisions that these reasons for obedience no longer apply. With regard to the particular decision restricting free speech, we seem to be forced to say that while there are democratic reasons for disobeying (to restore the fair compromise) there are also democratic reasons for obeying. If there is a clash here, all one can say is that both factors must be taken into account. Perhaps they cancel each other out, or perhaps, as I am inclined to think, freedom of speech is such a fundamental requirement that any reasonable chance of restoring it outweighs the reasons for obedience. In any case, I do not think that this clash indicates any serious inconsistency in democratic principles. The same kind of conflict of reasons may be found in very simple political doctrines. If an absolute monarch were to make an irrevocable grant of all his powers to an elected assembly, the absolutist principle that one ought to obey only the hereditary monarch could be cited both for and against obedience to the decision. This problem can arise in respect of any sovereign decision-procedure, because sovereignty involves the power to modify or change altogether the decision-procedure in operation. If it be decided by decision-procedure X that decision-procedure Y should be instituted, this will always lead to a dilemma for someone who has championed X against Y.

What is true of the right to freedom of speech is also true, for the same reasons, of any other right essential to the operation of a decision-procedure like that of the third association. Among these are the right to vote or stand for office, or the right to freedom of association and peaceful assembly, and so on. More complete lists of the rights essential to democracy can be found in any standard text on the subject.[2] As there is some controversy over the details, I will avoid giving a complete list. . . . In general, then, the very nature of the democratic process involves the existence of rights, the violation of which invalidates the reasons for obedience to which the democratic process normally gives rise. Strictly speaking, the violation will (unless it is a violation of the right to vote) invalidate only the reason for obedience derived from fair compromise, and not that derived from voluntary participation; but if the fair compromise has ceased to operate, there will be little point in participating.

If the question be put: who is to decide when a right essential to democracy has been violated? the answer can only be: the individual. As we saw in considering the problem of minorities, the decision as to the fairness of the decision-procedure cannnot be left to the decision-procedure itself. The only other possible solution, that of setting up some body independent of the decision-procedure, is not, in practice, a real possibility. Ultimately such bodies must be under the control of the decision-procedure, for someone must appoint the members of the body. The Supreme Court of the United States, for instance, has never really been an effective guardian of minority rights against the majority—it has generally followed public thinking after a decent interval.[3]

When we turn to rights which are not essential to a system of government sufficiently like that of our third model to give rise to the special reasons for obedience, the situation is different. Among the rights of this sort which people have demanded are the right of freedom of worship, the right to attend the same schools as people of other races, the right to equal pay, and the right to have sexual intercourse with persons of one's own sex. (The violation of some of these rights might, of course, be part of a policy of discrimination against a minority which would, as explained earlier, be incompatible with fair compromise.) The right to life can be construed either broadly or narrowly, so that it may or may not be essential to democratic government. Broadly construed, the right to life would prohibit capital punishment under any circumstances. A violation of this right, say in cases of murder, would not be contrary to democratic principles. On a more narrow construction of the right to life, only some arbitrary taking of life would count as a breach. Needless to say, some arbitrary killing would destroy the basis of democracy—the killing of those who held certain views must be at least as contrary to democratic principles as the banning of those views! So just when a right is essential to democracy and when not will require judgement. Once we have decided that a right is not essential to democracy, however, it is clear that the violation of such rights does not destroy the basis of the democratic reasons for obedience. Again, I emphasize that the violation of non-essential rights may be so serious as to justify disobedience despite the democratic reasons for obedience; my point is only that in this case the disobedience is 'despite' these reasons. When the rights violated are essential to democracy, there is no need for the democratic reasons to be overridden, and so a less serious violation may justify disobedience. . . .

Notes

---

1. E. Malatesta, *Anarchy* (Freedom Press, London, 7th ed., 1942), p. 35.

2. One such list can be found in R. A. Dahl, *Polyarchy* (Yale U.P., New Haven and London, 1971), p. 3.

3. See R. A. Dahl, *Pluralist Democracy in the United States: Conflict and Consent* (Rand McNally, Chicago, 1967), ch. 6.

The Justification of Democracy

Carl Cohen

Carl Cohen argues that the case for democratic government rests on neither its ability to behave like a market nor on the salutary effects of political participation. Instead, he claims, democracy is justified by the ideal of equality. Beginning with Aristotle's account of equality, he argues that a voice in the political process is a good which must be distributed equally. To establish this, he considers and rejects two attempts to avoid the conclusion: that people may be denied equal concern and that they may be denied equal standing. Though there are real and enormous differences among people there is nonetheless one sense in which all are equal: we each have only one life to lead, and therefore have an equal stake in the political community. And not only does each have an equal stake, but unlike a classroom, for example, each also is entitled to equal membership or standing.

The Enterprise

By "democracy" I mean that form of community government in which the members of a community may participate equally in making directive decisions which concern them all. This definition needs clarification, of course; most of the issues it raises—the meaning of community, the dimensions of participation, the problems of representation, and so on—I bypass here. Supposing there is general agreement on the fundamental proposition that democratic government is government *by the people*, government of a community by the body of its members, I now open the question: why have it?

To this question many rational answers may

From Carl Cohen, "The Justification of Democracy," *The Monist*, Vol. 55 (January 1971), pp. 1–19. Reprinted by permission of *The Monist*.

be given. My object here is to present one such reply in some detail. . . .

The Argument Outlined

The defense of democracy which follows proceeds in two phases. In the first I shall try to show what would be required to justify democratic government in *any* given community context. This I call the justifiability of democracy in general. In the second phase I shall try to show how democratic government can be justified in the context of the *political* community. This I call the justification of democracy in the body politic. The expression "the justification of political democracy," I avoid because the phrase "political democracy" suggests, incorrectly, that there are kinds of democracy of which the political is one. In fact there are different *spheres* in which democracy may be operative, of which the political is one.

The justifiability of democracy in general

rests essentially upon one moral principle likely to meet with universal acceptance: that equals should be treated equally. This is a formal principle purely; it says nothing about who are or are not equals. Therefore, any effort using this principle to justify democracy in a particular community or kind of community needs to be supplemented by argument showing that the members of that community (or kind of community) are indeed equal in the necessary relevant sense.

The justification of democracy in the body politic requires that this supplementary argument be provided specifically with reference to the political community. To do this it will be necessary to maintain that there is one fundamental respect in which all men are equal— all men because, in principle, any man may be a member of the body politic. And it will be necessary to maintain further that that respect in which all men are equal is so related to the political community that it serves to justify democracy in that community.

Three key principles, then, will be discussed in the following two sections; each is crucial to justificatory arguments used in defense of democracy. They are:

(1) That equals should be treated equally.
(2) That all men are equal in one fundamental respect.
(3) That the respect in which all men are equal is precisely that necessary to justify democracy in the body politic.

The Justification of Democracy in General

That equals should be treated equally is a basic principle of distributive justice. So fundamental is this principle and so universally accepted that it is likely to be thought of as at least part of what is normally meant by justice, part of what is meant by "giving to every one his due." It is not my present purpose to defend this principle. Rather I aim to show that, supposing its truth, democracy is generally justifiable for those communities in which certain equalities are realized.

From the time of Aristotle, at least, there has been wide agreement that "persons who are equal should have assigned to them equal things." But a principle so general in formulation cannot be applied until supplemented by specific claims about actual equalities, and about what equalities are relevant in a particular context. No sooner do we assert the general principle than, as Aristotle continues, "there arises a question which must not be overlooked. Equals and unequals—yes; but equals and unequals in *what?*" (*Politics* III, 12, 1282b).

It is largely the result of fundamental disagreement on these questions—*who* are equal, and equal in *what*—that attitudes toward democracy and social policy in general have varied so over the ages. In the assignment of any given set of goods, tangible or intangible, justice requires that equals be assigned equal portions. But for the just assignment of a particular set of goods some equalities and inequalities will be important, and some will be irrelevant. Aristotle makes this point crisply:

> It is possible to argue that offices and honors ought to be distributed unequally [i.e., that superior amounts should be assigned to superior persons] on the basis of superiority *in any respect whatsoever*—even though there were similarity, and no shadow of any difference in every other respect. . . . If this argument were accepted, the mere fact of a better complexion, or greater height, or any other such advantage, would establish a claim for a greater share of political rights to be given to its possessor. But is not the argument obviously wrong? To be clear that it is, we have only to study the other arts and sciences. If you were dealing with a number of flute-players who were equal in their art, you would not assign them flutes on the principle that the better born should have a greater amount. Nobody will play the better for being better born; . . . If our point is not yet plain, it can be made so if we push it still futher. Let us suppose a man who is superior to others in flute-playing, but far inferior in birth and beauty. Birth and beauty may be greater goods than ability to play the flute, and those who possess them may, upon balance, surpass the flute-player more in these qualities than he surpasses them in his flute-playing; but the fact remains that *he* is the man who ought to get the better supply of flutes. (*Politics,* III, 12, 1282b.)

The point is that where an equality (or inequality) among men is not properly relevant to the use of the goods to be distributed (as noble birth is irrelevant to flute-playing ability) that equality (or inequality) ought not affect the allocation.

Furthermore, Aristotle argues, it must be the case that some equalities (or inequalities) are relevant to a given allocation while others are not. For if we could not distinguish the relevant from the irrelevant we should have to weigh *all* equalities and inequalities in making the allocation. But to suppose that we can weigh them all is to suppose that every quality of a person is commensurable with every other—and that is plainly false. One man exceeds another in height but is exceeded by him in wealth. Now if it were possible to say in the particular case that A excels B in height to a greater degree than B excels A in wealth, we seem committed to the position that, in general, it is possible to measure the relative merits of height and wealth. But this is absurd. There is no degree of height equal or even properly comparable to a degree of wealth. So, depending on the goods to be assigned, it may be the one, or the other, or neither of these respects in which the equality or inequality of A and B is to be measured. (*Politics,* III, 12, 1283a).

These arguments are compelling and their conclusions correct. To achieve a just distribution of a given set of goods in a given community, we must distinguish relevant from irrelevant equalities and inequalities, and weigh only the former in making the allocation.

Now, selecting the most just form of government for a given community may be viewed as a problem of distributive justice within that community. The task is one of deciding to whom, and in what degree, the right to participate in making decisions which affect the whole should be given. Alternative government forms may be conceived as alternative patterns of distribution of a special good—that good being the right to a voice in community decision-making.

A democratically governed community is one in which that right is distributed to all members equally. What would justify this pattern of distribution for any given community? Two claims would have to be made good: first,

that equals should be treated equally; and second, that all members of that community are equal in the respect(s) properly relevant to the allocation of the right to participate in government.

To show that these are the claims the justification of democracy requires (and to make clearer what is involved in them) we may suppose a genuine community—Xcom—of which nothing is at first known save that it has a specified membership. If now we must choose a form of government for Xcom, nothing further being known about the members of Xcom, there is a strong presumption in favor of democracy. By hypothesis we have no information that could justify the unequal distribution of rights of participation. So far as we know, the members of Xcom are equals; at least they are equals in being members of Xcom. Regarding the right to a voice in the affairs of Xcom we have no rational way to justify any preference among them. The choice of any alternative to democracy entails that preference be given to some over others; upon him who would give such preference lies the obligation to justify such preference.

How might one seek to meet that obligation? Were one to deny that all the members of Xcom have an equal right to a voice in its affairs, he would be forced to claim either that the members of Xcom are unequal in some fundamental and relevant respect, or that, although equal, they should not be treated equally. The latter claim no one is likely to make or to accept. The denial that democracy in a given community is just will be defended by trying to show the important and relevant inequalities among its members. Where such claims of inequality cannot be made good we reject the denial, and view the preference of some to others as ungrounded and unjust. All of which is to say that we invariably do believe that equals ought to be treated equally. And we are likely to act on the presumption that where important and relevant inequalities cannot be shown, the members of a community are entitled to equal treatment with regard to the right to participate in common affairs.

There are two kinds of inequality which might be used to justify the denial of the equal right of members of a community to participate in their government. These are: inequalities of *concern,* and inequalities of *standing.* I discuss these in turn.

Inequalities of Concern.

Inequalities of Concern. Every member of a community, by virtue of being a member of it, has a stake in the outcome of the decisions of that community. He is concerned in the result; if it affects the community it affects him as one of its constituents. But, of course the outcome need not concern all members equally. Each member (inequalities of standing aside) is entitled to some voice in the outcome in which he has a stake; each would be entitled to an equal voice only if the stake of each were equal, or nearly so. Where it is clear that some members have a much larger stake in the outcome of the decision-making process than do others, we are faced with inequalities of concern. In such cases the basic principle, that equals should be treated equally, calls for a stronger voice to be given to those more greatly concerned in the result. The classic illustration is that of shareholders in a private corporation, to whom votes are assigned on the basis of the number of shares owned. If equals are to be treated equally, one's voice in the government of any community of which he is a member should be proportionate to his relative stake in the outcome of its decisions.

A vital qualification must accompany this conclusion, however. There are many cases in which inequalities of concern must, as a practical matter, be disregarded. Sometimes it may seem clear that some in the community have a greater interest (material or spiritual) in the outcome of certain decisions than do others. Yet it may be impossible or wholly infeasible to identify those having a greater interest, or to measure the differences of interest, and hence it may be impossible to assign differing rights of participation justly. The only practical course in dealing with such cases is to treat as a class the many decisions facing the community, then to attend to those equalities and inequalities that can be pretty clearly determined and which are relevant to that whole class of decisions. Therefore we normally and properly weigh such factors as registered membership in the community, or the number of shares owned, while ignoring equalities and inequalities we cannot reasonably decide upon.

Inequalities of Standing.

Inequalities of Standing. The claim of a community member to an equal voice in the government of that community supposes not only that his concern in the results of its decisions is roughly equal to that of all other members, but supposes also that the nature of his membership in that community is fundamentally the same as that of every other membership. The large shareholder in a corporation may claim a voice proportionate to the number of his shares just when all shareholders are shareholders in precisely the same sense. If that is in doubt we must look to the nature of the claimant's shares, to their "class," and should they differ in kind from the rest his claim to a voice proportionate to the number of his shares may not prove valid. The claim to equal treatment supposes equality of kind as well as equality of interest. But many communities have members in different categories, memberships of different kinds. Where these different categories of membership can be specified, and the differences are relevant to the right to participate, the principle that equals should be treated equally will not serve to justify participation proportionate to interest only. In such communities, even supposing equality of concern, democracy may not be justifiable because of inequalities in standing.

Some illustrations from everyday experience will serve to confirm this analysis. There are communities in which we recognize an essential inequality with respect to the nature of the membership of their members; in these we are likely to think democracy inappropriate, or applicable only in limited degree or special cases. The family community is an excellent case in point. Minor children are likely to have a stake at least equal to that of the parent in the outcome of many decisions that the family must make. But while parent and child are both members of that community, their memberships are of different category, and it is rarely believed that important family decisions should be reached by majority vote. Where the obligations which arise out of such decisions fall chiefly on the parents, children may be listened to with respect, and may be properly overruled. On the other hand, there may be circumstances in which all the members of the family have not only an essentially equal stake, but have as well an essentially like membership with regard to the issue to be decided. What shall be the destination of a day's outing? What kind of dog shall the family acquire? On such questions we may deem it appropriate to count the vote of parent and child equally.

Classroom situations exhibit similar disparities of standing in a community. We do not normally permit full democracy in the classroom, even though the stake of the pupil in some of the decisions made may be as great or greater than that of the teacher. The clear inequality of status in that community justifies unequal voice in its government. Where this difference between instructor and student is enormous—as in primary school classes—we think democracy largely absurd as a way of making classroom decisions. Where the gap between instructor and student has greatly narrowed—as in a graduate seminar in philosophy—we are likely to think that a good measure of democracy can be justified.

Turning the matter about, whenever we begin with the assumption that a community, whatever its size or function, is essentially a community of equals, all having an essentially equal stake in its affairs, we are likely to insist upon an equal voice for each in the making of its directive decisions. The members of a chess club have, as members, precisely equal standing within that community and a concern roughly equal in its joint affairs; each may therefore claim, as a matter of justice, an equal voice in deciding whether the club shall hold a tournament or not. Fraternal orders tend to be highly democratic internally (however discriminatory they may be in choosing members) just because the significance of membership is confraternity—equal status in a social group. In any group so organized the equality enjoyed by members *as* members is a paramount feature of that community. This is often the reason membership in some "exclusive" club is prized; believing the members of that club superior to the mass, the member (or potential member) regards membership in it as a badge of equality with its other members. And in treating membership as a symbol of equality within that community he is correct.

Therefore democracy is readily justified within fraternal communities, and is almost universally practiced—internally—by them.

To this point the argument has been concerned only with democracy in general—with what would have to be established regarding any community to justify democracy in it. In general we may conclude that:

First. In any community, if the members have an equal concern in the outcome of community decisions, and have an equal standing as community members, they are equal in the respects relevant to the assignment of the right to participate in the government of that community.

Second. If the principle be accepted, that equals should be treated equally, and the members of any community are equal in the respects relevant to the assignment of the right to participate in government, democracy in the community is justified. . . .

I turn now to the core of the matter. What is the sense of the principle of human equality upon which the justification of democracy in the body politic depends? It is, simply, that beneath all the undeniable differences among men there is in every human being an element, or aspect, or essential quality which justifies our treating him as the equal of every other in the largest sphere of human life.

In the *Fundamental Principles of the Metaphysics of Morals* Immanuel Kant distinguishes the possession of *value* from the possession of *dignity*. "Whatever has a value can be replaced by something else which is *equivalent* in value; whatever, on the other hand, is above all value, and therefore admits of no equivalent, has a dignity." So commodities which satisfy human wants and needs have a market value; what appeals to human tastes (even in the absence of need) may be said to have emotional or imaginative value. But some things in the world cannot be measured on any scale of values; they are invaluable, priceless. That is the case with every human being. One man may be a better cook than another, or a better student or legislator, and in restricted spheres of conduct we may and often must appraise their relative merit. But *as men* they do not have relative merit; for what has relative merit may, insofar as it has that merit, be replaced by another like entity with equal or greater merit.

A good cook may be replaced by a better cook; a good legislator by one at least his equal in legislation. But *as a person* no human being can possibly be replaced by another. What entitles him to a place in this sphere is simply his having human dignity; it is a quality intrinsic to his being. Just this thought is expressed in the now commonplace remark that the dignity of every human being must be respected. Dignity here connotes not pride or manner, but the intrinsic worthiness of every human being, without regard to his intelligence, skills, talents, rank, property, or beliefs. Who affirms the principle of human equality normally asserts the universal possession of dignity in this sense.

A paradox arises here. It seems to be a feature of things equal to one another that they are mutually substitutable, interchangeable. But if all men are equal in possessing dignity just that interchangeability is being denied with respect to them. The paradox is resolved simply by distinguishing the sense of equality here employed from the sense in which equal things are verified as equal by measurement. In this latter sense replaceable elements in a machine or system are equal to their replacements. And if human equality were of a kind to be so verifiable we should be rightly astounded if some, at least, did not measure out different from others. But it is an irrelevant objection to the principle of human equality that there is no empirical respect in which all men measure out the same. If true it would only show that this equality must lie beyond or beneath any qualities empirically measurable. If all men are equal they are so in possessing an intrinsic dignity which does not admit of any relative evaluation.

John Dewey wrote:

> In social and moral matters, equality does not mean mathematical equivalence. It means rather the inapplicability of considerations of greater and less, superior and inferior. It means that no matter how great the quantitative differences of ability, strength, position, wealth, such differences are negligible in comparison with something else—the fact of individuality, the manifestation of something irreplaceable. It means, in short, a world in which an existence must be reckoned with on its own account, not as something capable of

equation with and transformation into something else. It implies, so to speak, a metaphysical mathematics of the incommensurable in which each speaks for itself and demands consideration on its own behalf. (*Characters and Events*, Vol. II, p. 854)

And Walter Lippmann has put the matter more colloquially:

> There is no worldly sense in this feeling [of ultimate equality and fellowship with all others], for it is reasoned from the heart: 'there you are, sir, and there is your neighbor. You are better born than he, you are richer, you are stronger, you are handsomer, nay, you are better, wiser, kinder, and more likeable; you have given more to your fellow men and taken less than he. By any and every test of intelligence, of virtue, of usefulness, you are demonstrably a better man than he, and yet—absurd as it sounds—these differences do not matter, for the last part of him is untouchable and incomparable, and unique and universal.' Either you feel this or you do not; when you do not feel it, the superiorities that the world acknowledges seem like mountainous waves at sea; when you do feel it they are slight and impermanent ripples upon a vast ocean. Men were possessed by this feeling long before they had imagined the possibility of democratic government. They spoke of it in many ways, but the essential quality of feeling is the same from Buddha to St. Francis to Whitman . . .

> There is felt to be a spiritual reality behind and independent of the visible character and behavior of a man. We have no scientific evidence that this reality exists, and in the nature of things we can have none. But we know, each of us, in a way too certain for doubting, that, after all the weighing and comparing and judging of us is done, there is something left over which is the heart of the matter. (*Men of Destiny*, pp. 49–50.)

Lippmann catches well the spirit of human equality; but when he suggests that the real differences among men "do not matter" he makes too strong a claim. These differences do matter; they are of high importance and make life worth living; they are the frequent objects of our attention and deserve to be. What is true is that these differences can be fully understood and appreciated only against the background of an underlying equality.

A rough analogy may be drawn between

this problem and the metaphysical problem of change for pre-Socratic Greek philosophers. Heracliteans are said to have suggested that all is flux, that everything in the world is constantly changing in all respects. But Heraclitus himself well realized that everything cannot be always changing in every respect. A completely universal flux would be nothing but chaos; some regularity there must be if change is to be understood as change. So he chose fire as a symbol of the universal stuff—a thing which changes constantly and yet remains itself. His student Cratylus, not so perceptive, is reputed to have denied all stability whatever, and was thereupon forced to deny that any meaningful communication can take place. Since he could not consistently communicate this denial, of course, he was reduced, according to the legend, to the waving of his little finger. The lesson is clear; the reality and significance of change can only be grasped against a background of at least relative permanence. If nothing whatever is stable the world is reduced to a flashing chaos of scenes of which no real sense can be made. Change and stability imply one another; the one without the other would be unintelligible.

So likewise in the case of equality and difference among men. That all men are equal in every way, or should be, is as false and foolish as the claim that nothing ever changes, or should change. But as change requires a backdrop of stability to be understood, so also do the differences among men require a backdrop of essential equality if they are to be understood and dealt with intelligently.

Here Walter Lippmann's metaphor—that the differences among men may be treated as mountainous waves or slight ripples—may be pressed instructively. He is wrong in suggesting that whether a real difference among men be dealt with as a wave or a ripple depends wholly on whether we feel an ultimate equality with our fellows. Our feelings have no effect upon the sea, real or metaphorical. But Lippmann is essentially right in suggesting that the same phenomenon may be of major or minor importance to us, depending upon the nature and object of our activity. Waves don't become less mighty by thinking them so; in the task of making our way from place to place on the ocean's surface they can be awful obstacles,

and each may have to be dealt with individually, as the sailor rounding the Horn can testify. For the oceanographer, however, whose attention is directed at the ocean as a whole, and whose aim is the understanding of its behavior in general, the differences among particular waves fade into insignificance, their common features being the focus of his interest.

So likewise with human differences and equality. Differences among men are real and enormous; no attitude on our part will alter that. In the task of accomplishing practical objectives, as individual persons moving in a world of persons, we encounter these differences as helps or hindrances in the most forceful ways. They must often be dealt with individually; they can be serious obstacles at times, and some may even prove insurmountable. The differences among men, in a human world, make all the difference. But when we change the nature of our interest, when our object is not the accomplishment of particular ends but the understanding of the whole community of men and their common problems, it is the features common to humanity which command attention, while the differences among men fade in significance. Whether it is the inequalities among men, therefore, or the equality they share which ought to be the focus of our attention must depend largely upon the nature of our interests and aims. Human differences important in one context may be insignificant in another; human equality entirely unnoticed in some contexts may be crucial in others.

We come now to the second hurdle in justifying democracy for the body politic. Supposing that the possession of dignity is the fundamental respect in which all men are equal, does equality in that respect justify the equal right of men to participate in their government? Allowing that equals should be treated equally, does *this* kind of equality justify *that* kind of equal treatment? Showing that it does requires again two stages. First, I shall argue that human equality as described above gives to every man an equal *concern* in the political community. Second, I shall argue that human equality as described above gives to every man an equal *standing* in the political community.

Stage One. Every community has some reason for being. The common pursuit of some objectives held in common is the unifying principle of every community, and hence of every political community. But the political community is importantly different from all other communities in being, within its domain, universally inclusive. Within it all other communities of interest are organized and all other human ends are pursued. Because of this inclusive nature, the objectives every political community can be said to have are of the most general sort. It aims to achieve what is in the interest of all its members; particular ends arise only out of this general service function. When, therefore, it appears necessary to formulate the purposes of the body politic, the most general concepts are employed—the public interest, the common weal, the general good. So the *Constitution of the United States* was ordained to " . . . establish Justice, insure domestic Tranquility, provide for the common defense, promote the general Welfare, and secure the Blessings of Liberty. . . ." In short, the purpose of the political community is to help meet the universal needs of men living together.

Precisely because these needs are universal every man has an equal concern in the effort to meet them. Every man has an equal concern in the establishment of justice, the protection of liberty, and the promotion of general welfare, because these goals are crucial to the pursuit of all his other ends, and hence crucial to the conduct of his own life. Every man has a life to lead; it is a life unique, irreplaceable, having dignity but no price. In living such a life all men are equal, and that is why they have, every single one, an equal stake in the decisions of the community whose general purpose is the protection and improvement of the lives of its members. In summary: the special and inclusive nature of the political community gives to every man an equal concern in the outcome of its decisions.

On precisely this ground we deny (in a democracy) that some have a right to a stronger voice in government than others. We may admit that in some respects the interests of one segment of the community may be more seriously affected than those of other segments by certain decisions. So it was long believed, even in countries now professing democracy, that the right to participate should be the prerogative only of those with property, or other significant economic stake in the community. Similarly, a university education was long believed to entitle one to a louder voice in government than those not so educated. But now it is generally agreed that differences in economic interests and education do not justify such discrimination. However great these differences may be they are relatively unimportant when compared with the interests shared equally by all. Whatever his rank or wealth, every man has not only a stake in the political community, but equally with all others the highest stake; for it is his life which is under that government, and that is a matter which concerns no citizen less than any other. Insofar as his having a stake entitles him to a voice in the outcome, his having an equal stake entitles him to an equal voice.

So Colonel Rainboro, in the Putney Debates of 1647, concerning the award of the franchise to English soldiers, argued eloquently:

> Really, I think the poorest he that is in England hath a life to live as the richest he, and therefore truly I think it is clear that every man that is to live under a government ought first by his own consent to put himself under that government, and I do think that the poorest man in England is not at all bound in a strict sense to that government that he hath not had a voice to put himself under. (Cited in Lindsay, *The Modern Democratic State,* p. 118.)

Stage Two. Not only an equal *stake*, but as well an equal *standing* in the political community must be shown if democracy is to be justified within it. It is precisely upon this issue that much of the traditional debate over the rightness of democracy has centered.

As the most inclusive of organized human communities, the political must comprise all, or virtually all, of the human inhabitants of a given geographical area; occasional exceptions to this (the cases of aliens, minors, convicts, etc.) will be given special justification. Within its physical domain the political community is essentially universal. Every man, by virtue of his being a man, is entitled to membership in some polity; the man without a country is a puzzling anomaly. Furthermore, one's membership in his polity has no ground other than that he is a man. The origin and foundation of his membership is—equally with all others—the simple fact that he was born or lives there, just as the others do. Our common practice is silent testimony to this principle of universal membership. Barring deliberate changes, we say everyone is a citizen of a state who is born on its territory, or (where patrimony takes precedence over domicile) we may say that he is a citizen who is born the son of a citizen. We do not require that he be born rich, or healthy, or clever, but only that he be born there or in that family, and that when he comes to maturity he be not lacking in essential human characteristics. These established, his citizenship, his equal membership in the political community, is unquestioned.

This is why the respect in which all men are equal does justify their equal standing in the political community. That standing is their standing as members, and as a member of the polity each man is exactly the equal of the rest. The dignity and irreplaceability of his human life entitles him to a membership in the body politic essentially no different from the membership enjoyed by any other citizen.

Earlier illustrations may be recalled to advantage. Communities in which membership arises from different sources—the family consisting of parents and children, or the classroom in which sit students and teacher—exhibit a fundamental dissimilarity in the nature of membership enjoyed by their members. Student and teacher are both members of the classroom community, but they are not members on the same ground; they acquire their membership in very different ways requiring very different qualifications; even the authority which certifies their membership is likely to be different. Members of chess clubs or fraternal orders, on the other hand, however different in some respects, are exactly equal with respect to the nature of their membership in that club or society. Whatever their playing skill or social graces, they are, as members of these communities, of equal standing. The political community—although of incomparably greater importance—is essentially of the latter sort. It is essentially one whose members are members equally, and whose membership rests upon a common foundation. In the case of the political community the chief element of that foundation is their common humanity. . . .

Political Equality and Majority Rule

Peter Jones

Peter Jones begins with a survey of the various justifications given on behalf of the "majority principle," which he interprets to mean that decisions should be adopted that receive a majority of the votes cast. Rejecting consequentialist justifications, he goes on to consider various arguments claiming to show that democratic processes are intrinsically fair or just. He focuses, in particular, on the idea that the majority principle can be defended by an appeal to equality. This leads to a discussion of minority rights and of various limitations on the majority principle, including the possibility that it leads to "persistent minorities." Jones concludes with a discussion of various related issues including the distinction between votes as expressions of interests and judgments about what is right.

From Peter Jones, "Political Equality and Majority Rule" in *The Nature of Political Theory*, D. Miller and L. Siedentop, eds. (Clarendon: Oxford University Press, 1983), pp. 155–182. © Peter Jones. Some footnotes omitted.

Disputes concerning democracy often seem fruitless exercises in assertion and counter-assertion. Given the favourable connotations that now attach to the adjective 'democratic', it is not surprising that politicians have manipulated its meaning as suits their purposes. Political theorists have neither the same need to exploit, nor therefore the same excuse for exploiting, the rhetorical potentialities of the term. Yet they seem no more agreed upon what democracy is, nor any less keen to defend their preferred definitions. Argument over the correct usage of 'democracy' and 'democratic' is not entirely pointless since there are criteria by which some uses can be judged more justified than others and by which still others can be dismissed as misuses. But these criteria still leave scope for disagreement and they do not tell us what, if anything, is so special about democracy.

Whatever democracy is, it is not self-justifying. If someone declared himself 'against justice', we would infer either that he intended some sort of irony or else that he had no understanding of what justice meant. There is nothing similarly puzzling, let alone incomprehensible, about someone's declaring himself 'against democracy'. Even those of us who are 'for' democracy may not be so unreservedly; we may believe it to be the right or best decision procedure for some sorts of decision but not for others. Democracy then is something that can be argued both for and against and, when it is argued for, quite different sorts of argument can be offered in its support. Granted this, instead of dealing with disputes over democracy as though they were mere battles of definition, it is more profitable to establish people's reasons for preferring the decision procedure that they deem 'democratic' so that the argument can become one about those reasons and what they imply. Even where different reasons are offered in support of the same general conception of democracy, they may still imply differences of detail and emphasis.

It is with how different justifications bear upon one prominent 'detail' of democracy, its decision rule, that I shall be concerned in this paper. More particularly, my concern is with the status of the majority principle and with the issues raised by 'persistent minorities', that is, by groups of individuals who invariably find themselves on the losing side. Although I shall have to engage in a good deal of preliminary skirmishing, the issue I shall eventually confront is whether persistent minorities should regard their position as unfair or merely unfortunate.

When I use the term 'democracy' I shall have in mind a very simple and, I hope, uncontroversial model: an association of people who enjoy equal rights of participation in their decision procedure and who vote directly upon issues. By the 'majority principle' or 'majority rule' I shall mean simply the rule that a proposal should be adopted if it receives the support of at least 50 per cent +1 of the votes cast. My excuse for using this simple model is that the general principle of what I have to say is unaffected by the complexities and modifications exhibited by actual 'democratic' political systems and there is no point in complicating the argument unnecessarily. Moreover, the argument I develop applies not only to the state but also to other associations for which democracy is thought the right or desirable form of decision procedure, and my simple model is less far removed from the reality of many such non-state associations.

Justifying Democracy

Why should democracy be regarded as the right or desirable decision procedure for some, if not all, associations? One sort of answer is consequentialist in character. It posits a condition as desirable and then commends democracy because it is the decision procedure which is guaranteed to produce that desirable condition or which is more likely to do so than any alternative decision procedure. Thus democracy has been defended because it results in wise policies, a just society, a free society, decisions which promote the public interest or the common good, which respect individual rights, which promote science and intellectual activity, and so on. The list is limited only by one's resourcefulness in enumerating the good things of life and the conviction with which one is able to argue that democracy will promote them.[1] Each of these justifications can also be urged in defence of the majority principle. Why should the vote of the majority be decisive? Because it will promote, or is most likely to promote, this or that desirable result.

Consequentialist justifications of the type I have instanced focus upon the intrinsic quality of democratic decisions. However, there is another type of consequentialist justification in which the appeal is not to the desirable content of democratic decisions but to the benefits that flow from the way in which those decisions are reached. Perhaps the most widely used justification of this sort is that particularly associated with J. S. Mill: the argument that, in participating in the decisions that are to govern his life, an individual is improved both intellectually and morally.[2] Claims that people are more ready to respect decisions reached democratically and that democracy has an integrative effect upon a community are also examples of this second type of consequentialist justification.

It is less easy to relate this second sort of consequentialist justification to any specific decision rule such as the majority principle. Clearly it implies widespread participation and participation implies the possibility of having an influence upon decisions. That, however, need not be of any specific type. Mill, for example, thought that his arguments for participation did not necessarily entail that participants should be granted equal voting rights.

Consequentialist justifications of democracy have an obvious rationale. It would be surprising if one's approval or disapproval of a form of government took no account of the quality of government that one could expect from it. Nevertheless there are a number of reasons why one might be less than wholly satisfied with justifying democracy in this way. (These reasons apply with less force to one sort of consequentialist justification: the utilitarian justification of democracy in terms of the maximization of happiness or want-satisfaction. I shall deal with utilitarianism later.) Firstly, consequentialist justifications are contingent in character. They involve empirical assertions which may or may not hold true. For example, whether a society which respects certain sorts of individual right is a 'good' society is not an empirical question; whether a democratic system of government will ensure such a society most definitely is. The simple confidence with which some writers are prepared to make such empirical assertions in justifying democracy is, to say the least, quite remarkable. Moreover, given that consequentialist justifications have this contingent character, they do not constitute principled commitments to democracy as such. If it turned out that the desired result would be better achieved by a non-democratic system of government, then we should abandon democracy.

Secondly, and relatedly, consequentialist justifications fail to account for our sense that democracy constitutes a fair decision procedure. That is, they do not accommodate the idea that, irrespective of what decisions are made, a democratic system constitutes a fairer way of making decisions than one in which some are excluded from the process of decision-making and others are accorded a privileged status. More particularly, consequentialist justifications cannot provide a satisfactory account of the idea of an equal *right* of participation. The assertion of a right makes the focus of concern the well-being of the individual right-holder. Thus the assertion of a right to vote entails construing a vote as of benefit to the individual voter and the removal of that right as a disbenefit to him. In consequentialist justifications of democracy, the establishment of equal voting rights is justified simply as a means to a desirable collective end. If that collective end required unequal or selective voting rights there could be no ground for complaint. Even where the attainment of a collective end did require equal voting rights, the removal of those rights from an individual or group of individuals would be construed as a harm to society at large (because it endangered the attainment of the collective end) rather than as an injustice to the disfranchised individuals. Yet the arbitrary disfranchisement of a group of individuals is typically thought of as an infringement of *their* (pre-legal) rights, as an injustice to them in particular rather than merely a harm to society in general.

Thirdly, of less significance but still worth

mentioning, democracy is a form of decision procedure thought appropriate to many associations other than the state. Several of the consequentialist justifications offered in support of democracy have little or no relevance to these non-state associations. For example, if a gardening club or a rambling association or a film society has a democratic constitution, it is unlikely to apologize for this by appeals to the promotion of justice or freedom. It may regard its democratic constitution as *embodying* ideas of justice and freedom but that is a different matter.

How else then might democracy be justified? The answer is clearly implied in the shortcomings of consequentialist justification. The alternative is to appeal to a principle which entails that democracy is the inherently right or fair way of making decisions. Here there is not a prospective appeal to a desirable consequence but a retrospective appeal to a principle which predicates the intrinsic rightness or fairness of the democratic process itself. When equality is appealed to not merely as a feature of democratic institutions but as a reason for having those institutions, democracy is being justified in this way. It is to the justification of democracy by way of equality that I shall give most of my attention. It is not the only form of non-consequentialist justification of democracy that there can be. If one believed that democracy was the divinely approved form of government (as some have believed in the past and, for all I know, as some may still believe now) that would clearly afford a non-consequentialist justification of democracy. Justifications which stress 'self-determination' will also usually be of this type. However, the appeal to equality is perhaps more frequently heard than any other.

Equality and the Majority Principle

In a moment, I want to look at what sort of principle of equality can justify political equality. But since my interest is ultimately in the decision rule that a democracy should adopt, let me first of all indicate the very simple way

in which the majority principle is often justified by way of equality. Political equality entails that each should have an equal right of participation and, in particular, that each should have a vote and that each vote should count equally. If there is a clash of preferences and if each vote is to count equally, then the proposal preferred by the majority must be adopted. To allow the will of the minority to prevail would be to give greater weight to the vote of each member of the minority than to the vote of each member of the majority, thus violating political equality. This argument can be used not only in defence of absolute majorities but also in defence of relative majorities if, for some reason, an absolute majority is unattainable.

If we accept the spirit of this argument, does it require our unqualified acceptance of the majority principle? There are two widely canvassed limitations upon the majority principle which must be mentioned, though I mention them largely to emphasize their separateness from a third sort of limitation upon which I shall dwell.

1. Majority Rule and Minority Rights

People often want to assert individual or minority rights as restrictions upon the scope of majority preference. Is this compatible with the argument from equality?

In answering this we need to distinguish between democratic and non-democratic rights. By 'democratic rights' I understand those rights which are integral to the democratic process. Obviously these include the right to vote but also rights such as freedom of expression and freedom of association in so far as these are essential for an individual's participation in the democratic process. Anyone committed to democracy and to the rule of the majority of a pre-defined demos must require the maintenance of those rights. One reason is that those rights are sanctioned by the principle of equality which sanctions the majority principle itself. Another is that a majority which removes the democratic rights of part of a demos impairs the claim of future majorities to be majorities of that demos.

The case of non-democratic rights is perhaps more contentious. Rights such as the right of freedom of worship or the right to a fair trial rest upon some ground other than their being essential to the democratic process and are intended to limit the scope of that process. These rights are often called minority rights but that is misleading since they are usually rights ascribed to every individual in a community and not only to a specific minority. Presumably they are labelled minority rights because they are conceived as safeguards against possible ravages of the majority. As long as these rights are universal to each member of a demos, I cannot see how they can be impugned on grounds of equality. It is sometimes implied that the inhibition of majority preference by individual rights constitutes an inequality in favour of a minority. But the inequality involved in universal rights is not an inequality of persons, but an inequality in the status attributed to certain goods and is an inequality enjoyed by everyone.

This is not to say that democracy requires that such rights be recognized or respected. On the contrary, there would be nothing 'undemocratic' about their denial, removal, or infringement, although these might well be objectionable on other grounds. I am holding only that a society which restricts the scope of the democratic process, and therefore the will of the majority, by the institution of individuals rights cannot be faulted on grounds of equality alone.

2. Apathetic Majorities and Intense Minorities

A second complication in moving from political equality to majority rule concerns intensity of preference. It is often considered a defect of the majority principle that it merely counts preferences and takes no account of the different intensities with which those preferences are held. It is not obviously right or desirable that the very mild preferences of a 52 per cent 'apathetic majority' should prevail over the strongly held preferences of a 48 per cent 'intense minority'. Certainly any justification of democracy in terms of maximizing satisfactions implies that account should be taken of the intensity as well as the number of preferences. Nor would it be difficult to argue

that equality allows, if it does not require, that account be taken of intensity of preference. If individuals are treated equally in respect of the criterion of intensity, the egalitarian *qua* egalitarian has no reason to complain.

There are large problems in devising procedures which take reliable account of intensity of preference and much disagreement about the sensitivity of Western representative democracies to differing intensities of preference. But, for the moment, my concern is only with whether it is right, in principle, to take account of intensity of preference. A feature of this criterion which may make one hesitate about it at this level is its subjectivity. Some people seem to feel more strongly than others about almost everything. Some become excited without good reason; others fail to become excited when they have good reason. Taking account of intensity of preference may therefore favour over-sensitive busybodies to the disadvantage of long-suffering stoics. The point here is not that recognized by Dahl: that overt behaviour may not always be a reliable indicator of individuals' states of mind. Rather it is that, even if X undoubtedly feels more strongly than Y, it is not clear that X should get his way if his strength of feeling seems 'unreasonable'. This element of subjectivity can be avoided by reformulating the principle in terms of interests, so that ideally a decision procedure would take account of the extent to which individuals' interests were affected beneficially or adversely even when this did not coincide with the sensitivities manifested by the individuals themselves. Certainly if the principle upon which political equality rests is that of an equal claim to the promotion of one's interests (as I shall argue), that implies that interests should be weighed as well as heads counted.

A further point of principle is that the case for taking account of intensity depends upon how the democratic process is conceived. If one thinks of it as computing wants or interests, there is a case for weighing as well as counting these. If, on the other hand, one takes a consequentialist view of democracy in which votes represent judgements rather than preferences, intensity may be irrelevant. As Rawls points out, those who have stronger feelings on an issue may do so because of their ignorance or prejudice, while those who have weaker feelings may do so because of their better appreciation of the complexities of the issue.[3] In other words, intensity of feeling is not a reliable indicator of quality of judgement.

However, having made these qualifications, there is clearly a strong case for allowing considerations of intensity to modify the majority principle (in so far as this is practicable), and a case which has more rather than less to be said for it in terms of equality of treatment.

What Principle of Equality?

Before taking up a third and more radical qualification of the majority principle, I want to return to the issue of equality itself and the principle which underlies a commitment to political equality.

Since democracy is a decision procedure, it may seem that the principle of equality relevant to democracy must be one concerning people's capacities as decision-makers. And, indeed, there are writers who assert or imply that adherence to democracy entails a presumption of the equality of competence of individuals on political matters. This presumption can be more or less strong. In its strongest form, the claim would be simply that people *are* equally competent to make political decisions. A slightly weaker claim would be that, although there are differences in competence between individuals, those differences are too slight to matter. A still weaker claim would be that, although some are more competent than others, those differences are insufficiently obvious for there to be agreement on who is more competent than whom and that therefore we have to treat people as if they were equally competent, even though they are not. Thus Singer suggests that the reason for rejecting Mill's proposal for plural votes for those with superior education and intelligence 'is not that it would be obviously unfair to give more votes to better qualified people, but rather that it would be impossible to get every-

one to agree on who was to have the extra votes'. Thus, 'one person, one vote', represents a sort of practical compromise.[4]

One reason, possibly the main reason, why people have been induced to make these claims is that, historically, the most common objection to democracy has been the alleged incompetence of the many. This objection implies that the right to govern is dependent upon one's competence and, if the democrat accepts that implied premiss, he has to make his case in those terms. Nevertheless, this is an unpromising and unnecessary line of argument for a democrat to pursue. Firstly, the assertion of equality of political competence is an empirical one and one that it is difficult to find convincing. Secondly, it is not usually accepted that competence is a quality which, of itself, generates rights. Consider, for example, how we distinguish between being *in* authority and being *an* authority. To be in authority is to possess a right to determine the conduct of others. To be an authority is to be distinguished by one's competence on a matter but not therefore to be *in* a position of authority on that matter; that is, it does not give you an automatic right to decide on behalf of others. Others may be well advised to heed you, but you have no right to control their conduct and they have no duty to conform to your injunctions merely in virtue of your superior wisdom. Thirdly, if equality of competence were to figure at all in a justification of democracy, it would seem that it could figure only as an empirical presumption in a consequential justification and not as an autonomous justificatory principle.

The argument from equality is much more plausible if it focuses not upon people's qualities as *producers* of decisions but on their qualities as *consumers* of decisions.[5] The members of an association are each subject to the decisions of the association. They therefore each have an interest in the decisions that the association makes. Moreover, it is often, though not always, true that each member is equally interested in the decisions of the association. This can be true whether the members of the association are pursuing some collective purpose through the association or (as may be the case in a political association) simply making rules which provide a framework within which they can pursue their individual purposes. Even then, it may not be that each member is equally affected by each and every decision; a particular decision may affect some more than others and that is why it may be appropriate to weigh individuals' interests or to measure the intensities of their preferences. But we may still be able to say that, taking all decisions in the round, taking the 'set' of all decisions, any member is as interested in the outcomes of the decision procedure as any other. In particular it would seem reasonable to say this of individuals as members of states.

This account of the position of individuals as members of associations is partly analytic and partly empirical. It is not, or not obviously, moral. To derive a prescription for an egalitarian decision procedure we have to introduce an egalitarian principle. However, that principle need not be a particularly specific or strong principle of equality—simply one that entails that, *ceteris paribus*, the well-being of one person is to be valued as much as that of another. A principle such as the principle of equal human worth as elaborated by Gregory Vlastos would fit the bill.[6] For Vlastos an individual's worth is not the same as his merit. 'Merit' takes in all of those qualities by which we grade people. By contrast individuals' 'worth' is 'the value which persons have simply because they are persons'. It is because we attribute worth equally to persons *qua* persons that we hold that 'one man's well-being is as valuable as any other's'.[7] Following a principle such as this we may say that, where individuals' interests or wants are equally at stake (and that is the only relevant consideration), each has an equal claim to have his interests promoted or his wants satisfied. This, in turn, implies that a decision procedure should be structured so that it respects the equal claim of each to have his interests promoted or his wants satisfied. ('His' here is, of course, meant to be sexless.) Thus a decision procedure is fair in so far as it respects equally this equal claim of each; unfair in so far as it does not.

The presumption that people's interests *are* equally at stake in the decision arena is as important to this conclusion as a principle of equal human worth. If some people's interests were more greatly at stake than others, then the principle of equal human worth would not

merely allow but would require that account should be taken of those differences of interest. There are cases where the members of an association have different degrees of interest in the association, where the decision procedure reflects those differences, and where that arrangement seems perfectly acceptable. For example, in general terms, there is nothing unfair or otherwise objectionable about the shareholders of a company holding votes in proportion to the number of shares that they hold.

Even now, the argument for democracy is not entirely complete. Given that each individual is equally interested in the decisions of an association, that interest may be interpreted as no more than that decisions should be, as far as possible, what he wants them to be. In that case we can move straight to the inference that the decision procedure should afford an equal opportunity for the expression of wants and take equal account of those wants. Alternatively, acknowledging the conceptual distinction between interests and wants (even if an individual's interests have, ultimately, to connect with his wants), one might argue entirely in terms of the interests of individuals. The democrat would then have to confront the well-worn objection that a benevolent and informed despotism could promote the interests of a people as well, if not better than, a democracy. The usual reply to that objection is that we may presume that each individual is the best judge of his own interests. In fact the more relevant presumption is that each is the best promoter or, in Mill's words, the best 'guardian' of his interest since it benefits him nothing if his interest is better judged by another but then ignored. However, this is not the only strategy open to the democrat. He might argue that whatever an individual's competence as judge of his own interests, he and he alone has the right to be the final arbiter of that interest. I shall not assess the merits of either argument, partly because that would be a lengthy and probably inconclusive business, but mainly because that assessment is at some distance from my chief concern: the limits of majoritarianism. I shall simply presume that the care of each individual's interest is properly left in his own hands.

Majority Satisfaction and Proportionate Satisfaction

From the principles and presumptions that I have outlined we can derive the characteristic features of democracy, at least in its simple form: an equal right to vote, to participate in discussion, to place items on the agenda, and so on. Some might argue that this equalitarian position requires not only that these rights should be formally available to all, but also that socio-economic conditions should be adjusted to ensure that these rights constitute genuinely equal opportunities rather than merely formal entitlements. In addition it might be supposed that we can derive the majority principle in the way that I have already indicated. Individuals' interests or wants are to count equally, therefore votes are to count equally; if votes count equally and if there is a conflict of votes, then the votes of the majority must prevail. But is such an inference valid? Consider the following example.

There is a street whose residents control and pay for the amenities of the street and who decide democratically what those amenities shall be. Each resident has a vote and the vote of the majority is always decisive. They have three issues to decide upon, each of which they reckon equally important.

1. Whether to have asphalt or paved sidewalks. Asphalt is ugly but cheap. Paving stones are pleasant but more expensive.
2. Whether to keep the existing gas lighting which is picturesque and in keeping with the character of the street or to replace it with electric street-lighting which would be garish but provide the same amount of lighting more cheaply.
3. Whether to improve the appearance of the street by planting trees or to save money and plant no trees.

Two-thirds of the residents are economizers; one-third are aesthetes. Thus when each vote is taken the economizers win, the aesthetes lose. The street has asphalt instead of paved side-walks, electric instead of gas lighting, and no trees. Is that result satisfactory?

If we took any decision in isolation the answer would be yes both for an orthodox utilitarian and for someone who adhered to the principle of equality that I have outlined. Utility has been maximized and each individual's wants or interests have been valued equally. But consider the decisions as a group. Again the utilitarian would find nothing to object to particularly if we assume, as seems reasonable in the example I have given, that successive wins do not have a declining marginal utility for the winning majority. Provided social utility has been maximized, it is of no concern to the utilitarian that, in each decision, it is the same individuals who have had their utilities promoted and the same individuals who have not.

However, this must be of concern to the democrat who is a democrat because he adheres to the principle of equality that I have outlined. He cannot be satisfied that the interests or wants of the members of a community are consistently opposed in a ratio of 2:1 but consistently satisfied in a ratio of 3:0. Those individuals who make up the persistent minority can properly complain that repeated applications of the majority principle are not consistent with their equal entitlement as individuals to want-satisfaction or interest-promotion. If that entitlement were respected the aesthetes would get their way on one of the three issues.

It might be objected that there is no justification for treating the three decisions as a group. Each is an independent decision, each individually meets the requirements of equality, and it should be accepted as merely fortuitous that the same people win or lose in each of the three decisions. That objection cannot be sustained. What links the three decisions is that each is part of a process of want-satisfaction or interest-promotion. Want-satisfaction or interest-promotion is a good and a good capable of different distributions which, in turn, can be examined in the light of distributive principles. The democratic process allocates that good and it is quite legitimate to assess the overall distribution of the good even though that distribution is made by way of a number of separate decisions. If, having made such an assessment, we discover that some individuals have received all of that good and others have received none, we have good reason to doubt that the equal claim of each individual to the promotion of his interests has been respected.[8]

This, of course, relates to an essential and oft-noted difference between principles such as equality or fairness on the one hand and utilitarianism on the other. Equality and fairness are distributive principles, whereas the maximization of social utility is an aggregative principle to which distributive considerations are entirely subordinate. It is true that utilitarians would generally follow Bentham's injunction that each should count for one and no more than one. But that is no more than a working assumption to be following in maximizing aggregate utility and, at most, yields a principle of impersonality or 'anonymity'. Maximizing social utility may entail taking equal account of each individual's interest, but that does not make it the same exercise as distributing satisfactions fairly.

It is for this reason that I have avoided a formula that is often presented in discussions of this sort: that each person is entitled to equal consideration or, more specifically, that each person's interest should be considered equally. The trouble with this formula is that it is not clear what it requires. Dahl, for example, gives the following as a principle which a procedure must satisfy to be 'democratic'.

> *Equal Consideration for all members:* No distribution of socially allocated entities, whether actions, forbearances, or objects, is acceptable if it violates the principle that the good or interest of each member is entitled to equal consideration.[9]

But how demanding is this principle supposed to be? If 'equal consideration' requires merely 'taking equally into account', the utilitarian can claim to consider interests equally in maximizing social utility. If, on the other hand, 'equal consideration' means that equal claims of interest should be equally met, the principle sets a test which the utilitarian cannot pass—except in those few cases where, by a happy chance, maximizing utility coincides with meeting equal claims equally. Elsewhere in the same essay, Dahl enunciates another principle that is fundamental to procedural democracy:

'equally valid claims justify equal shares'.[10] He apparently thinks that 'this elementary principle of fairness' amounts to very little—'it falls just short of a tautology'. But it is just such an 'elementary' principle that a utilitarian cannot acknowledge. He can claim to consider interests equally in respect of the goal of maximum social utility; what he cannot do is to acknowledge the equal satisfaction of equal claims as a goal in its own right, for maximizing aggregate utility is not guaranteed to redeem each individual's equal claim to interest-promotion.

Procedural Fairness and Equality of Opportunity

A possible counter to my argument against majoritarianism is that a system in which people have equal chances or opportunities is compatible with the egalitarian principle I have outlined, and that decision by majority vote constitutes a system of equal chance or opportunity. I would accept the first proposition but not the second.

Suppose a group of individuals agreed to make the decisions which applied to them collectively by way of a lottery. For every issue there would be a lottery in which each individual held one and only one ticket. The individual who held the winning ticket for a particular issue would have the right to decide on that issue on behalf of the whole group. Thus, for any issue, each individual *qua* individual would have an equal chance of being the decider. The odds in favour of any particular proposal being adopted would be proportionate to the number of individuals who favoured that alternative in the total group. However, the fairness of the lottery system would not depend upon its tendency, over time, to produce decisions roughly in proportion to the wishes of different sections of the population. Rather the procedure could be said to be inherently fair; it would be an example of what Rawls calls 'pure procedural justice'.[11] The mere fact that each individual's ticket counts for one and no more than one can be regarded as enough to satisfy the equal claim of each to want-satisfaction.

However, decision by majority vote cannot properly be represented as a lottery of this sort. When individuals enter the decision arena they may be ignorant of one another's preferences and therefore ignorant of whether they will be in the majority or the minority. In addition, they may be ignorant of one another's preferences on future issues. Indeed, they are likely to be ignorant of their own preferences on future issues since they will not know what all of those issues will be and therefore will not yet have formed preferences on them. But ignorance is not randomness; it is merely ignorance. That people are ignorant of the total configuration of preferences on all future issues, and therefore ignorant of how often they will find themselves in the majority or minority, does not mean that decision by majority vote amounts to a lottery in which people have equal chances of winning.

This may seem too short a way with majoritarianism. Have I not overlooked an important equality commonly claimed for majoritarian democracy: the equal opportunity of each to persuade the majority to his point of view? If the entitlement of each individual to that opportunity is respected, should that not remove our reservations about majoritarianism? There are at least three reasons why it should not. Firstly, a majority may simply be intransigent and not open to persuasion. Secondly, there are many issues—particularly those which arise from conflicting interests or wants—which are not really matters for persuasion. I do not know how the aesthetes in my street example could produce reasons which would 'persuade' the economizers to change their preferences. (Issues which arise from conflicting judgements are a different matter which I shall consider separately in a moment.) Thirdly, this sort of equality presupposes what is at issue: the majority principle. Persuading the majority is simply set as the condition of a competition in which people have an equal opportunity to participate. That people have an equal right to participate in that competition does nothing to establish that the competition is itself satisfactory, that persuading the majority ought always to be the condition of promoting interests or satisfying wants.

What if people consent to majority rule, if not directly then indirectly by joining an association in which the majority principle is already an established part of the constitution? Does that not render majority rule fair? The problems involved in holding that people 'consent' to be members of states are well known. However, I have said that my reservations about majority rule apply equally to many non-state associations and we would normally have no qualms about describing membership of most of those associations as 'voluntary'. That people have consented to a form of government rather than having it imposed upon them must count for something. Nevertheless, it is still possible to assess the fairness of an argument independently of whether it has received the consent of those to whom it applies. Consider, for example, a lottery in which there are two sorts of ticket—one for Blacks, the other for Whites. All tickets are sold at the same price but those sold to Blacks carry half the chance of winning as those sold to Whites. All are aware of this and no one is obliged to buy a ticket, so that when a Black buys a ticket he does so freely and is therefore a 'consenting' participant in the lottery. Even so, it seems quite reasonable to say that, as far as Black participants are concerned, the lottery is unfair. Notice that if consent were a sufficient condition of fairness, we would have to describe as fair not just majority rule but *any* arrangement to which people consented no matter how morally grotesque it might be. Thus, even where people have consented to be governed according to the majority principle, we may still say that that principle can work unfairly, though we may also feel that there is little reason to protest on behalf of a persistent minority that has, more or less wittingly, consented to the position in which it finds itself.

Conclusion

The conclusion that I wish to draw from all that I have said will be obvious: where majority rule results in persistent minorities those minorities have reason to complain that they are being treated unfairly. This is a simple and perhaps unsurprising statement but it is one that democratic theorists have been remarkably reluctant to make. The common assumption seems to be that a democratic minority can legitimately complain only in two sorts of circumstance: (1) if its rights are infringed or if in some other way it is persecuted, oppressed, or exploited; (2) if its special interests are overridden by an 'apathetic majority'. If a minority is persistently on the losing side, but can make neither of these complaints, its position is usually regarded as merely unfortunate rather than unfair.

Certainly persistent minorities are thought to be 'bad' or 'unhealthy' for a democracy. For one thing, persistent minorities are likely to become increasingly reluctant to bend to the majority's will. For another, persistent majorities, it is said,[12] are likely to abuse their position. Where there are fluctuating majorities, the individual who is in the majority today knows that he will be in the minority tomorrow. He therefore has an incentive not to abuse his majority position lest he, in turn, is abused when he is in the minority. The members of a persistent majority have no such incentive to play fair by the minority. However, neither of these points questions the fairness of majoritarianism itself. Both are simply empirical assertions about the way in which persistent majorities and minorities endanger the satisfactory working of democratic institutions, whereas I have tried to argue that a persistent minority has reason to complain in terms of the very principle of equality that underlies democracy.

Some Consequent Issues

1. Democracy and the Majority Principle

Am I therefore saying that majoritarianism is 'undemocratic'? Any such assertion would contradict the main import of the remarks with which I began this paper. I have simply argued that one major justification for democracy, the argument from equality, is not always compatible with one typical feature of democratic systems—decision by majority vote. However, where majorities fluctuate so that want-satisfaction is fairly distributed, majority rule is unobjectionable in terms of that argument. Moreover, as I have indicated, there are other justifications of democracy, many of which are, at least in principle, quite compatible with straight-forward majority rule.

2. Proportionate Returns and Equal Returns

Is the conclusion that I have drawn from my premises sufficiently radical? I have argued for proportionate levels of satisfaction but it might be thought that I should be arguing for equal levels of satisfaction. Suppose there were 100 individuals who were opposed 99 to 1 on every issue and the majority of 1 was always the same individual. If the decisions were taken on 100 issues then, on my argument, the group of 99 would get their way 99 times and the lone dissenter would get his way once. Yet each member of the 99 is no less 'rewarded' by a winning vote merely because he shares it with 98 others. Should not the majority of 99 and the minority of 1 each get their way 50 per cent of the time? Assuming that each issue was equally significant, each member of the community would then enjoy equal levels of satisfaction or utility.

A committed egalitarian might well argue that this would be the right outcome. Nevertheless, it is not the outcome required by my premises. I have argued that where individuals are equally interested in the outcomes of a decision procedure, that procedure should value their interests equally. If we regard a vote as a political purchasing power, then each individual's vote should constitute the same sum of political money. No one should be required to spend that money for a nil return but neither should anyone be able to claim a larger sum of political money than anyone else. To allow the persistent minority of 1 to get his way as often as the persistent majority of 99 would be equivalent to giving him 99 times as much political purchasing power as any individual in the majority. The members of the 99 could then protest that their interests were not being given the same status as those of the lone dissenter.

This point is perhaps illustrated more graphically when it arises in relation to a single decision. Imagine a group of individuals are voting on a public good. Since the good will be equally available to each, it is agreed that each should be taxed equally in order to finance it. However, there can be more or less of the public good and the members of the group are divided over how much of their income they want to devote to it and therefore over how much of the public good there should be. The group is made up of four individuals whose preferences are as follows: A, B, and C each want 3 units, D wants 1 unit. Decision by majority vote would result in 3 units of the public good. My principle is taking equal account of the preferences of each individual would entail adopting the average preference: 2.5 units. The equivalent of giving equal weight to the preferences of the lone dissenter as to the collective preferences of the 99 in my earlier example, would be to observe that A, B, and C each have the same preference and to hold that that preference should therefore enter the calculation only once. Thus the decision would be that there should be only 2 units of the public good. It is true that, if this were the decision, D would suffer no greater disutility than A or B or C. However, A, B, and C could quite properly protest that they were then being treated unfairly since each of them is a distinct individual with distinct, if identical, wants, yet the decision to have only 2 units of the public good gives only a third of the value to each of their wants as to those of D.

3. Preferences and Judgements

My argument has been developed entirely in terms of decisions on whose interests are to be promoted or whose wants satisfied, and that is a crucial feature of the argument. Sometimes votes are interpreted not as expressions of interests or wants (i.e. preferences) but as judgements—judgements about what is right, true, efficacious, etc. Unfortunately writers on democracy are inclined to describe the democratic process either entirely in terms of preferences or entirely in terms of judgements, whereas in most associations some decisions are of one kind and some of the other. Is majoritarianism subject to the criticisms I have made where votes express judgements rather than preferences?

The example of a jury shows clearly that it is not. A jury is a body in which a decision has to receive the support of a majority, although in this case the majority has to be at least 10 to 2. Imagine I am one of twelve members of a jury which judges 12 cases. In each case there is disagreement amongst the jurors and in each case I find myself in the minority of 2. Even so it would be quite misplaced for me to complain that my fellow-jurors were treating me unfairly and that my judgement should prevail on at least one of the 12 cases. The reason is simple. The purpose of a jury is to judge guilt or innocence and not to distribute goods amongst the jurors themselves. I may complain that my fellow-jurors are making the wrong judgements and that the innocent are being convicted and the guilty going free; but I cannot complain that they are being unjust *to me* in not deferring to my judgement on at least one occasion.

A jury is a special sort of body but this point is not at all special to juries. If votes express judgements and nothing but judgements— judgements about what is true or false, right or wrong, expedient or inexpedient—then they are necessarily disinterested. I can therefore have no interest in my judgement's prevailing over those of others merely because it is *my* judgement. This is so not only where my judgements bear only upon others (as in a jury) but also where my judgements bear upon myself. Consider a decision which is not about whose interest is to be promoted but simply about how a desired result is best achieved. We all agree that X is desirable and the vote is simply upon the most effective way of securing X. If every individual's vote, including my own, expresses a judgement and only a judgement on that issue then, as I have said, I have no interest in my judgement prevailing simply because it is my judgement. I have an interest in the right or best judgement prevailing, but that is a different matter. Of course, if I had reason to suppose that my judgement were superior to that of others then I would have an interest in its being given greater weight, simply because it was more likely to be right. But then everyone else would have the same interest in my judgement's being given greater weight. By the same token, if there was reason to suppose that my judgement was inferior to those of others then I, as well as everyone else, would have an interest in its being given less weight.

Thus the argument from an equal claim to want-satisfaction or interest-promotion against simple majoritarianism does not apply where votes express pure judgements. One might still have reservations about majoritarianism where votes are of this kind, but these would be reservations of a different sort.

It would be convenient if the issue of preferences and judgements could be dismissed so easily. Unfortunately there are a number of considerations which muddy the simple clarity of the distinction I have drawn. For one thing, the distinction between preferences and judgements may not always be easy to apply in practice, Considerations of personal interest will often intrude into votes that are ostensibly pure judgements. In addition there are some issues which are not clearly either issues of preferences or issues of judgement. Votes on abortion, blood sports, pornography, the interests of future generations, are likely to straddle this distinction. The distinction is likely to be most difficult to maintain where decisions are of a moral rather than a purely technical nature. Nevertheless, it remains true that the argument that I have developed up till now applies only if, and in so far as, individuals can be shown to have an interest in their votes being decisive.

Suppose that an issue is clearly one of pure judgement. I have argued that an individual then has no interest in account being taken of his judgement simply because it is *his* judgement. This simple view may be insufficiently sensitive to the realities of human relationships. David Miller has argued that 'in modern societies political equality has come to symbolise the basic human equality between the members of a given community in such a way that everyone who is excluded from, or treated unequally in, the political realm will suffer a loss of self-respect'. The claim for equal voting rights is 'essentially a claim for status'.[13] If this is true then an individual can have an interest in his being granted an equal

voice in matters of judgement, for his self-esteem may be no less damaged by having his judgements discounted than by having his preferences ignored. In Rawls's theory . . . [i]f some individuals held less than equal political rights that would 'have the effect of publicly establishing their inferiority' which would be 'humiliating and destructive of self-esteem'.[14] However there is not a simple logical link between these arguments for political equality and the reservations I have expressed about the majority principle. The constraints that equality of status places upon the decision rule that a society may adopt would seem to be entirely dependent upon what the members of that society feel is compatible with their being accorded equal respect. In particular, since the relevant interest here is not an interest in the outcomes of the decision procedure but simply an interest in being a participant in that procedure, there may be no serious tension between equality of status and majority rule.

A somewhat different matter is the 'psychic' interest that an individual may have in his judgement's prevailing. People often have a considerable emotional investment in their opinions and are consequently gratified when their views prevail and displeased when they do not. Our estimation of these feelings may vary—'worthy' if they derive from a concern to see right done, 'unworthy' if they are merely the self-gratification of victory or the pique of defeat. Either way, there are obvious reasons why this sort of utility should be ignored by decision procedures. To mention but one, if they were not ignored, we could be faced with an embarrassing choice between the decision rule which distributed psychic satisfactions fairly (or maximised such satisfactions, if that was our concern) and the rule which seemed most likely to yield the right substantive decision. (The same dilemma may confront those who emphasize the importance of political equality to equality of social status. The decision rule which is most desirable in terms of equal status may not be the rule that is most likely to yield the correct result.)

Finally, consider the following case. The members of an association have to make a number of decisions, each of which is concerned not with what they want but with what they believe to be right. On each decision there is disagreement and each member is equally convinced that his judgement is correct: that is, each is equally unconvinced that the judgement of any other member or members is superior to his own. There is no independent source of wisdom to which the members can resort, nor is there any shared conviction that a particular decision rule, such as majority vote, is likely to issue in the right answers. How should the members resolve their disagreements?

The answer suggested by Peter Singer is by a decision procedure in which each member has an equal voice.[15] This is not because an equal franchise is required by an equal right of self-government or by other principles of equality, appeal to which Singer abjures.[16] Rather it is because, in these circumstances, 'one person, one vote' constitutes a 'fair compromise'. Each member is convinced that he is right, but each has to recognize that this is equally true of every other member. A democratic decision procedure 'makes it possible for everyone to refrain from acting on his own judgement about particular issues without giving up more than the theoretical minimum which it is essential for everyone to give up in order to achieve the benefits of a peaceful solution to disputes'.[17] Singer also apparently accepts that 'one person, one vote' entails decision by majority vote. The majority principle should be embraced therefore, not because it is likely to issue in correct judgements, but because it is part of the fair compromise.

This is not a case in which disputes can be represented as conflicts of interest. Each member is impelled solely by his wish to see right done together with his sincere conviction that he knows what is right. Indeed, what a member judges to be right could run counter to his personal interests. Nevertheless, since, for Singer, the merit of democracy consists in its fairness, albeit its 'compromise' fairness, rather than in its propensity to produce right answers, the logic of proportionality would seem to apply just as strongly in this kind of case as in cases of conflicting interests. This is especially so where conflicting judgements are consistently those of fixed majorities and minorities. Singer recognizes that his argument may run into trouble where there are permanent majorities and minorities. However,

he believes that the fairness of the compromise holds provided that a permanent majority does not use its votes to the constant disadvantage of the minority.[18] What he fails to recognize is that the logic of his argument requires not merely that the minority be treated fairly in whatever decisions the majority makes but that a fair proportion of decisions should be made *by* that minority.[19]

4. *From Principle to Practice*

My chief concern has been to consider what constitutes fair treatment of minorities by a decision procedure and, in particular, to explain why we should (and often do) feel unhappy about the position of persistent minorities under majority rule. However, what I have said raises some important practical issues. One of these, which I shall have to leave undiscussed, is how the plight of persistent minorities under majority rule affects their obligation to conform to the decisions of the many. More particularly, how would the answer to this question be affected by whether, and to what extent, membership of an association was voluntary? Another practical issue is how the principle of proportionality can be implemented. Again this is a subject which requires more attention than I can give to it here, but I can hardly escape without saying something about the problem of implementation.

If life were always as simple as in my street example, implementing the principle of proportionality would present no great difficulty. For example, the residents could first reveal their preferences on the three issues of sidewalks, street-lighting, and trees. Noticing that there was a consistent division of 2:1 on each issue, they could then agree that the aesthetes should get their way on one of the issues. That would still leave the question of which of the three issues should go the minority's way. This could be determined randomly. Alternatively, if the minority held slightly more intense preferences or the majority slightly less intense preferences on one of the issues, that would provide a rationale for selecting that issue as the one on which the minority should get its way.

Unfortunately, life is not usually so simple

either in the state or in associations which confront fewer and less complex issues than the state. There are four obvious difficulties that are likely to arise in any attempt to implement the principle of proportionality.

1. Issues are not always as easily separable as in the street example. If the residents decide upon asphalt rather than paved sidewalks that is unlikely to pre-empt their choice between gas or electric lighting and trees or no trees. But issues are often more interrelated than these so that one cannot extend a measure of satisfaction to everyone and still have a coherent set of decisions. (However, this may also be a problem under the majority rule where there are fluctuating majorities.)
2. The membership of majorities and minorities is unlikely to be absolutely stable on all issues. This does not make the principle of proportionality either irrelevant or inapplicable but it does make its application more complicated.
3. It is not enough merely to count wins and losses. Account also has to be taken of the different importances of issues and therefore of the different importances of wins and losses. This can be done, but again it complicates matters considerably.
4. A decision process is often 'open-ended' in that there is no point at which it is obviously appropriate to call a halt while one takes account of and adjusts for the total distribution of wins and losses to date.

The principle of proportionality is widely, though not universally, accepted as the correct principle for one aspect of modern democratic systems: representation. The problems of implementation that I have listed may go some way to explaining people's reluctance to apply the same principle to decisions upon issues. There are fairly simple ways in which the principle can be implemented, albeit in a rough and ready fashion. In associations which prefer (and can afford) to reach decisions by agreement and accommodation rather than by simple votes, deference can be, and often is, paid to the principle of proportionality. What I have said also indicates that 'power-sharing', such as has been tried (unsuccessfully) in Northern Ireland, can be looked upon as

more than a shabby compromise which departs from the 'truly democratic' principle of majority rule. However, a precise implementation of the principle would require a voting system which continually adjusted individuals' voting powers to take account of how often they have been on the winning and losing sides, the proportions involved, and the different importances of the issues voted upon.

No doubt such a voting system could be devised but it is difficult to see how it could be other than cumbersome, complex, and time-consuming in its application. Thus those who recognize the claims of proportionality might still conclude that these have to be sacrificed in the interest of efficient and coherent decision-making. Nevertheless, it is still worth establishing that a sacrifice is involved and that the majority principle is not always consistent with the principle that inspires our commitment to political equality.

Notes

---

1. For [an] example of justifications of this kind, see Carl Cohen. *Democracy* (Athens, University of Georgia Press, 1971), ch. 14.

2. J. S. Mill, *Utilitarianism, Liberty and Representative Government* (London, Dent, 1910), pp. 202–18. See also Carole Pateman, *Participation and Democratic Theory* (Cambridge, Cambridge University Press, 1970).

3. Rawls, *Theory of Justice*, pp. 230–1, 361.

4. Peter Singer, *Democracy and Disobedience* (Oxford, Oxford University Press, 1973), pp. 34–5.

5. The argument of the next few paragraphs is similar in many respects to the more detailed argument of Carl Cohen, *Democracy*, ch. 15.

6. Gregory Vlastos, 'Justice and Equality' in Richard B. Brandt (ed.), *Social Justice* (Englewood Cliffs, N.J., Prentice-Hall, 1962), pp. 31–72.

7. Ibid., pp. 48, 51.

8. I say only 'good reason to doubt' to allow for the possibility that this result could be the outcome of the sort of lottery that I consider in the next section. Another objection to my argument here might be that what I have presented as three separate issues could be equally well re-

garded as a single issue: should the street have the cheapest or the most pleasant amenities? However, part of the thrust of the argument I develop here is that, wherever it is practicable to divide up issues so that a fairer satisfaction of preferences becomes possible, this should be done.

9. Robert A. Dahl, 'Procedural Democracy' in Peter Laslett and James Fishkin (eds.), *Philosophy, Politics and Society*, 5th series (Oxford, Basil Blackwell, 1979), p. 125. See also Stanley I. Benn, 'Egalitarianism and the Equal Consideration of Interests' in J. Roland Pennock and John W. Chapman (eds.), *Nomos IX: Equality* (New York, Atherton Press, 1967).

10. Dahl, 'Procedural Democracy', p. 99. Dahl himself refrains from deriving any specific decision rule from either principle of equality; ibid., pp. 101–2.

11. Rawls, *Theory of Justice*, p. 86.

12. e.g. by Madison in *The Federalist*, No. 10 and by Cohen, *Democracy*, pp. 71–4.

13. David Miller, 'Democracy and Social Justice' in Pierre Birnbaum, Jack Lively, and Geraint Parry

(eds.), *Democracy, Consensus and Social Contract* (London, Sage, 1978), pp. 92, 95–6.

14. Rawls, *Theory of Justice*, pp. 234, 544–5.

15. Singer, *Democracy and Disobedience*, pp. 30–41.

16. Ibid., pp. 26–30.

17. Ibid., p. 32.

18. Ibid., pp. 42–5.

19. Nelson, *On Justifying Democracy*, pp. 22–4, criticizes Singer's general approach to democracy on the ground that, where a decision is about what is right, what matters is not the intrinsic fairness of a decision procedure, but its probability of producing the correct outcome. 'If there are independent standards for evaluating legislation, and if the procedure most likely to produce legislation acceptable by those standards is not a fair compromise, then, in fact, we ought to adopt this unfair procedure.' (p. 24.) But his criticism is of no force in the circumstances that Singer contemplates: if there is no generally agreed standard for assessing outcomes and therefore no agreed standard for assessing decision procedures in terms of outcomes, how are we to proceed?

Procedural Equality in Democratic Theory

Charles Beitz

In this essay Charles Beitz explores further the connections between democratic procedures and equality. His particular focus is on what he terms the "principle of procedural equality"—the claim that each citizen should have an equal opportunity to influence the outcomes of the legislative process. His argument is that various attempts to justify that principle have failed. Notions of equal concern and respect and of giving equal weight to each person's interests cannot justify procedural equality, he claims, nor can it be supported by considerations of fairness (as Peter Singer argued) or on the basis of its capacity to produce political stability. His own defense of democratic procedures is provided in the next selection.

From Charles Beitz, "Procedural Equality in Democratic Theory: A Preliminary Inquiry." Reprinted by permission of New York University Press from *Liberal Democracy*, NOMOS XXV, edited by J. Roland Pennock and John W. Chapman. Copyright © 1983 by New York University, pp. 59–91.

According to a widely held contemporary view, the legislative mechanism of representative democracy should conform to the *principle of procedural equality:* each citizen is to have a fundamental right to an equal opportunity to influence the outcomes of the legislative process.[1] The interpretation of this principle evokes considerable disagreement. In this paper, however, I shall set this question aside.[2] Instead, I would like to explore the prior question of whether the principle can be given a plausible justification.

Offhand, this might appear to be a pointless, or at least an unnecessary, exercise, since for several reasons it may seem obvious that democrats must be procedural egalitarians. Some will regard the principle as true by definition; that is, they will suppose that a political system simply is not a democracy if its legislative procedures are not egalitarian. However, this is probably false, and in in any case it is not very illuminating. It is probably false because there is a natural conception of representative democracy from which nothing definite follows about the distribution of relative influence within democratic procedures. In this conception, the central feature of representative democracy is an electoral mechanism that enables citizens to influence the choice of legislation by participating periodically in the choice of legislators.[3] It would be consistent with this conception, for example, for all citizens to be entitled to vote, but for some to have more votes than others. In any case, it would not be very illuminating to rule out such possibilities by definitional fiat. It is better to regard the distribution and extent of opportunities to participate as posing normative problems in their own right about how the structural details of representative democracy should be arranged.

Another reason it might seem plausible that democrats should be egalitarians is this. Nearly everyone agrees that political democracy, of all the familiar forms of government, most completely embodies an egalitarian ideal, and that its egalitarianism explains (or helps explain) why it is the best form of government. But it is far from clear what is involved in such an ideal, and thus it is uncertain in what sense democratic institutions should answer to it or why their egalitarian features should recom-

mend them to us. The principle of procedural equality resolves this indeterminacy by identifying a precise interpretation of political equality that imposes definite requirements on institutional forms. Obviously, however, the precision and clarity of a principle are not in themselves reasons to accept it. (Indeed, in some contexts we might even regard these properties as invitations to error.) They will recommend a principle only if there are already strong independent considerations in its favor.

In this essay, I shall question whether such reasons can be advanced. My thesis is that it is more difficult than it may seem to give a philosophically compelling defense of the persistent modern conviction that citizens of representative democracies have fundamental rights that their institutions be procedurally egalitarian. I shall not actually argue that the principle of procedural equality is false; indeed, something like it may well be true, at least for the range of cases in which we are most likely to be interested. Rather, I wish to suggest that the most philosophically basic connection between democracy and equality is to be sought elsewhere than in the formal elements of democratic procedures, and that the appropriate distributive characteristics of these procedures should be worked out from this more fundamental point of view.

I

The principle of procedural equality specifies that every citizen is to have a fundamental right to an equal opportunity to influence the outcomes of the legislative process. While a complete analysis of the principle's meaning is not necessary for present purposes, it may be helpful, to fix ideas, to offer a few preliminary observations.

The principle refers to a *fundamental* right to procedural equality: procedural inequalities are impermissible even when they are likely to produce more desirable results than those that would occur under procedural equality. This is an important part of the view I wish to criticize. It assigns a special status to the principle that makes it inappropriate to treat procedural equality merely as one among many considerations that must be balanced or compromised in the design of representative institutions. Thus, for example, the principle of procedural equality rules out from the start the system of plural voting advocated by J. S. Mill;[4] even if (as seems unlikely) Mill were correct in his empirical hypothesis that plural voting would produce legislation satisfying the utility principle, as he understood it, the system would still be unacceptably inegalitarian. Similarly, the principle forbids inequalities in the apportionment of population among legislative districts, even when this is an unavoidable consequence of the effort to realize an ostensibly desirable purpose such as conformity of district lines to pre-existing political boundaries.[5] From the point of view I want to examine, procedural equality is morally basic.

The principle of procedural equality should be distinguished from the principle that each person's interests should receive equal weight in the legislative process. The latter—call it the principle of equal consideration—is result-oriented in the sense that its subject is the relationship between the set of individual interests in a society and the distribution of interest satisfaction resulting from the outcomes produced by the society's legislative institutions. Given an interpretation of the principle of equal consideration (e.g., a social welfare function), the system of representation is to be set up in whatever way promises to yield outcomes maximally satisfying it.[6] The concern for processes is indirect, deriving from the more basic concern for acceptable outcomes. By contrast, the principle of procedural equality is directly process-oriented. Its concern is not (as with equal consideration) the distributive characteristics of political outcomes themselves; rather, it is the distribution of control over the mechanism that produces these outcomes.

The importance of this distinction does not derive only from the fact that procedural equality and equal consideration are not equivalent principles. They may not even be consistent. The view that egalitarian procedures tend to produce results that are in some sense egalitarian is a substantive position requiring an argument. (In the next section, I suggest some reasons to doubt that this position is correct.)

Finally, it should be noted that the principle of procedural equality is indifferent about some questions apparently involving the relative legislative power of individuals and groups. The most important of these arise primarily within representation systems employing separate election districts. A traditional objection to these systems is that they give rise to inequalities in representation resulting from the existence of superfluous majorities and unrepresented minorities within districts.[7] Moreover, since districting systems allow the composition of the legislature to be affected by the distribution of voters across districts, they can produce distortions at the legislative level. Such distortions are familiar in cases of gerrymandering, in which the deliberate manipulation of district boundaries enables a party to gain legislative representation disproportionate to its share of the popular vote; of course similar distortions can come about accidentally.

Although the existence of such distortions is often seen as evidence of procedural inequality, this is not necessarily so. Indeed, one sense of procedural equality (one common in the literature on voting power) is perfectly consistent with distortions in representation of these kinds. Let us say that a representation system satisfies procedural equality if it accords to every voter an equal a priori probability of influencing any particular legislative choice.[8] This criterion will be satisfied whenever the following two conditions are true: (1) each voter has an equal a priori probability of casting the decisive vote (that is, roughly, of making the difference between victory and defeat) in electing the legislator or legislators representing his district; (2) each legislator has an equal a priori probability of casting the decisive vote on any matter coming before the legislature.[9] Clearly, it is fully consistent with these conditions that there be superfluous majorities and unrepresented minorities within districts. Furthermore, neither condition imposes any restriction on how district boundaries should be drawn beyond the requirement of equal population (or, perhaps, equal numbers of qualified voters).[10] Finally, neither condition imposes any restriction on the structure of the representation system beyond the requirements that every district return the same number of representatives to the legislature, and that each representative have an equally weighted vote.[11] These conditions can be satisfied in an extremely wide variety of districting systems, resulting in many different patterns of representation at the legislative level.[12]

This contention is not paradoxical. The principle of procedural equality refers to the distribution of *opportunities* for political influence (that is, of *potential* influence) rather than of *actual* influence. The potential influence that a procedural arrangement confers on any individual can be calculated without knowing how that person or any other person will use the opportunities defined by the arrangement. The extent of one's potential influence depends only on the structure of the procedures themselves. This is not generally true of actual influence, however. A person's actual influence, understood as the probability that he will, in fact, be successful in getting the legislation he wants (or, as the value, to him, of his procedural opportunities) also depends on how he exercises his opportunities and on how others exercise theirs. For example, in a committee in which each member casts one vote and the majority rules, my potential influence equals that of every other member; but if my interests are opposed to everyone else's, my actual influence is zero (assuming that everyone votes his or her interests).

If the subject of procedural equality is taken to be the distribution of potential rather than actual influence, then members of a group that returns fewer than its proportionate share of legislators cannot complain of procedural inequality provided that their votes had an equal a priori probability of being decisive in each district. Their complaint, rather, may be that their votes had less value than the votes of others: under the circumstances (given the district boundaries and the distribution of voter interests across boundaries), their interests are likely to be less well served by the legislature than those of others. Of course, arrangements that give rise in this way to arbitrary variations in the value of a vote may be open to moral criticism for a number of reasons. For ex-

ample, it might be claimed that such arrangements violate a principle of equal actual influence (although it is not clear that political procedures in any moderately complex society could ever satisfy this principle). More plausibly, perhaps, they may violate a principle of proportional representation for groups.[13] Whether any such principle can be given a persuasive justification is a question that I shall not pursue here, except to observe that the considerations involved are distinct from those associated with procedural equality.

II

The foregoing observations leave open a number of difficult problems about the interpretation of the principle of procedural equality, but I do not believe that anything in the criticisms to be advanced below turns on them. Thus, we may ask whether good reasons support the principle as a constraint on the structure of representative institutions.

A likely reply is that procedural equality is required by the deeper principle that institutions should treat persons as equals, or, in Dworkin's phrase, as equally deserving of concern and respect.[14] The difficulty, of course, lies in formulating the deeper principle with sufficient precision to yield definite implications about the distribution of opportunities for political influence. I shall comment on two different, although possibly consistent, formulations.

What is intended might be that procedural equality expresses public recognition of (or embodies institutionally the principle of) equal respect for the autonomy of persons. Political institutions, it might be said, should avoid interfering with, and when possible should contribute to, their citizens' respect for themselves and for one another as persons equally capable of making deliberate choices about their own situations, and of carrying out these choices in action.[15]

The idea of respect for autonomy is frequently appealed to in more general justifications of democracy. In that context it has several aspects, each of which connects with democratic institutions in a different way. Most obviously, that opportunities to influence political decisions are available to everyone ensures that those so motivated will be enabled to defend their interests and to promote their ideals. They will be able to exercise some degree of control over aspects of their lives affected by political decisions, and need not passively accept those decisions as *faits accomplis* that are beyond challenge. Further, since democratic politics requires public discussion and debate, it supports a political culture with incentives for investigation and criticism of government, and for the public presentation of opposing political views. Such a culture both encourages and enables the exercise of the faculties of judgment and choice. Finally, democratic politics creates an environment in which persons confront each other not only to manipulate but to persuade, and so must take seriously each other's nature as a rational being. In this sense, public recognition of rights of participation is a form of "communal acknowledgement of individual worth," providing grounds for the belief that one is regarded by others as a person whose opinions and choices have intrinsic importance.[16]

Although claims like these play an important role in the general justification of democracy, they do not appear to lend support to the principle of procedural equality as well. First, procedural equality does not seem necessary to ensure that citizens will regard themselves as sharing in control rather than as objects of manipulation by an alien power. As Mill observed, this consideration requires that everyone have *some* opportunity to participate in political decision-making; it is not obvious that these opportunities should therefore be equal, particularly if other considerations making for equality are widely accepted.[17] Similarly, the distinctive political culture of democracy seems to be consistent with some amount of political inequality. The essential condition here seems to be that political competition be extensive enough to generate a continuing interest in having available independent sources of information and criticism regarding a government's activities, and to create recurring situations in which engagement in argument and persuasion will be necessary to compete effectively for power. In both cases, institutions must be sufficiently open to allow conflicting positions to be represented, but it is not obviously necessary that every citizen have an equal opportunity to influence outcomes.

Some forms of inequality are clearly objectionable for other reasons related to respect for autonomy. Consider, for example, the white primary or the use of unequal election districts to dilute the influence of blacks. Such inequalities not only work to the detriment of the disadvantaged group but will also be experienced by them as demeaning. The visible dilution of influence will appear as an insult. This may be true even when there is good reason to believe (which is lacking in the examples cited) that those who are disadvantaged by the inequality will benefit in the long run: the inequality itself comes to symbolize the paternalistic superiority of those advantaged by it. But not every procedural inequality has this effect; few, for example, feel insulted or degraded by the patent inequality of representation in the U.S. Senate. This suggests that inequalities in the voting system that work to the detriment of identifiable groups will be regarded as insulting in the presence of other social practices that single out those same groups for invidiously discriminatory treatment, but not necessarily otherwise. Other types of procedural inequality (for example, limitations on access to the ballot) seem even less immediately degrading, again at least insofar as the inequalities do not reflect discriminatory practices elsewhere in society. Here there is an asymmetry in the basis of procedural equality: considerations associated with respect for autonomy furnish stronger objections to inequalities that reinforce existing patterns of unacceptable social discrimination than to inequalities that are, in this respect, benign.

But it may be objected that this formulation of the argument from equal consideration is too subjective; what is important is not only that persons have equal self-respect, but that their equal self-respect be rational in view of how their interests are treated by their institutions. This objection introduces a second formulation of the argument, for now it is claimed that political institutions treat persons as equals only when the decisions reached give equal weight to each person's interests. Some such criterion is the basis of the arguments for democracy offered by Bentham and James Mill, and by various contemporary "economic" theorists of democracy (insofar as they are concerned with normative issues). Now it is not clear offhand how this criterion should be interpreted. There are minimal and maximal interpretations. The first—which underpins utilitarian theories of democracy—is that decisions (or, more exactly, a sufficiently long string of decisions) should maximize the overall or average increase in satisfaction; the second, that decisions should (in the long run) yield equal increments in satisfaction for each person. These interpretations are obviously very different. Other interpretations of the equal weight formula might also be suggested, as well as alternative standards of distributive equity based on an objective ranking of sources of satisfaction . . . and mixed views in which a satisfaction-maximizing principle is constrained by an objective "welfare floor."[18]

While equal-weight formulae initially appear to be especially appropriate in democracies (because each evaluates decisions according to a standard in which, in an obvious sense, each person counts for one) I do not believe that this appearance survives scrutiny. Whatever superficial plausibility attaches to equal-weight formulae is likely to dissolve once it is recognized that these formulae govern the distribution of *increments* in satisfaction resulting from political decisions rather than aggregate levels of satisfaction. If the antecedent distribution is unacceptable, ensuring that increments are equal will only perpetuate an unacceptable distribution.[19]

Nevertheless, let us assume for the sake of argument that some form of the incremental equal-weight formulae provides the most adequate substantive standard for assessing the outcomes of political decision procedures. With suitable modifications our conclusions will apply to other outcome-oriented standards as well. The question is whether egalitarian procedures are sufficient to guarantee that the outcomes will be acceptable from this point of view.

The answer is that they are not. Whether egalitarian procedures will produce egalitarian outcomes depends on whether various further conditions are met in the society in which the procedures operate. As Barry has argued, outcomes that are egalitarian in the maximal sense are likely to result from egalitarian procedures (specifically one person, one vote majoritarian legislative procedures with binary choices, but the result can be generalized) only when two conditions are met: "(1) on each issue, each of those who are in the majority stands on the average to gain as much satisfaction from the law as each of those in the minority stands to lose from it; and (2) on each issue there is an independent probability for each person of being in the majority that is equal to the proportion of the total number in the majority on that issue."[20] A third condition is also needed: all (first order) preferences are equally represented in the decision process. (Suppose that we divide the members of a society into groups on the basis of similarities of preference among the options available in an election. All preferences would be equally represented if the voting rates of all groups were equal.)[21]

Barry's first condition is a weakened version of the idea that each preference must represent an equal opportunity for producing satisfaction (one fulfilled preference adds as much as another to the total amount of satisfaction in society). Without this condition, fulfillment of the majority's preferences might not produce a greater gain in satisfaction than fulfillment of the minority's preferences. The first condition, therefore, might be said to hold that there are no *intense* minorities. The second condition reflects the pluralist idea that the diversity of interests in society and the presence of many cross-cutting cleavages guarantee that electoral majorities will be constantly shifting, giving each person in the long run an equal chance of being in the majority more than half of the time. Otherwise there is no assurance that in the long run satisfaction will be distributed equally throughout society. This condition might be said to hold that there are no *permanent* minorities. The third condition is more straightforward: it ensures that the electoral system will accurately register the distribution of preferences. To maintain the parallelism, although with some exaggeration, we might say that this condition holds that there are no *silent* minorities.

Egalitarian procedures guarantee egalitarian results in the maximal sense only if society satisfies all three conditions. But surely few (if any) modern democracies satisfy all three conditions. Therefore, in few (if any) modern democracies could the principle of procedural equality be justified by appeal to the principle of equal consideration. The case for procedural equality is not much strengthened by switching to the minimal interpretation of the equal weight criterion. While we could drop the second condition, the first and third would still be necessary, and these in themselves are too demanding for almost any large contemporary democratic society. Matters only get worse if some other equity standard (such as Rawls's difference principle) is substituted for either version of the incremental equal-weight criterion. Since such standards distinguish between legitimate claims and expressed preferences, the required social conditions would be more rather than less demanding than those we have considered.

In practice, any effort to tailor democratic procedures to specific distributional results will be subject to formidable uncertainties about the political behavior of citizens, as well as to variations in the many other socioeconomic conditions that affect political outcomes. These factors are fluid and it is unlikely that much can be said in general about the relation between alternative configurations of procedures and the distributive characteristics of the resulting decisions. In itself this uncertainty might argue for procedural equality a "focal point solution"[22] to the problem of procedural design. But this is only to say that equality serves as a first approximation of the optimal distribution of opportunities for participation, and that the burden of proof lies with those who advocate procedural inequalities for outcome-oriented reasons.

Even if we accept the equal-weight criterion as a standard for assessing political decisions, therefore, it does not necessarily follow that the distribution of opportunities for political influence should conform to the principle of procedural equality. It is true that procedural equality has historically served as a goal of political reform, but if these reflections are correct this is more likely to be justified by the

tendency of egalitarian procedures to improve the distribution of benefits and burdens relative to that produced under the old regime. This is a second respect in which the argument based on the principle of equal consideration is asymmetrical, since procedural inequalities might be permissible if reasonably calculated to produce further improvements in the quality of political outcomes, assessed from the point of view of whatever interpretation of the principle is adopted.

III

The defects in the two views just considered may be traced to the fact that each holds procedural equality to be instrumental to the satisfaction of the more basic principle of treating persons as equals. In each case empirical premises are needed to connect the more basic principle with procedural equality, and in each case these empirical premises do not appear to be true. Indeed, in each case it is even possible to imagine circumstances in which procedural *in*equalities might be necessary to treat persons as equals (as Mill's advocacy of plural voting illustrates).

It might be thought, however, that procedural equality has intrinsic rather than instrumental value. Perhaps its importance derives from considerations of fairness that override the types of result-oriented considerations discussed above. Such a view seems to represent a widely held intuition. Can reasons be given to back it up?

One plausible account is suggested by an analogy taken with minor changes from Barry.[23] Imagine a railway car which has not been designated either "smoking" or "no smoking" and assume that each of the passengers either wants to smoke or objects to others smoking in the car. Assume also that no other seats are available aboard the train. Finally, suppose that the consequences of failure to agree on a rule about smoking would be such that no one would prefer it to either "smoking" or "no smoking." Now one might think that decisive reasons dictate one decision or the other; but it seems likely that any such reasons would be disputed by those on the other side. Where there are "no presumptions as to merits," Barry suggests that the only decision procedure that has a chance of acceptance all around is one based on procedural equality: each person casts one vote and the majority rules.[24]

This might be true in the following sort of case. It may be that none of the passengers believes that decisive reasons dictate one or the other decision; each regards his or her preference simply as an arbitrary taste, none believes that much damage would be done by either possible outcome of the decision process, and so on. There are "no presumptions as to merits" in the sense that no individual passenger entertains any view about which decision would be best on the merits. In this case each might reason that deciding by majority vote is the best decision procedure, because it will satisfy the greater number of preferences, and no preference has more to be said for it than any other. Now of course this case has few interesting political analogs, and it is clearly not the sort of case that Barry intends. However, if the description of the case is brought closer to the circumstances Barry imagines (and is thereby made more realistic), his conclusion becomes more problematic. According to the amended description, each passenger does have a reasoned belief about which decision would be best, but these beliefs conflict. Each has presumptions as to merits, but *shared* presumptions as to merits are insufficient to generate agreement. Here it is harder to accept majority voting on the grounds that it satisfies the greater number of preferences. Why should those who turn out to be in the minority think it a good thing to satisfy preferences that are unreasonable from their point of view?[25]

Where not only preferences but also the reasons underlying them conflict, a more elaborate explanation of the fairness of procedural equality will be required. One might say that agreement on egalitarian decision procedures represents a compromise that is reasonable when some decision procedure is needed and agreement on the merits of conflicting claims is unlikely to be reached.

Peter Singer advances such an account of procedural equality as a criticism of Mill's plu-ral voting proposal: "Assuming that we did believe Mill's system of voting to be perfectly fair," we should still have to recognize "that it would be impossible to get everyone to agree on who was to have the extra votes." Thus, "it would be wise to put aside beliefs about what would be perfectly fair, and settle for the sort of compromise represented by 'one man, one vote'. . . . As a fair compromise, [this principle] is greatly preferable to a 'fight to the finish' over each controversial issue."[26]

Without questioning the wisdom of procedural equality as a strategic accommodation to the threat of chaos, I do not believe that its "fairness," if based on such a compromise, can carry much moral weight. Certainly this "fairness" is insufficient to justify the claim that equal rights to influence political outcomes are fundamental in the sense of being immune in principle from adjustment to obtain desirable patterns of outcomes. For the criterion of "fairness as a compromise" is simply that it is accepted all around: the features in virtue of which a procedural arrangement is fair are set by what those who will be bound to its results will accept, given that everyone prefers *some* decision procedure to none at all. No independent standard of fairness can be invoked to persuade or criticize someone who refused to accept procedural equality, and nothing in principle prohibits dispensing special favors or procedural advantages to such a hold-out if that were the only way to get him or her to go along. More importantly, nothing prohibits procedural inequalities that yield desirable results if the compliance of a sufficient number of those affected could somehow be guaranteed.

But perhaps it will be objected that this criticism caricatures the ideas of fairness as a compromise by assimilating it too closely to the equilibrium point in a bargaining situation. Not just any compromise counts as fair, it might be said; at a minimum, we want to exclude compromises arrived at under such threats as that of noncompliance in the case of the hold-out imagined above. Here, the idea of a hypothetical agreement suggests itself. Suppose, to return to our railway car, that the passengers were asked what procedure for group decision-making they *would* agree to if they were required to agree without knowing that one matter for decision would be the question of smoking versus no smoking. Surely *then* they would accept procedural equality.

This may true, but it does not salvage the account of fairness as a compromise. The force of arguments concerning what people would have agreed to, when in fact they have not agreed to anything, depends on the reasons any particular agreement would have been reached.[27] It is these reasons that explain the significance that should be attached to the claim that certain people would have agreed to some principle. Hence, we need to consider why procedural equality would be accepted by the passengers in our railway car. There are two interesting possibilities: either the agreement would be the result of a compromise (some procedure is required and this is the only one that everyone would accept), or it would be the result of a convergence of individual judgments about what procedure is antecedently most likely to produce acceptable decisions. If the former, then our earlier problem returns at a new level: the terms of the compromise, and hence its fairness, will merely reflect the balance of bargaining power among the passengers. This may have strategic, but it does not have moral, importance. (Simply to stipulate that bargaining power is equal will not help, since this merely smuggles in the conclusion that requires justification. Moreover, it is not clear that procedural equality would be agreed to even if bargaining power *were* equal; some other principle might be Pareto superior [i.e. might benefit at least one without worsening anybody's situation—ED.] to it.) If the latter, then it needs to be argued that the requisite convergence would indeed emerge, and this will turn out to depend on empirical assumptions like those considered earlier; for example, that cleavages among the passengers are not so deep that one group would have reason to expect permanently to be in the minority. In any event on the latter view the fairness of procedural equality would not consist in its compromise character but in its conduciveness to acceptable results, a position that, for reasons already discussed, is not likely to make good the claim that procedural equality is fundamental.

Perhaps there are other ways of defending procedural equality as a fundamental requirement of fairness; if so, there are reasons to doubt that they would be successful. Assertions that some procedural arrangements are fair invite the question of why *those* arrangements should have a special claim on our support. If one wishes to maintain that fairness is morally fundamental, this question must be answered by showing that the favored procedures have a characteristic whose value is both overriding and independent of considerations about results. But then the further question arises of why the indicated characteristic has overriding value. Simply to respond that procedural fairness has *intrinsic* value is unsatisfying when the choice among alternative procedures makes a difference in the expected results and independent standards for evaluating these results are available. This is particularly true when the requirements of procedural fairness are in dispute. The value of fairness should be susceptible to some more compelling explanation than is provided by the unanalyzed claim that its value is intrinsic. But any other response—including the effort to bring to bear a principle of respect for persons—seems to collapse into an argument from desirable results.[28]

IV

A last argument for procedural equality, which I shall call the argument from liberal stability, can be seen as the residue of Singer's conception of fairness as a compromise once the misleading moral connotations of "fairness" are stripped away. If one were in the position to design political institutions, other things equal, one would want to find ways to encourage compliance with the laws and to promote social order with the least coercive interference in individual lives. One possibility—that pursued by Rousseau in *The Social Contract*—is to constrain the decision-making system so that its outcomes will be (and will be regarded as) in the interests of most of the people most of the time. But this is unrealistic in complex and diverse societies. Another possibility is to build into the system procedural devices that will elicit popular support even when particular decisions disappoint some interests.

A familiar part of the justification of representative government relies on something like the argument from liberal stability. As Barry puts it,

> The most important point about a system of elections for representatives is that it provides an intelligible and determinate answer to the question why these particular people, rather than others perhaps equally well or better qualified, should run the country . . . [O]nce the idea of the natural equality of all men has got about, claims to rule cannot be based on natural superiority. Winning an election is a basis for rule that does not conflict with equality. Indeed, it might be said to flow from it. For if quality is equal (or, as Hobbes more exactly put it, quality must be taken to be equal as a condition of peace) the only differentiating factor left is quantity. . . . Justification for rule in terms of the specific achievements of the government lacks this essential feature of determinateness. Others can always claim that their performance would be superior, and who is to say it would not be?[29]

As I understand him, Barry does not hold that there *are* no objective moral principles for assessing the performance (or expected performance) of representatives. Rather, the idea is that people are likely to disagree about what these principles require and how they should be applied. Moreover, few are likely to allow that some person or group, by virtue of intelligence, birth, or position, is better qualified than anyone else to arbitrate among contending principles. These observations are to be regarded as generalizations from political sociology. Their function in Barry's argument is to define an empirical condition that must be satisfied by any form of government reasonably likely to be voluntarily supported by the bulk of its population.

If this interpretation of the argument is correct, then it is not simply the "determinateness" of representative systems that recommends them. Many systems for choosing public officials are determinate in the ordinary sense of giving an unambiguous answer to the question of who should rule. Indeed, some non-electoral systems are both determinate and consistent with "natural equality" (selec-

tion by lot, for example). What recommends representative government, on this view, must be that it is more likely than any other form of government, in the context of prevailing political attitudes, to elicit continuing popular support.

It is clear that this view rests on several nontrivial empirical premises, but let us grant for the sake of argument at least this much: in modern industrial societies and in normal circumstances, representative institutions with a universal franchise are more likely than any other kind of political institutions to elicit the willing support of their people. The question I would like to explore is whether considerations of liberal stability should incline us to the more exacting position that representative institutions should be procedurally egalitarian.

This depends on the political attitudes of the members of a given society, particularly the extent to which their acceptance of democratic procedures is based on the perception that those procedures are equally open to all. Some such perception probably plays a role in explaining the stability of most modern democracies; if not, at least it is likely that the type and extent of procedural inequalities that any given population will accept are limited. However, the area of indeterminacy seems to be large; while "the idea of the natural equality of all men"[30] has been about for several centuries, procedural equality is a more recent innovation. In the U.S., striking inequalities continue to be tolerated in the less obvious segments of the electoral system (e.g., access to the ballot, campaign financing) with no discernable adverse effect on public acceptance of political decisions. Indeed, it is sometimes said that considerations of liberal stability militate against procedural equality in some of its aspects. For example, some writers argue that the kinds of procedural inequalities that favor two-party as against multi-party (or no-party) systems make for higher levels of acceptance of political decisions by creating incentives for compromise in the pre-election stage of political competition.[31] Therefore, it appears that at least some procedural inequalities are compatible with, and may even be required for, public acceptance of the outcomes produced by democratic procedures. Other, perhaps more striking, inequalities might become compatible with liberal stability if norms and expectations shift; for example, if it came to be thought that some group had been systematically deprived of its appropriate share of social benefits and that some procedural inequality was a suitable remedy. Thus, while considerations of stability place limits on the distributional characteristics of procedural arrangements in democratic systems, these limits are historically variable and do not obviously favor thorough-going procedural equality.

V

The arguments I have criticized appear to represent the most common reasons for accepting the principle of procedural equality. Since there may be other, more persuasive arguments, it would be claiming too much to say that the principle has been shown to be incorrect. Nevertheless, I hope to have raised doubts about the view that procedural equality is a fundamental right, and thus, about the understanding of the democratic ideal that interprets its egalitarian element wholly in procedural terms. Similarly, I hope to have made it plausible that the justification (not to say the rationale) of many of the movements that have historically pressed for egalitarian procedural reforms is to be sought in the redress of substantive inequities in law and society rather than in the realization of some intrinsically important, fundamental procedural right.

It would require another paper to develop an alternative view about the connection between democracy and equality and to explain what such a view implies for controversies about procedural design. Here, I can only indicate briefly and schematically how one might proceed. The alternative view would locate the egalitarian element at a more abstract level: for example, an ideally equal democracy might be said to be one which treats its citizens as moral equals, or perhaps (in the formula cited earlier) as persons equally deserving of concern and respect.[32] Again, this is not very illuminating. To unpack such a formula, one needs a democratic theory in the

wider sense, one which addresses substantive problems of liberty and distributive justice. Problems of procedural design—the issues of democratic theory in its narrower sense— would be worked out with reference to these broader concerns. A theory specifying rules to govern procedural design that was instrumental in this way would inevitably be more complex than that associated with procedural equality; it could not proceed from one basic principle, but would, instead, express a compromise among multiple basic concerns (such as respect for autonomy, distributive justice, and stability) as seen from the point of view of citizens conceived as moral equals.[33] Its application would necessarily involve more extensive reference to empirical considerations. As I have suggested, an instrumental view might recommend different institutional requirements for different contexts, and circumstances can be imagined in which it might not only allow but require inegalitarian procedural arrangements. But procedural inequalities that were justified from this broader point of view would not be *unacceptably* inegalitarian; rather, they would be necessary to ensure that persons would be treated as the moral equals that they are.

Notes

For their critical reactions to previous drafts, I am grateful to David Hoekema, J. Roland Pennock, Thomas Scanlon, Mark Wicclair, and the members of the Yale Legal Theory Workshop, among whom Owen Fiss was especially helpful. The early stages of my work on democratic theory were supported by a Rockefeller Foundation Humanities Fellowship.

1. In formulations differing mainly in details, the principle is endorsed in many recent works of democratic theory. See, e.g., Carole Pateman, *Participation and Democratic Theory* (Cambridge: Cambridge University Press, 1970), p. 43; John Rawls, *A Theory of Justice* (Cambridge: Harvard University Press, 1971), p. 221; Jack Lively, *Democracy* (Oxford: Basil Blackwell, 1975), pp. 8, 16; Amy Gutmann, *Liberal Equality* (Cambridge: Cambridge University Press, 1980), pp. 180–81.

The principle plays an important role, as well, in American constitutional law. It is evoked, for example, by Chief Justice Warren's declaration in *Reynolds v. Sims*, 377 U.S. 533 (1963), that "the fundamental principle of representative government," "the clear and strong command of our Constitution's Equal Protection Clause," "the heart of Lincoln's vision of 'government of the people, by the people, [and] for the people,' " is "substantially equal legislative representation for all citizens. . . ." *Ibid*, at 560, 568. With respect to the size of election districts, the *Reynolds* Court held further that deviations from absolute equality would be acceptable if "based on legitimate considerations incident to the effectuation of a rational state policy." *Ibid.*, at 579. Contrast the more restrictive language of *Wesberry v. Sims*, 376 U.S. 1 (1964): "As nearly as is practicable, one man's vote in a congressional election is to be worth as much as another's" *Ibid.*, at 7–8. A generous reading of all of the election cases, taken together, might allow a more nuanced position than that described here to be attributed to the Court. See, e.g., Laurence H. Tribe, *American Constitutional Law* (Mineola, N.Y.: Foundation Press, 1978), pp. 737–61.

2. There is a particularly illuminating analysis of the possibilities in Jonathan W. Still, "Political Equality and Election Systems," *Ethics* 91, no. 3 (April 1981), pp. 375–94.

3. Such a view derives from Joseph Schumpeter. *Capitalism, Socialism, and Democracy,* 3d ed. (New York: Harper and Bros., 1950), p. 269.

4. Mill suggested that persons of greater intelligence (measured by level of education) be given extra votes, since their political judgment was likely to be superior. J. S. Mill, *Considerations on Representative Government* [1861] (Indianapolis: Liberal Arts Press, 1958), ch. 8, pp. 136–37.

5. This position is maintained, for example, in Justice Brennan's majority opinion in *Kirkpatrick v. Preisler*, 394 U.S. 526 (1969).

6. See Ronald Rogowski, "Representation in Political Theory and in Law," *Ethics* 91, no. 3 (April 1981), p. 397, and the references cited there.

7. Thus, Mill remarked that "In a really equal democracy. . . . [a] majority of the electors would always have a majority of representatives, but a minority of the electors would always have a minority of the representatives. Man for man they would be as fully represented as the major-

ity." *Considerations on Representative Government,* ch. 7, p. 103.

8. The phrase "a priori probability" may be misleading. The probabilities intended are not literally a priori: they are defined against an information base including all relevant features of the actually existing voting arrangements, with the exception that each voter is assigned an equal chance of choosing any of the alternatives available to him. These probabilities are a priori in the special sense that they express the chance that each voter would have of being decisive on an issue if he were equally likely to take any available position on that issue.

9. This is a crude formulation of the standard view in the literature on voting power. It derives from L. S. Shapley and Martin Shubik, "A Method for Evaluating the Distribution of Power in a Committee System," *American Political Science Review* 48, no. 3 (September 1954), pp. 787–92. See also John H. Banzhaf III, "Weighted Voting Doesn't Work: A Mathematical Analysis," *Rutgers Law Review* 19 (Winter 1965), pp. 317–43; and Alvin I. Goldman, "On the Measurement of Social Power," *Journal of Philosophy* 71, no. 8 (May 2, 1974), pp. 231–52.

10. As Dixon puts it, "all districting is gerrymandering" in the sense that the pattern of legislative representation by group or party will always be affected by the system of districting, even when the system is perfectly egalitarian, and whether the effect is intended or accidental. Robert G. Dixon, *Democratic Representation* (New York: Oxford University Press, 1968), p. 462.

11. For the last point, see Banzhaf, "Weighted Voting Doesn't Work," and the same author's "Multi-Member Electoral Districts—Do They Violate the 'One Man, One Vote' Rule?," *Yale Law Journal* 75, no. 8 (July 1966), pp. 1309–38.

12. See Edward R. Tufte, "The Relationship between Seats and Votes in Two-Party Systems," *American Political Science Review* 67, no. 2 (June 1973), pp. 540–54.

13. As Dixon suggests. *Democratic Representation,* p. 463. An argument of this general form is also given in Justice White's majority opinion in *White v. Regester*, 412 U.S. 755 (1973), at 765–69 (multimember districts held unacceptable when they deny adequate legislative representation to groups which were subjects of past discrimination).

14. Ronald M. Dworkin, *Taking Rights Seriously* (Cambridge: Harvard University Press, 1977), pp. 180–83.

15. "Whether it be in the field of individual or social activity, men are not recognizable as men unless, in any given situation, they are using their minds to give direction to their behavior." Alexander Meiklejohn, *Political Freedom* (New York: Harper and Brothers, 1960), p. 13.

16. Lively, *Democracy*, pp. 134–35.

17. Mill, *Considerations on Representative Government*, ch. 8, p. 137.

18. Such a principle is suggested by R. M. Hare, "Rawls's Theory of Justice—II," *Philosophical Quarterly* 23, no. 93 (July 1978), pp. 241–51.

19. A more serious problem—which we need not pursue here—is the reliance of the equal-weight formulae on interests as indices of individual positions rather than on some more objective standard. For a discussion, see Thomas M. Scanlon, "Preference and Urgency," *Journal of Philosophy* 72, no. 19 (November 6, 1975), pp. 655–99.

20. Brian Barry, "Is Democracy Special?," *Philosophy, Politics, and Society*, Fifth Series, ed. Peter Laslett and James Fishkin (New Haven: Yale University Press, 1979), pp. 176–77. It is neglect of these presuppositions that explains G. E. M. Anscombe's peculiar findings in "On the Frustration of the Majority by Fulfillment of the Majority's Will," *Analysis* 36, no. 4 (June 1976), pp. 161–68.

21. This condition is particularly important in view of evidence that participation rates vary with social class in most western democracies. See Sidney Verba, Norman Nie, and Jae-On Kim, *Participation and Political Equality* (Cambridge: Cambridge University Press, 1978), esp. ch. 4.

22. The phrase is Thomas Schelling's. *The Strategy of Conflict* (Cambridge: Harvard University Press, 1960), pp. 57ff.

23. Brian Barry, *Polical Argument* (London: Routledge and Kegan Paul, 1965), p. 312.

24. *Ibid.*

25. This thought is the source of Wollheim's "paradox" of democracy. Richard Wollheim, "A Paradox in the Theory of Democracy," *Philoso-phy, Politics, and Society*, Second Series, ed. Peter Laslett and W. G. Runciman (Oxford: Basil Blackwell, 1962), pp. 71–87.

26. Peter Singer, *Democracy and Disobedience* (New York: Oxford University Press, 1973), p. 35; the order of the phrases has been changed.

27. As Dworkin points out in his review of Rawls's *A Theory of Justice*. See *Taking Rights Seriously*, pp. 150–83.

28. For a helpful further discussion of this last point, see William N. Nelson, *On Justifying Democracy* (London: Routledge and Kegan Paul, 1980), pp. 17–33.

29. Barry, "Is Democracy Special?," p. 193.

30. *Ibid.*

31. For example, Maurice Duverger, *Political Parties*, trans. B. and R. North (London: Methuen, 1954), pp. 216–28, 403–12; Gabriel A. Almond, "Introduction," in G. A. Almond and James S. Coleman, *The Politics of the Developing Areas* (Princeton: Princeton University Press, 1960), esp. pp. 33–45. For a discussion, see Leon Epstein, *Political Parties in Western Democracies* (New York: Praeger, 1967), pp. 73–76.

32. In *On Justifying Democracy*, William N. Nelson defines a similar view. He argues that the most compelling justification of democracy is that it is more likely than any other system for making political decisions to yield just legislation. *Ibid.*, pp. 100–21. While I believe that Nelson is correct in regarding the justification of democracy in instrumental terms, his view is too narrow in concentrating only on the quality of the legislation that democratic systems produce. It is also important that democracies have, historically, been most hospitable to a variety of personal liberties, and that their political cultures have supported the development of habits of critical inquiry and independent judgment about public affairs.

33. An example of a theory of this kind is that developed in Rawls's *A Theory of Justice*. However, Rawls's own discussion of political justice is too abstract, and at some points too ambiguous, to yield clear guidance for many problems of procedural design. *Ibid.*, pp. 221–34.

Complex Proceduralism

Charles Beitz

Despite the concerns he expressed in the preceding section, Charles Beitz believes that political equality is the key to understanding democracy. What features must a political system possess if it is to treat its citizens equally, he asks. His central claim is that equality demands that institutions providing for political participation be justifiable to all citizens, based on the interest they have arising out of their membership in the political community. The three most important of these "interests," he argues, are recognition, equitable treatment, and deliberative responsibility. Democratic procedures are fair since people having these interests would have no reasonable basis to reject the procedures. Beginning with a discussion of the social contract and its connections with this approach, he goes on to discuss each of those three interests citizens have. Democratic procedures, he claims, provide the best chance of achieving just laws that are consistent with a public recognition of each citizen's status as an equal. Beitz concludes with a brief discussion of the contrasts between his theory and other defenses of democracy.

As Hobbes recognized, the members of political society occupy two distinct roles: they are both the "makers" and the "matter" of government, its agents and its objects, its producers and its consumers.[1] Each role constitutes a point of view from which political arrangements can be judged. Hobbes's innovation was to relegate persons conceived as "makers" to a hypothetical act of "authorization" establishing a form of government where there is no place for participation in the choice of leadership or policy, no occasion for political deliberation, no sharing of information, no compromise, no voting, indeed no organized *public* life at all. The measure of a government's success, according to Hobbes, is its ability to induce its people to accept the conception of their political identity implicit in this vision— to accept, that is, the legitimacy of institutions designed to replace the desire to participate in public life with a desire to enjoy a felicitous private one. A government that succeeds in protecting the lives and promoting the satisfaction of the private desires of its people does all that they can reasonably require of it.[2]

The democratic ideal stands in contrast to Hobbes's vision. Its aspiration is a form of government continuously justifiable from both points of view. That political decisions take fair account of each person's prospects is not enough; for, in theory at least, this could be the case in a perfectly impartial dictatorship. As a generic form, democracy is distinguished from the other traditional forms of government by provisions for the regular participation of its citizens in political decisions. The "making" of policy is a shared function of the many, not the exclusive province of one or a few. The uniqueness of democratic forms lies in the fact that the set of rulers and the set of the ruled—the "makers" and the "matter" of politics—for the most part coincide.

This fact defines the philosophical problem to which a theory of political equality is a response, and it explains why any adequate theory must be complex. Popular participation in political decisions is possible only within an institutional framework that organizes and regulates it. But many such frameworks can be imagined, and the basic idea of democracy— that the people should rule—is too protean to settle the choice among them. A theory of political equality must resolve this indeterminacy by identifying the features that institutions for political participation should possess if they can truly be said to treat citizens as equals.

An adequate solution to this problem must be complex because the status of democratic citizenship is complex. The terms of participation in democratic politics should be fair to persons conceived as citizens. However, as both the "makers" and the "matter" of politics, citizens occupy multiple roles and so can judge their institutions from more than one point of view. We must not suppose that the interests of citizens conceived from one of these points of view will always harmonize with their interests conceived from the other or that an effort to secure one kind of interest will not put the other in jeopardy. For example, we can hardly assume a priori that the conditions of participation that would be optimal for the making of responsible judgments about public affairs will be the same as those that would generate political outcomes that would be best for those to whom they apply. Indeed, we must not suppose that either of these points of view, taken separately, defines a single consistent set of aims; either could dissolve on examination into a series of disparate, and potentially conflicting, concerns. It would be a mistake to assume (though in the end, it may prove to be true) that fairness to persons conceived as citizens names a simple, univocal criterion. We may understand it better as a complex criterion that brings together a plurality of values corresponding to both the active and the passive dimensions of citizenship.

Outline of the Theory

. . . I turn here to the more constructive task of formulating an alternative theory that takes account of these lessons. In form, the theory I shall set forth is a hybrid version of the procedural theory; thus, it differs not only from best result and popular will theories but also from simple versions of proceduralism that identify fair participation with procedural equality. To distinguish it from these other views, I call this theory *complex proceduralism*.

The central idea is this. Institutions for

participation should be justifiable to each citizen, taking into account the interests that arise from both aspects of citizenship. We should be able to regard the terms of participation as the object of an agreement that it would be reasonable to expect every citizen to accept. Institutions that satisfy this condition can be said to be egalitarian in the deepest sense: being equally justifiable to each of their members, they recognize each person's status as an equal citizen.

The notion of reasonable agreement is an application of the idea of a social contract to the subject of political equality. As we shall see, this idea has normative consequences: it will rule out any arrangement for participation in political decisions for which no justification of the appropriate form is plausibly available. However, this is not likely to be enough to settle many practical disputes about the structure of democratic institutions. Often, what is at issue is not the *form* of the justification but its *content;* various reasons might be advanced to show why some arrangement is acceptable to all, and the question is whether these reasons ought to be seen as compelling. Hence, the formal conception of contractualist justification needs to be supplemented by a generalized account of the kinds of reasons we are prepared to recognize as grounds for refusing to accede to any particular arrangements for participation.

In complex proceduralism, this account is provided by a doctrine of *regulative interests of citizenship.* These are higher-order interests that represent within the theory the plurality of regulative concerns that arise in connection with the complex status of democratic citizenship. Paramount among these are interests in *recognition, equitable treatment,* and *deliberative responsibility.* Each defines a category of interest it would be reasonable to take into account in assessing the arrangements for participation. Taking the formal and the substantive elements of the theory together, complex proceduralism holds that *the terms of participation are fair if no one who had these ("regulative") interests and who was motivated by a desire to reach agreement with others on this basis could reasonably refuse to accept them.*

Unlike best result and popular will theories, complex proceduralism does not seek criteria for identifying the uniquely best or most desirable institutions; its aim is to identify grounds on which some of the feasible arrangements might reasonably be ruled out. To put it somewhat differently, it seeks criteria that any procedural arrangement should satisfy in order to be regarded as acceptable. . . .

The Idea of a Social Contract

A more detailed account of complex proceduralism should provide an explanation of both its formal and its substantive elements and of the important relationship between them.

Beginning with the social contract framework, there are three questions. First, in view of the variety of interpretations of the contract idea, why adopt so informal a conception as that employed in complex proceduralism? For example, why not impose informational constraints (a "veil of ignorance") on the parties to the agreement? Second, why should we take any interest in the contract idea, so understood? In particular, how is it connected to the traditional aspirations of democratic reform? Third, what is the normative force of this idea? What difference does it make that our conception of political fairness is based on contractualist reasoning rather than on reasoning of some other kind?

There are many ways to understand the idea of a social contract, each importantly different from the others. Later we will note some of the differences; for the moment we concentrate on the common elements. The social contract doctrine is first of all a view about the form that the justification of political principles should take. Like other moral conceptions, contractualism holds that principles should be justifiable from the perspective of everyone affected by them. What is special in contractualism is the attempt to understand this perspective as that of several distinct individuals, combined so that the separateness of each person's point of view is retained. In the classical social contract theories, this idea was expressed metaphorically in the requirement that the original agreement be unani-

mous. To remove the metaphor, we might say, following Scanlon, that contractualism regards moral principles as principles that "no one could reasonably reject as a basis for informed, unforced general agreement," provided they were moved by a desire to reach such an agreement.[3]

The requirement of unanimity reflects what might be called a distributive conception of justification: contractualist principles should be reasonable from each individual point of view. By way of comparison, views in the tradition of classical utilitarianism embody an aggregative conception: the perspective of everyone affected is interpreted as that of society at large, and principles are held to be justified when they are shown to be better, for the community as a whole, than any others, even if from some individual perspectives they appear less reasonable than some alternatives. Thus, although aggregative conceptions hold that principles should be acceptable from the perspective of society, this does not imply that they should be acceptable from the perspective of everyone, taken seriatim. In contrast to contractualist conceptions, utilitarian views might therefore be seen as an application of the idea of rule by the majority.[4] . . .

So understood, the contract doctrine describes a conception of justification that is particularly compatible with the aspirations of modern democratic culture. The Leveller defense of an expanded suffrage was perhaps the first important attempt to invoke these aspirations on behalf of political reform. Commenting on Colonel Rainsborough's famous words, Lindsay wrote: "The poorest has his own life to *live*, not to be managed or drilled or used by other people."[5] The poorest and the richest are equally responsible for the conduct of their own lives and the choice of an individual good and should have equal authority over the public decisions that affect them. Of course, this aspiration would be fully realized only if unanimous consent were required for political decisions and then only if there were grounds for supposing that the status quo ante were itself unanimously accepted; otherwise, someone might find himself coerced to accept, or at least to accommodate himself to, political decisions affecting the conduct of his life that were taken without his consent. Contractualism arises in democratic theory once it is acknowledged that this degree of agreement will not normally obtain on political matters; indeed, it will not normally obtain even at the level of constitutional choice. The most that can be hoped is that institutions will be compatible with principles that no one could reasonably reject, supposing that they were motivated by a desire to find principles that each could justify to everyone else. Then, when someone complains that a procedural arrangement may disappoint her interests, it can be replied that this is the unavoidable result of acting on principles that her fellow citizens could reasonably expect her to accept. Institutions that can be justified in this way come as close as possible to the ideal of respect for each person's final authority over the conduct of her own life.

There are many ways of interpreting the contract idea for normative purposes consistently with this understanding of the source of its appeal. For example, there are more and less formal conceptions, which differ according to the degree to which the background and setting of the original agreement are constrained by counterfactual assumptions about the knowledge, interests, and motivation of the parties. Rawls's theory is an instance of a relatively formal view, which proceeds by offering an account of the circumstances of agreement with sufficient normative content to enable principles to be derived, ideally, by deduction. On the other hand, the theory described by Scanlon is considerably less formal; the parties are imagined to be motivated by a desire to come to agreement but are otherwise conceived as having the knowledge and interests of the actual persons whom they represent. The theory consists of a generalized description of the point of view from which the justification of principles is to be sought and invites substantive argument about the reasons that would be sufficient to justify someone who took up this point of view in rejecting any particular principle. Because the structure of the theory incorporates less normative content than more formal views, it is less determinate in its consequences.

In this sense, complex proceduralism is a relatively informal conception. One reason for adopting such a formulation is that any theory that included sufficient constraints to resolve the main institutional problems concerning political fairness would seem excessively artificial. Another is that the more informal view facilitates a clearer presentation of the considerations relevant to various interpretations of fair participation, and it forces the resolution of conflicts among these considerations into the open, so to speak, rather than allowing them to be concealed within the structure of a more formal theory.

Complex proceduralism is not, however, without significant normative content. We stipulate that the parties have certain regulative interests, that these are higher-order interests in the sense of being controlling in matters of procedural choice, and that the parties are motivated by a desire to reach an agreement that no one who had *these* interests would have sufficient reason to reject in preference to any feasible alternative. These assumptions are clearly significant additions, for they limit the range of considerations that the parties can be imagined to bring to bear on the choice of political procedures. Later, we will consider the basis of these constraints. For the moment, the point to stress is that complex proceduralism is nonetheless an informal view in at least two respects. First, in the construction of the contract situation we do not attempt to correct for the influence of knowledge of people's natural endowments or social situation by imposing informational limitations like the "veil of ignorance." It is true that the regulative interests have a similar effect but only to the extent of preventing the parties from seeking procedural advantages for themselves that conflict with these interests which all are assumed to share. Counterfactual assumptions are made about the motivation of the parties but not about their knowledge of individual circumstance and social context, which is allowed to influence judgments about procedural fairness from the start. Second, no attempt is made to frame the contract situation so that the technical devices of the theory of rational choice can be brought to bear. Thus, for example, there is no claim that the interests of the parties can be represented as individual utility functions or that their reasoning can be meaningfully described as maximizing the satisfaction of these interests.

Whereas the first point shows that in complex proceduralism the interests that explain agreement function as substantive constraints on the deliberations of the parties rather than as structural elements of the model itself, the second indicates that the problem of combining these interests to yield a decision on any particular issue of procedural design must be treated as a freestanding moral issue to be worked out more or less intuitively in a way that takes account of the historical circumstances in which the procedures are to operate. By leaving so much to be worked out by moral reasoning of the ordinary kind, we forbear from representing the agreement, so to speak, as the output of an axiomatic decision procedure or from claiming that the model is capable of generating by its own rules determinate decisions in the choices facing the parties.

These remarks provide answers to the first two of our questions about the contract idea—why we should interpret it so informally and why, so interpreted, its consequences should matter to us. However, the effect is to make the third question—about the normative force of contractualism—more pressing. For in view of what I have said thus far, the following objection will arise. The substantive elements of the theory—that is, the regulative interests—appear to do all of the normative work. These interests furnish the main basis for resolving disputes about procedural design; the contractualist framework seems not to contribute anything of its own. One might therefore wonder why it should not be seen as empty: a mere formality serving only to rationalize conclusions that would be fully determined by the regulative interests alone.

The answer to this objection has two parts. First, there is no need to deny that the doctrine of regulative interests has normative content. However, to grant this is not also to agree that the contract idea is empty. As a contractualist view, complex proceduralism holds that institutions should be justifiable to *each* person who comes under their sway; it should be possible to say to each person that the terms of participation are acceptable from her own point of view, given her social and historical circumstances, when this point of view is conceived as that of an equal citizen of a democratic society. [I]t may be relevant, but it can-

not be enough, that institutions yield outcomes that are best for society at large or that they generate decisions that accord with a technical construction of the popular will. For neither condition ensures that each citizen would have reason to accept the institutions when they are regarded from her own point of view. This would be true even if what is "best for society at large" could somehow be interpreted as a function of the regulative interests: complex proceduralism does not seek to maximize the aggregate, societywide level of satisfaction of these interests. It is true that by postulating a set of higher-order interests that motivate the choices of the parties, we restrict the bounds of possible agreement. But what is being restricted are the bounds of possible *agreement:* it is the set of procedural arrangements one could reasonably expect each of his fellow citizens to accept. There is no reason to believe that arrrangements that satisfy this requirement will normally, if ever, yield the highest level of interest-satisfaction in society at large.

Second, and more basically, the regulative interests themselves stand in need of justification. Otherwise, the claim that they should be assigned a privileged position in reasoning about political fairness would seem arbitrary: we would have provided no special reason to care about them. I have said that these interests represent within the theory various elements of an ideal of democratic citizenship. But this ideal is not, so to speak, imposed on the theory from the outside; as we shall see, the theory seeks to provide an account of its appeal by connecting it with values we are prepared to accept as reasonable grounds for objecting to a procedural arrangement. The regulative interests themselves have a contractualist justification. Their prominence within the theory is not, therefore, an indication that the contractualist framework is normatively empty; indeed, it is only by accepting the framework that their prominence can be accounted for.

Regulative Interests of Citizenship

An explanation of the interests in recognition, equitable treatment, and deliberative responsibility should specify their content and show why it is reasonable to regard them in furnishing grounds for refusing to accept a procedural regime.

Imagine that citizens could meet to establish the terms of participation that their institutions should embody. We assume that the institutions are generically democratic [*i.e. that some form of universal participation is adopted*—ED.]; the question is not whether people should be entitled to participate in political decisions but how the mechanism of participation is to be arranged. What kinds of considerations would it be reasonable to take into account in assessing the alternatives?

It would be convenient if a catalog of these considerations could be exhibited as a systematic deduction from some more abstract and widely accepted conception of democratic citizenship. As no such deduction presents itself, we must proceed inductively, attempting to construct such a conception from more particularistic judgments. Thus, we might reflect on various procedural arrangements that would be widely agreed to be objectionable. We may regard such cases as *paradigmatic*[6] of procedural unfairness; they are ones about which most people's judgments converge. They might include, for example, weighted voting by race, systems of representation that favor certain minority interests (say, those of the landed gentry), unrestricted majority rule and the idea of majority tyranny, ballot access regulations that exclude popular candidates or positions from consideration, or imbalances in election campaign resources that give a decisive advantage to incumbents.

In considering each case, we should try to explain at a general level the reasons that would justify someone in objecting to the procedural arrangement in question. Any such explanation must be *constructive*. That is, we do not aim for a description of the actual basis of people's objections to the kinds of unfairness found in the paradigmatic cases; instead, we seek an account that seems maximally plausible in view of the characteristics of the case at hand, keeping in mind the desire to produce a more general conception of political fairness that coheres with the accounts that can be provided for the other cases as well. Accordingly, judgments about the reasonableness of objections to paradigmatic cases of unfairness will

normally have a two-level structure. First, a weight must be assigned to the interest motivating the objection (the "harm"), reflecting its objective importance or urgency. By "objective" I mean, roughly, that the weight of the harm should reflect the degree of importance or urgency one could expect others in society to accord to it. It is not sufficient to rely on an agent's own subjective valuations; someone who detests being awake while the sun shines should have less weight attached to his objection to daytime voting hours than someone whose fourteen-hour-a-day job keeps him at work from dawn to dusk, even if each attaches equal subjective importance to his objection. Second, the harm must be compared with the harms to other interests that might be anticipated under the feasible alternative arrangements, again taking into account their objective importance. For, clearly, supposing that everyone is moved by a desire to reach *some* agreement, it would not be reasonable to refuse to accept an institutional arrangement, even if it would do harm, if the alternatives would be even worse.

The three categories of values I have identified as regulative interests arise from reflection about paradigmatic cases of procedural unfairness. Each interest represents a type of reason that would justify someone in refusing to accept a procedural arrangement.

The interest in *recognition* involves the public status or identity that procedural roles assign to those who occupy them. Political procedures define the terms on which citizens recognize each other as participants in public deliberation and choice. In the extreme case, when some people are excluded entirely from any public role (as, for example, with the wholesale denial of the franchise to blacks in the antebellum South), it has been said that those excluded "are not publicly recognized as persons at all" and might be described as "socially dead."[7] Something similar occurs when procedural roles are assigned in a way that conveys social acceptance of a belief in the inferiority or lesser merit of one group as distinct from others—as, for example, with racially weighted voting or efforts to dilute the votes of racial minorities through the use of gerrymandering techniques. Those singled out as less worthy are demeaned and insulted; they are encouraged to feel that patterns of disrespect that exist in society at large enjoy official sanction. It would be reasonable for anyone to object to procedural arrangements that had this effect. This is not simply because, from a subjective point of view, it is unpleasant or painful to be assigned a demeaning role in public procedures, although this is certainly true. The objection has a more objective foundation—not because it rests on some transcendent or immutable standard of value, but rather because it is a fixed point in a democratic culture that public institutions should not establish or reinforce the perception that some people's interests deserve less respect or concern than those of others simply in virtue of their membership in one rather than another social or ascriptive group. The political roles defined by democratic institutions should convey a communal acknowledgment of equal individual worth.

Because it bears so directly on the definition of the procedural roles in which people participate in public decisions, the interest in recognition corresponds to the point of view of citizens as "makers." The interest in *equitable treatment* corresponds instead to that of citizens as "matter." The basic idea is that citizens might reasonably refuse to accept institutions under which it was predictable that their actual interests—that is, the satisfaction of their needs and the success of their projects—would be unfairly placed in jeopardy, at least if there were alternatives that would avoid these effects without imposing even worse risks on others. Normally, we rely on democratic mechanisms themselves to guard against the oppressive use of state power; however, recognizing that these may not always be sufficient, we are prepared to supplement them with further constraints such as a bill of rights, judicial review, and the like. Without these further protections, democratic forms might reasonably be seen as so dangerous as to be unacceptable.

The idea of equitable treatment is difficult to render more precisely primarily because it is uncertain how the notion of an interest's being "unfairly placed in jeopardy" should be interpreted. It seems clear that procedural interpretations will not suffice; one ought not to say, for example, that a person's interests are unfairly jeopardized when institutions accord the person less than an equal share in power or influence over the relevant class of decisions. This follows from our earlier observations about power: many manipulable factors can affect a person's prospects in a procedural regime; the extent of his power is only one (and ordinarily not the most important) of these. As the example of entrenched minorities illustrates, one's interests might be placed in great jeopardy even when power is equal. The interest in equitable treatment needs a more substantive interpretation.

One possibility is to identify equitable treatment with the principle that political decisions should aim to generate equal increments of preference- or interest-satisfaction. However, here we face a familiar difficulty: whereas any such principle must presuppose that the *ex ante* distribution was morally satisfactory, as a general matter we have no reason to believe this. People would not necessarily be justified in objecting to participatory mechanisms that lead to unequal increments in preference- or interest-satisfaction if the inequalities worked to the benefit of those whose most urgent needs would otherwise be placed in jeopardy. Suppose, for example, that a choice was to be made between two systems of legislative representation, each of which guaranteed everyone equal procedural opportunities to influence the choice of representatives. If those with the greater or more urgent needs would tend to do better in one system than in the alternative, those who would fare worse in that system could not reasonably complain simply because another system would be better for them. Since what is at issue is the contribution of particular decisions to each person's global situation rather than the distributive characteristics of individual political decisions viewed in isolation, there seems to be no alternative to relying on substantive views concerning social justice to render a complete account. Political decisions could then be said to satisfy the interest in equitable treatment when, over time, they promote (or do not systematically detract from) a distribution that accords with the requirements of justice, which are themselves to be worked out from a point of view in which each person's prospects are taken equally into account.

It may be surprising that a theory of political fairness should incorporate a concern for the substantive characteristics of political outcomes. For people's conceptions of equity differ; if the present view were widely accepted, then disagreement about the meaning of political fairness would be endemic. But this hardly seems consistent with the notion that a main function of the idea of fairness is to regulate the social processes through which substantive disagreements are adjudicated, or at least, compromised.

In response, there are two points. First, it is no misrepresentation of our pre-theoretical views about political fairness to hold that result-oriented considerations sometimes play a role. Consider, for example, the traditional democratic concern about the dangers of majority tyranny and the protection of minority rights. The idea that fair institutions should contain safeguards against the oppressive use of state power by popular majorities would be incomprehensible unless the concept of oppression had some substantive content. Moreover, as a matter of descriptive accuracy, it does not seem wrong to characterize some procedural disputes as reflections of underlying disagreements about the nature of the outcomes that procedures should produce. The account I have offered recognizes this by relativizing the requirements of fairness to underlying views about acceptable results. (To say this is not *also* to say that the underlying disagreeements are incapable of principled resolution.)

Second, the direction of political decisions is determined by a great variety of factors, among which the structure of the system of political participation plays at best a subordinate role. It is unrealistic to think that, by a series of fine manipulations of this structure, small improvements in the distributive characteristics of political outcomes could often be guaranteed. Hence, the interest in equitable treatment is likely to operate more selectively and at a greater remove. It will justify a refusal to accept an institutional scheme mainly when it seems likely that the scheme will give rise to (or perpetuate) serious and recurring injustices and when there is an alternative available that would be less likely to do so without introducing countervailing harms of other kinds. Thus, in the context of reasoning about

political procedures, the interest in equitable treatment will normally appear as an interest in safeguarding one's urgent or vital interests in the face of the threat that they might be systematically subordinated to the competing but less urgent claims of others. While there may be considerable disagreement in society about conceptions of social justice and the common good, it seems likely that the prospects of convergence are greatest in connection with the most vital of human interests. So, although the chances that substantive disagreement will generate procedural controversy cannot be ruled out, they need not pose too great a difficulty.

Now the central virtue of democratic forms is that, in the presence of a suitable social background, they provide the most reliable means of reaching substantively just political outcomes consistently with the public recognition of the equal worth or status of each citizen.[8] Democratic forms succeed in achieving this aim, when they succeed at all, less because they aggregate existing preferences efficiently than because they foster a process of public reflection in which citizens can form political views in full awareness of the grounds as well as the content of the (possibly competing) concerns of others.[9] It is a mistake to conceive democracy as a crude hydraulic device, moving society in the direction of the greater power. Instead, we must understand it as a deliberative mechanism that frames the formation and revision of individual political judgments in a way likely to elicit outcomes that treat everyone's interests equitably. The characteristics of preference-aggregating devices are clearly significant for an assessment of the fairness of the system as a whole, but they should be seen as parts of a larger deliberative framework.

These observations illustrate the significance of the third regulative interest, in *deliberative responsibility:* democratic institutions should embody a common (and commonly acknowledged) commitment to the resolution of political issues on the basis of public deliberation that is adequately informed, open to the expression of a wide range of competing views, and carried out under conditions in which these views can be responsibly assessed. This is important for reasons connected with both of the points of view characteristic of citizenship. Citizens conceived as participants in public decisions (Hobbes's "makers") will wish to regard their judgments as the most reasonable ones possible under the circumstances; such judgments should be formed in light of the relevant facts and should be defensible in the face of the conflicting views held by others in the community. If individual judgment could not be seen as justifiable in this way, it would be indistinguishable from prejudice; and this should be intolerable for anyone who takes seriously her responsibility for her own beliefs. On the other hand, for citizens conceived as the objects of public policy (its "matter"), the awareness that institutions encourage responsible deliberation is a necessary basis of confidence in the integrity of political decisions and, indeed, of the system of participation itself. Without this, the supposed tendency of democratic mechanisms to elicit equitable outcomes would be no more than a pious hope, and an important ground of the stability of democratic regimes would be lacking.

The interest in deliberative responsibility has two elements, which may be in conflict. The first is openness: deliberation should not be constrained by the exclusion of positions that would gain substantial support if they were sufficiently exposed to public scrutiny. Thus, someone might reasonably object if widely supported candidates or positions were excluded from the political arena by such mechanisms as restrictive ballot access regulations or a distribution of campaign resources that gave some parties or positions a decisive advantage in access to the principal fora of public debate. Such an objection would be reasonable partly because exclusionary provisions could prevent people from representing their own interests in public deliberation; but even if this were not the case, exclusion of positions widely held by others would be objectionable because it would suppress information and points of view that would be essential for all citizens in reaching responsible judgments about the public good. The other element involves the quality of the deliberative process itself: the conditions of public deliberation should be favorable to the thoughtful consideration and comparative assessment of all of the positions represented. Citizens should

be enabled to reach political judgments on the basis of an adequately informed and reflective comparison of the merits of the contending positions. Only then will they have reason to conduct themselves as cooperating members of a public deliberative enterprise, to exercise the capacities for judgment and choice in the public realm, and to regard others as similarly equipped and motivated.

Both elements are part of the nature of responsible deliberation. The potential for conflict arises from the fact that the conditions of public deliberation may be maximally favorable to the thoughtful assessment of the alternatives only if the number of alternatives to be considered is not too large. There is no guarantee that the range of alternatives that elicit nontrivial numbers of adherents will always fall within this limit. The interest in seeing a wide range of positions represented argues for openness, but the interest in conditions of public deliberation in which political judgments can be adequately informed and reflective argues, at least under some circumstances, for constraint. It is not easy to generalize about how such conflicts are most appropriately to be reconciled. In practice, any reconciliation will be heavily influenced by local considerations concerning the context in which the conflict arises and the impact that one or another way of resolving it seems likely to have on satisfaction of the other regulative interests. However such conflicts are resolved (and they may of course not arise at all), the interest in deliberative responsibility clearly expresses an important requirement on the choice of institutions for political participation and one which is distinct from those embodied in the other regulative interests.

The interests I have identified function within the theory as the criteria by which political institutions and procedures are to be assessed when they are regarded from each person's point of view. Although it would be surprising if things were otherwise, there is no claim that all citizens, in fact, conceive themselves as having these interests or are motivated to accord them a controlling position in actual political deliberation. This fact gives rise to an objection we have already anticipated: why not regard the regulative interests as no more than an arbitrary selection from the much wider range of values reflected in people's actual aims and preferences? And why endow them with a higher-order status, so that they eclipse people's more particularistic concerns in informing judgments about procedural design?

The answer is that these interests give theoretical expression to certain aspects of a normative conception of democratic citizenship, which is implicit in our ordinary judgments about political fairness and which we are prepared to accept as determining in matters of procedural choice. The list of regulative interests, and their interpretations, is derived from a consideration of cases of procedural unfairness that we may regard as paradigmatic. The diversity of the interests reflects the complexity of the status of membership in a democratic society, and the desire to realize this status on terms compatible with a similar realization by everyone else is taken to be the fundamental motivation for concern about procedural fairness. If the distinctive egalitarianism of the view is found in its contractualist framework, its distinctive idealism lies in this motivational aspect.

Finally, as I have suggested, a choice among institutions must rest on a consideration of how the alternatives affect all three kinds of interests. However, there is no reason to believe that the regulative interests will always coincide; indeed, it would be surprising if they did not occasionally conflict. A possible response would be to deny that, under the circumstances, *any* institutions could be fair. Perhaps there are cases so extreme that this is what we must say. However, this need not always be true: a degree of sacrifice in one interest may be a reasonable expectation, particularly when it is made up by gains in another. Because the regulative interests are irreducibly plural, it is unlikely that any systematic mechanism can be set forth for reconciling conflicts; one is forced to rely on an intuitive balancing of competing values. This is not an insuperable difficulty, particularly when the range of interests that enter at the foundational level is restricted and the grounds of their importance are reasonably clear. In part 2, [*omitted here*—ED.] I shall illustrate this by considering how complex proceduralism applies to several controversial

problems of institutional design. Here, I note a related point. One must recall that we are driven to adopt a theory like complex proceduralism by a recognition of the diversity of the considerations it seems natural to take into account in assessing political institutions. It is neglect of some of these, and excessive concentration on others, that gives rise to the critical defects of more conventional theories of political equality. The need to rely on intuitive comparisons of conflicting and irreducible interests may seem less than satisfactory from a theoretical point of view, but it is an unavoidable reflection in democratic theory of the variety of ways in which political institutions touch people's lives.

Contrasts with Other Views

Complex proceduralism differs from [other] views . . . in several respects. First, the form of proceduralism I have sketched is not in any straightforward sense instrumentalist. Fair terms of participation are not conceived as those most likely to succeed at producing outcomes that strike some independently identified target, whether this is described in terms of the substantive characteristics of desirable political decisions or the relationship of the decisions actually taken to the political preferences held by the people. Of course, both types of concerns may play a role in complex proceduralism, but this role is neither definitive nor morally basic; there are always further questions about why a given kind of outcome-oriented concern should matter and how it should be balanced against the other regulative concerns with which it may conflict.

Moreover, as I have emphasized, there is no a priori reason to assume that these interests will always be complementary, and it may be necessary to balance them against one another. Now the weights it would be appropriate to assign to these interests when they conflict may depend in part on a society's historical circumstances. For example, the interest in protecting against the political effects of racial bigotry and prejudice will be more weighty where its legacy is more pronounced.

Hence, the theory contains some residual indeterminacy. Of course, the application of any abstract conception of political fairness will require some reference to the circumstances of the society in question. What is different about complex proceduralism is where, within the theory, historical considerations play a role: here they may enter at the foundational level of the theory—in judgments about appropriate weights for the regulative interests—as well as at the level of application. In other words, the theory's conception of fairness may itself remain partially indeterminate until the context of its application is taken into account. This does not seem to me to be objectionable; in fact, it might be seen as a virtue of a theory of political equality that it takes account of historical considerations in a way that more faithfully represents their actual effects on intuitive judgments about fair participation.

Third, this theory is primarily negative. It does not attempt to describe ideal conditions that institutions should strive to satisfy; rather, it seeks an account of the forms of unfairness that they should strive to avoid. (Of course, it need not follow that considerations of fairness *operate* only negatively, for example, by ruling out institutions with this or that objectionable feature; sometimes the avoidance of unfairness requires institutional provisions that might be characterized as affirmative.) I believe this feature of the theory is consistent with the characteristic role of political equality in controversy about the structure of democratic institutions: it is invoked more often to support criticism of the established order than as a description of a constructive ideal. Moreover, I believe that it accords with our intuitions about a variety of questions of policy: when a particular procedure is uncontroversially unfair, it is frequently possible to give an account of the reasons for the unfairness without committing oneself to a view about the nature of a uniquely preferable alternative.

This points to a fourth contrast in other theories.[10] According to at least the more familiar versions of the best result and popular will theories, there is always a uniquely best solution (or, in the case of indifference, class of solutions) to the problem of social choice. Thus, the fact that under certain circumstances a decision procedure operating on the same utility or preference information might produce either of two (or more) inconsistent outcomes must be deeply embarrassing: it shows either that there is some deficiency in the theory or that under these circumstances the ideal of fair participation is unattainable. . . . A consequence of the negative character of complex proceduralism is that its requirements may be satisfied in more than one way; several institutional structures, each perhaps likely to have different or even inconsistent political results, may be equally fair. But this need not be cause for concern. Because institutions are not evaluated simply with respect to the outcomes they are likely to produce, it is no occasion for unease, for example, that institutions that are equally fair according to the theory might generate inconsistent outcomes given identical information about people's preferences. This is not to say that it will never be occasion for concern *within* the theory: if, for example, considerations of stability indicate that institutions should normally produce outcomes that bear a predictable relationship to the political preferences in society, then the possibility that a particular decision procedure may give rise to inconsistency will count against that procedure. It will be one among many factors to be taken into account in comparing that procedure with the feasible alternatives. Moreover, the fact that several institutional configurations may be equally fair does not mean that they will be equally desirable overall; for example, considerations relevant to the vitality of political culture might incline toward one or another alternative. What complex proceduralism requires is that these considerations operate within the range of equally fair alternatives. It is no reason for embarrassment that there may be more than one of these.

Notes

---

1. Thomas Hobbes, *Leviathan* [1651] (New York: Collier Books, 1962), pp. 19, 229 (the passages occur in the "Author's Introduction" and chap. 28). The centrality of the distinction in Hobbes's

thought was first made clear to me by Michael Walzer in a lecture presented in Princeton in 1973.

2. This is reflected in Hobbes's conception of the social contract as an undertaking in which people surrender their power to a sovereign (an "alienation" contract), rather than as one in which their power is merely "loaned," subject to certain conditions on its use (an "agency" contract). For this distinction, see Jean Hampton, *Hobbes and the Social Contract Tradition* (Cambridge: Cambridge University Press, 1986), pp. 3–4, 256–79.

3. T. M. Scanlon, "Contractualism and Utilitarianism," in *Utilitarianism and Beyond,* ed. Amartya Sen and Bernard Williams (Cambridge: Cambridge University Press, 1982), p. 110. My interpretation of the social contract idea is greatly indebted to this article throughout.

4. Thomas Nagel, "Equality," in *Mortal Questions* (Cambridge: Cambridge University Press, 1979), p. 112.

5. A. D. Lindsay, *The Essentials of Democracy,* Lectures on the William J. Cooper Foundation of Swarthmore College (Philadelphia: University of Pennsylvania Press, 1929), p. 13 (emphasis in original).

6. The term is used this way by Ronald Dworkin: *Law's Empire* (Cambridge: Harvard University Press, 1986), p. 75.

7. John Rawls, "Justice as Fairness: Political not Metaphysical," *Philosophy & Public Affairs* 14 (1985), p. 243. For the idea of "social death," see Orlando Patterson, *Slavery and Social Death* (Cambridge: Harvard University Press, 1982).

8. This is a comparative judgment; it need not presuppose any very optimistic noncomparative view about the tendency of democratic institutions to produce just outcomes.

9. As Pericles famously (if, perhaps, self-servingly) put it, ". . . instead of looking on discussion as a stumbling-block in the way of action, we think it an indispensable preliminary to any wise action at all. . . ." Thucydides. *The Peloponnesian War,* trans. John H. Finley, Jr. (New York: Modern Library, 1951), II.40, p. 105.

10. I am grateful to Thomas Scanlon for pointing this out.

5

Workplace
Democracy

The Case of Pullman, Illinois

Michael Walzer

Unlike political philosophers who seek universal principles of justice applicable to all societies, Walzer contends political argument must take place within a particular community with its own history and tradition. Different communities will view the goods it distributes, including political power, wealth, jobs and status, in different ways. These different types of goods are given social meanings that determine how they should be distributed, so that punishment should be distributed according to whether it is deserved, university places according to merit, jobs according to the needs of employers, economic wealth according to the free market, and health care and other basic necessities according to need based on membership. Each category should thus be distributed in accord with its own "internal logic." But while that is our ideal, it is sometimes not realized: one good, for example, wealth, may be used to acquire goods in another sphere, for example, by purchasing political power through vote-buying or places in a university through donations. In the following selection from his book, Walzer discusses the ways in which political power and property are related. Arguing that industrial democracy is just as important as political democracy, he focuses on the company town of Pullman, Illinois. Ownership of property cannot be allowed to dominate politics. There is no relevant difference between a factory and a town that could justify democracy in the town but not the factory.

Ownership is properly understood as a certain sort of power over things. Like political power, it consists in the capacity to determine destinations and risks—that is, to give things away or to exchange them (within limits) and also to keep them and use or abuse them, freely deciding on the costs in wear and tear. But ownership can also bring with it various sorts and degrees of power over people. The extreme case is slavery, which far exceeds the usual forms of political rule. I am concerned here, however, not with the actual possession, but only with the control, of people—mediated by the possession of things; this is a kind of power closely analogous to that which the state exercises over its subjects and disciplinary institutions over their inmates. Ownership also has effects well short of subjection. People engage with one another, and with institutions too, in all sorts of ways that reflect the momentary inequality of their economic positions. I own such-and-such book, for example, and you would like to have it; I am free to decide whether to sell or lend or give it to you or keep it for myself. We organize a factory commune and conclude that so-and-so's skills do not suit him for membership. You gather your supporters and defeat me in the competition for a hospital directorship. Their company squeezes out ours in intense bidding for a city contract. These are examples of brief encounters. I see no way to avoid them except through a political arrangement that systematically replaces the encounters of men and women with what Engels once called "the administration of things"—a harsh response to what are, after all, normal events in the spheres of money and office. But what sovereignty entails, and what ownership sometimes achieves (outside its sphere), is sustained control over the destinations and risks of other people; and that is a more serious matter. . . .

George Pullman was one of the most successful entrepreneurs of late nineteenth century America. His sleeping, dining, and parlor cars made train travel a great deal more comfortable than it had been, and only somewhat more expensive; and on this difference of degree, Pullman established a company and a fortune. When he decided to build a new set of factories and a town around them, he insisted that this was only another business venture. But he clearly had larger hopes: he dreamed of a community without political or economic unrest—happy workers and a strike-free plant.[1] He clearly belongs, then, to the great tradition of the political founder, even though, unlike Solon of Athens, he didn't enact his plans and then go off to Egypt, but stayed on to run the town he had designed. What else could he do, given that he owned the town?

Pullman, Illinois, was built on a little over four thousand acres of land along Lake Calumet just south of Chicago, purchased (in seventy-five individual transactions) at a cost of eight hundred thousand dollars. The town was founded in 1880 and substantially completed, according to a single unified design, within two years. Pullman (the owner) didn't just put up factories and dormitories, as had been done in Lowell, Massachusetts, some fifty years earlier. He built private homes, row houses, and tenements for some seven to eight thousand people, shops and offices (in an elaborate arcade), schools, stables, playgrounds, a market, a hotel, a library, a theater, even a church: in short, a model town, a planned community. And every bit of it belonged to him.

> A stranger arriving at Pullman puts up at a hotel managed by one of Mr. Pullman's employees, visits a theater where all the attendants are in Mr. Pullman's service, drinks water and burns gas which Mr. Pullman's water and gas works supply, hires one of his outfits from the manager of Mr. Pullman's livery stable, visits a school in which the children of Mr. Pullman's employees are taught by other employees, gets a bill charged at Mr. Pullman's bank, is unable to make a purchase of any kind save from some tenant of Mr. Pullman's, and at night he is guarded by a fire department every member of which from the chief down is in Mr. Pullman's service.[2]

This account is from an article in the *New York Sun* (the model town attracted a lot of attention), and it is entirely accurate except for the line about the school. In fact, the schools of

Pullman were at least nominally run by the elected school board of Hyde Park Township. The town was also subject to the political jurisdiction of Cook County and the State of Illinois. But there was no municipal government. Asked by a visiting journalist how he "governed" the people of Pullman, Pullman replied, "We govern them in the same way a man governs his house, his store, or his workshop. It is all simple enough.[3] Government was, in his conception, a property right; and despite the editorial "we," this was a right singly held and singly exercised. In his town, Pullman was an autocrat. He had a firm sense of how its inhabitants should live, and he never doubted his right to give that sense practical force. His concern, I should stress, was with the appearance and the behavior of the people, not with their beliefs. "No one was required to subscribe to any set of ideals before moving to [Pullman]." Once there, however, they were required to live in a certain way. Newcomers might be seen "lounging on their doorsteps, the husband in his shirt-sleeves, smoking a pipe, his untidy wife darning, and half-dressed children playing about them." They were soon made aware that this sort of thing was unacceptable. And if they did not mend their ways, "company inspectors visited to threaten fines."[4]

Pullman refused to sell either land or houses—so as to maintain "the harmony of the town's design" and also, presumably, his control over the inhabitants. Everyone who lived in Pullman (Illinois) was a tenant of Pullman (George). Home renovation was strictly controlled; leases were terminable on ten days' notice. Pullman even refused to allow Catholics and Swedish Lutherans to build churches of their own, not because he opposed their worship (they were permitted to rent rooms), but because his conception of the town called for one rather splendid church, whose rent only the Presbyterians could afford. For somewhat different reasons, though with a similar zeal for order, liquor was available only in the town's one hotel, at a rather splendid bar, where ordinary workers were unlikely to feel comfortable.

I have stressed Pullman's autocracy; I could also stress his benevolence. The housing he provided was considerably better than that generally available to American workers in the

1880s; rents were not unreasonable (his profit margins were in fact quite low); the buildings were kept in repair; and so on. But the crucial point is that all decisions, benevolent or not, rested with a man, governor as well as owner, who had not been chosen by the people he governed. Richard Ely, who visited the town in 1885 and wrote an article about it for *Harper's Monthly* called it "unAmerican . . . benevolent, well-wishing feudalism."[5] But that description wasn't quite accurate, for the men and women of Pullman were entirely free to come and go. They were also free to live outside the town and commute to work in its factories, though in hard times Pullman's tenants were apparently the last to be laid off. These tenants are best regarded as the subjects of a capitalist enterprise that has simply extended itself from manufacturing to real estate and duplicated in the town the discipline of the shop. What's wrong with that?

I mean the question to be rhetorical, but it is perhaps worthwhile spelling out the answer. The inhabitants of Pullman were guest workers, and that is not a status compatible with democratic politics. . . .

Ely argued that Pullman's ownership of the town made its inhabitants into something less than American citizens: "One feels that one is mingling with a dependent, servile people." Apparently, Ely caught no intimations of the great strike of 1894 or of the courage and discipline of the strikers.[6] He wrote his article early on in the history of the town; perhaps the people needed time to settle in and learn to trust one another before they dared oppose themselves to Pullman's power. But when they did strike, it was as much against his factory power as against his town power. Indeed, Pullman's foremen were even more tyrannical than his agents and inspectors. It seems odd to study the duplicated discipline of the model town and condemn only one half of it. Yet this was the conventional understanding of the time. When the Illinois Supreme Court in 1898 ordered the Pullman Company (George Pullman had died a year earlier) to divest itself of all property not used for manufacturing purposes, it argued that the ownership of a town, but not of a company, "was incompatible with the theory and spirit of our institutions."[7] The town had to be governed democratically—not so much because ownership made the inhabitants servile, but because it forced them to fight for rights they already possessed as American citizens.

It is true that the struggle for rights in the factory was a newer struggle, if only because factories were newer institutions than cities and towns. I want to argue, however, that with regard to political power democratic distributions can't stop at the factory gates. The deep principles are the same for both sorts of institution. This identity is the moral basis of the labor movement—not of "business unionism," which has another basis, but of every demand for progress toward industrial democracy. It doesn't follow from these demands that factories can't be owned; nor did opponents of feudalism say that land couldn't be owned. It's even conceivable that all the inhabitants of a (small) town might pay rent, but not homage, to the same landlord. The issue in all these cases is not the existence but the entailments of property. What democracy requires is that property should have no political currency, that it shouldn't convert into anything like sovereignty, authoritative command, sustained control over men and women. After 1894, at least, most observers seem to have agreed that Pullman's ownership of the town was undemocratic. But was his ownership of the company any different? The unusual juxtaposition of the two makes for a nice comparison.

They are not different because of the entrepreneurial vision, energy, inventiveness, and so on that went into the making of Pullman sleepers, diners, and parlor cars. For these same qualities went into the making of the town. This, indeed, was Pullman's boast: that his " 'system' which had succeeded in railroad travel, was now being applied to the problems of labor and housing."[8] And if the application does not give rise to political power in the one case, why should it do so in the other?*

---

*But perhaps it was Pullman's expertise, not his vision, energy, and so on, that justified his autocratic rule. Perhaps factories should be assimilated to the category of disciplinary institutions and run by scientific managers. But the same argument might be made for towns. Indeed, professional managers are often hired by town councils; they are subject, however, to the authority of the elected councilors. Factory managers are subject, though often ineffectively, to the authority of owners. And so the question remains: Why owners rather than workers (or their elected representatives)?

Nor are the two different because of the investment of private capital in the company. Pullman invested in the town, too, without thereby acquiring the right to govern its inhabitants. The case is the same with men and women who buy municipal bonds: they don't come to own the municipality. Unless they live and vote in the town, they cannot even share in decisions about how their money is to be spent. They have no political rights; whereas residents do have rights, whether they are investors or not. There seems no reason not to make the same distinction in economic associations, marking off investors from participants, a just return from political power.

Finally, the factory and the town are not different because men and women come willingly to work in the factory with full knowledge of its rules and regulations. They also come willingly to live in the town, and in neither case do they have full knowledge of the rules until they have some experience of them. Anyway, residence does not constitute an agreement to despotic rules even if the rules are known in advance; nor is prompt departure the only way of expressing opposition. There are, in fact, some associations for which these last propositions might plausibly be reversed. A man who joins a monastic order requiring strict and unquestioning obedience, for example, seems to be choosing a way of life rather than a place to live (or a place to work). We would not pay him proper respect if we refused to recognize the efficacy of his choice. Its purpose and its moral effect are precisely to authorize his superior's decisions, and he can't withdraw that authority without himself withdrawing from the common life it makes possible. But the same thing can't be said of a man or a woman who joins a company or comes to work in a factory. Here the common life is not so all-encompassing and it does not require the unquestioning acceptance of authority. We respect the new worker only if we assume that he has not sought out political subjection. Of course, he encounters foremen and company police, as he knew he would; and it may be that the success of the enterprise requires his obedience, just as the success of a city or a town requires that citizens obey public officials. But in neither case would we want to say (what we might say to the novice monk): if

you don't like these officials and the orders they give, you can always leave. It's important that there be options short of leaving, connected with the appointment of the officials and the making of the rules they enforce. . . .

[T]he political community is . . . a common enterprise, a public place where we argue together over the public interest, where we decide on goals and debate acceptable risks. All this was missing in Pullman's model town, until the American Railway Union provided a forum for workers and residents alike.

From this perspective, an economic enterprise seems very much like a town, even though—or, in part, because—it is so unlike a home. It is a place not of rest and intimacy but of cooperative action. It is a place not of withdrawal but of decision. If landlords possessing political power are likely to be intrusive on families, so owners possessing political power are likely to be coercive of individuals. Conceivably the first of these is worse than the second, but this comparison doesn't distinguish the two in any fundamental way; it merely grades them. Intrusiveness and coercion are alike made possible by a deeper reality—the usurpation of a common enterprise, the displacement of collective decision making, by the power of property. And for this, none of the standard justifications seems adequate. Pullman exposed their weaknesses by claiming to rule the town he owned exactly as he ruled the factories he owned. Indeed, the two sorts of rule are similar to one another, and both of them resemble what we commonly understand as authoritarian politics. The right to impose fines does the work of taxation; the right to evict tenants or discharge workers does (some of) the work of punishment. Rules are issued and enforced without public debate by appointed rather than by elected officials. There are no established judicial procedures, no legitimate forms of opposition, no channels for participation or even for protest. If this sort of thing is wrong for towns, then it is wrong for companies and factories, too.

Imagine now a decision by Pullman or his heirs to relocate their factory/town. Having paid off the initial investment, they see richer ground elsewhere; or, they are taken with a new design, a better model for a model town, and want to try it out. The decision, they claim, is theirs alone since the factory/town is theirs alone; neither the inhabitants nor the workers have anything to say. But how can this be right? Surely to uproot a community, to require large-scale migration, to deprive people of homes they have lived in for many years; these are political acts, and acts of a rather extreme sort. The decision is an exercise of power; and were the townspeople simply to submit, we would think they were not self-respecting citizens. What about the workers?

What political arrangements should the workers seek? Political rule implies a certain degree of autonomy, but it's not clear that autonomy is possible in a single factory or even in a group of factories. The citizens of a town are also the consumers of the goods and services the town provides; and except for occasional visitors, they are the only consumers. But workers in a factory are producers of goods and services; they are only sometimes consumers, and they are never the only consumers. Moreover, they are locked into close economic relationships with other factories that they supply or on whose products they depend. Private owners relate to one another through the market. In theory, economic decisions are non-political, and they are coordinated without the interventions of authority. Insofar as this theory is true, worker cooperatives would simply locate themselves within the network of market relations. In fact, however, the theory misses both the collusions of owners among themselves and their collective ability to call upon the support of state officials. Now the appropriate replacement is an industrial democracy organized at national as well as local levels. But how, precisely, can power be distributed so as to take into account both the necessary autonomy and the practical linkage of companies and factories? The question is often raised and variously answered in the literature on workers' control. I shall not attempt to answer it again, nor do I mean to deny its difficulties; I only want to insist that the sorts of arrangements required in an industrial democracy are not all that different from those required in a political democracy. Unless they are independent states, cities and towns are never fully autonomous; they have no absolute authority even over the goods and services they produce for internal consumption. In the United States today, we enmesh them in a federal structure and regulate what they can do in the areas of education, criminal justice, environmental use, and so on. Factories and companies would have to be similarly enmeshed and similarly regulated (and they would also be taxed). In a developed economy, as in a developed polity, different decisions would be made by different groups of people at different levels of organization. The division of power in both these cases is only partly a matter of principle; it is also a matter of circumstance and expediency. . . .

Notes

1. Stanley Buder, *Pullman: An Experiment in Industrial Order and Community Planning, 1880–1930* (New York, 1967).

2. Ibid., pp. 98–99.

3. Ibid., p. 107.

4. Ibid., p. 95; see also William M. Carwardine, *The Pullman Strike,* intro. Virgil J. Vogel (Chicago, 1973), chaps. 8, 9, 10.

5. Richard Ely, quoted in Buder, *Pullman,* p. 103.

6. Ibid.; see also Carwardine, *Pullman Strike,* chap. 4.

7. Carwardine, *Pullman Strike,* p. xxxiii.

8. Buder, *Pullman,* p. 44.

The Right to Democracy within Firms

Robert Dahl

Democracy is sometimes thought applicable only to political processes, so that control by a minority of owners over economic enterprises is not regarded as incompatible with the underlying ideals of democratic government. In the preceding selection Michael Walzer disputed that, claiming that the case for democracy is as strong in the factory as in the city. In this essay, taken from his recent book, Robert Dahl begins with some brief comments on the effects of economic inequality on democracy and on the question whether economic enterprises make decisions that are binding on workers the same way governmental decisions bind citizens. Dahl then considers various objections, practical and theoretical, which might be brought against his proposal to democratize economic enterprises.

Democracy and the Economic Order

Ownership and control of firms affects political inequality in two ways that are closely related but rather different. First, ownership and control contribute to the creation of great differences among citizens in wealth, income, status, skills, information, control over information and propaganda, access to political leaders, and, on the average, predictable life chances, not only for mature adults but also for the unborn, infants, and children. After all due qualifications have been made, differences like these help in turn to generate significant inequalities among citizens in their capacities and opportunities for participating as political equals in *governing the state*.

Second, and even more obvious, with very few exceptions the internal governments of economic enterprises are flatly undemocratic both de jure and de facto. Indeed, genuine political equality has been rejected by Americans as a proper principle of authority within firms. Hence the ownership and control of

From Robert Dahl, *A Preface to Economic Democracy* (Berkeley, CA: University of California Press, 1985), pp. 55, 75, 101, 113–115, 117–124, 128–135. Copyright © 1985 by the Regents of the University of California. Reprinted by permission.

enterprises creates enormous inequalities among citizens in their capacities and opportunities for participating in *governing economic enterprises*. . . .

Even if we were to assume that everyone has a fundamental moral right to private property, it would not follow that economic enterprises should be privately owned. Even if we were to assume that economic enterprises should be privately owned, it would not follow that they should be owned privately and managed in the interests of shareholders—much less managed in the interests of managers. We cannot leap from my entitlement to secure possession of the shirt on my back or the cash in my pocket to a fundamental moral right to acquire shares in IBM and therewith the standard rights of ownership that shareholdings legally convey.

But, one may object, isn't property a natural right, as Locke contended? Don't we have a moral right to life, liberty, and property?

To assert that private property is a natural right, standing alone, is to say close to nothing at all. To begin with, the truth of the assertion is certainly not self-evident. Moreover, even if it were true, a natural right to property might conflict with other natural rights. From the bald assertion of property as a natural right we cannot know whether it is subordinate to a natural right to self-government, as Jefferson thought. . . .

If property is distributed in a highly unequal fashion, a conflict will tend to arise between democracy and property rights. The obvious republican solution was to ensure, somehow, that property be distributed more or less evenly. In the United States, the ideology of agrarian democratic republicanism promised a unique form of that solution: Factors largely external to the political process—principally a vast supply of cheap land—would ensure that economic resources would be so widely diffused as to promote and sustain a satisfactory approximation to political equality.

As it turned out, however, this solution proved to be historically ephemeral. The new social and economic order that gradually replaced the American agrarian society in the course of the nineteenth century did not spontaneously generate the equality of condition so sharply emphasized by Tocqueville as a fundamental characteristic of American agrarian society. On the contrary, the new order produced enormous differences in wealth, income, status, and power. Clearly a solution to the classical republican problem could no longer depend on the accidental existence of a factor, like land, that was mainly exogenous to the political process. . . .

Are Decisions Binding?

[C]an the assumptions . . . justifying the democratic process reasonably be applied to economic enterprises? For example, do economic enterprises make decisions that are *binding* on workers in the same way that the government of the state makes decisions that citizens are compelled to obey? After all, laws made by the government of a state can be enforced by physical coercion, if need be. In a democratic state, a minority opposed to a law is nevertheless compelled to obey it. But a firm, it might be said, is nothing more than a sort of market within which people engage in voluntary individual exchanges: workers voluntarily exchange their labor in return for wages paid by the employer. Decisions made by the government of a firm and by the government of the state, however, are in some crucial respects more similar than this classical liberal interpretation allows for. Like the government

of the state, the government of a firm makes decisions that apply uniformly to all workers or a category of workers: decisions governing the place of work, time of work, product of work, minimally acceptable rate of work, equipment to be used at work, number of workers, number (and identity) of workers laid off in slack times—or whether the plant is to be shut down and there will be no work at all. These decisions are enforced by sanctions, including the ultimate sanction of firing.

Have I now understated the difference? Unlike citizens of a state, one might object, workers are not *compelled* to obey managerial decisions; their decision to do so is voluntary. Because a worker may choose to obey the management or not, because he is free to leave the firm if he prefers not to obey, and because he cannot be punished by management for leaving, some would argue that his decision to obey is perfectly free of all compulsion.

But an objection along these lines exaggerates the differences between a worker's subjection to decisions made by the government of a firm and a citizen's subjection to decisions made by the government of the state. Take a local government. A citizen who does not like a local ordinance is also "free" to move to another community. Indeed, if a citizen does not want to obey her country's laws, she is "free"—at least in all democratic countries—to leave her country. Now if a citizen were perfectly free to leave, then citizenship would be wholly voluntary; for if a citizen found "voice" unsatisfactory, she could freely opt for "exit." But is not "exit" (or exile) often so costly, in every sense, that membership is for all practical purposes compulsory—whether it requires one to leave a country, a municipality, or a firm? If so, then the government of a firm looks rather more like the government of a state than we are habitually inclined to believe: because exit is so costly, membership in a firm is not significantly more voluntary or less compulsory than citizenship in a municipality or perhaps even in a country.

In fact, citizenship in a democratic state is in one respect more voluntary than employment in a firm. Within a democratic country, citizens may ordinarily leave one municipality and automatically retain or quickly acquire full rights of citizenship in another. Yet even

though the decisions of firms, like the decisions of a state, can be enforced by severe
sanctions (firing), unlike a citizen of a democratic state, one who leaves a firm has no right
to "citizenship" (that is, employment) in another.

Like a state, then, a firm can also be viewed
as a political system in which relations of power exist between governments and the governed. If so, is it not appropriate to insist that
the relationship between governors and governed should satisfy the criteria of the democratic process—as we properly insist in the domain of the state? . . .

Equality in Firms

The government of large American corporations [can] be seen as a form of guardianship.
Although managers are nominally selected by
a board of directors, which in turn is nominally chosen by and legally accountable to
stockholders, in reality new managers are typically co-opted by existing management which
also, in practice, chooses and controls its own
board of directors. Guardianship has also been
the ideal of many socialists, particularly the
Fabians. In this view the managers of state-
owned enterprises were to be chosen by state
officials, to whom the top managers were to be
ultimately responsible. In most countries, in
fact, nationalized industries are governed by
some such scheme. One could easily dream up
still other meritocratic alternatives.

Thus in theory and practice both corporate
capitalism and bureaucratic socialism have rejected the principle of equality for economic
enterprises; explicitly or by implication they
uphold guardianship. [*By the principle of equality Dahl means that all adult members are assumed
to be qualified to make decisions affecting the
group.*—Ed.] Because of the overwhelming
weight of existing institutions and ideologies,
probably most people, including many
thoughtful people, will find it hard to believe
that employees are qualified to govern the enterprises in which they work. However, in considering whether the strong principle of equality holds for business firms, it is important to

keep two points in mind. First, while we may
reasonably compare the ideal or theoretically
possible performance of one system with the
ideal or theoretical performance of another,
we cannot reasonably compare the actual performance of one with the ideal performance
of another. Although a good deal of the discussion of self-governing enterprises that follows is necessarily conjectural, my aim is to
compare the probable performance of self-
governing enterprises with the actual performance of their current principal alternative, the modern privately owned corporation.

Second, . . . the principle of equality does
not require that citizens be equally competent
in every respect. It is sufficient to believe that
citizens are qualified enough to decide which
matters do or do not require binding collective
decisions (e.g., which matters require general
rules); of those that do require binding collective decisions, citizens are competent to decide whether they are themselves sufficiently
qualified to make the decisions collectively
through the democratic process; and on matters they do not feel competent to decide for
themselves, they are qualified to set the terms
on which they will delegate these decisions to
others.

Except in exceedingly small firms, employees would surely choose to delegate some
decisions to managers. In larger firms, they
would no doubt elect a governing board or
council, which in the typical case would probably be delegated the authority to select and
remove the top executives. Except in very
large enterprises, the employees might constitute an assembly for "legislative" purposes—
to make decisions on such matters as the workers choose to decide, to delegate matters they
prefer not to decide directly, and to review
decisions on matters they had previously delegated as well as the conduct of the board and
the managers in other ways. In giant firms,
where an assembly would suffer all the in-
firmities of direct democracy on an excessively
large scale, a representative government
would have to be created.

Given the passivity of stockholders in a
typical firm, their utter dependency on information supplied by management, and the
extraordinary difficulties of contesting a managerial decision, it seems to me hardly open to

doubt that employees are on the whole as well qualified to run their firms as are stockholders, and probably on average a good deal more. But of course that is not really the issue, given the separation of ownership from control. . . . A recent . . . study reports that 64 percent of the 200 largest nonfinancial American corporations are controlled by inside management and another 17 percent by inside management with an outside board, or altogether 81 percent of the total, with 84 percent of the assets and 82 percent of the sales. Although the percentage of management-controlled firms might be less among smaller firms, the question remains whether workers are as qualified to govern economic enterprises as managers who gain their position by co-option—thus producing a sort of co-optive guardianship.

This question raises many of the familiar and ancient issues of democracy versus guardianship, including the grounds for believing that the putative guardians possess superior knowledge about what is best for the collectivity, and also superior virtue—the will or predisposition to seek that good. It is important therefore to distinguish knowledge about the *ends* the enterprise should seek from technical knowledge about the best *means* for achieving those ends. As to ends, the argument might be made that self-governing enterprises would produce lower rates of savings, investment, growth, and employment than the society might rationally (or at least reasonably) prefer. As to means, it might be contended that self-governing enterprises would be less likely to supply qualified management and for this and other reasons would be less efficient than stockholder-owned firms like American corporations.

Ends: Savings, Investment, Growth, and Employment

How then would a system of self-governing enterprises affect savings, investment, employment, and growth? For example, would workers vote to allocate so much of enterprise earnings to wages that they would sacrifice investment in new machinery and future efficiencies? Would firms run democratically by their employees be more shortsighted than firms run hierarchically by managers? American corporate managers are frequently criticized nowadays for an excessive emphasis on short-run as against long-run returns. Would self-governing enterprises accentuate the sacrifice of deferred to immediate benefits, to the disadvantage and contrary to the collective preferences of their society? If so, would not the particular interests of workers in an enterprise conflict with the general interest?

Purely theoretical analysis by economists, whether critics or advocates of worker-managed firms, is ultimately inconclusive. Advocates of self-management agree that in contrast to conventional firms in which managers seek to maximize total profit for shareholders, the worker-members of self-governing firms would seek to maximize the per capita income of the members. In view of this, some critics reason, members would have no incentive to expand savings, production, employment, or investment unless the effect were to increase their own per capita earnings; and they would have a definite incentive not to do so if they expected that by doing so they would reduce their own earnings. These critics therefore conclude that in some situations in which a conventional firm would expand in order to increase returns to shareholders, worker-managed firms would not.*

Advocates of self-governing firms reply that in an economy of self-governing firms, the problem of employment is theoretically distinguishable from the problem of investment and growth. In the theoretical scenario just sketched out, expanding employment is a

*One theoretical argument can be illustrated as follows. Assume a firm with 100 members, a daily output of 100 units—each selling at $200 a unit, and costs for nonlabor inputs (equipment, buildings, materials, etc.) of $150 a unit. The total return available for distribution to workers is $5,000, or $50 per member. Assume that by doubling the workforce (and thus membership), output would rise to 150 units at the same unit cost. Although the amount available for distribution to members would rise to $7,500, the share of each member would fall to $37.50. Thus (unless they were altruists) the members would be unwilling to expand their firm's employment and membership. If, however, they were legally permitted to, they might try to hire additional workers at a wage low enough to protect their own current earnings; in our example, such a wage would have to be less than $25.

problem only at the level of the individual firm. At the level of the economy, however, it would be dealt with by ensuring ease of entry for new firms. If unemployment existed and enterprises failed to respond to rising demand for their product by expanding employment, new firms would do so; hence both investment and employment would increase. As to investment, except in the circumstances just described, members of a self-managed enterprise would have strong incentives to invest, and thus to save, whenever by doing so they would increase the surplus available for distribution to themselves.

In the real world, however, these comparisons between theoretical models do not take us very far. As Peter Jay remarks:

So far we have been comparing the rational investment behavior of workers' cooperatives with the rational behavior of idealized capital enterprises working according to textbook optimization. If we actually lived in the latter world, we would hardly be considering the problem discussed in this paper at all.[1]

Turning then to the domain of practical judgment, it seems likely that in the real world, self-governing enterprises might stimulate as much savings, investment, and growth as American corporate enterprises have done, and perhaps more, because workers typically stand to incur severe losses from the decline of a firm. If we permit ourselves to violate the unenforceable injunction of some welfare economists against interpersonal comparisons, we can hardly deny that the losses incurred by workers from the decline of a firm are normally even greater than those investors suffer; for it is ordinarily much easier and less costly in human terms for a well-heeled investor to switch in and out of the securities market than for a worker to switch in and out of the job market. A moderately foresightful worker would therefore be as greatly concerned with long-run efficiencies as a rational investor or a rational manager, and perhaps more so.

This conjecture is supported by at least some cases in which, given the opportunity, workers have made significant short-term sacrifices in wages and benefits in order to keep their firm from collapsing. They did so, for example, at both Chrysler Corporation and

the Rath Packing Company. And when workers own the company their incentive to sacrifice in order to save it is all the stronger. As a worker in one of the plywood co-ops put it, "If things get bad we'll all take a pay cut. You don't want to milk the cow, because if you milk the cow, there's nothing left. And *we* lose the company."[2]

Perhaps an even more relevant example is that of Mondragon, a complex of more than 80 worker co-operatives in Spain. During a period in which the Spanish economy was expanding generally, the sales of the Mondragon cooperatives grew at an impressive rate, averaging 8.5 percent from 1970 to 1979. Their market share increased from less than 1 percent in 1960 to over 10 percent in 1976. The percentage of gross value added through investment by the cooperatives between 1971 and 1979 averaged 36 percent, nearly four times the average rate of industry in the heavily industrialized Basque province in which Mondragon is located. Moreover, when a recession in the Spanish economy led to declining profits in 1981, "investment [was] squeezed, but the workers [were] prepared to make sacrifices to keep their jobs, digging into their own pockets to keep the balance sheets in shape." [*The Economist*, 31 October 1981, p. 84.] Members chose to contribute more capital rather than cut their wages. Thus the members of one co-op voted to increase their individual capital contributions by amounts that ranged from $570 to $1,700, depending on wage level. Nor have the self-managed enterprises of Yugoslavia on the whole followed the theoretical model advanced by critics of self-management. Though the causes are complex, with some exceptions they have not sacrificed investment to current income but, on the contrary, have maintained very high levels of investment. . . .

[I]t is not inconceivable that workers might enter into a social contract that would require them to provide funds for investment, drawn from payrolls, in return for greater control over the government of economic enterprises. If self-governing enterprises proved to be better matched to the incentives of workers than hierarchically run firms, and thus more efficient, a system of self-governing enterprises might be a prescription for economic growth that would surpass even Japan's success—and leave recent American performance far behind.

Means: Managerial Skills

A disastrous assumption of revolutionaries, exhibited with stunning naivete in Lenin's *State and Revolution,* is that managerial skills are of trivial importance, or will arise spontaneously, or will be more than compensated for by revolutionary enthusiasm. The historical record relieves one of all need to demonstrate the foolishness of such an assumption. The question is obviously not whether self-governing enterprises would need managerial abilities, but whether workers and their representatives would select and oversee managers less competently than is now the case in American corporations, which are largely controlled by managers whose decisions are rarely open to serious challenge, except when disaster strikes, and not always even then. If a system of self-governing enterprises were established it would be wise to provide much wider opportunities than now exist in any country for employees to learn some of the tools and skills of modern management. One source of the Mondragon cooperatives' success lies in the prominence they have assigned to education, including technical education at advanced professional levels. As a result, they have developed their own managers. In the United States, at least, a significant proportion of both blue- and white-collar workers, often the more ambitious and aggressive among them, aspire to supervisory and managerial positions but lack the essential skills. Efficiency and economic growth flow from investments in human capital every bit as much as from financial capital, and probably more. A system of self-governing enterprises would be likely to heighten—not diminish—efforts to improve a country's human capital.

If in the meanwhile skilled managers are in short supply, self-governing enterprises will have to compete for their services, as does Puget Sound Plywood, a worker-owned cooperative. The president and members of the board of trustees are elected by and from the members, who all receive the same pay. However, the president and board in turn select a general manager from outside the membership "because he can command pay that is far in excess of what he could realize as a shareholder [i.e., as a worker-member]. . . . The qualifications for being a general manager are not what one would normally gain from working in a plywood mill. So we usually employ the best person we can find in the industry."[3]

Means: Efficiency

Unless self-governing enterprises were less competent in recruiting skilled managers, they should be no less efficient in a narrow sense than American corporations at present. And unless they were more likely to evade the external controls of competition and regulation, they should not be less efficient in a broader sense. I have suggested why it is reasonable to expect neither of these deficiencies to occur.

Yet if self-governing enterprises can be as efficient as orthodox firms, why have they so often failed? As everyone familiar with American and British labor history knows, the late nineteenth century saw waves of short-lived producer cooperatives in Britain and in the United States. Their quick demise convinced trade union leaders that in a capitalist economy unionism and collective bargaining held out a much more realistic promise of gains for workers than producer cooperatives. In both countries, and in Europe as well, labor and socialist movements largely abandoned producer cooperatives as a major short-run objective. Most academic observers, including labor economists and social historians, concluded that the labor-managed firm was a rejected and forlorn utopian idea irrelevant to a modern economy.

In recent years, however, a number of factors have brought about a reassessment of the relevance of the older experience. These include the highly unsatisfactory performance of both corporate capitalism and bureaucratic socialism, whose failings have stimulated a search for a third alternative; the introduction and survival—despite severe difficulties—of self-management in Yugoslavia; some stunning successes, such as the U.S. plywood cooperatives and the Mondragon group; formal economic analysis showing how a labor-managed market economy would theoretically satisfy efficiency criteria; growing awareness of the need to reduce the hierarchical structure of the workplace and increase participation by workers in order to increase productivity; and the seeming success of many new arrangements for worker participation, control, or ownership in Europe and the United States.

In sum, it has become clear that many failed labor-managed firms had been doomed not by inherent weaknesses but by remediable ones, such as shortages of credit, capital, and managerial skills. Moreover, in the past, producer cooperatives have usually been organized in the worst possible circumstances, when employees desperately attempt to rescue a collapsing company by taking it over—often during a recession. It is hardly surprising that workers may fail to save a firm after management has already failed. What is surprising is that workers' cooperatives have sometimes succeeded where private management has failed. For example, it was from the failure of privately owned companies that some of the plywood co-ops started.

I have also mentioned the Mondragon producer cooperatives in Spain as an example of success. They include their nation's largest manufacturer of machine tools as well as one of its largest refrigerator manufacturers. During a period of a falling Spanish economy and rising unemployment, between 1977 and 1981, employment in the Mondragon co-ops increased from 15,700 to about 18,500. Unless they are denied access to credit—the Mondragon complex has its own bank—self-governing enterprises have a greater resiliency than American corporations. For in times of stringency when an orthodox private firm would lay off workers or shut down, the members of a self-governing enterprise can decide to reduce their wages, curtail their share of the surplus, if any, or even contribute additional capital funds, as at Mondragon. As these and other cases show, self-governing enterprises are likely to tap the creativity, energies, and loyalties of workers to an extent that stockholder-owned corporations probably never can, even with profit-sharing schemes.

Although rigorous comparisons of the relative efficiencies of labor-managed and con-

ventional corporations are difficult and still fairly uncommon, the best analysis of a broad range of experiences in a number of different countries appears to support these conclusions: participation by workers in decision-making rarely leads to a decline of productivity; far more often it either has no effect or results in an increase in productivity.

How Much Internal Democracy?

Often the effects of more democratic corporate structures have been greatly exaggerated by both advocates and opponents. Yet just as the democratization of the authoritarian structures of centralized monarchies and modern dictatorships has transformed relations of authority and power in the government of states, so there is every reason to believe that the democratization of the government of modern corporations would profoundly alter relations of authority and power in economic enterprises. Relationships of governors to governed of a sort that Americans have insisted on for two hundred years in the public governments of the state would be extended to the hitherto private governments in the economy.

If too often exaggerated, it is nonetheless a grievous mistake to underestimate the importance of democratic institutions in the domain of the state. It is similarly a mistake to underestimate the importance of authoritarian corporate institutions in the daily lives of working people. . . .

Conclusion

My arguments in this chapter have shown, I think, that the main objections to democratizing economic enterprises are not adequately supported by analysis and evidence. It is not true that self-governing enterprises would violate a superior right to private ownership. It is not true that the assumptions justifying the democratic process in the government of the state do not apply to economic enterprises. Nor is it true that democracy in an economic enterprise would be a sham. If these objections are invalid, then a country committed to [democracy] would choose to extend democracy to economic enterprises. The prevailing view among the people of such a country might be something like this:

If democracy is justified in governing the state, then it is also justified in governing economic enterprises. What is more, if it cannot be justified in governing economic enterprises, we do not quite see how it can be justified in governing the state. Members of any association for whom the assumptions of the democratic process are valid have a *right* to govern themselves by means of the democratic process. If, as we believe, those assumptions hold among us, not only for the government of the state but also for the internal government of economic enterprises, then we have a *right* to govern ourselves democratically within our economic enterprises. Of course, we do not expect that the introduction of the democratic process in the government of economic enterprises will make them perfectly democratic or entirely overcome the tendencies toward oligarchy that seem to be inherent in all large human organizations, including the government of the state. But just as we support the democratic process in the government of the state despite substantial imperfections in practice, so we support the democratic process in the government of economic enterprises despite the imperfections we expect in practice. We therefore see no convincing reasons why we should not exercise our right to the democratic process in the government of enterprises, just as we have already done in the government of the state. And we intend to exercise that right.

Notes

1. Peter Jay, "The Workers Cooperative Economy" in *The Political Economy of the Third World: Cooperation and Participation.* A. Clayre, ed. (Oxford: Oxford Univ. Press, 1980), p. 20.

2. Daniel Zwerdling, *Workplace Democracy* (New York: Harper and Row, 1980), p. 101.

3. Leamon J. Bennett, "When Employees Run the Company: An Interview with Leamon Bennett," *Harvard Business Review* 57 (January-February), pp. 81–82, 85.

6

Democracy and the Law

Beyond Carolene Products: A Critique of Process-Based Theories of Constitutional Interpretation

Bruce Ackerman

Judicial review—the power of judges to invalidate laws passed by elected officials in the name of a two-hundred-year-old Constitution—seems to many to be at odds with the democratic ideal of self-government. Why should today's majority be limited by language adopted so long ago? And what gives judges the right to impose their own values on the majority, as they often do when the Constitution's meaning is unclear?

In response to these problems, legal scholars sometimes point to "footnote four" of an otherwise un-important 1938 case, U.S. v. Carolene Products. *In that case the Supreme Court suggested that rather than working* against *democratic ideals, judicial review should be used only to assure that the political process is genuinely democratic:*

> [4] There may be narrower scope for operation of the presumption of constitutionality when legislation appears on its face to be within a specific prohibition of the Constitution, such as those of the first ten amendments, which are deemed equally specific when held to be embraced within the Fourteenth . . .
>
> It is unnecessary to consider now whether legislation which restricts those political processes which can ordinarily be expected to bring about repeal of undesirable legislation, is to be subjected to more exacting judicial scrutiny under the general prohibitions of the Fourteenth Amendment than are most other types of legislation . . .
>
> Nor need we enquire whether similar considerations enter into the review of statutes directed at particular religious . . . or national . . . or racial minorities . . . ; whether prejudice against discrete and insular minorities may be a special condition, which tends seriously to curtail the operation of those political processes ordinarily to be relied upon to protect minorities, and which may call for a correspondingly more searching judicial inquiry.

While it deferred to the legislature in this case, the Court suggested that in the future it would limit itself to "policing by the process of representation" as one commentator described the Carolene Products *approach. Footnote four suggests three important ways the Court meets that responsibility. First, the Justices must assure that everybody is able to exercise the franchise and that each vote has roughly equal weight. In that vein, the Court has struck down the poll tax, invalidated residency requirements for voting, and required legislative redistricting. But democratic government cannot function without a robust, open political debate, so freedom of speech and the press provide the second critical role for the Court. Justices, with the responsibility to police the political process, must prevent those in power from stifling opposition voices.*

Carolene Products *added the third component to the process-based theory of judicial review: Justices must see that laws do not reflect prejudice against "discrete and insular minorities." Consistent with this, the Fourteenth Amendment's promise that states will not deny citizens "equal protection" of the law has been interpreted to forbid school segregation as well as many other forms of discrimination. Having assured a fair voting process, robust and open political debate, and prejudice-free outcomes, then the Court should keep out of the process and let the majority govern. Only then, can the Court be assured it is not overstepping its legitimate authority by acting contrary to basic democratic principles.*

This process-based approach to judicial review has attracted both supporters and critics, and contin-ues to exert considerable influence on legal thinking. In the following essay, Bruce Ackerman focuses on the problems with the last of the Carolene Products *recommendations: that the Court protect democracy by assuring that laws are not motivated by prejudice against discrete and insular minorities. In the course of his argument Ackerman discusses the nature of pluralistic political bargaining, the dangers posed by prejudice, and the possibility that Justices might avoid value judgments in exercising judicial review.*

From Bruce Ackerman, "Beyond *Carolene Products*," 98 *Harvard Law Review* 713 (1985).

I. The Promise of Carolene Products

*"[P]rejudice against discrete and insular minorities may be a special condition . . . curtail[ing] the operation of those political processes ordinarily to be relied upon to protect minorities, and [so] may call for a correspondingly more searching judicial inquiry."**

These famous words, appearing in the otherwise unimportant *Carolene Products* case, came at a moment of extraordinary vulnerability for the Supreme Court. They were written in 1938. The Court was just beginning to dig itself out of the constitutional debris left by its wholesale capitulation to the New Deal a year before. With the decisive triumph of the activist welfare state over the Old Court, an entire world of constitutional meanings, laboriously built up over two generations, had come crashing down upon the Justices' heads. Indeed, the Court had been so politically discredited by its constitutional defense of laissez-faire capitalism that it was hardly obvious whether *any* firm ground remained upon which to rebuild the institution of judicial review. How, then, to begin the work of reconstruction?

Only once before had the Court confronted a similar challenge. Just as the triumphant New Deal Democrats had destroyed the laissez-faire constitutionalism of *Lochner v. New York,* so too a triumphant Republican Congress had destroyed the slavocratic constitutionalism of *Dred Scott v. Sanford* after the Civil War. Just as many contemporary observers doubted the institutional independence—let alone the constitutional importance—of the Supreme Court during Reconstruction, nobody could be confident about the future of judicial review in the aftermath of the Court-packing crisis.

Only one thing was clear. If the Court were to reassert itself after the Great Depression, it could not do so through the same constitutional rhetoric with which it had rehabili-

*United States v. Carolene Prods. Co., 304 U.S. 144, 152 n.4 (1938).

tated itself after the Civil War. During the long period between Reconstruction and New Deal, the Court had risen to the heights of power by insisting upon the fundamental right of free men to pursue their private aims in a free market system. Yet it was precisely this ideological elixir, which had given the judiciary new life after the Civil War, that proved nearly fatal during the constitutional birth agony of the activist welfare state. *If* the Court were to build a new foundation for judicial review, it would need an entirely new constitutional rhetoric—one that self-consciously recognized that the era of laissez-faire capitalism had ended.

Against this historical background, we may glimpse the promise of *Carolene Products.* Rather than look back longingly to a repudiated constitutional order, *Carolene* brilliantly endeavored to turn the Old Court's recent defeat into a judicial victory. As far as *Carolene* was concerned, lawyers could dispense with their traditional effort to organize their concern for individual rights through a constitutional rhetoric glorifying private property and free contract. Instead, *Carolene* proposed to make the ideals of the victorious activist Democracy serve as a primary foundation for constitutional rights in the United States.

Fifty years onward, the basic idea is familiar, but it requires restatement if we are to examine it carefully. *Carolene* promises relief from the problem of legitimacy raised whenever nine elderly lawyers invalidate the legislative decisions of a majority of our elected representatives. The *Carolene* solution is to seize the high ground of democratic theory and establish that the challenged legislation was produced by a profoundly defective process. By demonstrating that the legislative decision itself resulted from an undemocratic procedure, a *Carolene* court hopes to reverse the spin of the countermajoritarian difficulty. For it now may seem that the original legislative decision, not the judicial invalidation, suffers the greater legitimacy deficit.

Assume, for example, that the people of a state, after excluding blacks from the polls, elect an all-white legislature that proceeds to enact some classic Jim Crow legislation. Under the *Carolene* approach, the court does not purport to challenge the substantive value judgments underlying the legislative decision; instead, it simply denies that the Jim Crow statute would have emerged from a fair and open political process in which blacks were allowed to participate. In essence, the court is trumping the statutory conclusions of the deeply flawed real-world legislature by appealing to the hypothetical judgment of an ideally democratic legislature.

No wonder, then, that *Carolene Products* seemed so promising in 1938. Not only did it point the Supreme Court toward the path of racial justice and minority rights, but it also explained why the new road to minority rights was fundamentally different from the old road to property rights that had so recently led the Court to the brink of self-destruction. Whereas the Old Court had protected property owners who enjoyed ample opportunity to safeguard their own interests through the political process, the New Court would accord special protection to those who had been deprived of their fair share of political influence.

No less significantly, the *Carolene* Court sketched its new mission in exceptionally broad strokes. It did not limit its prospective intervention to the straightforward cases in which blacks or other unpopular groups were excluded from the polls or denied other fundamental rights of political expression. *Carolene* suggested an enduring role for the judiciary, one that would continue even after every adult American had secured his right to participate in politics. To take the case that will serve as a paradigm in this essay: the *Carolene* footnote suggests that, even in a world in which blacks voted no less frequently than whites, and in which election districts strictly conformed to the Court's reapportionment decisions, blacks would still possess, by virtue of their discreteness and insularity, a disproportionately small share of influence on legislative policy—a disproportion of such magnitude as to warrant the judicial conclusion that a fair democratic process would have generated outcomes systematically more favorable to minority interests. This suggestion, moreover, animates countless modern discussions—judicial as well as academic—in which the political weakness of "discrete and insular minorities" is a crucial, if unexamined, premise in the elaboration of intricate con-

stitutional doctrines. I shall argue, however, that the *Carolene* formula cannot withstand close scrutiny.

Given the unsettling character of this thesis, it is best to begin by emphasizing its limits. My critique applies exclusively to the paradigm case I have just described, and *not* to the cruder case in which blacks—or other racial or religious minorities—are excluded from the voting booth or deterred from exercising their fundamental rights to speak freely and organize politically. During *Carolene*'s first half-century, it was these brutal efforts at political exclusion that rightly were of central constitutional concern. Nothing I say is intended to deny the obvious unconstitutionality involved in excluding minorities from the nation's political life.

My concern here, however, is with the future, not the past. Although America has by no means worked itself clear of past practices of political exclusion, it is not visionary to hope that we will indeed put this grim aspect of history behind us and that, during the next generation, we will inhabit a world that increasingly resembles my paradigm case: a world in which, despite the existence of pervasive social prejudice, minorities can and do participate in large numbers within the normal political process. In light of this prospect, a reappraisal of *Carolene* is a pressing necessity: its approach to minority rights is profoundly shaped by the old politics of exclusion and yields systematically misleading cues within the new participatory paradigm.

Indeed, if we fail to rethink *Carolene*'s dictum about discrete and insular minorities, we will succeed only in doing two different kinds of damage. On the one hand, we will fail to do justice to the very racial and religious groups that *Carolene* has done so much to protect in the past half-century. By tying their rights to an increasingly unrealistic model of politics, we will place them on the weakest possible foundation. On the other hand, we will fail to do justice to *Carolene*'s basic insight into the problem posed by prejudice in a pluralist democracy. The end of the politics of exclusion hardly implies that pluralist democracy now functions fairly; it does mean, however, that the groups most disadvantaged by pluralism in the future will be different from those excluded under the old regime. The victims of sexual discrimination or poverty, rather than racial or religious minorities, will increasingly constitute the groups with the greatest claim upon *Carolene*'s concern with the fairness of pluralist process.

To demonstrate the need for doctrinal reorientation, I shall examine separately each of *Carolene*'s four operative terms: (1) prejudice, (2) discrete, (3) insular, and (4) minorities. It is by means of these four terms that *Carolene* hopes to identify groups that have been unconstitutionally deprived of their fair share of democratic influence. As America moves toward the participatory paradigm, however, judges can no longer expect these familiar concepts to operate in a way that will allow courts to solve the problem of countermajoritarianism. To explain why, I have found it helpful to examine *Carolene*'s four basic terms in reverse order from the way they appear in the standard litany. A concluding section glimpses the path of reconstruction that lies ahead.

II. Discrete and Insular Minorities?

The *Carolene* formula limits its attention to the asserted political weakness of minorities and fails to consider the analogous case of a politically ineffective majority. In view of *Carolene*'s larger ambition to deflect the countermajoritarian difficulty, this is an especially odd omission. Consider again the paradigm case: blacks are participating no less frequently than whites in a political system that satisfies the standards for electoral fairness elaborated in the Court's modern decisions. Despite these formal safeguards, imagine that an all-white legislature manages to get elected, and then enacts a series of laws prohibiting interracial marriage and forbidding interracial adoptions. Would we be less concerned about this outcome if we completed the scenario by assuming that blacks amounted to 75 percent, rather than 12 percent, of the relevant electorate?

Of course not. Indeed, the existence of a commanding black majority would encourage us to intensify our search for a set of structural factors that somehow allowed whites to dominate the ostensibly democratic political process. *Carolene* casually disregards the easiest case for finding a substantive defect in a formally fair electoral process: the case in which organizational difficulties have prevented a commanding majority of the population from influencing the ongoing flow of legislative decisions. After all, if democracy means anything, it means a regime designed to further the majority's basic interests; that is certainly not what is going on in the case we have hypothesized.

A. The Principle of Minority Acquiescence

If we begin with the easy case of an ineffective majority, we can also begin to see how much harder it is to justify the *Carolene* concern for ineffective minorities. To put the point simply, minorities are *supposed* to lose in a democratic system—even when they want very much to win and even when they think (as they often will) that the majority is deeply wrong in ignoring their just complaints. This principle—call it the principle of minority acquiescence—is absolutely central to democratic theory. Of course, a minority may not be denied its right to participate within a democratic framework. Although it must acquiesce in current legislative decisions, it is fully entitled to use all its political resources to induce a future legislative majority to accede to its demands. But *Carolene* promises minorities more than formal rights: it asserts that they are sometimes entitled to demand substantive victory now, not merely the chance of victory later.

The problem this promise raises is all the more acute because *Carolene* refuses to accept the solution that countless others have embraced. It is easy to solve the problem of majority rule by positing the existence of minority rights that are so fundamental as to trump the value of democratic rule itself. Indeed, as the *Carolene* Court was well aware, it is *too* easy to solve the problem in this way. Faced with the political repudiation of *Lochner*'s natural rights jurisprudence, the Court was determined to build another foundation for the protection of minority rights: why not redefine the concept of democracy itself in a way that would support the notion that minorities *do* have a right to win some of the time?

B. The Pluralist Solution

While the courts speak vaguely of "those political processes ordinarily relied upon to protect minorities," generations of American political scientists have filled in the picture of pluralist democracy presupposed by *Carolene*'s distinctive argument for minority rights. According to this familiar view, it is a naive mistake to speak of democracy as if it involved rule by a single, well-defined majority over a coherent and constant minority. Instead, normal American politics is pluralistic: myriad pressure groups, each typically representing a fraction of the population, bargain with one another for mutual support.

Once this picture of pluralistic politics is accepted, the stage has been set for the rehabilitation of *Carolene*'s concern with ineffective minorities. We may now find that there is something about certain minority groups—call them *Carolene* or *C*-groups—that makes it especially difficult for them to strike bargains with potential coalition partners. As a consequence, *C*-groups will find themselves in politically ascendant coalitions much less often than will otherwise comparable groups. Over time, then, *C*-groups will achieve less than their "fair share" of influence upon legislation. And it is for this reason, the pluralist concludes, that *Carolene* rightly suggests that judicial protection for *C*-groups can be defended in a manner responsive to the countermajoritarian difficulty afflicting judicial review. By intervening on behalf of *C*-groups, a *Carolene* court merely produces the substantive outcomes that the *C*-group would have obtained through politics if it had not been so systematically disadvantaged in the ongoing process of pluralist bargaining.

It thus appears, at first glance, that a *Carolene* court can draw upon a well-developed body of pluralist political science to support its special protection of minority rights. When we move beyond intuition to analysis, however, the pluralist argument is full of traps for the unwary. First, it is by no means clear that our

Constitution wholeheartedly endorses the bargaining theory of democracy.* Second, all that pluralist theory explains is why minority groups can expect to influence legislative outcomes some of the time; it is something very different to explain why minorities may dress up these expectations in the language of constitutional rights and demand judicial protection for them.

I shall defer these fundamental points to the concluding section. My focus here is on a central doctrinal difficulty that persists even if *Carolene*'s pluralist foundations are secure. This problem concerns the indiscriminate standard according to which *Carolene* proposes to regulate the judicial protection of *C*-groups. In the common legal understanding, *Carolene* is generally taken to imply that the same level of strict judicial scrutiny should apply to legislation affecting each and every *C*-group. But the pluralist model cannot justify such a uniform judicial approach.

Consider, for example, an American constituency that includes 12 percent blacks and .5 percent Jehovah's Witnesses among its population. Doubtless, both groups will be encouraged by the pluralist vision of democracy, since it suggests that neither group will inexorably be excluded from the pluralist bazaar. Nonetheless, it should be plain that these two groups have absolutely no reason to find the prospect of pluralist bargaining *equally* gratifying. To the contrary, the fact that blacks greatly outnumber Witnesses is bound to play an important role in any plausible bargaining theory. Thus, even if the two groups could somehow be compensated for their *Carolene* disadvantages, the Witnesses could not reasonably expect to win substantive victories nearly as often as the blacks.

To put the point more generally, a bargaining approach to *Carolene* does not suggest that each *C*-group has a right to be treated identically to all other *C*-groups in the legislative process. Instead, the decisive thought-experiment should involve the comparison of a particular *C*-group with a hypothetical minority that I shall call an unencumbered or

*See Ackerman, *The Storrs Lectures: Discovering the Constitution*, 93 YALE L.J. 1013 (1984) (arguing that pluralism is only one aspect of the American constitutional tradition); *infra* pp. 741–43.

U-group. In each comparison, the relevant *U*-group should be supposed to contain the same proportion of the population as the *C*-group that invokes the Court's protection; the *U*-group differs, however, in that it is unencumbered by the bargaining disadvantages that unconstitutionally burden the *C*-group. Thus, the *Carolene* question for blacks entails a comparative analysis of the bargaining expectations of a 12 percent minority unencumbered by those structural impediments that unconstitutionally impair blacks' bargaining position in the ongoing pluralist process, while the question for Jehovah's Witnesses involves a comparison with a much smaller *U*-group.

Such thought-experiments will most naturally result in a sliding scale of *Carolene* concern. On one end of the scale are groups consisting of ineffective majorities or very large minorities that find themselves disadvantaged in the political process by some constitutionally impermissible barrier to bargaining. In cases involving these "major minorities," a court can be quite confident that a comparable *U*-group would have a decisive impact on the terms of pluralistic legislation. In the middle of the *Carolene* scale are "middling minorities" in the 10 to 20 percent range. Here there is less reason for a court to expect that a *U*-group of comparable size would radically change the terms of political trade, though its influence would be very substantial in many plausible contexts. And finally, on the other end of the scale, there are groups so small as to elicit little solicitude from courts concerned with correcting the failures of democratic bargaining. When faced with "minor minorities" of .01 percent, for example, a judge might well be unmoved by the enumeration of *Carolene* factors that would generate substantial concern in the case of middling minorities, not to mention major minorities. For the fact is that a *U*-group of .01 percent has little to expect from a democratic political process, unless it is very lucky, or exceptionally adept, in the bargaining process. This point is essential to the responsible elaboration of *Carolene Products*—whose promise, be it recalled, is to permit courts to evade the thrust of the countermajoritarian difficulty by appealing over the

heads of real-world legislatures to the hypothetical outcomes of a purified democratic process.

There is, then, an inevitably uneasy relationship between *Carolene*'s pluralist approach to democracy and the judicial protection of minority rights. The tension reaches the breaking point in the proverbial case of a minority of one: when the solitary citizen, having little to expect from pluralist bargaining, challenges the invasion of his fundamental rights by the normal political process.*

My aim here, though, is to work out the doctrinal implications of the *Carolene* formula rather than to criticize its foundations. So let us focus our attention upon those groups, ranging from middling minorities to encumbered majorities, whose role in the bargaining process might well have a significant impact on the ongoing stream of legislative decisions. How does *Carolene* propose to determine whether a group suffers from severe enough bargaining disadvantages to merit special protection? In other words, how are we supposed to distinguish a *C*-group from a *U*-group?

III. Discrete and Insular Minorities?

As in the case of its failure to consider the rightful claims of politically ineffective majorities, *Carolene* disdains the easy case in its eagerness to pronounce on harder ones. A dispassionate survey of the relevant literature does not reveal a single-minded concern with the political weakness of *insular* minorities. Instead, it expresses a pervasive anxiety over the way in which inequalities of *wealth* distort the operation of a democratic process formally based upon egalitarian principles.

I do not suggest that every thoughtful

*Of course, *Carolene*'s defense of judicial review is not limited to the pluralist rationale developed in this section. In particular, *Carolene* raises the prospect of judicial intervention in cases involving "a specific prohibition of the Constitution, such as those in the first ten amendments." For a critique of this alternative approach to the protection of individual rights, see [section VI below.]

democrat believes that a systematic effort to check the influence of wealth is an indispensable condition of democratic legitimacy. There are respectable arguments—though I am thoroughly unconvinced by them—to support the claim that any effort to purge our regime of its plutocratic vices would prove worse than the disease itself. For the present, however, I need not evaluate these claims on their merits. It is. enough that I make my point explicitly conditional: if, as *Carolene* plainly supposes, it is legitimate to move beyond a purely formal conception of democratic rule, we should begin building a substantive conception of undue influence by considering the disproportionate impact wealth has on American politics. It is here where the easy case for undemocratic influence may be established.

Yet, as we all know, *Carolene* does not assert that prejudice against "impoverished and uneducated minorities" may call for a more searching judicial inquiry. Instead, it professes a concern for the status of "discrete and insular minorities." This way of framing the issue has strongly influenced the judicial understanding of American democracy over the past half-century. Thus, although modern courts regularly express concern about the bargaining position of discrete and insular minorities, they often react skeptically to the very idea that legislatures may constitutionally attempt to curb the influence of wealth over formally democratic processes.

It is too kind to *Carolene*, however, to regard it as yet another example of the American judiciary's eagerness to emphasize the symptom while ignoring the disease. Even when considered as an exercise in symptomatology, *Carolene* is utterly wrongheaded in its diagnosis. Other things being equal, "discreteness and insularity" will normally be a source of enormous bargaining advantage, not disadvantage, for a group engaged in pluralist American politics. Except for special cases, the concerns that underlie *Carolene* should lead judges to protect groups that possess the opposite characteristics from the ones *Carolene* emphasizes—groups that are "anonymous and diffuse" rather than "discrete and insular." It is these groups that both political science and

American history indicate are systematically disadvantaged in a pluralist democracy.

A. *The Free-Rider Problem*

To see my point, start with insularity and consider a thought-experiment suggested by the previous argument. Imagine two groups, *I* and *D*, of equal size (say each accounts for 12 percent of the population). The members of one group, the *I*'s, are distributed in an insular way, concentrated in a single massive island within the sea of American life; the *D*'s, on the other hand, are diffused evenly throughout the sea. Is it really so clear that, by virtue of their diffusion throughout American life, the *D*'s will gain systematic advantages over the *I*'s in the normal course of pluralist politics?

Hardly. To begin with the basics, a political interest gains a great advantage if its proponents can form a well-organized lobby to press their cause in the corridors of power. Yet the construction of a pressure group is no easy task. The main obstacle is the familiar free-rider problem. Simply because a person would find his interests advanced by the formation of a pressure group, it does not follow that he will spend his own scarce time and energy on political organization. On the contrary, from each individual's selfish viewpoint, abstaining from interest-group activity is a "heads-I-win-tails-you-lose" proposition. If only a few people adopt the do-nothing strategy, the do-nothings will free-ride on the successful lobbying effort of others. If free-riding becomes pervasive, things will not improve much if a single member of the group adds his money and time to the floundering political effort. Either way, it pays for a selfish person to remain a free rider even if he has a lot to gain from concerted lobbying. For this reason, many interests remain ineffectively organized even in pressure-group America. How, then, does a minority's insularity affect the probability that it will break through the free-rider barrier and achieve organizational effectiveness?

Far from being a patent disadvantage, insularity can help *I*-groups in at least four different ways, all of which depend upon a single sociological assumption that we should identify at the outset: however oppressed the *I*'s may be in other respects, they have not been prevented from building up a dense communal life for themselves on their tight little island. Thus, wherever an *I* looks, he will find himself in businesses and churches, schools and labor unions, composed largely of people speaking in distinctively *I*-accents about the daily problems of social life. This fundamental fact will generate a whole series of advantages for *I*-members who seek to organize for political purposes.

First, insularity will help breed sentiments of group solidarity. Given an *I*'s daily immersion in social realities that reaffirm his group identity, the typical *I* will conceive his *I*-ness as something much more than an incidental fact about himself. Instead, *I*-ness will serve as a fundamental feature of self-identity—one that will encourage each *I* to view the political activities of the group from a perspective that transcends the purely instrumental. Thus, when a black or a Jew gives $25 to the NAACP or the Anti-Defamation League, he is not merely, or even principally, gambling that his small bit of money will perceptibly increase his chance of enjoying the fruits of future lobbying victories. Rather, the contribution is a means by which the donor can symbolize the seriousness of his own commitment to his *I*-ness. By contributing to the group cause, I demonstrate to myself, as well as others, that I am serious about the values I profess to hold. Here, at last, is one commodity—group identification—that is immune from the free-rider problem: for if I do not give even a few dollars to the group cause, can I plausibly say, even to myself, that I take my *I*-ness seriously?

But insularity does more than engender the sentiment of group solidarity that encourages symbolic contributions—contributions that, when multiplied thousands of times, add up to very substantial resources for the interest group receiving them. It also aids the *I*-group in a second way by providing it with a new range of social sanctions to impose upon would-be free riders. An *I* who refuses to contribute to his interest group cannot expect this fact to be kept secret from his fellow *I*'s—news travels fast along the grapevine in an insular community. Thus, the shirker cannot reason-

ably hope to evade the moral disapproval of other *I*'s when they learn that he has failed to do his fair share to support the group cause. This stigma may not only lead to embarrassment, but may also result in very concrete material disadvantages in an *I*'s day-to-day dealings with his fellow group members. Only by uprooting himself from his insular community can an *I* hope to escape the opprobrium his free-riding may engender. In contrast, a member of a diffuse *D*-group need not suffer such severe dislocation in order to avoid the disapproval of his fellow group members. Instead, he may insulate himself from their displeasure by assimilating into the majoritarian mainstream—undoubtedly a costly process, but typically less costly than the social stigma heaped on the free-riding *I*. In short, as compared to an *I*, a *D* is both less likely to view his group membership as fundamental to his self-identity and less likely to suffer severe sanctions at the hands of his fellow group members if he fails to do his fair share to support their common objectives.

B. Organizational Costs

It follows, then, that the average *I* is more likely to contribute his time and money to the group cause than is an otherwise comparable *D*. Yet this conclusion tells only half the story: not only will an *I*-group receive more resources from its constituency, but *I*'s will also find it cheaper to organize themselves for effective political action. First, the dense communications network generated by insularity dramatically reduces one of the heaviest costs involved in effective political lobbying: the cost of communicating with a mass membership. To get its messages out to its constituency, an insular political group can often avail itself of the communications channels already established by the group's churches, businesses, or labor unions. In contrast, a *D*-group must somehow locate and reach people who interact with one another much less frequently and who have fewer channels already established for the cheap transmission of *D*-group concerns.

Second, the organic character of insular life greatly reduces the costs of selecting credible political leaders. The *I*-group can draw upon a pool of people who have already earned the respect of their fellow *I*'s in other communal contexts: ministers and rabbis, successful lawyers, businessmen, union leaders. In contrast, even if *D*-group members manage to overcome the communications barrier, they must often take the risk of selecting political leaders who have not been tested and observed in other leadership settings.

C. *Insularity and Congressional Influence*

So insularity is an asset, both in increasing a group's political resources and in reducing its organizational costs. Yet before we render an overall assessment, we must consider the way insularity is likely to affect the attitude of the people upon whom all the bargaining pressure must ultimately be brought to bear: politicians seeking to gain, and retain, elective office. Here we must refine our definitions if we are to make analytic progress. Thus far, I have used "insularity" to refer to the tendency of group members to interact with great frequency in a variety of social contexts. If the term is conceived in this sociological way, people who live far apart from one another may still be members of a single *I*-group, especially under modern conditions. Conversely, it is easy for people living cheek by jowl to fail to qualify as an insular minority from a sociological point of view.

We have reached a point, however, where it is necessary to introduce an explicitly geographic concept of insularity into the discussion—for the simple reason that geography is of the first importance in assessing a group's influence within the American political system. For present purposes, it will suffice to restrict our speculations to two simple geographic alternatives. On the one hand, our sociologically insular minority might also be geographically insular: concentrated in a relatively small number of places in the United States. On the other hand, geographic insularity might not accompany sociological insularity. Indeed, at the limit, the *I*-group might be evenly spread over the fifty states and 435 congressional districts. For heuristic purposes, let us begin with the alternative that is empirically less common, but analytically more tractable. Suppose that an *I*-group is distributed in a geographically diffuse way: if it contains 12 percent of the national population, it accounts for 12 percent of each congressional district. Now compare this geographically diffuse *I*-group with a *D*-group that is both sociologically and geographically diffuse. Other things being equal, which group is more likely to succeed in influencing Congressmen?

The previous analysis suggests that the *I*-group will probably have greater influence. Such a group is more likely to form a political lobby peopled by credible leaders who remain in close touch with the insular constituency they represent. When such lobbyists threaten a Congressman with electoral retribution, they can expect a respectful hearing. Even if the interest-group leaders can influence only 10 to 20 percent of their 12 percent of the population, no sensible politician would lightly forfeit 1 to 2 percent of the vote. Of course, if it happens that the *I*-group's interests are diametrically opposed to those of other groups within a Congressman's electoral coalition, a reelection-maximizing politician might decide to ignore the *I*-group's demands. Yet his reluctance to forsake the group will be greater than it would be if he were dealing with a comparable *D*-group. The *D*-group is less likely to have a well-organized lobby to press its cause. It is also less likely to have the communications network necessary for the lobby's leaders credibly to threaten Congressmen with the prospect of electoral retribution. In short, even if the *I*-group is distributed evenly throughout the nation, it has a greater ability to exert political influence through the ultimate currency of democratic politics: votes on election day.

This conclusion is reinforced when we turn to the more realistic case in which the middling *I*-group is distributed very unevenly throughout the country. In this scenario, a middling minority could reasonably expect to be a local majority—or at least a decisive voting bloc—in 20 to 30 congressional districts. For the representatives of these districts, the support of the *I*-group amounts to nothing less than the stuff of political survival. In fact, for all our *Carolene* talk about the powerlessness of insular groups, we are perfectly aware of the enormous power such voting blocs have in

American politics. The story of the protective tariff is, I suppose, the classic illustration of insularity's power in American history. Over the past half-century, we have been treated to an enormous number of welfare-state variations on the theme of insularity by the farm bloc, the steel lobby, the auto lobby, and others too numerous to mention. In this standard scenario of pluralistic politics, it is precisely the diffuse character of the majority forced to pay the bill for tariffs, agricultural subsidies, and the like, that allows strategically located Congressmen to deliver the goods to their well-organized local constituents. Given these familiar stories, it is really quite remarkable to hear lawyers profess concern that insular interests have too little influence in Congress. Instead, the American system typically deprives *diffuse* groups of their rightful say over the course of legislative policy. If there is anything to *Carolene Products,* then, it cannot be a minority's insularity, taken by itself—something more must be involved.

IV. <u>Discrete</u> *and Insular Minorities?*

Could that something be the "discreteness" of a *Carolene* minority?

I begin with a question because it is not obvious whether most constitutional lawyers endow the word "discrete" with independent significance in their understanding of the *Carolene* doctrine. Nonetheless, we can conceive the term in a way that adds something important to the overall formula. I propose to define a minority as "discrete" when its members are marked out in ways that make it relatively easy for others to identify them. For instance, there is nothing a black woman may plausibly do to hide the fact that she is black or female. Like it or not, she will have to deal with the social expectations and stereotypes generated by her evident group characteristics. In contrast, other minorities are socially defined in ways that give individual members the chance to avoid easy identification. A homosexual, for example, can keep her sexual preference a very private affair and thereby

avoid much of the public opprobrium attached to her minority status. It is for this reason that I shall call homosexuals, and groups like them, "anonymous" minorities and contrast them with "discrete" minorities of the kind paradigmatically exemplified by blacks.

This way of defining terms allows us to complement our analysis of insularity in a natural way. While the insularity-diffuseness continuum measures the intensity and breadth of *intra*group interaction, the discreteness-anonymity continuum measures the ease with which people *outside* a group can identify group members. It should be plain that these two continua are not invariably associated with one another. Blacks, for example, are both discrete and insular, whereas women are discrete yet diffuse; homosexuals are anonymous but may be somewhat insular, whereas the poor are both relatively anonymous and diffuse. Because there is no necessary correlation between discreteness and insularity, I shall treat discreteness as a distinct subject for analysis and consider how a group's place on the discreteness-anonymity continuum can be expected to add to, or detract from, its probable political influence.

Carolene takes a straightforward position on this question. In its view, discreteness is a political liability. Once again, however, the only thing that is obvious is that this is not obvious. The main reason why has been elegantly developed in Albert Hirschman's modern classic, *Exit, Voice and Loyalty* (1970). The book's title refers to three nonviolent ways of responding to an unsatisfactory situation: if you dislike something, you may try to avoid it (exit), you may complain about it (voice), or you may grin-and-hope-for-improvement (loyalty). Although these three responses may be related to one another in a number of ways, the relationship between two of them—exit and voice—is of special relevance here. People do not respond to a bad situation by engaging in a random pattern of avoidance and protest. Instead, according to Hirschman, an inverse relationship obtains: the more exit, the less voice, and vice versa. The reason for this is straightforward: the easier it is to avoid a bad situation, the less it will seem worthwhile to complain, and vice versa.

This inverse relationship holds significant implications for the relative political strength of minorities at different points on the discreteness-anonymity scale. If you are a black in America today, you know there is no way you can avoid the impact of the larger public's views about the significance of blackness. Because exit is not possible, there is only one way to do something about disadvantageous racial stereotypes: complain about them. Among efficacious forms of complaint, the possibility of organized political action will surely rank high.

This is not to say, of course, that individual blacks, or members of other discrete minorities, will necessarily lend their support to interest-group activity. They may, instead, succumb to the temptations of free-riding and thus deprive the group of vital political resources. But even if discreteness is no cure-all for selfishness, it does free a minority from the organizational problem confronting an anonymous group of comparable size. To see my point, compare the problem faced by black political organizers with the one confronting organizers of the homosexual community. As a member of an anonymous group, each homosexual can seek to minimize the personal harm due to prejudice by keeping his or her sexual preference a tightly held secret. Although this is hardly a fully satisfactory response, secrecy does enable homosexuals to "exit" from prejudice in a way that blacks cannot. This means that a homosexual group must confront an organizational problem that does not arise for its black counterpart: somehow the group must induce each anonymous homosexual to reveal his or her sexual preference to the larger public and to bear the private costs this public declaration may involve.

Although some, perhaps many, homosexuals may be willing to pay this price, the fact that each must individually choose to pay it means that this anonymous group is less likely to be politically efficacious than is an otherwise comparable but discrete minority. For, by definition, discrete groups do not have to convince their constituents to "come out of the closet" before they can engage in effective political activity. So it would seem that *Carolene Products* is wrong again: a court concerned with pluralist bargaining power should be more, not less,

attentive to the claims of anonymous minorities than to those of discrete ones.

V. Prejudice

But surely it is time to stop playing *Hamlet* without the Prince. The whole point of *Carolene*'s concern with "discrete and insular minorities" cannot be understood, I am sure you are thinking, without grasping the final term of the formula: prejudice. Indeed, it has been one of my aims to provoke precisely this reaction. By detailing all the ways discrete and insular minorities gain political advantage over diffuse and anonymous groups, I have meant to emphasize how heavy a burden the idea of prejudice must carry in the overall argument for *Carolene Products*. The burden is of two kinds: one empirical, the other conceptual. To take them one at a time, I shall defer all problems involved in conceptualizing prejudice so that we may first focus upon the empirical side of the matter.

A. Questions of Fact

Carolene's empirical inadequacy stems from its underinclusive conception of the impact of prejudice upon American society. It is easy to identify groups in the population that are not discrete and insular but that are nonetheless the victims of prejudice, as that term is commonly understood. Thus, the fact that homosexuals are a relatively anonymous minority has not saved the group from severe prejudice. Nor is sexism a nonproblem merely because women are a diffuse, if discrete, majority. Prejudice is generated by a bewildering variety of social conditions. Although some *Carolene* minorities are seriously victimized, they are not the only ones stigmatized; nor is it obvious that all *Carolene* minorities are stigmatized more grievously than any other non-*Carolene* group. Why should the concern with "prejudice" justify *Carolene*'s narrow fixation upon "discrete and insular" minorities?

The answer seemed easy in a world in which members of the paradigmatic *Carolene* minority group—blacks—were effectively barred from voting and political participation.

Something is better than nothing: whatever the organizational problems engendered by anonymity and diffuseness, surely they are not nearly so devastating as total disenfranchisement. As we turn toward the future, however, it is far less clear that such selective perception makes constitutional sense. Nonetheless, I shall give *Carolene* the benefit of the doubt by sketching a "pariah" model of the political process in which *Carolene*'s emphasis on the fate of discrete and insular minorities will still seem empirically plausible.* As we move beyond the pariah model, however, anonymous or diffuse minorities will increasingly emerge as the groups that can raise the most serious complaints of pluralist disempowerment.

1. *The Pariah Model*. Assume a polity in which middling minorities—in the 10 to 20 percent range—attain majority status in a significant number of congressional districts because of the way their insularity interacts with the geographic biases of the American political system. Nonetheless, the minority representatives these groups elect are entirely ineffective in Congress—because all remaining Congressmen refuse to bargain with them in any way. Thus, imagine that you are a nonminority Congressman trying to get a legislative coalition together to support a bill of central importance to your district. After extensive wheeling and dealing, you come within 20 votes of your goal, but the only possible source of support remaining is a bloc of 25 minority Congressmen. Despite your fervent desire to pass the bill for your district, you do not even try to interest them in joining your legislative coalition. Defeat of your priority bill is preferable to victory with the aid of congressional pariahs. And so you grin and bear it as your bill goes down to defeat, thanks to your refusal to deal.

Sound implausible? Nonetheless, there are conditions in which a nonminority Congressman, concerned with maximizing his chances

of reelection, might treat his minority brethren like complete pariahs: Imagine, for example, that a majority Congressman's constituency were *so* prejudiced against the discrete and insular minority that *no* legislative benefit the Congressmen might deliver would, in their eyes, compensate them for the ideological affront they would suffer from seeing their Representative soliciting minority support. The magnitude of this prejudice must be very great indeed to preempt concern for practical matters. Moreover, this condition, let us call it "preemptive prejudice," must pervade a very substantial number of congressional districts before the pariah model is applicable. Yet it is only by indulging in something like these strong empirical assumptions that *Carolene* can claim that the effects of prejudice *plainly* outweigh the political advantages enjoyed by minorities that are discrete and insular.

2. *Beyond the Pariah Model*. Once we deny the general empirical validity of the pariah model, our assessment of the political impact of a discrete and insular group will invariably be more complex. Such a minority may be expected to bring to the bargaining process an asset that many diffuse and anonymous groups lack—namely, 20 to 25 Representatives devoted to the energetic pursuit of the minority's interests. Whether this substantial bargaining advantage is completely negated by prejudice will depend upon many particular institutional factors that will change from decade to decade, if not day to day—facts, moreover, that the Supreme Court of the United States would have special difficulties elaborating upon in a judicial opinion.

It is within this context that I turn to a very different approach to *Carolene* presented by John Hart Ely in his important work, *Democracy and Distrust* (1980). . . . Quite simply, our efforts in bargaining theory have led us to expect that "middling minorities" of the "discrete and insular" kind will elect a significant number of Representatives—say 20 to 25— who are extremely responsive to their interests. As long as these politicians are not treated like pariahs, they can become a potent legislative force—trading votes with other legislators to further the objectives of their

---

*Even within this "pariah" model, however, it is possible that some anonymous or diffuse groups might be as politically disadvantaged by prejudice as any discrete and insular minority. The point of sketching the pariah model is simply to describe a political system in which *Carolene*'s narrow focus, although not necessarily correct, becomes "empirically plausible."

own constituents. Thus, if minority politicians also harbor "we-they" prejudices, the legislative dynamic will inevitably be far more complex than Ely allows. Rather than remorselessly reflecting a monochromatic view of social reality, legislation will be the joint product of different "we-they" prejudices held by the different politicians sitting around the legislative bargaining table. This is more than diffuse or anonymous minorities can expect: *their* representatives may not even *be* at the bargaining table. . . .

Although *Democracy and Distrust* does not contain a fully developed analysis of minority legislative power, it does hint at an approach different from the one I advance here. Dean Ely suggests that minority politicians may suffer from a distinctive psychological affliction: while other Congressmen act on "we-they" prejudices in favor of their own constituents, minority politicians may accept the very stereotypes they should be challenging. If this point were conceded, Ely's argument would take on a self-sealing quality: no matter how actively minority representatives participated in the bargaining process, they would only reinforce, and never challenge, prevailing prejudices. . . .

I believe . . . that an appeal to "false consciousness" cannot be elaborated in a way that makes constitutional sense.

The first question to ask about "false consciousness" is an empirical one: will the rising generation of minority politicians in fact passively accept debasing stereotypes? I see no reason to project such a grim image upon our future. To the contrary, the classic prejudices are under vigorous challenge by powerful voices emerging from a broad range of discrete and insular communities. This is not to say, of course, that minority-group representatives will unanimously agree about matters of public policy. But I do not believe it useful to analyze these inevitable—and often reasonable—disagreements by labeling one or another group of disputants as the victims of "false consciousness."

The second question is: even if some social psychologist could "prove" the existence of false consciousness, should the Supreme Court transform this social phenomenon into an assumption of constitutional law? We are

dealing here not with an academic scientific inquiry, but with a question of institutional relationships. In branding minority politicians as victims of "false consciousness" on the pages of the *United States Reports*, the Supreme Court would be consigning them to a peculiarly demeaning constitutional status. Henceforth, they—and they alone—would be deemed constitutionally incapable of discharging the representative functions of democratically elected legislators. Such a declaration would make a mockery of *Carolene*'s promise. Rather than attempting to approximate the results of a perfect pluralist democracy, the Court would be protecting minority rights by emphatically impugning the capacity of these very same minorities to engage in democratic politics at all.

Once we reject the appeal to false consciousness, I see no way to avoid reformulating *Carolene*'s implications if it is to serve the needs of a polity moving beyond the pariah model. This doctrinal reorientation, it bears repeating, does *not* suppose that we have reached a point in our history in which prejudice against discrete and insular minorities has become a thing of the past. Instead, it simply recognizes that many of these groups can deal with the problem politically in ways that other victims of prejudice may be powerless to match. It is the members of anonymous or diffuse groups who, in the future, will have the greatest cause to complain that pluralist bargaining exposes them to systematic—and undemocratic— disadvantage.

B. Questions of Value

But *Carolene*'s failure to recognize the political predicament of anonymous or diffuse groups that are victims of prejudice is only half the problem; the other half is more conceptual, but no less troubling. The idea of "prejudice" is simply unequal to the task assigned it within the overall *Carolene* analysis. Recall that *Carolene*'s promise is a form of argument that allows a court to say that it is purifying the democratic process rather than imposing its own substantive values upon the political branches. And yet it is just this process orientation that is at risk when a *Carolene* court undertakes to identify the prejudices that entitle a group to special protection from the vagaries of pluralist politics. One person's "prejudice" is, notoriously, another's "principle." How, then, do we identify a group for *Carolene* protection without performing the substantive analysis of constitutional values that *Carolene* hopes to avoid?

The kind of answer required is clear enough. To redeem *Carolene*'s promise, the judicial identification of a prejudice cannot depend upon the substance of the suspect view, but must turn on the way in which legislators come to hold their belief. The process-oriented argument goes something like this: although each of us cannot always expect to convince our legislators, we can at least insist that they treat our claims with respect. At the very least, they should thoughtfully consider our moral and empirical arguments, rejecting them only after conscientiously deciding that they are inconsistent with the public interest. If a group fails to receive this treatment, it suffers a special wrong, one quite distinct from its substantive treatment on the merits. And it is this purely processual kind of prejudice that constitutes the grievance *Carolene* courts may endeavor to remedy without engaging in the suspect task of prescribing substantive values.

Of course, no one imagines that it will be easy for the courts to act effectively on behalf of the victims of purely processual prejudice. To the contrary, a rich and provocative literature describes the difficulties involved in legislative mind reading. For present purposes, I shall assume that the partisans of the process approach can solve these problems in one way or another. My own objections to the enterprise arise only after these threshold difficulties have been overcome. Thus, I shall assume that judges can accurately gauge the quality of legislative deliberation behind a statute, and I shall ask you to speculate about what they would find if they deployed their high-powered techniques on a representative range of legislation.

To begin with the obvious: judges would find that a lot of purely processual prejudice does exist in the case of classic discrete and insular minorities. There are plenty of racial

and religious bigots who have never stopped for a moment to consider the arguments and interests on the other side. But this obvious fact is hardly sufficient to justify *Carolene*'s selective focus on discrete and insular minorities. The critical question, instead, is whether purely processual prejudice is more characteristic in this context than in the political treatment of other interests and opinions. What of the prejudice middle-class legislators may have toward the poor? Heterosexuals toward homosexuals? More fundamentally, are we right to assume that only those *opposed* to "progressive" causes can be processually prejudiced?

Let me propose a test case. Imagine that . . . a group of conservative legalists becomes sincerely convinced that *Brown v. Board of Education* . . . does not deserve its place as a cornerstone of our constitutional law. Acting on this conviction, the group begins a campaign advocating a constitutional amendment to repeal *Brown* and generates some modest interest among conservatives across the country. Arriving in Washington, D.C., with their legal process arguments elaborately developed, the group proceeds to the lobbies of Congress. How do you think the group would be received? Would most Representatives be willing and able to confront the . . . arguments with a thoughtful defense of our constitutional commitment to equality? Or would they respond in a *processually* prejudiced fashion—peremptorily brushing aside the . . . arguments with a catch-phrase or two that fails to join issue?

This is, in principle, an empirical question—though, like many others, it will never get a good empirical answer. Nonetheless, if my study of politics has taught me anything, I would not expect the agitating [conservatives] to receive a processually unprejudiced response on Capitol Hill. As far as I can tell, any large representative assembly will contain a bewildering variety of human types—from the elaborately thoughtful to the superficially unquestioning. It is simply self-congratulatory to suppose that the members of our own persuasion have reached their convictions in a deeply reflective way, whereas those espousing opinions we hate are superficial. Instead, a thoughtful judge can expect to find an abundance of stereotype-mongers and knee-jerks on *all* sides of *every* important issue—as well as many who have struggled their way to more considered judgments. Given the complexity of the human comedy, a judge is bound on a fool's errand if he imagines that the good guys and bad guys of American politics can be neatly classified according to the seriousness with which they have considered opposing points of view. Processual prejudice is a pervasive problem in the American political system.

But if this is right, *Carolene* cannot justify its concern with discrete and insular minorities without calling on judges to engage in a very different kind of judgment, one dealing with the *substance* of racial and religious prejudice. In doing so, the judge need not try to play the elaborate psychological and political guessing game required to assess the extent to which a statute is the product of a prejudiced refusal to give a respectful hearing to disfavored interests and opinions. Instead, she proceeds to a more familiar judicial inquiry into the nature of the substantive reasons that might plausibly justify the legislature's assertion of authority. If the only plausible reasons for the statute's enactment offend substantive constitutional principles, the groups aggrieved by the statute are declared victims of "prejudice"; if not, not. Although this judicial inquiry into the rational foundations of a statute may sometimes require a focused inquiry into the data available to, or even the subjective opinions of, particular public officials, the critical legal question is of a very different kind: why are the political principles endorsed by some groups judicially recognized as vindicating the constitutionality of a statute, while others are viewed as inadmissible "prejudices" delegitimating a statute's claim to constitutionality?

If *Carolene* somehow hoped to find a shortcut around this substantive inquiry into constitutional values, its journey was fated to fail from the outset. The difference between the things we call "prejudice" and the things we call "principle" is in the end a substantive moral difference. And if the courts are authorized to protect the victims of certain "prejudices," it can only be because the Constitution has placed certain normative judgments beyond the pale of legitimacy.

From Critique to Reconstruction

. . . Against [its] historical background, the *Carolene* Court was absolutely right to emphasize the special vulnerability of discrete and insular minorities, as well as the fundamental importance of ensuring their effective participation in the democratic process. After a generation of renewed struggle for civil rights, however, it no longer follows that the discreteness or insularity of a group will continue to serve as a decisive disadvantage in the ongoing process of pluralist bargaining. Rather than find this fact embarrassing, constitutional lawyers ought to be proud of it. It suggests that, despite the racial and religious prejudices that still haunt our society, Americans *have* made some progress toward a more just polity.

It will be a tragedy, however, if the progress we have made serves to justify a refusal to develop and extend *Carolene's* concern with the integrity of pluralist process to contemporary conditions. Long after discrete and insular minorities have gained strong representation at the pluralist bargaining table, there will remain many other groups who fail to achieve influence remotely proportionate to their numbers: groups that are discrete and diffuse (like women), or anonymous and somewhat insular (like homosexuals), or *both* diffuse and anonymous (like the victims of poverty). If we are to treat *Carolene* as something more than a tired formula, constitutional lawyers must develop paradigms that detail the systematic disadvantages that undermine our system's legitimacy in dealing with the grievances of these diffuse or anonymous groups.

At the same time that we enrich the capacity of constitutional law to perfect pluralist democracy, we must also reaffirm a second fundamental mission for judicial review: to expound the ultimate limits imposed on pluralist bargaining by the American constitutional system. In the exercise of this critical function, the courts insist that, for all our plural differences, We the People of the United States *do* have a set of fundamental commitments that bind us together in ways that our interest-group representatives are not normally elected to modify. It is this idea of higher law that must be taken with renewed seriousness if we are to sustain judicial protection for racial and religious minorities in the coming generation. Although, as we have seen, the *Carolene* effort to protect minorities ultimately required the elaboration of substantive constitutional principles, the *Carolene* tradition's reliance on bad political science has made it seem possible to avoid the sustained inquiry into democratic theory that substantive judicial review entails. More particularly, *Carolene*'s focus on pluralist bargaining has subtly encouraged the belief that pluralism is the alpha and the omega of the American constitutional system, and that any effort by the courts to challenge the substantive values generated by legislative compromise is necessarily antidemocratic.

We must repudiate this reduction of the American Constitution to a simple system of pluralist bargaining if we are to reassert the legitimacy of the courts' critical function. Although the bargaining model captures an important aspect of American politics, it does not do justice to the most fundamental episodes of our constitutional history. We make a mistake, for example, to view the enactment of the Bill of Rights and the Civil War Amendments as if they were outcomes of ordinary pluralist bargaining. Instead, these constitutional achievements represent the highest legal expression of a different kind of politics—one characterized by mass mobilization and struggle that, after experiences like the Revolution and the Civil War, yielded fundamental principles transcending the normal processes of interest-group accommodation. It is only by reasserting the relevance of this tradition of constitutional politics, as I have called it, that we shall gain the necessary perspective to put pluralist bargaining in its place as one—but only one—form of American democracy, and the lesser form at that.

Not that the *Carolene* tradition—or *Carolene* itself—is entirely oblivious to the limits of pluralist bargaining. Indeed, it was just this issue that initially provoked Chief Justice Hughes to press for a revision of *Carolene* in the opinion-writing process. While Justice Stone's early draft had focused exclusively on the pluralist perfection rationale, the Chief Justice believed that something essential was missing in the case for judicial review. In response to this expression of concern, Justice Stone added a first paragraph to footnote four that takes our higher-law tradition more explicitly into account. Thus, before addressing the pluralist themes we have considered here, *Carolene* noted that "the presumption of constitutionality" may also be overcome "when legislation appears on its face to be within a specific prohibition of the Constitution, such as those of the first ten amendments."

In calling the Bill of Rights "specific," Justice Stone doubtless wished to emphasize that the Court had learned its lesson in 1937 and would not use the Constitution's grand abstractions to revive the laissez-faire capitalism of the *Lochner* era. Nonetheless, by framing its pledge of judicial restraint in this way, *Carolene* added a distortion of its own. For it intimated that the judicial process of articulating the nature of our higher law values can be reduced to a mechanical effort to apply "specific" constitutional rules to predetermined facts. Such a position requires judges to repudiate the main line of modern American legal thought, which—from Pound to Dworkin—is one long elaboration of the inadequacies of mechanical jurisprudence. Even more fundamentally, it trivializes the nature of the American people's higher-law achievement. Our Constitution does not even attempt to provide a detailed set of rules that might suggest the possibility of pseudomechanical application. Instead, our higher law tradition gains its distinctive character precisely by speaking in abstract and general terms about the nature of our basic rights. Hence, in endowing the Bill of Rights with a false "specificity," *Carolene* not only proffered a misleading and unattainable picture of responsible judicial decisionmaking. It also diverted us from the main question: having cleared away the laissez-faire debris of the *Lochner* era, can we still reconstruct, out of authoritative sources, a legally cogent set of higher-law principles that can continue to govern the pluralist process in the name of We the People?

The point of this essay is not to answer this question, but to convince you that it needs asking if we are to preserve the constitutional rights of discrete and insular minorities during the coming decades. I do not believe that the weaknesses in *Carolene*'s defense of minority rights will long remain a professional secret locked in the pages of the *Harvard Law Review.* Instead, *Carolene*'s errors will become increasingly apparent on the surface of American political life. Thanks largely to the achievements of the generation that looked to *Carolene* for inspiration, black Americans today are generally free to participate in democratic politics—and do so by the millions in every national election.* Moreover, the predicted consequences of the discreteness and insularity of black voters are beginning to be obvious at every level of American government. From City Hall to Capitol Hill, black politicians now aggressively represent their constituencies in the citadels of power.** Similarly, religious organizations are increasingly involved in pressure-group politics.

I am not suggesting that America is on the way to becoming a religious and racial utopia. Despite their political gains, blacks still suffer under the weight of grossly disproportionate economic, educational, and social disadvantage, as well as sheer racial prejudice. In light of these facts, it is far too early to say that we have redeemed the promise of the thirteenth and fourteenth amendments. In contrast to black political mobilization, the heightened involvement of organized religion can readily undermine our substantive constitutional legacy—threatening the very values

*In the congressional elections of 1982, voting participation among whites was 50%; among blacks, 43%. *See* BUREAU OF THE CENSUS, U.S. DEP'T OF COMMERCE, VOTING AND REGISTRATION IN THE ELECTION OF NOVEMBER 1982, at vi (1983) (P-20, No. 383).

**"Between 1965 and 1982, the number of black elected officials increased tenfold, from about 500 to more than 5,100. . . . Blacks have now been elected to every major category of public office except the presidency, vice presidency, and governorship. . . ." T. CAVANAGH & D. STOCKTON, BLACK ELECTED OFFICIALS AND THEIR CONSTITUENCIES 2 (1983) at l. Blacks have made the most substantial gains at the local level: in 1982, there were 465 black county officials, 2,451 elected blacks at the municipal level, and 563 in the judiciary or in law enforcement. *Id.* at 2. For the data on black Representatives in Congress, see note 35.

of religious toleration and free exercise to which our higher law is committed.

Yet as long as we use *Carolene* rhetoric to express our constitutional concerns with racial equality and religious freedom, we will find ourselves saying things that are increasingly belied by political reality. While constitutional lawyers decry the political powerlessness of discrete and insular groups, representatives of these interests will be wheeling and dealing in the ongoing pluralist exchange—winning some battles, losing others, but plainly numbering among the organized interests whose electoral power must be treated with respect by their bargaining partners and competitors. Gradually, this clash between constitutional rhetoric and political reality can have only one result. As time goes by, the constitutional center will not hold: the longer *Carolene* remains at the core of the constitutional case for judicial review, the harder lawyers will find it to convince themselves, let alone others, that judicial protection for the rights of "discrete and insular minorities" makes constitutional sense.

For those who are constitutional conservatives in the deepest sense, and who look upon our tradition of civil liberties as one of the greatest achievements of American law, the challenges are clear. On the one hand, if we are to remain faithful to *Carolene*'s concern with the fairness of pluralist politics, we must repudiate the bad political science that allows us to ignore those citizens who have the most serious complaints: the anonymous and diffuse victims of poverty and sexual discrimination who find it most difficult to protect their fundamental interests through effective political organization. On the other hand, we must explain to our fellow Americans that there are constitutional values in our scheme of government even more fundamental than perfected pluralism—most notably, those that bar prejudice against racial and religious minorities. If we persist in holding these rights hostage to pluralist theory, we shall only end up mocking the proud role that *Carolene* has played in the pursuit of constitutional values over the past half-century. By failing to adapt *Carolene*'s constitutional theory to a changing political reality, we shall have passively allowed the Constitution's profound concern for racial equality and religious freedom to be trivialized into a transparent apologia for the status quo.

Constitutional Cases

Ronald Dworkin

Ronald Dworkin's work has had a large impact on the related fields of philosophy of law and political philosophy. One of the topics he has been most concerned to address is the role of judges, particularly the legitimacy of judicial review in a constitutional democracy where elected representatives make law. In the following essay he defends judicial activism against those who argue judges should defer to elected branches whenever there is controversy about a law's constitutionality. The latter view, which he terms judicial restraint, could be defended on one of two grounds: skepticism about the existence of moral rights and deference to elected branches. Dworkin considers, and rejects, each of these defenses of judicial restraint, concluding that genuine democracy and judicial activism are compatible.

I.

When Richard Nixon was running for President he promised that he would appoint to the Supreme Court men who represented his own legal philosophy, that is, who were what he called "strict constructionists." . . .

Nixon claimed that his opposition to the Warren Court's desegregation decisions, and to other decisions it took, were not based simply on a personal or political distaste for the results. He argued that the decisions violated the standards of adjudication that the Court should follow. The Court was usurping, in his views, powers that rightly belong to other institutions, including the legislatures of the various states whose school systems the Court sought to reform. . . .

I shall argue that there is in fact no coherent philosophy to which such politicians may consistently appeal. . . .

From Ronald Dworkin, *Taking Rights Seriously* (Cambridge: Harvard University Press, 1978). © 1978 by Ronald Dworkin.

Nixon is no longer president, and his crimes were so grave that no one is likely to worry very much any more about the details of his own legal philosophy. Nevertheless in what follows I shall use the name "Nixon" to refer, not to Nixon, but to any politician holding the set of attitudes about the Supreme Court that he made explicit in his political campaigns. There was, fortunately, only one real Nixon, but there are, in the special sense in which I use the name, many Nixons.

What can be the basis of this composite Nixon's opposition to the controversial decisions of the Warren Court? He cannot object to these decisions simply because they went beyond prior law, or say that the Supreme Court must never change its mind. Indeed the Burger Court itself seems intent on limiting the liberal decisions of the Warren Court, like *Miranda*. The Constitution's guarantee of "equal protection of the laws," it is true, does not in plain words determine that "separate but equal" school facilities are unconstitutional, or that segregation was so unjust that heroic measures are required to undo its effects. But neither does it provide that as a matter of constitutional law the Court would be wrong to reach these conclusions. It leaves these issues to the Court's judgment. . . .

2.

The constitutional theory on which our government rests is not a simple majoritarian theory. The Constitution, and particularly the Bill of Rights, is designed to protect individual citizens and groups against certain decisions that a majority of citizens might want to make, even when that majority acts in what it takes to be the general or common interest. Some of these constitutional restraints take the form of fairly precise rules, like the rule that requires a jury trial in federal criminal proceedings or, perhaps, the rule that forbids the national Congress to abridge freedom of speech. But other constraints take the form of what are often called "vague" standards, for example, the provision that the government shall not deny men due process of law, or equal protection of the laws.

This interference with democratic practice requires a justification. The draftsmen of the Constitution assumed that these restraints could be justified by appeal to moral rights which individuals possess against the majority, and which the constitutional provisions, both "vague" and precise, might be said to recognize and protect.

The "vague" standards were chosen deliberately, by the men who drafted and adopted them, in place of the more specific and limited rules that they might have enacted. But their decision to use the language they did has caused a great deal of legal and political controversy, because even reasonable men of good will differ when they try to elaborate, for example, the moral rights that the due process clause or the equal protection clause brings into the law. They also differ when they try to apply these rights, however defined, to complex matters of political administration, like the educational practices that were the subject of the segregation cases.

The practice has developed of referring to a "strict" and a "liberal" side to these controversies, so that the Supreme Court might be said to have taken the "liberal" side in the segregation cases and its critics the "strict" side. Nixon has this distinction in mind when he calls himself a "strict constructionist." But

the distinction is in fact confusing, because it runs together two different issues that must be separated. Any case that arises under the "vague" constitutional guarantees can be seen as posing two questions: (1) Which decision is required by strict, that is to say faithful, adherence to the text of the Constitution or to the intention of those who adopted that text? (2) Which decision is required by a political philosophy that takes a strict, that is to say narrow, view of the moral rights that individuals have against society? Once these questions are distinguished, it is plain that they may have different answers. The text of the First Amendment, for example, says that Congress shall make *no* law abridging the freedom of speech, but a narrow view of individual rights would permit many such laws, ranging from libel and obscenity laws to the Smith Act.

In the case of the "vague" provisions, however, like the due process and equal protection clauses, lawyers have run the two questions together because they have relied, largely without recognizing it, on a theory of meaning that might be put this way: If the framers of the Constitution used vague language, as they did when they condemned violations of "due process of law," then what they "said" or "meant" is limited to the instances of official action that they had in mind as violations, or, at least, to those instances that they would have thought were violations if they had had them in mind. If those who were responsible for adding the due process clause to the Constitution believed that it was fundamentally unjust to provide separate education for different races, or had detailed views about justice that entailed that conclusion, then the segregation decisions might be defended as an application of the principle they had laid down. Otherwise they could not be defended in this way, but instead would show that the judges had substituted their own ideas of justice for those the constitutional drafters meant to lay down.

This theory makes a strict interpretation of the text yield a narrow view of constitutional rights, because it limits such rights to those recognized by a limited group of people at a fixed date of history. It forces those who favor a more liberal set of rights to concede that they are departing from strict legal authority, a departure they must then seek to justify by appealing only to the desirability of the results they reach.

But the theory of meaning on which this argument depends is far too crude; it ignores a distinction that philosophers have made but lawyers have not yet appreciated. Suppose I tell my children simply that I expect them not to treat others unfairly. I no doubt have in mind examples of the conduct I mean to discourage, but I would not accept that my "meaning" was limited to these examples, for two reasons. First I would expect my children to apply my instructions to situations I had not and could not have thought about. Second, I stand ready to admit that some particular act I had thought was fair when I spoke was in fact unfair, or vice versa, if one of my children is able to convince me of that later; in that case I should want to say that my instructions covered the case he cited, not that I had changed my instructions. I might say that I meant the family to be guided by the *concept* of fairness, not by any specific *conception* of fairness I might have had in mind.

This is a crucial distinction which it is worth pausing to explore. Suppose a group believes in common that acts may suffer from a special moral defect which they call unfairness, and which consists in a wrongful division of benefits and burdens, or a wrongful attribution of praise or blame. Suppose also that they agree on a great number of standard cases of unfairness and use these as benchmarks against which to test other, more controversial cases. In that case, the group has a concept of unfairness, and its members may appeal to that concept in moral instruction or argument. But members of that group may nevertheless differ over a large number of these controversial cases, in a way that suggests that each either has or acts on a different theory of *why* the standard cases are acts of unfairness. They may differ, that is, on which more fundamental principles must be relied upon to show that a particular division or attribution is unfair. In that case, the members have different conceptions of fairness.

If so, then members of this community who give instructions or set standards in the name of fairness may be doing two different things. First they may be appealing to the concept of fairness, simply by instructing others to act fairly; in this case they charge those whom they instruct with the responsibility of developing and applying their own conception of fairness as controversial cases arise. That is not the same thing, of course, as granting them a discretion to act as they like; it sets a standard which they must try—and may fail—to meet, because it assumes that one conception is superior to another. The man who appeals to the concept in this way may have his own conception, as I did when I told my children to act fairly; but he holds this conception only as his own theory of how the standard he set must be met, so that when he changes his theory he has not changed that standard.

On the other hand, the members may be laying down a particular conception of fairness; I would have done this, for example, if I had listed my wishes with respect to controversial examples or if, even less likely, I had specified some controversial and explicit theory of fairness, as if I had said to decide hard cases by applying the utilitarian ethics of Jeremy Bentham. The difference is a difference not just in the *detail* of the instructions given but in the *kind* of instructions given. When I appeal to the concept of fairness I appeal to what fairness means, and I give my views on that issue no special standing. When I lay down a conception of fairness, I lay down what I mean by fairness, and my view is therefore the heart of the matter. When I appeal to fairness I pose a moral issue; when I lay down my conception of fairness I try to answer it.

Once this distinction is made it seems obvious that we must take what I have been calling "vague" constitutional clauses as representing appeals to the concepts they employ, like legality, equality, and cruelty. The Supreme Court may soon decide, for example, whether capital punishment is "cruel" within the meaning of the constitutional clause that prohibits "cruel and unusual punishment." It would be a mistake for the Court to be much influenced by the fact that when the clause was adopted capital punishment was standard and unquestioned. That would be decisive if the framers of the clause had meant to lay down a particular conception of cruelty, because it would show that the conception did not extend so far. But it is not decisive of the different question the Court now faces, which is this:

Can the Court, responding to the framers' appeal to the concept of cruelty, now defend a conception that does not make death cruel?

Those who ignore the distinction between concepts and conceptions, but who believe that the Court ought to make a fresh determination of whether the death penalty is cruel, are forced to argue in a vulnerable way. They say that ideas of cruelty change over time, and that the Court must be free to reject out-of-date conceptions; this suggests that the Court must change what the Constitution enacted. But in fact the Court can enforce what the Constitution says only by making up its own mind about what is cruel, just as my children, in my example, can do what I said only by making up their own minds about what is fair. If those who enacted the broad clauses had meant to lay down particular conceptions, they would have found the sort of language conventionally used to do this, that is, they would have offered particular theories of the concepts in question.

Indeed the very practice of calling these clauses "vague," in which I have joined, can now be seen to involve a mistake. The clauses are vague only if we take them to be botched or incomplete or schematic attempts to lay down particular conceptions. If we take them as appeals to moral concepts they could not be made more precise by being more detailed.[1]

The confusion I mentioned between the two senses of "strict" construction is therefore very misleading indeed. If courts try to be faithful to the text of the Constitution, they will for that very reason be forced to decide between competing conceptions of political morality. So it is wrong to attack the Warren Court, for example, on the ground that it failed to treat the Constitution as a binding text. On the contrary, if we wish to treat fidelity to that text as an overriding requirement of constitutional interpretation, then it is the conservative critics of the Warren Court who are at fault, because their philosophy ignores the direction to face issues of moral principle that the logic of the text demands.

I put the matter in a guarded way because we may *not* want to accept fidelity to the spirit of the text as an overriding principle of constitutional adjudication. It may be more important for courts to decide constitutional cases in a manner that respects the judgments of other institutions of government, for example. Or it may be more important for courts to protect established legal doctrines, so that citizens and the government can have confidence that the courts will hold to what they have said before. But it is crucial to recognize that these other policies compete with the principle that the Constitution is the fundamental and imperative source of constitutional law. They are not, as the "strict constructionists" suppose, simply consequences of that principle.

3.

Once the matter is put in this light, moreover, we are able to assess these competing claims of policy, free from the confusion imposed by the popular notion of "strict construction." For this purpose I want now to compare and contrast two very general philosophies of how the courts should decide difficult or controversial constitutional issues. I shall call these two philosophies by the names they are given in the legal literature—the programs of "judicial activism" and "judicial restraint"—though it will be plain that these names are in certain ways misleading.

The program of judicial activism holds that courts should accept the directions of the so-called vague constitutional provisions in the spirit I described, in spite of competing reasons of the sort I mentioned. They should work out principles of legality, equality, and the rest, revise these principles from time to time in the light of what seems to the Court fresh moral insight, and judge the acts of Congress, the states, and the President accordingly. (This puts the program in its strongest form; in fact its supporters generally qualify it in ways I shall ignore for the present.)

The program of judicial restraint, on the contrary, argues that courts should allow the decisions of other branches of government to stand, even when they offend the judges' own sense of the principles required by the broad constitutional doctrines, except when these decisions are so offensive to political morality that they would violate the provisions on any plausible interpretation, or, perhaps, when a contrary decision is required by clear precedent. (Again, this put the program in a stark form; those who profess the policy qualify it in different ways.) . . .

We must now . . . notice a distinction between two forms of judicial restraint, for there are two different, and indeed incompatible, grounds on which that policy might be based.

The first is a theory of political *skepticism* that might be described in this way. The policy of judicial activism presupposes a certain objectivity of moral principle; in particular it presupposes that citizens do have certain moral rights against the state, like a moral right to equality of public education or to fair treatment by the police. Only if such moral rights exist in some sense can activism be justified as a program based on something beyond the judge's personal preferences. The skeptical theory attacks activism at its roots; it argues that in fact individuals have no such moral rights against the state. They have only such *legal* rights as the Constitution grants them, and these are limited to the plain and uncontroversial violations or public morality that the framers must have had actually in mind, or that have since been established in a line of precedent.

The alternative ground of a program of restraint is a theory of judicial *deference*. Contrary to the skeptical theory, this assumes that citizens do have moral rights against the state beyond what the law expressly grants them, but it points out that the character and strength of these rights are debatable and argues that political institutions other than courts are responsible for deciding which rights are to be recognized.

This is an important distinction, even though the literature of constitutional law does not draw it with any clarity. The skeptical theory and the theory of deference differ dramatically in the kind of justification they assume, and in their implications for the more general moral theories of the men who profess to hold them. These theories are so different that most American politicians can consistently accept the second, but not the first.

A skeptic takes the view, as I have said, that men have no moral rights against the state and

only such legal rights as the law expressly provides. But what does this mean, and what sort of argument might the skeptic make for his view? There is, of course, a very lively dispute in moral philosophy about the nature and standing of moral rights, and considerable disagreement about what they are, if they are anything at all. I shall rely, in trying to answer these questions, on a low-keyed theory of moral rights against the state. . . . Under that theory, a man has a moral right against the state if for some reason the state would do wrong to treat him in a certain way, even though it would be in the general interest to do so. So a black child has a moral right to an equal education, for example, if it is wrong for the state not to provide that education, even if the community as a whole suffers thereby.

I want to say a word about the virtues of this way of looking at moral rights against the state. A great many lawyers are wary of talking about moral rights, even though they find it easy to talk about what is right or wrong for government to do, because they suppose that rights, if they exist at all, are spooky sorts of things that men and women have in much the same way as they have non-spooky things like tonsils. But the sense of rights I propose to use does not make ontological assumptions of that sort: it simply shows a claim of right to be a special, in the sense of a restricted, sort of judgment about what is right or wrong for governments to do.

Moreover, this way of looking at rights avoids some of the notorious puzzles associated with the concept. It allows us to say, with no sense of strangeness, that rights may vary in strength and character from case to case, and from point to point in history. If we think of rights as things, these metamorphoses seem strange, but we are used to the idea that moral judgments about what it is right or wrong to do are complex and are affected by considerations that are relative and that change.

The skeptic who wants to argue against the very possibility of rights against the state of this sort has a difficult brief. He must rely, I think, on one of three general positions: (a) He might display a more pervasive moral skepticism, which holds that even to speak of an act being morally right or wrong makes no sense. If no act is morally wrong, then the government of North Carolina cannot be wrong to refuse to bus school children. (b) He might hold a stark form of utilitarianism, which assumes that the only reason we ever have for regarding an act as right or wrong is its impact on the general interest. Under that theory, to say that busing may be morally required even though it does not benefit the community generally would be inconsistent. (c) He might accept some form of totalitarian theory, which merges the interests of the individual in the good of the general community, and so denies that the two can conflict.

Very few American politicians would be able to accept any of these three grounds. Nixon, for example, could not, because he presents himself as a moral fundamentalist who knows in his heart that pornography is wicked and that some of the people of South Vietnam have rights of self-determination in the name of which they and we may properly kill many others.

I do not want to suggest, however, that no one would in fact argue for judicial restraint on grounds of skepticism; on the contrary, some of the best known advocates of restraint have pitched their arguments entirely on skeptical grounds. In 1957, for example, the great judge Learned Hand delivered the Oliver Wendell Holmes lectures at Harvard. Hand was a student of Santayana and a disciple of Holmes, and skepticism in morals was his only religion. He argued for judicial restraint, and said that the Supreme Court had done wrong to declare school segregation illegal in the *Brown* case. It is wrong to suppose, he said, that claims about moral rights express anything more than the speakers' preferences. If the Supreme Court justifies its decisions by making such claims, rather than by relying on positive law, it is usurping the place of the legislature, for the job of the legislature, representing the majority, is to decide whose preferences shall govern.

This simple appeal to democracy is successful if one accepts the skeptical premise. Of course, if men have no rights against the majority, if political decision is simply a matter of whose preferences shall prevail, then democracy does provide a good reason for leaving that decision to more democratic institutions than courts, even when these in-

stitutions make choices that the judges themselves hate. But a very different, and much more vulnerable, argument from democracy is needed to support judicial restraint if it is based not on skepticism but on deference, as I shall try to show.

4.

If Nixon holds a coherent constitutional theory, it is a theory of restraint based not on skepticism but on deference. He believes that courts ought not to decide controversial issues of political morality because they ought to leave such decisions to other departments of government. . . .

There is one very popular argument in favor of the policy of deference, which might be called the argument from democracy. It is at least debatable, according to this argument, whether a sound conception of equality forbids segregated education or requires measures like busing to break it down. Who ought to decide these debatable issues of moral and political theory? Should it be a majority of a court in Washington, whose members are appointed for life and are not politically responsible to the public whose lives will be affected by the decision? Or should it be the elected and responsible state or national legislators? A democrat, so this argument supposes, can accept only the second answer.

But the argument from democracy is weaker than it might first appear. The argument assumes, for one thing, that state legislatures are in fact responsible to the people in the way that democratic theory assumes. But in all the states, though in different degrees and for different reasons, that is not the case. In some states it is very far from the case. I want to pass that point, however, because it does not so much undermine the argument from democracy as call for more democracy, and that is a different matter. I want to fix attention on the issue of whether the appeal to democracy in this respect is even right in principle.

The argument assumes that in a democracy all unsettled issues, including issues of moral and political principle, must be resolved only by institutions that are politically responsible in the way that courts are not. Why should we accept that view of democracy? To say that that is what democracy means does no good, because it is wrong to suppose that the word, as a word, has anything like so precise a meaning. Even if it did, we should then have to rephrase our question to ask why we should have democracy, if we assume that is what it means. Nor is it better to say that that view of democracy is established in the American Constitution, or so entrenched in our political tradition that we are committed to it. We cannot argue that the Constitution, which provides no rule limiting judicial review to clear cases, establishes a theory of democracy that excludes wider review, nor can we say that our courts have in fact consistently accepted such a restriction. The burden of Nixon's argument is that they have.

So the argument from democracy is not an argument to which we are committed either by our words or our past. We must accept it, if at all, on the strength of its own logic. In order to examine the arguments more closely, however, we must make a further distinction. The argument as I have set it out might be continued in two different ways: one might argue that judicial deference is required because democratic institutions, like legislatures, are in fact likely to make *sounder* decisions than courts about the underlying issues that constitutional cases raise, that is, about the nature of an individual's moral rights against the state.

Or one might argue that it is for some reason *fairer* that a democratic institution rather than a court should decide such issues, even though there is no reason to believe that the institution will reach a sounder decision. The distinction between these two arguments would make no sense to a skeptic, who would not admit that someone could do a better or worse job at identifying moral rights against the state, any more than someone could do a better or worse job of identifying ghosts. But a lawyer who believes in judicial deference rather than skepticism must acknowledge the distinction, though he can argue both sides if he wishes.

I shall start with the second argument, that legislatures and other democratic institutions have some special title to make constitutional decisions, apart from their ability to make better decisions. One might say that the nature of this title is obvious, because it is always fairer to allow a majority to decide any issue than a minority. But that, as has often been pointed out, ignores the fact that decisions about rights against the majority are not issues that in fairness ought to be left to the majority. Constitutionalism—the theory that the majority must be restrained to protect individual rights—may be a good or bad political theory, but the United States has adopted that theory, and to make the majority judge in its own cause seems inconsistent and unjust. So principles of fairness seem to speak against, not for, the argument from democracy.

Chief Justice Marshall recognized this in his decision in *Marbury v. Madison,* the famous case in which the Supreme Court first claimed the power to review legislative decisions against constitutional standards. He argued that since the Constitution provides that the Constitution shall be the supreme law of the land, the courts in general, and the Supreme Court in the end, must have power to declare statutes void that offend that Constitution. Many legal scholars regard his argument as a *non sequitur,* because, they say, although constitutional constraints are part of the law, the courts, rather than the legislature itself, have not necessarily been given authority to decide whether in particular cases that law has been violated.[2] But the argument is not a *non sequitur* if we take the principle that no man should be judge in his own cause to be so fundamental a part of the idea of legality that Marshall would have been entitled to disregard it only if the Constitution had expressly denied judicial review.

Some might object that it is simple-minded to say that a policy of deference leaves the majority to judge its own cause. Political decisions are made, in the United States, not by one stable majority but by many different political institutions each representing a different constituency which itself changes its composition over time. The decision of one branch of government may well be reviewed by another branch that is also politically responsible, but to a larger or different constituency. The acts of the Arizona police which the Court held unconstitutional in *Miranda,* for example, were in fact subject to review by various executive boards and municipal and state legislatures of Arizona, as well as by the national Congress. It would be naïve to suppose that all of these political institutions are dedicated to the same policies and interests, so it is wrong to suppose that if the Court had not intervened the Arizona police would have been free to judge themselves.

But this objection is itself too glib, because it ignores the special character of disputes about individual moral rights as distinct from other kinds of political disputes. Different institutions do have different constituencies when, for example, labor or trade or welfare issues are involved, and the nation often divides sectionally on such issues. But this is not generally the case when individual constitutional rights, like the rights of accused criminals, are at issue. It has been typical of these disputes that the interests of those in political control of the various institutions of the government have been both homogeneous and hostile. Indeed that is why political theorists have conceived of constitutional rights as rights against the "state" or the "majority" as such, rather than against any particular body or branch of government. . . .

It does seem fair to say, therefore, that the argument from democracy asks that those in political power be invited to be the sole judge of their own decisions, to see whether they have the right to do what they have decided they want to do. That is not a final proof that a policy of judicial activism is superior to a program of deference. Judicial activism involves risks of tyranny; certainly in the stark and simple form I set out. It might even be shown that these risks override the unfairness of asking the majority to be judge in its own cause. But the point does undermine the argument that the majority, in fairness, must be allowed to decide the limits of its own power.

We must therefore turn to the other continuation of the argument from democracy, which holds that democratic institutions, like legislatures, are likely to reach *sounder* results about the moral rights of individuals than would courts. In 1969 the late Professor Alexander Bickel of the Yale Law School delivered his Holmes Lectures at Harvard and argued

for the program of judicial restraint in a novel and ingenious way. He allowed himself to suppose, for purposes of argument, that the Warren Court's program of activism could be justified if in fact it produced desirable results.[3] He appeared, therefore, to be testing the policy of activism on its own grounds, because he took activism to be precisely the claim that the courts have the moral right to improve the future, whatever legal theory may say. Learned Hand and other opponents of activism had challenged that claim. Bickel accepted it, at least provisionally, but he argued that activism fails its own test. . . .

What are we to make of Bickel's argument? His account of recent history can be, and has been, challenged. It is by no means plain, certainly not yet, that racial integration will fail as a long-term strategy; and he is wrong if he thinks that black Americans, of whom more still belong to the NAACP than to more militant organizations, have rejected it. No doubt the nation's sense of how to deal with the curse of racism swings back and forth as the complexity and size of the problem become more apparent, but Bickel may have written at a high point of one arc of the pendulum.

He is also wrong to judge the Supreme Court's effect on history as if the Court were the only institution at work, or to suppose that if the Court's goal has not been achieved the country is worse off than if it had not tried. Since 1954, when the Court laid down the principle that equality before the law requires integrated education, we have not had, except for a few years of the Johnson Administration, a national executive willing to accept that principle as an imperative. For the past several years we have had a national executive that seems determined to undermine it. Nor do we have much basis for supposing that the racial situation in America would now be more satisfactory, on balance, if the Court had not intervened, in 1954 and later, in the way that it did.

But there is a very different, and for my purpose much more important, objection to take to Bickel's theory. His theory is novel because it appears to concede an issue of principle to judicial activism, namely, that the Court is entitled to intervene if its intervention produces socially desirable results. But the concession is an illusion, because his sense of what is socially desirable is inconsistent with the presupposition of activism that individuals have moral rights against the state. In fact, Bickel's argument cannot succeed, even if we grant his facts and his view of history, except on a basis of a skepticism about rights as profound as Learned Hand's.

I presented Bickel's theory as an example of one form of the argument from democracy, the argument that since men disagree about rights it is safer to leave the final decision about rights to the political process, safer in the sense that the results are likely to be sounder. Bickel suggests a reason why the political process is safer. He argues that the endurance of a political settlement about rights is some evidence of the political morality of that settlement. He argues that this evidence is better than the sorts of argument from principle that judges might deploy if the decision were left to them.

There is a weak version of this claim, which cannot be part of Bickel's argument. This version argues that no political principle establishing rights can be sound, whatever abstract arguments might be made in its favor, unless it meets the test of social acceptance in the long run; so that, for example, the Supreme Court cannot be right in its views about the rights of black children, or criminal suspects, or atheists, if the community in the end will not be persuaded to recognize these rights.

This weak version may seem plausible for different reasons. It will appeal, for instance, to those who believe both in the fact and in the strength of the ordinary man's moral sense, and in his willingness to entertain appeals to that sense. But it does not argue for judicial restraint except in the very long run. On the contrary, it supposes what lawyers are fond of calling a dialogue between the judges and the nation, in which the Supreme Court is to present and defend its reflective view of what the citizen's rights are, much as the Warren Court tried to do, in the hope that the people will in the end agree.

We must turn, therefore, to the strong version of the claim. This argues that the organic political process will secure the genuine rights of men more certainly if it is not hindered by the artificial and rationalistic intrusion of the courts. On this view, the rights of blacks, suspects, and atheists will emerge through the process of political institutions responding to political pressures in the normal way. If a claim of right cannot succeed in this way, then for that reason it is, or in any event it is likely to be, an improper claim of right. But this bizarre proposition is only a disguised form of the skeptical point that there are in fact no rights against the state.

Perhaps, as Burke and his modern followers argue, a society will produce the institutions that best suit it only by evolution and never by radical reform. But rights against the state are claims that, if accepted, require society to settle for institutions that may not suit it so comfortably. The nerve of a claim of right, even on the demythologized analysis of rights I am using, is that an individual is entitled to protection against the majority even at the cost of the general interest. Of course the comfort of the majority will require some accommodation for minorities but only to the extent necessary to preserve order; and that is usually an accommodation that falls short of recognizing their rights.

Indeed the suggestion that rights can be demonstrated by a process of history rather than by an appeal to principle shows either a confusion or no real concern about what rights are. A claim of right presupposes a moral argument and can be established in no other way. Bickel paints the judicial activists (and even some of the heroes of judicial restraint, like Brandeis and Frankfurter, who had their lapses) as eighteenth-century philosophers who appeal to principle because they hold the optimistic view that a blueprint may be cut for progress. But this picture confuses two grounds for the appeal to principle and reform, and two senses of progress.

It is one thing to appeal to moral principle in the silly faith that ethics as well as economics moves by an invisible hand, so that individual rights and the general good will coalesce, and law based on principle will move the nation to a frictionless utopia where everyone is better off than he was before. Bickel attacks that vision by his appeal to history, and by his other arguments against government by principle. But it is quite another matter to appeal to principle *as* principle, to show, for example, that it is unjust to force black children to take their public education in black schools, even if a great many people *will* be worse off if the state adopt the measures needed to prevent this.

This is a different version of progress. It is moral progress, and though history may show how difficult it is to decide where moral progress lies, and how difficult to persuade others once one has decided, it cannot follow from this that those who govern us have no responsibility to face that decision or to attempt that persuasion.

5.

This has been a complex argument, and I want to summarize it. Our constitutional system rests on a particular moral theory, namely, that men have moral rights against the state. The difficult clauses of the Bill of Rights, like the due process and equal protection clauses, must be understood as appealing to moral concepts rather than laying down particular conceptions; therefore a court that undertakes the burden of applying these clauses fully as law must be an activist court, in the sense that it must be prepared to frame and answer questions of political morality. . . .

If we give the decisions of principle that the Constitution requires to the judges, instead of to the people, we act in the spirit of legality, so far as our institutions permit. But we run a risk that the judges may make the wrong decisions. Every lawyer thinks that the Supreme Court has gone wrong, even violently wrong, at some point in its career. If he does not hate the conservative decisions of the early 1930s, which threatened to block the New Deal, he is likely to hate the liberal decisions of the 1960s.

We must not exaggerate the danger. Truly unpopular decisions will be eroded because public compliances will be grudging, as it has been in the case of public school prayers, and because old judges will die or retire and be replaced by new judges appointed because they agree with a President who has been elected by the people. The decisions against the New Deal did not stand, and the more daring decisions of recent years are now at the mercy of the Nixon Court. Nor does the danger of wrong decisions lie entirely on the side of excess; the failure of the Court to act in the McCarthy period, epitomized by its shameful decision upholding the legality of the Smith Act in the *Dennis* case, may be thought to have done more harm to the nation than did the Court's conservative bias in the early Roosevelt period. . . .

Constitutional law can make no genuine advance until it isolates the problem of rights against the state and makes that problem part of its own agenda. That argues for a fusion of constitutional law and moral theory, a connection that, incredibly, has yet to take place. It is perfectly understandable that lawyers dread contamination with moral philosophy, and particularly with those philosophers who talk about rights, because the spooky overtones of that concept threaten the graveyard of reason. But better philosophy is now available than the lawyers may remember. Professor Rawls of Harvard, for example, has published an abstract and complex book about justice which no constitutional lawyer will be able to ignore.[4] There is no need for lawyers to play a passive role in the development of a theory of moral rights against the state, however, any more than they have been passive in the development of legal sociology and legal economics. They must recognize that law is no more independent from philosophy than it is from these other disciplines.

Notes

1. It is less misleading to say that the broad clauses of the Constitution "delegate" power to the Court to enforce its own conceptions of political morality. But even this is inaccurate if it suggests that the Court need not justify its conception by arguments showing the connections between its conception and standard cases, as described in the text. If the Court finds that the death penalty is cruel, it must do so on the basis of some principles or groups of principles that unite the death penalty with the thumbscrew and the rack.

2. I distinguish this objection to Marshall's argument from the different objection, not here relevant, that the Constitution should be interpreted to impose a legal *duty* on Congress not, for example, to pass laws abridging freedom of speech, but it should not be interpreted to detract from the legal *power* of Congress to make such a law valid if it breaks its duty. In this view, Congress is in the legal position of a thief who has a legal duty not to sell stolen goods, but retains legal power to make a valid transfer if he does. This interpretation has little to recommend it since Congress, unlike the thief, cannot be disciplined except by denying validity to its wrongful acts, at least in a way that will offer protection to the individuals the Constitution is designed to protect.

3. Professor Bickel also argued, with his usual very great skill, that many of the Warren Court's major decisions could not even be justified on conventional grounds, that is, by the arguments the Court advanced in its opinions. His criticism of these opinions is often persuasive, but the Court's failures of craftsmanship do not affect the argument I consider in the text. (His Holmes lectures were amplified in his book *The Supreme Court and the Idea of Progress*, 1970.)

4. *A Theory of Justice*, 1972. See Chapter 6.

Preferences and Politics

Cass R. Sunstein

In this article, Cass Sunstein returns to the question of the relationship between people's preferences and democratic government. He begins with a brief discussion of American constitutionalism's apparent commitment to respect citizens' private preferences and avoid enforcing, through government, one conception of the good life. He then goes on to defend the claim government may often legitimately override personal preferences. Sunstein's focus is on what he terms "endogenous" preferences, that is, preferences that are unstable and that adapt to a variety of changing circumstances. Next he distinguishes three types of private preferences that should be overridden: collective judgments, preferences that result from injustice, and preferences, such as those for addictive substances, where past consumption decisions have pernicious effects on current preferences. Sunstein concludes his essay with a discussion of the relevance of these conclusions for several constitutional issues: free speech (including hate speech and pornography) and proportional representation.

The drafting of the United States Constitution, it is often said, signaled a rejection of conceptions of politics founded on classical ideals in favor of a quite different modern view. The precise terms of the alleged shift are not altogether clear, but it is possible to identify the most prominent strands. The classical conception assumes a relatively homogeneous people and prizes active participation by the polity's citizenry. In the classical conception, the polity is self-consciously concerned with the character of the citizens; it seeks to inculcate in them and to profit from a commitment to the public good. Plato said that politics is the "art whose business it is to care for souls";[1] and under the classical conception, civic virtue, not private interest, is the wellspring of political behavior. Whether or not the state imposes a "comprehensive view"[2] on the nation, it relies relatively little on private rights to constrain government. The underly-

From Cass R. Sunstein, "Preferences and Politics," *Philosophy and Public Affairs*, Vol. 20 No. 1 (Winter 1991). Copyright © 1991 by Princeton University Press. Pp. 3–34 reprinted by permission of Princeton University Press. Some footnotes omitted.

1. *The Laws* 650b.

2. See John Rawls, "The Idea of an Overlapping Consensus," *Oxford Journal of Legal Studies* 7 (1987): 1–25.

ing vision of "republican" politics is one of frequent participation and deliberation in the service of decision, by the citizenry, about the sorts of values according to which the nation will operate.

In the modern account, by contrast, government is above all respectful of the divergent conceptions of the good held by its many constituents. People are taken as they are, not as they might be. Modern government has no concern with souls. Although electoral processes are ensured, no special premium is placed on citizen participation. Self-interest, not virtue, is understood to be the usual motivating force of political behavior. Politics is typically, if not always, an effort to aggregate private interests. It is surrounded by checks, in the form of rights, protecting private liberty and private property from public intrusion.

In this system, the goal of the polity is quite modest: the creation of the basic ground rules under which people can satisfy their desires and go about their private affairs. Much of this is famously captured in *The Federalist* No. 10, in which Madison redescribed the so-called republican problem of the corruption of virtue as the so-called liberal problem of the control of factions, which, as Madison had it, were inevitable if freedom was to be preserved.

In fact, the conventional division between the American founders and their classical predecessors is far too crude. The founders attempted to create a deliberative democracy, one in which the institutions of representation, checks and balances, and federalism would ensure a deliberative process among political equals rather than an aggregation of interests.[3] But respect for private preferences, rather than collective deliberation about public values or the good life, does seem to be a distinguishing feature of American constitutionalism. Indeed, the view that government should refuse to evaluate privately held beliefs about individual welfare, which are said to be irreducibly "subjective," links a wide range of views about both governmental structure and individual rights.

In this article I want to explore the question whether a contemporary democracy might not sometimes override the private preferences and beliefs of its citizens, not in spite of its salutary liberalism but because of it. It is one thing to affirm competing conceptions of the good; it is quite another to suggest that political outcomes must generally be justified by, or even should always respect, private preferences. A large part of my focus here is on the phenomenon of endogenous preferences. By this term I mean to indicate that preferences are not fixed and stable, but are instead adaptive to a wide range of factors—including the context in which the preference is expressed, the existing legal rules, past consumption choices, and culture in general. The phenomenon of endogenous preferences casts doubt on the notion that a democratic government ought to respect private desires and beliefs in all or almost all contexts. It bears on a number of particular problems as well, including the rationale for and extent of the constitutional protection accorded to speech; proportional representation and checks and balances; and the reasons for and limits of governmental regulation of the arts, broadcasting, and the environment. I take up these issues at several points in this article.

The argument proceeds in several stages. In Section I, I set forth some fairly conventional ideas about welfare and autonomy, in conjunction with the endogeneity of desires, in order to argue against the idea that government ought never or rarely to override private preferences. In Section II, I contend that in three categories of cases, private preferences, as expressed in consumption choices, should be overridden. The first category involves what I call collective judgments, including considered beliefs, aspirations for social justice, and altruistic goals; the second involves preferences that have adapted to undue limitations in available opportunities or to unjust background conditions; the third points to intrapersonal collective action problems that, over a lifetime, impair personal welfare. In all of these cases, I suggest, a democracy should be free and is perhaps obliged to override private preferences. In Section III, I make

---

3. Indeed, participants in the liberal tradition, in its classical forms, emphasized the need for deliberation in government and placed a high value on political virtue. Many liberals do not take private preferences as the basis for social choice, without regard to their sources and consequences, or to the reasons that might be offered in their support. See my "Beyond the Republican Revival," *Yale Law Journal* 97 (1988): 1539–89.

some remarks about the relevance of these claims to several current issues of constitutional controversy. These include proportional representation in politics and governmental regulation of the speech "market," including rights of access to the media, democratic controls on the electoral process, hate speech, and pornography.

I Against Subjective Welfarism

Should a constitutional democracy take preferences as the basis for political choice? In contemporary politics, law, and economics, the usual answer is affirmative. Modern economics, for example, is dominated by a conception of welfare based on the satisfaction of existing preferences, as measured by willingness to pay; in politics and law, something called "paternalism" is disfavored in both the public and private realms. But the idea that government ought to take preferences as the basis for political decisions is a quite modern one. This is not to say that the idea is without foundations. Partly a function of the perceived (though greatly overstated) difficulty of making interpersonal comparisons of utility, the idea is also a product of the epistemological difficulties of assessing preferences in terms of their true connection with individual welfare, and, perhaps most of all, the genuine political dangers of allowing government to engage in such inquiries.

The constellation of ideas that emerges from these considerations has been exceptionally influential. It embodies a conception of political justification that might be described as "subjective welfarism."[4] On this

4. I am grateful to Joshua Cohen for this formulation. I will not explore the complexities of the notion of "preference" here. I mean to refer simply to choices, mostly as these are observed in market behavior. This understanding of course captures the economic notion of "revealed preference" and also is a foundational part of subjective welfarism as I understand it. . . .

If the notion of preference is intended to refer to an internal psychological force, or to a supposed wellspring of action, difficulties of course abound: people have first-, second-, and nth order preferences, and their desires can be organized into many different categories, ranging from whimsy to considered judgments.

view, the government, even or perhaps especially in a democracy, should attend exclusively to conceptions of welfare as subjectively held by its citizens. A wide range of prominent approaches to politics turn out to be versions of subjective welfarism. These include, for example, certain forms of utilitarianism; the view that some version of Paretian efficiency ought to be treated as the foundational norm for political life; opposition to paternalism in public and private life; approaches to politics modeled on bargaining theory (rational or otherwise); and conceptions of politics that see the democratic process as an effort to aggregate individual preferences.

It is important to understand that subjective welfarism, thus defined, may or may not be accompanied by a broader notion that ethical and moral questions should generally be treated in welfarist or subjectivist terms. It is as a political conception, rather than an ethical one, that subjective welfarism underlies a wide range of approaches to public life, including ideas about institutional arrangements and individual or collective rights. What I want to argue here is that subjective welfarism, even as a political conception, is unsupportable by reference to principles of autonomy or welfare, the very ideas that are said to give rise to it.

The initial objection to the view that government should take preferences "as they are," or as the basis for political choice, is one of impossibility. Whether people have a preference for a commodity, a right, or anything else is in part a function of whether the government has allocated it to them in the first instance. There is no way to avoid the task of initially allocating an entitlement, and the decision to grant an entitlement to one person frequently makes that person value that entitlement more than if the right had been allocated to someone else. (It also makes other people value it less than they would otherwise.) Government must not only allocate rights to one person or another; it must also decide whether or not to make the right alienable through markets or otherwise. The initial allocation serves to reflect, to legitimate, and to reinforce social understandings about presumptive rights of ownership, and that allocation has an important causal connection to individual perceptions of the good or right in question.

For example, a decision to give employees a right to organize, farmers a right to be free from water pollution, or women a right not to be subjected to sexual harassment will have an impact on social attitudes toward labor organization, clean water, and sexual harassment. The allocation therefore has an effect on social attitudes toward the relevant rights and on their valuation by both current owners and would-be purchasers. And when preferences are a function of legal rules, the rules cannot be justified by reference to the preferences. Moreover, the initial assignment creates the basic "reference state" from which values and judgments of fairness are subsequently made, and those judgments affect preferences and private willingness to pay. Of course, a decision to make an entitlement alienable or inalienable (consider the right to vote or reproductive capacities) will have preference-shaping effects. Because of the preference-shaping effects of the rules of allocation, it is difficult to see how a government might even attempt to take preferences "as given" or as the basis for decisions in any global sense.

To some degree this concern might be put to one side. Surely there is a difference between a government that concerns itself self-consciously and on an ongoing basis with private preferences and a government that sets up the basic rules of property, contract, and tort, and then lets things turn out however they may. If this distinction can be sustained, disagreements about the relationship between politics and preferences turn on competing notions of autonomy or freedom on the one hand and welfare on the other. Subjective welfarism is founded on the claim that an approach that treats preferences as sovereign is most likely to promote both individual freedom, rightly conceived, and individual or social welfare.

It will be useful to begin with welfare. Even if one accepted a purely welfarist view, one might think that the process of promoting welfare should take place not by satisfying current preferences but by promoting those preferences and satisfying them to such an extent as is consonant with the best or highest conception of human happiness. This view is connected with older (and some current) forms of utilitarianism; it also has roots in Aristotle.

Here one does not take existing preferences as given, and one does not put all preferences on the same plane. A criterion of welfare remains the ultimate one, but the system is not focused solely on preference satisfaction, since it insists that welfare and preference satisfaction are entirely different things.

A central point here is that preferences are shifting and endogenous rather than exogenous, and as a result are a function of current information, consumption patterns, legal rules, and general social pressures. An effort to identify welfare with preference satisfaction would be easier to understand if preferences were rigidly fixed at some early age, or if learning were impossible; if this were so, democratic efforts to reflect on, change, or select preferences would breed only frustration. But because preferences are shifting and endogenous, and because the satisfaction of existing preferences might lead to unhappy or deprived lives, a democracy that treats all preferences as fixed will lose important opportunities for welfare gains.

With respect to welfare, then, the problem posed by the endogeneity of preferences is not the origin of desires but their malleability. At least if the relevant cases can be confidently identified in advance, and if collective action can be justified by reference to particular good reasons, the argument for democratic interference will be quite powerful. Respect for preferences that have resulted from unjust background conditions and that will lead to human deprivation or misery hardly appears the proper course for a liberal democracy.[5]

5. The objection here is not solely that preferences are endogenous to state action of some sort. As discussed in more detail below, the fact of endogeneity is not in itself an argument for democratic control of preferences. The argument is instead that misery that is a product of unjust background conditions calls for collective change. A subjectively satisfactory status quo produced by unjust background conditions will also call for change in some settings, for reasons taken up below. I do not deal with the possibility that subjective unhappiness that is a product of just background conditions also calls for governmental action, except insofar as an intrapersonal collective action problem is involved.

Moreover, to say that a preference is endogenous is not to say that it is a mere whim or fancy, or highly malleable. Some preferences are in fact relatively stable, even if they are a function of legal rules, social

(footnote continued next page)

For example, legal rules prohibiting or discouraging addictive behavior may have significant advantages in terms of welfare. Regulation of heroin or cigarettes (at least if the regulation can be made effective) might well increase aggregate social welfare, by decreasing harmful behavior, removing the secondary effects of those harms, and producing more healthful and satisfying lives. Similarly, governmental action relating to the environment, broadcasting, or culture—encouraging or requiring, for example, protection of beautiful areas, broadcasting about public issues, high-quality programs, or public support of artistic achievement—may in the end generate (or, better, prevent obstacles to the generation of) new preferences, providing increased satisfaction and in the end producing considerable welfare gains. The same may well be true of antidiscrimination measures, which affect the desires and attitudes of discriminators and victims alike. A system that takes existing private preferences as the basis for political choice will sacrifice important opportunities for social improvement on welfarist criteria. This point was a crucial one in the early stages of utilitarian thought; it has been lost more recently with the shift from older forms of welfarism to the idea of "revealed preferences."

Moreover, the satisfaction of private preferences, whatever their content and origins, does not respond to a persuasive conception of liberty or autonomy. The notion of autonomy should refer instead to decisions reached with a full and vivid awareness of available opportunities, with reference to all relevant information, and without illegitimate or excessive constraints on the process of preference formation. When these conditions are not met, decisions should be described as unfree or nonautonomous; for this reason it is most difficult to identify autonomy with preference satisfaction. If preferences are a product of

available information, existing consumption patterns, social pressures, and governmental rules, it seems odd to suggest that individual freedom lies exclusively or by definition in preference satisfaction, or that current preferences should, on grounds of autonomy, be treated as the basis for settling political issues. It seems even odder to suggest that all preferences should be treated equally, independently of their basis and consequences, or of the reasons offered in their support.

For purposes of autonomy, then, governmental interference with existing desires may be justified because of problems in the origins of those desires. Welfare-based arguments that invoke endogeneity tend to emphasize the malleability of preferences after they are formed; arguments based on autonomy stress what happens before the preferences have been created, that is, the conditions that gave rise to them. Because of this difference, the two arguments will operate along different tracks; and in some cases autonomy-based arguments will lead to conclusions different from those that would emerge from arguments based on welfare. In many cases, however, considerations of autonomy will argue powerfully against taking preferences as the basis for social choice.

Consider, for example, a decision to purchase dangerous foods, consumer products, or cigarettes by someone unaware of the (serious) health risks; an employer's decision not to hire blacks because of a background of public and private segregation or racial hostility in his community; a person who disparages or has no interest in art and literature because the culture in which he has been reared centers mainly around television; a decision of a woman to adopt a traditional gender role because of the social stigma attached to refusing to do so; a decision not to purchase cars equipped with seat belts or not to wear a motorcycle helmet produced by the social pressures imposed by one's peer group; a lack of interest in environmental diversity resulting from limitation of one's personal experiences to industrialized urban areas; a decision not to employ blacks at a restaurant because of fear of violence from whites.

These examples are different from one another. The source of the problem varies in

(continued footnote)

pressures, or existing institutions. A high degree of stability, and great resistance to change, will counsel against efforts at changing preferences, certainly on welfare grounds, and perhaps on grounds of autonomy as well (though even stable preferences may be nonautonomous, as in the case of rigid adaptations to an unjust status quo). In the face of extremely stable preferences, democratic efforts at change will merely breed resentment and frustration on the part of the objects of those efforts.

each. But in all of them, the interest in liberty or autonomy does not call for governmental inaction, even if that were an intelligible category. Indeed, in many or perhaps all of these cases, regulation removes a kind of coercion.

One goal of a democracy, in short, is to ensure autonomy not merely in the satisfaction of preferences, but also, and more fundamentally, in the processes of preference formation. John Stuart Mill himself was emphatic on this point, going so far as to suggest that government itself should be evaluated in large measure by its effects on the character of the citizenry.[6] The view that freedom requires an opportunity to choose among alternatives finds a natural supplement in the view that people should not face unjustifiable constraints on the free development of their preferences and beliefs. It is not altogether clear what such a view would require—a point to which I will return. At the very least, however, it would see a failure of autonomy, and a reason for collective response, in beliefs and preferences based on insufficient information or opportunities.

Governmental action might also be justified on grounds of autonomy when the public seeks to implement, through democratic processes culminating in law, widely held social aspirations or collective desires. Individual consumption choices often diverge from collective considered judgments: people may seek, through law, to implement a democratic decision about what courses to pursue. If so, it is ordinarily no violation of autonomy to allow those considered judgments to be vindicated by governmental action. Collective aspirations or considered judgments, produced by a process of deliberation on which competing perspectives are brought to bear, reflect a conception of political freedom having deep roots in the American constitutional tradition. On this view, political autonomy can be found in collective self-determination, as citizens decide, not what they "want," but instead who they are, what their values are, and what those values require. What they "want" must be supported by reasons.

To summarize: On the thinnest version of the account offered thus far, the mere fact that preferences are what they are is at least

sometimes and perhaps generally an insufficient justification for political action. Government decisions need not be and in some cases should not be justified by reference to preferences alone. More broadly, a democratic government should sometimes take private preferences as an object of regulation and control—an inevitable task in light of the need to define initial entitlements—and precisely in the interest of welfare and autonomy. Of course, there are serious risks of overreaching here, and there must be some constraints (usually denominated "rights") on this process. Checks laid down in advance are an indispensable part of constitutional government. Those checks will include, at a minimum, basic guarantees of political liberty and personal security, and such guarantees may not be [compromised] by processes of collective self-determination. I return to this point below.

II Democratic Rejection of Revealed Preferences: A Catalogue

In this section, I attempt to particularize the claims made thus far by cataloguing cases in which considerations of autonomy and welfare justify governmental action that subjective welfarism would condemn. In all of these cases, I claim that participants in a liberal government ought to be concerned with whether its citizens are experiencing satisfying lives and that the salutary liberal commitment to divergent conceptions of the good ought not to be taken to disable government from expressing that concern through law. The cases fall into three basic categories.

A. Collective Judgments and Aspirations

Citizens in a democratic polity might act to embody in law not the preferences that they hold as private consumers, but instead what might be described as collective judgments, including aspirations or considered reflections. Measures of this sort are a product of deliberative processes on the part of citizens

---

6. See Mill, *Considerations on Representative Government.*

and representatives. In that process, people do not simply determine what they "want." The resulting measures cannot be understood as an attempt to aggregate or trade off private preferences.

I. *Politics, Markets, and the Dependence of Preferences on Context.* Frequently political choices cannot easily be understood as a process of aggregating prepolitical desires. Some people may, for example, support nonentertainment broadcasting on television, even though their own consumption patterns favor situation comedies; they may seek stringent laws protecting the environment or endangered species, even though they do not use the public parks or derive material benefits from protection of such species; they may approve of laws calling for social security and welfare even though they do not save or give to the poor; they may support antidiscrimination laws even though their own behavior is hardly race- or gender-neutral. The choices people make as political participants are different from those they make as consumers. Democracy thus calls for an intrusion on markets.

The widespread disjunction between political and consumption choices presents something of a puzzle. Indeed, it sometimes leads to the view that market ordering is undemocratic and that choices made through the political process are a preferable basis for social ordering.

A generalization of this sort is far too broad in light of the multiple breakdowns of the political process and the advantages of market ordering in many arenas. Respect for private markets is an important way of respecting divergent conceptions of the good and is thus properly associated with individual liberty. Respect for markets is also an engine of economic productivity, an important individual and collective goal. But it would be a mistake to suggest, as some do, that markets always reflect individual choice more reliably than politics; or that democratic choices differ from consumption outcomes only because of confusion, as voters fail to realize that they must ultimately bear the costs of the programs they favor; or that voting patterns merely reflect a willingness to seek certain goods so long as other people are footing the bill.

Undoubtedly, consumer behavior is sometimes a better or more realistic reflection of actual preferences than is political behavior. But in light of the fact that preferences depend on context, the very notion of a "better reflection" of "actual" preferences is a confusing one; there is no such thing as an "actual" (in the sense of unitary or acontextual) preference in these settings. Moreover, the difference might be explained by the fact that political behavior reflects a variety of influences that are distinctive to the context of politics, and that justify according additional weight to what emerges through the political setting.

These influences include four closely related phenomena. First, citizens may seek to implement individual and collective aspirations in political behavior but not in private consumption. As citizens, people may seek the aid of the law to bring about a social state that they consider to be in some sense higher than what emerges from market ordering. Second, people may, in their capacity as political actors, attempt to satisfy altruistic or other-regarding desires, which diverge from the self-interested preferences sometimes characteristic of markets. Third, political decisions might vindicate what might be called metapreferences or second-order preferences. People have wishes about their wishes, and sometimes they try to vindicate those second-order wishes, including considered judgments about what is best, through law. Fourth, people may precommit themselves, in democratic processes, to a course of action that they consider to be in the general interest. The adoption of a constitution is itself an example of a precommitment strategy.

Three qualifications are necessary here. First, some of these objections might be translated into the terms of subjective welfarism. Some preferences, after all, are most effectively expressed in democratic arenas, and that expression can be supported precisely on the grounds that they are subjectively held and connected to a certain form of individual and collective welfare. My broader point, however, is that political choices will reflect a kind of deliberation and reasoning, transforming values and perceptions of interests, that is often inadequately captured in the marketplace. It is this point that amounts to a rejection or at least a renovation of subjective welfarism as a political conception. It is here that democracy becomes something other than an aggregative mechanism, that politics is seen to be irreducible to bargaining, and that prepolitical "preferences" are not taken as the bedrock of political justification.

Second, to point to these various possibilities is not at all to deny that market or private behavior frequently reflects considered judgments, altruism, aspirations, or far more complex attitudes toward diverse goods than are captured in conventional accounts of preference structures. There are countless counterexamples to any such claim. All I mean to suggest is that divergences between market and political behavior will sometimes be attributable to phenomena of the sort I have described.

Third, a democratic system must be built on various safeguards to ensure that its decisions are in fact a reflection of deliberative processes of the sort described here. Often, of course, such processes are distorted by the fact that some groups are more organized than others, by disparities in wealth and influence, and by public and private coercion of various kinds. I am assuming here that these problems have been sufficiently overcome to allow for a favorable characterization of the process.

2. *Explanations.* Thus far I have suggested that people may seek, through law, to implement collective desires that diverge from market choices. Is it possible to come up with concrete explanations for the differences? There are a number of possibilities.

First, the collective character of politics, which permits a response to collective action problems, is critical here. People may not want to implement their considered judgments, or to be altruistic, unless there is assurance that others will be bound to do so as well. More simply, people may prefer not to contribute to a collective benefit if donations are made individually, with no guarantee that others will participate; but their most favored system, obtainable only or best through democratic forms, might be one in which they contribute if (but only if) there is assurance that others will do so as well. Perhaps people feel ashamed if others are contributing and they are not. Perhaps they feel victimized if they are contributing and others are not. In any case, the

satisfaction of aspirations or altruistic goals will sometimes have the characteristics of the provision of public goods or the solution of a prisoner's dilemma.

Second, the collective character of politics might overcome the problem, discussed below, of preferences and beliefs that have adapted, at least to some extent, to an unjust status quo or to limits in available opportunities.[7] Without the possibility of collective action, the status quo may seem intractable, and private behavior, and even desires, will adapt accordingly. But if people can act in concert, preferences might take on a quite different form. Consider social movements involving the environment, labor, and race and sex discrimination. The collective action problem thus interacts with aspirations, altruistic desires, second-order preferences, and precommitment strategies. All of these are most likely to be enacted into law if an apparatus such as democratic rule is available to overcome collective action problems.

Third, social and cultural norms might incline people to express aspirational or altruistic goals more often in political behavior than in markets. Such norms may press people, in their capacity as citizens, in the direction of a concern for others or for the public interest.

Fourth, the deliberative aspects of politics, bringing additional information and perspectives to bear, may affect preferences as expressed through governmental processes. A principal function of a democratic system is to ensure that through representative or participatory processes, new or submerged voices, or novel depictions of where interests lie and what they in fact are, are heard and understood. If representatives or citizens are able to participate in a collective discussion of (for example) broadcasting or levels of risk in the workplace, they might well generate a far fuller and richer picture of diverse social goods, and of how they might be served, than can be provided through individual decisions as registered in the market. It should hardly be surprising if preferences, values, and perceptions of both individual and collective welfare are changed as a result of that process.

Fifth, and finally, consumption decisions

7. Cf. Mill's discussion of the ability of regimes to create active or passive characters, in *Considerations on Representative Government.*

are a product of the criterion of private willingness to pay, which creates distortions of its own. Willingness to pay is a function of ability to pay, and it is an extremely crude proxy for utility or welfare. Political behavior removes this distortion—which is not to say that it does not introduce distortions of new kinds.

3. Qualifications. Arguments from collective desires are irresistible if the measure at issue is adopted unanimously. But more serious difficulties are produced if (as is usual) the law imposes on a minority what it regards as a burden rather than a benefit. Suppose, for example, that a majority wants to require high-quality television and to ban violent and dehumanizing shows, but that a significant minority wants to see the latter. (I put the First Amendment questions to one side.) It might be thought that those who perceive a need to bind themselves, or to express an aspiration, should not be permitted to do so if the consequence is to deprive others of an opportunity to satisfy their preferences.

The foreclosure of the preferences of the minority is unfortunate, but in general it is difficult to see what argument there might be for an across-the-board rule against collective action of this sort. If the majority is prohibited from vindicating its considered judgments through legislation, an important arena for democratic self-government will be eliminated. The choice is between the considered judgments of the majority and the preferences (and perhaps judgments as well) of the minority. On the other hand, the foreclosure of the minority should probably be permitted only when less restrictive alternatives, including private arrangements, are unavailable to serve the same end.

Of course, the argument for democratic outcomes embodying collective judgments is not always decisive. It is easy to imagine cases in which that argument is weak. Consider a law forbidding atheism or agnosticism, or barring the expression of unpatriotic political displays. And while I cannot provide in this space a full discussion of the contexts in which the case for democratic outcomes is overcome, it might be useful to describe, in a preliminary way, three categories of cases in which con-

straints on collective judgments seem especially appropriate.

First, if the particular choice foreclosed has some special character, and especially if it is a part of deliberative democracy itself, it is appropriately considered a right, and the majority has no authority to intervene. Political expression and participation are prime examples. The equal political rights of members of the minority, as citizens, should be respected even if a general aspiration, held by the majority, argues for selective exclusions. So, too, other rights fundamental to autonomy or welfare—consider consensual sexual activity—ought generally to be off-limits to government.

Second, some collective desires might be objectionable or a product of unjust background conditions. A collective judgment that racial intermarriage is intolerable could not plausibly be justified even if it is said to reflect a collective social aspiration. To explain why, it is of course necessary to offer an argument challenging that judgment and invoking principles of justice. Such an argument might itself involve notions of autonomy or welfare. However that may be, the example suggests that the collective judgment must not be objectionable on moral grounds.

Third, some collective desires might reflect a special weakness on the part of the majority: consider a curfew law, or perhaps prohibition. In such circumstances, a legal remedy might remove desirable incentives for private self-control, have unintended side effects resulting from the "bottling-up" of desires, or prove unnecessary in light of the existence of alternative remedies. When any one of these three concerns arises, the case for protection of collective judgments is implausible. But in many contexts, these concerns are absent, and democratic controls initiated on these grounds are justified.

B. Excessive Limitations in Opportunities or Unjust Background Conditions

Citizens in a democracy might override existing preferences in order to foster and promote diverse experiences, with a view to providing broad opportunities for the formation of preferences and beliefs and for distance on and critical scrutiny of current desires. This goal usually supports private ordering and freedom of contract as well. But it calls for collective safeguards when those forces push toward homogeneity and uniformity, as they often do in industrialized nations. Here the argument for governmental controls finds a perhaps ironic origin in Mill. Such controls are necessary to cultivate divergent conceptions of the good and to ensure a degree of reflection on those conceptions.

A system that took this goal seriously could start from a range of different foundations. It might find its roots in the principles that underlie a deliberative democracy itself. Here the notions of autonomy and welfare would be defined by reference to the idea of free and equal persons acting as citizens in setting up the terms of democratic life. That idea will impose constraints on the sorts of preferences and beliefs that a political system would be permitted to inculcate. Perhaps more controversially, the system could be regarded as embodying a mild form of liberal perfectionism. Such a system would see the inculcation of critical and disparate attitudes toward prevailing conceptions of the good as part of the framework of a liberal democracy. Liberal education is of course the principal locus of this concern, but the principles embodied in liberal education need not be confined to the school system. Still another foundation would be Aristotelian. Here the governing goal would be to ensure that individual capacities and capabilities are promoted and not thwarted by governmental arrangements. And this set of ideas, a different kind of perfectionism, is not so dramatically different from Mill's version of utilitarianism.

If government can properly respond to preferences that are based on limitations in available opportunities, it might well undertake aggressive initiatives with respect to the arts and broadcasting: subsidizing public broadcasting, ensuring a range of disparate programming, or calling for high-quality programming not sufficiently provided by the marketplace. Indeed, the need to provide diverse opportunities for preference formation suggests reasons to be quite skeptical of unrestricted markets in communication and broadcasting. There is a firm theoretical justification for governmental regulation here, including the much-criticized, and now largely abandoned, "fairness doctrine," which required broadcasters to cover controversial issues and to give equal time to competing views. In view of the inevitable effects of programming on character, beliefs, and even conduct, it is hardly clear that governmental "inaction" is always appropriate in a constitutional democracy. Indeed, the contrary seems true. I take up this issue in more detail below.

Market behavior is sometimes based on an effort to reduce cognitive dissonance by adjusting to undue limitations in current practices and opportunities. When this is so, respect for preferences seems unjustified on grounds of autonomy and under certain conditions welfare as well. Preferences might be regarded as nonautonomous insofar as they are reflexively adaptive to unjust background conditions, and collective responses to such preferences might yield welfare gains.[8] The point has significant implications. For example, workers appear to underestimate the risks of hazardous activity partly in order to reduce the dissonance that would be produced by an accurate understanding of the dangers of the workplace. Democratic controls might produce gains in terms of both welfare and autonomy.

Similar ideas help account for principles of antidiscrimination. In general, the beliefs of both beneficiaries and victims of existing injustice are affected by dissonance-reducing strategies. The phenomenon of blaming the victim has distinct cognitive and motivational foundations: the strategy of blaming the victim, or assuming that an injury or an inequality was deserved or inevitable, permits nonvictims or members of advantaged groups to re-

8. There is a difference between self-conscious adaptation to an intractable status quo and the sorts of processes I am describing. If a person without musical talent decides to counteract and revise a desire to be a world-famous pianist, it would be odd to find that (healthy) decision to be inconsistent with personal autonomy. The cases under discussion involve a reflexive process based on a socially produced absence of sufficient opportunities. Of course, the notion of sufficient opportunities itself requires a baseline; every system contains limited opportunties.

duce dissonance by enabling them to maintain that the world is just—a pervasively, insistently, and sometimes irrationally held belief. The reduction of cognitive dissonance is a powerful motivational force, and it operates as a significant obstacle to the recognition of social injustice or irrationality.

Victims also participate in dissonance-reducing strategies, including the lowering of their own self-esteem to accommodate both the fact of victimization and the belief that the world is essentially just. Sometimes it is easier to assume that one's suffering is warranted than that it has been imposed cruelly or by chance. Consider here the astonishing fact that after a draft lottery, participants decided that the results of the purely random process, whether favorable or not, were deserved. The phenomenon of blaming the victim also reflects the "hindsight effect," through which people unjustifiably perceive events as having been more predictable than they in fact were, and therefore suggest that victims or disadvantaged groups should have been able to prevent the negative outcome. All of these phenomena make reliance on existing or revealed preferences highly problematic in certain contexts.

There is suggestive evidence to this effect in the psychological literature in this area. Some work here reveals that people who engage in cruel behavior begin to devalue the objects of their cruelty; observers tend to do the same. Such evidence bears on antidiscrimination law in general. Certain aspects of American labor and race discrimination law can be understood as a response to the basic problem of distorted beliefs and preferences. For example, the Supreme Court has emphatically rejected freedom-of-choice plans as a remedy for school segregation.[9] Such plans would simply permit whites and blacks to send their children to whichever school they wished. The Court's rejection of such plans might well be puzzling to proponents of subjective welfarism, but the outcome becomes more reasonable if it is seen as based in part on the fact that, in this area, preferences and beliefs have conspicuously

grown up around and adapted to the segregative status quo. Under these circumstances, freedom of choice is no solution at all; indeed, in view of the background and context the term seems an oxymoron.

In labor law as well, American law rejects freedom of contract and freedom of choice in order to protect collective bargaining. Some of this legislation must stand on a belief that private preferences have been adaptive to a status quo skewed against unionization. Special steps are therefore necessary in order to encourage collective bargaining, which also, of course, overcomes the prisoner's dilemma faced by individual workers, and therefore facilitates collective deliberation on the conditions of the workplace.

Poverty itself is perhaps the most severe obstacle to the free development of preferences and beliefs. Programs that attempt to respond to the deprivations faced by poor people—most obviously by eliminating poverty, but also through broad public education and regulatory efforts designed to make cultural resources generally available regardless of wealth—are fully justified in this light. They should hardly be seen as objectionable paternalism or as unsupportable redistribution. Indeed, antipoverty efforts are tightly linked with republican efforts to promote security and independence in the interest of creating the conditions for full and equal citizenship.

Sometimes, of course, preferences are only imperfectly adapted. At some level there is a perception of injury, but a fear of social sanctions or a belief that the cause is intractable prevents people from seeking redress. Here the collective character of politics, permitting the organization of numerous people, can be exceedingly helpful.

Standing by itself, the fact that preferences are shifting and endogenous is hardly a sufficient reason for the imposition of democratic controls. All preferences are to some degree dependent on existing law and current opportunities, and that fact cannot be a reason for governmental action without creating a license for tyranny. The argument for democratic controls in the face of endogenous preferences must rely on a belief that welfare or autonomy will thereby be promoted. Usually

9. See Green v. County School Bd., 391 U.S. 430 (1968), and Paul Gewirtz, "Choice in the Transition," *Columbia Law Review* 86 (1986): 728–98.

governmental interference should be avoided. But far too often, the salutary belief in respect for divergent conceptions of the good is transformed into an unwillingness to protect people from either unjust background conditions or a sheer lack of options.

The actual content of democratic controls here will of course be controversial, and it probably should begin and usually end with efforts to provide information and to increase opportunities. Thus, for example, governmentally required disclosure of risks in the workplace is a highly laudable strategy. In a few cases, however, these milder initiatives are inadequate, and other measures are necessary. A moderately intrusive strategy could involve economic incentives, which might take the form of tax advantages or cash payments. For example, the government might give financial inducements to day-care centers as a way of relieving child-care burdens. Such a system might well be preferable to direct transfers of money to families, a policy that will predictably lead many more women to stay at home. In view of the sources and consequences of the differential distribution of child-care burdens, it is fully legitimate for the government to take steps in the direction of equalization. The most intrusive option, to be used rarely, is direct coercion, as in the case of governmentally mandated use of safety equipment.

The category of democratic responses to endogenous preferences of this sort overlaps with that of measures that attempt to protect collective aspirations. Frequently, aspirations form the basis for laws that attempt to influence processes of preference formation.

C. Intrapersonal Collective Action Problems

There is also a case for democratic controls on existing preferences when such preferences are a function of past acts of consumption and when such acts alter desires or beliefs in such a way as to cause long-term harm. In such cases, the two key facts are that preferences are endogenous to past consumption decisions and that the effect of those decisions on current preferences is pernicious. For government to act in this context, it is important that

it be confident of its conclusions; in the face of uncertainty, freedom of choice is appropriate here. An absence of information on the part of the private actors is usually a necessary condition for collective controls.

Regulations of addictive substances, myopic behavior, and habits are familiar examples. In the case of an addiction, the problem is that the costs of nonconsumption increase dramatically over time as the benefits of consumption remain constant or fall sharply. The result is that the aggregate costs, over time or over a life, of consumption exceed the aggregate benefits, even though the initial consumption choice provides benefits that exceed costs. Individual behavior that is rational for each individual consumption choice ultimately leads people into severely inferior social states. In such cases, people, if fully informed, would in all likelihood not want to choose the good in the first place. Governmental action is a possible response.

Menahem Yaari offers the example of a group of traders attempting to induce alcoholism in an Indian tribe.[10] At the outset, alcoholic beverages are not extremely valuable to consumers. The consumers are willing to buy only for a low price, which the traders accept. But as a result of consumption, the value of the beverages to the consumers steadily increases to the point where they are willing to pay enormous sums to obtain them. Thus the traders are able "to manoevre the Indian into a position where rationality conflicts with Pareto-efficiency, i.e., into a position where to be efficient is to be irrational and to be rational is to be inefficient. . . . [T]he disadvantage, for an economic unit, of having endogenously changing tastes is that, even with perfect information and perfect foresight, the unit may find itself forced to follow an action which, by the unit's own standards, is Pareto-dominated."

Because of the effect over time of consumption on preferences, someone who is addicted to heroin is much worse off than he would have been had he never started, even though the original decision to consume was not irra-

10. Menahem Yaari, "Endogenous Changes in Tastes: A Philosophical Discussion," in *Decision Theory and Social Ethics: Issues in Social Choice,* ed. Hans Gottinger and Werner Leinfellner (Boston: D. Reidel, 1978), pp. 59–98.

tional in terms of immediate costs and benefits. Statutes that regulate addictive substances respond to a social belief, grounded on this consideration, that the relevant preferences should not be formed in the first place.

We might describe this situation as involving an intrapersonal collective action problem, in which the costs and benefits, for a particular person, of engaging in an activity change dramatically over time. A central point here is that consumption patterns induce a significant change in preferences, and in a way that makes people worse off in the long run. In the case of addictions, there will also be interconnections between intrapersonal collective action problems and preferences and beliefs that are adaptive to unjust background conditions, at least as a general rule. (Yaari's own example, involving whites trading alcohol with native Americans, is a prime example.) The problem of drug addiction is hardly distributed evenly throughout the population, and the process of addiction is in large part a response to social institutions that severely limit and condition the range of options.

While addiction is the most obvious case, it is part of a far broader category. Consider, for example, myopic behavior, defined as a refusal, because the short-term costs exceed the short-term benefits, to engage in activity having long-term benefits that dwarf long-term costs. Another kind of intrapersonal collective action problem is produced by habits, in which people engage in behavior because of the subjectively high short-term costs of changing their behavior, regardless of the fact that the long-term benefits exceed the long-term costs. *Akrasia,* or weakness of the will, has a related structure, and some laws respond to its individual or collective forms.

For the most part, problems of this sort are best addressed at the individual level or through private associations, which minimize coercion; but social regulation is a possible response. Statutes that subsidize the arts or public broadcasting, or that discourage the formation of some habits and encourage the formation of others, are illustrations. There are similar arguments for compulsory recycling programs (the costs of participation in which decrease substantially over time, and often turn

into benefits) and for democratic restrictions on smoking cigarettes.

The problem with collective controls in this context is that they are unlikely to be fine-tuned. They will often sweep up so many people and circumstances as to create serious risks of abuse. In some settings, however, citizens will be able to say with confidence that the effect of consumption on preferences will lead to severe welfare or autonomy losses. In such cases democratic controls are justified.

III   Examples

A. The Frontiers of Free Speech Law: The Fairness Doctrine, Campaign Speech, Hate Speech, and Pornography

The most important issues in the contemporary law of free expression have produced cleavages between groups and ideas that were previously closely allied. Thus the First Amendment has been invoked, with considerable vigor and passion, on behalf of cigarette companies seeking to advertise their products; corporations attempting to influence electoral outcomes; people engaged in racial hate speech; pornographers; and large networks objecting to a private right of access to broadcasting or to other efforts to promote quality and diversity in the media. The effort to invoke the First Amendment is increasingly resisted—often, ironically, on the theory that it runs counter to the goals of deliberative democracy and free expression itself—by individuals and groups formerly associated with an absolutist or near-absolutist position against governmental regulation of speech.

These debates raise exceedingly complex issues, and I can only touch on them briefly here. The complexities are increased by the fact that a system dedicated to freedom of expression ought to be highly sensitive to the idea that speech alters preferences and beliefs. It should also find that process to be one to which a democracy is generally quite receptive. As Justice Louis D. Brandeis wrote in what is probably the most distinguished judicial opinion in the entire history of free expression, "the fitting remedy for evil counsels is good ones. . . . If there be time to expose through discussion the falsehood and fallacies, to avert the evil by the processes of education, the remedy to be applied is more speech, not enforced silence."[11]

Justice Brandeis's statement notwithstanding, I want to suggest that attention to the endogenous character of preferences and to the considerations traced thus far provides some basis for receptivity to democratic controls in this context.

I. *The Fairness Doctrine*. There is a growing consensus that the government should not concern itself with the airwaves and that total reliance on private markets and consumer preferences is the appropriate strategy for government. On this view, broadcasting should be treated like soap, cereal, or any other commodity. Indeed, there is a growing consensus that this result is ordained by the First Amendment. But if the claims made here are persuasive, the consensus is misguided. The meaning of the First Amendment is a function of competing views about what sort of relation between government and markets will best promote democratic deliberation. Lawyers (and not a few nonlawyers) have an unfortunate habit of thinking that the meaning of the First Amendment precedes rather than postdates that inquiry.

The consequence of market-based strategies in broadcasting is a system in which most viewers see shows that rarely deal with serious problems; are frequently sensationalistic, prurient, dehumanizing, or banal; reflect and perpetuate a bland, watered-down version of the most conventional views about politics and morality; are influenced excessively by the concerns of advertisers; produce an accelerating "race to the bottom" in terms of the quality and quantity of attention that they require and encourage; and are often riddled with violence, sexism, and racism. It simply defies belief to suggest that such shows do not affect the preferences and even the character of the citizenry. Is it so clear that a constitutional democracy ought to consider itself unable to

respond to this situation? Is it so clear that a First Amendment enacted in order to ensure democratic self-determination bars a democratic corrective here?

In my view, the considerations marshaled thus far suggest that citizens in a constitutional democracy ought to be conceded, and ought to exercise, the power to engage in a wide range of controls. If welfare and autonomy provide the governing criteria, large gains might be expected from such controls. All three of the categories I have described argue in favor of some form of regulation. Democratic controls would probably reflect collective desires, which deserve respect. They would respond to the fact that in spite of the large number of channels, the current regulatory regime diminishes genuine options, to the detriment of both welfare and autonomy; they would also counteract a kind of intrapersonal collective action problem faced by many of those habituated to the broadcasting status quo.

Such controls might permit the government to regulate advertising on television, certainly for children, but for others as well; to require broadcasters to pay attention to public affairs, as in, for example, an hour of compulsory programming per night; to ban gratuitous or prurient violence on television, especially when it is sexualized; to require, as a condition for licensing, a subsidy to public television; and to impose a broad fairness doctrine, in the form not only of an obligation of attention to important issues but also a chance to speak for divergent sides. The evident dangers notwithstanding, there would be a wide range of collective and external benefits from such controls, which would thus carry forward a strand of the liberal tradition that calls for governmental action in such cases.

At least in principle, rights of private access to the media for differing positions and associated kinds of controls ought to be considered congenial to the free speech guarantee. Surely this is so if that guarantee is understood as a protection of a deliberative process centered on public values rather than of a "marketplace." The First Amendment need not be seen as an obstacle to such efforts. If anything, the existing system might be thought to raise serious constitutional questions. A system in

11. Whitney v. California, 274 U.S. 357, 377 (1927).

which access to the media, with its inevitable consequences for the shaping of preferences and beliefs, is made dependent on private willingness to pay raises genuine problems for free expression.

2. Campaign Regulation. It would not be difficult to argue that a variety of regulations on the electoral process are necessary both to promote a deliberative process among political equals and to ensure that the deliberative process is a genuine one. Properly conceived, such efforts would be highly congenial to the purposes of the free speech guarantee. Both restrictions on campaign contributions—to eliminate the distorting effects of wealth—and qualitative measures to reduce the "soundbite" phenomenon and to promote more in the way of reflective discussion hold considerable promise.

Currently, however, there is a large if ironic obstacle to such efforts: the First Amendment. The Supreme Court has generally been unreceptive to governmental efforts to regulate electoral campaigns.[12] In the key passage in *Buckley v. Valeo,* the Court said that "the concept that government may restrict the speech of some elements of our society in order to enhance the relative voice of others is wholly foreign to the first amendment."[13] It is crucial to note here that the Court did not say that the effort to promote deliberation among political equals was insufficiently weighty or inadequately promoted by the legislation at hand. Instead the Court said, far more broadly, that the effort was constitutionally illegitimate.

Under the approach suggested here, campaign regulation would be treated more hospitably. In view of the effects of wealth on the formation of political beliefs, and the corrosive consequences of some forms of electioneering, democratic controls on the process might be welcomed. The First Amendment might be understood not as a guarantor of unrestricted speech "markets," and much less as a vehicle for the translation of economic inequalities into political ones, but instead as

an effort to ensure a process of deliberation that would, under current conditions, be promoted rather than undermined through regulatory measures. This is so especially if citizens in a democratic polity support regulation of the electoral process in order to pursue their desire for a well-functioning deliberative process.

Of course, there are great risks here, and any regulatory efforts must be carefully monitored to ensure that they do not act as incumbent protection bills or as serious constraints on speech that should instead be encouraged. But the issue is far more complex, from the standpoint of the First Amendment itself, than existing law allows.

3. Violent Pornography and Hate Speech. Many Western democracies, including those firmly committed to freedom of speech, regulate speech that casts contempt on identifiable social groups (hate speech). Some such democracies also control sexually explicit speech, especially when it associates sex and violence. These controls have been justified on mixed grounds of human dignity, community morality, and sexual equality. In the United States, the precise status of such restrictions remains unclear. Probably the best account of current law is that hate speech is protected, as is most speech that associates sex and violence, even if that speech is not conceivably part of a serious exchange of ideas but instead qualifies as pornography.

The cases of hate speech and pornography raise somewhat different problems. Hate speech is self-consciously directed toward an issue of public concern; it is conspicuously and intentionally political in nature. Violent pornography is of course political too, in the sense that it has political origins and consequences. But it cannot be thought to be a self-conscious contribution to democratic deliberation about public issues. In this way it differs from misogynist speech of a more straightforward sort, where the political content is explicit. In terms of its connection to the First Amendment, pornography should probably be thought to fall in the same category as commercial speech, libel of private persons, bribes, and conspiracies. The reason is that most pornography does not amount to an effort to contribute to

12. See Buckley v. Valeo, 424 U.S. 1 (1976), and First National Bank of Boston v. Bellotti, 435 U.S. 765 (1978).
13. 424 U.S. at pp. 48–49.

deliberation on matters of public interest, even if that category is broadly conceived, as it should be. Expression that is not central to the free speech principle counts as speech, but it is entitled to a lesser degree of protection. It may be regulated, not on a whim, but on a basis of demonstration of harm that is weaker than that required for political speech.

Should the First Amendment be taken to disable government from regulating hate speech and pornography? The affirmative answer of current law may well be unsound. Both of these forms of speech have serious and corrosive effects on beliefs and desires. Both have the additional and unusual characteristic of denying victimized groups the right to participate in the community as free and equal persons. With respect to certain kinds of violent pornography, there are especially severe consequences in terms of how men and women perceive sexuality, how men perceive women, and how women perceive themselves. One need not believe that the regulation of violent pornography would eliminate sexual violence or even do a great deal to produce sexual equality in order to recognize that the pervasiveness of material that associates sex with violence has a variety of harmful social consequences.

The case for regulation of these forms of speech is strongest when the relevant speech is pervasive, when it causes tangible harm, and when it falls outside the category of speech that is guaranteed First Amendment protection unless there is a demonstration of unavoidable, imminent, and serious danger. The considerations marshaled here suggest that at least certain forms of violent pornography ought to be regulated, and that perhaps in certain restricted settings, hate speech may be an appropriate subject of democratic controls as well.

B. Proportional Representation

In recent years, there has been a revival of interest in systems of proportional or group representation, both for disadvantaged groups and perhaps generally as well. There is a solid constitutional pedigree for such systems, notwithstanding the constant and emphatic rejections, by the Supreme Court, of

constitutionally based arguments for representation of members of racial minority groups. Despite the rigidity of the one person—one vote formula, with its majoritarian and individualistic overtones, group representation has always been a feature of American constitutionalism.[14]

Moreover, the basic constitutional institutions of federalism, bicameralism, and checks and balances share some of the appeal of proportional representation, and owe their origins in part to notions of group representation. These institutions proliferate the points of access to government, increasing the ability of diverse groups to influence policy, multiplying perspectives in government, and improving deliberative capacities. In this respect, they ensure something in the way of group representation, at least when compared with unitary systems. Of course, both the separation of powers and bicameralism grew in part out of efforts to promote representation of diverse groups: bicameralism allowed representation of both the wealthy and the masses, while the notion of separation derived from (though it also repudiated) notions of mixed government, which was designed to ensure a measure of representation of groups defined in social and economic terms.

Proportional representation might be designed, as in its Western European forms, to ensure representation in the legislature of all those groups that are able to attain more than a minimal share of the vote. In another form, the system might be an effort to ensure that members of disadvantaged groups are given the power to exert influence on political outcomes. In America, the Voting Rights Act goes far in this direction for blacks.

There are serious problems with both of these efforts, and I do not mean to evaluate them in detail here. I do suggest that efforts to ensure proportional representation become much more acceptable if they are justified on

---

14. At the time of the framing, for example, geography was thought to define distinct communities with distinct interests; representation of the states as such seemed only natural. It would not be impossible to argue that racial and ethnic groups (among others) are the contemporary analogues to groups that were defined in geographical terms during the founding period.

grounds that do not take existing preferences as the basis for governmental decisions and if they emphasize the preference-shaping effects of discussion and disagreement in politics.[15] The argument here is that deliberative processes will be improved, not undermined, if mechanisms are instituted to ensure that multiple groups have access to the process and are actually present when decisions are made. Proportional or group representation, precisely by having this effect, would ensure that diverse views are expressed on an ongoing basis in the representative process, where they might otherwise be excluded.

In this respect, proportional or group representation could be regarded as a kind of second-best solution for the real-world failures of Madisonian deliberation. And the primary purpose of access is not to allow each group to have its "piece of the action"—though that is not entirely irrelevant—but instead to ensure that the process of deliberation is not distorted by the mistaken appearance of a common set of interests on the part of all concerned. In this incarnation, proportional representation is designed to increase the likelihood that political outcomes will incorporate some understanding of all perspectives. That process should facilitate the healthy expression of collective values or aspirations and the scrutiny of preferences adaptive to unjust background conditions or limited opportunities.

For this reason, proportional representation may be the functional analogue of the institutions of checks and balances and federalism, recognizing the creative functions of disagreement and multiple perspectives for the governmental process. In this sense there is continuity between recent proposals for pro-

portional representation and some of the attractive features of the original constitutional regime. Indeed, Hamilton himself emphasized that in a system of checks and balances, the "jarring of parties . . . will promote deliberation."[16] If this is so, proportional representation is most understandable in a democracy that does not take existing preferences as the basis for social choice but instead sees the broadest form of deliberation, covering ends as well as means, as a central ingredient in democratic politics.

IV Conclusion

A constitutional democracy should not be self-consciously concerned, in a general and comprehensive way, with the souls of its citizens. Under modern conditions, liberal constraints on the operation of the public sphere and a general respect for divergent conceptions of the good are indispensable. At the same time, it would be a grave mistake to characterize liberal democracy as a system that requires existing preferences to be taken as the basis for governmental decisions and that forbids citizens, operating through democratic channels, from enacting their considered judgments into law, or from counteracting, through the provision of opportunities and information, preferences and beliefs that have adjusted to an unjust status quo. Ironically, a system that forecloses these routes—and that claims to do so in the name of liberalism or democracy—will defeat many of the aspirations that gave both liberalism and democracy their original appeal, and that continue to fuel them in so many parts of the world.

15. In part this is Mill's defense of such efforts. See *Considerations on Representative Government.*

16. *The Federalist No.* 70.

Civil Disobedience and Legal Obligation

John Rawls

Few if any twentieth century philosophers have had as much influence on political philosophy as John Rawls. His seminal work, A Theory of Justice, *is an attempt to revise the social contract tradition and to defend it against its major rivals. There Rawls argues that principles governing the constitution and laws enacted under it should be chosen behind a "veil of ignorance" in which people ignore their social class, race, and religion, as well as any other facts that are morally arbitrary and that, if known, would allow the laws to be tailored so as to advantage one group over another. He calls the theory "justice as fairness" because the veil of ignorance (corresponding to the traditional social contract) assures that principles chosen are fair.*

In the following essay, John Rawls discusses the related questions of civil disobedience and legal obligation, both within the context of social contract theory. Democracy has been defended in various ways, and, as we have seen in other selections, it is often claimed that laws chosen by democratic procedures have special claim to legitimacy. Others, however, defend democracy based on the more modest claim that the laws emerging from such a process will tend to be more just than ones chosen by a ruling elite, that the laws will promote the general interest, or that popular participation in politics has salutary effects on citizens. For Rawls, the most basic question to be asked of any political regime is whether it is just, not whether its leaders are popularly elected. Though he supports the electoral process, he does so in the context of a larger theory of justice. But even assuming a just constitution providing for regular elections, there is no assurance that laws enacted in accordance with its procedures will be just. Nonetheless, he argues, citizens have an obligation to obey laws enacted under a just constitution based on the "principle of fairness." He concludes with a discussion of the role of civil disobedience in a constitutional democracy, including the circumstances in which it would be justified.

Introduction

I should like to discuss briefly, and in an informal way, the grounds of civil disobedience in a constitutional democracy. Thus, I shall limit my remarks to the conditions under which we may, by civil disobedience, properly oppose legally established democratic authority; I am not concerned with the situation under other kinds of government nor, except incidentally, with other forms of resistance.

From John Rawls, "The Justification of Civil Disobedience" in *Civil Disobedience,* Hugo Bedau, editor (New York: Pegasus, 1969) and "Legal Obligation and the Duty of Fair Play" in *Law and Philosophy,* Sidney Hook, editor (New York: New York University Press, 1968). Reprinted by permission of the author. Some footnotes omitted.

My thought is that in a reasonably just (though of course not perfectly just) democratic regime, civil disobedience, when it is justified, is normally to be understood as a political action which addresses the sense of justice of the majority in order to urge reconsideration of the measures protested and to warn that in the firm opinion of the dissenters the conditions of social cooperation are not being honored. This characterization of civil disobedience is intended to apply to dissent on fundamental questions of internal policy, a limitation which I shall follow to simplify our question.

The Social Contract Doctrine

It is obvious that the justification of civil disobedience depends upon the theory of political obligation in general, and so we may appropriately begin with a few comments on this question. The two chief virtues of social institutions are justice and efficiency, where by the efficiency of institutions I understand their effectiveness for certain social conditions and ends the fulfillment of which is to everyone's advantage. We should comply with and do our part in just and efficient social arrangements for at least two reasons: first of all, we have a natural duty not to oppose the establishment of just and efficient institutions (when they do not yet exist) and to uphold and comply with them (when they do exist); and second, assuming that we have knowingly accepted the benefits of these institutions and plan to continue to do so, and that we have encouraged and expect others to do their part, we also have an obligation to do our share when, as the arrangement requires, it comes our turn. Thus, we often have both a natural duty as well as an obligation to support just and efficient institutions, the obligation arising from our voluntary acts while the duty does not.

Now all this is perhaps obvious enough, but it does not take us very far. Any more particular conclusions depend upon the conception of justice which is the basis of a theory of political obligation. I believe that the appropriate conception, at least for an account of political obligation in a constitutional democracy, is that of the social contract theory from which so much of our political thought derives. If we are careful to interpret it in a suitably general way, I hold that this doctrine provides a satisfactory basis for political theory, indeed even for ethical theory itself, but this is beyond our present concern.[1] The interpretation I suggest is the following: that the principles to which social arrangements must conform, and in particular the principles of justice, are those which free and rational men would agree to in an original position of equal liberty; and similarly, the principles which govern men's relations to institutions and define their natural duties and obligations are the principles to which they would consent when so situated. It should be noted straightway that in this interpretation of the contract theory the principles of justice are understood as the outcome of a hypothetical agreement. They are prin-

ciples which would be agreed to if the situation of the original position were to arise. There is no mention of an actual agreement nor need such an agreement ever be made. Social arrangements are just or unjust according to whether they accord with the principles for assigning and securing fundamental rights and liberties which would be chosen in the original position. This position is, to be sure, the analytic analogue of the traditional notion of the state of nature, but it must not be mistaken for a historical occasion. Rather it is a hypothetical situation which embodies the basic ideas of the contract doctrine; the description of this situation enables us to work out which principles would be adopted. I must now say something about these matters.

The contract doctrine has always supposed that the persons in the original position have equal powers and rights, that is, that they are symmetrically situated with respect to any arrangements for reaching agreement, and that coalitions and the like are excluded. But it is an essential element (which has not been sufficiently observed although it is implicit in Kant's version of the theory) that there are very strong restrictions on what the contracting parties are presumed to know. In particular, I interpret the theory to hold that the parties do not know their position in society, past, present, or future; nor do they know which institutions exist. Again, they do not know their own place in the distribution of natural talents and abilities, whether they are intelligent or strong, man or woman, and so on. Finally, they do not know their own particular interests and preferences or the system of ends which they wish to advance: they do not know their conception of the good. In all these respects the parties are confronted with a veil of ignorance which prevents any one from being able to take advantage of his good fortune or particular interests or from being disadvantaged by them. What the parties do know (or assume) is that Hume's circumstances of justice obtain: namely, that the bounty of nature is not so generous as to render cooperative schemes superfluous nor so harsh as to make them impossible. Moreover, they assume that the extent of their altruism is limited and that, in general, they do not take an interest in one another's interests. Thus, given the special features of the original position, each man tries to do the best he can for himself by insisting on principles calculated to protect and advance his system of ends whatever it turns out to be.

I believe that as a consequence of the peculiar nature of the original position there would be an agreement on the following two principles for assigning rights and duties and for regulating distributive shares as these are determined by the fundamental institutions of society: first, each person is to have an equal right to the most extensive liberty compatible with a like liberty for all; second, social and economic inequalities (as defined by the institutional structure or fostered by it) are to be arranged so that they are both to everyone's advantage and attached to positions and offices open to all. In view of the content of these two principles and their application to the main institutions of society, and therefore to the social system as a whole, we may regard them as the two principles of justice. Basic social arrangements are just insofar as they conform to these principles, and we can, if we like, discuss questions of justice directly by reference to them. But a deeper understanding of the justification of civil disobedience requires, I think, an account of the derivation of these principles provided by the doctrine of the social contract. Part of our task is to show why this is so. . . .

The Grounds of Compliance with an Unjust Law

If we assume that in the original position men would agree both to the principle of doing their part when they have accepted and plan to continue to accept the benefits of just institutions (the principle of fairness), and also to the principle of not preventing the establishment of just institutions and of upholding and complying with them when they do exist, then the contract doctrine easily accounts for our having to conform to just institutions. But how does it account for the fact that we are normally required to comply with unjust laws as well? The injustice of a law

is not a sufficient ground for not complying with it any more than the legal validity of legislation is always sufficient to require obedience to it. Sometimes one hears these extremes asserted, but I think that we need not take them seriously.

An answer to our question can be given by elaborating the social contract theory in the following way. I interpret it to hold that one is to envisage a series of agreements as follows: first, men are to agree upon the principles of justice in the original position. Then they are to move to a constitutional convention in which they choose a constitution that satisfies the principles of justice already chosen. Finally they assume the role of a legislative body and guided by the principles of justice enact laws subject to the constraints and procedures of the just constitution. The decisions reached in any stage are binding in all subsequent stages. Now whereas in the original position the contracting parties have no knowledge of their society or of their own position in it, in both a constitutional convention and a legislature, they do know certain general facts about their institutions, for example, the statistics regarding employment and output required for fiscal and economic policy. But no one knows particular facts about his own social class or his place in the distribution of natural assets. On each occasion the contracting parties have the knowledge required to make their agreement rational from the appropriate point of view, but not so much as to make them prejudiced. They are unable to tailor principles and legislation to take advantage of their social or natural position; a veil of ignorance prevents their knowing what this position is. With this series of agreements in mind, we can characterize just laws and policies as those which would be enacted were this whole process correctly carried out.

In choosing a constitution the aim is to find among the just constitutions the one which is most likely, given the general facts about the society in question, to lead to just and effective legislation. The principles of justice provide a criterion for the laws desired; the problem is to find a set of political procedures that will give this outcome. I shall assume that, at least under the normal conditions of a modern state, the best constitution is some form of democratic regime affirming equal political liberty and using some sort of majority (or other plurality) rule. Thus it follows that on the contract theory a constitutional democracy of some sort is required by the principles of justice. At the same time it is essential to observe that the constitutional process is always a case of what we may call imperfect procedural justice: that is, there is no feasible political procedure which guarantees that the enacted legislation is just even though we have (let us suppose) a standard for just legislation. In simple cases, such as games of fair division, there are procedures which always lead to the right outcome (assume that equal shares is fair and let the man who cuts the cake take the last piece). These situations are those of perfect procedural justice. In other cases it does not matter what the outcome is as long as the fair procedure is followed: fairness of the process is transferred to the result (fair gambling is an instance of this). These situations are those of pure procedural justice. The constitutional process, like a criminal trial, resembles neither of these; the result matters and we have a standard for it. The difficulty is that we cannot frame a procedure which guarantees that only just and effective legislation is enacted. Thus even under a just constitution unjust laws may be passed and unjust policies enforced. Some form of the majority principle is necessary but the majority may be mistaken . . .

It should be observed that the majority principle has a secondary place as a rule of procedure which is perhaps the most efficient one under usual circumstances for working a democratic constitution. The basis for it rests essentially upon the principles of justice and therefore we may, when conditions allow, appeal to these principles against unjust legislation. . . .

Legal Obligation and the Duty of Fair Play

. . . I shall assume, as requiring no argument, that there is, at least in a society such as ours, a moral obligation to obey the law, although it may, of course, be overridden in certain cases by other more stringent obligations. I shall assume also that this obligation must rest on some general moral principle; that is, it must depend on some principle of justice or upon some principle of social utility or the common good, and the like. Now, it may appear to be a truism, and let us suppose it is, that a moral obligation rests on some moral principle. But I mean to exclude the possibility that the obligation to obey the law is based on a special principle of its own. After all, it is not, without further argument, absurd that there is a moral principle such that when we find ourselves subject to an existing system of rules satisfying the definition of a legal system, we have an obligation to obey the law; and such a principle might be final, and not in need of explanation, in the way in which the principles of justice or of promising and the like are final. I do not know of anyone who has said that there is a special principle of legal obligation in this sense. Given a rough agreement, say, on the possible principles as being those of justice, of social utility, and the like, the question has been on which of one or several is the obligation to obey the law founded, and which, if any, has a special importance. I want to give a special place to the principle defining the duty of fair play.

In speaking of one's obligation to obey the law, I am using the term "obligation" in its more limited sense, in which, together with the notion of a duty and of a responsibility, it has a connection with institutional rules. Duties and responsibilities are assigned to certain positions and offices, and obligations are normally the consequence of voluntary acts of persons, and while perhaps most of our obligations are assumed by ourselves, through the making of promises and the accepting of benefits, and so forth, others may put us under obligation to them (as when on some occasion they help us, for example, as children). I should not claim that the moral grounds for our obeying the law is derived from the duty of fair-play except insofar as one is referring to an obligation in this sense. It would be incorrect to say that our duty not to commit any of the legal offenses, specifying crimes of violence is based on the duty of fair play, at least entirely. These crimes involve wrongs as such, and with such offenses, as with the vices of cruelty and greed, our doing them is wrong independently of there being a legal system the benefits of which we have voluntarily accepted. . . .

Some have thought that there is ostensibly a paradox of a special kind when a citizen, who votes in accordance with his moral principles (conception of justice), accepts the majority decision when he is in the minority. Let us suppose the vote is between two bills, A and B each establishing an income tax procedure, rates of progression, or the like, which are contrary to one another. Suppose further that one thinks of the constitutional procedure for enacting legislation as a sort of machine that yields a result when the votes are fed into it—the result being that a certain bill is enacted. The question arises as to how a citizen can accept the machine's choice, which (assuming that B gets a majority of the votes) involves thinking that B ought to be enacted when, let us suppose, he is of the declared opinion that A ought to be enacted. For some the paradox seems to be that in a constitutional democracy a citizen is often put in a situation of believing that both A and B should be enacted when A and B are contraries: that A should be enacted because A is the best policy, and that B should be enacted because B has a majority—and moreover, and this is essential, that this conflict is different from the usual sort of conflict between prima facie duties.

There are a number of things that may be said about this supposed paradox, and there are several ways in which it may be resolved, each of which brings out an aspect of the situation. But I think the simplest thing to say is to deny straightway that there is anything different in this situation than in any other situation where there is a conflict of prima facie principles. The essential of the matter seems to be as follows: (1) Should A or B be enacted and implemented, that is, administered? Since it is supposed that everyone accepts the outcome of the vote, within limits, it is appropriate to put the enactment and implementation together. (2) Is A or B the best policy? It is assumed that everyone votes according to his political opinion as to which is the best policy and that the decision as to how to vote is not based on personal interest. There is no special conflict in this situation: the citizen who knows that he will find himself in the minority be-

lieves that, taking into account only the relative merits of A and B as prospective statutes, and leaving aside how the vote will go, A should be enacted and implemented. Moreover, on his own principles he should vote for what he thinks is the best policy, and leave aside how the vote will go. On the other hand, given that a majority will vote for B, B should be enacted and implemented, and he may know that a majority will vote for B. These judgments are relative to different principles (different arguments). The first is based on the person's conception of the best social policy; the second is based on the principles on which he accepts the constitution. The real decision, then, is as follows: A person has to decide, in each case where he is in the minority, whether the nature of the statute is such that, given that it will get, or has got, a majority vote, he should oppose its being implemented, engage in civil disobedience, or take equivalent action. In this situation he simply has to balance his obligation to oppose an unjust statute against his obligation to abide by a just constitution. This is, of course, a difficult situation, but not one introducing any deep logical paradox. Normally, it is hoped that the obligation to the constitution is clearly the decisive one.

Although it is obvious, it may be worthwhile mentioning, since a relevant feature of voting will be brought out, that the result of a vote is that a rule of law is enacted, and although given the fact of its enactment, everyone agrees that it should be implemented, no one is required to believe that the statute enacted represents the best policy. It is consistent to say that another statute would have been better. The vote does not result in a statement to be believed: namely, that B is superior, on its merits, to A. To get this interpretation one would have to suppose that the principles of the constitution specify a device which gathers information as to what citizens think should be done and that the device is so constructed that it always produces from this information the morally correct opinion as to which is the best policy. If in accepting a constitution it was so interpreted, there would, indeed, be a serious paradox: for a citizen would be torn between believing, on his own principles, that A is the best policy, and believing at the same time that

B is the best policy as established by the constitutional device, the principles of the design of which he accepts. This conflict could be made a normal one only if one supposed that a person who made his own judgment on the merits was always prepared to revise it given the opinion constructed by the machine. But it is not possible to determine the best policy in this way, nor is it possible for a person to give such an undertaking. . . .

Now to turn to the main problem, that of understanding how a person can properly find himself in a position where, by his own principles, he must grant that, given a majority vote, B should be enacted and implemented even though B is unjust. There is, then, the question as to how it can be morally justifiable to acknowledge a constitutional procedure for making legislative enactments when it is certain (for all practical purposes) that laws will be passed that by one's own principles are unjust. It would be impossible for a person to undertake to change his mind whenever he found himself in the minority; it is not impossible, but entirely reasonable, for him to undertake to abide by the enactments made, whatever they are, provided that they are within certain limits. But what more exactly are the conditions of this undertaking?

First of all, it means, as previously suggested, that the constitutional procedure is misinterpreted as a procedure for making legal rules. It is a process of social decision that does not produce a statement to be believed (that B is the best policy) but a rule to be followed. Such a procedure, say involving some form of majority rule, is necessary because it is certain that there will be disagreement on what is the best policy. This will be true even if we assume, as I shall, that everyone has a similar sense of justice and everyone is able to agree on a certain constitutional procedure as just. There will be disagreement because they will not approach issues with the same stock of information, they will regard different moral features of situations as carrying different weights, and so on. The acceptance of a constitutional procedure is, then, a necessary political device to decide between conflicting legislative proposals. If one thinks of the constitution as a fundamental part of the scheme of social cooperation, then one can say that if the constitution is just, and if one has accepted the benefits of its working and intends to continue doing so, and if the rule enacted is within certain limits, then one has an obligation, based on the principle of fair play, to obey it when it comes one's turn. In accepting the benefits of a just constitution one becomes bound to it, and in particular one becomes bound to one of its fundamental rules: given a majority vote in behalf of a statute, it is to be enacted and properly implemented.

The principle of fair play may be defined as follows. Suppose there is a mutually beneficial and just scheme of social cooperation, and that the advantages it yields can only be obtained if everyone, or nearly everyone, cooperates. Suppose further that cooperation requires a certain sacrifice from each person, or at least involves a certain restriction of his liberty. Suppose finally that the benefits produced by cooperation are, up to a certain point, free: that is, the scheme of cooperation is unstable in the sense that if any one person knows that all (or nearly all) of the others will continue to do their part, he will still be able to share a gain from the scheme even if he does not do his part. Under these conditions a person who has accepted the benefits of the scheme is bound by a duty of fair play to do his part and not to take advantage of the free benefit by not cooperating. The reason one must abstain from this attempt is that the existence of the benefit is the result of everyone's effort, and prior to some understanding as to how it is to be shared, if it can be shared at all, it belongs in fairness to no one.

Now I want to hold that the obligation to obey the law, as enacted by a constitutional procedure, even when the law seems unjust to us, is a case of the duty of fair play as defined. It is, moreover, an obligation in the more limited sense in that it depends upon our having accepted and our intention to continue accepting the benefits of a just scheme of cooperation that the constitution defines. In this sense it depends on our own voluntary acts. Again, it is an obligation owed to our fellow citizens generally: that is, to those who cooperate with us in the working of the constitution. It is not an obligation owed to public officials, although there may be such obligations. That it is an obligation owed by citizens to one another is shown by the fact that they are entitled to be indignant with one another for failure to comply. Further, an essential condition of the obligation is the justice of the constitution and the general system of law being roughly in accordance with it. Thus the obligation to obey (or not to resist) an unjust law depends strongly on there being a just constitution. Unless one obeys the law enacted under it, the proper equilibrium, or balance, between competing claims defined by the constitution will not be maintained. Finally, while it is true enough to say that the enactment by a majority binds the minority, so that one may be bound by the acts of others, there is no question of their binding them in conscience to certain beliefs as to what is the best policy, and it is a necessary condition of the acts of others binding us that the constitution is just, that we have accepted its benefits, and so forth. . . .

Now recall that the question is this: How is it possible that a person, in accordance with his own conception of justice, should find himself bound by the acts of another to obey an unjust law (not simply a law contrary to his interests)? Put another way: Why, when I am free and still without my chains, should I accept certain a priori conditions to which any social contract must conform, a priori conditions that rule out all constitutional procedures that would decide in accordance with my judgment of justice against everyone else? To explain this, we require two hypotheses: that among the very limited number of procedures that would stand any chance of being established, none would make my decision decisive in this way; and that all such procedures would determine social conditions that I judge to be better than anarchy. Granting the second hypothesis, I want to elaborate on this in the following way: the first step in the explanation is to derive the principles of justice that are to apply to the basic form of the social system and, in particular, to the constitution. Once we have these principles, we see that no just constitutional procedure would make my judgment as to the best policy decisive. It is not simply that, among the limited number of procedures

actually possible as things are, no procedure would give me this authority. The point is that even if such were possible, given some extraordinary social circumstances, it would not be just. (Of course it is not possible for everyone to have this authority). Once we see this, we see how it is possible that within the framework of a just constitutional procedure to which we are obligated, it may nevertheless happen that we are bound to obey what seems to us to be and is an unjust law. Moreover, the possibility is present even though everyone has the same sense of justice (that is, accepts the same principles of justice) and everyone regards the constitutional procedure itself as just. Even the most efficient constitution cannot prevent the enactment of unjust laws if, from the complexity of the social situation and like conditions, the majority decides to enact them. A just constitutional procedure cannot foreclose all injustice; this depends on those who carry out the procedure.

To summarize, . . . our moral obligation to obey the law is a special case of the duty of fair play. This means that the legal order is construed as a system of social cooperation to which we become bound because: first, the scheme is just (that is, it satisfies the two principles of justice), and no just scheme can ensure against our ever being in the minority in a vote; and second, we have accepted, and intend to continue to accept, its benefits. If we failed to obey the law, to act on our duty of fair play, the equilibrium between conflicting claims, as defined by the concept of justice, would be upset. The duty of fair play is not, of course, intended to account for its being wrong for us to commit crimes of violence, but it is intended to account, in part, for the obligation to pay our income tax, to vote, and so on. . . .

The Place of Civil Disobedience in a Constitutional Democracy

We are now in a position to say a few things about civil disobedience. I shall understand it to be a public, nonviolent, and conscientious act contrary to law usually done with the intent to bring about a change in the policies or laws of the government.[2] Civil disobedience is a political act in the sense that it is an act justified by moral principles which define a conception of civil society and the public good. It rests, then, on political conviction as opposed to a search for self or group interest; and in the case of a constitutional democracy, we may assume that this conviction involves the conception of justice (say that expressed by the contract doctrine) which underlies the constitution itself. That is, in a viable democratic regime there is a common conception of justice by reference to which its citizens regulate their political affairs and interpret the constitution. Civil disobedience is a public act which the dissenter believes to be justified by this conception of justice and for this reason it may be understood as addressing the sense of justice of the majority in order to urge reconsideration of the measures protested and to warn that, in the sincere opinion of the dissenters, the conditions of social cooperation are not being honored. For the principles of justice express precisely such conditions, and their persistent and deliberate violation in regard to basic liberties over any extended period of time cuts the ties of community and invites either submission or forceful resistance. By engaging in civil disobedience a minority leads the majority to consider whether it wants to have its acts taken in this way, or whether, in view of the common sense of justice, it wishes to acknowledge the claims of the minority.

Civil disobedience is also civil in another sense. Not only is it the outcome of a sincere conviction based on principles which regulate civic life, but it is public and nonviolent, that is, it is done in a situation where arrest and punishment are expected and accepted without resistance. In this way it manifests a respect for legal procedures. Civil disobedience expresses disobedience to law within the limits of fidelity to law, and this feature of it helps to establish in the eyes of the majority that it is indeed conscientious and sincere, that it really is meant to address their sense of justice.[3] Being completely open about one's acts and being willing to accept the legal consequences of one's conduct is a bond given to make good one's sincerity, for that one's deeds are conscientious is not easy to demonstrate to another or even before oneself. No doubt it is possible to imagine a legal system in which conscientious belief that the law is unjust is accepted as a defense for noncompliance, and men of great honesty who are confident in one another might make such a system work. But as things are such a scheme would be unstable: we must pay a price in order to establish that we believe our actions have a moral basis in the convictions of the community.

The nonviolent nature of civil disobedience refers to the fact that it is intended to address the sense of justice of the majority and as such it is a form of speech, an expression of conviction. To engage in violent acts likely to injure and to hurt is incompatible with civil disobedience as a mode of address. Indeed, an interference with the basic rights of others tends to obscure the civilly disobedient quality of one's act. Civil disobedience is nonviolent in the further sense that the legal penalty for one's action is accepted and that resistance is not (at least for the moment) contemplated. Nonviolence in this sense is to be distinguished from nonviolence as a religious or pacifist principle. While those engaging in civil disobedience have often held some such principle, there is no necessary connection between it and civil disobedience. For on the interpretation suggested, civil disobedience in a democratic society is best understood as an appeal to the principles of justice, the fundamental conditions of willing social cooperation among free men, which in the view of the community as a whole are expressed in the constitution and guide its interpretation. Being an appeal to the moral basis of public life, civil disobedience is a political and not primarily a religious act. It addresses itself to the common principles of justice which men can require one another to follow and not to the aspirations of love which they cannot. Moreover by taking part in civilly disobedient acts one does not foreswear indefinitely the idea of forceful resistance; for if the appeal against injustice is repeatedly denied, then the majority has declared its intention to invite submission or resistance and the latter may conceivably be justified even in a democratic regime.

We are not required to acquiesce in the crushing of fundamental liberties by democratic majorities which have shown themselves blind to the principles of justice upon which justification of the constitution depends.

The Justification of Civil Disobedience

So far we have said nothing about the justification of civil disobedience, that is, the conditions under which civil disobedience may be engaged in consistent with the principles of justice that support a democratic regime. Our task is to see how the characterization of civil disobedience as addressed to the sense of justice of the majority (or to the citizens as a body) determines when such action is justified.

First of all, we may suppose that the normal political appeals to the majority have already been made in good faith and have been rejected, and that the standard means of redress have been tried. Thus, for example, existing political parties are indifferent to the claims of the minority and attempts to repeal the laws protested have been met with further repression since legal institutions are in the control of the majority. While civil disobedience should be recognized, I think, as a form of political action within the limits of fidelity to the rule of law, at the same time it is a rather desperate act just within these limits, and therefore it should, in general, be undertaken as a last resort when standard democratic processes have failed. In this sense it is not a normal political action. When it is justified there has been a serious breakdown; not only is there grave injustice in the law but a refusal more or less deliberate to correct it.

Second, since civil disobedience is a political act addressed to the sense of justice of the majority, it should usually be limited to substantial and clear violations of justice and preferably to those which, if rectified, will establish a basis for doing away with remaining injustices. For this reason there is a presumption in favor of restricting civil disobedience to violations of the first principle of justice, the principle of equal liberty, and to barriers which contravene the second principle, the principle of open offices which protects equality of opportunity. It is not, of course, always easy to tell whether these principles are satisfied. But if we think of them as guaranteeing the fundamental equal political and civil liberties (including freedom of conscience and liberty of thought) and equality of opportunity, then it is often relatively clear whether their principles are being honored. After all, the equal liberties are defined by the visible structure of social institutions; they are to be incorporated into the recognized practice, if not the letter, of social arrangements. When minorities are denied the right to vote or to hold certain political offices, when certain religious groups are repressed and others denied equality of opportunity in the economy, this is often obvious and there is no doubt that justice is not being given. However, the first part of the second principle which requires that inequalities be to everyone's advantage is a much more imprecise and controversial matter. Not only is there a problem of assigning it a determinate and precise sense, but even if we do so and agree on what it should be, there is often a wide variety of reasonable opinion as to whether the principle is satisfied. The reason for this is that the principle applies primarily to fundamental economic and social policies. The choice of these depends upon theoretical and speculative beliefs as well as upon a wealth of concrete information, and all of this mixed with judgment and plain hunch, not to mention in actual cases prejudice and self-interest. Thus unless the laws of taxation are clearly designed to attack a basic equal liberty, they should not be protested by civil disobedience; the appeal to justice is not sufficiently clear and its resolution is best left to the political process. But violations of the equal liberties that define the common status of citizenship are another matter. The deliberate denial of these more or less over any extended period of time in the face of normal political protest is, in general, an appropriate object of civil disobedience. We may think of the social system as divided roughly into two parts, one which incorporates the fundamental equal liberties (including equality of opportunity) and another which embodies social and economic policies properly aimed at promoting the advantage of everyone. As a rule civil disobedience is best limited to the former where the appeal to justice is not only more definite and precise, but where, if it is effective, it tends to correct the injustices in the latter.

Third, civil disobedience should be restricted to those cases where the dissenter is willing to affirm that everyone else similarly subjected to the same degree of injustice has the right to protest in a similar way. That is, we must be prepared to authorize others to dissent in similar situations and in the same way, and to accept the consequences of their doing so. Thus, we may hold, for example, that the widespread disposition to disobey civilly clear violations of fundamental liberties more or less deliberate over an extended period of time would raise the degree of justice throughout society and would insure men's self-esteem as well as their respect for one another. Indeed, I believe this to be true, though certainly it is partly a matter of conjecture. As the contract doctrine emphasizes, since the principles of justice are principles which we would agree to in an original position of equality when we do not know our social position and the like, the refusal to grant justice is either the denial of the other as an equal (as one in regard to whom we are prepared to constrain our actions by principles which we would consent to) or the manifestation of a willingness to take advantage of natural contingencies and social fortune at his expense. In either case, injustice invites submission or resistance; but submission arouses the contempt of the oppressor and confirms him in his intention. If straightway, after a decent period of time to make reasonable political appeals in the normal way, men were in general to dissent by civil disobedience from infractions of the fundamental equal liberties, these liberties would, I believe, be more rather than less secure. Legitimate civil disobedience properly exercised is a stabilizing device in a constitutional regime, tending to make it more firmly just.

Sometimes, however, there may be a complication in connection with this third condition. It is possible, although perhaps unlikely, that there are so many persons or groups with a sound case for resorting to civil disobedience (as judged by the foregoing criteria) that dis-

order would follow if they all did so. There might be serious injury to the just constitution. Or again, a group might be so large that some extra precaution is necessary in the extent to which its members organize and engage in civil disobedience. Theoretically the case is one in which a number of persons or groups are equally entitled to and all want to resort to civil disobedience, yet if they all do this, grave consequences for everyone may result. The question, then, is who among them may exercise their right, and it falls under the general problem of fairness. I cannot discuss the complexities of the matter here. Often a lottery or a rationing system can be set up to handle the case; but unfortunately the circumstances of civil disobedience rule out this solution. It suffices to note that a problem of fairness may arise and that those who contemplate civil disobedience should take it into account. They may have to reach an understanding as to who can exercise their right in the immediate situation and to recognize the need for special constraint.

The final condition, of a different nature, is the following. We have been considering when one has a right to engage in civil disobedience, and our conclusion is that one has this right should three conditions hold: when one is subject to injustice more or less deliberate over an extended period of time in the face of normal political protests; where the injustice is a clear violation of the liberties of equal citizenship; and provided that the general disposition to protest similarly in similar cases would have acceptable consequences. These conditions are not, I think, exhaustive but they seem to cover the more obvious points; yet even when they are satisfied and one has the right to engage in civil disobedience, there is still the different question of whether one should exercise this right, that is, whether by doing so one is likely to further one's ends. Having established one's right to protest one is then free to consider these tactical questions. We may be acting within our rights but still foolishly if our action only serves to provoke the harsh retaliation of the majority; and it is likely to do so if the majority lacks a sense of justice, or if the action is poorly timed or not well designed to make the appeal to the sense of justice effective. It is easy to think of instances of this sort, and in each case these practical questions have to be faced. From the standpoint of the theory of political obligation we can only say that the exercise of the right should be rational and reasonably designed to advance the protester's aims, and that weighing tactical questions presupposes that one has already established one's right, since tactical advantages in themselves do not support it.

Conclusion: Several Objections Considered

In a reasonably affluent democratic society justice becomes the first virtue of institutions. Social arrangements irrespective of their efficiency must be reformed if they are significantly unjust. No increase in efficiency in the form of greater advantages for many justifies the loss of liberty of a few. That we believe this is shown by the fact that in a democracy the fundamental liberties of citizenship are not understood as the outcome of political bargaining nor are they subject to the calculus of social interests. Rather these liberties are fixed points which serve to limit political transactions and which determine the scope of calculations of social advantage. It is this fundamental place of the equal liberties which makes their systematic violation over any extended period of time a proper object of civil disobedience. For to deny men these rights is to infringe the conditions of social cooperation among free and rational persons, a fact which is evident to the citizens of a constitutional regime since it follows from the principles of justice which underlie their institutions. The justification of civil disobedience rests on the priority of justice and the equal liberties which it guarantees.

It is natural to object to this view of civil disobedience that it relies too heavily upon the existence of a sense of justice. Some may hold that the feeling for justice is not a vital political force, and that what moves men are various other interests, the desire for wealth, power, prestige, and so on. Now this is a large question the answer to which is highly conjectural and each tends to have his own opinion. But

there are two remarks which may clarify what I have said: first, I have assumed that there is in a constitutional regime a common sense of justice the principles of which are recognized to support the constitution and to guide its interpretation. In any given situation particular men may be tempted to violate these principles, but the collective force in their behalf is usually effective since they are seen as the necessary terms of cooperation among free men; and presumably the citizens of a democracy (or sufficiently many of them) want to see justice done. Where these assumptions fail, the justifying conditions for civil disobedience (the first three) are not affected, but the rationality of engaging in it certainly is. In this case, unless the costs of repressing civil dissent injures the economic self-interest (or whatever) of the majority, protest may simply make the position of the minority worse. No doubt as a tactical matter civil disobedience is more effective when its appeal coincides with other interests, but a constitutional regime is not viable in the long run without an attachment to the principles of justice of the sort which we have assumed.

Then, further, there may be a misapprehension about the manner in which a sense of justice manifests itself. There is a tendency to think that it is shown by professions of the relevant principles together with actions of an altruistic nature requiring a considerable degree of self-sacrifice. But these conditions are obviously too strong, for the majority's sense of justice may show itself simply in its being unable to undertake the measures required to suppress the minority and to punish as the law requires the various acts of civil disobedience. The sense of justice undermines the will to uphold unjust institutions, and so a majority despite its superior power may give way. It is unprepared to force the minority to be subject to injustice. Thus, although the majority's action is reluctant and grudging, the role of the sense of justice is nevertheless essential, for without it the majority would have been willing to enforce the law and to defend its position. Once we see the sense of justice as working in this negative way to make established injustices indefensible, then it is recognized as a central element of democratic politics.

Finally, it may be objected against this account that it does not settle the question of who is to say when the situation is such as to justify civil disobedience. And because it does not answer this question, it invites anarchy by encouraging every man to decide the matter for himself. Now the reply to this is that each man must indeed settle this question for himself, although he may, of course, decide wrongly. This is true on any theory of political duty and obligation, at least on any theory compatible with the principles of a democratic constitution. The citizen is responsible for what he does. If we usually think that we should comply with the law, this is because our political principles normally lead to this conclusion. There is a presumption in favor of compliance in the absence of good reasons to the contrary. But because each man is responsible and must decide for himself as best he can whether the circumstances justify civil disobedience, it does not follow that he may decide as he pleases. It is not by looking to our personal interests or to political allegiances narrowly contrued, that we should make up our mind. The citizen must decide on the basis of the principles of justice that underlie and guide the interpretation of the constitution and in the light of his sincere conviction as to how these principles should be applied in the circumstances. If he concludes that conditions obtain which justify civil disobedience and conducts himself accordingly, he has acted conscientiously and perhaps mistakenly, but not in any case at his convenience.

In a democratic society each man must act as he thinks the principles of political right require him to. We are to follow our understanding of these principles, and we cannot do otherwise. There can be no morally binding legal interpretation of these principles, not even by a supreme court or legislature. Nor is there any infallible procedure for determining what or who is right. In our system the Supreme Court, Congress, and the President often put forward rival interpretations of the Constitution. Although the Court has the final say in settling any particular case, it is not immune from powerful political influence that may change its reading of the law of the land. The Court presents its point of view by reason and argument; its conception of the Constitution must, if it is to endure, persuade men of its soundness. The final court of appeal is not the Court, or Congress, or the President, but the electorate as a whole. The civilly disobedient appeal in effect to this body. There is no danger of anarchy as long as there is a sufficient working agreement in men's conceptions of political justice and what it requires. That men can achieve such an understanding when the essential political liberties are maintained is the assumption implicit in democratic institutions. There is no way to avoid entirely the risk of divisive strife. But if legitimate civil disobedience seems to threaten civil peace, the responsibility falls not so much on those who protest as upon those whose abuse of authority and power justifies such opposition.

Notes

1. By the social contract theory I have in mind the doctrine found in Locke, Rousseau, and Kant. I have attempted to give an interpretation of this view in: "Justice as Fairness," *Philosophical Review* (April, 1958); "Justice and Constitutional Liberty," *Nomos,* VI (1963); "The Sense of Justice," *Philosophical Review* (July, 1963).

2. Here I follow H. A. Bedau's definition of civil disobedience. See his "On Civil Disobedience," *Journal of Philosophy* (October, 1961).

3. For a fuller discussion of this point to which I am indebted, see Charles Fried, "Moral Causation," *Harvard Law Review* (1964).

Voting Influence and Reapportionment

Reynolds v. Sims
377 U.S. 533 (1964)

The U.S. Supreme Court, under the leadership of Chief Justice Earl Warren, exerted a profound influence on American politics during the 1950s and 1960s. Desegregation and school prayer were widely discussed, of course, as were cases aimed to protect the rights of people accused of crimes. But the Warren Court also changed the face of U.S. political practices with a series of voting cases extending the franchise beyond anything that had been seen before.

The Constitution left issues of voting qualifications and practices almost entirely to the states to decide. The one exception is Article I, which provides that everybody who is allowed to vote for members of the largest state legislative body must also be allowed to vote in Congressional elections. Mention of elections in different constitutional Amendments prevents disenfranchisement based on race (fifteenth), gender (nineteenth), age (twenty-sixth) and ability to pay a poll tax (twenty-fourth). So when the Warren Court confronted the failure of state legislatures to reapportion themselves it did so largely on a clean slate.

In a series of cases announced the same day in 1964, the Supreme Court invalidated the apportionment schemes in eight states, including Alabama and Colorado. The leading case is Reynolds v. Sims. *A group of Alabama citizens challenged their state's scheme for determining the size of election districts, which had not changed since the census of 1900. According to the 1960 census, population in Alabama's senate districts varied from 15,000 to 634,000 and its house districts from 6,700 to 104,000. The district court had rejected several state reapportionment proposals that would still have allowed wide variations in population and ordered implementation of its own reapportionment plan. For different reasons, both the private citizens and the state appealed to the Supreme Court.*

Chief Justice Warren delivered the opinion of the Court. . . . Undeniably the Constitution of the United States protects the right of all qualified citizens to vote, in state as well as in federal elections. A consistent line of decisions by this Court in cases involving attempts to deny or restrict the right of suffrage has made this indelibly clear. . . . And history has seen a continuing expansion of the scope of the right of suffrage in this country. The right to vote freely for the candidate of one's choice is of the essence of a democratic society, and any restrictions on that right strike at the heart of representative government. And the right of suffrage can be denied by a debasement or dilution of the weight of a citizen's vote just as effectively as by wholly prohibiting the free exercise of the franchise. . . .

A predominant consideration in determining whether a State's legislative apportionment scheme constitutes an invidious discrimination violative of rights asserted under the Equal Protection Clause is that the rights allegedly impaired are individual and personal in nature. . . . Undoubtedly, the right of suffrage is a fundamental matter in a free and democratic society. Especially since the right to exercise the franchise in a free and unimpaired manner is preservative of other basic civil and political rights, any alleged infringement of the right of citizens to vote must be carefully and meticulously scrutinized. . . . [I]n Yick Wo v. Hopkins [1886] the Court referred to "the political franchise of voting" as "a fundamental political right, because preservative of all rights."

Legislators represent people, not trees or acres. Legislators are elected by voters, not farms or cities or economic interests. As long as ours is a representative form of government, and our legislatures are those instruments of government elected directly by and directly representative of the people, the right to elect legislators in a free and unimpaired fashion is a bedrock of our political system. . . . Weighting the votes of citizens differently, by any method or means, merely because of where they happen to reside, hardly seems justifiable. . . .

State legislatures are, historically, the fountainhead of representative government in this country. . . . But representative government is in essence self-government through the medium of elected representatives of the people, and each and every citizen has an inalienable right to full and effective participation in the political processes of his State's legislative bodies. Most citizens can achieve this participation only as qualified voters through the election of legislators to represent them. Full and effective participation by all citizens in state government requires, therefore, that each citizen have an equally effective voice in the election of members of his state legislature. Modern and viable state government needs, and the Constitution demands, no less.

Logically, in a society ostensibly grounded on representative government, it would seem reasonable that a majority of the people of a State could elect a majority of that State's legislators. To conclude differently, and to sanction minority control of state legislative bodies, would appear to deny majority rights in a way that far surpasses any possible denial of minority rights that might otherwise be thought to result. Since legislatures are responsible for enacting laws by which all citizens are to be governed, they should be bodies which are collectively responsive to the popular will. And the concept of equal protection has been traditionally viewed as requiring the uniform treatment of persons standing in the same relation to the governmental action questioned or challenged. With respect to the allocation of legislative representation, all voters, as citizens of a State, stand in the same relation regardless of where they live. Any suggested criteria for the differentiation of

citizens are insufficient to justify any discrimination, as to the weight of their votes, unless relevant to the permissible purposes of legislative apportionment. Since the achieving of fair and effective representation for all citizens is concededly the basic aim of legislative apportionment, we conclude that the Equal Protection Clause guarantees the opportunity for equal participation by all voters in the election of state legislators. Diluting the weight of votes because of place of residence impairs basic constitutional rights under the Fourteenth Amendment just as much as invidious discriminations based upon factors such as race. . . .

We hold that, as a basic constitutional standard, the Equal Protection Clause requires that the seats in both houses of a bicameral state legislature must be apportioned on a population basis. Simply stated, an individual's right to vote for state legislators is unconstitutionally impaired when its weight is in a substantial fashion diluted when compared with votes of citizens living in other parts of the State. . . .

[We] find the federal analogy inapposite and irrelevant to state legislative districting schemes. Attempted reliance on the federal analogy appears often to be little more than an after-the-fact rationalization offered in defense of maladjusted state apportionment arrangements. . . .

The system of representation in the two Houses of the Federal Congress is one ingrained in our Constitution, as part of the law of the land. It is one conceived out of compromise and concession indispensable to the establishment of our federal republic. Arising from unique historical circumstances, it is based on the consideration that in establishing our type of federalism a group of formerly independent States bound themselves together under one national government. . . .

Political subdivisions of States—counties, cities, or whatever—never were and never have been considered as sovereign entities. Rather, they have been traditionally regarded as subordinate governmental instrumentalities created by the State to assist in the carrying out of state governmental functions. . . . The relationship of the States to the Federal Government could hardly be less analogous. . . .

We do not believe that the concept of bicameralism is rendered anachronistic and meaningless when the predominant basis of representation in the two state legislative bodies is required to be the same—population. A prime reason for bicameralism, modernly considered, is to insure mature and deliberate consideration of, and to prevent precipitate action on, proposed legislative measures. Simply because the controlling criterion for apportioning representation is required to be the same in both houses does not mean that there will be no differences in the composition and complexion of the two bodies. Different constituencies can be represented in the two houses. One body could be composed of single-member districts while the other could have at least some multimember districts. The length of terms of the legislators in the separate bodies could differ. The numerical size of the two bodies could be made to differ, even significantly, and the geographical size of districts from which legislators are elected could also be made to differ. And apportionment in one house could be arranged so as to balance off minor inequities in the representation of certain areas in the other house. . . .

[T]he Equal Protection Clause requires that a State make an honest and good faith effort to construct districts, in both houses of its legislature, as nearly of equal population as is practicable. We realize that it is a practical impossibility to arrange legislative districts so that each one has an identical number of residents, or citizens, or voters. Mathematical exactness or precision is hardly a workable constitutional requirement. . . .

So long as the divergences from a strict population standard are based on legitimate considerations incident to the effectuation of a rational state policy, some deviations from the equal-population principle are constitutionally permissible. . . . But neither history alone, nor economic or other sorts of group interests, are permissible factors in attempting to justify disparities from population-based representation. Citizens, not history or economic interests, cast votes. Considerations of area alone provide an insufficient justification for deviations from the equal-population principle. Again, people, not land or trees or pastures, vote. Modern developments and improvements in transportation and communications make rather hollow, in the mid-1960's, most claims that deviations from population-based representation can validly be based solely on geographical considerations. . . .

Voting Influence and Reapportionment

Lucas v. Forty-fourth General Assembly
377 U.S. 713 (1964)

A second of the eight reapportionment cases decided along with Reynolds *was* Lucas v. Forty-fourth General Assembly. *In a 1962 referendum the people of Colorado had chosen between two amendments, each of which provided an alternative method for reapportionment of its state legislature. Amendment Eight called for both the state House of Representatives and the Senate to be apportioned on a "population basis." That amendment was defeated by a vote of 305,700 to 172,725. Amendment Seven was approved by an almost identical margin of the Colorado electorate, and a majority of voters in every county. It provided for apportionment of the House of Representatives on the basis of population, but maintained the existing apportionment in the Senate, which was based on a combination of population and other factors. A three-judge Appeals Court panel had already upheld Amendment Seven, but the Supreme Court reversed. Chief Justice Warren wrote the opinion of the Court, and Justice Stewart dissented. Justice Harlan's dissent applied to* Lucas *as well as to* Reynolds.

Chief Justice Warren delivered the opinion of the Court. Although the initiative device provides a practicable political remedy to obtain relief against alleged legislative malapportionment, an individual's constitutionally protected right to cast an equally weighted vote cannot be denied even by a vote of a majority of a State's electorate, if the apportionment scheme adopted by the voters fails to measure up to the requirements of the Equal Protection Clause. [A] citizen's constitutional rights can hardly be infringed simply because a majority of the people choose that it be.

Justice Stewart dissenting. First, says the Court, it is "established that the fundamental principle of representative government in this country is one of equal representation for equal numbers of [people]." [But] this "was not the colonial system, it was not the system chosen for the national government by the Constitution, it was not the system exclusively or even predominantly practiced by the States at the time of adoption of the Fourteenth Amendment, it is not predominantly practiced by the States today."* Secondly, says the Court, unless legislative districts are equal in population, voters in the more populous districts will suffer a 'debasement' amounting to a constitutional injury. [I] find it impossible to understand how or why a voter in California, for instance, either feels or is less a citizen than a voter in Nevada, simply because, despite their population disparities, each of those States is represented by two United States Senators.

[My] own understanding of the various theories of representative government is that no one theory has ever commanded unanimous [assent]. But even if it were thought that

the rule announced today by the Court is, as a matter of political theory, the most desirable, [I] could not join in the fabrication of a constitutional mandate which imports and forever freezes one theory of political thought into our Constitution, and forever denies to every State any opportunity for enlightened and progressive innovation. . . .

Representative government is a process of accommodating group interests through democratic institutional arrangements. . . . Appropriate legislative apportionment, therefore, should ideally be designed to insure effective representation in the State's legislature, in cooperation with other organs of political power, of the various groups and interests making up the electorate. In practice, of course, this ideal is approximated in the particular apportionment system of any State by a realistic accommodation of the diverse and often conflicting political forces operating within the State.

[The] fact of geographic districting, the constitutional validity of which the Court does not question, carries with it an acceptance of the idea of legislative representation of regional needs and interests. Yet if geographical residence is irrelevant, as the Court suggests, and the goal is solely that of equally 'weighted' votes, I do not understand why the Court's constitutional rule does not require the abolition of districts and the holding of all elections at large.*

The fact is, of course, that population factors must often to some degree be subordinated in devising a legislative apportionment plan which is to achieve the important goal of ensuring a fair, effective, and balanced representation of the regional, social, and eco-

---

*See also Bickel, *The Supreme Court and Reapportionment,* in Reapportionment in the 1970's, 57, 58–59 (Polsby ed. 1971): "[A] rigorous majoritarianism is not what our institutions rest [on]. American government [includes] a Supreme Court which wields political power and [is] not elected at all. Our government includes a Senate [in] which each state, regardless of population, has an equal vote that not even a duly enacted and ratified constitutional amendment can, without its own consent, deprive it of. Our government includes a House of Representatives in which each state has at least one vote, even though the whole state may be (as some are) considerably smaller in population than the average congressional district."

*Even with legislative districts of exactly equal voter population, 26% of the electorate (a bare majority of the voters in a bare majority of the districts) can, [by] the kind of theoretical mathematics embraced by the Court, elect a majority of the legislature under our simple majority electoral system. Thus, the Court's constitutional rule permits minority rule.

Students of the mechanics of voting systems tell us that if all that matters is that votes count equally, the best vote-counting electoral system is proportional representation in statewide elections. [B]ecause electoral systems are intended to serve functions other than satisfying mathematical theories, [however,] proportional representation has not been widely adopted.

nomic interests within a State. And the further fact is that throughout our history the apportionments of State Legislatures have reflected the strongly felt American tradition that the public interest is composed of many diverse interests, and that in the long run it can better be expressed by a medley of component voices than by the majority's monolithic command. [I] think the cases should be decided by application of accepted principles of constitutional adjudication under the Equal Protection Clause [and that] demands but two basic attributes of any plan of state legislative apportionment. First, it demands that, in the light of the State's own characteristics and needs, the plan must be a rational one. Secondly, it demands that the plan must be such as not to permit the systematic frustration of the will of a majority of the electorate of the State. . . .

[In] the Colorado House, the majority unquestionably [rules]. It is true, that, as a matter of theoretical arithmetic, a minority of 36% of the voters could elect a majority of the Senate, but this percentage has no real meaning in terms of the legislative process. [N]o possible combination of Colorado senators from rural districts, even assuming arguendo that they would vote as a bloc, could control the Senate. To arrive at the 36% figure, one must include [a] substantial number of urban [districts].

[T]he people living in each of [the state's] four regions have interests unifying themselves and differentiating them from those in other regions. Given these underlying facts, certainly it was not irrational to conclude [that] planned departures from a strict per capita standard of representation were a desirable way of assuring [that] districts should be small enough in area, in a mountainous State like Colorado, where accessibility is affected by configuration as well as compactness of districts, to enable each senator to have firsthand knowledge of his entire district and to maintain close contact with his constituents. . . .

[I]f per capita representation were the rule in both houses of the Colorado Legislature, counties having small populations would have to be merged with larger counties having totally dissimilar interests. Their representatives would not only be unfamiliar with the problems of the smaller county, but the interests of the smaller counties might well be totally submerged to the interests of the larger counties with which they are joined. . . .*

The present apportionment, adopted overwhelmingly by the people [is] entirely rational, [and] the majority has consciously chosen to protect the minority's interests, and under the liberal initiative provisions of the Colorado Constitution, it retains the power to reverse its decision to do so. Therefore, there can be no question of frustration of the basic principle of majority rule.

***Justice Harlan, dissenting in both* Reynolds *and* Lucas.** . . . Stripped of aphorisms, the Court's argument boils down to the assertion that appellees' right to vote has been invid-

---

*Under *Reynolds,* could Colorado still give such counties "effective representation" by permitting them each to have a representative in the legislature, but granting that legislator only a fractional vote determined on a population basis (or granting him a full vote but giving legislators from larger counties a more heavily weighted vote)? Consider Dixon, *Reapportionment Perspectives: What is Fair Representation?,* 51 A.B.A.J. 319, 322 (1965): "[W]eighted voting may be nullified for several reasons. One of the most important reasons would be the consideration that one man casting nineteen votes is not as effective in terms of representation as nineteen separate voices (or lobbyists). Another would be that nineteen men separately elected would provide more opportunity for expression of divergent views. [B]oth of these arguments involve going beyond the simple mathematical tenor of the Supreme Court's 'one-man, one-vote' decisions. They involve putting reapportionment in the context of the actual complexities of representation—and the difficulties in determining what is fair and effective representation." Does this objection go similarly to fractional voting? If not, should fractional voting also extend to committee voting? Assignment to committee? Compensation? What else?

What about a system of cumulative voting? Consider Note, *Apportionment Problems in Local Government,* 49 Not.D.Law. 671, 683–84 (1974): "[E]ach elector has as many votes as there are representatives to be elected from the area at large, and he may cast his votes in any combination for the candidates on the slate. If there are three candidates to be elected, the voter may cast all three votes for one candidate, or give one candidate two votes and give another candidate one vote, or give one vote to each of three candidates. The three candidates with the highest number of votes are the winners. [Where] there are several positions to be filled minority groups can easily achieve a voice by running only a few candidates (or only one) and then voting in blocs. In this manner cumulative voting becomes very much like proportional representation."

iously "debased" or "diluted" by systems of apportionment which entitle them to vote for fewer legislators than other voters, an assertation which is tied to the Equal Protection Clause only by the constitutionally frail tautology that "equal" means "equal."

Had the Court paused to probe more deeply into the matter, it would have found that the Equal Protection Clause was never intended to inhibit the States in choosing any democratic method they pleased for the apportionment of their legislatures. This is shown by the language of the Fourteenth Amendment taken as a whole, by the understanding of those who proposed and ratified it, and by the political practices of the States at the time the Amendment was adopted. . . .

Although the Court—necessarily, as I believe—provides only generalities in elaboration of its main thesis, its opinion nevertheless fully demonstrates how far removed these problems are from fields of judicial competence. Recognizing that "indiscriminate districting" is an invitation to "partisan gerrymandering," the Court nevertheless excludes virtually every basis for the formation of electoral districts other than "indiscriminate districting." . . . : (1) history; (2) "economic or other sorts of group interests"; (3) area; (4) geographical considerations; (5) a desire "to insure effective representation for sparsely settled areas"; (6) "availability of access of citizens to their representatives"; (7) theories of bicameralism (except those approved by the Court); (8) occupation; (9) "an attempt to balance urban and rural power"; (10) the preference of a majority of voters in the State.

So far as presently appears, the *only* factor which a State may consider, apart from numbers, is political subdivisions. But even "a clearly rational state policy" recognizing this factor is unconstitutional if "population is submerged as the controlling consideration. . . ."

I know of no principle of logic or practical or theoretical politics, still less any con-

stitutional principle, which establishes all or any of these exclusions. . . . So far as the Court says anything at all on this score, it says only that "legislators represent people, not trees or acres"; that "citizens, not history or economic interests, cast votes"; that "people, not land or trees or pastures, vote." All this may be conceded. But it is surely equally obvious, and, in the context of elections, more meaningful to note that people are not ciphers and that legislators can represent their electors only by speaking for their interests—economic, social, political—many of which do reflect the place where the electors live. The Court does not establish, or indeed even attempt to make a case for the proposition that conflicting interests within a State can only be adjusted by disregarding them when voters are grouped for purposes of representation.

Finally, these decisions give support to a current mistaken view of the Constitution and the constitutional function of this Court. This view, in a nutshell, is that every major social ill in this country can find its cure in some constitutional "principle," and that this Court should "take the lead" in promoting reform when other branches of government fail to act. The Constitution is not a panacea for every blot upon the public welfare, nor should this Court, ordained as a judicial body, be thought of as a general haven for reform movements. The Constitution is an instrument of government, fundamental to which is the premise that in a diffusion of governmental authority lies the greatest promise that this Nation will realize liberty for all its citizens. This Court, limited in function in accordance with that premise, does not serve its high purpose when it exceeds its authority, even to satisfy justified impatience with the slow workings of the political process. For when, in the name of constitutional interpretation, the Court *adds* something to the Constitution that was deliberately excluded from it, the Court in reality substitutes its view of what should be so for the amending process. . . .

Representation and Groups

City of Mobile v. Bolden
446 U.S. 55 (1980)

The city of Mobile, Alabama has been governed since 1911 by a City Commission made up of three elected commissioners. Rather than dividing the city into three districts, Mobile residents elected all three in an at-large voting process. The result is that no black has won a seat on the council, despite a large African-American population. In this case the Court considered and rejected a claim that the voting procedures, followed in Mobile (and in many other cities as well), unconstitutionally dilute the voting power of blacks.

Justice Stewart delivered the opinion of the Court. [Justice Stewart first observed that the "claim that at-large electoral schemes" violate the equal protection clause " 'is rooted in their winner-take-all aspects, their tendency to submerge minorities.' " Stewart noted that, despite this feature, multimember legislative districts "are not unconstitutional per se." Rather, he maintained, they are invalid only if their purpose is "invidiously to minimize or cancel out the voting potential of racial or ethnic minorities." "A plaintiff," in other words, "must prove that the disputed plan was 'conceived or operated' as [a] purposeful devic[e] to further [racial] discrimination." Stewart explained that this "burden of proof is simply one aspect of the basic principle that only if there is purposeful discrimination can there be a violation of the Equal Protection Clause." To illustrate, Stewart pointed to Gomillion v. Lightfoot, 364 U.S. 339 (1960), in which the Court had invalidated a "racially motivated gerrymander of municipal boundaries"; White v. Register, 412 U.S. 755 (1973), in which the Court had invalidated a multimember district plan which minimized the voting strength of blacks and Mexican-Americans where it was proved that "the political processes [were] not equally open to participation by the group[s] in question"; and Wright v. Rockefeller, 376 U.S. 52 (1964), in which the Court had sustained a state congressional reapportionment statute against claims that the district lines had been racially gerrymandered, because the plaintiffs had failed to prove that the legislature had been "motivated by racial considerations." Applying the intent standard, Stewart concluded that "the evidence [falls] far short of showing that the appellants 'conceived or operated [a] purposeful devic[e] to further racial [discrimination].' "—ED.]

We turn finally to the arguments advanced in [Mr.] Justice Marshall's dissenting opinion. The theory [appears] to be that every "political group," or at least every such group that is in the minority, has a federal constitutional right to elect candidates in proportion to its numbers. Moreover, a political group's "right" to have its candidates elected is said to be a "fundamental interest," the infringement of which may be established without proof that a State has acted with the purpose of impairing anybody's access to the political process. This dissenting opinion finds the "right" infringed in the present case because no Negro has been elected to the Mobile City Commission.

Whatever appeal the dissenting opinion's view may have as a matter of political theory, it is not the law. The Equal Protection Clause [does] not require proportional representation as an imperative of political organization. The entitlement that the dissenting opinion assumes to exist simply is not to be found in the Constitution of the United States.

It is of course true that a law that impinges upon a fundamental right [is] presumptively unconstitutional. [And it is true] that the Equal Protection Clause confers a substantive right to participate in elections on an equal basis

---

with other qualified voters. See [Dunn v. Blumstein; Reynolds v. Sims]. But this right to equal participation in the electoral process does not protect any "political group," however defined, from electoral defeat.

The dissenting opinion erroneously discovers the asserted entitlement to group representation within the "one person, one vote" principle of Reynolds v. Sims, supra, and its progeny. [The] Court [there] recognized that a voter's right to "have an equally effective voice" in the election of representatives is impaired where representation is not apportioned substantially on a population basis. [There] can be, of course, no claim that the "one person, one vote" principle has been violated in this case, because the city of Mobile is a unitary electoral district and the Commission elections are conducted at large. It is therefore obvious that nobody's vote has been "diluted" in the sense in which that word was used in the *Reynolds* case. [It] is, of course, true that the right of a person to vote on an equal basis with other voters draws much of its significance from the political associations that its exercise reflects, but it is an altogether different matter to conclude that political groups themselves have an independent constitutional claim to representation.* . . .

[Reversed and remanded.]

*It is difficult to perceive how the implications of the dissenting opinion's theory of group representation could rationally be cabined. Indeed, certain preliminary practical questions immediately come to mind: Can only members of a minority of the voting population in a particular municipality be members of a "political group"? How large must a "group" be to be a "political group"? Can any "group" call itself a "political group"? If not, who is to say which "groups" are "political groups"? Can a qualified voter belong to more than one "political group"? Can there be more than one "political group" among white voters (e.g., Irish-American, Italian-American, Polish-American, Jews, Catholics, Protestants)? Can there be more than one "political group" among nonwhite voters? Do the answers to any of these questions depend upon the particular demographic composition of a given city? Upon the total size of its voting population? Upon the size of its governing body? Upon its form of government? Upon its history? Its geographic location? The fact that even these preliminary questions may be largely unanswerable suggests some of the conceptual and practical fallacies in the constitutional theory espoused by the dissenting opinion, putting to one side the total absence of support for that theory in the Constitution itself.

Justice Stevens concurring in the judgment.

. . . In my view, there is a fundamental distinction between state action that inhibits an individual's right to vote and state action that affects the political strength of various groups that compete for leadership in a democratically governed community. That distinction divides so-called vote dilution practices into two different categories "governed by entirely different constitutional considerations."

In the first category are practices such as poll taxes or literacy tests that deny individuals access to the ballot. Districting practices that make an individual's vote in a heavily populated district less significant than an individual's vote in a smaller district also belong in that category. [Such] practices must be tested by the strictest of constitutional standards. . . .

This case does not fit within the first category. [Rather,] this case draws into question a political structure that treats all individuals as equals but adversely affects the political strength of a racially identifiable group. . . .

Whatever the proper standard for identifying an unconstitutional gerrymander may be, [it] must apply equally to all forms of political gerrymandering—not just to racial gerrymandering. [This follows] from the very nature of a gerrymander. By definition, gerrymandering involves drawing district boundaries (or using multimember districts or at-large elections) in order to maximize the voting strength of those loyal to the dominant political faction and to minimize the strength of those opposed to it. In seeking the desired result, legislators necessarily make judgments about the probability that the members of certain identifiable groups, whether racial, ethnic, economic, or religious, will vote in the same way. The success of the gerrymander from the legislators' point of view, as well as its impact on the disadvantaged group, depends on the accuracy of those predictions.

A prediction based on a racial characteristic is not necessarily more reliable than a prediction based on some other group characteristic. Nor, since a legislator's ultimate purpose in making the prediction is political in character, is it necessarily more invidious or benign than a prediction based on other group characteristics.* In the line-drawing process, racial, religious, ethnic, and economic gerrymanders are all species of political gerrymanders. . . .

My conclusion that the same standard should be applied to racial groups as is applied to other groups leads me also to conclude that the standard cannot condemn every adverse impact on one or more political groups without spawning more dilution litigation than the judiciary can manage. [Nothing] comparable to the mathematical yardstick used in apportionment cases is available to identify the difference between permissible and impermissible adverse impacts on the voting strength of political groups.

[Today], the plurality [holds] that the primary, if not the sole, focus of the inquiry must be on the intent of the political body responsible for making the districting decision. [I] do not believe that it is appropriate to focus on the subjective intent of the decisionmakers.

In my view [a challenged scheme should be invalidated if three objective factors are present]: (1) [it] was manifestly not the product of a routine or a traditional political decision; (2) it [has] a significant adverse impact on a minority group; and (3) it [is] unsupported by any neutral justification and thus [is] either totally irrational or entirely motivated by a desire to curtail the political strength of the minority. . . .

[In] this case, if the commission form of government in Mobile were extraordinary, or if it were nothing more than a vestige of history, with no [rational] justification, it would surely violate the Constitution [because of] its adverse impact on black voters plus the absence of any legitimate justification for the system. [And this would be so] without reference to the subjective intent of the political body that has refused to alter it.

Conversely, I [am] persuaded that a political decision that affects group voting rights may be valid even if it can be proved that irrational or invidious factors have played some part in its enactment or retention. The [process of] drawing political boundaries [inevitably] involves a series of compromises among different group interests. If the process is to work, it must reflect an awareness of group interests and it must tolerate some attempts to advantage or to disadvantage particular segments of the voting populace. [The] standard cannot, therefore, be so strict that any evidence of a purpose to disadvantage a bloc of voters will justify a finding of "invidious discrimination"; otherwise, the facts of political life would deny legislatures the right to perform the districting function. Accordingly, a political decision that is supported by valid and articulable justifications cannot be invalid simply because some participants in the decisionmaking process were motivated by a purpose to disadvantage a minority group.

The decision to retain the commission form of government in Mobile, Ala., is such a decision. [The] fact that these at-large systems characteristically place one or more minority groups at a significant disadvantage in the struggle for political power cannot invalidate all such systems. Nor can it be the law that such systems are valid when there is no evidence that they were instituted or maintained for discriminatory reasons, but that they may be selectively condemned on the basis of the subjective motivation of some of their supporters. A contrary view "would spawn endless litigation" [and] would entangle the judiciary in a voracious political thicket.

In sum, I believe we must accept the choice to retain Mobile's commission form of government as constitutionally permissible even though that choice may well be the product of mixed motivation, some of which is invidious. . . .

Justice Marshall dissenting. . . . "[O]nly if there is purposeful discrimination," announces the plurality, "can there be a violation of the Equal Protection Clause of the Fourteenth Amendment." That proposition is plainly overbroad. It fails to distinguish between two distinct lines of equal protection decisions: those involving suspect classifications, and those involving fundamental rights. . . .

Under the Equal Protection Clause, if a classification "impinges upon a fundamental right [strict] judicial scrutiny" is required, regardless of whether the infringement was

---

*Thus, for example, there is little qualitative difference between the motivation behind a religious gerrymander designed to gain votes on the abortion issue and a racial gerrymander designed to gain votes on an economic issue.

intentional. [There is] a fundamental right to equal electoral participation that encompasses protection against vote dilution. Proof of discriminatory purpose is, therefore, not required to support a claim of vote dilution. . . .

[The] equal protection problem attacked by the "one person, one vote" principle is [one] of vote dilution: under *Reynolds,* each citizen must have an "equally effective voice" in the election of representatives. In the present cases, the alleged vote dilution, though caused by the combined effects of the electoral structure and social and historical factors rather than by unequal population distribution, is analytically the same concept: the unjustified abridgment of a fundamental right. . . .

The plurality's response is that my approach amounts to nothing less than a constitutional requirement of proportional representation for groups. [I] explicitly reject the notion that the Constitution contains any such requirement. The constitutional protection against vote dilution [does] not extend to those situations in which a group has merely failed to elect representatives in proportion to its share of the population. To prove unconstitutional vote dilution, the group is also required to carry the far more onerous burden of demonstrating that it has been effectively fenced out of the political process. Typical of the plurality's mischaracterization of my position is its assertion that I would provide protection against vote dilution for "every 'political group,' or at least every such group that is in the minority." The vote-dilution doctrine can logically apply only to groups whose electoral discreteness and insularity allow dominant political factions to ignore them. In short, the distinction between a requirement of proportional representation and the discriminatory-effect test I espouse is by no means a difficult one, and it is hard for me to understand why the plurality insists on ignoring it.

The plaintiffs [proved] that no Negro had ever been elected to the Mobile City Commission, despite the fact that Negroes constitute about one-third of the electorate, and that the persistence of severe racial bloc voting made it highly unlikely that any Negro could be elected at large in the foreseeable future. [The] plaintiffs convinced the District Court

that Mobile Negroes were unable to use alternative avenues of political influence. They showed that Mobile Negroes still suffered pervasive present effects of massive historical official and private discrimination, and that the City Commission had been quite unresponsive to the needs of the minority community. [Negroes] are grossly underrepresented on city boards and committees. [The] city's distribution of public services is racially discriminatory. . . .

[The] protection against vote dilution [serves] as a minimally intrusive guarantee of political survival for a discrete political minority that is effectively locked out of governmental decisionmaking processes.* [The] doctrine is a simple reflection of the basic principle that the Equal Protection Clause protects "[t]he right of a citizen to equal representation and to have his vote weighted equally with those of all other citizens." [*Reynolds.*] . . .

[Even if] it is assumed that proof of discriminatory intent is necessary to support the vote-dilution claims in these cases, the question becomes what evidence will satisfy this requirement.

I would apply the common-law foreseeability presumption to the present cases. [Because] the foreseeable disproportionate impact was so severe, the burden of proof should have shifted to the defendants, and they should have been required to show that they refused to modify the districting schemes in spite of, not because of, their severe discriminatory effect. Reallocation of the burden of proof is especially appropriate in these cases, where the challenged state action infringes the exercise of a fundamental right. The defendants would carry their burden of proof only if they

---

*It is at this point that my view most diverges from the position expressed by my Brother Stevens. He would strictly scrutinize state action having an adverse impact on an individual's right to vote. In contrast, he would apply a less stringent standard to state action diluting the political influence of a group. The facts of the present cases, however, demonstrate that severe and persistent racial bloc voting, when coupled with the inability of the minority effectively to participate in the political arena by alternative means, can effectively disable the individual Negro as well as the minority community as a whole. In these circumstances, Mr. Justice Stevens' distinction between the rights of individuals and the political strength of groups becomes illusory.

showed that they considered submergence of the Negro vote a detriment, not a benefit, of the multimember systems, that they accorded minority citizens the same respect given to whites, and that they nevertheless decided to maintain the systems for legitimate reasons. . . .

The plurality [fails] to recognize that the maintenance of multimember districts in the face of foreseeable discriminatory consequences strongly suggests that officials are blinded by "racially selective sympathy and indifference." Like outright racial hostility, selective racial indifference reflects a belief that the concerns of the minority are not worthy of the same degree of attention paid to problems perceived by whites. When an interest as fundamental as voting is diminished along racial lines, a requirement that discriminatory purpose must be proved should be satisfied by a showing that official action was produced by this type of pervasive bias. . . .

Voting Qualifications

Kramer v. Union Free School District
395 U.S. 621 (1969)

Voting is treated by the Supreme Court as a fundamental interest. If a law infringes on it the Court applies the same sort of heightened scrutiny as classifications based on race. Prior to this case, Kramer v. Union Free School District, *the Court had struck down a Virginia poll tax of $1.50, saying that wealth is "not germane to one's ability to participate intelligently in the electoral process." (Harpur v. Virginia Board of Elections, 1966). In* Kramer, *the Court assessed a New York law which provided that residents could vote in school district elections only if they own or lease taxable property within the district or else have children enrolled in local public schools. (Property taxes were used to finance the district's school system.)*

Chief Justice Warren delivered the opinion of the Court. In this case we are called on to determine whether §2012 of the New York Education Law is constitutional. The legislation provides that in certain New York school districts residents who are otherwise eligible to vote in state and federal elections may vote in the school district election only if they . . . [are] either (1) . . . the owner or lessee of taxable real property located in the district, (2) . . . the spouse of one who owns or leases qualifying property, or (3) . . . the parent or guardian of a child enrolled for a specified time during the preceding year in a local district school. . . .

In determining whether or not [this] law violates the Equal Protection Clause, . . . we must give the statute a close and exacting examination. . . . Any unjustified discrimination in determining who may participate in political affairs or in the selection of public officials undermines the legitimacy of representative government.

. . . [S]tatutes granting the franchise to residents on a selective basis always pose the danger of denying some citizens any effective voice in the governmental affairs which substantially affect their lives. Therefore, if a challenged state statute grants the right to vote to some bona fide residents of requisite age and citizenship and denies the franchise to others, the Court must determine whether the exclusions are necessary to promote a compelling state interest.

And, for these reasons, the deference usually given to the judgment of legislators does not extend to decisions concerning which resident citizens may participate in the election of legislators and other public officials. Those decisions must be carefully scrutinized by the Court to determine whether each resident citizen has, as far as is possible, an equal voice in the selections. Accordingly, when we are reviewing statutes which deny some residents the right to vote, the general presumption of constitutionality afforded state statutes and the traditional approval given state classifications if the Court can conceive of a "rational basis" for the distinctions made are not applicable. The presumption of constitutionality and the approval given "rational" classifications in other types of enactments are based on an assumption that the institutions of state government are structured so as to represent fairly all the people. However, when the challenge to the statute is in effect a challenge of this basic assumption, the assumption can no longer serve as the basis for presuming constitutionality. And, the assumption is no less under attack because the legislature which decides who may participate at the various levels of political choice is fairly elected. Legislation which delegates decision making to bodies elected by only a portion of those eligible to vote for the legislature can cause unfair representation. Such legislation can exclude a minority of voters from any voice in the decisions just as effectively as if the decisions were made by legislators the minority had no voice in selecting.

The need for exacting judicial scrutiny of statutes distributing the franchise is undiminished simply because, under a different statutory scheme, the offices subject to election might have been filled through appointment. . . .

Besides appellant and others who similarly live in their parents' homes,* the statute also disenfranchises the following persons (unless they are parents or guardians of children enrolled in the district public school): senior citizens and others living with children or relatives; clergy, military personnel, and others who live on tax-exempt property; boarders and lodgers; parents who neither own nor lease qualifying property and whose children are too young to attend school; parents who

*"Appellant is a 31-year-old college-educated stockbroker who lives in his parents' home. . . . He is a citizen of the United States and has voted in federal and state elections since 1959."

neither own nor lease qualifying property and whose children attend private schools. . . . All members of the community have an interest in the quality and structure of public education, appellant says, and he urges that "the decisions taken by local boards . . . may have grave consequences to the entire population." Appellant also argues that the level of property taxation affects him, even though he does not own property, as property tax levels affect the price of goods and services in the community.

We turn therefore to question whether the exclusion is necessary to promote a compelling state interest. First, appellees argue that the State has a legitimate interest in limiting the franchise in school district elections to "members of the community of interest"—those "primarily interested in such elections." Second, appellees urge that the State may reasonably and permissibly conclude that "property taxpayers" (including lessees of taxable property who share the tax burden through rent payments) and parents of the children enrolled in the district's schools are those "primarily interested" in school affairs.

We do not understand appellees to argue that the State is attempting to limit the franchise to those "subjectively concerned" about school matters. Rather, they appear to argue that the State's legitimate interest is in restricting a voice in school matters to those "directly affected" by such decisions. The State apparently reasons that since the schools are financed in part by local property taxes, persons whose out-of-pocket expenses are "directly" affected by property tax changes should be allowed to vote. Similarly, parents of children in school are thought to have a "direct" stake in school affairs and are given a vote.

Appellees argue that it is necessary to limit the franchise to those "primarily interested" in school affairs because "the ever increasing complexity of the many interacting phases of the school system and structure make it extremely difficult for the electorate fully to understand the whys and wherefores of the detailed operations of the school system." Appellees say that many communications of school boards and school administrations are sent home to the parents through the district pupils and are "not broadcast to the general public"; thus, nonparents will be less informed than parents. Further, appellees argue, those who are assessed for local property taxes (either directly or indirectly through rent) will have enough of an interest "through the burden on their pocketbooks, to acquire such information as they may need." . . .

Whether classifications allegedly limiting the franchise to those resident citizens "primarily interested" deny those excluded equal protection of the laws depends, inter alia, on whether all those excluded are in fact substantially less interested or affected than those the statute includes. In other words, the classifications must be tailored so that the exclusion of appellant and members of his class is necessary to achieve the articulated state goal.[1] Section 2012 does not meet the exacting standard of precision we require of statutes which selectively distribute the franchise. The classifications in §2012 permit inclusion of many persons who have, at best, a remote and indirect interest in school affairs and, on the other hand, exclude others who have a distinct and direct interest in the school meeting decisions.[2]

Nor do appellees offer any justification for the exclusion of seemingly interested and informed residents—other than to argue that the §2012 classifications include those "whom the State could understandably deem to be the most intimately interested in actions taken by the school board." . . . The requirements of §2012 are not sufficiently tailored to limiting the franchise to those "primarily interested" in school affairs to justify the denial of the franchise to appellant and members of his class. . . .

Justice Stewart dissenting. . . . [T]he appellant explicitly concedes, as he must, the validity of voting requirements relating to resi-

1. Of course, if the exclusions are necessary to promote the articulated state interest, we must then determine whether the interest promoted by limiting the franchise constitutes a compelling state interest. We do not reach that issue in this case.
2. For example, appellant resides with his parents in the school district, pays state and federal taxes and is interested in and affected by school board decisions; however, he has no vote. On the other hand, an uninterested unemployed young man who pays no state or federal taxes, but who rents an apartment in the district, can participate in the election.

dence, literacy, and age. Yet he argues—and the Court accepts the argument—that the voting qualifications involved here somehow have a different constitutional status. I am unable to see the distinction.

Clearly a State may reasonably assume that its residents have a greater stake in the outcome of elections held within its boundaries than do other persons. Likewise, it is entirely rational for a state legislature to suppose that residents, being generally better informed regarding state affairs than are nonresidents, will be more likely than nonresidents to vote responsibly. And the same may be said of legislative assumptions regarding the electoral competence of adults and literate persons on the one hand, and of minors and illiterates on the other. It is clear, of course, that lines thus drawn cannot infallibly perform their intended legislative function. Just as "[i]lliterate people may be intelligent voters," nonresidents or minors might also in some instances be interested, informed, and intelligent participants in the electoral process. Persons who commute across a state line to work may well have a great stake in the affairs of the State in which they are employed; some college students under 21 may be both better informed and more passionately interested in political affairs than many adults. But such discrepancies are the inevitable concomitant of the line drawing that is essential to law making. So long as the classification is rationally related to a permissible legislative end, therefore—as are residence, literacy, and age requirements imposed with respect to voting—there is no denial of equal protection.

Thus judged, the statutory classification involved here seems to me clearly to be valid. New York has made the judgment that local educational policy is best left to those persons who have certain direct and definable interests in that policy: those who are either immediately involved as parents of school children or who, as owners or lessees of taxable property, are burdened with the local cost of funding school district operations. True, persons outside those classes may be genuinely interested in the conduct of a school district's business—just as commuters from New Jersey may be genuinely interested in the outcome of a New York City election. But . . . I see no way to justify the conclusion that the legislative classification involved here is not rationally related to a legitimate legislative purpose.

With good reason, the Court does not really argue the contrary. Instead, it strikes down New York's statute by asserting that the traditional equal protection standard is inapt in this case, and that a considerably stricter standard—under which classifications relating to "the franchise" are to be subjected to "exacting judicial scrutiny"—should be applied. But the asserted justification for applying such a standard cannot withstand analysis. . . .

The voting qualifications at issue have been promulgated, not by Union Free School District No. 15, but by the New York State Legislature, and the appellant is of course fully able to participate in the election of representatives in that body. There is simply no claim whatever here that the state government is not "structured so as to represent fairly all the people," including the appellant. . . . The appellant is eligible to vote in all state, local and federal elections in which general governmental policy is determined. He is fully able, therefore, to participate not only in the processes by which the requirements for school district voting may be changed, but also in those by which the levels of state and federal financial assistance to the District are determined. He clearly is not locked into any self-perpetuating status of exclusion from the electoral process.

. . . The appellant's status is merely that of a citizen who says he is interested in the affairs of his local public schools. If the Constitution requires that he must be given a decision-making role in the governance of those affairs, then it seems to me that any individual who seeks such a role must be given it. For as I have suggested, there is no persuasive reason for distinguishing constitutionally between the voter qualifications New York has required for its Union Free School District elections and qualifications based on factors such as age, residence, or literacy.

Campaign Financing

Buckley v. Valeo
424 U.S. 1 (1976)

Many of the selections in this volume have raised problems associated with the influence of money and power on the democratic political process. Congress made an attempt to deal with the problem with the Federal Election Campaign Act of 1971. For certain federal offices that act limited both the contributions *individuals could make on behalf of specific candidates and the campaign* expenditures *of candidates. It also established a system of public funding of Presidential campaigns and a reporting procedure for expenditures and contributions above specified levels. The act was challenged on grounds it violated freedom of speech, a challenge the Court accepted with respect to expenditure limitations but not contribution limits.* Per Curiam *indicates all Justices agreed.*

Per Curiam. These appeals present constitutional challenges to the key provisions of the Federal Election Campaign Act of 1971 (Act), and related provisions of the Internal Revenue Code of 1954, all as amended in 1974. . . .

[The] statutes at issue [contain] the following provisions: (a) individual political contributions [and expenditures] "relative to a clearly identified candidate" are limited, [and] campaign spending by candidates for various federal offices [are] subject to prescribed limits; (b) contributions and expenditures above certain threshold levels must be reported and publicly disclosed; (c) a system for public funding of Presidential campaign activities is established; [and] (d) a Federal Election Commission is established to administer and enforce the legislation. . . .

Contribution and Expenditure Limitations

The intricate statutory scheme adopted by Congress to regulate federal election campaigns includes restrictions on political contributions and expenditures that apply broadly to all phases of and all participants in the election process. The major contribution and expenditure limitations in the Act prohibit individuals from contributing more than $25,000 in a single year or more than $1,000 to any single candidate for an election campaign and from spending more than $1,000 a year "relative to a clearly identified candidate." Other provisions restrict a candidate's use of personal and family resources in his campaign and limit the overall amount that can be spent by a candidate in campaigning for federal office. . . .

A. General Principles

The Act's contribution and expenditure limitations operate in an area of the most fundamental First Amendment activities. Discussion of public issues and debate on the qualifications of candidates are integral to the operation of the system of government established by our Constitution. . . .

The interests served by the Act include restricting the voices of people and interest groups who have money to spend and reducing the overall scope of federal election campaigns. Although the Act does not focus on the ideas expressed by persons or groups subject to its regulations, it is aimed in part at equalizing the relative ability of all voters to affect electoral outcomes by placing a ceiling on expenditures for political expression by citizens and groups. . . .

Nor can the Act's contribution and expenditure limitations be sustained, as some of the parties suggest, by reference to the con-

stitutional principles reflected in [earlier] decisions. [Earlier cases] involved place or manner restrictions on legitimate modes of expression—picketing, parading, demonstrating, and using a soundtruck. The critical difference between this case and those time, place, and manner cases is that the present Act's contribution and expenditure limitations impose direct quantity restrictions on political communication and association by persons, groups, candidates, and political parties in addition to any reasonable time, place, and manner regulations otherwise imposed.[1]

A restriction on the amount of money a person or group can spend on political communication during a campaign necessarily reduces the quantity of expression by restricting the number of issues discussed, the depth of their exploration, and the size of the audience reached.[2] This is because virtually every means of communicating ideas in today's mass society requires the expenditure of money. . . .

The expenditure limitations contained in the Act represent substantial rather than merely theoretical restraints on the quantity and diversity of political speech. . . .

By contrast with a limitation upon expenditures for political expression, a limitation upon the amount that any one person or group may contribute to a candidate or political committee entails only a marginal restriction upon the contributor's ability to engage in free communication, [for] it permits the symbolic expression of support evidenced by a contribution but does not in any way infringe the contributor's freedom to discuss candidates and issues. . . .

---

1. The nongovernmental appellees argue that just as the decibels emitted by a sound truck can be regulated consistently with the First Amendment, [*Kovacs*], the Act may restrict the volume of dollars in political campaigns without impermissibly restricting freedom of speech. [This] comparison underscores a fundamental misconception. The decibel restriction upheld in *Kovacs* limited the *manner* of operating a soundtruck, but not the *extent* of its proper use. By contrast, the Act's dollar ceilings restrict the extent of the reasonable use of virtually every means of communicating information. . . .

2. Being free to engage in unlimited political expression subject to a ceiling on expenditures is like being free to drive an automobile as far and as often as one desires on a single tank of gasoline.

Given the important role of contributions in financing political campaigns, contribution restrictions could have a severe impact on political dialogue if the limitations prevented candidates and political committees from amassing the resources necessary for effective advocacy. There is no indication, however, that the contribution limitations imposed by the Act would have any dramatic adverse effect on the funding of campaigns and political associations.[3] The overall effect of the Act's contribution ceilings is merely to require candidates and political committees to raise funds from a greater number of persons and to compel people who would otherwise contribute amounts greater than the statutory limits to expend such funds on direct political expression, rather than to reduce the total amount of money potentially available to promote political expression. . . .

In sum, although the Act's contribution and expenditure limitations both implicate fundamental First Amendment interests, its expenditure ceilings impose significantly more severe restrictions on protected freedoms of political expression and association than do its limitations on financial contributions.

B. Contribution Limitations

. . . It is unnecessary to look beyond the Act's primary purpose—to limit the actuality and appearance of corruption resulting from large individual financial contributions—in order to find a constitutionally sufficient justification for the $1,000 contribution limitation. [The] increasing importance of the communications media and sophisticated mass-mailing and polling operations to effective campaigning make the raising of large sums of money an ever more essential ingredient of an effective candidacy. To the extent that large contributions are given to secure a political quid pro quo from current and potential office holders, the integrity of our system of representative democracy is undermined. . . .

Of almost equal concern [is] the appearance of corruption stemming from [the] opportuni-

ties for abuse inherent in a regime of large individual financial contributions. [Congress] could legitimately conclude that the avoidance of the appearance of improper influence [is] "critical [if] confidence in the system of representative Government is not to be [eroded]."
. . .

Appellants contend that the contribution limitations must be invalidated because bribery laws and narrowly drawn disclosure requirements constitute a less restrictive means of dealing with "proven and suspected quid pro quo arrangements." But laws making criminal the giving and taking of bribes deal with only the most blatant and specific attempts of those with money to influence governmental action. And while disclosure requirements serve [many salutary purposes] Congress was surely entitled to conclude that disclosure was only a partial measure, and that contribution ceilings were a necessary legislative concomitant to deal with the reality or appearance of corruption. . . .

We find that, under the rigorous standard of review established by our prior decisions, the weighty interests served by restricting the size of financial contributions to political candidates are sufficient to justify the limited effect upon First Amendment freedoms caused by the $1,000 contribution ceiling.

[Appellants argue further, however,] that the contribution limitations work [an] invidious discrimination between incumbents and [challengers].[4] [But] there is [no] evidence

3. Statistical findings agreed to by the parties reveal that approximately 5.1% of the $73,483,613 raised by the 1,161 candidates for Congress in 1974 was obtained in amounts in excess of $1,000. . . .

4. In this discussion, we address only the argument that the contribution limitations alone impermissibly discriminate against nonincumbents. We do not address the more serious argument that these limitations, in combination with the limitation on expenditures [invidiously] discriminate against major-party challengers and minor-party candidates.

Since an incumbent is subject to these limitations to the same degree as his opponent, the Act, on its face, appears to be evenhanded. The appearance of fairness, however, may not reflect political reality. Although some incumbents are defeated in every congressional election, it is axiomatic that an incumbent usually begins the race with significant advantages. [In some circumstances] the overall effect of the contribution and expenditure limitations enacted by Congress could foreclose any fair opportunity of a successful challenge.

However, since we decide, infra, that the ceilings on [expenditures] are unconstitutional under the First Amendment, we need not express any opinion with regard to the alleged invidious discrimination resulting from the full sweep of the legislation as enacted.

[that] contribution limitations [discriminate] against major-party challengers to incumbents, [and although] the charge of discrimination against minor-party and independent candidates is more troubling, [the] record provides no basis for concluding that the Act invidiously disadvantages such candidates. [Indeed, in some circumstances] the restriction would appear to benefit minor-party and independent candidates relative to their major-party opponents because major-party candidates receive far more money in large contributions. . . .

In view of these considerations, we conclude that the impact of the Act's $1,000 contribution limitation on major-party challengers and on minor-party candidates does not render the provision unconstitutional on its face.

[For similar reasons, the Court also upheld the $5,000 limit on contributions by "political committees," the limits on volunteers' incidental expenses, and the $25,000 limit on total political contributions by an individual during a single calendar year.]

C. Expenditure Limitations

The Act's expenditure ceilings impose direct and substantial restraints [on] the quantity of campaign speech by individuals, groups, and candidates. The restrictions, while neutral as to the ideas expressed, limit political expression "at the core of our electoral process and of the First Amendment freedoms." . . .

We find that the governmental interest in preventing corruption and the appearance of corruption is inadequate to justify §608(e)(1)'s ceiling on independent expenditures. §608(e)(1) prevents only some large expenditures. So long as persons and groups eschew expenditures that in express terms advocate the election or defeat of a clearly identified candidate, they are free to spend as much as they want to promote the candidate and his views. The exacting interpretation of the statutory language necessary to avoid unconstitutional vagueness thus undermines the limitation's effectiveness. . . .

It is argued . . . [that] governmental interest in equalizing the relative ability of individuals [to] influence the outcome of elections [justifies the] expenditure ceiling. But the concept

that government may restrict the speech of some [in] order to enhance the relative voice of others is wholly foreign to the First Amendment, which was designed "to secure 'the widest possible dissemination of information from diverse and antagonistic sources.' " [The] First Amendment's protection against governmental abridgment of free expression cannot properly be made to depend on a person's financial ability to engage in public discussion. [Section] 608(e)(1)'s [expenditure] limitation is unconstitutional under the First Amendment.

The Act also [limits] expenditures by a candidate "from his personal funds, or the personal funds of his immediate family, in connection with his campaigns during any calendar year." . . .

The ceiling on personal expenditures by candidates on their own [behalf] imposes a substantial restraint on the ability of persons to engage in protected First Amendment expression. The candidate, no less than any other person, has a First Amendment right to engage in the discussion of public issues and [to] advocate his own election. . . .

The [interest] in equalizing the relative financial resources of candidates competing for elective office is clearly not sufficient to justify the provision's infringement of fundamental First Amendment rights. . . .

Section 608(c) places limitations on overall campaign expenditures by candidates seeking nomination for election and election to federal office. . . .

No governmental interest that has been suggested is sufficient to justify the restriction on the quantity of political expression imposed by §608(c)'s campaign expenditure limitations. [The] interest in alleviating the corrupting influence of large contributions is served by the Act's contribution limitations and disclosure provisions, [and the] interest in equalizing the financial resources of candidates [is not a] convincing justification for restricting the scope of federal election campaigns. [The] campaign expenditure ceilings appear to be designed primarily to [reduce] the allegedly skyrocketing costs of political campaigns. [But the] First Amendment denies government the power to determine that spending to promote one's political views is wasteful, excessive, or unwise. In the free society ordained by our Constitution it is not the government, but the people—individually as citizens and candidates and collectively as associations and political committees—who must retain control over the quantity and range of debate on public issues in a political campaign.

For these reasons we hold that §608(c) is constitutionally invalid.

Justice White concurring in part and dissenting in part. . . . I dissent [from] the Court's view that the expenditure limitations [violate] the First Amendment. . . .

The congressional judgment [was that expenditure limitations are necessary] to counter the corrosive effects of money in federal election campaigns. [The] Court strikes down [§608(e)], strangely enough claiming more [knowledge] as to what may improperly influence candidates than is possessed by the majority of Congress that passed this bill and the President who signed it. [I] would take the word of those who know—that limiting independent expenditures is essential to prevent transparent and widespread evasion of the contribution limits. . . .

The Court also rejects Congress' judgment manifested in §608(c) that the federal interest in limiting total campaign expenditures by individual candidates justifies the incidental effect on their opportunity for effective political speech. I disagree. . . .

[The] argument that money is speech and that limiting the flow of money to the speaker violates the First Amendment proves entirely too much. Compulsory bargaining [has] increased the labor costs of those who publish newspapers, [and] taxation directly removes from company coffers large amounts of money that might be spent on larger and better newspapers. [But] it has not been suggested [that] these laws, and many others, are invalid because they siphon [off] large sums that would otherwise be available for communicative activities.

[The] judgment of Congress was that reasonably effective campaigns could be conducted within the limits established by the Act. [There] is no sound basis for invalidating the expenditure limitations, so long as the purposes they serve are legitimate and sufficiently substantial, which in my view they are.

[Expenditure] ceilings reinforce the contribution limits and help eradicate the hazard of corruption. [Without] limits on total expenditures, campaign costs will [inevitably] escalate, [creating an incentive to accept unlawful contributions. Moreover,] the corrupt use of money by candidates is as much to be feared as the corrosive influence of large contributions. There are many illegal ways of spending money to influence elections. [The] expenditure limits could play a substantial role in preventing unethical practices. There just would not be enough of "that kind of money" to go around. . . .

It is also important to [restore] public confidence in federal elections. It is critical to obviate [the] impression that federal elections are purely and simply a function of money. [The] ceiling on candidate expenditures represents the considered judgment of Congress that elections are to be decided among candidates none of whom has overpowering advantage by reason of a huge campaign war chest. [This] seems an acceptable purpose and the means chosen a commonsense way to achieve it. . . .

I also disagree with the Court's judgment that §608(a), which limits the amount of money that a candidate or his family may spend on his campaign, violates the Constitution. [By] limiting the importance of personal wealth, §608(a) helps to assure that only individuals with a modicum of support from others will be viable candidates. [This] would tend to discourage any notion that the outcome of elections is primarily a function of money. Similarly, §608(a) tends to equalize access to the political arena, encouraging the less wealthy [to] run for political office. [Congress] was entitled to determine that personal wealth ought to play a less important role in political campaigns than it has in the past. Nothing in the First Amendment stands in the way of that determination. . . .

Justice Marshall concurring in part and dissenting in part. [The] Court invalidates §608(a), [which limits the amount a candidate may spend from personal or family funds], as violative of the candidate's First Amendment Rights. [I] disagree.

[The] perception that personal wealth wins elections may not only discourage potential candidates without significant personal wealth from entering the political arena, but also undermine public confidence in the integrity of the electoral process.[5]

The concern that candidacy for public office not become, or appear to become, the exclusive province of the wealthy assumes heightened significance when one considers the impact of §608(b), which the Court today upholds. That provision prohibits contributions from individuals and groups to candi-

5. "In the Nation's seven largest States in 1970, 11 of the 15 major senatorial candidates were millionaires. The four who were not millionaires lost their bid for election." . . .

dates in excess of $1,000, and contributions from political committees in excess of $5,000. While the limitations on contributions are neutral there can be no question that large contributions generally mean more to the candidate without a substantial personal fortune to spend on his campaign. Large contributions are the less wealthy candidate's only hope of countering the wealthy candidate's immediate access to substantial sums of money. [Section §608(a) thus provides] some symmetry to a regulatory scheme that otherwise enhances the natural advantage of the wealthy. . . .

7

Critical Perspectives

Capitalism and Democracy

Joshua Cohen and Joel Rogers

To understand capitalist democracy, argue Cohen and Rogers, it is essential to appreciate the importance of the system's being capitalist *as well as* democratic. *Although democratic, in the sense that workers can exercise political rights, capitalist democracies are limited in two respects. First, the rights which workers exercise are formal and procedural rather than substantive, while the distribution of resources that occurs in capitalism has a decisive impact on even those procedural rights. The second restraint, termed by the authors a "demand constraint," means that capitalist democracies direct the exercise of political rights to the satisfaction of certain interests but not others. Part of its stability, they argue, rests the system's ability to satisfy the desires that it creates. Consideration of these two constraints leads to a wide-ranging discussion of the many ways capitalism influences the real-world operations of democratic political systems.*

How can one make sense of something as complex as a social system? There are so many different aspects of such systems, and no clear way of deciding in advance which are important and which are not. . . . In considering the basic structure of the American system we will begin by abstracting from many of its most distinctive features. Some of these features, like the famous American devotion to canned beer and professional football, are obviously peripheral to the basic operation of its political and economic order. . . . The most profound characteristics of the American system, we will argue, are provided by its structure as a capitalist democracy, a structure it shares with virtually all of the world's most advanced industrial states. We order our analysis first by considering this structure as a framework for domestic politics, and then by considering it at the level of international relations. . . .

To describe the American system as a capitalist democracy is in part to indicate the presence within a single social order of private property, labor markets, and private control of investment decisions on the one hand, and such formal organizations of political expression as political parties and regular elections on the other. But the nature of capitalist democracy is not captured by merely listing these forms of economic and political organization. Capitalist democracy is not a system in which a capitalist economy persists alongside a democratic political system, each unaffected by the other. Nor is it a system in which capitalism and democracy are only temporarily joined in an unstable structure of inner antagonism, each striving to forsake the other. Capitalist democracy is neither just capitalism, nor just democracy, nor just some combination of the two that does not change its component parts. Indeed even to think of such separate "parts" is to miss the vital integrity of the system.

Capitalist democracy is different from plain capitalism, since workers possess political rights. Along with rights of speech and association, they can vote, join or form political parties, and engage in a number of other actions in the political arena which can influence the behavior of capital by influencing state policies. By using their vote, for example, workers can promote politicians committed to maintaining higher levels of employment, or punish those who are not so committed. The legality of such political action reduces its cost and thereby increases its likelihood. But the presence of political rights can also enhance

From Joshua Cohen and Joel Rogers, *On Democracy* (Harmondsworth Middlesex: Penguin Books, 1983) pp. 48–73. Reprinted by permission. Some footnotes omitted.

the ability of workers to engage in forms of opposition outside the arenas of formal politics. It can, for example, enhance their ability to form trade unions or other secondary organizations from which to press further political demands.* While no gain is guaranteed, everything else being equal, capitalist democracy's provision of political rights creates more favorable conditions for the material gain of workers than do other kinds of capitalist regimes, such as fascism or bureaucratic authoritarianism.

But if capitalist democracy is not just capitalism, still less is it just democracy. In a capitalist democracy the exercise of political rights is constrained in two important ways. In the first place, the political rights granted to all citizens, workers among others, are formal or procedural, and not substantive. That is, they do not take into account in their own form and application the inequalities in the distribution of resources, characteristic of capitalism, which decisively affect the exercise of political rights and importantly limit their power of expression. Both an unemployed worker and a millionaire owner of a major television station enjoy the same formal right of free speech, but their power to express and give substance to that right are radically different. We will return to this "resource constraint" below.

But before considering in detail the role played by the resource constraint in the normal course of politics, a second constraint needs to be introduced. Capitalist democracy does not only rest on the material inequalities that limit the effective expression of the formal rights it guarantees. Capitalist democracy also tends to direct the exercise of political rights toward the satisfaction of certain interests. This structuring of political demand, or what we shall call the "demand constraint," is crucial to the process of consent. The problem highlighted by the demand constraint might be put this way. It is clear that within capitalist democracies there are profound un-

derlying structural inequalities that shape the normal course of politics. What is less clear is how that normal course is possible at all. How is it that politics in a capitalist democracy can proceed at all without the underlying inequalities themselves becoming a central object of political conflict? Why do people consent? This is a central question for anyone whose interest in understanding capitalist democracy is informed by a desire to transform it.

Two answers to the question of consent are familiar. According to the first sort of account, determined opposition to capitalist democracy is stifled by force or fear in anticipation of the use of force. People go along because they know that if they did not go along they would be beaten up or killed. The second sort of account relies upon some kind of mass delusion as the explanation of consent, although there is much disagreement about the precise source of that delusion. Sometimes it is said to derive from "false consciousness," sometimes just from an innate inability to understand. Many may find these explanations satisfactory in themselves. Others may think that there is no alternative account that is not simply an apologetic rationalization for existing inequality.

Finding neither explanation adequate, we wish to offer a nonapologetic alternative. The central thesis of this alternative is that capitalist democracy is in some measure capable of satisfying the interests encouraged by capitalist democracy itself, namely, interests in short-term material gain. Capitalist democracy is capable of satisfying the standards of rational calculation encouraged by its structure. To observe this is to note again that capitalist democracy is a system. It rewards and thereby promotes certain sorts of interests and patterns of behavior based on those interests, and given those interests and patterns of behavior it is capable of providing satisfaction. Though fear and delusion no doubt play a role, consent is based on narrowly defined calculations of private advantage, calculations which together comprise a norm of "economic rationality."

Specifying a social norm in this way should not be confused with more ambitious claims about human motivation, a point we shall re-

*To underscore this common interaction between the exercise of explicitly political liberties such as suffrage and the exercise of classic associational and expressive liberties such as the liberties of assembly and speech, we shall refer to *all* such universal formal liberties as "political rights."

turn to later. To say that economic rationality is especially important within capitalist democracy is not to say that it is the only interest that people have in general, or that it is the only motivation ever expressed or acted upon within capitalist democracy, or that reasoning about action is in principle limited to calculations of material gain. It is merely to claim that calculation of economic interest has a special importance in capitalist democracy because it is especially encouraged by the system, and its pursuit tends to reproduce that system over time.

To develop this thesis about interests, and explore the workings of the demand constraint, we will consider two points: (1) how capitalist democracy tends to reduce political conflict to conflict over short-term material advantage; and (2) the concomitant difficulties associated with any attempt to move out of this system to a materially more satisfying form of social organization.

Capitalism is a form of economic organization in which profit provides the motive for investment and investment decisions are preeminently the decisions of competing units of capital. Capitalists earn profits by, among other things, hiring labor at wages that permit the extraction of profit. Those whom they hire typically have no other assets than their ability to work.

As a result of their control of investment, the satisfaction of the interests of capitalists is a necessary condition for the satisfaction of all other interests within the system. This is not a polemical remark but a straightforward point about the logic of interest satisfaction within a capitalist structure. Failing to satisfy the interests of capitalists means failing to secure them adequate profits. But if profits are insufficient, there will be no investment. If there is no investment, then there is no production or employment. If there is no production or employment, then workers whose principal resource is their capacity to produce starve to death. This is the famous "bottom line." It might be objected that this conclusion is too harsh, since modern capitalist democracies protect workers against such a fate through the provision of unemployment insurance and other assistance programs. But such an objection misses the mark. All such welfare mea-

sures are themselves dependent upon tax revenues, and if people are not working those revenues soon begin to dry up. There must be production for employment. There must be investment for production. And there must be an expectation of profit for investment. The requirement of profitable accumulation is not eliminated by the "welfare state."

Under capitalism, therefore, the welfare of workers remains structurally secondary to the welfare of capitalists, and the well-being of workers depends directly on the decisions of capitalists. The interests of capitalists appear as general interests of the society as a whole, the interests of everyone else appear as merely particular, or "special."

In fact, the dependence of workers on capitalists runs even deeper. As the source of funds for investment, profits are the social form characteristic of capitalism in which present resources are withheld for future production. But for wage earners this form of withholding or "saving" provides no guarantee of future benefit or return. While present profits are a necessary condition for future well-being, they are not a sufficient condition. Material uncertainty remains in the society, since investment decisions remain out of the reach of social control. Profits can be consumed, used for financial speculation, diverted to rare coins, race horses and antique cars, or used for productive investment outside the economy from which they were extracted. And even if profits are reinvested in some form in the domestic economy, such investment does not per se guarantee material improvement to wage earners. Profits made in Factory A can be diverted to a new Factory B within the same economy, but employing different workers. Or profits made in Factory A can be used to automate Factory A completely, throwing workers out of work.

There is then a characteristic economic rationality to the actions of workers specifically encouraged by capitalism. In the face of material uncertainties arising from continued dependence on the labor market under conditions of the private control of investment, it makes sense for workers to struggle to increase their wages.

As indicated earlier, in a capitalist democracy, workers' struggles to improve their mate-

rial position are aided by the existence of political rights. Given the potential material benefit
deriving from the exercise of such rights, and
given the pervasive material uncertainty for
workers characteristic of capitalism, it makes
sense that workers' use of political rights be
directed toward the achievement of material
ends. The structure of capitalist democracy
thus effectively encourages the reduction of
politics to striving over material gain. In addition to acting outside the framework of formal
politics, workers can take action *within* that
framework aimed either at improving their
material position directly or enhancing their
capacity to make and enforce material demands in other arenas. Workers can vote for
social programs such as Social Security, unemployment insurance, or Medicaid and Medi-
care to protect themselves from poverty and
the extremities of unemployment. They can
rally around more ambitious programs of economic stabilization, such as the Humphrey-
Hawkins Bill or various full employment acts,
or they can press for the passage of laws easing
the constraint on their own organization, such
as the Wagner Act that legalized the formation
of trade unions. What a capitalist democracy
provides are specifically political means
whereby workers can try to capture some of
the benefits of past "savings," and thus generally reduce their material uncertainty. But
material uncertainty remains. Indeed, to say
that material uncertainty over the future is
never eliminated in a capitalist democracy is
really only to restate a defining characteristic
of that system. For future uncertainty to be
eliminated (leaving aside the uncertainty of
nature), workers would have to control investment themselves. Such control violates the
very definition of capitalism as a form of economic organization in which investment decisions are preeminently the decisions of competing capitals. The reproduction of capitalist democracy reconstitutes material uncertainty, and thus reconstitutes the conditions
that encourage the reduction of political demand to the defense or promotion of material
interests.

It might be objected that we have simply
begged the question of consent by neglecting
the most important possibility of all, namely,
that workers might use their political rights to
contest the basic structure of capitalist democracy. Workers might exercise their rights of
association and suffrage by forming political
parties and voting for programs that call for
the transformation of the entire social order.
They might demand the construction of a society that was not defined by conditions
structuring demand toward the overcoming of
material uncertainty. Given the structure of
capitalist democracy, it may be economically
rational to use political rights for short-term
material gain. But in what sense is it rational to
consent to that basic structure itself, and not
pursue transformative struggle?

Thinking through the conditions of demand formation within capitalist democracy
reveals the obstacles to such collective action.
Capitalist democracy encourages economic
calculation through the generation of conditions of material uncertainty. But economic
calculation leads rationally to a rejection of
more radical longer-term struggles against
capitalism itself. Short-term material improvement is the preferred aim of materially based
conflict within a capitalist democracy because
of the different requirements and competing
logics of short-term pursuits and longer-term
struggles, and the rational pursuit of material
advantage within capitalist democracy thus
leads to a less radical and less global pursuit of
short-term material gain.

Why this is the case might be clarified by
considering the dimensions of short-term as
against longer-term struggles. Short-term
struggles are relatively easy to coordinate. One
can even engage in them all by oneself. One
can try to get a raise or a promotion by flatter-
ing the boss, or working late in the evening, or
discreetly suggesting that someone is not doing his or her job as well as "someone else"
might. Short-term struggles are often recognized and licensed by the state, as in enabling
legislation for the formation of trade unions as
bargaining representatives for workers, or
penalties imposed on employers for failing to
bargain with those representatives. In addition
to relative ease of coordination and potential
for official recognition, short-term struggles
always have the advantage of relative clarity of
aims. While there might be debate and sharp

disagreement about *how much* to demand, there is not the same problem of determining *what sorts* of demands to make, as is commonly the case in longer-term struggles. This is true even for militant short-term struggles to alter the conditions under which material benefits are bargained for within a capitalist democracy, as in struggles to organize unions or to form a party of labor. Even in these cases, the scope of debate is reduced by the fact that the more basic organization of political and economic arenas is held fixed, and the relative clarity of purpose facilitates the struggle.

Where successful, the cumulative effect of short-term struggles can be materially very satisfying. Some people say that capitalism cannot improve workers' material well-being. This is simply not true. It is often the case that individual workers do better than they have done in the past. And this can be the case even if not all workers are better off. Even during times of recession, some people get raises. Even if wages overall are dropping, it may be the case that a strong union can get better wages for its members. Having encouraged the reduction of political conflict to struggle over material interest, capitalist democracy provides many avenues to and examples of short-term satisfaction of those interests. In so doing, capitalist democracy more specifically encourages the reduction of politics to striving for *short-term* material gain.

It might still be argued that while it is rational for individual workers to try to improve their position within capitalist democracy, the only way for all workers to improve their material position steadily would be by struggling together to overthrow capitalism. This may indeed be true, but at almost any given point it is also true that it would be economically irrational for individual workers to engage in such a struggle. In contemplating the costs of such a long-term fight, individual workers face a familiar problem of collective action. Far from there being an "invisible hand" that guides their individually rational choices to the best collective outcome, the structure in which they find themselves yields less than optimal social results from their isolated but economically rational decisions. While we reserve a more complete exploration

of this point about collective action for our discussion of the "resource constraint," a few observations on the problem are directly pertinent here.

In considering social struggle, individual workers lack information about how other workers will behave. Other workers or groups of workers may choose not to join the struggle, or they may abandon it at a later point. Undertaking a long-term battle against capitalism under such conditions of uncertainty means that individual workers do not know how great their personal burden of the costs of that struggle will be. It therefore makes sense for individuals to try to get as much as they can for themselves in the short run before even contemplating cooperation with others in the longer term. But the achievement of short-run material satisfaction often makes it irrational to engage in more radical struggle, since that struggle is by definition directed against those institutions which provide one's current gain.

Thus the situation in which workers make their decisions leads them rationally, on the basis of material interest, to choose not to struggle against capitalism. The long-term production of consent within capitalist democracy is based on just such short-term decisions to consent to capitalist production. The system can provide workers with short-term material satisfaction, and workers participate in the system to assure that satisfaction. And even when, as is not infrequently the case, capitalism is failing to deliver material benefits, rational calculation does not mandate a longer-term transformative conflict. Individual workers may hope that the burdens of decline will not fall on them. They may calculate that protecting existing gains from further erosion is more likely to deliver benefits than engaging in a costly and in any case uncertain long-term effort. And if they are organized, their organizations, designed to deliver short-term benefits under better conditions, are likely to be ill-suited to the enterprise of radical transformation.

The integrity of capitalist democracy indicated by the demand constraint can be underscored by exploring the process of its disruption. Let us assume for the sake of argument that all workers solved their problems of information and coordination and came together to radically contest the system. What would happen? Assuming that such contestation was motivated exclusively by interests in short-term material gain, no transition to a more materially satisfying social order could be completed under democratic conditions. This may seem like an implausibly strong assertion, but it follows from the nature of collective action within capitalist democracy.

Fighting for total system transformation carries many costs. People often get killed. Internal resistance from capitalists is substantial. External pressures are often exerted by international lending agencies or hostile states. When the people of Chile elected a socialist government, President Nixon said he wanted to disrupt the internal workings of the Chilean state, drive down the price of copper on the world market, and generally crush Chile's economy. Helped along by many powerful people, he soon got his wish.

But let us again make an improbable assumption, this time that there is no violence, or internal subversion, or external subversion. Even in such a scenario, one cost that always accompanies a transition out of capitalist democracy is economic crisis. As workers try to change the basis of economic institutions from profit to something else, capitalists withdraw their capital. It makes sense for them to withdraw, since they can no longer be assured of making profits, and even if the state offers them guarantees, their future position is uncertain. But if investment stops, chaos results. Unemployment increases. Redistributional measures and state compensation of jobless workers must increase. Inflation then increases. Borrowing needs become greater, and yet more difficult to satisfy. Credit-worthiness is impaired by the new weakness of the economy. The currency is debased on international markets, making debt payments more difficult to satisfy. And so on.

Consider what this means. Economic crisis means that short-term material interests suffer. But if support for the project of transition is motivated by short-term material interests, then at the point of economic crisis, support will begin to vanish. Within the coalition seeking transition, sharp splits will open if the appeal of that coalition is based on the satisfaction of short-term material interests. These splits and defections will become overwhelming long before a democratic transition can be completed. Under democratic conditions the transition will be halted or reversed.

It might be argued that workers would see their material gain in longer terms, but that is to forget that capitalist democracy ceaselessly structures the articulation and satisfaction of demand toward short-term gain. The point again underscores the status of capitalist democracy as a system.

The integrity and relative stability of capitalist democracy indicated by the demand constraint permits and encourages a more normal course of operation based on compromise between workers and capitalists. The most general conditions of such compromise follow directly from the conditions of stability of capitalist democracy itself. Workers must "agree" not to enforce wage demands that preclude profits. Capitalists must "agree" to invest a sufficient share of profits to provide for future well-being. Of course, an important asymmetry remains between the concessions of the two classes. Workers are agreeing to something they are doing now, namely, restraining wages. Capitalists are agreeing to do something in the future, namely, invest a sufficient share of profits. Uncertainty and conflict are never fully eliminated, and any compromise therefore remains an unstable one. But so long as the terms of a compromise are kept, it permits the satisfaction of the material interests of both workers and capitalists within the structural inequality that defines capitalism.

Within the boundaries just described, there is a range of possible outcomes pertaining to both the shares of product distributed between capitalists and workers and to the direction of profit to productive investment. Both Sweden and the United States are capitalist democracies, for example, but Sweden is much more a "welfare state" than the United States, and is currently experimenting with a variety of attempted controls on the disposition of profits. In terms of both distribution and production, the Swedish and U.S. cases yield different results. The range of possible outcomes within the boundary conditions of capitalist democracy provides yet another source of uncertainty and possible conflict within the system. At any given point, the outcome achieved along this range is importantly determined by the relative power of workers and capitalists, including their degree and forms of organization and their willingness to engage in conflict at all. In determining this balance, the first constraint on the exercise of political rights, the "resource constraint" mentioned earlier, figures prominently.

We can begin our discussion of the resource constraint by noting that the ability to take advantage of the formally equal political rights characteristic of capitalist democracy is not only a function of an individual's own resources. It also depends upon the ability of large numbers of individuals who share common interests to coordinate their actions in pursuit of those interests. The ability to coordinate, however, requires more than shared enthusiasm or convergent interests. Successful coordination commonly requires the expenditure of material resources and the availability of strategic information. Everything else being equal, coordination is easier to achieve for small groups than for larger ones, and the likelihood of its occurrence varies directly with the probability of its success.

On each of these dimensions, capitalists have advantages over workers. They have enormous fixed and liquid assets. They already know a great deal about their own operations, the conditions in their industry, and the economic situation more generally, all of which is information essential to their own economic performance, and all of which makes them relatively better informed and hence more efficient political actors. They operate as a relatively limited number of units, often of colossal size. Their importance to the economy guarantees their access to key decision-makers, including public officials and other capitalists, and together importance and access increase the likelihood that they will get what they want.

These advantages of assets, structurally based information, limited numbers, and access to key decision-makers are cumulative in their effect. The presence of accumulated reserves lowers the costs of political action. Good information makes the target of political action more clearly visible. Together, informa-tion and assets reduce both the need for and the relative cost of acquiring further resources. From this position of initial strength, coordination is further facilitated, made less costly, by the relatively limited number of actors involved. Importance to the economy and access to other decision-makers finally ensures that action will be given due regard. When capitalists are upset, they make a loud noise. When they walk, they make a booming sound. And when they need to talk to someone, someone answers the phone.

The operation of such cumulative processes cannot be detailed here. But some of their essential features may be highlighted by exploring a typical scenario of the interaction of workers and capitalists within a system of formal political equality. Let us begin with an accurate assumption of initial gross inequalities in resource distribution. Let us assume, too, on the basis of our discussion of the demand constraint, that actors within the political arena behave in economically rational ways. In deciding how to act they must consider not only the potential benefits of a course of action, but also both the likelihood of success and costs of the action, including the cost of foregoing *other* courses of action. Economic rationality dictates that an action should be undertaken if and only if the expected value of the benefits of the action exceeds the expected value of the full range of costs. What happens within such a system of political conflict?

Two problems will be examined here. The first is a problem of information; the second, of bargaining and coordination.

We can begin to explore the information problem by stating the obvious. Under the workings of formal representative democracy, political decisions are always made under conditions of uncertainty. Politicians do not have perfect information about the wishes of voters, even assuming that they want to represent them accurately, and voters do not have perfect information about the future behavior of politicians, or about the costs and benefits of the programs for which they stand, even assuming complete fidelity to articulated programs. Several things follow from this. The lack of information clouds the decision process, and the "transparency" necessary to fully efficient representative decision-making is not achieved. But this is especially true for those the scarcity of whose resources precludes their regular or easy acquisition of costly information.

Rational economic motivation applied to questions of information acquisition dictates that information should be acquired only if the marginal cost of that information is exceeded by the marginal benefits gained by action on that information. For most citizens, there is virtually no costly acquisition of political information that satisfies this condition. Policy choices rarely present the average citizen with opportunities for great personal gain, and the average citizen is in any case almost powerless to affect any policy choice alone. The small expected benefit, discounted by the ineffectiveness of personal action, is virtually always outweighed by the costs of acquiring relevant information. Citizens therefore choose, rationally, to limit their acquisition of information to that information which can be obtained at zero cost. They choose a strategy of "rational ignorance." Virtually the only information that satisfies the conditions of zero cost is that which is supplied "free" by advertisers, lobbyists, and the like. This information, however, is by no means objective. Its very supply derives from the interest private decision-makers with a large stake in the outcome of a particular decision have in trying to influence that decision in a direction beneficial to themselves.

The constraints voters place on their own acquisition of information, and the special interest that motivates the supply of "free" information by producer groups, result in distortions in the consideration of issues of public policy. It makes sense, for example, for the private individuals who will benefit from a taxpayer subsidy of a $37 billion Alaska natural gas pipeline to spend hundreds of thousands of dollars lobbying and advertising to influence that decision, but it makes no sense for any individual taxpayer to spend any amount of time or money acquiring the information needed to make a correct decision about the pipeline. In the same way, it makes sense for sugar growers to spend money lobbying for import restrictions on sugar, because for sugar growers that decision is of monumental im-

portance, but it makes no sense for individual consumers of sugar to spend time or money acquiring information or organizing around the import question. For the average consumer, a small increase in the price of a pound of sugar is outweighed by the costs of acquiring information. If on the other hand there is another producer group with a very large stake in the price of sugar, for example the manufacturers of soft drinks, who purchase tons and tons of sugar each week, such information acquisition and organization does make sense. The same might be said of disputes between the construction industry and the makers of high-priced domestic steel, or between aluminum can manufacturers and bottle factory owners, or between savings and loan associations and commercial banks. Because of the many divisions among producers, such situations are common. It is often the case that different producer groups take turns bombarding the public with misleading information. This is called "national debate."

In a system of formal political equality, the information problem thus compounds economic inequality by guaranteeing a systematic bias in the information upon which public decisions are made. The bias is systematic in the sense that it is always weighted toward producers and against consumers, toward capitalists and against workers, and correspondingly affects the resulting decisions. It is worth noting again that such a bias is generated within this system *because* all the important actors— producer lobbyists and advertisers, politicians and voters—are behaving in economically rational ways. The information problem thus helps to generate further inequalities even without the additional impetus produced by the tremendous direct payoffs, bribes, campaign contributions, and backdoor pledges that place the stamp of private dominance on the American public arena. Once those additional practices are factored in, of course, the inequalities become greater still.

The second major aspect of the resource constraint concerns the process of group mobilization and bargaining. The bargaining of groups within the political system further compounds economic and political inequality because of the persistence of so-called free-rider problems. The free-rider problem is a problem of collective action. It arises from the existence of "public" or "collective" goods whose provision benefits all members of a group, and whose "consumption" by any member of the group does not preclude consumption by any other. Such goods are relatively common. A harbor lighthouse, for example, benefits all sailors navigating the harbor, and the fact that one sailor is helped by the lighthouse ("consumes" its benefits) does not mean that another cannot be helped as well. There is however a difficulty in providing for such collective goods, since individuals who are economically motivated have little or no incentive to contribute voluntarily to their provision. This is true even when the individuals would derive benefits from the goods. Not contributing ensures zero costs, but does not exclude receipt of the benefits that may be achieved through the contributions of others. One's own contribution, on the other hand, does not guarantee that the good will be made available. It thus ensures the presence of costs but not the receipt of benefits. Given a free choice, it makes sense to take a "free ride" on the backs of others.

Free-rider problems are important because collective goods are commonly the object of bargaining or struggle in the political system. The sugar import restrictions mentioned earlier provide one example of such group benefits. If import restrictions are imposed, they benefit all domestic sugar growers. Another example would be clean air. If clean air standards are enacted and enforced, everyone breathes easier. National defense, street lights, public parks, and public education are all similar goods in that consumption of the good by one person does not preclude consumption by another.

The examples indicate that collective goods comprise many of the most familiar objects of political concern, but they also underscore the fact that where collective goods are provided they are usually provided through the state. In the political arena, the free-rider problem most commonly and directly arises as a problem of mobilizing people to make demands upon the state for the provision of some particular collective good. It is here that there are significant differences between workers and capitalists. While the free-rider problem confronts all attempts to mobilize in pursuit of collective goods, the force of the problem depends on the size of the group, the resources available to those who wish to organize, the relative improvement brought about by the benefits struggled for, and the certainty of achieving those benefits through concerted action. If the group is small, it is easier to coordinate. If the benefits are large, there is more initial incentive to join in their pursuit. If the benefits are certain, the cost of achieving them can be allocated more rationally. If initial resources are high, then potential free riders can be coerced into joining the struggle or rewarded by others for not disrupting it. While any mobilization offers opportunities for participation, the participation of the rational economic actor may follow on receiving "an offer he couldn't refuse." In all these respects, capitalists have advantages over workers. They can more easily solve their free-rider problems.

If the information problem thus tends to distort public debate, the free-rider problem tends to bias the pattern of public expenditures and benefits. Everything else being equal, more specific benefits applicable to small groups of powerful actors are easier to organize for and extract from the state than benefits which will accrue to much larger groups in the political system. Everything else being equal, getting a tax writeoff for the ten largest oil companies is easier to organize and achieve than getting clean air for everyone, getting preferential trade treatment for the steel industry is easier than getting safe working conditions for the workers in that industry, getting a favorable antitrust decree for a particular class of firms is easier than getting restrictions on runaway shops.

This bias toward more specific expenditures and benefits has a differentiated impact on workers and capitalists. This is not only because capitalists can more readily solve their free-rider problems in the pursuit of more particular collective benefits, but because their greater initial resources enable them to compensate for the failure of the political system to provide adequate public goods. A rich person is less critically affected by the absence of decent public schools, or effective police protection, or attractive public recreational facilities than a poor person. Rich people can afford to send their children to private schools, or can hire bodyguards or private security forces, or purchase a private beach house or ski condo, all with a relatively small impact on overall resources. The poor person cannot. This difference in impact of the free-rider problem upon capitalists and upon workers compounds the structural inequality with which we began our discussion of the resource constraint. It closes the circle of those constraints.

But it closes another circle as well. Because the formal political system cannot fully redress initial inequalities, because it tends to reproduce and compound them over time, it continues to generate those conditions of material uncertainty that first lead individuals to accede to the reduction of politics to short-term material striving. This is where we began our discussion of the formation of political demand in a capitalist democracy, and we are led back to that starting point again. Along with all the other problems of resource inequality and organization, the free-rider problem effectively encourages individuals to find a personal way out. But that personal way out only reproduces on its own terms the short-term strivings for material satisfaction which give the free-rider problem force. The free-rider problem encourages the pursuit of particular material benefits by small groups or individuals. Need it be noted again that those are precisely the sorts of pursuits encouraged by capitalist democracy?

The free-rider problem again underscores the problem of motivation within capitalist democracy, a problem mentioned at the beginning of the discussion of the demand and resource constraints. We entered a caveat then about the consideration of motivation within those constraints. Having completed our discussion of the constraints, we return to that caveat now. At the time, we said that capitalist democracy encourages certain sorts of interests and patterns of behavior, precisely the sorts that lead to the reproduction of capitalist democracy. But we also observed that those interests and patterns do not exhaust all motivations that people have, nor even all motivations evident within a capitalist democracy. How are these points consistent? How is

the acknowledgment of the diversity of human motivations compatible with our insistence on the central role of economic rationality in the operation of capitalist democracy?

The question of compatibility is important for at least two reasons. First, unless there is some way of acknowledging the presence of concerns other than those of short-term material gain, our account of human beings is manifestly implausible. The fact is simply too obvious to be dwelt upon that virtually all people are moved by any number of feelings, desires, and aspirations other than economic maximizing. But the question is important as well for the same reason that the question of consent is important. For those whose interest in understanding capitalist democracy is informed by a desire to transform it, the presence of powerful concerns other than short-term material striving is crucial. As our discussion of transition problems indicated, a democratic movement out of capitalist democracy is impossible in the absence of other such concerns.

But while the compatibility problem is of supreme importance, it is not so very difficult to solve. Everyday life and experience indicate innumerable ways in which diverse motivations are channeled or structured into patterns of behavior compatible with capitalist democracy. In developing this point we consider two sorts of structuring. One involves the pursuit of means to fixed and determinate ends, the other involves reasoning about the ends of actions themselves. Again, the aim of the discussion is not to provide a theory of human nature or a full account of the springs of human action as expressed in capitalist democracy. The point rather is to show that the account of consent and stability offered earlier is not rooted in a perverse inattention to the familiar diversity of human motivation, and that it remains robust even in the face of motivational facts that do not fit with the basic account of economic rationality.

The first sort of structuring can be described as seeking money as a means to other things. Money is the "universal equivalent." It can be exchanged for any other good, and other goods commonly cannot be had without it. Wishing to pursue other goods thus commonly leads to an interest in money. Consider a familiar situation. Let us make the safe assumption that parents love their children, that they want the "best of life" for their children, and that they recognize that the best of life costs money. Parents will then be led to struggle for money under the conditions of uncertainty characteristic of capitalist democracy. They may work longer and harder hours to get the savings needed to pay for college for their children, or to pay for dance lessons, music lessons, chemistry sets, or the rental of prom tuxedos and formal gowns. What motivates parents to work harder to acquire the money to pay for these many things is not greed, but love for their children. Or consider the example of those who want to write poetry. To write poetry they need peace and quiet, and time to take advantage of their peace and quiet. But to get peace, time, and quiet, they need money. "The spirit must become flesh."

These examples and countless others underscore a familiar point. The pursuit of non-material concerns—the love of children, the love of poetry—is commonly conditional on the availability of material resources, and therefore conditional on conforming to the rules of those arenas in which such resources become available. This does not require greediness or any particular affection for the rules themselves. But within capitalist democracy, it does typically require dependence on labor markets, and such dependence binds the initial motivation to an interest in short-term material gain.

The second sort of structuring can be described as "institutionally constrained deliberation about ends." Even within a capitalist democracy it is of course possible to view social activity as other than merely a way to secure the material prerequisites of private satisfactions. Social activities can be valued for their own sake. They might be valued as expressing one's talents, enhancing the general welfare, or simply being the morally correct things to do. If such noninstrumental attachments motivate behavior within capitalist democracy, which they sometimes do, then our previous account of consent and stability is incomplete. Without addressing the question of the extent to which such attachments are operative in social activity, we can still explore how serious this incompleteness is.

Consider someone interested in finding a social outlet for his nonmaterial aspirations. Because those aspirations are themselves typically indefinite and unclear, such situations present a twofold problem. In addition to the task of finding an outlet for the aspirations there is the task of specifying the aspirations themselves in greater clarity and detail. Both the finding and the specifying commonly take place through available institutions. If one wants to promote solidarity among working people, for example, one is commonly encouraged to work for a union, and to identify the promotion of solidarity with the achievement of higher wages for union members. If one wants recognition for a talent, one is commonly encouraged to make that talent commercially viable, and to identify the exercise and acknowledgment of that talent with its commercially viable form. If one wants to express love in a gift, one is commonly encouraged to make the gift an expensive one, and to identify gifts of love with expensive gifts. If one's love extends to one's country, one is commonly encouraged to fight in imperialist wars, and to identify patriotism with the willingness to fight in such wars. None of this is to say that all union officials have forsaken the ideals of solidarity, that those who use their talents commercially do not truly value those talents for their intrinsic merit, that there are no feelings of love between those who exchange expensive gifts, or that all patriots are imperialists. It is, however, to observe that if certain institutions contribute to the stability of an order, it is not surprising to find that those institutions come to exhaust the variety of institutional outlets available for the expression of interests. And if acting through those institutions is systematically rewarded and accorded respect, it is not surprising to find people realizing their aspirations through those outlets and coming to specify their aspirations in terms of them.

Finally, it might be asked why reasoning about means or ends should be so willing to accommodate the existing structures of social choice. What prevents people from judging the existing arenas of social activity as inadequate, confining, or even degrading? The answer is that many do judge them so. Alienation is not unfamiliar. And sometimes there is determined resistance to the structure of social opportunity and reward. But however familiar alienation is, consent and not resistance is the norm. Thus the original question persists. Why do people consent? But answering *that* question would simply require repeating everything we have said up to this point. Material uncertainty gives encouragement to beginning any activity with a small hoard of cash. The equivalent status of money recommends that the pursuit of nonmaterial aspirations begin with the pursuit of material means. The difficulty of coordinating more transformative struggles, together with the ability of capitalist democracy to "deliver the goods," encourages the search for private forms of satisfaction. Reasoning about ends is constrained by the existing models of social expression, and these are themselves existing models because they contribute to and are compatible with the continued existence of capitalist democracy.

To say that capitalist democracy is a system is not merely to claim that it is stable *on the assumption* of economic rationality. The claim to the status of a system also involves the strong claim that capitalist democracy can take many different people with diverse motivations and effectively bend them to engage in certain shared patterns of consensual behavior with which they will at least partly identify and which they find at least in some measure rewarding. At the level of individual acculturation, this is commonly called "growing up."

We argued earlier that the production of consent within capitalist democracy encourages a normal course of operation based on compromise between workers and capitalists. While the terms of such compromises are largely determined by the aggregate balance of power between workers and capitalists, the compromises are themselves organized through and enforced by the state. When the conditions of compromise are thus organized and enforced, the state is sometimes said to be performing its "legitimate functions," such as the "defense of national security," "the administration of justice," or "the promotion of the general welfare." But these functions are not universal or eternal, and they do not drop from the sky. The content and manner of their performance varies significantly over time. And often, as in the case of the "welfare

function" assumed by modern states, there is enduring conflict over whether these functions are appropriate ends of state action at all. In fact the state's famous functions are more usefully thought of as arising from the requirements of compromise itself. Their terms and conditions mimic the terms and conditions of the compromise. In performing its functions, the state tirelessly reiterates the terms of the compromise just reached, and it does so on the basis of the distribution and mobilization of power that led to the enactment of that compromise. It expresses and enforces the compromise, and is itself the product of previous conflict and compromise. The state in a capitalist democracy may thus be thought of both as an outcome and an expression of material conflict. In any of its particular forms, themselves determined by the content of the compromise it is currently enforcing, the state holds together as a set of particular institutions and practices only so long as the compromise upon which it is founded holds together.

Upholding a compromise or organizing the terms of a new one is the central domestic condition of regime stability in a capitalist democracy. This may be seen as a threefold requirement. The state must provide conditions such that capitalists will continue to invest. It must make some sort of deal with labor such that the conditions of profitable accumulation are satisfied. And it must ensure broad consent to its own use of coercion in enforcing these agreements by demonstrating its own legitimacy.

Aside from the legitimacy that derives from its "fair" enforcement of the existing compromise (the rule of law), state legitimacy is secured under capitalist democracy by winning elections. Electoral viability is determined through a system of party competition whose structure and content, like everything else within capitalist democracy, reflect the aggregate balance of power between workers and capitalists and their preferred methods of organization. The rules on party competition and financing, the number of parties, the methods of counting the ballots of voters in "winner take all" or proportional representation schemes, the commitment of the state to the registration of voters, and the enlistment of citizens in the actual processes of formal politics are all examples of such structure and content, which vary widely from regime to regime.

Satisfying this threefold requirement provides the framework for national politics within capitalist democracy. Through its institutions the state may facilitate the organization and continued viability of a democratic capitalist regime. But it is not by itself the decisive factor in ensuring the reproducibility of such a system. While the continued reorganization of the terms and conditions of relations between workers and capitalists requires and is achieved through the institutions of the state, those institutions do not themselves control the conditions of reorganization.

Such considerations of the nature and limitations of the state underscore the limitations of class compromise itself. Since the basic condition for compromise within the structure of class subordination that marks capitalist democracy is the satisfaction of the interests of capitalists in profitable accumulation, compromise is subject to disruption whenever the conditions of such accumulation are undermined. The conditions of profitable accumulation are several. Wages must not be too "high" and markets must clear. In addition, capitalists must keep their cost conditions competitive, that is, their productivity relative to other capitalists must be maintained. When these conditions are absent, there are profitability problems. And when there are profitability problems, symptoms of those problems appear in all arenas of a capitalist democracy, because all action within such orders is materially conditioned. While not all action is undertaken in pursuit of material advantage, all action depends on material resources. Profitability problems result in a short-fall of those resources for a variety of actors and institutions, including the state, and may result in the breakdown of a compromise, and its reordering. While such breakdowns occur within particular states, however, there is no reason to conclude from this that the problems from which they ensue can be explained solely in terms of conditions within the domestic system. Demand-side problems can arise on international markets, as when a recession or protectionist policies in another state restrict foreign demand. Supply-side problems can be posed by international competitors whose wages are significantly lower, or whose labor productivity is significantly higher. Such problems have become all the more frequent with the development of an increasingly integrated world economy. . . .

Feminism and Democracy

Carole Pateman

In this essay Carole Pateman argues that democratic theorists' most serious failure is their exclusion of women and women's oppression from their deliberations. Focusing on the work of J. S. Mill and social contract theorists as well as her own book on participatory democracy, she argues that feminist criticisms of marriage and women's social condition cannot any longer be ignored, for they raise serious objections to any democratic theory. It is no longer possible for political theorists to deny the connection between the private, economic world of the family and the public one. Defenders of participatory theories in particular need to weigh these concerns, given their commitment to replace hierarchy with an educated and independent citizenry.

From Carole Pateman, "Feminism and Democracy" in *Democratic Theory and Practice*, Graeme Duncan, editor (Cambridge: Cambridge University Press, 1985), pp. 204–217. Reprinted by permission.

A feminist might dispose briskly of the subject of this essay. For feminists, democracy has never existed; women have never been and still are not admitted as full and equal members and citizens in any country known as a 'democracy'. A telling image that recurs throughout the history of feminism is of liberal society as a series of male clubs—usually, as Virginia Woolf points out in *Three Guineas*, distinguished by their own costumes and uniforms—that embrace parliament, the courts, political parties, the military and police, universities, workplaces, trade unions, public (private) schools, exclusive Clubs and popular leisure clubs, from all of which women are excluded or to which they are mere auxiliaries. Feminists will find confirmation of their view in academic discussions of democracy which usually take it for granted that feminism or the structure of the relationship between the sexes are irrelevant matters. The present volume at least acknowledges that feminism might have something significant to say to democratic theorists or citizens, albeit in a token paper by a token woman writer. In the scope of a short essay it is hardly possible to demolish the assumption of two thousand years that there is no incompatibility between 'democracy' and the subjection of women or their exclusion from full and equal participation in political life. Instead, I shall indicate why feminism provides democracy—whether in its existing liberal guise or in the form of a possible future participatory or self-managing democracy—with its most important challenge and most comprehensive critique.

The objection that will be brought against the feminists is that after a century or more of legal reforms and the introduction of universal suffrage women are now the civil and political equals of men, so that feminism today has little or nothing to contribute to democratic theory and practice. This objection ignores much that is crucial to an understanding of the real character of liberal democratic societies. It ignores the existence of widespread and deeply held convictions, and of social practices that give them expression, that contradict the (more or less) formally equal civic status of women. The objection is based on the liberal argument that social inequalities are irrelevant to political equality. Thus, it has to ignore the problems that have arisen from the attempt to universalize liberal principles by extending them to women while at the same time maintaining the division between private and political life which is central to liberal democracy, and is also a division between women and men. If liberal theorists of democracy are content to avoid these questions, their radical critics, along with advocates of participatory democracy, might have been expected to confront them enthusiastically. However, although they have paid a good deal of attention to the class structure of liberal democracies and the way in which class inequality undercuts formal political equality, they have rarely examined the significance of sexual inequality and the patriarchal order of the liberal state for a democratic transformation of liberalism. Writers on democracy, whether defenders or critics of the status quo, invariably fail to consider, for example, whether their discussions of freedom or consent have any relevance to women. They implicitly argue as if 'individuals' and 'citizens' are men.

It is frequently overlooked how recently democratic or universal suffrage was established. Political scientists have remained remarkably silent about the struggle for womanhood suffrage (in England there was a continuous organized campaign for 48 years from 1866 to 1914) and the political meaning and consequences of enfranchisement. Women's position as voters also appears to cause some difficulty for writers on democracy. Little comment is excited, for example, by Schumpeter's explicit statement, in his extremely influential revisionist text, that the exclusion of women from the franchise does not invalidate a polity's claim to be a 'democracy'. In Barber's fascinating account of direct democracy in a Swiss canton, womanhood suffrage (gained only in 1971) is treated very equivocally. Barber emphasizes that women's enfranchisement was 'just and equitable'—but the cost was 'participation and community'. Assemblies grew unwieldy and participation diminished, atomistic individualism gained official recognition and the ideal of the citizen-soldier could no longer be justified.[1] The reader is left wondering whether women should not have sacrificed their just demand for the sake of men's citizenship. Again, in

Verba, Nie and Kim's recent cross-national study of political participation it is noted, in a discussion of the change in Holland from compulsory to voluntary voting, that 'voting rights were universal'. The footnote, on the same page, says that in both electoral systems there was 'a one man one vote system'.[2] Did women vote? Unrecognized historical ironies abound in discussions of democracy. Feminists are frequently told today that we must not be offended by masculine language because 'man' really means 'human being', although when, in 1867 in support of the first women's suffrage bill in Britain, it was argued that 'man' (referring to the householder) was a generic term that included women the argument was firmly rejected. Another recent example of the way in which women can be written out of democratic political life can be found in Margolis' *Viable Democracy*. He begins by presenting a history of 'Citizen Brown', who is a man and who, we learn, in 1920 obtained 'his latest major triumph, the enfranchisement of women'.[3] Thus the history of women's democratic struggles disappears and democratic voting appears as the sole creation—or gift—of men.

Such examples might be amusing if they were not symptomatic of the past and present social standing of women. Feminism, liberalism and democracy (that is, a political order in which citizenship is universal, the right of each adult individual member of the community) share a common origin. Feminism, a general critique of social relationships of sexual domination and subordination and a vision of a sexually egalitarian future, like liberalism and democracy, emerges only when individualism, or the idea that individuals are by nature free and equal to each other, has developed as a universal theory of social organization. However, from the time, three hundred years ago, when the individualist social contract theorists launched the first critical attack on patriarchalism the prevailing approach to the position of women can be exemplified by the words of Fichte who asks:

Has woman the same rights in the state which man has? This question may appear ridiculous to many. For if the only ground of all legal rights is reason and freedom, how can a dis-

tinction exist between two sexes which possess both the same reason and the same freedom?

He replies to this question as follows:

Nevertheless, it seems that, so long as men have lived, this has been differently held, and the female sex seems not to have been placed on a par with the male sex in the exercise of its rights. *Such a universal sentiment must have a ground, to discover which was never a more urgent problem than in our days.*[4]

The anti-feminists and anti-democrats have never found this 'urgent problem' difficult to solve. Differential rights and status have been and are defended by appeal to the 'natural' differences between the sexes, from which it is held to follow that women are subordinate to their fathers or husbands and that their proper place is in domestic life. The argument from nature stretches back into mythology and ancient times (and today often comes dressed up in the scientific garb of sociobiology) and its longevity appears to confirm that it informs us of an eternal and essential part of the human condition. But, far from being timeless, the argument has specific formulations in different historical epochs and, in the context of the development of liberal-capitalist society, it appears in a form which obscures the patriarchal structure of liberalism beneath the ideology of individual freedom and equality.

It is usually assumed that the social contract theorists, and Locke in particular, provided the definitive counter to the patriarchal thesis that paternal and political power are one and the same, grounded in the natural subjection of sons to fathers. Locke certainly drew a sharp distinction between natural or familial ties and the conventional relations of political life, but although he argued that sons, when adult, were as free as their fathers and equal to them, and hence could only justifiably be governed with their own consent, it is usually 'forgotten' that he excluded women (wives) from this argument. His criticism of the patriarchalists depends upon the assumption of natural individual freedom and equality, but only men count as 'individuals'. Women are held to be born to subjection. Locke takes it for granted that a woman will, through the marriage contract, always agree to place herself in subordination to her husband. He agrees with the patriarchalists that wifely subjection has 'a Foundation in Nature' and argues that in the family the husband's will, as that of the 'abler and the stronger', must always prevail over 'that of his wife in all things of their common Concernment'.[5] The contradiction between the premise of individual freedom and equality, with its corollary of the conventional basis of authority, and the assumption that women (wives) are naturally subject has since gone unnoticed. Similarly, there has been no acknowledgement of the problem that if women are naturally subordinate, or born into subjection, then talk of their consent or agreement to this status is redundant. Yet this contradiction and paradox lie at the heart of democratic theory and practice. The continuing silence about the status of wives is testament to the strength of the union of a transformed patriarchalism with liberalism. For the first time in history, liberal individualism promised women an equal social standing with men as naturally free individuals, but at the same time socio-economic developments ensured that the subordination of wives to husbands continued to be seen as natural, and so outside the domain of democratic theorists or the political struggle to democratize liberalism.

The conviction that a married woman's proper place is in the conjugal home as a servant to her husband and mother to her children is now so widespread and well established that this arrangement appears as a natural feature of human existence rather than historically and culturally specific. The history of the development of the capitalist organization of production is also the history of the development of a particular form of the sexual division of labour (although this is not the history to be found in most books). At the time when the social contract theorists attacked the patriarchal thesis of a natural hierarchy of inequality and subordination, wives were not their husband's equals, but nor were they their economic depend[e]nts. Wives, as associates and partners in economic production, had an independent status. As production moved out of the household, women were forced out of the trades they controlled and wives became dependent on their husbands for subsistence or competed for individual wages in certain areas

of production.[6] Many working-class wives and mothers have had to continue to try to find paid employment to ensure the survival of their families, but by the mid-nineteenth century the ideal, the natural and respectable, mode of life had come to be seen as that of the middle-class, breadwinning paterfamilias and his totally dependent wife. By then the subjection of wives was complete; with no independent legal or civil standing they had been reduced to the status of property, as the nineteenth-century feminists emphasized in their comparisons of wives to the slaves of the West Indies and American South. Today, women have won an independent civil status and the vote; they are, apparently, 'individuals' as well as citizens—and thus require no special attention in discussions of democracy. However, one of the most important consequences of the institutionalization of liberal individualism and the establishment of universal suffrage has been to highlight the practical contradiction between the formal political equality of liberal democracy and the social subordination of women, including their subjection as wives within the patriarchal structure of the institution of marriage.

It is indicative of the attitude of democratic theorists (and political activists) towards feminism that John Stuart Mill's criticism of the argument from (women's) nature, and the lessons to be learned from it, are so little known. The present revival of the organized feminist movement has begun to rescue *The Subjection of Women* from the obscurity into which Mill's commentators have pushed it, although it provides a logical extension of the arguments of his academically acceptable *On Liberty*. The *Subjection* is important for its substantive argument, but also because the ultimately contradictory position that Mill takes in the essay illustrates just how radical feminist criticism is, and how the attempt to universalize liberal principles to both sexes pushes beyond the confines of liberal democratic theory and practice.

In *The Subjection* Mill argues that the relation between women and men, or, more specifically, between wives and husbands, forms an unjustified exception to the liberal principles of individual rights, freedom and choice, to the principles of equality of opportunity and the allocation of occupational positions by merit that, he believes, now govern other social and political institutions. In the modern world, consent has supplanted force and the principle of achievement has replaced that of ascription—except where women are concerned. Mill writes that the conjugal relation is an example of 'the primitive state of slavery lasting on, . . . It has not lost the taint of its brutal origin' (p. 130).[7] More generally, the social subordination of women is 'a single relic of an old world of thought and practice, exploded in everything else' (p. 146). Mill opens *The Subjection* with some pertinent comments on the difficulty feminists face in presenting an intellectually convincing case. Domination by men is rooted in long-standing customs, and the idea that male supremacy is the proper order of things derives from deep feelings and sentiments rather than rationally tested beliefs (and, it might be added, men have a lot to lose by being convinced). Thus feminists must not expect their opponents to 'give up practical principles in which they have been born and bred and which are the basis of much of the existing order of the world, at the first argumentative attack which they are not capable of logically resisting' (p. 128). Mill is very conscious of the importance of the appeal to nature. He notes that it provides no criterion to differentiate the subordination of women from other forms of domination because all rulers have attempted to claim a grounding in nature for their position. He also argues that nothing at all can be said about the respective natures of women and men because we have only seen the sexes in an unequal relationship. Any differences in their moral and other capacities will become known when men and women can interact as independent and equal rational beings.

However, despite Mill's vigorous attack on the appeal to custom and nature he ultimately falls back on the very argument that he has carefully criticized. His failure consistently to apply his principles to domestic life has been noted by recent feminist critics, but it is less often pointed out that his inconsistency undermines his defence of womanhood suffrage and equal democratic citizenship. The central argument of *The Subjection* is that husbands must be stripped of their legally-sanctioned

despotic powers over their wives. Most of the legal reforms of the marriage law that Mill advocated have now been enacted (with the significant exception of marital rape, to which I shall return), and the implications of his unwillingness to extend his criticism to the sexual division of labour within the home are now fully revealed. Mill argues that because of their upbringing, lack of education and legal and social pressures, women do not have a free choice whether or not to marry: 'wife' is the only occupation open to them. But although he also argues that women must have equal opportunity with men to obtain a proper education that will enable them to support themselves, he assumes that, if marriage were reformed, most women would *not* choose independence.

Mill states that it is generally understood that when a woman marries she has chosen her career, like a man when he chooses a profession. When a woman becomes a wife, 'she makes choice of the management of a household, and the bringing up of a family, as the first call on her exertions, . . . she renounces, . . . all [occupations] not consistent with the requirement of this' (p. 179). Mill is reverting here to ascriptive arguments and the belief in women's natural place and occupation. He is falling back on the ancient tradition of patriarchal political theory that, as Susan Okin has shown in *Women in Western Political Thought* (Princeton, 1979), asserts that whereas men are, or can be, many things, women are placed on earth to fulfil one function only; to bear and rear children. Mill neatly evades the question of how, if women's task is prescribed by their sex, they can be said to have a real choice of occupation, or why equal opportunity is relevant to women if marriage itself is a 'career'. Mill compares an egalitarian marriage to a business partnership in which the partners are free to negotiate their own terms of association, but he relies on some very weak arguments, which run counter to liberal principles, to support his view that equality will not disturb the conventional domestic division of labour. He suggests that the 'natural arrangement' would be for wife and husband each to be 'absolute in the executive branch of their own department . . . any change of system and principle requiring the consent of both' (p.

169). He also suggests that the division of labour between the spouses could be agreed in the marriage contract—but he assumes that wives will be willing to accept the 'natural' arrangement. Mill notes that duties are already divided 'by consent . . . and general custom' (p. 170) modified in individual cases; but it is exactly 'general custom', as the bulwark of male domination, that he is arguing against in the body of the essay. He forgets this when he suggests that the husband will generally have the greater voice in decisions as he is usually older. Mill adds that this is only until the time of life when age is irrelevant; but when do husbands admit that this has arrived?[8] He also forgets his own arguments when he suggests that more weight will be given to the views of the partner who brings the means of support, disingenuously adding 'whichever this is' when he has already assumed that wives will 'choose' to be dependent by agreeing to marry.

Anti-feminist movements and propagandists in the 1980s also claim that the domestic division of labour supported by Mill is the only natural one. They would not be disturbed by the implications of this arrangement for the citizenship of women but advocates of democracy should be. Mill championed womanhood suffrage for the same reasons that he supported votes for men; because it was necessary for self-protection or the protection of individual interests and because political participation would enlarge the capacities of individual women. The obvious problem with his argument is that women as wives will largely be confined to the small circle of the family and its daily routines and so will find it difficult to use their vote effectively as a protective measure. Women will not be able to learn what their interests are without experience outside domestic life. This point is even more crucial for Mill's arguments about political development and education through participation. He writes (p. 237) in general terms of the elevation of the individual 'as a moral, spiritual and social being' that occurs under free government, but this is a large claim to make for the periodic casting of a vote (although the moral transformation of political life through enfranchisement was a central theme of the womanhood suffrage move-

ment). Nor did Mill himself entirely believe that this 'elevation' would result from the suffrage alone. He writes that 'citizenship', and here I take him to be referring to universal suffrage, 'fills only a small place in modern life, and does not come near the daily habits or inmost sentiments' (p. 174). He goes on to argue that the family, 'justly constituted', would be the 'real school of the virtues of freedom'. However, this is as implausible as the claim about the consequences of liberal democratic voting. A patriarchal family with the despotic husband at its head is no basis for democratic citizenship; but nor, *on its own*, is an egalitarian family. Mill argues in his social and political writings that only participation in a wide variety of institutions, especially the workplace, can provide the political education necessary for active, democratic citizenship. Yet how can wives and mothers, who have 'chosen' domestic life, have the opportunity to develop their capacities or learn what it means to be a democratic citizen? Women will therefore exemplify the selfish, private beings, lacking a sense of justice or public spirit, that result when an individual is confined to the narrow sphere of everyday family life.[9] Mill's failure to question the apparently natural division of labour within the home means that his arguments for democratic citizenship apply only to men.

It might be objected that it is unreasonable and anachronistic to ask of Mill, writing in the 1860s, that he criticize the accepted division of labour between husband and wife when only very exceptional feminists in the nineteenth century were willing to question the doctrine of the separate spheres of the sexes. But if that objection is granted,[10] it does not excuse the same critical failure by contemporary democratic theorists and empirical investigators. Until the feminist movement began, very recently, to have an impact on academic studies not only has the relation between the structure of the institution of marriage and the formal equality of citizenship been ignored, but women citizens have often been excluded from empirical investigations of political behavior and attitudes or merely referred to briefly in patriarchal not scientific terms.[11] A reading of *The Subjection* should long ago have placed these matters in the forefront of discussions of democracy. Perhaps the appearance of empirical findings showing, for example, that even women active in local politics are inhibited from running for office because of their responsibility for child-care and a belief that office-holding is not a proper activity for women,[12] will be taken more seriously than the feminist writings of even eminent philosophers.

The problems surrounding women's citizenship in the liberal democracies may have been sadly neglected, but the failure of democratic theorists to confront the woman and wife question runs much deeper still. Democratic citizenship, even if interpreted in the minimal sense of universal suffrage in the context of liberal civil rights, presupposes the solid foundation of a practical, universal recognition that all members of the polity are social equals and independent 'individuals', having all the capacities implied by this status. The most serious failure of contemporary democratic theory and its language of freedom, equality, consent, and of the individual, is that women are so easily and inconspicuously excluded from references to the 'individual'. Thus the question never arises whether the exclusion reflects social and political realities. One reason why there is no consciousness of the need to ask this question is that democratic theorists conventionally see their subject-matter as encompassing the political or public sphere, which for radical theorists includes the economy and the workplace. The sphere of personal and domestic life—the sphere that is the 'natural' realm of women—is excluded from scrutiny. Despite the central role that consent plays in their arguments democratic theorists pay no attention to the structure of sexual relations between men and women and, more specifically, to the practice of rape and the interpretation of consent and non-consent which define it as a criminal offence. The facts about rape are central to the social realities which are reflected in and partly constituted by our use of the term 'individual'.

Among Mill's criticism of the despotic powers of nineteenth-century husbands is a harsh reminder that a husband had the legal right to rape his wife. Over a century later a husband still has that right in most legal jurisdictions.

Locke excludes women from the status of 'free and equal individual' by his agreement with the patriarchal claim that wives were subject to their husbands by nature; the content of the marriage contract confirms that, today, this assumption still lies at the heart of the institution of marriage. The presumed consent of a woman, in a free marriage contract, to her subordinate status gives a voluntarist gloss to an essentially ascribed status of 'wife'. If the assumption of natural subjection did not still hold, liberal democratic theorists would long ago have begun to ask why it is that an ostensibly free and equal individual should *always* agree to enter a contract which subordinates her to another such individual. They would long ago have begun to question the character of an institution in which the initial agreement of a wife deprives her of the right to retract her consent to provide sexual services to her husband, and which gives him the legal right to force her to submit. If contemporary democratic theorists are to distance themselves from the patriarchal assumptions of their predecessors they must begin to ask whether a person can be, at one and the same time, a free democratic citizen and a wife who gives up a vital aspect of her freedom and individuality, the freedom to refuse consent and say 'no' to the violation of the integrity of her person.

A woman's right of refusal of consent is also a matter of more general importance. Outside of marriage rape is a serious criminal offence, yet the evidence indicates that the majority of offenders are not prosecuted. Women have exemplified the beings whom political theorists have regarded as lacking the capacities to attain the status of individual and citizen or to participate in the practice of consent, but women have, simultaneously, been perceived as beings who, in their personal lives, always consent, and whose explicit refusal of consent can be disregarded and reinterpreted as agreement. This contradictory perception of women is a major reason why it is so difficult for a woman who has been raped to secure the conviction of her attacker(s). Public opinion, the police and the courts are willing to identify enforced submission with consent, and the reason why this identification is possible is that it is widely believed that if a woman says 'no' her words have no meaning, since she 'really' means 'yes'. It is widely regarded as perfectly reasonable for a man to reinterpret explicit rejection of his advances as consent.[13] Thus women find that their speech is persistently and systematically invalidated. Such invalidation would be incomprehensible if the two sexes actually shared the same status as 'individuals'. No person with a secure, recognized standing as an 'individual' could be seen as someone who consistently said the opposite of what they meant and who, therefore, could justifiably have their words reinterpreted by others. On the other hand, invalidation and reinterpretation are readily comprehensible parts of a relationship in which one person is seen as a natural subordinate and thus has an exceedingly ambiguous place in social practices (held to be) grounded in convention, in free agreement and consent.

Political theorists who take seriously the question of the conceptual foundations and social conditions of democracy can no longer avoid the feminist critique of marriage and personal life. The critique raises some awkward and often embarrassing questions, but questions that have to be faced if 'democracy' is to be more than a men's club writ large and the patriarchal structure of the liberal democratic state is to be challenged. The assumptions and practices which govern the everyday, personal lives of women and men, including their sexual lives, can no longer be treated as matters remote from political life and the concerns of democratic theorists. Women's status as 'individuals' pervades the whole of their social life, personal and political. The structure of everyday life, including marriage, is constituted by beliefs and practices which presuppose that women are naturally subject to men—yet writers on democracy continue to assert that women and men can and will freely interact as equals in their capacity as enfranchised democratic citizens.

The preceding argument and criticism is relevant to discussions of both liberal democracy and participatory democracy, but particularly to the latter. Liberal theorists continue to claim that the structure of social relations and social inequality is irrelevant to political equality and democratic citizenship, so they are no more likely to be impressed by feminists than by any other radical critics. Advocates of parti-

cipatory democracy have been reluctant to take feminist arguments into account even though these arguments are, seen in one light, an extension of the participatory democratic claim that 'democracy' extends beyond the state to the organization of society. The resistance to feminism is particularly ironical because the contemporary feminist movement has, under a variety of labels, attempted to put participatory democratic organization into practice.[14] The movement is decentralized, anti-hierarchical and tries to ensure that its members collectively educate themselves and gain independence through consciousness-raising, participatory decision-making and rotation of tasks and offices.

Feminists deny the liberal claim that private and public life can be understood in isolation from each other. One reason for the neglect of J. S. Mill's feminist essay is that his extension of liberal principles to the institution of marriage breaches the central liberal separation, established by Locke, between paternal and political rule; or between the impersonal, conventional public sphere and the family, the sphere of natural affection and natural relations. Proponents of participatory democracy have, of course, been willing to challenge commonplace conceptions of the public and the private in their discussions of the workplace, but this challenge ignores the insights of feminism. It is rarely appreciated that the feminists and participatory democrats see the division between public and private very differently. From the feminist perspective participatory democratic arguments remain within the patriarchal-liberal separation of civil society and state; domestic life has an exceedingly ambiguous relation to this separation, which is a division within public life itself. In contrast, feminists see domestic life, the 'natural' sphere of women, as private, and thus as divided from a public realm encompassing both economic and political life, the 'natural' arenas of men.[15]

By failing to take into account the feminist conception of 'private' life, by ignoring the family, participatory democratic arguments for the democratization of economic life have neglected a crucial dimension of democratic social transformation (and I include my *Participation and Democratic Theory* here). It is difficult to find any appreciation of the significance of the integral relation between the domestic division of labour and economic life, or the sexual division of labour in the workplace, let alone any mention of the implications of the deeper matters touched on in this essay, in writings on industrial democracy. It is the feminists, not the advocates of workplace democracy, who have investigated the very different position of women workers, especially married women workers, from that of male employees. Writers on democracy have yet to digest the now large body of feminist research on women and paid employment or to acknowledge that unless it is brought into the centre of reflection, debate and political action, women will remain as peripheral in a future participatory 'democracy' as they are at present in liberal democracies.

I have drawn attention to the problem posed by the assumption that women's natural place is a private one, as wife and mother in the home, for arguments about the educative and developmental consequences of political participation. It might be argued that this problem is much less pressing today than in Mill's time because many married women have now entered the public world of paid employment and so they, if not housewives, already have their horizons widened and will gain a political education if enterprises are democratized. In Australia, for example, in 1977 women formed 35% of the labour force and 63% of these women were married.[16] The reality behind the statistics, however, is that women's status as workers is as uncertain and ambiguous as our status as citizens and both reflect the more fundamental problem of our status as 'individuals'. The conventional but implicit assumption is that 'work' is undertaken in a workplace, not within the 'private' home, and that a 'worker' is male—someone who has his need for a clean place of relaxation, clean clothes, food and care of his children provided for him by his wife. When a wife enters paid employment it is significant for her position as 'worker' that no one asks who performs these services for her. In fact, married women workers do two shifts, one in the office or factory, the other at home. A large question arises here why members of enterprises who are already burdened with two jobs should be eager to take on the new

responsibilities, as well as exercise the opportunities, that democratization would bring.

The relative importance of the two components of the wife's double day, and so the evaluation of women's status as workers, is reflected, as Eisenstein notes, in the popular use of 'the term "working mother" which simultaneously asserts women's first responsibility to motherhood and her secondary status as worker'.[17] Again, the question has to be asked how workers of secondary status could, without some very large changes being made, take their place as equal participants in a democratized workplace. The magnitude of the changes required can be indicated by brief reference to three features of women's (paid) worklife. The sexual harassment of women workers is still a largely unacknowledged practice but it reveals the extent to which the problem of sexual relations, consent and women's status as 'individuals' is also a problem of the economic sphere.[18] Secondly, women still have to win the struggle against discrimination by employers and unions before they can participate as equals. Finally, it has to be recognized that the workplace is structured by a sexual division of labour which poses still further complex problems for equality and participation. Women are segregated into certain occupational categories ('women's work') and they are concentrated in non-supervisory and low-skilled and low-status jobs. It is precisely workers in such jobs that empirical research has shown to be the least likely to participate.

The example of the workplace, together with the other examples discussed in this essay, should be sufficient to show the fundamental importance to democratic theory and practice of the contemporary feminist insistence that personal and political life are integrally connected. Neither the equal opportunity of liberalism nor the active, participatory democratic citizenship of *all* the people can be achieved without radical changes in personal and domestic life. The struggles of the organized feminist movement of the last 150 years have achieved a great deal. An exceptional woman can now become Prime Minister—but that particular achievement leaves untouched the structure of social life of unexceptional women, of women as a social category. They remain in an uncertain position as individuals, workers and citizens, and popular opinion echoes Rousseau's pronouncement that 'nature herself has decreed that women, . . . should be at the mercy of man's judgement'.[19] The creation of a free and egalitarian sexual and personal life is the most difficult to achieve of all the changes necessary to build a truly democratic society precisely because it is not something remote from everyday life that can be applauded in abstract slogans while life, and the subjection of women, goes on as usual. Democratic ideals and politics have to be put into practice in the kitchen, the nursery and the bedroom; they come home, as J. S. Mill wrote (p. 136) 'to the person and hearth of every male head of a family, and of everyone who looks forward to being so'. It is a natural biological fact of human existence that only women can bear children, but that fact gives no warrant whatsoever for the separation of social life into two sexually defined spheres of private (female) existence and (male) public activity. This separation is ultimately grounded in the mistaken extension of the argument from natural necessity to child-rearing. There is nothing in nature that prevents fathers from sharing equally in bringing up their children, although there is a great deal in the organization of social and economic life that works against it. Women cannot win an equal place in democratic productive life and citizenship if they are deemed destined for a one ascribed task, but nor can fathers take an equal share in reproductive activities without a transformation in our conception of 'work' and of the structure of economic life.

The battle joined three hundred years ago when the social contract theorists pitted conventionalist arguments against the patriarchalists' appeal to nature is far from concluded, and a proper, democratic understanding of the relation of nature and convention is still lacking. The successful conclusion of this long battle demands some radical reconceptualization to provide a comprehensive theory of a properly democratic practice. Recent feminist theoretical work offers new perspectives and insights into the problem of democratic theory and practice, including the question of individualism and participatory democracy, and an appropriate conception of 'political' life.[20] It has been hard to imagine what a democratic

form of social life might look like for much of the past century. Male-dominated political parties, sects and their theoreticians have attempted to bury the old 'utopian' political movements which are part of the history of the struggle for democracy and women's emancipation, and which argued for prefigurative forms of political organization and activity. The lesson to be learnt from the past is that a 'democratic' theory and practice that is not at the same time feminist merely serves to maintain a fundamental form of domination and so makes a mockery of the ideals and values that democracy is held to embody.

Notes

1. B. R. Barber, *The Death of Communal Liberty* (Princeton, Princeton University Press, 1974), p. 273. The comment on citizen-soldiers is very revealing. There is no reason why women should not be armed citizens and help defend the *patrie* (as guerrilla fighters and armies have shown). However, one of the major arguments of the anti-suffragists in Britain and the U.S.A. was that the enfranchisement of women would fatally weaken the state because women by nature were incapable of bearing arms. I have commented on these issues in C. Pateman, 'Women, Nature and the Suffrage', *Ethics*, 90: 4 (1980), pp. 564–75. Some other aspects of the patriarchal argument from nature are discussed below.

2. S. Verba, N. Nie and J.-O. Kim, *Participation and Political Equality* (Cambridge, Cambridge University Press, 1978), p. 8.

3. M. Margolis, *Viable Democracy* (Harmondsworth, Penguin, 1979), p. 9.

4. J. G. Fichte, *The Science of Rights*, trans. A. E. Kroeger (London, Trubner, 1889), 'Appendix', §3.1, p. 439 (my emphasis).

5. J. Locke, *Two Treatises of Government*, 2nd edn, ed. P. Laslett (Cambridge, Cambridge University Press, 1967), I, §47, 48; II, §82.

6. For amplification of these necessarily brief comments see T. Brennan and C. Pateman, ' "Mere Auxiliaries to the Commonwealth": Women and the Origins of Liberalism', *Political Studies*, 27 (1979), pp. 183–200: R. Hamilton, *The Liberation of Women: A Study of Patriarchy and*

Capitalism (London, Allen and Unwin, 1978); H. Hartmann, 'Capitalism, Patriarchy and Job Segregation by Sex', *Signs*, I: 3, Pt 2 (1976), pp. 137–70: A. Oakley, *Housewife* (Harmondsworth, Penguin, 1976), Chs. 2 and 3.

7. Page references in the text are to J. S. Mill, 'The Subjection of Women', in J. S. Mill and H. Taylor, *Essays on Sex Equality*, ed. A. Rossi (Chicago, Chicago University Press, 1970).

8. It is worth noting that Mill implicitly distinguishes between the actions and beliefs of individual husbands and the power given to 'husbands' over 'wives' within the structure of the institution of marriage. He notes that marriage is not designed for the benevolent few to whom the defenders of marital slavery point, but for every man, even those who use their power physically to ill-treat their wives. This important distinction is still frequently overlooked today when critics of feminism offer examples of individual 'good' husbands personally known to them.

9. Mill, and many other feminists, see the lack of a sense of justice (a consequence of confinement to domestic life) as the major defect in women's characters. The assertion that the defect is natural to women is central to the belief—ignored by writers on democracy—that women are inherently subversive of political order and a threat to the state; on this question see C. Pateman, ' "The Disorder of Women": Women, Love and the Sense of Justice', *Ethics*, 91: I (1980), pp. 20–34.

10. It need not be granted. *The Subjection* owes a good deal to William Thompson's (much neglected) *Appeal of One Half the Human Race, Women, Against the Pretensions of the Other Half, Men, to Retain them in Political, and Hence in Civil and Domestic, Slavery* (New York, Source Book Press, 1970), originally published in 1825. Thompson was very willing to question these matters in his vision of a cooperative–socialist and sexually egalitarian future.

11. For an early critique see, for example, M. Goot and E. Reid, 'Women and Voting Studies: Mindless Matrons or Sexist Scientism', *Sage Professional Papers in Contemporary Sociology*, I (1975); more recently, for example, J. Evans, 'Attitudes to Women in American Political Science', *Government and Opposition*, 15: I, (1980), pp. 101–14.

12. M. M. Lee, 'Why Few Women Hold Public Office: Democracy and Sexual Roles', *Political Science Quarterly*, 91 (1976), pp. 297–314.

13. A detailed discussion of the paradoxical manner in which political theorists have treated women's consent, and references to the empirical evidence on which these comments are based, can be found in C. Pateman, 'Women and Consent', *Political Theory*, 8: 2, (1980), pp. 149–68. In some legal jurisdictions, for example the States of New South Wales, South Australia and Victoria in Australia, rape within marriage is now a criminal offence. Legal reform is extremely welcome, but the wider social problem remains; one of the saddest conclusions I reached during my research was that rather than rape being 'a unique act that stands in complete opposition to the consensual relations that ordinarily obtain between the sexes . . . rape is revealed as the extreme expression of, or an extension of, the accepted and "natural" relation between men and women' (p. 161).

14. On the other hand, the experience of women in the 'participatory democratic' New Left was a major impetus to the revival of the feminist movement. The New Left provided an arena for political action, the development of skills, and was ideologically egalitarian—but it remained male supremacist in its organization and, especially, its personal relations: see S. Evans, *Personal Politics* (New York, Knopf, 1979).

15. For some comments on the ambiguous place of the family, see my ' "The Disorder of Women" ': on the wider question of public and private, see C. Pateman, 'Feminist Critiques of the Public–Private Dichotomy', in *Conceptions of the Public and Private in Social Life*, ed. S. Benn and G. Gaus (London, Croom Helm, forthcoming).

16. A steady increase in the employment of married women has been one of the most striking features of the post-war development of capitalism. However, it is worth re-emphasizing that (working-class) wives have always been in the paid workforce. In Britain in 1851 about a quarter of married women were employed (Oakley, *op. cit.*, p. 44). Moreover, domestic service, until the late 1930s, was a major occupation for (usually single) women. One reason that Mill is able to overlook the fundamental importance of wives' (private) childrearing duties for their public sta-

tus is that middle-class mothers had other women to look after their children; similarly, upper- and middle-class suffragettes could go to prison secure in the knowledge that domestic servants were caring for their homes and children (on this point see J. Liddington and J. Norris, *One Hand Tied Behind Us: The Rise of the Women's Suffrage Movement* (London, Virago, 1978)).

17. Z. R. Eisenstein, *The Radical Future of Liberal Feminism* (New York, Longman, 1980), pp. 207–8.

18. On sexual harassment see, for example, C. A. Mackinnon, *Sexual Harassment of Working Women* (New Haven, Conn., Yale University Press, 1979).

19. J.-J. Rousseau, *Emile*, trans. B. Foxley (London, Dent, 1911), p. 328.

20. See, for example, the discussion by R. P. Petchesky, 'Reproductive Freedom: Beyond "A Woman's Right to Choose" ', *Signs*, 5: 4 (1980), pp. 661–85.

Further Reading

Arthur, John. *The Unfinished Constitution*. Belmont, CA: Wadsworth Publishing Co. (1989).

Barber, Benjamin R. *Strong Democracy*. Berkeley: University of California Press (1984).

Barry, Brian. *Theories of Justice*. Berkeley: University of California Press (1989).

Beitz, Charles R. *Political Equality*. Princeton: Princeton University Press (1989).

Brennan, Geoffrey and Lomasky, Loren E., eds. *Politics and Process: New Essays in Democratic Thought*. Cambridge: Cambridge University Press (1989).

Choper, Jesse H. *Judicial Review and the National Political Process*. Chicago: The University of Chicago Press (1980).

Coleman, Jules L. *Markets, Morals and the Law*. Cambridge: Cambridge University Press (1988).

Dahl, Robert A. *A Preface to Democratic Theory*. Chicago: University of Chicago Press (1956).

—— *A Preface to Economic Democracy*. Berkeley: University of California Press (1985).

Duncan, Graeme, ed. *Democratic Theory and Practice*. Cambridge: Cambridge University Press (1983).

Dworkin, Ronald. *Taking Rights Seriously*. Cambridge: Harvard University Press (1977).

Elster, Jon and Hylland, Aanund, eds. *Foundations of Social Choice Theory*. Cambridge: Cambridge University Press (1986).

Ely, John. *Democracy and Distrust*. Cambridge: Harvard University Press (1980).

Gould, Carol C. *Rethinking Democracy*. Cambridge: Cambridge University Press (1988).

Graham, Keith. *The Battle of Democracy*. Totowa, NJ: Barnes & Noble (1986).

Gutmann, Amy. *Liberal Equality*. Cambridge: Cambridge University Press (1980).

Hamlin, Alan and Philip Petit. *The Good Polity: Normative Analysis of the State*. Oxford: Basil Blackwell (1989).

Hayek, Friedrich A. *The Constitution of Liberty*. Chicago: Henry Regnery Co. (1960).

Kariel, Henry S., ed. *Frontiers of Democratic Theory*. New York: Random House (1970).

Laslett, Peter and Fishkin, James, eds. *Philosophy, Politics and Society*, 5th Series. New Haven: Yale University Press (1979).

Lively, Jack and Rees, John, eds. *Utilitarian Logic and Politics*. Oxford: Clarendon Press (1978).

Macpherson, C. B. *Democratic Theory*. Oxford: Clarendon Press (1973).

Nelson, William N. *On Justifying Democracy*. London: Routledge & Kegan Paul (1989).

Pateman, Carole. *Participation and Democratic Theory*. Cambridge: Cambridge University Press (1970).

Pennock, J. Roland. *Democratic Political Theory*. Princeton: Princeton University Press (1979).

Pennock, J. Roland and Chapman, John W. *Constitutionalism*, NOMOS XX. New York: New York University Press (1979).

—— *Liberal Democracy*, NOMOS XXV New York: New York University Press (1983).

—— *Participation in Politics*, NOMOS XVI. Lieber-Atherton (1975).

—— *Representation*, NOMOS X. Lieber-Atherton (1968).

Pitkin, Hanna. *Representation*. New York: Atherton Press (1969).

Rawls, John. *A Theory of Justice*. Cambridge: Harvard University Press (1971).

Rowley, Charles K. *Democracy and Public Choice*. London: Basil Blackwell (1987).

Ryker, William. *Liberalism Against Populism*. San Francisco: W. H. Freeman & Co. (1982).

Singer, Peter. *Democracy and Disobedience*. Oxford: Clarendon Press (1973).

Sunstein, Cass R. "Beyond the Republican Revival," *Yale Law Journal* 97 (1988).

—— "Preferences and Politics" *Philosophy and Public Affairs* Vol. 20 No. 1 (Winter, 1991).

Walzer, Michael. "Political Decision-making and Political Education," *Political Theory and Political Education*. Princeton: Princeton University Press (1980).

—— *Spheres of Justice*. New York: Basic Books (1983).